English Romantic Poets

Titles in the CRITICAL COSMOS series include

AMERICAN FICTION

American Fiction through 1914
American Fiction, 1914–1945
American Fiction, 1946–1965
American Fiction, 1966 to the Present
American Jewish Literature
American Women Novelists and Short
  Story Writers
Black American Fiction

AMERICAN POETRY, DRAMA, AND PROSE

American Drama to 1945
American Drama 1945 to the Present
American Poetry through 1914
American Poetry, 1915–1945
American Poetry, 1946–1965
American Poetry, 1966 to the Present
American Prose and Criticism to 1945
American Prose and Criticism, 1945 to
  the Present
American Women Poets
Black American Poetry

BRITISH LITERATURE THROUGH 1880

British Drama: 18th and 19th Centuries
Eighteenth-Century Fiction and Prose
Eighteenth-Century Poetry
Elizabethan and Jacobean Drama
Elizabethan Poetry
Elizabethan Prose and Fiction
English Romantic Fiction and Prose
English Romantic Poetry
Medieval Literature
Seventeenth-Century Poetry
Seventeenth-Century Prose
Victorian Fiction
Victorian Poetry
Victorian Prose

FRENCH LITERATURE

French Drama through 1915
French Fiction through 1915
French Poetry through 1915
French Prose and Criticism through 1789
French Prose and Criticism, 1790 to the
  Present
Modern French Drama
Modern French Fiction
Modern French Poetry
Modern French Prose and Criticism

GERMAN LITERATURE

German Drama through 1915
German Fiction through 1915
German Poetry through 1915
German Prose and Criticism through 1915
Modern German Drama
Modern German Fiction
Modern German Poetry
Modern German Prose and Criticism

MODERN BRITISH AND COMMONWEALTH LITERATURE

Anglo-Irish Literature
British Prose, 1880–1914
British World War I Literature
Canadian Fiction
Canadian Poetry and Prose
Commonwealth Poetry and Fiction
Contemporary British Drama, 1946 to the
  Present
Contemporary British Fiction, 1946 to the
  Present
Contemporary British Poetry
Contemporary British Prose
Edwardian and Georgian Fiction,
  1880–1914
Edwardian and Georgian Poetry,
  1880–1914
Modern British Drama, 1900–1945
Modernist Fiction, 1920–1945
Modern Poetry and Prose, 1920–1945

OTHER EUROPEAN AND LATIN AMERICAN LITERATURE

African Anglophonic Literature
Dadaism and Surrealism
Italian Drama
Italian Fiction
Italian Poetry
Jewish Literature: The Bible through 1945
Modern Jewish Literature
Modern Latin American Fiction
Modern Scandinavian Literature
Modern Spanish Fiction
Modern Spanish and Latin American
  Poetry
Russian Drama
Russian Fiction
Russian Poetry
Scandinavian Literature through 1915
Spanish Fiction through 1927
Spanish Poetry through 1927

THE CRITICAL COSMOS SERIES

English Romantic Poets

Edited and with an introduction
by *HAROLD BLOOM*
Sterling Professor of the Humanities
Yale University

CHELSEA HOUSE PUBLISHERS ◇ 1986
New York ◇ *New Haven* ◇ *Philadelphia*

© 1986 by Chelsea House Publishers, a division
of Chelsea House Educational Communications, Inc.
    133 Christopher Street, New York, NY 10014
    345 Whitney Avenue, New Haven, CT 06511
    5014 West Chester Pike, Edgemont, PA 19028

Printed and bound in the United States of America

∞The paper used in this publication meets the minimum
requirements of the American National Standard for
Permanence of Paper for Printed Library Materials,
Z39.48-1984.

Library of Congress Cataloging-in-Publication Data
The English romantic poets.

    (The Critical cosmos series)
    Bibliography: p.
    Includes index.
    1. English poetry—19th century—History and
criticism. 2. Romanticism—England. 3. Blake, William,
1757–1827—Criticism and interpretation. I. Bloom,
Harold. II. Series: Critical cosmos.
PR590.E48 1986   821'.7'09   86-6057
ISBN 0-87754-976-1

Contents

Editor's Note

This volume gathers together a representative selection of the best criticism devoted to the six major English Romantic poets, arranged first by date of birth of poet, then within each group by the date of publication of the essay. I am indebted to Peter Childers for his assistance in editing this book. The editor's introduction traces the patterns by which the rhetoric and topoi of the Romance genre internalize themselves in the High Romantics.

The Blake section opens with an essay by Northrop Frye, written nearly twenty years after the publication of his major book on Blake. Frye's essay is an intricate guide to the levels of meaning of Blake's systematic myths. The analysis of *Jerusalem* by the editor seeks to relate the troubling form of that poem to the structure of its central precursor text, the Book of Ezekiel. The late Thomas Weiskel's essay departs from overly system-bound views of Blake to examine the critique of transcendence which is another aspect of Blake's vitalism.

The sequence devoted to William Wordsworth begins with Frederick A. Pottle's classic exposition of Wordsworth's endeavor to keep his eye steadily upon the natural object. Pottle's critical stance is then transposed by Geoffrey H. Hartman's vision of how Wordsworth composed his "romance of nature" through an original mode of negation. In Paul H. Fry's fine close reading of the Intimations Ode, the contradictory nature of the Great Ode and the generic problems inherent in all of Wordsworth's best odes are persuasively examined.

M. H. Abrams, in the first essay in the Coleridge section, gives a full account of the grand conceptual image "A Light in Sound." Angus Fletcher provides an analysis of Coleridgean threshold personifications, which is followed by E. S. Shaffer's profoundly learned excavation of the origins of "Kubla Khan" in Coleridge's abandoned vision of a projected epic on the fall of Jerusalem.

The Byron section begins with G. Wilson Knight's eloquent rumination on Byron's central conflict, "torn between history and tragic insight." Leslie Brisman then offers a remarkable reading of *Cain* and an equally perceptive account of *Lara*, each as a prelude to a brief consideration of *Manfred*. A still younger generation of Byron critics is represented here by Sheila Emerson, whose reading of *Childe Harold* III is a distinguished instance of an eclectic version of our contemporary "language"-oriented criticism of poetry.

The section on Percy Bysshe Shelley begins with the editor's comprehensive introduction to a volume of Shelley's poetry, which reflects the debate of the 1950s and early 1960s as to Shelley's aesthetic eminence. This debate passed away with the Age of Eliot and the New Criticism that he inspired (F. R. Leavis, Allen Tate, W. H. Auden were the principal anti-Shelleyans), but it prepared the way for a more advanced criticism of Shelley. Frederick A. Pottle's masterly reading of *Prometheus Unbound* sets Shelley's cognitive skepticism against his heart's pervasive desires, exposing a dialectical interplay that never ceased in Shelley's work. In his reading of *The Triumph of Life*, the late Paul de Man makes a distinguished attempt to deconstruct the image of Rousseau in the text of Shelley's last poem.

Walter Jackson Bate, the precursor of all Keats criticism subsequent to him, begins the sequence of essays on Keats. Negative capability, which Keats named as his ideal poetic stance, is uniquely Bate's subject. A more European and dialectical mode of negation is ascribed to Keats by Paul de Man, in a remarkable general overview of Keats's achievement both as poet and as theorist. The editor's own essay, concluding this book, centers upon the "Ode to Psyche" and *The Fall of Hyperion*.

Introduction

Freud, in an essay written sixty years ago on the relation of the poet to daydreaming, made the surmise that all aesthetic pleasure is forepleasure, an "incitement premium" or narcissistic fantasy. The deepest satisfactions of literature, on this view, come from a release of tensions in the psyche. That Freud had found, as almost always, either part of the truth or at least a way to it, is clear enough, even if a student of Blake or Wordsworth finds, as probably he must, this Freudian view to be partial, reductive, and a kind of mirror-image of the imagination's truth. The deepest satisfactions of reading Blake or Wordsworth come from the realization of new ranges of tensions in the mind, but Blake and Wordsworth both believed, in different ways, that the pleasures of poetry were only forepleasures, in the sense that poems, finally, were scaffoldings for a more imaginative vision, and not ends in themselves. I think that what Blake and Wordsworth do for their readers, or can do, is closely related to what Freud does or can do for his, which is to provide both a map of the mind and a profound faith that the map can be put to a saving use. Not that the uses agree, or that the maps quite agree either, but the enterprise is a humanizing one in all three of these discoverers. The humanisms do not agree either; Blake's is apocalyptic, Freud's is naturalistic, and Wordsworth's is—sometimes sublimely, sometimes uneasily—blended of elements that dominate in the other two.

Freud thought that even romance, with its element of play, probably commenced in some actual experience whose "strong impression on the writer had stirred up a memory of an earlier experience, generally belonging to childhood, which then arouses a wish that finds a fulfillment in the work in question, and in which elements of the recent event and the old memory should be discernible." Though this is a brilliant and comprehensive thought, it seems inadequate to the complexity of romance, particularly in the period during which romance as a genre, however displaced, became again the dominant form, which is to say the age of Romanticism. For English-speaking readers, this age may be defined as extending from the childhood of Blake and Wordsworth to the present moment. Convenience dictates that we distinguish the High Romantic period proper, during which a half-dozen major English poets did their work, from the generations that have come after them, but the distinction is difficult to justify critically.

Freud's embryonic theory of romance contains within it the potential for an adequate account of Romanticism, particularly if we interpret his "memory of an earlier experience" to mean also the recall of an earlier insight, or yearning, that may not have been experiential. The immortal longings of the child, rather variously interpreted by Freud, Blake, and Wordsworth, may not be at the roots of romance, historically speaking, since those roots go back to a psychology very different from ours, but they do seem to be at the sources of the mid-eighteenth-century revival of a romance consciousness, out of which nineteenth-century Romanticism largely came.

J. H. Van den Berg, whose introduction to a historical psychology I find crucial to an understanding of Romanticism, thinks that Rousseau "was the first to view the child as a child, and to stop treating the child as an adult." Van den Berg, as a doctor, does not think this was necessarily an advance: "Ever since Rousseau the child has been keeping its distance. This process of the child and adult growing away from each other began in the eighteenth century. It was then that the period of adolescence came into existence." Granting that Van den Berg is broadly correct (he at least attempts to explain an apparent historical modulation in consciousness that few historians of culture care to confront), then we are presented with another in a series of phenomena, clustering around Rousseau and his age, in which the major change from the Enlightenment to Romanticism manifested itself. Changes in consciousness are of course very rare, and no major synthesizer has come forth as yet, from any discipline, to demonstrate to us whether Romanticism marks a genuine change in consciousness or not. From the Freudian viewpoint, Romanticism is an "illusory therapy" (I take the phrase from Philip Rieff), or what Freud himself specifically termed an "erotic illusion." The dialectics of Romanticism, to the Freudians, are mistaken or inadequate, because the dialectics are sought in Schiller or Heine or in German Romantic philosophy down to Nietzsche, rather than in Blake or the English Romantics after him. Blake and Coleridge do not set intellect and passion against one another, any more than they arrive at the Freudian simplicity of the endless conflict between Eros and Thanatos. Possibly because of the clear associations between Jung and German Romanticism, it has been too easy for Freudian intellectuals to confound Romanticism with various modes of irrationalism. Though much contemporary scholarship attempts to study English and Continental Romanticism as a unified phenomenon, it can be argued that the English Romantics tend to lose more than they gain by such study.

Behind Continental Romanticism there lay very little in the way of a congenial native tradition of major poets writing in an ancestral mode, particularly when compared to the English Romantic heritage of Spenser, Shakespeare, and Milton. What allies Blake and Wordsworth, Shelley and Keats, is their strong mutual conviction that they are reviving the true English tradition of poetry, which they thought had vanished after the death of Milton and had reappeared in diminished form, mostly after the death of Pope, in admirable but doomed poets like Chatterton, Cowper, and Collins, victims of circumstance and of their own false dawn of Sensibility. It is in this highly individual sense that English Romanticism legitimately can be called, as traditionally it has been, a revival of romance. More than a revival, it is an internalization of romance, particularly of the quest variety, an internalization made for more than therapeutic purposes, because made in the name of a humanizing hope that approaches apocalyptic intensity. The poet takes the patterns of quest-romance and transposes them into his own imaginative life, so that the entire rhythm of the quest is heard again in the movement of the poet himself from poem to poem. M. H. Abrams brilliantly traces these patterns of what he calls "the apocalypse of imagination." As he shows, historically they all directly stem from English reactions to the French Revolution, or to the intellectual currents that had flowed into the Revolution. Psychologically, they stem from the child's vision of a more titanic universe that the English Romantics were so reluctant to abandon. If adolescence was a Romantic or Rousseauistic phenomenon of consciousness, its concomitant was the very secular sense of being twice-born that is first discussed in the fourth chapter of *Émile*, and then beautifully developed by Shelley in his visionary account of Rousseau's second birth, in the concluding movement of *The Triumph of Life*. The pains of psychic maturation become, for Shelley, the potentially saving though usually destructive crisis when the imagination confronts its choice of either sustaining its own integrity or yielding to the illusive beauty of nature.

The movement of quest-romance, before its internalization by the High Romantics, was from nature to redeemed nature, the sanction of redemption being the gift of some external spiritual authority, sometimes magical. The Romantic movement is from nature to the imagination's freedom (sometimes a reluctant freedom), and the imagination's freedom is frequently purgatorial, redemptive in direction but destructive of the social self. The high cost of Romantic internalization, that is, of finding paradises within a renovated man, tends to manifest itself in the arena of self-consciousness. The quest is to widen consciousness as well as intensify it, but the quest is shadowed by a spirit that tends to narrow consciousness to an acute preoccupation with self. This shadow of imagination is solipsism, what Shelley calls the Spirit of Solitude or *Alastor*, the avenging daimon who is a baffled residue of the self, determined to be compensated for its loss of natural assurance, for having been awakened from the merely given condition that to Shelley, as to Blake, was but the sleep of death-in-life. Blake calls this spirit of solitude a Spectre, or the genuine Satan, the Thanatos or death-impulse in every natural man. Modernist poetry in English organized itself, to an excessive extent, as a supposed revolt against Romanticism, in the mistaken hope of escaping this inwardness (though it was unconscious that this was its prime motive). Modernist poetry learned better, as its best work, the last phases of W. B. Yeats and Wallace Stevens, abundantly shows, but criticism until recently was tardy in catching up, and lingering misapprehensions about the Romantics still abide. Thus, Irving Howe, in an otherwise acute essay on literary Modernism, says of the Romantic poets that "they do not surrender the wish to discover in the universe a network of spiritual meaning which, however precariously, can enclose their selves." This is simply not true of Blake or Wordsworth or Shelley or Keats, nor is the statement of Marius Bewley's that Howe quotes approvingly, that the Romantics' central desire is "to merge oneself with what is greater than oneself." Indeed, both statements are excellent guides to what the major Romantics regarded as human defeat or a living death, as the despairing surrender of the imagination's autonomy. Since neither Howe nor Bewley is writing as an enemy of the Romantics, it is evident that we still need to clear our mind of Eliotic cant on this subject.

Paul de Man terms this phenomenon the post-Romantic dilemma, observing that every fresh attempt of Modernism to go beyond Romanticism ends in the gradual realization of the Romantics' continued priority. Modern poetry, in English, is the invention of Blake and of Wordsworth, and I do not know of a long poem written in English since then that is either as legitimately difficult or as rewardingly profound as *Jerusalem* or *The Prelude*. Nor can I find a modern lyric, however happily ignorant its writer, that develops beyond or surmounts its debt to Wordsworth's great trinity of "Tintern Abbey," "Resolution and Independence," and the Intimations Ode. The dreadful paradox of Wordsworth's greatness is that his uncanny originality, still the most astonishing break with tradition in the language, has been so influential that we have lost sight of its audacity and its arbitrariness. In this, Wordsworth strongly resembles Freud, who rightly compared his own intellectual revolution to those of Copernicus and Darwin. Van den Berg quietly sees "Freud, in the desperation of the moment, turning away from the present, where the cause of his patients' illnesses was located, to the past; and thus making them suffer from the past and making our existence akin to their suffering. It was not necessary." Is Van den Berg right? The question is as crucial for Wordsworth and Romanticism as it is for Freud and psychoanalysis. The most searching critique of Romanticism that I know is Van den Berg's critique of Freud, particularly the description of "The Subject and His Landscape":

> Ultimately the enigma of grief is the libido's inclination toward exterior things. What prompts the libido to leave the inner self? In 1914 Freud asked himself this question—the essential question of his psychology, and the essential question of the psychology of the twentieth century. His answer ended the process of inte-

riorization. It is: the libido leaves the inner self when the inner self has become too full. In order to prevent it from being torn, the I has to aim itself on objects outside the self;" . . . ultimately man must begin to love in order not to get ill." So that is what it is. Objects are of importance only in an extreme urgency. Human beings, too. The grief over their death is the sighing of a too-far-distended covering, the groaning of an overfilled inner self.

Wordsworth is a crisis-poet, Freud a crisis-analyst; the saving movement in each is backward into lost time. But what is the movement of loss, in poet and in analyst? Van den Berg's suggestion is that Freud unnecessarily sacrificed the present moment, because he came at the end of a tradition of intellectual error that began with the extreme Cartesian dualism, and that progressively learned to devalue contact between the self and others, the self and the outer world, the self and the body. Wordsworth's prophecy, and Blake's, was overtly against dualism; they came, each said, to heal the division within man, and between man and the world, if never quite between man and man. But Wordsworth, the more influential because more apparently accessible of the two (I myself would argue that he is the more difficult because the more problematic poet), no more overcame a fundamental dualism than Freud did. Essentially this was Blake's complaint against him; it is certainly no basis for us to complain. Wordsworth made his kind of poetry out of an extreme urgency, and out of an overfilled inner self, a Blakean Prolific that nearly choked in an excess of its own delights. This is the Egotistical Sublime of which Keats complained, but Keats knew his debt to Wordsworth, as most poets since do not.

Wordsworth's Copernican revolution in poetry is marked by the evanescence of any subject but subjectivity, the loss of what a poem is "about." If, like the late Yvor Winters, one rejects a poetry that is not "about" something, one has little use for (or understanding of) Wordsworth. But, like Van den Berg on Freud, one can understand and love Wordsworth, and still ask of his radical subjectivity: was it necessary? Without hoping to find an answer, one can explore the question so as to come again on the central problem of Romantic (and post-Romantic) poetry: what, for men without belief and even without credulity, is the spiritual form of romance? How can a poet's (or any man's) life be one of continuous allegory (as Keats thought Shakespeare's must have been) in a reductive universe of death, a separated realm of atomized meanings, each discrete from the next? Though all men are questers, even the least, what is the relevance of quest in a gray world of continuities and homogenized enterprises? Or, in Wordsworth's own terms, which are valid for every major Romantic, what knowledge might yet be purchased except by the loss of power?

Frye, in his theory of myths, explores the analogue between quest-romance and the dream: "Translated into dream terms, the quest-romance is the search of the libido or desiring self for a fulfillment that will deliver it from the anxieties of reality but will still contain that reality." Internalized

romance, and *The Prelude* and *Jerusalem* can be taken as the greatest examples
of this kind, traces a Promethean and revolutionary quest, and cannot be
translated into dream terms, for in it the libido turns inward into the self.
Shelley's *Prometheus Unbound* is the most drastic High Romantic version of
internalized quest, but there are more drastic versions still in our own age,
though they present themselves as parodistic, as in the series of marvelous
interior quests by Stevens, that go from *The Comedian As the Letter C* to the
climactic *Notes Toward a Supreme Fiction*. The hero of internalized quest is
the poet himself, the antagonists of quest are everything in the self that
blocks imaginative work, and the fulfillment is never the poem itself but
the poem beyond that is made possible by the apocalypse of imagination.
"A timely utterance gave that thought relief" is the Wordsworthian formula
for the momentary redemption of the poet's sanity by the poem already
written, and might stand as a motto for the history of the modern lyric
from Wordsworth to Hart Crane.

The Romantics tended to take Milton's Satan as the archetype of the
heroically defeated Promethean quester, a choice in which modern criticism
has not followed them. But they had a genuine insight into the affinity
between an element in their selves and an element in Milton that he would
externalize only in a demonic form. What *is* heroic about Milton's Satan is
a real Prometheanism and a thoroughly internalized one; he can steal only
his own fire in the poem, since God can appear as fire, again in the poem,
only when he directs it against Satan. In Romantic quest the Promethean
hero stands, finally quite alone, upon a tower that is only himself, and his
stance is all the fire there is. This realization leads neither to nihilism nor
to solipsism, though Byron plays with the former and all fear the latter.

The dangers of idealizing the libido are of course constant in the life
of the individual, and such idealizations are dreadful for whole societies,
but the internalization of quest-romance had to accept these dangers. The
creative process is the hero of Romantic poetry, and imaginative inhibitions,
of every kind, necessarily must be the antagonists of the poetic quest. The
special puzzle of Romanticism is the dialectical role that nature had to take
in the revival of the mode of romance. Most simply, Romantic nature poetry, despite a long critical history of misrepresentation, was an anti-nature
poetry, even in Wordsworth, who sought a reciprocity or even a dialogue
with nature, but found it only in flashes. Wordsworthian nature, thanks
to Arnold and the critical tradition he fostered, has been misunderstood,
though the insights of recent critics have begun to develop a better interpretative tradition founded on A. C. Bradley's opposition to Arnold's view.
Bradley stressed the strong side of Wordsworth's imagination, its Miltonic
sublimity, which Arnold evidently never noticed, but which accounts for
everything that is major in *The Prelude* and in the central crisis lyrics associated with it. Though Wordsworth came as a healer, and Shelley attacked
him in "Mont Blanc" for attempting to reconcile man with nature, there is
no such reconciliation in Wordsworth's poetry, and the healing function
is performed only when the poetry shows the power of the mind over

outward sense. The strength of renovation in Wordsworth resides only in the spirit's splendor, in what he beautifully calls "possible sublimity" or "something evermore about to be," the potential of an imagination too fierce to be contained by nature. This is the force that Coleridge sensed and feared in Wordsworth, and is remarkably akin to that strength in Milton that Marvell urbanely says he feared, in his introductory verses to *Paradise Lost*. As Milton curbed his own Prometheanism, partly by showing its dangers through Satan's version of the heroic quest, so Wordsworth learned to restrain his, partly through making his own quest-romance, in *The Prelude*, an account of learning both the enormous strength of nature and nature's wise and benevolent reining-in of its own force. In the covenant between Wordsworth and nature, two powers that are totally separate from each other, and potentially destructive of the other, try to meet in a dialectic of love. "Meet" is too hopeful, and "blend" would express Wordsworth's ideal and not his achievement, but the try itself is definitive of Wordsworth's strangeness and continued relevance as a poet.

If Wordsworth, so frequently and absurdly called a pantheist, was not questing for unity with nature, still less were Blake, Shelley, and Keats, or their darker followers in later generations, from Beddoes, Darley, and Wade down to Yeats and Lawrence in our time. Coleridge and Byron, in their very different ways, were oddly closer both to orthodox Christian myth and to pantheism or some form of nature-worship, but even their major poems hardly approximate nature poetry. Romantic or internalized romance, especially in its purest version of the quest form, the poems of symbolic voyaging that move in a continuous tradition from Shelley's *Alastor* to Yeats's *The Wanderings of Oisin*, tends to see the context of nature as a trap for the mature imagination. This point requires much laboring, as the influence of older views of Romanticism is very hard to slough off. Even Northrop Frye, the leading romance theorist we have had at least since Ruskin, Pater, and Yeats, says that "in Romanticism the main direction of the quest of identity tends increasingly to be downward and inward, toward a hidden basis or ground of identity between man and nature." The directional part of this statement is true, but the stated goal I think is not. Frye still speaks of the Romantics as seeking a final unity between man and his nature, but Blake and Shelley do not accept such a unity as a goal, unless a total transformation of man and nature can precede unity, while Wordsworth's visions of "first and last and midst and without end" preserve the unyielding forms both of nature and of man. Keats's closest approach to an apocalyptic vision comes when he studies Moneta's face, at the climax of *The Fall of Hyperion*, but even that vision is essentially Wordsworthian, seeing as it does a perpetual change that cannot be ended by change, a human countenance made only more solitary in its growing alienation from nature, and a kind of naturalistic entropy that has gone beyond natural contraries, past "the lily and the snow." Probably only Joyce and Stevens, in later Romantic tradition, can be termed unreconstructed naturalists, or naturalistic humanists. Late Romantics as various as Eliot, Proust, and Shaw all break through uneasy natural contexts, as though sexuality was antithetical to the imagination, while Yeats, the very last of the High Romantics, worked out an elaborate sub-myth of the poet as antithetical quester, very much in the mode of Shelley's poetry. If the goal of Romantic internalization of the quest was a wider consciousness that would be free of the excesses of self-consciousness, a consideration of the rigors of experiential psychology will show, quite rapidly, why nature could not provide adequate context. The program of Romanticism, and not just in Blake, demands something more than a natural man to carry it through. Enlarged and more numerous senses are necessary, an enormous virtue of Romantic poetry clearly being that it not only demands such expansion but begins to make it possible, or at least attempts to do so.

The internalization of romance brought the concept of nature, and poetic consciousness itself, into a relationship they had never had before the advent of Romanticism in the later eighteenth century. Implicit in all the Romantics, and very explicit in Blake, is a difficult distinction between two modes of energy, organic and creative (Orc and Los in Blake, Prometheus bound and unbound in Shelley, Hyperion and Apollo in Keats, the Child and the Man, though with subtle misgivings, in Wordsworth). For convenience, the first mode can be called Prometheus and the second "the Real Man, the Imagination" (Blake's phrase, in a triumphant letter written when he expected death). Generally, Prometheus is the poet-as-hero in the first stage of his quest, marked by a deep involvement in political, social, and literary revolution, and a direct, even satirical attack on the institutional orthodoxies of European and English society, including historically oriented Christianity, and the neoclassic literary and intellectual tradition, particularly in its Enlightenment phase. The Real Man, the Imagination, emerges after terrible crises in the major stage of the Romantic quest, which is typified by a relative disengagement from revolutionary activism, and a standing-aside from polemic and satire, so as to re-center the arena of search within the self and its ambiguities. In the Prometheus stage, the quest is allied to the libido's struggle against repressiveness, and nature is an ally, though always a wounded and sometimes a withdrawn one. In the Real Man, the Imagination stage, nature is the immediate though not the ultimate antagonist. The final enemy to be overcome is a recalcitrance in the self, what Blake calls the Spectre of Urthona, Shelley the unwilling dross that checks the spirit's flight, Wordsworth the sad perplexity or fear that kills or, best of all, the hope that is unwilling to be fed, and Keats, most simply and perhaps most powerfully, the Identity. Coleridge calls the antagonist by a bewildering variety of names since, of all these poets, he is the most hagridden by anxieties, and the most humanly vulnerable. Byron and Beddoes do not so much name the antagonist as they mock it, so as to cast it out by continuous satire and demonic farce. The best single name for the antagonist is Keats's Identity, but the most traditional is the Selfhood, and so I shall use it here.

Only the Selfhood, for the Romantics as for such Christian visionaries as Eckhart before them, burns in Hell. The Selfhood is not the erotic principle, but precisely that part of the erotic that cannot be released in the dialectic of love, whether between man and man, or man and nature. Here the Romantics, all of them, I think, even Keats, part company with Freud's dialectics of human nature. Freud's beautiful sentence on marriage is a formula against which the Romantic Eros can be tested: "A man shall leave father and mother—according to the Biblical precept—and cleave to his wife; then are tenderness and sensuality united." By the canons of internalized romance, that translates: a poet shall leave his Great Original (Milton, for the Romantics) and nature—according to the precept of Poetic Genius—and cleave to his Muse or Imagination; then are the generous and solitary halves united. But, so translated, the formula has ceased to be Freudian and has become High Romantic. In Freud, part of the ego's own self-love is projected onto an outward object, but part always remains in the ego, and even the projected portion can find its way back again. Somewhere Freud has a splendid sentence that anyone unhappy in love can take to heart: "Object-libido was at first ego-libido and can be again transformed into ego-libido," which is to say that a certain degree of narcissistic mobility is rather a good thing. Somewhere else Freud remarks that all romance is really a form of what he calls "family-romance"; one could as justly say, in his terms, that all romance is necessarily a mode of ego-romance. This may be true, and in its humane gloom it echoes a great line of realists who culminate in Freud, but the popular notion that High Romanticism takes a very different view of love is a sounder insight into the Romantics than most scholarly critics ever achieve (or at least state). All romance, literary and human, is founded upon enchantment; Freud and the Romantics differ principally in their judgment as to what it is in us that resists enchantment, and what the value of that resistance is. For Freud it is the reality-principle, working through the great disenchanter, reason, the scientific attitude, and without it no civilized values are possible. For the Romantics, this is again a dialectical matter, as two principles intertwine in the resistance to enchantment, one "organic," an anxiety-principle masquerading as a reality-principle and identical to the ego's self-love that never ventures out to others, and the other "creative," which resists enchantment in the name of a higher mode than the sympathetic imagination. This doubling is clearest in Blake's mythology, where there are two egos, the Spectre of Urthona and Los, who suffer the enchantments, real *and* deceptive, of nature and the female, and who resist, when and where they can, on these very different grounds. But, though less schematically, the same doubling of the ego into passive and active components is present in the other poets wherever they attempt their highest flights and so spurn the earth. The most intense effort of the Romantic quest is made when the Promethean stage of quest is renounced and the purgatorial crisis that follows moves near to resolution. Romantic purgatory, by an extraordinary displacement of earlier mythology, is found just beyond the earthly paradise, rather than just before it, so that the imagination is tried by nature's best aspect. Instances of the interweaving of purgatory and paradise include nearly everything Blake says about the state of being he calls Beulah and the whole development of Keats, from *Endymion* with its den or cave of Quietude on to the structure of *The Fall of Hyperion* where the poet enjoys the fruit and drink of paradise just before he has his confrontation with Moneta, whose shrine must be reached by mounting purgatorial stairs.

Nothing in Romantic poetry is more difficult to comprehend, for me anyway, than the process that begins after each poet's renunciation of Prometheus; for the incarnation of the Real Man, the Imagination, is not like psychic maturation in poets before the Romantics. The love that transcends the Selfhood has its analogues in the renunciatory love of many traditions, including some within Christianity, but the creative Eros of the Romantics is not renunciatory though it is self-transcendent. It is, to use Shelley's phrasing, a total going-out from our own natures, total because the force moving out is not only the Promethean libido but rather a fusion between the libido and the active or imaginative element in the ego; or simply, desire wholly taken up into the imagination. "Shelley's love poetry," as a phrase, is almost a redundancy, Shelley having written little else, but his specifically erotic poems, a series of great lyrics and the dazzling *Epipsychidion*, have been undervalued because they are so very difficult, the difficulty being the Shelleyan and Romantic vision of love.

Blake distinguished between Beulah and Eden as states of being, the first being the realm of family-romance and the second of apocalyptic romance, in which the objects of love altogether lose their object-dimension. In family-romance or Beulah, loved ones are not confined to their objective aspect (that would make them denizens of Blake's state of Generation or mere Experience), but they retain it nevertheless. The movement to the reality of Eden is one of recreation or better, of knowledge not purchased by the loss of power, and so of power and freedom gained *through* a going-out of our nature, in which that last phrase takes on its full range of meanings. Though Romantic love, particularly in Wordsworth and Shelley, has been compared to what Charles Williams calls the Romantic theology of Dante, the figure of Beatrice is not an accurate analogue to the various Romantic visions of the beloved, for sublimation is not an element in the movement from Prometheus to Man. There is no useful analogue to Romantic or imaginative love, but there is a useful contrary, in the melancholy wisdom of Freud on natural love, and the contrary has the helpful clarity one always finds in Freud. If Romantic love is the sublime, then Freudian love is the pathetic, and truer of course to the phenomenon insofar as it is merely natural. To Freud, love begins as ego-libido, and necessarily is ever after a history of sorrow, a picaresque chronicle in which the ever-vulnerable ego stumbles from delusion to frustration, to expire at last (if lucky) in the compromising arms of the ugliest of Muses, the reality-principle. But the saving dialectic of this picaresque is that it is better thus, as there is no satisfaction in satisfaction anyway, since in the Freudian view all erotic partners are somewhat inadequate replacements for the initial sexual objects, parents. Romantic love, to Freud, is a particularly intense version of the longing for the mother, a love in which the imago is loved, rather than the replacement. And Romantic love, on this account, is anything but a dialectic of transformation, since it is as doomed to overvalue the surrogate as it compulsively overvalues the mother. Our age begins to abound in late Romantic "completions" of Freud, but the Romantic critiques of him, by Jung and Lawrence in particular, have not touched the strength of his erotic pessimism. There is a subtly defiant attempt to make the imago do the work of the imagination by Stevens, particularly in the very Wordsworthian *The Auroras of Autumn*, and it is beautifully subversive of Freud, but of course it is highly indirect. Yet a direct Romantic counter-critique of Freud's critique of Romantic love emerges from any prolonged, central study of Romantic poetry. For Freud, there is an ironic loss of energy, perhaps even of spirit, with every outward movement of love away from the ego. Only pure self-love has a perfection to it, a stasis without loss, and one remembers again Van den Berg's mordant observation on Freud: "Ultimately the enigma of grief is the libido's inclination toward exterior things." All outward movement, in the Freudian psychodynamics, is a fall that results from "an overfilled inner self," which would sicken within if it did not fall outward, and downward, into the world of objects and of other selves. One longs for Blake to come again and rewrite *The Book of Urizen* as a satire on this cosmogony of love. The poem would not require that much rewriting, for it now can be read as a prophetic satire on Freud, Urizen being a superego certainly overfilled with itself, and sickening into a false creation or creation-fall. If Romantic love can be castigated as "erotic illusion," Freudian love can be judged as "erotic reduction," and the prophets of the reality-principle are in danger always of the Urizenic boast:

> I have sought for a joy without pain,
> For a solid without fluctuation
> Why will you die O Eternals?
> Why live in unquenchable burnings?

The answer is the Romantic dialectic of Eros and Imagination, unfair as it is to attribute to the Freudians a censorious repressiveness. But, to Blake and the Romantics, all available accounts of right reason, even those that had risen to liberate men, had the disconcerting tendency to turn into censorious moralities. Freud painfully walked a middle way, not unfriendly to the poetic imagination, and moderately friendly to Eros. If his myth of love is so sparse, rather less than a creative Word, it is still open both to analytic modification and to a full acceptance of everything that can come out of the psyche. Yet it is not quite what Philip Rieff claims for it, as it does not erase "the gap between therapeutic rationalism and self-assertive romanticism." That last is only the first stage of the Romantic quest, the one this discussion calls Prometheus. There remains a considerable gap between the subtle perfection to which Freud brought therapeutic rationalism and the mature Romanticism that is self-transcendent in its major poets.

There is no better way to explore the Real Man, the Imagination, than to study his monuments: *The Four Zoas, Milton,* and *Jerusalem; The Prelude* and the *Recluse* fragment; *The Ancient Mariner* and *Christabel; Prometheus Unbound, Adonais,* and *The Triumph of Life;* the two *Hyperions; Don Juan; Death's Jest-Book;* these are the definitive Romantic achievement, the words that were and will be, day and night. What follows is only an epitome, a rapid sketch of the major phase of this erotic quest. The sketch, like any that attempts to trace the visionary company of love, is likely to end in listening to the wind, hoping to hear an instant of a fleeting voice.

The internalization of quest-romance made of the poet-hero not a seeker after nature but after his own mature powers, and so the Romantic poet turned away, not from society to nature, but from nature to what was more integral than nature, within himself. The widened consciousness of the poet did not give him intimations of a former union with nature or the Divine, but rather of his former selfless self. One thinks of Yeats's Blakean declaration: "I'm looking for the face I had / Before the world was made." Different as the major Romantics were in their attitudes toward religion, they were united (except for Coleridge) in *not* striving for unity with anything but what might be called their Tharmas or id component, Tharmas being the Zoa or Giant Form in Blake's mythology who was the unfallen human potential for realizing instinctual desires, and so was the regent of Innocence. Tharmas is a shepherd-figure, his equivalent in Wordsworth being a number of visions of man against the sky, of actual shepherds Wordsworth had seen in his boyhood. This Romantic pastoral vision (its pictorial aspect can be studied in the woodcuts of Blake's Virgil series, and in the work done by Palmer, Calvert, and Richmond while under Blake's influence) is Biblical pastoralism, but not at all of a traditional kind. Blake's Tharmas is inchoate when fallen, as the id or appetite is inchoate, desperately starved and uneasily allied to the Spectre of Urthona, the passive ego he has projected outward to meet an object-world from which he has been severed so unwillingly. Wordsworth's Tharmas, besides being the shepherd image of human divinity, is present in the poet himself as a desperate desire for continuity in the self, a desperation that at its worst sacrifices the living moment, but at its best produces a saving urgency that protects the imagination from the strong enchantments of nature.

In Freud the ego mediates between id and superego, and Freud had no particular interest in further dividing the ego itself. In Romantic psychic mythology, Prometheus rises from the id, and can best be thought of as the force of libido, doomed to undergo a merely cyclic movement from appetite to repression, and then back again; any quest within nature is thus at last irrelevant to the mediating ego, though the quest goes back and forth through it. It is within the ego itself that the quest must turn, to engage the antagonist proper, and to clarify the imaginative component in the ego by its strife of contraries with its dark brother. Frye, writing on Keats, calls the imaginative ego *identity-with* and the selfhood ego *identity-as*, which clarifies Keats's ambiguous use of "identity" in this context. Geoffrey H. Hartman, writing on Wordsworth, points to the radical Protestant analogue to the Romantic quest: "The terror of discontinuity or separation enters, in fact, as soon as the imagination truly enters. In its restraint of vision, as well as its peculiar nakedness before the moment, this resembles an extreme Protestantism, and Wordsworth seems to quest for 'evidences' in the form of intimations of continuity." Wordsworth's greatness was in his feeling the terror of discontinuity as acutely as any poet could, yet overcoming this terror nevertheless, by opening himself to vision. With Shelley, the analogue of the search for evidences drops out, and an Orphic strain takes its place, as no other English poet gives so continuous an impression of relying on almost literal inspiration. Where Keats knew the Selfhood as an attractive strength of distinct identity that had to be set aside, and Wordsworth as a continuity he longed for yet learned to resist, and Blake as a temptation to prophetic wrath and withdrawal that had to be withstood, Shelley frequently gives the impression of encountering no enchantment he does not embrace, since every enchantment is an authentic inspiration. Yet this is a false impression, though Yeats sometimes received it, as in his insistence that Shelley, great poet as he certainly was, lacked a Vision of Evil. The contrary view to Yeats is that of C. S. Lewis, who held that Shelley, more than any other "heathen" poet (the word is from Lewis), drove home the truth of Original Sin. Both views are mistaken. For Shelley, the Selfhood's strong enchantment, stronger even than it is for the other Romantics, is one that would keep him from ever concluding the Prometheus phase of the quest. The Selfhood allies itself with Prometheus against the repressive force Shelley calls Jupiter, his version of Blake's Urizen or Freud's superego. This temptation calls the poet to perpetual revolution, and Shelley, though longing desperately to see the tyrannies of his time overturned, renounces it at the opening of *Prometheus Unbound* in the Imagination's name. Through his renunciation, he moves to overturn the tyranny of time itself.

There are thus two main elements in the major phase of Romantic quest, the first being the inward overcoming of the Selfhood's temptation, and the second the outward turning of the triumphant Imagination, free of further internalizations, though "outward" and "inward" become cloven fictions or false conceptual distinctions in this triumph, which must complete a dialectic of love by uniting the Imagination with its bride, a transformed, ongoing creation of the Imagination rather than a redeemed nature. Blake and Wordsworth had long lives, and each completed his version of this dialectic. Coleridge gave up the quest, and became only an occasional poet, while Byron's quest, even had he lived into middle age, would have become increasingly ironic. Keats died at twenty-five, and Shelley at twenty-nine; despite their fecundity, they did not complete their development, but their death-fragments, *The Fall of Hyperion* and *The Triumph of*

Life, prophesy the final phase of the quest in them. Each work breaks off with the Selfhood subdued, and there is profound despair in each, particularly in Shelley's, but there are still hints of what the Imagination's triumph would have been in Keats. In Shelley, the final despair may be total, but a man who had believed so fervently that the good time would come had already given a vision of imaginative completion in the closing act of *Prometheus Unbound*, and we can go back to it and see what is deliberately lacking in *The Triumph of Life*. What follows is a rapid attempt to trace the major phase of quest in the four poets, taking as texts *Jerusalem* and *The Prelude*, and the *Fall* and *Triumph*, these two last with supplementary reference to crucial earlier erotic poems of Keats and Shelley.

Of Blake's long poems the first, *The Four Zoas*, is essentially a poem of Prometheus, devoting itself to the cyclic strife between the Promethean Orc and the moral censor, Urizen, in which the endless cycle between the two is fully exposed. The poem ends in an apocalypse, the explosive and Promethean "Night the Ninth, Being The Last Judgment," which in itself is one of Blake's greatest works, yet from which he turned when he renounced the entire poem (by declining to engrave it). But not before he attempted to move the entire poem from the Prometheus stage to the Imagination, for Blake's own process of creative maturation came to its climax while he worked on *The Four Zoas*. The entrance into the mature stage of the quest is clearly shown by the different versions of "Night the Seventh," for the later one introduces the doubling of the ego into Spectre of Urthona and Los, Selfhood or *Identity-As*, and Imagination or *Identity-With*. Though skillfully handled, it was not fully clarified by Blake, even to himself, and so he refused to regard the poem as definitive vision. Its place in his canon was filled, more or less, by the double-romance *Milton* and *Jerusalem*. The first is more palpably in a displaced romance mode, involving as it does symbolic journeys downward to our world by Milton and his emanation or bride of creation, Ololon, who descend from an orthodox Eternity in a mutual search for one another, the characteristic irony being that they could never find one another in a traditional heaven. There is very little in the poem of the Prometheus phase, Blake having already devoted to that a series of prophetic poems, from *America* and *Europe* through *The Book of Urizen* and on to the magnificent if unsatisfactory (to him, not to us) *The Four Zoas*. The two major stages of the mature phase of quest dominate the structure of *Milton*. The struggle with the Selfhood moves from the quarrel between Palamabron (Blake) and Satan (Hayley) in the introductory Bard's Song on to Milton's heroic wrestling match with Urizen, and climaxes in the direct confrontation between Milton and Satan on the Felpham shore, in which Milton recognizes Satan as his own Selfhood. The recognition compels Satan to a full epiphany, and a subsequent defeat. Milton then confronts Ololon, the poem ending in an epiphany contrary to Satan's, in what Blake specifically terms a preparation for a going-forth to the great harvest and vintage of the nations. But even this could not be Blake's final Word; the quest in *Milton* is primarily Milton's and not Blake's, and the quest's antagonist is still somewhat externalized. In *Jerusalem*, *The Prelude's* only rival as the finest long poem of the nineteenth century, Blake gives us the most comprehensive single version of Romantic quest. Here there is an alternation between vision sweeping outward into the nightmare world of the reality-principle, and a wholly inward vision of conflict in Blake's ego, between the Spectre and Los. The poet's antagonist is himself, the poem's first part being the most harrowing and tormented account of genius tempted to the madness of self-righteousness, frustrate anger, and solipsistic withdrawal, in the Romantic period. Blake-Los struggles on, against this enchantment of despair, until the poem quietly, almost without warning, begins to move into the light of a Last Judgment, of a kind passed by every man upon himself. In the poem's final plates (Blake's canonical poems being a series of engraved plates), the reconciliation of Los and his emanative portion, Enitharmon, begins, and we approach the completion of quest.

Though Blake, particularly in *Jerusalem*, attempts a continuity based on thematic juxtaposition and simultaneity, rather than on consecutiveness, he is in such sure control of his own procedure that his work is less difficult to summarize than *The Prelude*, a contrast that tends to startle inexperienced readers of Blake and of Wordsworth. *The Prelude* follows a rough, naturalistic chronology through Wordsworth's life down to the middle of the journey, where it, like any modern reader, leaves him, in his state of preparation for a further greatness that never came. What is there already, besides the invention of the modern lyric, is a long poem so rich and strange it has defied almost all description.

The Prelude is an autobiographical romance that frequently seeks expression in the sublime mode, which is really an invitation to aesthetic disaster. *The Excursion* is an aesthetic disaster, as Hazlitt, Byron, and many since happily have noted, yet there Wordsworth works within rational limits. *The Prelude* ought to be an outrageous poem, but its peculiar mixture of displaced genre and inappropriate style *works*, because its internalization of quest is the inevitable story for its age. Wordsworth did not have the Promethean temperament, yet he had absolute insight into it, as *The Borderers* already showed. In *The Prelude*, the initial quest phase of the poet-as-Prometheus is diffuse but omnipresent. It determines every movement in the growth of the child's consciousness, always seen as a violation of the established natural order, and it achieves great power in Book VI, when the onset of the French Revolution is associated with the poet's own hidden desires to surmount nature, desires that emerge in the great passages clustered around the Simplon Pass. The Promethean quest fails, in one way in the Alps when chastened by nature, and in another with the series of shocks to the poet's moral being when England wars against the Revolution, and the Revolution betrays itself. The more direct Promethean failure, the poet's actual abandonment of Annette Vallon, is presented only indirectly in the 1805 *Prelude*, and drops out completely from the revised, posthumously published *Prelude* of 1850, the version most readers encounter. In his crisis,

Wordsworth learns the supernatural and superhuman strength of his own imagination, and is able to begin a passage to the mature phase of his quest. But his anxiety for continuity is too strong for him, and he yields to its dark enchantment. The Imagination phase of his quest does not witness the surrender of his Selfhood and the subsequent inauguration of a new dialectic of love, purged of the natural heart, as it is in Blake. Yet he wins a provisional triumph over himself, in Book XII of *The Prelude*, and in the closing stanzas of "Resolution and Independence" and the Great Ode. And the final vision of *The Prelude* is not of a redeemed nature, but of a liberated creativity transforming its creation into the beloved:

> Prophets of Nature, we to them will speak
> A lasting inspiration, sanctified
> By reason, blest by faith: what we have loved
> Others will love, and we will teach them how;
> Instruct them how the mind of man becomes
> A thousand times more beautiful than the earth
> On which he dwells, above this frame of things.

Coleridge, addressed here as the other Prophet of Nature, renounced his own demonic version of the Romantic quest (clearest in the famous triad of "Kubla Khan," *Christabel*, and *The Ancient Mariner*), his wavering Prometheanism early defeated not so much by his Selfhood as by his Urizenic fear of his own imaginative energy. It was a high price for the release he had achieved in his brief phase of exploring the romance of the marvelous, but the loss itself produced a few poems of unique value, the "Dejection" Ode in particular. These poems show how Coleridge preceded Wordsworth in the invention of a new kind of poetry that shows the mind in a dialogue with itself. The motto of this poetry might well be its descendant Stevens's "The mind is the terriblest force in the world, father, / Because, in chief, it, only, can defend / Against itself. At its mercy, we depend / Upon it." Coleridge emphasizes the mercy, Wordsworth the saving terror of the force. Keats and Shelley began with a passion closer to the Prometheus phase of Blake than of Wordsworth or Coleridge. The fullest development of Romantic quest, after Blake's mythology and Wordsworth's exemplary refusal of mythology, is in Keats's *Endymion* and Shelley's *Prometheus Unbound*. In this second generation of Romantic questers the same first phase of Prometheanism appears, as does the second phase of crisis, renounced quest, overcoming of the Selfhood, and final movement toward imaginative love, but the relation of the quest to the world of the reality-principle has changed. In Blake, dream with its ambiguities centers in Beulah, the purgatorial lower paradise of sexuality and benevolent nature. In Wordsworth, dream is rare, and betokens either a prolepsis of the imagination abolishing nature or a state the poet calls "visionary dreariness," in which the immediate power of the mind over outward sense is so great that the ordinary forms of nature seem to have withdrawn. But in Keats and Shelley, a polemical Romanticism matures, and the argument of the dream with reality becomes an equivocal one. Romanticism guessed at a truth our doctors begin to measure; as infants we dream for half the time we are asleep, and as we age we dream less and less while we sleep. The doctors have not yet told us that utterly dreamless sleep directly prophesies or equals death, but it is a familiar Romantic conceit, and may prove to be true. We are our imaginations, and die with them.

Dreams, to Shelley and Keats, are not wish-fulfillments. It is not Keats but Moneta, the passionate and wrong-headed Muse in *The Fall of Hyperion*, who first confounds poets and dreamers as one tribe, and then overreacts by insisting they are totally distinct, and even sheer opposites, antipodes. Freud is again a clear-headed guide; the manifest and latent content of the dream can be distinct, even opposite, but in the poem they come together. The younger Romantics do not seek to render life a dream, but to recover the dream for the health of life. What is called real is too often an exhausted phantasmagoria, and the reality-principle can too easily be debased into a principle of surrender, an accommodation with death-in-life. We return to the observation of Van den Berg, cited earlier; Rousseau and the Romantics discovered not only the alienation between child and adult, but the second birth of psychic maturation or adolescence. Eliot thought that the poet of *Adonais* and *The Triumph of Life* had never "progressed" beyond the ideas and ideals of adolescence, or at least of what Eliot had believed in his *own* adolescence. Every reader can be left to his own judgment of the relative maturity of *Ash Wednesday* and *The Witch of Atlas*, or *The Cocktail Party* and *The Cenci*, and is free to formulate his own dialectics of progression.

The Promethean quest, in Shelley and in Keats, is from the start uneasy about its equivocal ally, nature, and places a deeper trust in dream, for at least the dream itself is not reductive, however we reduce it in our dissections. Perhaps the most remarkable element in the preternatural rapidity of maturation in Keats and Shelley is their early renunciation of the Prometheus phase of the quest, or rather, their dialectical complexity in simultaneously presenting the necessity and the inherent limitation of this phase. In *Alastor*, the poem's entire thrust is at one with the poet-hero's self-destruction; this is the cause of the poem's radical unity, which C. S. Lewis rightly observed as giving a marvelous sense of the poet's being at one with his subject. Yet the poem is also a daimonic shadow in motion; it shows us nature's revenge upon the imagination, and the excessive price of the quest in the poet's alienation from other selves. On a cosmic scale, this is part of the burden of *Prometheus Unbound*, where the hero, who massively represents the bound prophetic power of all men, rises from his icy crucifixion by refusing to continue the cycles of revolution and repression that form an ironic continuity between himself and Jupiter. Demogorgon, the dialectic of history, rises from the abyss and stops history, thus completing in the macrocosmic shadow what Prometheus, by his renunciation, inaugurates in the microcosm of the individual imagination, or the liberating dream taken up into the self. Shelley's poetry after this does not maintain the celebratory strain of Act IV of his lyrical drama. The way again is down and out, to a purgatorial encounter with the Selfhood, but the Selfhood's temptations, for Shelley, are subtle and wavering, and mask themselves in the forms of the ideal. So fused become the ideal and these masks that Shelley, in the last lines he wrote, is in despair of any victory, though it is Shelley's Rousseau and not Shelley himself who actually chants:

> thus on the way
> Mask after mask fell from the countenance
> And form of all; and long before the day
>
> Was old, the joy which waked like heaven's glance
> The sleepers in the oblivious valley, died;
> And some grew weary of the ghastly dance,
>
> And fell, as I have fallen, by the wayside—

For Shelley, Rousseau was not a failed poet, but rather the poet whose influence had resulted in an imaginative revolution, and nearly ended time's bondage. So, Rousseau speaks here not for himself alone, but for his tradition, and necessarily for Coleridge, Wordsworth, and the Promethean Shelley as well, indeed for poetry itself. Yet, rightly or wrongly, the image Shelley leaves with us, at his end, is not this falling-away from quest but the image of the poet forever wakeful amidst the cone of night, illuminating it as the star Lucifer does, fading as the star, becoming more intense as it narrows into the light.

The mazes of romance, in *Endymion*, are so winding that they suggest the contrary to vision, a labyrinthine nature in which all quest must be forlorn. In this realm, nothing narrows to an intensity, and every passionate impulse widens out to a diffuseness, the fate of Endymion's own search for his goddess. In reaction, Keats chastens his own Prometheanism, and attempts the objective epic in *Hyperion*. Hyperion's self-identity is strong but waning fast, and the fragment of the poem's Book III introduces an Apollo whose self-identity is in the act of being born. The temptation to go on with the poem must have been very great, after its magnificent beginnings, but Keats's letters are firm in renouncing it. Keats turns from the enchantments of Identity to the romance-fragment *The Fall of Hyperion*, and engages instead the demon of subjectivity, his own poetic ambitions, as Wordsworth had done before him. Confronted by Moneta, he meets the danger of her challenge not by asserting his own Identity, but by finding his true form in the merged identity of the poethood, in the high function and responsibilities of a Wordsworthian humanism. Though the poem breaks off before it attempts the dialectic of love, it has achieved the quest, for the Muse herself has been transformed by the poet's persistence and integrity. We wish for more, necessarily, but only now begin to understand how much we had received, even in this broken monument.

I have scanted the dialectic of love, in all of these poets. Romantic love, past its own Promethean adolescence, is not the possessive love of the natural heart, which is the quest of Freudian Eros, moving always in a tragic rhythm out from and back to the isolate ego. That is the love Blake explicitly rejected:

> Let us agree to give up Love
> And root up the Infernal Grove
> Then shall we return and see
> The worlds of happy Eternity
>
> Throughout all Eternity
> I forgive you you forgive me.

The Infernal Grove grows thick with virtues, but these are the selfish virtues of the natural heart. Desire for what one lacks becomes a habit of possession, and the Selfhood's jealousy murders the Real Man, the Imagination. All such love is an entropy, and as such Freud understood and accepted it. We become aware of others only as we learn our separation from them, and our ecstasy is a reduction. Is this the human condition, and love only its mitigation?

> To cast off the idiot Questioner who is always questioning,
> But never capable of answering.

Whatever else the love that the full Romantic quest aims at may be, it cannot be a therapy. It must make all things new, and then marry what it has made. Less urgently, it seeks to define itself through the analogue of each man's creative potential. But it learns, through its poets, that it cannot define what it is, but only what it will be. The man prophesied by the Romantics is a central man who is always in the process of becoming his own begetter, and though his major poems perhaps have been written, he as yet has not fleshed out his prophecy, nor proved the final form of his love.

Blake: The Keys to the Gates

Northrop Frye

The criticism of Blake, especially of Blake's prophecies, has developed in direct proportion to the theory of criticism itself. The complaints that Blake was "mad" are no longer of any importance, not because anybody has proved him sane, but because critical theory has realized that madness, like obscenity, is a word with no critical meaning. There are critical standards of coherence and incoherence, but if a poem is coherent in itself the sanity of its author is a matter of interest only to the more naive type of biographer. Those who have assumed that the prophecies are incoherent because they have found them difficult often use the phrase "private symbolism." This is also now a matter of no importance, because in critical theory there is no such thing as private symbolism. There may be allegorical allusions to a poet's private life that can only be interpreted by biographical research, but no set of such allusions can ever form a poetic structure. They can only be isolated signposts, like the allusions to the prototypes of the beautiful youth, dark lady, and rival poet which historians and other speculative critics are persuaded that they see in the Shakespeare sonnets.

When I first embarked on an intensive study of Blake's prophecies, I assumed that my task was to follow the trail blazed by Foster Damon's great book, and take further steps to demonstrate the coherence of those poems. My primary interests, like Damon's were literary, not occult or philosophical or religious. Many other writers had asserted that while the prophecies were doubtless coherent enough intellectually, they would turn out to depend for their coherence on some extra-poetic system of ideas. A student interested in Blake's prophecies as poems would have to begin by rejecting this hypothesis, which contradicts all Blake's views about the primacy of art and the cultural disaster of substituting abstractions for art.

From *Some British Romantics: A Collection of Essays*. © 1966 by the Ohio State University Press. Originally entitled "The Keys to the Gates."

But as I went on, I was puzzled and annoyed by a schematic quality in these prophecies that refused to dissolve into what I then regarded as properly literary forms. There were even diagrams in Blake's own designs which suggested that he himself attached a good deal of value to schematism, and such statements as "I must create a system." Perhaps, then, these critics I had begun by rejecting were right after all: perhaps Blake was not opposed to abstraction but only to other people's abstractions, and was really interested merely in expounding some conceptual system or other in an oblique and allegorical way. In any event, the schematic, diagrammatic quality of Blake's thought was there, and would not go away or turn into anything else. Yeats had recognized it; Damon had recognized it; I had to recognize it. Like Shelley, Blake expressed an abhorrence of didactic poetry but continued to write it.

This problem began to solve itself as soon as I realized that poetic thought is inherently and necessarily schematic. Blake soon led me, in my search for poetic analogues, to Dante and Milton, and it was clear that the schematic cosmologies of Dante and Milton, however they got into Dante and Milton, were, once they got there, poetic constructs, examples of the way poets think, and not foreign bodies of knowledge. If the prophecies are normal poems, or at least a normal expression of poetic genius, and if Blake nevertheless meant to teach some system by them, that system could only be something connected with the principles of poetic thought. Blake's "message," then, is not simply *his* message, nor is it an extra-literary message. What he is trying to say is what he thinks poetry is trying to say: the imaginative content implied by the existence of an imaginative form of language. I finished my book in the full conviction that learning to read Blake was a step, and for me a necessary step, in learning to read poetry, and to write criticism. For if poetic thought is inherently schematic, criticism must be so too. I began to notice that as soon as a critic confined himself to talking seriously about literature, his criticism tightened up and took on a systematic, even a schematic, form.

The nature of poetic "truth" was discussed by Aristotle in connection with action. As compared with the historian, the poet makes no specific or particular statements: he gives the typical, recurring, or universal event, and is not to be judged by the standards of truth that we apply to specific statements. Poetry, then, does not state historical truth, but contains it: it sets forth what we may call the *myth* of history, the kind of thing that happens. History itself is designed to record events, or, as we may say, to provide a primary verbal imitation of events. But it also, unconsciously perhaps, illustrates and provides examples for the poetic vision. Hence we feel that *Lear* or *Macbeth* or *Oedipus Rex*, although they deal almost entirely with legend rather than actual history, contain infinite reserves of historical wisdom and insight. Thus poetry is "something more philosophical" than history.

This last observation of Aristotle's has been of little use to critics except as a means of annoying historians, and it is difficult to see in what sense

Anacreon is more philosophical than Thucydides. The statement is best interpreted, as it was by Renaissance critics, schematically, following a diagram in which poetry is intermediate between history and philosophy, pure example and pure precept. It follows that poetry must have a relation to thought paralleling its relation to action. The poet does not think in the sense of producing concepts, ideas or propositions, which are specific predications to be judged by their truth or falsehood. As he produces the mythical structures of history, so he produces the mythical structures of thought, the conceptual frameworks that enter into and inform the philosophies contemporary with him. And just as we feel that the great tragedy, if not historical, yet contains an infinity of the kind of meaning that actual history illustrates, so we feel that great "philosophical" poetry, if not actually philosophical, contains an infinity of the kind of meaning that discursive writing illustrates. This sense of the infinite treasures of thought latent in poetry is eloquently expressed by several Elizabethan critics, and there is perhaps no modern poet who suggests the same kind of intellectual richness so immediately as Blake does.

Blake, in fact, gives us so good an introduction to the nature and structure of poetic thought that, if one has any interest in the subject at all, one can hardly avoid exploiting him. There are at least three reasons why he is uniquely useful for this purpose. One is that his prophecies are works of philosophical poetry which give us practically nothing at all unless we are willing to grapple with the kind of poetic thought that they express. Another is that Blake also wrote such haunting and lucid lyrics, of which we can at first say little except that they seem to belong in the center of our literary experience. We may not know why they are in the center, and some readers would rather not know; but for the saving remnant who do want to know, there are the prophecies to help us understand. The third reason is Blake's quality as an illustrator of other poets. If a person of considerable literary experience is reading a poem he is familiar with, it is easy for him to fall—in fact it is very difficult for him not to fall—into a passive habit of not really reading the poem, but merely of spotting the critical clichés he is accustomed to associate with it. Thus, if he is reading Gray's "Ode on the Death of a Favorite Cat," and sees the goldfish described as "angel forms," "genii of the stream," and with "scaly armour," his stock response will start murmuring: "Gray means fish, of course, but he is saying so in terms of eighteenth-century personification, Augustan artificiality, his own peculiar demure humour," and the like. Such a reading entirely obliterates Gray's actual processes of poetic thought and substitutes something in its place that, whatever it is, is certainly not poetry or philosophy, any more than it is history. But if he is reading the poem in the context of Blake's illustrations, Blake will compel him to see the angel forms, the genii of the stream, and the warriors in scaly armour, as well as the fish, in such a way as to make the unvisualized clichés of professional reading impossible, and to bring the metaphorical structure of the poem clearly into view.

I am suggesting that no one can read Blake seriously and sympathetically without feeling that the keys to poetic thought are in him, and what follows attempts to explain how a documentation of such a feeling would proceed. I make no claim that I am saying anything here that I have not said before, though I may be saying it in less compass.

EASTERN GATE: TWOFOLD VISION

The structure of metaphors and imagery that informed poetry, through the Middle Ages and the Renaissance, arranged reality on four levels. On top was heaven, the place of the presence of God: below it was the proper level of human nature, represented by the stories of the Garden of Eden and the Golden Age; below that was the physical world, theologically fallen, which man is in but not of: and at the bottom was the world of sin, death and corruption. This was a deeply conservative view of reality in which man, in fallen nature, was confronted with a moral dialectic that either lowered him into sin or raised him to his proper level. The raising media included education, virtue, and obedience to law. In the Middle Ages, this construct was closely linked with similar constructs in theology and science. These links weakened after the sixteenth century and eventually disappeared, leaving the construct to survive only in poetry, and, even there, increasingly by inertia. It is still present in Pope's *Essay on Man*, but accompanied with a growing emphasis on the limitation of poetic objectives. This limitation means, among other things, that mythopoeic literature, which demands a clear and explicit framework of imagery, is in the age of Pope and Swift largely confined to parody.

As the eighteenth century proceeded, the imaginative climate began to change, and we can see poets trying to move toward a less conservative structure of imagery. This became a crucial problem when the French Revolution confronted the Romantic poets. No major poet in the past had been really challenged by a revolutionary situation except Milton, and even Milton had reverted to the traditional structure for *Paradise Lost*. Blake was not only older than Wordsworth and Coleridge, but more consistently revolutionary in his attitude: again, unlike most English writers of the period, he saw the American Revolution as an event of the same kind as its French successor. He was, therefore, the first English poet to work out the revolutionary structure of imagery that continues through Romantic poetry and thought to our own time.

At the center of Blake's thought are the two conceptions of innocence and experience, "the two contrary states of the human soul." Innocence is characteristic of the child, experience of the adult. In innocence, there are two factors. One is an assumption that the world was made for the benefit of human beings, has a human shape and a human meaning, and is a world in which providence, protection, communication with other beings, including animals, and, in general, "mercy, pity, peace and love," have a genuine function. The other is ignorance of the fact that the world is not like this. As the child grows up, his conscious mind accepts "experience," or reality without any human shape or meaning, and his childhood innocent vision, having nowhere else to go, is driven underground into what we should call the subconscious, where it takes an essentially sexual form. The original innocent vision becomes a melancholy dream of how man once possessed a happy garden, but lost it forever, though he may regain it after he dies. The following diagram illustrates the process as well as the interconnection of *Songs of Innocence and Experience*, *The Marriage of Heaven and Hell*, and the early political prophecies *The French Revolution* and *America* in Blake's thought:

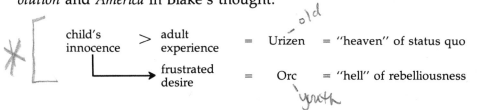

In place of the old construct, therefore, in which man regains his happy garden home by doing his duty and obeying the law, we have an uneasy revolutionary conception of conscious values and standards of reality sitting on top of a volcano of thwarted and mainly sexual energy. This construct has two aspects, individual or psychological, and social or political. Politically, it represents an ascendant class threatened by the growing body of those excluded from social benefits, until the latter are strong enough to overturn society. Psychologically, it represents a conscious ego threatened by a sexually-rooted desire. Thus the mythical structure that informs both the psychology of Freud and the political doctrines of Marx is present in *The Marriage of Heaven and Hell*, which gives us both aspects of the Romantic movement: the reaction to political revolution and the manifesto of feeling and desire as opposed to the domination of reason.

In the associations that Blake makes with Urizen and Orc, Urizen is an old man and Orc a youth: Urizen has the counterrevolutionary color white and Orc is a revolutionary red. Urizen is therefore associated with sterile winter, bleaching bones, and clouds; Orc with summer, blood, and the sun. The colors white and red suggest the bread and wine of a final harvest and vintage, prophesied in the fourteenth chapter of Revelation. Orc is "underneath" Urizen, and underneath the white cliffs of Albion on the map are the "vineyards of red France" in the throes of revolution. In a map of Palestine, the kingdom of Israel, whose other name, Jacob, means usurper, sits on top of Edom, the kingdom of the red and hairy Esau, the rightful heir. Isaiah's vision of a Messiah appearing in Edom with his body soaked in blood from "treading the winepress" of war, haunts nearly all Blake's prophecies. There are many other associations; perhaps we may derive the most important from the following passage in *America* [Blake's punctuation is retained]:

The terror answered: I am Orc, wreath'd round the accursed
	tree:
The times are ended: shadows pass the morning gins to break;
The fiery joy, that Urizen perverted to ten commands,
What night he led the starry hosts thro' the wide wilderness:
That stony law I stamp to dust: and scatter religion abroad
To the four winds as a torn book, & none shall gather the
	leaves:
But they shall rot on desart sands, & consume in bottomless
	deeps:
To make the desarts blossom, & the deeps shrink to their
	fountains,
And to renew the fiery joy, and burst the stony roof.
That pale religious letchery, seeking Virginity,
May find it in a harlot, and in coarse-clad honesty
The undefil'd tho' ravish'd in her cradle night and morn:
For every thing that lives is holy, life delights in life:
Because the soul of sweet delight can never be defil'd.
Fires inwrap the earthly globe, yet man is not consumd:
Amidst the lustful fires he walks: his feet become like brass,
His knees and thighs like silver, & his breast and head like
	gold.

At various times in history, there has been a political revolution sym-bolized by the birth or rebirth of Orc, the "terrible boy": each one, however, has eventually subsided into the same Urizenic form as its predecessor. Orc is the human protest of energy and desire, the impulse to freedom and to sexual love. Urizen is the "reality principle," the belief that knowledge of what is real comes from outside the human body. If we believe that reality is what we bring into existence through an act of creation, then we are free to build up our own civilization and abolish the anomalies and injustices that hamper its growth; but if we believe that reality is primarily what is "out there," then we are condemned, in Marx's phrase, to study the world and never to change it. And the world that we study in this way we are compelled to see in the distorted perspective of the human body with its five cramped senses, not our powers of perception as they are developed and expanded by the arts. Man in his present state is so con-structed that all he can see outside him is the world under the law. He may believe that gods or angels or devils or fairies or ghosts are also "out there," but he cannot see these things: he can see only the human and the subhuman, moving in established and predictable patterns. The basis of this vision of reality is the world of the heavenly bodies, circling around automatically and out of reach.

One early Orc rebellion was the Exodus from Egypt, where Orc is represented by a pillar of fire (the "fiery joy") and Urizen by a pillar of cloud, or what *Finnegans Wake* calls "Delude of Israel." Orc was a human society of twelve (actually thirteen) tribes; Urizen, a legal mechanism symbolized by the twelvefold Zodiac with its captive sun, which is why Urizen is said to have "led the starry hosts" through the wilderness. The eventual victory of Urizen was marked by the establishing of Aaron's priesthood (the twelve stones in his breastplate symbolized the Zodiac as well as the tribes, according to Josephus), and by the negative moral law of the Decalogue, the moral law being the human imitation of the automatism of natural law. The final triumph of Urizen was symbolized by the hanging of the brazen serpent (Orc) on the pole, a form of the "accursed tree," and recalling the earlier association of tree and serpent with the exile of Adam into a wilderness, as well as anticipating the Crucifixion.

Jesus was another Orc figure, gathering twelve followers and starting a new civilization. Christian civilization, like its predecessors, assumed the Urizenic form that it presented so clearly in Blake's own time. This historical perversion of Christianity is studied in *Europe*, where Enitharmon, the Queen of Heaven, summons up twelve starry children, along with Orc as the captive sun, to reimpose the cult of external reality, or what Blake calls natural religion, on Christendom. With the Resurrection, traditionally symbolized by a red cross on a white ground, Jesus made a definitive step into reality: the revolutionary apocalypse Blake hopes for in his day is a second coming or mass resurrection, which is why resurrection imagery is prominently displayed in *America*. Now, at the end of European civilization, comes another rebellion of Orc in America, bearing on its various banners a tree, a serpent, and thirteen red and white stripes. The spread of this rebellion to Europe itself is a sign that bigger things are on the way.

The Israelites ended their revolt in the desert of the moral law: now it is time to reverse the movement, to enter the Promised Land, the original Eden, which is to Israel what Atlantis is to Britain and America. The Promised Land is not a different place from the desert, but the desert itself transformed (Blake's imagery comes partly from Isa. 35, a chapter he alludes to in *The Marriage of Heaven and Hell*). The "deeps shrink to their fountains" because in the apocalypse there is no more sea: dead water is transformed to living water (as in Ezekiel's vision, Ezek. 47:8). The spiritual body of risen man is sexually free, an aspect symbolized by the "lustful fires" in which he walks. Man under the law is sexually in a prison of heat without light, a volcano: in the resurrection he is unhurt by flames, like the three Hebrews in Nebuchadnezzar's furnace who were seen walking with the son of God. According to *The Marriage of Heaven and Hell*, Jesus became Jehovah after his death, and Jehovah, not Satan, is the one who dwells in flaming fire. The risen man, then, is the genuine form of the metallic statue of Nebuchadnezzar's dream, without the feet of clay that made that statue an image of tyranny and the cycle of history.

The Resurrection rolled the stone away covering the tomb ("burst the stony roof"). The stone that covers the tomb of man under the law is the vast arch of the sky, which we see as a concave "vault of paved heaven" (a phrase in the early "Mad Song") because we are looking at it from under the "stony roof" of the skull. The risen body would be more like the shape of one of Blake's Last Judgment paintings, with an "opened centre" or radiance of light on top, in the place which is the true location of heaven. Finally, the entire Bible or revelation of the divine in and to man can be read either as the charter of human freedom or as a code of restrictive and negative moral commands. Orc proposes to use Urizen's version of the holy book as fertilizer to help make the desert blossom: what he would do, in other words, is to internalize the law, transform it from arbitrary commands to the inner discipline of the free spirit.

NORTHERN GATE: SINGLE VISION

The optimistic revolutionary construct set up in Blake's early prophecies is found again in Shelley, whose Prometheus and Jupiter correspond to Orc and Urizen. But in later Romanticism, it quickly turns pessimistic and once more conservative, notably in Schopenhauer, where the world as idea, the world of genuine humanity, sits on top of a dark, threatening, and immensely powerful world as will. A similar construct is in Darwin and Huxley, where the ethical creation of human society maintains itself precariously against the evolutionary force below it. In Freud, civilization is essentially an anxiety structure, where the "reality principle," Blake's Urizen, must maintain its ascendancy somehow over the nihilistic upthrusts of desire. It may permit a certain amount of expression to the "pleasure principle," but not to the extent of being taken over by it. And in Blake, if every revolt of Orc in history has been "perverted to ten commands," the inference seems to be that history exhibits only a gloomy series of cycles, beginning in hope and inevitably ending in renewed tyranny. In Blake's later prophecies, we do find this Spenglerian view of history, with a good many of Spengler's symbols attached to it.

The cyclical movement of history is summarized by Blake in four stages. The first stage is the revolutionary birth of Orc; the second, the transfer of power from Orc to Urizen at the height of Orc's powers, accompanied by the binding or imprisoning of Orc; the third, the consolidating of "natural religion" or the sense of reality as out there, symbolized by Urizen exploring his dens; the fourth, a collapse and chaos symbolized by the crucifixion of Orc, the hanging of the serpent on the dead tree. This fourth stage is the one that Blake sees his own age entering, after the triumph of natural religion or "Deism" in the decades following Newton and Locke. It is an age characterized by mass wars (Isaiah's treading of the winepress), by technology and complex machinery, by tyranny and "empire" (imperialism being the demonic enemy of culture), and by unimaginative art, especially in architecture. The central symbol of this final phase is the labyrinthine desert in which the Mosaic exodus ended. Jesus spent forty days in the desert, according to Mark, "with the wild beasts": the passage from empire to ruin, from the phase of the tyrant to the phase of the wild beast, is symbolized in the story of Nebuchadnezzar, whose metamorphosis is illustrated at the end of *The Marriage of Heaven and Hell*. The figure of Ijim in *Tiriel* has a parallel significance.

As Blake's symbolism becomes more concentrated, he tends to generalize the whole cycle in the conception of "Druidism." The Druids, according to Blake's authorities, worshipped the tree and the serpent, the Druid temple of Avebury, illustrated on the last plate of *Jerusalem*, being serpent-shaped; and they went in for orgies of human sacrifice which illustrate, even more clearly than warfare, the fact that the suppression or perversion of the sexual impulse ends in a death wish (I am not reading modern conceptions into Blake here, but following Blake's own symbolism). This "Druid" imagery is illustrated in the following passage from *Europe*, describing the reaction of the tyrannical "King" or guardian angel of the reactionary Albion and his councillors to the American revolution and kindred portents of apocalyptic disaffection:

> In thoughts perturb'd they rose from the bright ruins silent
>   following
> The fiery King, who sought his ancient temple serpent-form'd
> That stretches out its shady length along the Island white.
> Round him roll'd his clouds of war; silent the Angel went,
> Along the infinite shores of Thames to golden Verulam.
> There stand the venerable porches that high-towering rear
> Their oak-surrounded pillars, form'd of massy stones, uncut
> With tool: stones precious: such eternal in the heavens,
> Of colours twelve, few known on earth, give light in the opake,
> Plac'd in the order of the stars, when the five senses whelm'd
> In deluge o'er the earth-born man: then turn'd the fluxile eyes
> Into two stationary orbs, concentrating all things.
> The ever-varying spiral ascents to the heavens of heavens
> Were bended downward, and the nostrils golden gates shut,
> Turn'd outward barr'd and petrify'd against the infinite . . .
>
> Now arriv'd the ancient Guardian at the southern porch.
> That planted thick with trees of blackest leaf, & in a vale
> Obscure, inclos'd the Stone of Night; oblique it stood, o'erhung
> With purple flowers and berries red: image of that sweet south
> Once open to the heavens and elevated on the human neck,
> Now overgrown with hair and cover'd with a stony roof:
> Downward 'tis sunk beneath th' attractive north, that round the
>   feet
> A raging whirlpool draws the dizzy enquirer to his grave.

It is an intricate passage, but it all makes sense. The serpent temple of Avebury is identified with the white-cliffed Albion in its final Druid phase. It is centered at Verulam, which, as the site of a Roman camp, a "Gothic" cathedral, and the baronial title of Bacon, takes in the whole cycle of British civilization. As we approach the temple, it appears to be a Stonehenge-like circle of twelve precious stones, "plac'd in the order of the stars," or symbolizing the Zodiac. The imagery recalls the similar decadence of Israel in the desert: the twelve Zodiacal gems of Aaron's breastplate have been mentioned, and the Israelites also built megalithic monuments on which they were forbidden to use iron (Jos. 8:31), hence "uncut with tool," iron being in Blake the symbol of Los the blacksmith, the builder of the true city of gems (Isa. 54:16).

The central form of Druid architecture is the trilithic cromlech or dolmen, the arch of three stones. According to Blake, the two uprights of this arch symbolize the two aspects of creative power, strength and beauty, or sublimity and pathos, as he calls them in the *Descriptive Catalogue*, the horizontal stone being the dominant Urizenic reason. Human society presents this arch in the form of an "Elect" class tyrannizing over the "Reprobate," the unfashionable artists and prophets who embody human sublimity, and the "Redeemed," the gentler souls who are in the company of the beautiful and pathetic. This trilithic structure reappears in such later militaristic monuments as the Arch of Titus: in its "Druid" form, it is illustrated with great power in *Milton*, Plate 6, and *Jerusalem*, Plate 70. In the former, the balancing rock in front may represent the "Stone of Night" in the above passage. To pass under this arch is to be subjugated, in a fairly literal sense, to what is, according to the *Descriptive Catalogue*, both the human reason and the "incapability of intellect," as intellect in Blake is always associated with the creative and imaginative. Another form of tyrannical architecture characteristic of a degenerate civilization is the pyramid, representing the volcano or imprisoning mountain under which Orc lies. Blake connects the pyramids with the servitude of the Israelites among the brick-kilns and the epithet "furnace of iron" (1 Kings 8:51) applied to Egypt in the Bible. The association of pyramids and fire is as old as Plato's pun on the word πύρ.

The temple of Verulam is a monument to the fall of man, in Blake the same event as the deluge and the creation of the world in its present "out there" form. This form is that of the law, the basis of which is revolution in its mechanical sense of revolving wheels, the symbol of which is the *ouroboros*, the serpent with its tail in its mouth (indicated in a passage omitted above). We see the world from individual "opake" centers, instead of being identified with a universal Man who is also God, who created what we see as alien to us, and who would consequently see his world from the circumference instead of the center, the perspective reinstated in man by the arts. Such a God-Man would be "full of eyes," like the creatures of Ezekiel's vision, and by an unexpected but quite logical extension of the symbolism, Blake makes him full of noses too. Burning meat to gods on altars, after all, does assume that gods have circumferential noses.

The "Stone of Night," the opposite of the "lively stones" (1 Pet. 2:5) of the genuine temple, is an image of the human head, the phrase "stony roof" being repeated from the passage in *America* quoted above. It is in the south because the south is the zenith, the place of the sun in full strength in Blake's symbolism. Now it is covered with purple flowers and red berries, probably of the nightshade: the colors are those of the dying god, which is what Orc (usually Luvah in this context) comes to be in Blake's later poems. The Stone of Night has fallen like a meteor through the bottom or nadir of existence, represented by the north, and now has the same relation to its original that a gravestone has to a living body. We may compare the "grave-plot" that Thel reached when she passed under the "northern bar," and the black coffin which is the body of the chimney sweep (and the enslaved Negro, who also belongs in the "southern clime"). Blake's imagery of the north combines the magnetic needle and the legend of the northern maelstrom, the latter supplying a demonic parody of the ascending spiral image on the altar.

From the perspective of single vision, then, our original diagram of buried innocence trying to push its way into experience has to be completed by the death in which all life, individual or historical, ends. Death in Blake's symbolism is Satan, the "limit of Opacity," reduction to inorganic matter, who operates in the living man as a death wish or "accuser" of sin. His source in the outer world is the sky, Satan being the starry dragon of Rev. 12:4. Blake identifies this dragon with the Covering Cherub of Ezek. 28, and the Covering Cherub again with the angel trying to keep us out of the Garden of Eden. Thus the sky is, first, the outward illusion of reality that keeps us out of our proper home; second, the macrocosmic Stone of Night, the rock on top of man's tomb designed to prevent his resurrection; and third, the circumference of what Blake calls the "Mundane Shell," the world as it appears to the embryonic and unborn imagination. Thus:

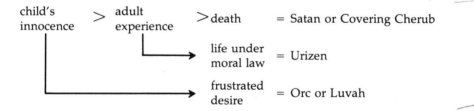

Ordinary human life, symbolized in Blake first by "Adam" and later by "Reuben," oscillates between the two submerged states.

The conception of Druidism in Blake, then, is a conception of human energy and desire continuously martyred by the tyranny of human reason, or superstition. The phrase "dying god" that we have used for Luvah suggests Frazer, and Blake's Druid symbolism has some remarkable anticipations of Frazer's *Golden Bough* complex, including the mistletoe and the oak. The anticipations even extend to Frazer's own unconscious symbolism: the colors of the three states above are, reading up, red, white, and black; and Frazer's book ends with the remark that the web of human thought has been woven of these three colors, though the status of the white or scientific one in Blake is very different. The following passage from *Jerusalem* 66 illustrates Blake's handling of sacrificial symbolism:

The Daughters of Albion clothed in garments of needle work
Strip them off from their shoulders and bosoms, they lay aside
Their garments, they sit naked upon the Stone of trial.
The knife of flint passes over the howling Victim: his blood
Gushes & stains the fair side of the fair Daughters of Albion.
They put aside his curls: they divide his seven locks upon
His forehead: they bind his forehead with thorns of iron,
They put into hand a reed, they mock, Saying: Behold
The King of Canaan, whose are seven hundred chariots of iron!
They take off his vesture whole with their Knives of flint:
But they cut asunder his inner garments: searching with
Their cruel fingers for his heart, & there they enter in pomp,
In many tears: & there they erect a temple & an altar:
They pour cold water on his brain in front, to cause
Lids to grow over his eyes in veils of tears: and caverns
To freeze over his nostrils, while they feed his tongue from
    cups
And dishes of painted clay.

The imagery combines the mockery and passion of Jesus with features from
Aztec sacrifices, as Blake realizes that the two widely separated rituals mean
essentially the same thing. In the Mexican rites, the "vesture whole" is the
skin, not the garment, and the heart is extracted from the body, not merely
pierced by a spear as in the Passion. As the passage goes on, the victim
expands from an individual body into a country: that is, he is beginning
to embody not merely the dying god, but the original universal Man, Albion, whose present dead body is England. The veils and caverns are
religious images derived from analogies between the human body and the
landscape. Serpent worship is for Blake a perennial feature of this kind of
superstition, and the victim is fed from dishes of clay partly because, as
Blake says in *The Everlasting Gospel*, "dust & Clay is the Serpent's meat."
An early Biblical dying-god figure is that of Sisera, the King of Canaan,
whose murder at the hands of Jael suggests the nailing down of Jesus and
Prometheus; and the reference to "needle work" in the first line also comes
from Deborah's war song. The role given to the Daughters of Albion shows
how clearly Blake associates the ritual of sacrifice, many features of which
are repeated in judicial executions, with a perversion of the erotic instinct;
and in fact Blake is clearer than Frazer about the role of the "white goddess"
in the dying god cult, the Cybele who decrees the death of Attis.

SOUTHERN GATE: THREEFOLD VISION

The conception of a cycle common to individual and to historical life is the
basis of the symbolism of several modern poets, including Yeats, Joyce in
Finnegans Wake, and Graves in *The White Goddess*. In its modern forms, it
usually revolves around a female figure. *The Marriage of Heaven and Hell*
prophesies that eventually the bound Orc will be set free and will destroy

the present world in a "consummation," which means both burning up and the climax of a marriage. When the marriage is accomplished "by an improvement of sensual enjoyment," the world of form and reason will be possessed by energy and desire, and will be their "outward bound or circumference" instead of a separate and therefore tyrannizing principle. One would think then that a female figure would be more appropriate for the symbolism of the world of form than the aged and male Urizen.

In traditional Christian symbolism, God the Creator is symbolically male, and all human souls, whether of men or of women, are creatures, and therefore symbolically female. In Blake, the real man is creating man; hence all human beings, men or women, are symbolically male. The symbolic female in Blake is what we call nature, and has four relations to humanity, depending on the quality of the vision. In the world of death, or Satan, which Blake calls Ulro, the human body is completely absorbed in the body of nature—a "dark Hermaphrodite," as Blake says in "The Gates of Paradise." In the ordinary world of experience, which Blake calls Generation, the relation of humanity to nature is that of subject to object. In the usually frustrated and suppressed world of sexual desire, which Blake calls Beulah, the relation is that of lover to beloved, and in the purely imaginative or creative state, called Eden, the relation is that of creator to creature. In the first two worlds, nature is a remote and tantalizing "female will"; in the last two she is an "emanation." Human women are associated with this female nature only when in their behavior they dramatize its characteristics. The relations between man and nature in the individual and historical cycle are different, and are summarized in "The Mental Traveller," a poem as closely related to the cyclical symbolism of twentieth-century poetry as Keats's "La Belle Dame Sans Merci" is to pre-Raphaelite poetry.

"The Mental Traveller" traces the life of a "Boy" from infancy through manhood to death and rebirth. This Boy represents humanity, and consequently the cycle he goes through can be read either individually and psychologically, or socially and historically. The latter reading is easier, and closer to the center of gravity of what Blake is talking about. The poem traces a cycle, but the cycle differs from that of the single vision in that the emphasis is thrown on rebirth and return instead of on death. A female principle, nature, cycles in contrary motion against the Boy, growing young as he grows old and vice versa, and producing four phases that we may call son and mother, husband and wife, father and daughter, ghost (Blake's "spectre") and ghostly bride (Blake's "emanation"). Having set them down, we next observe that not one of these relations is genuine: the mother is not really a mother, nor the daughter really a daughter, and similarly with the other states. The "Woman Old," the nurse who takes charge of the Boy, is Mother Nature, whom Blake calls Tirzah, and who ensures that everyone enters this world in the mutilated and imprisoned form of the physical body. The sacrifice of the dying god repeats this symbolism, which is why the birth of the Boy also contains the symbols of the Passion (we should compare this part of "The Mental Traveller" with the end of *Jerusalem* 67).

As the Boy grows up, he subdues a part of nature to his will, which thereupon becomes his mistress: a stage represented elsewhere in the Preludium to *America*. As the cycle completes what Yeats would call its first gyre, we reach the opposite pole of a "Female Babe" whom, like the newborn Boy, no one dares touch. This female represents the "emanation" or accumulated form of what the Boy has created in his life. If she were a real daughter and not a changeling, she would be the Boy's own permanent creation, as Jerusalem is the daughter of Albion, "a City, yet a Woman"; and with the appearance of such a permanent creation, the cycle of nature would come to an end. But in this world all creative achievements are inherited by someone else and are lost to their creator. This failure to take possession of one's own deepest experience is the theme of "The Crystal Cabinet" (by comparing the imagery of this latter poem with *Jerusalem* 70 we discover that the Female Babe's name, in this context, is Rahab). The Boy, now an old man at the point of death, acquires, like the aged king David, another "maiden" to keep his body warm on his deathbed. He is now in the desert or wilderness, which symbolizes the end of a cycle, and his maiden is Lilith, the bride of the desert, whom Blake elsewhere calls the Shadowy Female. The Boy as an old man is in an "alastor" relation to her: he ought to be still making the kind of creative effort that produced the Female Babe, but instead he keeps seeking his "emanation" or created form outside himself, until eventually the desert is partially renewed by his efforts, he comes again into the place of seed, and the cycle starts once more.

A greatly abbreviated account of the same cycle, in a more purely historical context, is in the "Argument" of *The Marriage of Heaven and Hell*. Here we start with Rintrah, the prophet in the desert, the Moses or Elijah or John the Baptist, who announces a new era of history; then we follow the historical cycle as it makes the desert blossom and produces the honey of the Promised Land. We notice how, as in the time of Moses, water springs up in the desert and how Orc's "red clay" puts life on the white bones of Urizen. Eventually the new society becomes decadent and tyrannical, forcing the prophet out into the desert once more to begin another cycle.

The poem called "The Gates of Paradise," based on a series of illustrations reproduced in the standard edition of Blake, describes the same cycle in slightly different and more individualized terms. Here conception in the womb, the mutilation of birth which produces the "mother's grief," is symbolized by the caterpillar and by the mandrake. The mandrake is traditionally an aphrodisiac, a plant with male and female forms, an opiate, the seed of hanged men, a "man-dragon" that shrieks when uprooted (i.e., born), and recalls the frustrated sunflower of the *Songs of Experience*. The association of the mandrake with the mother in Gen. 30:14 is the main reason why Blake uses "Reuben" instead of "Adam" as the symbol of ordinary man in *Jerusalem*. The embryo then takes on the substance of the four elements and the four humors that traditionally correspond to them, of which "Earth's Melancholy" is the dominant one. Then the infant is born and grows into an aggressive adolescent, like the Boy in "The Mental Traveller" binding nature down for his delight. This attitude divides nature into a part that is possessed and a part that eludes, and the separation indicates that the boy in this poem also is bound to the cyclical movement. The youth then collides with Urizen, the spear in the revolutionary left hand being opposed to the sword of established order in the right. The caption of this emblem, "My Son! My Son!", refers to Absalom's revolt against David. Orc is not the son of Urizen, but Absalom, hung on a tree (traditionally by his golden hair, like the mistletoe: cf. *The Book of Ahania*, II, 9) is another dying god or Druid victim.

The other plates are not difficult to interpret: they represent the frustration of desire, the reaction into despair, and the growing of the youthful and rebellious Orc into a wing-clipping Urizen again. Finally the hero, like the early Tiriel and like the Boy of "The Mental Traveller" in his old age, becomes a wandering pilgrim making his way, like the old man in the Pardoner's Tale, toward his own death. He enters "Death's Door," the lower half of a design from Blair's *Grave* omitting the resurrection theme in the upper half, and is once more identified with Mother Nature, with a caption quoted from Job 17:14. The Prologue asks us why we worship this dreary womb-to-tomb treadmill as God—that is, why we think of God as a sky-god of automatic order, when this sky-god is really Satan, the corpse of God. The Epilogue returns to the same attack, and concludes by calling Satan "The lost traveller's Dream under the Hill." Apart from the general theme of the dreaming traveller which is common to this poem and to "The Mental Traveller" (where the "mental" travelling is done by the poet and reader, not the hero), there is a more specific allusion to the passage in *The Pilgrim's Progress* where Christian, after falling asleep under Hill Difficulty and losing his roll, is forced to retrace his steps like the Israelites in the desert, to whom Bunyan explicitly refers.

The passage from death to rebirth is represented in Blake's symbolism by Tharmas, the power of renewing life. The ability of the individual to renew his life is resurrection, and the resurrection is a break with the cycle, but in ordinary life such a renewal takes place only in the group or species, and within the cycle. Tharmas is symbolized by the sea, the end and the beginning of life. As the original fall of man was also the deluge, we are in this world symbolically under water, our true home being Atlantis, or the Red Sea, which the Israelites found to be dry land. Tharmas and Orc are the strength and beauty, the sublime and the pathetic, the uprights of the Druid trilithon already mentioned, with Urizen, the anti-intellectual "reason," connecting them. Thus:

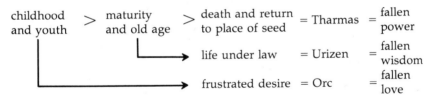

WESTERN GATE: FOURFOLD VISION

In *The Marriage of Heaven and Hell*, Blake presents the revolutionary vision of man as a self-centered anxious ego sitting on top of a rebellious desire, and he associates the emancipating of desire with the end of the world as we know it. The Proverbs of Hell say: "He who desires but acts not, breeds pestilence." Putting desire into action does not lead to anarchy, for the fires of Orc are "thought-creating": what it does lead to is an apocalypse in which "the whole creation will be consumed and appear infinite and holy, whereas it now appears finite & corrupt." But when we read other works of Blake, we begin to wonder if this "Voice of the Devil" tells the whole story. Blake certainly means what he says in *The Marriage of Heaven and Hell*, but that work is a satire, deriving its norms from other conceptions. As we read further in Blake, it becomes clear that the emancipating of desire, for him, is not the cause but the effect of the purging of reality. There was some political disillusionment as Blake proceeded—the perversion of the French Revolution into Napoleonic imperialism, the strength of the reactionary power in Britain, the continued ascendancy of the slave-owners in America, and a growing feeling that Voltaire and Rousseau were reactionaries and not revolutionaries were the main elements in it—but although this leads to some changes in emphasis in later poems, there is no evidence that he was ever really confused about the difference between the apocalyptic and the historical versions of reality.

Blake dislikes any terminology which implies that there are two perceivers in man, such as a soul and a body, which perceive different worlds. There is only one world, but there are two kinds of things to be done with it. There is, first, what Blake calls the natural vision, which assumes that the objective world is essentially independent of man. This vision becomes increasingly hypnotized by the automatic order and tantalizing remoteness of nature, creates gods in the image of its mindless mechanism, and rationalizes all evils and injustices of existence under some such formula as "Whatever is, is right." In extreme forms, this alienating vision becomes the reflection of the death wish in the soul, and develops annihilation wars like those of Blake's own time. Then there is the human vision, which takes the objective world to be the "starry floor," the bottom of reality, its permanence being important only as a stable basis for human creation. The goal of the human vision is "Religion, or Civilized Life such as it is in the Christian Church." This is a life of pure creation, such as is ascribed in Christianity to God, and which for Blake would participate in the infinite and eternal perspective of God. We note that Blake, like Kierkegaard, leads us toward an "either/or" dilemma, but that his terms are the reverse of Kierkegaard's. It is the aesthetic element for Blake which moves in the sphere of existential freedom; it is the ethical element which is the spectator, under the bondage of the law and the knowledge of good and evil.

We begin, then, with the view of an orthodox or moral "good," founded on an acceptance of the world out there, contrasted with the submerged "evil" desires of man to live in a world that makes more human sense. This vision of life turns out to be, when examined, a cyclical vision, completed by the more elaborate cycles just examined. But in addition to the cyclical vision there is also a dialectic, a separating-out of the two opposing human and natural visions. The categories of these visions are not moral good and evil, but life and death, one producing the real heaven of creation and the other the real hell of torture and tyranny. We have met one pole of this dialectic already in the conception of Satan, or death, as the only possible goal of all human effort from one point of view. The other pole is the impulse to transform the world into a human and imaginative form, the impulse that creates all art, all genuine religion, all culture and civilization. This impulse is personified by Blake as Los, the spirit of prophecy and creativity, and it is Los, not Orc, who is the hero of Blake's prophecies. Los derives, not from the suppressed desires of the individual child, but from a deeper creative impulse alluded to in Biblical myths about the unfallen state. These myths tell us that man's original state was not primitive, or derived from nature at all, but civilized, in the environment of a garden and a city. This unfallen state is, so to speak, the previous tree of which contemporary man is the seed, and the form he is attempting to recreate. Thus:

unfallen state	>	child's innocence	>	adult experience	= Urizen	= England	= Israel
			→	frustrated desire	= Orc	= France and America	= Edom
			→	creative power	= Los	= Atlantis	= Eden

It seems curious that, especially in the earlier prophecies, Los appears to play a more reactionary and sinister role than Urizen himself. We discover that it is Los, not Urizen, who is the father of Orc; Los, not Urizen, who actively restrains Orc, tying him down under Mount Atlas with the "Chain of Jealousy"; and Los who is the object of Orc's bitter Oedipal resentments. In the Preludium to *America*, he is referred to by his alternative name of Urthona, and there it is he and not Urizen who rivets Orc's "tenfold chains." These chains evidently include an incest taboo, for Orc is copulating with his sister in this Preludium. Evidently, as Blake conceives it, there is a deeply conservative element in the creative spirit that seems to help perpetuate the reign of Urizen. In fact certain functions given to Urizen in earlier prophecies are transferred to Los in later ones. According to William Morris, the joy that the medieval craftsman took in his work was so complete that he was able to accept the tyranny of medieval society: similarly, Blake is able to live in the age of Pitt and Nelson and yet be absorbed in building his palace of art on the "Great Atlantic Mountains," which will be here after the "Sea of Time and Space" above it is no more.

This principle that effective social action is to be found in the creation of art and not in revolution is, of course, common to many Romantics in Blake's period. It should not, however—certainly not in Blake—be regarded as a mere neurotic or wish-fulfillment substitute for the failure of revolution. Apart from the fact that the creation of art is a highly social act, Blake's conception of art is very different from the dictionary's. It is based on what we call the arts, because of his doctrine that human reality is created and not observed. But it includes much that we do not think of as art, and excludes much that we do, such as the paintings of Reynolds.

We notice that in "The Gates of Paradise" cycle there is one point at which there is a break from the cycle, the plate captioned "Fear & Hope are—Vision." and described in the commentary as a glimpse of "The Immortal Man that cannot Die." The corresponding point in "The Mental Traveller" comes in describing the form ("emanation") of the life that the Boy has been constructing, just before it takes shape as the elusive "Female Babe":

> And these are the gems of the Human Soul,
> The rubies & pearls of a lovesick eye,
> The countless gold of the akeing heart,
> The martyr's groan & the lover's sigh.

The curiously wooden allegory is not characteristic of Blake, but it recurs in *Jerusalem* 12, where the same theme is under discussion. Evidently, Blake means by "art" a creative life rooted in the arts, but including what more traditional language calls charity. Every act man performs is either creative or destructive. Both kinds seem to disappear in time, but in fact it is only the destructive act, the act of war or slavery or parasitism or hatred, that is really lost.

Los is not simply creative power, but the spirit of time: more accurately, he is the power that constructs in time the palace of art (Golgonooza), which is timeless. As Blake says in a grammatically violent aphorism, the ruins of time build mansions in eternity. The products of self-sacrifice and martyrdom and endurance of injustice still exist, in an invisible but permanent world created out of time by the imagination. This world is the genuine Atlantis or Eden that we actually live in. As soon as we realize that we do live in it, we enter into what Blake means by the Last Judgment. Most people do not make this act of realization, and those who do make it have the responsibility of being evangelists for it. According to Blake, most of what the enlightened can do for the unenlightened is negative: their task is to sharpen the dialectic of the human and natural visions by showing that there are only the alternatives of apocalypse and annihilation.

Blake obviously hopes for a very considerable social response to vision in or soon after his lifetime. But even if everybody responded completely and at once, the City of God would not become immediately visible: if it did, it would simply be one more objective environment. The real "heaven" is not a glittering city, but the power of bringing such cities into existence. In the poem "My Spectre around me," Blake depicts a figure like the Boy of "The Mental Traveller" in old age, searching vainly for his "emanation," the total body of what he can love and create, outside himself instead of inside. The natural tendency of desire (Orc) in itself is to find its object. Hence the effect of the creative impulse on desire is bound to be restrictive until the release of desire becomes the inevitable by-product of creation.

The real world, being the source of a human vision, is human and not natural (which means indefinite) in shape. It does not stretch away forever into the stars, but has the form of a single giant man's body, the parts of which are arranged thus:

Urizen = head = city
Tharmas = body = garden
Orc   = loins = soil or bed of love
Urthona = legs = underworld of dream and repose
(Los)

Except that it is unfallen, the four levels of this world correspond very closely to the four traditional levels that we find in medieval and Renaissance poetry. The present physical world, by the "improvement of sensual enjoyment," would become an integral part of nature, and so Comus' attempt to seduce the Lady by an appeal to "nature" would no longer be a seduction or a specious argument. But the really important distinction is that for earlier poets the two upper levels, the city and the garden, were divine and not human in origin, whereas for Blake they are both divine and human, and their recovery depends on the creative power in man as well as in God.

The difference between the traditional and the Blakean versions of reality corresponds to the difference between the first and the last plates of the Job illustrations. In the first plate, Job and his family are in the state of innocence (Beulah), in a peaceful pastoral repose like that of the twenty-third Psalm. They preserve this state in the traditional way, by obeying a divine Providence that has arranged it, and hence are imaginatively children. There is nothing in the picture that suggests anything inadequate except that, in a recall of a very different Psalm (137), there are musical instruments hung on the tree above. In the last plate, things are much as they were before, but Job's family have taken the instruments down from the tree and are playing them. In Blake, we recover our original state, not by returning to it, but by recreating it. The act of creation, in its turn, is not producing something out of nothing, but the act of setting free what we already possess.

Blake's *Jerusalem*:
The Bard of Sensibility
and the Form of Prophecy

Harold Bloom

Also out of the midst thereof came the likeness of four living creatures.
And this was their appearance; they had the likeness of a man.

—Ezek. 1:5

"The midst thereof" refers to "a fire infolding itself," in the Hebrew literally "a fire taking hold of itself," a trope for a series of fire-bursts, one wave of flame after another. Blake's *Jerusalem* has the form of such a series, appropriate to a poem whose structure takes Ezekiel's book as its model. *The Four Zoas*, like Young's *Night Thoughts*, is in the formal shadow of *Paradise Lost*, and *Milton* less darkly in the shadow of Job and *Paradise Regained*. In *Jerusalem*, his definitive poem, Blake goes at last for prophetic form to a prophet, to the priestly orator, Ezekiel, whose situation and sorrow most closely resemble his own.

Ezekiel is uniquely the prophet-in-exile, whose call and labor are altogether outside the Holy Land. Held captive in Babylon, he dies still in Babylon, under the tyrant Nebuchadnezzar, and so never sees his prophecy fulfilled:

> Thus saith the Lord God; In the day that I shall have cleansed you from all your iniquities I will also cause you to dwell in the cities, and the wastes shall be builded.
>
> And the desolate land shall be tilled, whereas it lay desolate in the sight of all that passed by.
>
> And they shall say, This land that was desolate is become like the garden of Eden; and the waste and desolate and ruined cities are become fenced, and are inhabited.

Everything in Ezekiel except this ultimate vision is difficult, more difficult than it at first appears. Blake's *Jerusalem* is less difficult than it first seems, even to the informed reader, but still is difficult. Both books share also a harsh plain style, suitable for works addressed to peoples in captivity.

From *The Ringers in the Tower: Studies in Romantic Tradition.* © 1971 by The University of Chicago. The University of Chicago Press, 1971.

41

Ezekiel, like *Jerusalem*, is replete with the prophet's symbolic actions, actions at the edge of social sanity, violence poised to startle the auditor into fresh awareness of his own precarious safety, and the spiritual cost of it. As early as *The Marriage of Heaven and Hell*, Blake invokes Ezekiel as one who heightens the contradictions of merely given existence:

> I then asked Ezekiel. why he eat dung, and lay so long on his right and left side? he answered the desire of raising other men into a perception of the infinite

The central image of Blake, from whenever he first formulated his mythology, is Ezekiel's; the *Merkabah*, Divine Chariot or form of God in motion. The Living Creatures or Four Zoas are Ezekiel's and not initially Blake's, a priority of invention that Blake's critics, in their search for more esoteric sources, sometimes evade. Ezekiel in regard to Blake's *Jerusalem* is like Homer in regard to the *Aeneid*: the inventor, the precursor, the shaper of the later work's continuities. From Ezekiel in particular Blake learned the true meaning of prophet, visionary orator, honest man who speaks into the heart of a situation to warn: if you go on so, the result is so; or as Blake said, a seer and not an arbitrary dictator.

I have indicated elsewhere the similarities in arrangement of the two books, and the parallel emphases upon individual responsibility and self-purgation. Here I want to bring the poets closer, into the painful area of the anxiety of influence, the terrible melancholy for the later prophet of sustained comparison with the precursor, who died still in the realm of loss, but in absolute assurance of his prophetic call, an assurance Blake suffered to approximate, in an isolation that even Ezekiel might not have borne. For Ezekiel is sent to the house of Israel, stiffened in heart and rebellious against their God, yet still a house accustomed to prophecy. God made Ezekiel as hard as adamant, the *shamir* or diamond-point of the engraver, and that was scarcely hard enough; Blake knew he had to be even harder, as he wielded his engraver's tool.

Jerusalem begins with the Divine Voice waking Blake at sunrise and "dictating" to him a "mild song," which Blake addresses in turn to Albion, the English Israel, at once Everyman and an exile, a sleeper in Beulah, illusive land of shades. When the Divine Voice orders Ezekiel to begin his ministry, the prophet has already had a vision of the four cherubim and their wheels, a manifestation of glory that sustains him in the trials ensuing. But Blake has never seen the Living Creatures of the *Merkabah*, his Four Zoas as one in the unity of a restored Albion. The fourth, final book of *Jerusalem* begins with a demonic parody of the *Merkabah*, with the Wheel of Natural Religion flaming "west to east against the current of/Creation." A "Watcher & a Holy-One," perhaps Ezekiel himself, "a watchman unto the house of Israel," identifies this antagonist image for Blake, who is afflicted throughout by demonic epiphanies, as Ezekiel was not. The form of Ezekiel's prophecy depends upon the initial vision, for the glory is thus revealed to him before his task is assigned, though the emphasis is on the *departure* of the *Merkabah*, interpreted by the great commentator David

Kimchi as a presage of the Lord's withdrawal from the Jerusalem Temple, thus abandoned to its destruction.

In the England of *Jerusalem*, everything that could be seen as an image of salvation has been abandoned to destruction. No poem could open and proceed in a profounder or more sustained despair, for the next level down is silence. The temptation of silence, as in the self-hatred of Browning's ruined quester, Childe Roland, type of the poet who has given up, is to turn, "quiet as despair," into the path of destruction. Blake's antagonist, in *Jerusalem*, is what destroys Browning's quester: selfhood. What menaces continued life for the imaginative man is the quality of his own despair:

> But my griefs advance also, for ever & ever without end
> O that I could cease to be! Despair! I am Despair
> Created to be the great example of horror & agony: also my
> Prayer is vain I called for compassion: compassion mocked,
> Mercy & pity threw the grave stone over me & with lead
> And iron, bound it over me for ever: Life lives on my
> Consuming: & the Almighty hath made me his Contrary
> To be all evil, all reversed & for ever dead: knowing
> And seeing life, yet living not; how can I then behold
> And not tremble; how can I be beheld & not abhorrd

The imaginative man's despair is the Spectre of Urthona, who speaks these lines, and who may be thought of as holding the same relation to Blake the poet as the Solitary of *The Excursion* has to Wordsworth the poet. For the Spectre of Urthona is every prophet's own Jonah, in full flight from vision for reasons more than adequate to our unhappy yet still not unpleasant condition as natural men. Though the Spectre of Urthona had his genesis, in Blake's work, as an initially menacing figure, he is very appealing in *Jerusalem*, and Blake's critics (myself included) have erred in slighting this appeal, and thus diminishing the force of Blake's extraordinary artistry. The Spectre of Urthona *is always right*, if the reductive truth of our condition as natural men be taken as truth. Nor is the poor Spectre unimaginative in his reductions; they are exuberant by their unqualified insistence at knowing by knowing the worst, particularly concerning the self and the sexual wars of the self and the other. What is most moving about the Spectre's reductive power is its near alliance with his continual grief. We are repelled by his "mockery & scorn" and his "sullen smile," but each time we hear him we see him also as one who "wiped his tears he washd his visage" and then told the terror of his truths:

> The Man who respects Woman shall be despised by Woman
> And deadly cunning & mean abjectness only, shall enjoy
>   them
> For I will make their places of joy and love, excrementitious.
> Continually building, continually destroying in Family feuds
> While you are under the dominion of a jealous Female
> Unpermanent for ever because of love & jealousy.
> You shall want all the Minute Particulars of Life

The form of prophecy cannot sustain such reductive, natural truths, for in the context of prophecy they are not true. When we listen to the Spectre of Urthona we hear a bard, but not a prophet, and the bard belongs to Blake's own literary age, the time of Sensibility or the Sublime. Blake's lifelong critique of the poets to whom he felt the closest affinity—Thomson, Cowper, Collins, Gray, Chatterton—culminates in *Jerusalem*. The Spectre of Urthona descends from the Los of the Lambeth books, and the Bard of Experience of the *Songs*, but is closer even than they were to the archetype Blake satirizes, the poet of Sensibility, the man of imagination who cannot or will not travel the whole road of excess to the palace of wisdom.

Martin Price, studying "the histrionic note" of mid-eighteenth-century poetry, emphasized the poet as both actor and audience in "the theatre of mind." Precisely this insight is our best starting-point in understanding the Spectre of Urthona, who is so unnerving because he appears always to be "watching with detachment the passions he has worked up in himself." The grand precursor of this histrionic kind of bard is the Satan of the early books of *Paradise Lost*, whose farewell to splendor, upon Mount Niphates, sums up the agony that makes so strange a detachment possible:

> to thee I call,
> But with no friendly voice, and add thy name
> O Sun, to tell thee how I hate thy beams. . .
>
> . . . .
>
> Me miserable! which way shall I flie
> Infinite wrauth, and infinite despair?
> Which way I flie is Hell, my self am Hell;
> And in the lowest deep a lower deep
> Still threatening to devour me opens wide,
> To which the Hell I suffer seems a Heav'n.

A detachment that can allow so absolute a consciousness of self-damnation has something Jacobean about it. What a Bosola or a Vendice sees at the end, by a flash of vision, Satan must see continuously and forever in the vast theater of his mind. There exists perpetually for Satan the terrible double vision of what was and what is, Eternity and the categories of mental bondage, the fallen forms of space and time. This twofold vision is the burden also of the Bard of Sensibility, but not of the prophet who has seen the *Merkabah*, or even studies in hope to see it, as does the Blake-Los of *Jerusalem*. Freedom for the prophet means freedom from the detachment of the histrionic mode; the prophet retains a sense of himself as actor, but he ceases to be his own audience. A passage from solipsism to otherness is made, the theater of mind dissolves, and the actor stands forth as orator, as a warner of *persons* (Ezek. 3:17–21). Should he fail to make this passage, he is reduced to the extreme of the histrionic mode, and becomes the singer-actor of his own Mad Songs, one of the "horrid wanderers of the deep" or a destined wretch "washed headlong from on board." I take the first of these phrases from Cowper's powerful, too-little known poem, "On The

Ice Islands" (dated 19 March 1799) and the second from the justly famous "The Castaway" (written evidently the following day). A year later and Cowper died, his death like his life a warning to Blake during his years at Hayley's Felpham (1800–1803) and a crucial hidden element in both *Milton* and *Jerusalem*, where Blake fights desperately and successfully to avoid so tragically wasted a death-in-life as Cowper's.

In "On The Ice Islands" Cowper translates his own Latin poem, "Montes Glaciales, In Oceano Germanica Natantes" (written 11 March 1799). The ice islands are "portents," with the beauty of treasure, but apocalyptic warnings nevertheless as they float in "the astonished tide." They appear almost to be volcano-births, yet are Winter's creations:

> He bade arise
> Their uncouth forms, portentous in our eyes.
> Oft as, dissolved by transient suns, the snow
> Left the tall cliff to join the flood below,
> He caught and curdled with a freezing blast
> The current, ere it reached the boundless waste.

This is, to Blake, his Urizen at work, a methodical demiurge who always blunders. In Cowper's phantasmagoria, this is the way things are, a Snow Man's vision, a violence from without that crumbles the mind's feeble defenses. To it, Cowper juxtaposes the creation of Apollo's summer vision:

> So bards of old
> How Delos swam the Ægean deep have told.
> But not of ice was Delos. Delos bore
> Herb, fruit, and flower. She, crowned with laurel, wore
> Even under wintry skies, a summer smile;
> And Delos was Apollo's favourite isle.
> But, horrid wanderers of the deep, to you,
> He deems Cimmerian darkness only due.
> Your hated birth he deigned not to survey,
> But, scornful, turned his glorious eyes away.

One remembers Blake's youthful "Mad Song," written at least twenty years earlier:

> Like a fiend in a cloud
>   With howling woe,
> After night I do croud,
>   And with night will go;
> I turn my back to the east,
> From whence comforts have increas'd;
> For light doth seize my brain
> With frantic pain.

Late in his life, long after the Felpham crisis, Blake looked back upon Cowper's madness. We do not know when Blake annotated Spurzheim's

Observations on . . . Insanity (London, 1817), and we perhaps cannot rely on the precise wording of the annotations as being wholly Blake's own rather than Yeats's, since the copy from which Yeats transcribed has been lost. But, to a student of Blake, the wording seems right:

> *Spurzheim*: ". . . the primitive feelings of religion may be misled and produce insanity . . ."

> *Blake*: "Cowper came to me & said. O that I were insane always I will never rest. Can you not make me truly insane. I will never rest till I am so. O that in the bosom of God I was hid. You retain health & yet are as mad as any of us all—over us all—mad as a refuge from unbelief—from Bacon Newton & Locke."

Spurzheim cites Methodism "for its supply of numerous cases" of insanity, and Blake begins his note by scrawling "Methodism &." The Spectre of Urthona has the same relation to Blake's Cowper that Los has to Blake's Ezekiel, and we will see more of the Spectre than we have seen if we keep in mind that he is both a poet of Sensibility and a kind of sin-crazed Methodist. Cowper ends "On The Ice Islands" by desperately warning the "uncouth forms" away:

> Hence! Seek your home, nor longer rashly dare
> The darts of Phoebus, and a softer air;
> Lest you regret, too late, your native coast,
> In no congenial gulf for ever lost!

The power of this, and of the entire poem, is in our implicit but over-whelming recognition of Cowper's self-recognition; he himself is such an ice island, and the uncongenial gulf in which he is lost is one with the "deeper gulfs" that end "The Castaway":

> No voice divine the storm allayed,
>   No light propitious shone,
> When, snatched from all effectual aid,
>   We perished, each alone:
> But I beneath a rougher sea,
> And whelmed in deeper gulfs than he.

Though Cowper's terror is his own, the mode of his self-destruction is akin to that of the Bard of Sensibility proper, Gray's Giant Form:

> "Fond impious Man, think'st thou yon sanguine cloud,
> Rais'd by thy breath, has quench'd the orb of day?
> To-morrow he repairs the golden flood,
> And warms the nations with redoubled ray,
> Enough for me: with joy I see
> The different doom our fates assign.
> Be thine despair, and scept'red care,

To triumph, and to die, are mine."
He spoke, and headlong from the mountain's height
Deep in the roaring tide he plung'd to endless night.

That is not the way the Spectre of Urthona ends:

Los beheld undaunted furious
His heavd Hammer; he swung it round & at one blow,
In unpitying ruin driving down the pyramids of pride
Smiting the Spectre on his Anvil & the integuments of his Eye
And Ear unbinding in dire pain, with many blows,
Of strict severity self-subduing, & with many tears labouring.

Then he sent forth the Spectre all his pyramids were grains
Of sand & his pillars; dust on the flys wing; & his starry
Heavens; a moth of gold & silver mocking his anxious grasp.

Cowper and the Bard drown to end an isolation, whether terrible or heroic; the theater of mind dissolves in the endless night of an original chaos, the abyss always sensed in the histrionic mode. The Spectre of Urthona is both shattered and unbound, his anxious grasp of self mocked by his selfhood's reduction to a fine grain, to the Minute Particulars of vision. Because he cannot face the hammering voice of the prophetic orator, the Spectre is at last divided "into a separate space," beyond which he cannot be reduced. The theater of mind is necessarily a Sublime theater of the Indefinite, but the prophet compels definite form to appear.

Jerusalem's quite definite form is the form of prophecy, Blake's mythologized version of the story of Ezekiel, even as the form of Revelation is demonstrated by Austin Farrer to be Saint John's mythologized rebirth of Ezekiel's images. When the visionary orator steps forward, he shares the courage of Gray's Bard, but goes further because his words are also acts. Emerson, in one of his eloquent journal broodings upon eloquence, fixes precisely this stance of Blake's Los:

> Certainly there is no true orator who is not a hero. His attitude in the rostrum, on the platform, requires that he counter-balance his auditory. He is challenger, and must answer all comers. The orator must ever stand with forward foot, in the attitude of advancing. His speech must be just ahead of the assembly, ahead of the whole human race, or it is superfluous. His speech is not to be distinguished from action.
>
> (*Journal*, June 1846)

Speech that is act cannot be reconciled with excessive self-consciousness; the prophetic mind is necessarily a mind no longer turned in upon itself. The man of Young's *Night Thoughts* ("I tremble at myself / And in myself am lost!") is succeeded by prophetic Man, the "identified" Human Form, as Blake exaltedly wishes him phrased. This transition, from representative man as poet of Sensibility, inhabiting the theater of mind, to prophetic Man, a transition made again in Wordsworth and in Shelley, is in Blake at least founded upon Biblical precedent. What drew Blake to Ezekiel is the denunciation, first made by that prophet, of the entire spiritual tradition of collective responsibility. As Buber remarks, "Ezekiel individualizes the prophetic alternative." The larger covenant has broken down, because the collectivity of Israel or Albion is no longer a suitable covenant partner.

For the theater of mind, though an Ulro-den of self-consciousness, is founded upon a collective Sublime. The man of Burke, Young, Gray, Cowper is still the universal man of humanist tradition, still the man Pope and Johnson longed to address. Wordsworth is enough of a Burkean to retain the outline of such a figure, but Blake knows that continuity to be broken down, and forever. Blake's God, like Ezekiel's, sends a "watchman" to admonish individuals, and Los, as that watchman, delivers a message that no collectivity is capable of hearing. The Sublime terror, founded as it is upon a universal anxiety, is dismissed by Blake as the Spectre's rhetoric, his deception of others, while the Sublime transport is similarly dismissed as the Spectre's sentimentality, or self-deception. "Los reads the Stars of Albion! the Spectre reads the Voids / Between the Stars." To see the Burkean Sublime is to see: "a Disorganized / And snowy cloud: brooder of tempests & destructive War."

The bounding outline, or organized vision, Blake rightly found in Ezekiel and the other prophets, who gave him the harsh but definite form in which *Jerusalem* is organized, perhaps even over-organized. The form of prophecy, particularly fixed in Ezekiel, is the unique invention of the writing prophets who sustained the destruction of the Northern kingdom and the subsequent Babylonian exile. Since the *nabi's* teaching emphasizes return, or salvation by renovation, the form the teaching takes emphasizes a process of return, the *Merkabah's* fire-bursts from within itself, a declaration that is also a performance. For the *Merkabah*, to surmise largely, is a giant image for the prophetic state-of-being, for the *activity of prophecy*, though it presents itself as something larger, as the only permitted (if daring) image of the divine imagelessness. If we think back to the first of the writing prophets, the sheep-breeder Amos, we find the *situation* of the *Merkabah* without its image. Prophecy comes among us as a sudden onslaught from a stranger, a divine judgment in a storm of human speech, circling in until it addresses itself against the house of Israel. The image favored by Amos is not the storm of the rushing chariot's own splendor, the wind that is the spirit, but the waters of judgment, a more Wordsworthian emblem than Blake could care to accept.

In the writing prophets between Amos and Ezekiel, the image of judgment or form of prophecy departs more and more from the natural. Hosea's emphasis is upon the land, but the land's faithlessness, the wife's whoredoms, presented as unnatural rather than all-too-natural, as they would be by Blake. Isaiah's vision of God's radiance, his *kabod* (wealth and glory), moves toward the vision of the *Merkabah*, subtly juxtaposing as it does the Divine Throne and the dethroned leper king Uzziah. Micah, a more vehement *nabi*, emphasizes the image of the glory's departure from the sanctuary, and is thus the true precursor of Jeremiah and Ezekiel, and through them of Blake. Jeremiah's great image, the potter's wheel upon which clay is molded into vessels, and marred vessels broken into clay again, is associated unforgettably with the prophet's own afflictions, an association which introduces into the prophetic form a new emphasis upon the *nabi* as person, but only insofar as the person is a vessel of God's message. In Ezekiel, the potter's wheel is taken up into the heavens in the wheels within wheels of the *Merkabah*, whose departure is at one with the advent of the prophet's inner afflictions, his intense personal sufferings.

Blake, a close and superb reader of the prophets, knew all this, better than we can know it because he knew also his election, following Milton, to the line of prophecy. But his immediate poetic tradition was the theater of mind, and he struggled throughout his writing life first partly to reconcile Sensibility and prophecy, and at last largely to disengage the lesser mode from the greater. In *Jerusalem*, the Bard is identified with the Spectre of Urthona, and the *nabi* not with Los or Blake, but with the Los-Blake-Jesus composite who achieves unified form at the poem's close. Cowper's suffering is not redressed, but rather is cast away, for Blake is concerned to distinguish it sharply from the suffering of the prophet, the more fruitful afflictions of Jeremiah and Ezekiel. And, since *Jerusalem* is even more purgatorial than *Milton*, the poem's main concern is to outline firmly the distinction between the two kinds of suffering *in Blake himself*. It is his *own* Spectre of Urthona who must be overcome, though the self-realization necessary for such harsh triumph depends upon his recognition that precisely this psychic component won out in the spirit of Cowper, and in other Bards of Sensibility.

Hayley, who patronized Cowper as he did Blake, extended his interest in what he took to be the "madness" of Bards to the *Jubilate Agno* of Smart, as we know from his correspondence with the Reverend Thomas Carwardine. We do not find in *Jerusalem*, with its powerful control of Blake's emotions, a pathos as immense and memorable as Smart's. The pathos of the Spectre compels a shudder more of revulsion than of sympathy; we are not humiliated by Smart's fate, or Cowper's, but we are by the Spectre's anguish. For the Spectre is rightly associated by Blake with Ezekiel's denunciation of "the dross of silver," the impure to be cast into the terrible refining furnace of Jerusalem-under-siege. Blake is singularly harsh toward the Spectre in *Jerusalem*, not only because it is at last wholly his own Spectre and so most menacing to him, but also because he is turning at last against some of his own deepest literary identifications, and so attempting to free himself from a poetic attitude powerfully attractive to him, whether in Cowper, Gray, Chatterton—whom he had admired overtly—or in lesser figures of the Sublime school.

But to cross over from Bard to *nabi*, from the theater of mind to the orator's theater of action, was not wholly a liberation for Blake's psyche. A different, a subtler anxiety than is incarnated by the Spectre, begins to manifest itself in *Jerusalem*. This is Blake's version of the anxiety of influence, which he had labored heroically to overcome in *Milton*. *Jerusalem* is not less in the Shadow of Milton (which Blake identified with Ezekiel's Covering Cherub) than *Milton* was, and is also in what we could call, following Blake, the Shadow of Ezekiel. To see and state clearly the hidden problem concerning Blake's degree of originality in his definitive poem, we need first to achieve a firmer sense of the poem's psychic cartography than is now available to us.

Freud, in *The Problem of Anxiety*, distinguishes anxiety from grief and sorrow, first by its underlying "increase of excitation" (itself a reproduction of the birth trauma) and then by its function, as a response to a situation of danger. Anxiety, he adds, can be experienced only by the ego, not by the id as "it is not an organization, and cannot estimate situations of danger." As for the superego, Freud declines to ascribe anxiety to it, without however explaining why. In Blake, the id (fallen Tharmas, or the Covering Cherub) does experience anxiety, and so does the superego (fallen Urizen or the Spectre of Albion, the Spectre proper). But Blake and Freud agree on the crucial location of anxiety, for the Blakean ego is Los, fallen form of Urthona, and the Spectre of Urthona is Los's own anxiety, the anxiety of what Yeats calls the faculty of *Creative Mind*. Yet Blake does distinguish the ego's anxiety from that of other psychic components. The Spectre of Urthona is neither the anxiety of influence, a peculiarly poetic anxiety that belongs to the Covering Cherub, with its sinister historical beauty of cultural and spiritual tradition, nor the anxiety of futurity, that belongs to fallen Urizen. Nor is it the sexual anxiety Blake assigns to Orc, the tormented libido burningly rising to a perpetual defeat. Los's anxiety is larger and more constant, resembling Kierkegaards's Concept of Dread, which must be why Northrop Frye ironically calls the Spectre of Urthona the first Existentialist. A desire for what one fears, a sympathetic antipathy, or walking oxymoron; so Kierkegaard speaks of Dread, and so we learn to see the Spectre of Urthona. To Kierkegaard, this was a manifestation of Original Sin; to Blake this manifests the final consequence of being one of Tirzah's children, a natural man caught on the spindle of Necessity.

If we combine the insights of Freud and Kierkegaard, then we approach the Spectre of Urthona's condition, though without wholly encompassing it. The missing element is the anxiety endemic in the theater of mind, or the ego's dread that it can never break through into action. To be fearful that one's words can never become deeds, and yet to desire only to continue in that fear, while remembering dimly the trauma of coming to one's separate existence, and sensing the danger (and excitation) of every threat to such separation: that horrible composite is the Spectre of Urthona's consciousness. Blake, who had known this internal adversary with a clarity only the prophets achieve, turns *Jerusalem* against him even as *Milton* was directed against the Covering Cherub, and as *The Four Zoas* identified its antagonist in fallen Urizen. But even the prophets must be all-too-human. Blake triumphs against his ego's Dread, and wards off again the Urizenic horror of futurity, yet becomes vulnerable instead throughout *Jerusalem* to the diffuse anxiety of influence, the *mimschach* or "wide-extending" Cherub. This baneful aspect of Poetic Influence produces the form of *Jerusalem*, which is the form of Ezekiel's prophecy twisted askew by too abrupt a swerve or *clinamen* away from Blake's model.

Ezekiel is both more methodical in arrangement and more prosaic in style than the writing prophets before him. Rabbi Fisch, in his Soncino edition of Ezekiel, notes the even balance of the prophet's divisions, between the siege and fall of Jerusalem and destruction of the kingdom, and the vision of a people's regeneration, twenty-four chapters being assigned to each. Blake might well have adopted this balance, but chose instead a darker emphasis. Ezekiel ends Chapter 24 with God's definitive establishment of His prophet as a sign, to those who have escaped destruction. "Thou shalt be a sign unto them; and they shall know that I am the Lord." At the close of 25 this formula is repeated, but as a prophecy against the Ammonites, with a grimly significant addition: ". . . and they shall know that I am the Lord, when I shall lay my vengeance upon them." For the prophet has moved from the fiction of disaster to the hope of renovation, a hope dependent upon the downfall of his people's enemies. He moves steadily toward comfort, and the vision of a rebuilt City of God. Blake's directly parallel movement is from Plate 50, end of Chapter 2, to Plate 53, start of Chapter 3 of *Jerusalem*. Plate 50 concludes with an antiphonal lament, of Erin and the Daughters of Beulah, imploring the Lamb of God to come and take away the remembrance of Sin. But Chapter 3 begins with Los weeping vehemently over Albion, and with our being reminded again that this lamenting, still ineffectual prophet is himself "the Vehicular Form of strong Urthona," that is, the *Merkabah* or Divine Chariot still in departure, still mourning in exile.

Throughout *Jerusalem*, no prophetic hint from Ezekiel is adopted if it might lead to what Blake could regard as a premature mitigation of fallen travail. I do not mean to question Blake's harshness, the necessity for his augmented sense of the prophet's burden. But the bitterness of presentation, the burden placed upon even the attentive and disciplined reader, may surpass what was necessary. At the close of Plate 3, addressing the Public, Blake declares his freedom from the "Monotonous Cadence" of English blank verse, even in Milton and Shakespeare:

> But I soon found that in the mouth of a true Orator such monotony was not only awkward, but as much a bondage as rhyme itself. I therefore have produced a variety in every line, both of cadences & number of syllables. Every word and every letter is studied and put into its fit place: the terrific numbers are reserved for the terrific parts—the mild & gentle, for the mild & gentle parts, and the prosaic, for inferior parts: all are necessary to each other.

Parodying Milton's defense of his refusal to use rhyme, Blake indicates his passage beyond Milton to the cadence of Isaiah and Ezekiel, the form of a true Orator. The defense of Blake's cadence has been conducted definitively by a formidable prosodist, John Hollander, in his essay on "Blake and the Metrical Contract," to which I can add nothing. In the passage above, Blake emphasizes, as against Milton, the prosody of the King James Version, which he does not distinguish from the Hebrew original. There is evidence that Blake, remarkably adept at teaching himself languages, had some Hebrew when he worked at *Jerusalem*, but his notions as to the variety of Biblical poetic numbers seem to go back to Lowth, as Smart's notions did also. This gave him a distorted sense of the metrical freedom of his great originals, a distortion that was an imaginative aid to him. Whether his distortion of larger prophetic forms was hindrance or action is my concern in the remainder of this essay.

Blake shies away from certain symbolic acts in Ezekiel that earlier had influenced him quite directly. It has never, I think, been noted that Blake's "London" has a precise source in Ezekiel:

> I wander thro' each charter'd street,
> Near where the charter'd Thames does flow.
> And mark in every face I meet
> Marks of weakness, marks of woe.

And the glory of the God of Israel was gone up from the cherub, whereupon he was, to the threshold of the house. And he called to the man clothed with linen, which had the writer's inkhorn by his side;

And the Lord said unto him, Go through the midst of the city, through the midst of Jerusalem, and set a mark upon the foreheads of the men that sigh and that cry for all the abominations that be done in the midst thereof.

Ezek. 9:3–4

> How the Chimney-sweepers cry
> Every blackning Church appalls,
> And the hapless Soldiers sigh,
> Runs in blood down Palace walls.

Those that sigh and cry are to be marked and spared, but those in Church and Palace are to be slain, as God pours out his fury upon Jerusalem, and upon London. Between Ezekiel and himself Blake is more than content to see an absolute identity. But, a decade or more later, the identity troubles him. If we contrast even the serene closes of Ezekiel and *Jerusalem*, where Blake directly derives from his precursor the *naming* of the City, we confront an identity straining to be dissolved:

And the name of the city from that day shall be "The Lord is there."

Ezek. 48:35

And I heard the Name of their Emanations they are named Jerusalem.

Jerusalem 99:5

"The Lord is there" because the promise of Ezekiel's prophecy is that the *Merkabah* will not depart again from His sanctuary. Jerusalem receives therefore a new name. Blake's promise is more restricted, and warier; the Judgment will restore London to Jerusalem, but Jerusalem will still be a smelting furnace of mind, subject to the alternation of Beulah and Eden, creative repose and the artist's activity. So the departed Chariot's Cherubim or restored Zoas are not invoked again at *Jerusalem's* close, as they are by Ezekiel in his final epiphany. For an apocalyptic poem, *Jerusalem* is remarkably restrained. Blake follows Ezekiel throughout, but always at a distance, for he needs to protect himself not only from the natural history of mind (which crippled the poets of Sensibility) but also from the too-rigorous Hebraic theism that would make his apocalyptic humanism impossible. *Jerusalem* does not accept the dualism of God and man, which is the only dualism sanctioned by the prophets, but which to them was less a dualism than a challenge to confrontation. Blake, who had held back from identifying himself wholly with Milton and Cowper, though he saw the Divine Countenance in them, kept himself distinct at last even from his prophetic precursor, Ezekiel, that he might have his own scope, but also that he might not be affrighted out of Eden the garden of God, though it be by "the anointed cherub that covereth."

Darkning Man: Blake's Critique of Transcendence

Thomas Weiskel

> And I will place within them as a guide
> My umpire conscience, whom if they will hear,
> Light after light well used they shall attain,
> And to the end persisting, safe arrive.
>
> O conscience! into what abyss of fears
> And horrors hast thou driven me; out of which
> I find no way, from deep to deeper plunged!
> —MILTON, *Paradise Lost*

At first look, the negative or Kantian sublime and the positive or egotistical sublime seem to be genuine contraries. Against the collapse of the sensible imagination, brought on by the noumenal reason's thirst for totality, we may plausibly set the imagination's exaltation—whether as the agency of immanence or as a projective, fictional power—in the egotistical sublime. The positive sublime is insured against the moment of sudden loss because its attachment to the object is from the start a secondary affair, a limited engagement protectively suffused with self-love. We have seen, [earlier], that the egotistical sublime evades or subverts dualism by declining to polarize thought and perception into a timeless, noumenal order and a finite, sensible world. The state of undifferentiated perception, as fact, memory, nostalgia, or fiction, is its touchstone.

Yet within the egotistical sublime we [find] both an essential instability and, ultimately, a principle of limitation. The logic of the egotistical sublime is dynamic but also perpetual: the "highest bliss" such minds can know is "the consciousness / Of Whom they are, habitually infused / Through every image and through every thought" (*Prelude* XIV. 114–16). The egotistical sublime is restless but repetitive, habit forming. The mind so deployed has "endless occupation . . . whether discursive or intuitive" but no chance of a leap through or beyond time. Wallace Stevens would expand the hour of "expressible bliss" into a month, a year, "a time / In which majesty is a mirror of the self," but in the section of "Notes" that immediately follows, he settles down to the chronic context of even such a claim:

> These things at least comprise
> An occupation, an exercise, a work,

From *The Romantic Sublime: Studies in the Structure and Psychology of Transcendence.* © 1976 by The Johns Hopkins University Press. Baltimore/London: The Johns Hopkins University Press, 1976.

A thing final in itself and, therefore, good:
One of the vast repetitions final in
Themselves and, therefore, good, the going round

And round and round, the merely going round,
Until merely going round is a final good,
The way wine comes at a table in a wood.

And we enjoy like men, the way a leaf
Above the table spins its constant spin,
So that we look at it with pleasure, look

At it spinning its eccentric measure. Perhaps,
The man-hero is not the exceptional monster,
But he that of repetition is most master.

In "Circles," Emerson speaks of man's "continual effort to raise himself above himself, to work a pitch above his last height," and finds his image for such ceaseless sublimating in the "generation of circles, wheel without wheel." The soul moves outward, bursting over each concentric orbit of limitation. But since the soul's self-transcendence is without term, the generation of circles itself succumbs to the circularity of succession: this is "the circular or compensatory character of every human action . . . the moral fact of the Unattainable . . . at once the inspirer and the condemner of every success." It is true that in "Compensation," Emerson excepts the soul—unjustifiably, it seems to me—from the universal "tax" or "penalty" of compensation. But the debt returns to be partially paid in "Circles," in the relativity of ceaseless supersession, if not in the proportional contraction of perception that we have argued. Because time will not relent, the ultimate form of activity in the egotistical sublime is circular. The negative sublime, on the contrary, suggests an infinite parallelism in which the perception of an object *as* sublime is a kind of parallax.

Readers of Blake will be tempted to recognize in Emerson's "generation of circles, wheel without wheel" and also in Stevens's "the going round, / And round and round, the merely going round" Blake's central imagery of fallen limitation, the circle of destiny or the mills of Satan. Emerson propounds an exuberance without a determinate object, so that the prolific soul of "Circles" seems more solipsistic than creative, and it is always subject to time. And repetition, however large the scope of its acts, is tantamount to disaster for Blake. "The same dull round even of a univer[s]e would soon become a mill with complicated wheels" (E, 2). [All Blake quotations are from *The Poetry and Prose of William Blake*, edited by David V. Erdman, with commentary by Harold Bloom. Doubleday and Co., 1970.] Blake's central conviction, dramatized in the career of his character Urizen, is that solipsism and the rational alienation of perception into mechanical regularity both result from the same imaginative disease. Blake is equally acute in diagnosing the negative sublime, of which Urizen is also in some respects the type. Both versions of transcendence are reduced, in Blake's radical therapy of culture, to one malaise of perception. Blake learned from Milton, if not from life, that the Fall is immensely and necessarily over-determined and that any definitive explanation is likely to turn into justification. What looks like indecision in the matter of a cause of the Fall is really the result of a technique in which distinct but correlative motives are superimposed. And about the results of the Fall Blake is definitive, though very complicated; best of all, he offers all the advantages of a perspective truly outside the Romantic sublime.

And some disadvantages as well. Blake is not, with all the distinguished scholarship, getting any easier to read. I used to think he was: with a little diligence the system could be mastered; the difficulty seemed conceptual, the very thing to engage the energetic compulsions of an ever-intellectualizing critic like the author of this book. But then I found myself at crucial points left outside the charmed circularity of Blakean hermeneutics, even playing with the vulgarity, Will the real Blake please appear? It would be ungenerous to cavil at the commentary, which nevertheless now illuminates and surrounds Blake like a hovering cherub. Blake has a way of turning his critics into apologists, and we still await the study at once fully informed, (a major project now), free from prejudice, *and* written from the proper distance. But it is not in the conditions of Blake's recent and spectacular academic success that the difficulty lies. The question is how to read Blake exoterically. He was certainly an ironic poet, rarely to be caught speaking in his own person; so there is an essential problem of tone which cannot be resolved by the application of a schematic calculus, however authentic. The emotions of his text look simple enough: pity, fear, grief, rage, jealousy, pain, joy—elemental stuff. But their permutations seem to make sense only conceptually. More rarely in Blake than in any other major poet does one have the sense that one has been there, at just that point of feeling. Or have we read him wrongly?

Consider the Zoas. One doesn't get far thinking of them exclusively as faculties or psychic agencies correlative to some other system such as Freud's. Each of the Zoas is a character in the specific sense that each is endowed with consciousness, whereas in Freud's system consciousness is ascribed only to a portion of the ego. The Zoas are states of mind and feeling as well as figures in a design. It is true that behind what seems to be an arbitrary turn in the careers of the Zoas, we nearly always find an analytic insight and not a realized moment of consciousness. But perhaps a subtler ear could discern the experiential correlative of the insight. We ought in any case to dispense with all the talk of "on one level" or the other; it's a tired metaphor that now stands in the way. I think the next great leap in the reading of Blake will come when we devise an interpretative language for the obscure contiguities of schematization and consciousness. At what point does a schema begin to be "lived"? Conversely, where does experience schematize itself or merge into the design it unconsciously plays out? This, in a sense, is our problem with Kant, whose concepts we are beginning to personify in the hope of finding a deeper structure beneath the subreptions of his logic.

After all this beating of the drum my reader will rightly hope for more than the confrontation of Blake and Kant which is our current agenda. Unfortunately, an authentic sounding of Blake lies outside the scope of this book, if not indeed of its author, for our subject is the Romantic poetics of sublimation, which Blake, quite literally, as the story goes, could not stomach. Yet I shall attempt to uncover something of Urizen's felt predicament in the moment of his fall, for it seems to me a version of the sublime moment. To the contemporary method of reading Blake entirely in his own terms I can only oppose a somewhat tendentious effort to think through, by way of Kant, the experience of self-consciousness which attends reason in the crisis of the sublime. A strong case can easily be made for Blake's enmity to the Romantic sublime on the "level" of art theory, and although this is not how we would engage Blake, his opinions as an aesthetician are worth a passing look as an introduction to his powerful concern with perception. Blake's views on the sublime as an aesthetic category are perfectly clear in his annotations to Reynolds's *Discourses*. He found Reynolds's work to be grounded on Burke's treatise on the sublime and the beautiful, which in turn was founded on the opinions of Newton and Locke, with whom Blake always associated Bacon. Reading all these men, he felt "Contempt and Abhorrence," for "They mock Inspiration & Vision" (E, 650). Blake uses the word *sublime* as a general honorific and obviously had no use for the distinction, fashionable after Burke (1757), between the sublime and the beautiful. His sublime is not the Romantic sublime. What piqued him most in Reynolds was praise of general conceptions and disdain of minuteness. And Burke's recommendation of obscurity seemed to him disastrous.

Minute Discrimination is Not Accidental All Sublimity is founded on Minute Discrimination

A Facility in Composing is the Greatest Power of Art & Belongs to None but the Greatest Artists, i.e. the Most Minutely Discriminating and Determinate

The Man who asserts that there is no Such Thing as Softness in Art & that every thing in Art is Definite & Determinate has not been told this by Practise but by Inspiration & Vision because Vision is Determinate & Perfect & he Copies That without Fatigue Every thing being Definite & determinate Softness is Produced Alone by Comparative Strength & Weakness in the Marking out of the Forms

Without Minute Neatness of Execution. The. Sublime cannot Exist! Grandeur of Ideas is founded on Precision of Ideas

Singular & Particular Detail is the Foundation of the Sublime

Distinct General Form Cannot Exist Distinctness is Particular Not General

Broken Colours & Broken Lines & Broken Masses are Equally Subversive of the Sublime

Obscurity is Neither the Source of the Sublime nor of any Thing Else

[E, 632–47]

As an annotator, Blake is delightfully sure of himself and gives no quarter. What seems perverse is his insistence that only when vision is determinate, minute, and particular does it conduct to or contain infinity. The eye which would "see a World in a Grain of Sand" (E, 481) must be a "Determinate Organ" (E, 627). Infinite perception must be distinguished from the perception of the "indefinite," which is Blake's version of mental hell. Blake is not merely wittily inverting the terms of contemporary aesthetic discourse. "It is not in Terms that Reynolds & I disagree Two Contrary Opinions can never by any Language be made alike" (E, 648). Nor is he, with Kant and the philosophers, worrying the phenomenological ambiguity of infinity. He conceived perception to be the fundamental index of consciousness, subsuming the primary and secondary degrees as formulated by Coleridge. It is an activity of which both object and image are merely phases or products. We have seen how the Wordsworthian "fade-out" signals a sublimation in which the formal properties of what is seen are dissolved and the residual otherness of the thing is alienated as indefinite substance. Here, for Blake, is the very crisis of man's Fall. In his view, the positive and negative sublimes turn out to be not genuine contraries but two versions of the same lapse, itself the negation of visionary perception. Blake's myth of the Fall is an analytic critique of sublimation.

THE PSYCHOPOLITICS OF REASON

What then can Blake tell us about the anxiety we suppose to be at work behind sublimation? We recall the defeat of the sensible imagination or phenomenal intellect in Kant's theory of the sublime. The nearest analogue in Blake to the "understanding" of the philosophers is Urizen, whose fall in Night III of Blake's manuscript epic *The Four Zoas* is suggestively parallel to the mind's self-alienation in Kant. Here first is Kant, at his most psychological, describing the crucial moment; the delight in the sublime is *negative*:

> that is to say it is a feeling of imagination by its own act depriving itself of its freedom by receiving a final determination in accordance with a law other than that of its empirical employment. In this

way it gains an extension and a power greater than that which it sacrifices. But the ground of this is concealed from it, and in its place it *feels* the sacrifice or deprivation, as well as its cause, to which it is subjected.

["Analytic of the Sublime"]

The imagination is evidently in an ambivalent position. It deprives itself "by its own act," and yet it passively receives its orders for this self-deprivation from the law of reason. As a proponent of sublimation, Kant would have it that the gain is greater than the sacrifice, but this is certainly not how it feels from the imagination's point of view. The imagination is here the victim of superior forces, and its self-mutilation can be explained only by the "cause"—fear. The text goes on to assert that

the *astonishment* which borders on terror, the awe and thrill of devout feeling, that takes hold of one . . . is not actual fear, but rather only an attempt to enter into it [fear] with the imagination, in order to feel the power of this faculty in combining the movement of the mind thereby aroused with its serenity, and of thus being superior to the nature within us, and therefore also to external nature, so far as the latter can have any influence upon our feeling of well-being.

The passage is not perspicuous; Kant's personification gets cloudy. It seems the imagination is exposed to fear in order to arouse its power, but this fear is at the same time sublimated or internalized in the wider consciousness of the mind as a whole. Thus, in its converted, ego-form, the power is lost to the imagination (hence the feeling of sacrifice and deprivation), but further, it is directed back against the imagination (the "nature within us") as a superior force. Kant's sublime celebrates the ingenious capacity of the ego to live off the energy and labor of another, who is kept ignorant of what is going on. The imagination can share in the power only by identifying with its superior and hence depriving itself by its own act.

I have gradually modulated into a Blakean politics of the psyche by intensifying Kant's hints of personification. Blake takes his psycho-political schemata much further into a properly mythopoeic dimension, a fact which may signal the presence of conceptual antinomies which the myth expresses without resolving. The Zoas fall into an obsession with power and face each other in a shifting series of master-slave confrontations. Urizen falls spectacularly when he rejects his emanation Ahania in a fit of what is now called male chauvinism. Schematically, the original condition of Ahania might be said to represent the unselfconscious unity of mind and object which attends creative intellectual work and that is the pleasure without which nothing of real value ever gets articulated. Ahania's own fall directly precedes and precipitates Urizen's and may be understood in a preliminary way as the well-known decline of such work into an alienating activity, so that its results confront the mind as an estranged reality over which the mind has no control and to which it must submit in a constant and fruitless sacrifice of mental energy. (Blake's doctrine of the emanation may be in-terpreted—apart from its esoteric provenance—in the analogous terms of the early, humanist Marx; indeed, the alienation of labor is a conspicuous theme in Romantic writers and is prominent in Schiller, Shelley, and of course Hegel.) As the third night of the *Four Zoas* opens, Ahania attempts to rescue her lord from the catastrophe engulfing his colleagues. She pleads with him to "Resume [his] fields of Light," apparently hoping, though she fears the worst, that the mind can retain its playful, creative powers in a world devoted to rack. Her plea is eloquent and far-sighted, but Urizen fails to understand and responds defensively:

She ended. [From] his wrathful throne burst forth the black hail
    storm

Am I not God said Urizen. Who is Equal to me
Do I not stretch the heavens abroad or fold them up like a
    garment

He spoke mustering his heavy clouds around him black opake

Then thunders rolld around & lightnings darted to & fro
His visage changd to darkness & his strong right hand came
    forth
To cast Ahania to the Earth he siezd her by the hair
And threw her from the steps of ice that froze around his
    throne

Saying Art thou also become like Vala. thus I cast thee out
Shall the feminine indolent bliss. the indulgent self of weariness
The passive idle sleep the enormous night & darkness of Death
Set herself up to give her laws to the active masculine virtue
Thou little diminutive portion that darst be a counterpart
Thy passivity thy laws of obedience & insincerity
Are my abhorrence. Wherefore hast thou taken that fair form
Whence is this power given to thee! once thou wast in my
    breast
A sluggish current of dim waters. on whose verdant margin
A cavern shaggd with horrid shades. dark and cool & deadly.
    where
I laid my head in the hot noon after the broken clods
Had wearied me. there I laid my plow & there my horses fed
And thou hast risen with thy moist locks into a watry image
Reflecting all my indolence my weakness & my death
To weigh me down beneath the grave into non Entity
Where Luvah strives scorned by Vala age after age wandering
Shrinking & shrinking from her Lord & calling him the Tempter
And art thou also become like Vala thus I cast thee out.
                            [42:18–43:22; E, 322]

Urizen's error is complex, as his defensive incoherence attests. He associates Ahania with weakness, but this is pure projection, an unconscious attempt to externalize and thereby to expel his own mental trouble. For it is Ahania who has called him to activity and lamented his paralysis. By gazing on futurity, in which he descries the dread Orc, Urizen has already lost the capacity for "present joy" (37:10); hence his very recollection of former pleasure is poisoned into a memory of "A cavern shaggd with horrid shades, dark and cool & deadly." Thinking is no longer even conceivably fun, for the pleasures of determinate intellect fall to the status of a "nature within us," which is erroneously identified with external nature, or Vala. Under the pressure of immense and unfamiliar anxiety, which springs from a fear of the future, the intellect is trying to concentrate—by concentrating itself. But this effort, heroic and pathetic at once, is doomed because Ahania is the source of all intellectual energy which does not emanate from anxiety. "Whence is this power given to thee!" asks the exasperated Urizen, as if he sensed that the very power he needs is being cut off by this self-mutilation. In this drastic sublimation, the determinate intellect or understanding aspires to superiority by alienating the "objective" imagining on which it is based. After this, the "King of Light" falls "down rushing, ruining, thundering, shuddering" into the state of generation. Blake locates ruin in precisely the same mental event that Kant would celebrate.

Blake's analytic of sublimation is shrewd enough to wrinkle the brow of any self-conscious literary intellectual. We stand to be valuably instructed, if not converted, by his spiritual economics, which are as severe as Freud's and yet argue for a vigorous mental activity not based on the paradox of reductive sublimation—the ceaseless contraction of "lower" into "higher" forms. On the whole, American intellectual culture is devoted to the ideology of the active ego, which can, so marvellously it seems, convert experience into the capital of power. In this context, Blake still has an antinomian aura, especially for those who take his rhetoric for his logic. There are many accounts of the Fall in Blake, and several critiques of sublimation in its sexual, political, and properly artistic guises. Each Fall involves a lapse, a failure or weakness like Urizen's weariness, and also an unjustified usurpation, an arrogation of exclusive power to one agency or faculty. Weakness releases the stuff of perception into an indeterminate otherness (as a refractory emanation) which is thus open for possession *by* another, and mental activity descends into a violent struggle for power jealously guarded and exercised. Blake fits the traditional and Miltonic theme of prideful usurpation into a psychological calculus of gain and loss, a law of compensation that runs through Generation. When any part of us is less creative than it could be, it immediately attempts to be more than it should, thereby becoming less than it was.

Consequently, we find the same ambiguity of cause in Blake's critique of the sublime that we found in Kant's analytic. There are several phases to Urizen's presumption, which is in each case proportionate to Albion's mental weariness. In Night I, Albion proposes to abandon the proper realm of thought (the South) to Luvah and announces his intention to invade the North, the domain of Urthona ("Earth-owner"), presumably in order to achieve an ownership to which he is originally not entitled; when Luvah objects, he departs secretly into the North anyway (21:16–35; 22:1–10; 32–37). The conflict between Urizen and Luvah is the immediate cause of Urthona's fall (22:16–31). Urizen aspires to the total possession or comprehension of the earth in the logical categories of the understanding—even at the cost of surrendering perceptional clarity to the passions. So, in Kant, the understanding and its correlative, the sensible imagination, attempt to comprehend in *one* intuition a multitude of discrete intuitions, even at the risk of an overextension of faculties and a consequent frustration, a feeling of sacrifice and deprivation. Kant's *Vernunft* ("higher reason") is a rich repository of indefinables, as its transmogrifications in subsequent idealism attest. To some extent it suggests both Urthona and the unfallen Tharmas, a principle of integration, but since it is conceived almost exclusively in negative terms, it is primarily what Blake logically calls a "Negation" or Spectre, a "Holy Reasoning Power" that "Negatives every thing" (E, 151). In Kant, as in Blake, Reason is obsessed with superiority and holiness, and demands awe.

In the moment of his fall, Urizen is turning into the Spectre as he "negatives" Ahania into Vala and abstracts himself from her. Ahania's attempt to forestall their mutual ruin is doomed not only by Urizen's defensiveness but also by her own naiveté, which must be explicated briefly if we wish to understand the negative sublime as a moment of feeling. Ahania presents a version of Albion's fall as a warning to Urizen, but she fails to see—in one of Blake's masterly ironies—how Urizen is already implicated in that fall:

> Then O my dear lord listen to Ahania, listen to the vision
> The vision of Ahania in the slumbers of Urizen
> When Urizen slept in the porch & the Ancient Man was smitten
>
> The Darkning Man walkd on the steps of fire before his halls
> And Vala walked with him in dreams of soft deluding slumber
> He looked up & saw thee Prince of Light thy splendor faded
> [*But saw not Los nor Enitharmon for Luvah hid them in shadow*]
>
> [*In a soft cloud Outstretch'd across, & Luvah dwelt in the cloud*]
>
> Then Man ascended mourning into the splendors of his palace
> Above him rose a Shadow from his wearied intellect
> Of living gold, pure, perfect, holy; in white linen pure he
>   hover'd
> A sweet entrancing self delusion, a watry vision of Man
> Soft exulting in existence all the Man absorbing

Man fell upon his face prostrate before the watry shadow
Saying O Lord whence is this change thou knowest I am
    nothing
And Vala trembled & covered her face, & her locks were spread
    on the pavement

I heard astonishd at the Vision & my heart trembled within me
I heard the voice of the Slumberous Man & thus he spoke
Idolatrous to his own Shadow words of Eternity uttering
O I am nothing when I enter into judgment with thee
If thou withdraw thy breath I die & vanish into Hades
If thou dost lay thine hand upon me behold I am silent
If thou withhold thine hand I perish like a fallen leaf
O I am nothing & to nothing must return again
If thou withdraw thy breath, behold I am oblivion

He ceasd: the shadowy voice was silent; but the cloud hoverd
    over their heads

[39:12–40:19; E, 320–21]

The uncorrupted Urizen may be dozing, but his Spectre is very much at work in this shadow in which the living gold of his unfallen form is draped in spectrous white. Just as in Kantian or "negative" thinking, from the defeated, "wearied intellect" rises a perfect, holy image of ultimacy, a "watry vision" without determinate outline—for, says Kant, the "inscrutability" of Reason's ideas "precludes all positive presentation." The Slumberous Man is made to echo the self-abnegating Psalm 143—"And enter not into judgment with thy servant: for in thy sight shall no man living be justified"—and also Psalm 104:

thou openest thine hand, they are filled with good.
Thou hidest thy face, they are troubled: thou takest away their
    breath, they die and return to their dust.

These very verses are quoted by Hegel as the consummate example of the negative sublime.

Ahania hopes that Urizen will reject the idolatry perpetrated while he "slept in the porch," but unknowingly she has exposed his project. (All of her vision may of course be understood as Urizen's moment of self-recognition, but so deeply is the original Urizen split that this further reduction has only theoretical significance at this point.) Urizen is dismayed at Ahania's vision (41:5–9, 18; 42:7–8), not because it recapitulates the fall, but because it reveals a countermyth to his own version of the fall—a myth which highlights his own role with an ingenuous clarity the more dangerous for being unconscious. In Urizen's view, Man fell because he became intellectually lazy and his "active masculine virtue" succumbed to Vala, "the feminine indolent bliss. The indulgent self of weariness"—what he hopes to avoid by casting out Ahania. Pleasure undermined self-discipline; in short, Man failed to sublimate. But Ahania's account of the fall suggests that sublimation is itself a creation of intellectual weariness (40:3), which in turn results from Man's commerce with Vala "in dreams of soft deluding slumber." From this point of view, Urizen's myth of the fall is totally incoherent because it proposes as a saving alternative the very sublimation which is the idolatrous result of mental failure.

Blake's irony is such that neither Urizen nor Ahania understands fully what is happening to the "Darkning Man." Ahania hopes naively that the intellect has retained its freedom and is not yet compromised in Man's fall; Urizen, however, refuses to see the fall for what it is and rejects its clear consequence even as he fails to take responsibility for his own role. His actions are secretive; they are concealed from the Darkning Man in just the way that the operations of the Kantian reason were hidden from the understanding. As Ahania's tale of the fall continues, the ironies, dramatic and allusive, rapidly thicken. Down from the shadowy cloud drops—unexpectedly—Luvah:

> And Lo that Son of Man, that shadowy Spirit of the Fallen One
> Luvah, descended from the cloud; In terror Albion rose
> Indignant rose the Awful Man & turnd his back on Vala
>
> . . . .
>
> And Luvah strove to gain dominion over the mighty Albion
> They strove together above the Body where Vala was inclos'd
> And the dark Body of Albion left prostrate upon the crystal
>   pavement
> Coverd with boils from head to foot. the terrible smitings of
>   Luvah
>
> Then frownd the Fallen Man & put forth Luvah from his
>   presence
> (I heard him:frown not Urizen:but listen to my Vision)
>
> Saying, Go & die the Death of Man for Vala the sweet
>   wanderer
> I will turn the volutions of your Ears outward; & bend your
>   Nostrils
> Downward; & your fluxile Eyes englob'd, roll round in fear
> Your withring Lips & Tongue shrink up into a narrow circle
> Till into narrow forms you creep. Go take your fiery way
> And learn what 'tis to absorb the Man you Spirits of Pity &
>   Love
>
> O Urizen why art thou pale at the visions of Ahania
> Listen to her who loves thee lest we also are driven away.
>   [41:2–4; 41:13–42:8; E, 321]

The allusion to Job identifies Luvah with Satan; as Satan is licensed by God to try Job, so Urizen is ultimately responsible for Luvah's descent, which fills Albion with terror—and then, significantly, with indignation. In Job's case, the boils come "from the sole of his foot to the crown of his head": Blake's reversed "from head to foot" nicely indicates the Urizenic nature of the affliction. The boils, traditionally signs of venereal disease, are identified in *Jerusalem* (21:3–5) as the "disease of Shame," which also covers from head to foot; Blake's illustration of the text in the Job series (6) shows Satan pouring his vial on Job's head, while Job's wife has custody of his feet and is ignored. Actually, we are informed by the excised lines ("*& Luvah dwelt in the cloud*") that the "watry vision of Man" which Albion worships is from the start a compound of Urizen and Luvah; its full explication, which is unnecessary here, would lead us to the heart of Blake's brilliant reading of Job—the claim that the demonic Satan and the jejune God of that text are both aspects of Job's erroneous theological imagination.

What Ahania's vision reveals is that the perceptional error of the Fallen Man is also a sexual crisis. This is a fundamental insight into the psychology of the negative sublime. The Fallen Man responds to sexual guilt by expelling his passional life into a grotesque naturalization. It now becomes possible to state the entire sequence of the fall, even at the risk of some reduction. The Darkning Man first conceives a slumberous passion for Vala; so the subject of the sublime is caught up by an appearance or prospect "out there" to such an extent that his faculties cease to function energetically and soon feel dwarfed and humiliated. From his "wearied intellect" rises an indeterminate image of perfection or totality; it is a negative projection, but since its origins are concealed from the imagination, the man worships it in self-abnegating awe. At this point Kant's account left unexplained the way in which consciousness rather suddenly ceased to inhabit the plight of the imagination and identified instead with the idea of totality, thereby recovering its self-respect by alienating the "nature within us." In Blake's vision this recovery has the look of an oedipal crisis "successfully" resolved—the very type of sublimation.

Luvah's presence in the cloud is not merely a function of wearied intellect but is also a fantasy which compensates for the passional frustration—the sacrifice and deprivation—which Man feels: it is an image of power. This power is, however, under Urizenic aegis, and it is now directed *against* Man; we remember how in Kant the reason used fear to induce awe for itself. In psychological terms, the passional force is introjected and felt first as fear and then as sexual guilt." In terror Albion rose / Indignant rose the Awful Man & turned his back on Vala." Albion's struggle with Luvah is not a competition for Vala but Man's attempt to suppress the passion he feels as shame. Ironically, Albion's inability to suppress shame leads him to expel desire itself (Luvah) and its object (Vala)—so that he may be "superior to the nature within . . . and therefore also to external nature." It is clear that this latter feat on Man's part is not quite what Urizen had in mind, for he is disturbed to hear it told: "Then frownd the Fallen Man & put forth Luvah from his presence / (I heard him:frown not Urizen: but listen to my Vision)."

The reader may share Urizen's perplexity over what looks like Albion's sudden reassertion of control over Luvah, but the sequence is psychologically true. In his indignation and struggle against the "Spirits of Pity & Love," Albion has in fact *over*identified with the holy specter he worshipped. Urizen is in the position of a father who, merely by trying to be perfect and godlike, has enforced a more drastic oedipal resolution upon his son than could have been anticipated—a common psychological pattern. Urizen wanted only to be worshipped by both Man and nature ("And Vala trembled & covered her face, & her locks were spread on the pavement"), and Luvah's mission (provocatively identified with the parousia in the epithet "Son of Man") was designed only to insure Albion's self-abrogation in nature. But because the power of the specter is derived as much from frustration as from a dream of totality, Albion's suppression of passion in effect accomplishes a negation more extreme than Urizen had realized was necessary. His response to Ahania, "Art thou also become like Vala. Thus I cast thee out," is in a sense an attempt to catch up with what Albion has already done. Ahania's vision reveals consequences to a Urizen who is still somewhat innocent—he hasn't yet wholly fallen, we remember.

Blake's analytic of sublimation is richly suggestive at a number of points. It helps us to fill in the affective mortar of Kant's structure and to account for some curious facts which emerge as we study speculations about the sublime. The peculiar combination of holy innocence and conspiratorial self-aggrandizement which may be detected in the career of Kant's reason is one such fact. The negative sublime begins with an excessive interest in nature and ends with an excessive disdain of nature, and again and again in reading the texts of the sublime—in Schiller, Schopenhauer, and even in the Wordsworth of *The Borderers*—we feel that this movement is compulsive. Reason and its cognates begin as a negative or dialectical alternative to human limitation, but such quasi-theological prestige begins to accumulate around the ideas of reason that in the end reason requires a total withdrawal from all natural connection. We shall later meet the pattern of oedipal overidentification as an element in the "daemonic" sublime. The immediate value of Blake's text is that it plays out a logic implicit in discursive theories of the sublime. We can read the affective logic of the sublime partly in Albion's fall and partly in Urizen's complicated state of self-knowledge.

The ultimate protagonist of the sublime in its third phase—the moment of self-recognition—speaks an extraordinary speech, a compound of anxiety and vaunting pride:

> Am I not God said Urizen. Who is Equal to me
> Do I not stretch the heavens abroad or fold them up like a
>   garment
> He spoke mustering his heavy clouds around him black opake
>   [42:19–21]

We are taken again to Hegel's chief instance of the negative sublime,

Psalm 104, where the Lord is addressed as He "who coverest [Himself] with light as with a garment; who stretchest out the heavens like a curtain." Urizen's role model is Jehovah himself, and the irony of the "heavy clouds . . . black opake" obviously cuts both ways. Urizen is also answering Luvah, who in the first Night had declined conspiracy with the bold claim: "Dictate to thy Equals, am not I / The Prince of all the hosts of Men nor Equal know in Heaven" (1.22:1–2; E, 307). But Luvah is no longer a threat— Albion has done Urizen's work for him—and Urizen has not yet focused his rage on Ahania. The ultimate object of his threatening rhetorical question is Albion. For Albion's drastic sublimation (a disaster from Blake's point of view), like Job's stubborn victory over Satan, in effect appears to accuse Urizen of being a soft god. Albion can turn against the nature within and without with a force that endangers the hegemony of Urizen, who still inhabits Beulah. Awe and terror, it seems, are not enough—because man can master his passions through indignant suppression. Kant in fact speaks directly to this situation. The mind which recognizes its own sublimity will not prostrate itself timorously before the Godhead; it will identify with that Godhead.

For Urizen this means that his original project—exploiting Man's passive turning outward to nature so that it yields a "watry vision of perfection"—is naive and is endangered by Man's withdrawal from any engagement with nature. The mind convinced of its own sublimity cannot in fact experience the awful or sublime moment, which is a discovery, a movement between two states: the overcoming of sense is necessarily predicated upon an engagement with the sensible. Unlike the positive sublime, whose ultimate form is repetitive and circular, the negative sublime theoretically aims toward a unique disillusionment—the unmasking of the "subreption" by which an object seems sublime. Ahania's narrative exhibits in the form of myth the tendency of the positive sublime to yield to the polarizing pressure that results in the negative sublime. Albion, of course, is not a real threat; he doesn't have the respect for himself that Urizen supposes; nothing suggests that he knows that "sweet entrancing self delusion, a watry vision of Man" is in fact "his own shadow." Albion is already worshiping Jehovah before Urizen has quite grown into his role. Albion lacks the self-consciousness of a potential protagonist of the sublime. This situation parallels the way reason operated on two levels of consciousness in Kant, the concealment which enables reason to discover its own power in an attitude of awe.

From an affective point of view, the salient feature of Ahania's vision is the coincidence it establishes between the obscuring of the Darkning Man's perception and the suppression of his desire. Blake's text enables us to confront a question that our own discussion has pretty much begged: are the two kinds of sublimation, perceptional and passional, really one, as we have implicitly claimed? Man's idolatrous awe changes to terror with the appearance of Luvah, "that Son of Man," whose arrival suggests (in addition to the oedipal introjection we have remarked) the realization of the judgment Man feared ("O I am nothing when I enter into judgment with thee"). Terror, we may surmise, is consistent with the Spectre's design, insofar as he is a separate will. (The subsequent indignation is Man's own contribution, a further fall into self-righteousness.) Urizen is not yet Jehovah until Man in effect makes him so. In Blake's technical terms, the Spectre represents a Pahad phase of God—the fifth "eye" which immediately precedes Jehovah. *Pahad* is translated "fear" or "terror" in the King James Version. He is invoked by Eliphaz, one of Job's comforters, in a passage cited by Burke as proof of his contention that obscurity is a cause of the sublime:

> But let it be considered that hardly any thing can strike the mind with its greatness, which does not make some sort of approach towards infinity; which nothing can do whilst we are able to perceive its bounds, but to see an object distinctly, and to perceive its bounds, is one and the same thing. A clear idea is therefore another name for a little idea. There is a passage in the book of Job amazingly sublime, and this sublimity is principally due to the terrible uncertainty of the thing described. *In thoughts from the visions of the night, when deep sleep falleth upon men, fear came upon me and trembling, which made all my bones to shake. Then a spirit passed before my face. The hair of my flesh stood up. It stood still,* but I could not discern the form thereof; *an image was before mine eyes; there was silence; and I heard a voice—Shall mortal man be more just than God?* We are first prepared with the utmost solemnity for the vision; we are first terrified, before we are let even into the obscure cause of our emotion; but when this grand cause of terror makes its appearance, what is it? is it not, wrapt up in the shades of its own incomprehensible darkness, more aweful, more striking, more terrible, than the liveliest description, than the clearest painting could possibly represent it?
>
> [*A Philosophical Enquiry into the Origin of Our Ideas of the Sublime and Beautiful*]

We have already met Burke's argument in its sophisticated Kantian form. What is indistinct is phenomenologically in-finite, and this leads to a hypostasized infinitude. Burke is not aware, although it would rescue his argument from a dubious premise of causality, that the "fear and trembling" is itself the indistinct spirit, i.e., Pahad. Blake's illustration of the text in the *Job* series (9) shows Pahad with his arms bound and concealed, which suggests most simply that he is powerless to judge right from left, right from wrong. Job is looking upward calmly at the nightmare invoked by Eliphaz, who is not looking at (i.e., reseeing) his own vision; the other comforters are frightened. In the margins are the forests of night (error) and the verses: "Shall mortal Man be more just than God? Shall a Man be more Pure than his Maker?" The irony is clear: Eliphaz's rhetorical questions, intended to frighten Job, have become for Job genuine questions. If this is God, then mortal man may well be more just and pure. Job's own error is a self-righteousness based on fallen categories. His state is closely analogous to what Urizen fears to be the case with Albion, who, as we have seen, is identified with Job in the third Night. Urizen is threatened to observe in Albion's expulsion of Luvah and Vala a man more just than God, purer than his Maker. Luvah-Satan having failed (ironically by conquest) to execute Urizen's naive design, Urizen must, like the God of *Job*, thunder his own anxiously rhetorical questions: "Am I not God . . . Who is Equal to me."

The point to be grasped in this confluence of texts is that the obscure image is terrible only to him who is conscious of guilt. It is a feeling of guilt that Eliphaz wishes in vain to force upon Job. Albion is already guilty with Vala, and the indistinct image of perfection arises to punish him. He feels this guilt, succumbs to a conviction of its justice, but then is able to suppress it by removing all desire (Luvah) and all occasion for desire (Vala). Like Kant's reason in its ultimate phase of self-congratulation, Albion is no longer exposed to terror. But the cost is great, for this sublimation dooms, among other things, natural religion and any connection to nature. The Kantian therapy is a drastic one; it logically ends in mental suicide. Behind the phenomenology of the sublime moment we begin to descry an immense and fascinating psychodrama.

The Eye and the Object
in the Poetry of Wordsworth

Frederick A. Pottle

This year, the centennial of Wordsworth's death, has seen the publication of a good many essays with some such title as "Wordsworth Today." The purpose of such essays has been to read and judge Wordsworth as though he were a contemporary poet, to decide what portion of his works is really available to present-day sensibility. My purpose is rather descriptive than judicial: I shall try to isolate qualities of Wordsworth's poetry that look as though they were going to be apparent to all historical varieties of sensibility, though the values assigned to them by different sensibilities may differ. And I think I can best get to what I want to say by the method of texts: by inviting you to consider two prose statements made by Wordsworth himself about poetry in general and his own poetry in particular. They are both from the famous Preface: "Poetry takes its origin from emotion recollected in tranquillity" and "I have at all times endeavoured to look steadily at my subject." It is my notion that the latter of these texts usually gets, if not a false, at least an impoverished interpretation; and that the two, taken together and rightly understood, go a long way towards placing Wordsworth in literary history.

At first sight it looks as though they were what Bacon calls "cross clauses": that is, they appear to be hopelessly contradictory. The natural image that rises in one's mind as one reads the statement "I have at all times endeavoured to look steadily at my subject" is that of an artist painting from a model or an actual landscape, and since Wordsworth's poetry contains a good deal of landscape, the meaning of his words would appear to be that he composed poetry while looking earnestly and steadily at the natural objects which he introduces into his poems. But if poetry takes its origin from emotion recollected in tranquillity, it is hard to see how this could have happened. In fact, the only way in which we can leave any

From *Yale Review* 40, no. 1 (September 1950). © 1950 by Yale University.

place for the actual model in poetry that starts from recollection is to suppose that after poetry *has* taken its origin, the poet goes back to natural objects and pores over them as he composes. And we know that Wordsworth did not do that. His normal practice, like that of other poets, was to paint without the model. He very seldom made a present joy the matter of his song, but rather turned habitually for the matter of poems to joys that sprang from hiding-places ten years deep.

More than that, a good many of his poems, including several of his finest, either have no basis in personal experience at all, or show autobiography so manipulated that the "subject" corresponds to nothing he ever saw with the bodily eye. His extensive critical writings deride matter-of-fact and speak over and over again of the power of the Imagination to modify and create. Yet there is a widespread belief that he was Nature's Boswell, in the old erroneous sense which defined Boswell as a man who followed Johnson about with a notebook, taking down his utterances on the spot. Actually, like Boswell, Wordsworth relied on memory, and says so quite explicitly. But then he says other things in which he appears to be vindicating the rightness of his poetry, not on the ground that it is well imagined, but on the ground that the things described in the poem really did happen in that fashion and in no other.

I do not mean merely the notes which he dictated in old age to Miss Fenwick. I mean such a passage as his impassioned defense of "The Leech Gatherer" against the mild and sisterly strictures of Sara Hutchinson, a defense made before the poem was published: "A young Poet in the midst of the happiness of Nature is described as overwhelmed by the thought of the miserable reverses which have befallen the happiest of all men, viz Poets—I think of this till I am so deeply impressed by it, that I consider the manner in which I was rescued from my dejection and despair almost as an interposition of Providence. . . . 'A lonely place, a Pond' 'by which an old man *was*, far from all house or home'—not stood, not sat, but *'was'*— the figure presented in the most naked simplicity possible. . . . I cannot conceive a figure more impressive than that of an old Man like this, the survivor of a Wife and ten children, travelling alone among the mountains and all lonely places, carrying with him his own fortitude, and the necessities which an unjust state of society has entailed upon him. . . . Good God! Such a figure, in such a place, a pious self-respecting, miserably infirm . . . Old Man telling such a tale!"

Who would believe from reading this that in real life (as we learn from his sister Dorothy's journal) Wordsworth met the old man, not on the lonely moor, but in the highway; that in real life the old man was not demonstrating resolution and independence by gathering leeches under great difficulties, but was begging? In short, that the narrative is from first to last an imaginative construction—the account of an imagined meeting between Wordsworth and the beggar as Wordsworth imagined him to have been before he was finally reduced to beggary?

What, then, are we to make of Wordsworth's boast that he endeavored at all times to look steadily at his subject? I shall try to answer the question by tracing the steps he followed in writing one of his most famous poems, "I wandered lonely as a cloud," commonly (though with no authority from Wordsworth) called "Daffodils." The starting point is the entry in Dorothy's journal for April 15, 1802. That entry is fairly long, but it is all good reading; and I have my reasons for not eliminating any of it.

"It was a threatening, misty morning, but mild. We set off after dinner from Eusemere. Mrs. Clarkson went a short way with us, but turned back. The wind was furious, and we thought we must have returned. We first rested in the large boat-house, then under a furze bush opposite Mr. Clarkson's. Saw the plough going in the field. The wind seized our breath. The Lake was rough. There was a boat by itself floating in the middle of the bay below Water Millock. We rested again in the Water Millock Lane. The hawthorns are black and green, the birches here and there greenish, but there is yet more of purple to be seen on the twigs. We got over into a field to avoid some cows—people working. A few primroses by the road-side—woodsorrel flower, the anemone, scentless violets, strawberries, and that starry, yellow flower which Mrs. C. calls pile wort. When we were in the woods beyond Gowbarrow Park we saw a few daffodils close to the water-side. We fancied that the lake had floated the seeds ashore, and that the little colony had so sprung up. But as we went along there were more and yet more; and at last, under the boughs of the trees, we saw that there was a long belt of them along the shore, about the breadth of a country turnpike road. I never saw daffodils so beautiful. They grew among the mossy stones about and about them; some rested their heads upon these stones as on a pillow for weariness; and the rest tossed and reeled and danced, and seemed as if they verily laughed with the wind, that blew upon them over the lake; they looked so gay, ever glancing, ever changing. This wind blew directly over the lake to them. There was here and there a little knot, and a few stragglers a few yards higher up; but they were so few as not to disturb the simplicity, unity, and life of that one busy highway. We rested again and again. The bays were stormy, and we heard the waves at different distances, and in the middle of the water, like the sea. Rain came on—we were wet when we reached Luff's, but we called in. Luckily all was chearless and gloomy, so we faced the storm—we *must* have been wet if we had waited—put on dry clothes at Dobson's. I was very kindly treated by a young woman, the landlady looked sour, but it is her way. She gave us a goodish supper, excellent ham and potatoes. We paid 7/—when we came away. William was sitting by a bright fire when I came downstairs. He soon made his way to the library, piled up in a corner of the window. He brought out a volume of Enfield's *Speaker*, another miscellany, and an odd volume of Congreve's plays. We had a glass of warm rum and water. We enjoyed ourselves, and wished for Mary. It rained and blew, when we went to bed. N. B. Deer in Gowbarrow Park like skeletons."

I said this was the starting point, for it is as near the raw matter of the poem as we can get. The true raw matter was certain perceptions—visual, auditory, tactile—which Wordsworth and his sister had on that windy April morning; and those we have no way of recovering. In Dorothy's entry this raw matter has already been grasped and shaped by a powerful imagination, and it has been verbalized. The entry is not a poem, because it contains a good deal of true but inconsequential statement (the rum and water, the volume of Congreve), but much of it is prefabricated material for a poem. And the fact is (though this is doctrine little heard of among men) that Wordsworth made grateful use of prefabricated material whenever he could get it of the right sort. As Professor Lane Cooper showed us long ago, he went regularly to books of travel for material of the right sort, but his best source was his sister's journal.

The function of the Imagination, as Wordsworth and Coleridge insisted, is, at the first level, to make sense out of the undifferentiated manifold of sensation by organizing it into individual objects or things; at the second, and specifically poetic, level, to reshape this world of common perception in the direction of a unity that shall be even more satisfactory and meaningful. Dorothy has made extensive use of the secondary or poetic imagination. Notice the devices by which she has unified and made sense of the experience of the daffodils. First, and most important, she has endowed them with human qualities. They are a social group engaged in busy concerted activity. The notion of the social group, the crowd (she does not actually use the word) is reinforced by her further figure of stragglers. Secondly, besides being active, the crowd of daffodils is happy: they look gay, they toss and reel and dance (their very activity is sport) and seem verily to laugh. And thirdly, some of the crowd have danced so hard that they are tired: they rest their heads upon the stones as on pillows.

Wordsworth recollected the scene in tranquillity and wrote his poem a full two years afterwards. He fixes on Dorothy's fine central perception of "the simplicity, unity, and life of that one busy highway," and condenses it into the one word "crowd." He takes over, too, her impression that the daffodils were "dancing," that they were "gay," that they were even "laughing." Ever since 1807, when Wordsworth published this poem, daffodils have danced and laughed, but there is nothing inevitable about it. The Greek myth of Narcissus is not exactly hilarious; and even Herrick, when he looked at a daffodil, saw something far from jocund:

> When a Daffadill I see
> Hanging down his head t'wards me,
> Guesse I may, what I must be:
> First, I shall decline my head;
> Secondly, I shall be dead;
> Lastly, safely buryed.

The literal, positivistic, "scientific" fact was that Wordsworth and his sister saw a large bed of wild daffodils beside a lake, agitated by a strong, cold spring wind. The rest is all the work of the imagination.

The mark of the poetic imagination is to simplify: to make the manifold of sensation more meaningful by reducing it to a number of objects which can actually be contemplated. Wordsworth continues Dorothy's process of simplification: he eliminates the bitterness of the wind, which is so prominent in her account; reduces the wind, in fact, to a breeze. It may appear here that he has simplified more than was necessary or wise. Shakespeare, in the most famous lines ever written about daffodils, kept the wind:

> Daffodils
> That come before the swallow dares, and take
> The winds of March with beauty.

Admittedly, it is a higher mode. Wordsworth, on some occasions, would have kept the wind, too; but to have kept it here would have made a more complex—if you will, a more tragic—poem than he felt like writing. He felt this poem as something very simple and very pure; when he came to publish it, he put it in a group called "Moods of My Own Mind." But he is impartial: as he throws out matter on the one hand because it is too serious, so he eliminates matter on the other because it is too playful. The prettiest thing in Dorothy's realization—her image of the daffodils pillowing their heads on the stones—drops out. He dispenses too with Dorothy's stragglers. He fastens on her central image of the dancing, laughing crowd, and lets everything else go.

But now the idea of the crowd calls for a modification, and a modification of a fundamental sort. The social glee of the crowd can be made more significant if it is set over against solitary joy; and so in the poem he makes himself solitary, which in literal fact he was not. He now has what for him is a promising situation. The solitariness of the poet and the sociability of the daffodils are set up as poles between which the poem discharges itself. I have said that the situation is for him a promising one. Everyone knows of Wordsworth's love of solitude, his conviction that the highest experiences came to him when he was alone. What we need constantly to remind ourselves of is that his theory assigned an only slightly lower value to the love of men in societies. (The subtitle of Book VIII of *The Prelude* is "Love of Nature Leading to Love of Mankind.") The trouble was that, though he had the best of intentions, he could never handle close-packed, present, human crowds in the mode of Imagination. If he were to grasp the life of a great city imaginatively, it had to be at night or early in the morning, while the streets were deserted; or at least in bad weather, when few people were abroad.

But in the figure of a bed of daffodils endowed with human characteristics, he can handle with feelings of approval and exhilaration the concept of a crowd, of ten thousand individuals packed close together. He begins and ends solitary: at the beginning, we may assume, filled with joy, but a joy somewhat solemn, somewhat cold and remote, as the symbol of the cloud indicates. He is surprised by the sensation of mere unmixed human gaiety and lightheartedness, yields to it, and finds it good; so good that ever after he can derive refreshment from the memory of the experience.

The progress towards explicit identification of the symbol is gradual. In the first stanza the flowers are "fluttering" (literal: the flowers are moved by the breeze); then "dancing" (the flowers are self-moved). By the end of the second stanza they are "tossing their heads in sprightly dance." (The flowers are self-moved and are having a wonderful time. "Dance" is the key-word: it occurs in either the last or the first line of each stanza.) Finally, but not till the third stanza is reached, we get the quite explicit series "glee," "gay," "jocund," "pleasure." Wordsworth is always (or almost always) explicit in this fashion: he tells you just how you are expected to take his figures. Of course it is the figures that do the work. No one can make us joyful by merely using the word "joy" or any of its synonyms. But there is impressive agreement among readers of all periods that by giving us a simple figure, reinforcing it by certain devices of varied iteration, and explicitly interpreting it, Wordsworth does evoke the emotion of joy.

We can now see what Wordsworth meant by looking steadily at his subject. So far as his subject is expressed in imagery drawn from nature (and that means in all his best poetry), there is implied a lifelong habit of close, detailed, and accurate observation of the objects composing the external universe. By "accurate" I mean something the same thing as "naturalistic," but not entirely so. Wordsworth scorned the merely analytic vision of the naturalist ("One that would peep and botanize / Upon his mother's grave"), because in his opinion that kind of apprehension empties the object of life and meaning by detaching it from its ground. "His theme is nature *in solido*," as Whitehead pointed out, "that is to say, he dwells on that mysterious presence of surrounding things, which imposes itself on any separate element that we set up as an individual for its own sake. He always grasps the whole of nature as involved in the tonality of the particular instance." But, except for those portions of the scientist's vision which require (let us say) dissection and magnification, there is little in the scientist's vision that Wordsworth misses. A *merely* matter-of-fact, an *exclusively* positivistic view of nature fills him with anger, but his own apprehension includes the matter-of-fact view without denying any of it. Dr. Leavis has perhaps put this more intelligibly when he remarks, as the chief virtue of Wordsworth's poetry, a "firm hold upon the world of common perception," though I myself should like to modify it, "in the mode of perception which has been common in Western civilization since some time in the late eighteenth century." In a literal, physiological sense, Wordsworth did look steadily at the natural objects that appear in his poetry.

But the subject he is talking about in the sentence in the Preface is not an object in external nature; and the eye that looks steadily is not the physical eye. The subject is a mental image and the eye is that inward eye which is the bliss of solitude. The mental image accompanies or is the source of the emotion recollected in tranquillity; it recurs in memory, not once but many times; and on each occasion he looks at it steadily to see what it *means*. Wordsworth in his best poetry does not start with an abstraction or a generalization, a divine commonplace which he wishes to illustrate. He starts with the mental image of a concrete natural object. He feels this object to be very urgent, but at first he does not know why. As he looks steadily at it, he simplifies it, and as he simplifies it, he sees what it means. He usually continues to simplify and interpret until the object becomes the correlative of a single emotion.

It is a great mistake to consider Wordsworth a descriptive poet. When he is writing in the mode of the Imagination, he never gives catalogues, in fact never provides a profusion of imagery. He employs few images. His images are firm and precise ("literal"), but they are very spare. Of the daffodils we are given nothing but their habit of growing in clumps, their color, and their characteristic movement when stirred by the wind. Wordsworth's method is not the method of beautification (Tennyson), nor the method of distortion (Carlyle); it is the method of transfiguration. The primrose by the river's brim remains a simple primrose but is also something more: it is a symbol (to use Hartley's quaint terminology) of sympathy, theopathy, or the moral sense.

We can also see now the main cause of Wordsworth's dissatisfaction with the poetry of Pope: "It is remarkable that, excepting the nocturnal Reverie of Lady Winchilsea, and a passage or two in the Windsor Forest of Pope, the poetry of the period intervening between the publication of the Paradise Lost and the Seasons does not contain a single new image of external nature; and scarcely presents a familiar one from which it can be inferred that the eye of the Poet had been steadily fixed upon his object, much less that his feelings had urged him to work upon it in the spirit of genuine imagination. To what a low state knowledge of the most obvious and important phenomena had sunk, is evident from the style in which Dryden has executed a description of Night in one of his Tragedies, and Pope his translation of the celebrated moonlight scene in the *Iliad*. A blind man, in the habit of attending accurately to descriptions casually dropped from the lips of those around him, might easily depict these appearances with more truth."

For Pope's usual method is the exact contrary of that which I have been describing. Pope starts with an abstraction or a generalization concerning human nature and then looks for a correlative in the world of nature apart from man. His habit of observation of external nature is not detailed and precise; indeed, he thinks it unimportant whether the "facts" of nature which he alleges in his illustrations are really facts or superstitions. The natural history of Pliny and the old bestiaries are as much grist to his mill as the latest papers of the Royal Society. He appears also to me to have at times no clear, detailed, and consistent mental picture of his own figures. To illustrate. In the couplet near the beginning of the *Essay on Man*,

> The latent tracts, the giddy heights explore
> Of all who blindly creep or sightless soar,

he means, I suppose, moles and birds of some sort. If so, in order to enforce his doctrine that "the proper study of mankind is man," he appears to be making use of the ancient and medieval notion that all birds except the eagle blind themselves by looking at the sun. Surely, by Pope's time it was generally known that high-flying birds are not "sightless"; that on the contrary they have telescopic vision?

When, in the same poem he says that man

> Touches some wheel, or verges to some goal,

I cannot convince myself that he could draw a diagram of the machine he has in mind. Or consider a famous passage from the Second Dialogue of the *Epilogue to the Satires*:

> Ye tinsel Insects! whom a Court maintains,
> That counts your Beauties only by your Stains,
> Spin all your Cobwebs o'er the Eye of Day!
> The Muse's wing shall brush you all away.

"Tinsel" to me means "shining or glittering like cheap metal foil," and my natural image of a "tinsel insect" would be some kind of beetle ("this Bug with gilded wings"). But the word can mean merely "pretentiously showy" and so may not have been intended to identify the kind of insects Pope has in mind. "Stains," however, can hardly mean anything else than moths or butterflies ("Innumerable of stains and splendid dyes, / As are the tiger-moth's deep damask'd wings"). But the trouble with that is that Pope's insects spin cobwebs, which no butterfly or moth can do. I think we shall do Pope no injustice if we conclude that his insects have the combined characteristics of beetles, moths, and spiders, and hence do not belong to any order known to naturalists.

Looking steadily at a subject, then, for Wordsworth means grasping objects firmly and accurately in the mode of common perception and then looking at them imaginatively. And we have not said all that needs to be said about the second half of the process. I have made a great deal of "I wandered lonely," and must add now that Wordsworth had doubts about putting that poem in the central group of his short pieces called "Poems of the Imagination." In the collected edition of 1815, where the grouping first appeared, he added the following note to "I wandered lonely": "The subject of these Stanzas is rather an elementary feeling and simple impression (approaching to the nature of an ocular spectrum) upon the imaginative faculty, than an *exertion* of it."

It is hard for us nowadays to understand why Blake, Wordsworth, Coleridge, and Shelley made such a fuss about the Imagination, and why Wordsworth and Coleridge labored so to distinguish the Imagination from the Fancy. Make no mistake about it; it was for them a matter of vital importance, nothing less than a vindication of their right to exist as poets. In the reigning psychology of Locke extended by Hartley, Imagination and Fancy—pretty much interchangeable terms—were handled as modes of memory. That in itself was proper enough, but there was a strong tendency to make a total and exclusive philosophy out of this mechanistic naturalism. Wordsworth and Coleridge were convinced that Imagination and Fancy were creative; and they wished to make Imagination not merely creative but a power for apprehending truth. It is a pity that neither of them was ever very clear on the subject. Perhaps the problem is too profound to allow of perfectly clear statement, but it is possible to be a lot clearer than either of them ever was. In particular, I should advise you to read carefully what Wordsworth says about Fancy in his Preface of 1815, but not to bother with what he says there about the Imagination, for it will only confuse you.

Fancy, he tells us, deals with images that are fixed, detailed, and sharply defined; its effects are "surprising, playful, ludicrous, amusing, tender, or pathetic." Furthermore (and most important) these effects are transitory because the deep relationships of things will not permit a serious, steady contemplation of them in that mode. Dorothy's charming image of the tired daffodils resting their heads on the stones was for Wordsworth an image of Fancy; her image of the daffodils as a busy crowd expressing social glee, an image of the Imagination. He did not disparage poetry of the Fancy, but he considered it inferior to poetry of the Imagination. He thought that an unfortunately large portion of Metaphysical poetry was fanciful rather than imaginative, because of the definiteness and fixity of its images; and he would probably have passed the same judgment on modern poetry. Imagination, in his opinion, gets at relationships that are true at the deepest level of experience.

He was, in short, a religious poet; and nothing for him is deeply imaginative unless it attains (I fall back on Hartley's terminology again) to theopathy and the moral sense. And since he was a mystic, subject to occasional mystic rapture, he felt that the deepest truth was not attained till the light of sense went out. He always connects deeply imaginative effects with the sense of infinity. So long as you can see sharply, clearly, with the kind and degree of detail that accompanies common perception, he might say, you should suspect that you are either engaged in merely practical activity or are resting in the mode of Fancy. You will know that you are dealing with Imagination when the edges of things begin to waver and fade out. In two brief texts he sums up the whole business far more satisfactorily than in the entire Preface devoted to the subject. The first is in the Sixth Book of *The Prelude* (he is speaking specifically of the Imagination):

> in such strength
> Of usurpation, when the light of sense
> Goes out, but with a flash that has revealed
> The invisible world, doth greatness make abode,
> There harbours; whether we be young or old,

> Our destiny, our being's heart and home,
> Is with infinitude, and only there;
> With hope it is, hope that can never die,
> Effort, and expectation, and desire,
> And something evermore about to be.

The second occurs in a letter to Walter Savage Landor, written January 21, 1824. Landor has said that he is disgusted with all books that treat of religion. Wordsworth replies that it is perhaps a bad sign in himself, but he has little relish for any other kind. "Even in poetry it is the imaginative only, viz., that which is conversant [with], or turns upon infinity, that powerfully affects me,—perhaps I ought to explain: I mean to say that, unless in those passages where things are lost in each other, and limits vanish, and aspirations are raised, I read with something too much like indifference."

It is not difficult by Wordsworth's own standards to establish the right of "I wandered lonely" to be considered an imaginative poem. The impression that the daffodils are joyous is not for him what Ruskin called pathetic fallacy. Under steady, prolonged, and serious contemplation daffodils can remain for him a symbol of joy because it is his faith (literally—no figure of speech) that every flower enjoys the air it breathes. Again, "I wandered lonely" is imaginative because the impression of joy deepens into *social* joy: since the daffodils stand for men in society, the poem attains to Sympathy on Hartley's ladder. But Wordsworth was not willing to rank it as an example of the higher exercise of the Imagination, because it lacks the fade-out. In it things only just begin to be lost in each other, and limits to vanish, and aspirations to be raised. He was quite aware of the fact that "I wandered lonely" is a very simple poem.

"The Solitary Reaper" has the degree of complexity necessary for full illustration of Wordsworth's theory.

> Behold her, single in the field,
> Yon solitary Highland Lass!
> Reaping and singing by herself;
> Stop here, or gently pass!
> Alone she cuts and binds the grain,
> And sings a melancholy strain;
> O listen! for the Vale profound
> Is overflowing with the sound.
>
> No Nightingale did ever chaunt
> More welcome notes to weary bands
> Of travellers in some shady haunt,
> Among Arabian sands:
> A voice so thrilling ne'er was heard,
> In spring-time from the Cuckoo bird,
> Breaking the silence of the seas
> Among the farthest Hebrides.

Will no one tell me what she sings?—
Perhaps the plaintive numbers flow
For old, unhappy, far-off things,
And battles long ago:
Or is it some more humble lay,
Familiar matter of to-day?
Some natural sorrow, loss, or pain,
That has been, and may be again?

Whate'er the theme, the Maiden sang,
As if her song could have no ending;
I saw her singing at her work,
And o'er the sickle bending;—
I listened, motionless and still;
And, as I mounted up the hill,
The music in my heart I bore,
Long after it was heard no more.

Here is what is for Wordsworth the optimum situation: solitude, in the single human figure against the landscape with more than a hint of dreariness in it; society, its affections and passions presented not directly but felt in the distanced, muted, managed form of song. Actual men in crowds are to him an unmanageable sight; a crowd of daffodils can stand for humanity if no more is called for than a gush of social joy; but this symbol will express the whole solemn mystery of human existence. The limits begin to vanish in the first stanza with the figure of the sound overflowing the rim of the vale.

The mystery of human existence: that is the first meaning of the bird metaphors of the second stanza. The reaper's song can stand for mystery because it is itself mysterious. Like the song of the nightingale and the song of the cuckoo, it is in a foreign tongue. It is one of those Gaelic occupational chants that go on and on like the drone of a bagpipe ("the maiden sang / As if her song could have no ending"): the poet feels it to be melancholy from its tone and rhythm, but he cannot understand the words. But he is also at work in other ways to make limits vanish: he pushes his boundaries out in space from Arabia to St. Kilda ("the farthest Hebrides"). And the third stanza, besides reinforcing "melancholy" by the more explicit "old, unhappy, far-off things, / And battles long ago" extends the boundaries in time: from "long ago" to "to-day," a plane of extension cutting across the plane of space. Again, we have the extension in human experience: from the unnatural sorrows of battles to the natural pain of everyday life. It is by devices such as these that Wordsworth transfigures the matter of common perception.

It would be perverse to attempt to identify the basic ideas of Wordsworth and Blake on the Imagination. Blake by his "double vision" no doubt meant much the same thing as did Wordsworth with his two ways of looking steadily at objects. Wordsworth might well have joined Blake's prayer to be kept from single vision and Newton's sleep. But Wordsworth believed that poetry must hold firm to the vision of the outward eye, and Blake, I think, wanted to relinquish the control of common perception altogether. "I assert for My Self that I do not behold the outward Creation & that to me it is hindrance & not Action; it is as the dirt upon my feet, No part of Me. . . . I question not my Corporeal or Vegetative Eye any more than I would Question a Window concerning a Sight. I look thro' it & not with it." Still, detached from Blake's private interpretations, his lines state very well what Wordsworth proposed:

> To see a World in a Grain of Sand
> And a Heaven in a Wild Flower,
> Hold Infinity in the palm of your hand
> And Eternity in an hour.

Wordsworth: The Romance of Nature and the Negative Way

Geoffrey H. Hartman

We know from "Tintern Abbey" that in certain "blessed" moods, the eye is quieted. Book XII of *The Prelude* relates that the tyranny of sight was, as well as "almost inherent in the creature," especially oppressive at a particular point in Wordsworth's life. This time coincided with an excessive sitting in judgment and may safely be identified with the period when the poet, disillusioned by the French Revolution and with Godwin, sought formal proof in everything till "yielding up moral questions in despair":

> I speak in recollection of a time
> When the bodily eye, in every stage of life
> The most despotic of our senses, gained
> Such strength in *me* as often held my mind
> In absolute dominion.
>
> (XII.127 ff.)

He refuses to enter upon abstruse argument to show how Nature thwarted such despotism by summoning all the senses to counteract each other; but his reflections lead him somewhat later in the same book to think of those "spots of time" which preserved and renovated him. One of them is the famous episode of the young boy, separated from his companion on a ride in the hills, dismounting out of fear and stumbling onto a murderer's gibbet, mouldered down, and of which nothing remained except the murderer's name carved nearby and kept clean because of local superstition:

> The grass is cleared away, and to this hour
> The characters are fresh and visible:
> A casual glance had shown them, and I fled,

From *The Unmediated Vision*, © 1954 by Yale University and © 1982 by Geoffrey H. Hartman, and from *Wordsworth's Poetry 1787–1814*, © 1964 by Yale University. Yale University Press, 1964. Originally entitled "The Romance of Nature and the Negative Way."

Faltering and faint, and ignorant of the road:
Then, reascending the bare common, saw
A naked pool that lay beneath the hills,
The beacon on the summit, and, more near,
A girl, who bore a pitcher on her head,
And seemed with difficult steps to force her way
Against the blowing wind. It was, in truth,
An ordinary sight.

(XII.244 ff.)

The nudity of such scenes has often been remarked and various hypotheses invented, for example that Wordsworth lacked sexual sensibility, saw in Nature a father substitute, etc. But a correct detailing of the characteristics of this moment would have to note first the cause of the faltering and fleeing, which is not so much the mouldered gibbet as the fresh and visible characters engraved by an unknown hand. The name evidently doesn't matter, only the characters as characters, and the effect on the boy is swift and out of proportion to the simple sight, a casual glance sufficing. Suggested first is the indestructibility of human consciousness, exemplified by the new characters, and after that the indestructibility of a consciousness in Nature, figured in the skeletal characters of a scene denuded of all color, sketched in a permanent black and white, yet capable of immense physical impact. The mystical chord is touched, and the eye overpowered by an intuition of characters affecting no single sense but compelling a comparison between the indestructibility of human consciousness and a physical indestructibility. The same effect will be found suggested in the second of the spots of time:

I sate half-sheltered by a naked wall;
Upon my right hand couched a single sheep,
Upon my left a blasted hawthorn stood;

(XII.299 ff.)

and the description of the characters of the great Apocalypse likewise starts with an intuition of indestructibility:

the immeasurable height
Of woods decaying, never to be decayed

(VI.623 ff.)

This, moreover, is coupled with a hint of the Last Judgment in the trumpeting of waterfalls that to the eye seem to possess the rigidity of rock,

The stationary blasts of waterfalls.

But before reaching a conclusion we should consider one more event, the most significant perhaps that enters through, yet overpowers, the eye. Wandering among London crowds the poet is smitten

> Abruptly, with the view (a sight not rare)
> Of a blind Beggar, who, with upright face,
> Stood, propped against a wall, upon his chest
> Wearing a written paper, to explain
> His story, whence he came, and who he was.
> Caught by the spectacle my mind turned round
> As with the might of waters; and apt type
> This label seemed of the utmost we can know,
> Both of ourselves and of the universe;
> And, on the shape of that unmoving man,
> His steadfast face and sightless eyes, I gazed.
> As if admonished from another world.
>
> (VII.638 ff.)

As in the gibbet scene, the poet emphasizes that the sight was ordinary and sudden, that is, having no intrinsic claim on the mind, nor worked up by meditation. But a greater similarity obtains between the two, though it is by no means complete. Both events focus on a label written by an impersonal hand. But whereas the characters in the one case seem indestructible, here the label is a sign of human impotence. Yet the superficial label clearly points to a set of deeper and indestructible characters, for the suggestion is that the lost eyes of the beggar were only like a piece of paper, a visual surface, and that, being removed, they leave the man more steadfast, fixed, eternal. We rediscover Wordsworth's constant concern with denudation, stemming from both a fear of visual reality and a desire for physical indestructibility. And the fine image of the mind turned by the spectacle as if with the might of waters, refers to that vast identity established throughout the poems of Wordsworth, an identity against sight, its fever and triviality, and making all things tend to the sound of universal waters; subduing the eyes by a power of harmony, and the reason by the suggestion of a Final Judgment which is God's alone. The intuition of indestructibility in the midst of decay, and the identity of the power in light with the power of sound ("by form or image unprofaned") are the two modes of a vision in which the mind knows itself almost without exterior cause or else as no less real, here, no less indestructible than the object of its perceptions.

II

Nature, for Wordsworth, is not an "object" but a presence and a power; a motion and a spirit; not something to be worshiped and consumed, but always a guide leading beyond itself. This guidance starts in earliest childhood. The boy of *Prelude* I is fostered alike by beauty and by fear. Through beauty, nature often makes the boy feel at home, for, as in the Great Ode, his soul is alien to this world. But through fear, nature reminds the boy from where he came, and prepares him, having lost heaven, also to lose nature. The boy of *Prelude* I, who does not yet know he must suffer this loss as well, is warned by nature itself of the solitude to come.

I have suggested elsewhere how the fine skating scene of the first book (425–63), though painted for its own sake, to capture the animal spirits of children spurred by a clear and frosty night, moves from vivid images of immediate life to an absolute calm which foreshadows a deeper and more hidden life. The Negative Way is a gradual one, and the child is weaned by a premonitory game of hide-and-seek in which nature changes its shape from familiar to unfamiliar, or even fails the child. There is a great fear, either in Wordsworth or in nature, of traumatic breaks: *Natura non facit saltus.*

If the child is led by nature to a more deeply meditated understanding of nature, the mature singer who composes *The Prelude* begins with that understanding or even beyond it—with the spontaneously creative spirit. Wordsworth plunges into *medias res*, where the *res* is Poetry, or Nature only insofar as it has guided him to a height whence he must find his own way. But Book VI, with which we are immediately concerned, records what is chronologically an intermediate period, in which the first term is neither Nature nor Poetry. It is Imagination in embryo: the mind muted yet also strengthened by the external world's opacities. Though imagination is with Wordsworth on the journey of 1790, nature seems particularly elusive. He goes out to a nature which seems to hide as in the crossing of the Alps.

The first part of this episode is told to illustrate a curious melancholy related to the "presence" of imagination and the "absence" of nature. Like the young Apollo in Keats's *Hyperion*, Wordsworth is strangely dissatisfied with the riches before him, and compelled to seek some other region:

> Where is power?
> Whose hand, whose essence, what divinity
> Makes this alarum in the elements,
> While I here idle listen on the shores
> In fearless yet in aching ignorance?
> [*Hyperion* III.103–7]

To this soft or "luxurious" sadness, a more masculine kind is added, which results from a "stern mood" or "underthirst of vigor"; and it is in order to throw light on this further melancholy that Wordsworth tells the incident of his crossing the Alps.

The stern mood to which Wordsworth refers can only be his premonition of spiritual autonomy, of an independence from sense-experience foreshadowed by nature since earliest childhood. It is the "underground" form of imagination, and *Prelude* II.315 ff. describes it as "an obscure sense / Of possible sublimity," for which the soul, remembering *how* it felt in exalted moments, but no longer *what* it felt, continually strives to find a new content. The element of obscurity, related to nature's self-concealment, is necessary to the soul's capacity for growth, for it vexes the latter toward self-dependence. Childhood pastures become viewless; the soul cannot easily find the source from which it used to drink the visionary power; and while dim memories of a passionate commerce with external things drive it more than ever to the world, this world makes itself more than ever inscrutable. The travelers' separation from their guides, then that of the road from the stream (VI.568), and finally their trouble with the peasant's words that have to be "translated," express subtly the soul's desire for a *beyond*. Yet only when poet, brook, and road are once again "fellow-travellers" (VI.622), and Wordsworth holds to Nature, does that reveal—a Proteus in the grasp of the hero—its prophecy.

This prophecy was originally the second part of the adventure, the delayed vision which compensates for his disappointment (the "Characters of the great Apocalypse," VI.617–40). In its original sequence, therefore, the episode has only two parts: the first term or moment of natural immediacy is omitted, and we go straight to the second term, the inscrutability of an external image, which leads via the gloomy strait to its renewal. Yet, as if this pattern demanded a substitute third term, Wordsworth's tribute to "Imagination" severs the original temporal sequence, and forestalls nature's renewal of the bodily eye with ecstatic praise of the inner eye.

The apocalypse of the gloomy strait loses by this the character of a *terminal* experience. Nature is again surpassed, for the poet's imagination is called forth, at the time of writing, by the barely scrutable, not by the splendid emotion; by the disappointment, not the fulfillment. This (momentary) displacement of emphasis is the more effective in that the style of VI.617 ff., and the very characters of the apocalypse, suggest that the hiding places of power cannot be localized in nature. Though the apostrophe to Imagination—the special insight that comes to Wordsworth in 1804—is a real peripety, reversing a meaning already established, it is not unprepared. But it takes the poet many years to realize that nature's "end" is to lead to something "without end," to teach the travelers to transcend nature.

The three parts of this episode, therefore, can help us understand the mind's growth toward independence of immediate external stimuli. The measure of that independence is Imagination, and carries with it a precarious self-consciousness. We see that the mind must pass through a stage where it experiences Imagination as a power separate from Nature, that the poet must come to think and feel as if by his own choice, or from the structure of his mind.

VI-a (557–91) shows the young poet still dependent on the immediacy of the external world. Imagination frustrates that dependence secretly, yet its blindness toward nature is accompanied by a blindness toward itself. It is only a "mute Influence of the soul, / An Element of nature's inner self" (1805, VIII.512–13).

VI-b (592–616) gives an example of thought or feeling that came from the poet's mind without immediate external excitement. There remains, of course, the memory of VI-a (the disappointment), but this is an internal feeling, not an external image. The poet recognizes at last that the power he has looked for in the outside world is really within and frustrating his search. A shock of recognition then feeds the very blindness toward the external world which helped to produce that shock.

In VI-c (617–40) the landscape is again an immediate external object of experience. The mind cannot separate in it what it desires to know and what it actually knows. It is a moment of revelation, in which the poet sees not as in a glass, darkly, but face to face. VI-c clarifies, therefore, certain details of VI-a and *seems* to actualize figurative details of VI-b. The matter-of-fact interplay of quick and lingering movement, of up-and-down per-plexities in the ascent (VI.567 ff.), reappears in larger letters; while the interchanges of light and darkness, of cloud and cloudlessness, of rising like a vapor from the abyss and pouring like a flood from heaven have entered the landscape bodily. The gloomy strait also participates in this actualization. It is revealed as the secret middle term which leads from the barely scrutable presence of nature to its resurrected image. The travelers who move freely with or against the terrain, hurrying upward, pacing downward, perplexed at crossings, are now led narrowly by the pass as if it were their rediscovered guide.

The Prelude, as history of a poet's mind, foresees the time when the "Characters of the great Apocalypse" will be intuited without the medium of nature. The time approaches even as the poet writes, and occasionally cuts across his narrative, the imagination rising up, as in Book VI, "Before the eye and progress of my Song" (version of 1805). This phrase, at once conventional and exact, suggests that imagination waylaid the poet on his mental journey. The "eye" of his song, trained on a temporal sequence with the vision in the strait as its final term, is suddenly obscured. He is momentarily forced to deny nature that magnificence it had shown in the gloomy strait, and to attribute the glory to imagination, whose interposition in the very moment of writing proves it to be a power more independent than nature of time and place, and so a better type "Of first, and last, and midst, and without end" (VI.640).

We know that VI-b records something that happened during compo-sition, and which enters the poem as a new biographical event. Wordsworth has just described his disappointment (VI-a) and turns in anticipation to nature's compensatory finale (VI-c). He is about to respect the original temporal sequence, "the eye and progress" of his song. But as he looks forward, in the moment of composition, from blankness toward revelation, a new insight cuts him off from the latter. The original disappointment is seen not as a test, or as a prelude to magnificence, but as a revelation in itself. It suddenly reveals a power—imagination—that could not be satisfied by anything in nature, however sublime. The song's progress comes to a halt because the poet is led beyond nature. Unless he can respect the natural (which includes the temporal) order, his song, at least as narrative, must cease. Here Imagination, not Nature (as in I.96 ff.), defeats Poetry.

This conclusion may be verified by comparing the versions of 1805 and 1850. The latter replaces "Before the eye and progress of my Song" with a more direct metaphorical transposition. Imagination is said to rise from the mind's abyss "Like an unfathered vapour that enwraps, / At once, some lonely traveller." The (literal) traveler of 1790 becomes the (mental) traveler at the moment of composition. And though one Shakespearean doublet has disappeared, another implicitly takes its place: does not imagination rise from "the dark backward and abysm of time" (*The Tempest*, I.ii.50)? The result, in any case, is a disorientation of time added to that of way; an apocalyptic moment in which past and future overtake the present; and the poet, cut off from nature by imagination, is, in an absolute sense, lonely.

The last stage in the poet's "progress" has been reached. The travelers of VI-a had already left behind their native land, the public rejoicing of France, rivers, hills, and spires; they have separated from their guides, and finally from the unbridged mountain stream. Now, in 1804, imagination separates the poet from all else: human companionship, the immediate scene, the remembered scene. The end of the *via negativa* is near. There is no more "eye and progress"; the invisible progress of VI-a (Wordsworth crossing the Alps unknowingly) has revealed itself as a progress independent of visible ends, or engendered by the desire for an "invisible world"— the substance of things hoped for, the evidence of things not seen. Wordsworth descants on the Pauline definition of faith:

> in such strength
> Of usurpation, when the light of sense
> Goes out, but with a flash that has revealed
> The invisible world, doth greatness make abode,
> There harbours; whether we be young or old,
> Our destiny, our being's heart and home,
> Is with infinitude, and only there;
> With hope it is, hope that can never die,
> Effort, and expectation, and desire,
> And something evermore about to be.
>
> (VI.599–608)

Any further possibility of progress for the poet would be that of song itself, of poetry no longer subordinate to the mimetic function, the experience faithfully traced to this height. The poet is a traveler insofar as he must respect nature's past guidance and retrace his route. He did come, after all, to an important instance of bodily vision. The way is the song. But the song often strives to become the way. And when this happens, when the song seems to capture the initiative, in such supreme moments of poetry as VI-b or even VI-c, the way is lost. Nature in VI-c shows "Winds thwarting winds, bewildered and forlorn," as if they too had lost their way. The apocalypse in the gloomy strait depicts a self-thwarting march and counter-march of elements, a divine mockery of the concept of the Single Way.

But in VI-c, nature still stands over and against the poet; he is still the observer, the eighteenth-century gentleman admiring a new manifestation of the sublime, even if the lo! or mark! is suppressed. He moves haltingly but he moves; and the style of the passage emphasizes continuities. Yet with the imagination athwart there is no movement, no looking before and after. The song itself must be the way, though that of a blinded man, who admits, "I was lost." Imagination, as it shrouds the poet's eye, also shrouds the eye of his song, whose tenor is nature guiding and fostering the power of song.

It is not, therefore, till 1804 that Wordsworth discovers the identity of his hidden guide. VI-c was probably composed in 1799, and it implies that Wordsworth, at that time, still thought nature his guide. But now he sees that it was imagination moving him by means of nature, just as Beatrice guided Dante by means of Virgil. It is not nature as such but nature indistinguishably blended with imagination that compels the poet along his Negative Way. Yet, if VI-b prophesies against the world of sense-experience, Wordsworth's affection and point of view remain unchanged. Though his discovery shakes the foundation of his poem, he returns after a cloudburst of verses to the pedestrian attitude of 1790, when the external world and not imagination seemed to be his guide ("Our journey we renewed, / Led by the stream," etc.). Moreover, with the exception of VI-b, imagination does not move the poet directly, but always through the agency of nature. The childhood "Visitings of imaginative power" depicted in Books I and XII also appeared in the guise or disguise of nature. Wordsworth's journey as a poet can only continue with eyes, but the imagination experienced as a power distinct from nature opens his eyes by putting them out. Wordsworth, therefore, does not adhere to nature because of natural fact, but despite it and because of human and poetic fact. Imagination is indeed an *awe-full* power.

III

Wordsworth's attempt to revive the Romance mode for a consciously Protestant imagination had no issue in his own poetry, or even in English poetry as a whole, which will follow the freer romances of Keats, Shelley, and Scott. But in America, where Puritanism still questioned the sacred and also secular rights of imagination, a similar development is found. The possibility of a consciously Protestant romance is what inspires or self-justifies Hawthorne, Melville, and Henry James. If the Christian poets of the Renaissance wondered how they could use Pagan forms and themes, the neo-Puritan writers wonder how they can use the Christian superstitions. Not only do we find the often directly presented schism between an old-world and a new-world imagination, in which the old world is, sometimes nobly, under the spell of "superstitious fancies strong," but the action centers on the manner in which a strange central apparition, a romance phenomenon, is imaginatively valued. In the European society in which she moves, James's Daisy Miller is a white doe, and there are those who do the gentle creature wrong, who kill her, in fact, by knowing her wrongly.

I have chosen, of course, a very simple case; but there is no need to ascend the scale of Jamesian or Melvillean fiction to the final white mystery. Wordsworth's scruples concerning the imagination are Puritan scruples even though they are gradually associated with Anglican thought.

That Wordsworth was seeking to develop a new kind of romance, one that would chasten our imaginations, is already suggested by the stanzas dedicating *The White Doe* to his wife. A moving personal document, they trace the history of his relation to romantic fiction. He describes his and Mary's love of Spenser, their innocent enjoyment of "each specious miracle." But then a "lamentable change"—the death of Wordsworth's brother—pierces their hearts:

> For us the stream of fiction ceased to flow,
> For us the voice of melody was mute.

Romance and realism are suddenly opposed. The truth is too harsh, and fiction is even blamed for deceiving the mind, for veiling reality with "the light that never was." Spenser, however, is so soothing, that he beguiles them once more, and the story of the Nortons, with its own "mild Una in her sober cheer," is composed.

But the death of Wordsworth's brother leaves its mark. Though Wordsworth returns to Spenser, the stream of fiction is troubled, it will never again flow lightly "in the bent of Nature." The poet seems to have interpreted his brother's death, like his father's, as a "chastisement" following an over-extension of imaginative hopes (cf. *Prelude* XII.309–16). The dream of happiness built on John's return was something *hyper moron*, secretly apocalyptic, or beyond the measure nature could fulfill. This is not to say that John's loss was the decisive cause for Wordsworth's decline as a poet— I have abjured speculation on this matter. Some speculations, however, are simply a way of describing the later poetry, and it is quite true that whether or not the decisive shock came in 1805, Wordsworth's mind is now much less inclined to "wanton" in "the exercise of its own powers . . . loving its own creation." If we compare his dedicatory stanzas to Mary with those Shelley wrote to *his* Mary and which preface *The Witch of Atlas*, the distance between one poet's lighthearted espousal of "visionary rhyme" and the other's weight of scruples becomes fully apparent. It is as if Shelley and Wordsworth had polarized Spenserian romance, the former taking its *dulce*, the latter, its *utile*.

It might not seem possible that the later poetry could be beset by even more scruples, but this is what happens. Wordsworth's attitude toward his mind's "exercise of its powers" suffers a further restraint. He begins to watch on *two* fronts: to be deluded that "the mighty Deep / Was even the gentlest of all gentle things" is as dangerous as to gaze into the bottomless abyss. He is now as careful about an idealizing impulse as about the apocalyptic intimation. The presence of a Sympathetic Nature, which is the one superstition for which he had kept his respect, for it is vital not only to poetry but also to human development, being a necessary illusion in the growth of the mind, this too is falling away. Yet the story of the white doe is his attempt to save the notion once more in some purer form. He knows that to give it up entirely is to return to a holy, but stern and melancholy, imagination.

Under the pressure of these many restraints, Wordsworth's mind has little chance to fall in love with or explore its own impressions. Self-discovery, which informs the meditative lyrics (the act of recall there is never a passive thing but verges on new and often disturbing intuitions) almost disappears. And, by a curious irony, the unpublished *Prelude*, which is his greatest testimony to the living mind, now discourages further self-exploration. Such later sentiments as:

> Earth prompts—Heaven urges; let us seek the light,
> Studious of that pure intercourse begun
> When first our infant brows their lustre won,
> [*Ecclesiastical Sonnets* Pt. III.46]

do not rely, in their weakness, on the external authority of the church, but on the internal authority of his own greatest poem, which is kept private, and as scripture to himself abets the flat reiteration of his ideas in a slew of minor poems. J. M. Murry is right in feeling that the later Wordsworth represents the process of self-discovery as much more orthodox from the beginning than it was; and Coleridge, severely disappointed by *The Excursion*, offers a similar diagnosis: Wordsworth's opinions, he said, were based on "self-established convictions" and did not have for readers in general the special force they had for the poet.

There are, nevertheless, strange happenings in the later poetry, which has a precarious quality of its own. Though Wordsworth no longer dallies with surmise, he cannot entirely forgo apocalyptic fancies, or the opposite (if more generous) error which attributes to nature a vital and continuous role in the maturing of the mind. The old imaginative freedoms continue to rise up, like Proteus or Triton, against the narrow-minded materialism of his time—a living Pagan is better than a dead Christian spirit. He is not beyond being surprised by his imagination. It continues to defy his censorship, even if he queries every fancy, every moment of "quickened subjectivity." I shall conclude by considering certain incidents from the later poetry that show in what relation to his own mind Wordsworth stands.

In 1820, thirty years after his journey through the Alps, he takes Mary and Dorothy to the Continent. Dorothy keeps her usual journal, to which he probably turned in composing the "memorials" of that tour. While in the valley of Chamonix (a place sacred to the poet) the travelers hear voices rising from the mountain's base and glimpse below them a procession making its way to the church. Dorothy describes the scene for us:

> [we saw] a lengthening Procession—the Priest in his robes—the host, and banners uplifted; and men following two and two;— and, last of all, a great number of females, in like order; the head and body of each covered with a white garment. The stream

continued to flow on for a long time, till all had paced slowly round the church. . . . The procession was grave and simple, agreeing with the simple decorations of a village church; the banners made no glittering shew; the Females composed a moving girdle round the Church; their figures, from head to foot, covered with one piece of white cloth, resembled the small pyramids of the Glacier, which were before our eyes; and it was impossible to look at one and the other without fancifully connecting them together. Imagine the *moving* Figures, like a stream of pyramids,—the white Church, the half-concealed Village, and the Glacier close behind, among pine-trees,—a pure sun shining over all! and remember that these objects were seen at the base of those enormous mountains, and you may have some faint notion of the effect produced upon us by that beautiful spectacle.

[Journal for September 16, 1820]

Wordsworth is inspired by this to a "progress poem" entitled "Processions. Suggested on a Sabbath Morning in the Vale of Chamouny" which traces the spirit of religious ceremonies from ancient times to the present. The Alps, archaic strongholds, allow him to recognize in Pagan ritual the impure basis of Christian pageantry. Shrill canticles have yielded to sober litanies; silver bells and pompous decorations to "hooded vestments fair"; and noisy feasts to an assembly breathing "a Spirit more subdued and soft." Moreover, as he looks on, another archaic vestige suggests itself, which is hinted at in Dorothy's account: that the procession is born of the mountain, like the white pillars above it. Indeed, the glacier columns, juxtaposed with the moving column of white figures, bring to mind the theory of Creation by Metamorphosis. The mountain, in this Blakean insight, is "men seen afar."

Wordsworth is strangely frightened at this—not at the mere thought of metamorphosis but at a reflexive knowledge connected with it. He realizes he has viewed more than a transformed archaic ritual, or ancient truth: he has seen the *source* of that truth in his mind's excited and spontaneous joining of the living stream of people to the frozen of nature. As in his greatest poetry, the mind is moved by itself after being moved by something external. He writes a stanza similar in tenor and directness to the apostrophe to Imagination in the sixth book of *The Prelude*, similar at least in its magnificent opening:

> Trembling, I look upon the secret springs
> Of that licentious craving in the mind
> To act the God among external things,
> To bind, on apt suggestion, or unbind;
> And marvel not that antique Faith inclined
> To crowd the world with metamorphosis,
> Vouchsafed in pity or in wrath assigned;
> Such insolent temptations wouldst thou miss,
> Avoid these sights; nor brood o'er Fable's dark abyss!

Wordsworth's reaction, visceral first, pontific later, differs from the usual religious decision to relinquish a profane subject or style. He does not say, in Herbert's sweet manner, farewell dark fables, or censor their use in Christian poetry. But he turns in the moment, and explicitly, from a power of his own mind without which poetry is not conceivable. It is not fabling merely, but "Fable's dark abyss"—the mind of man itself—he now fears to look on. He is afraid of fables because of their reaction on a mind that might brood too pregnantly on what they reveal of its power. Yet at the time of *The White Doe* he had still tried to "convert" a fable by purifying its superstition and cleansing its mystery: the doe is not a metamorphosed spirit and her powers of sympathy are due to natural not supernatural causes. What a difference, also, between this sacred tremor and his earlier, almost cavalier attitude toward all mythologies! In 1798, and again in 1814, he professes to be unalarmed at their conceptions because of the greater "fear and awe" that fall on him when he regards "the Mind of Man— / My haunt, and the main region of my song." He did not fear his fear then as he does now, trembling before his own creative will.

Wordsworth's diffidence is no sudden thing; we found it at the beginning of his career, and related it to an extraordinary, apocalyptic consciousness of self. At that time religion seemed to him too much a product of that same apocalyptic consciousness. Nature had to be defended against a supernatural religion as well as against the barren eye of Science. Was it ever meant, he asks,

> That this majestic imagery, the clouds
> The ocean and the firmament of heaven
> Should lie a barren picture on the mind?
> [addendum to "The Ruined Cottage"]

In the later poetry, however, religion has changed its role. It now protects rather than threatens nature. He begins to identify with the Anglo-Catholic concept of the *via media* his ideal of Nature, of England, even of Poetry. The poet, he had said in 1802, is "the rock of defence for human nature; an upholder and preserver, carrying everywhere with him relationship and love." He now sees the church as part of that rock: an *ecclesia* mediating by a divine principle of mercy the sterner demands of God, State, and Imagination, demands which have often threatened human nature, and led to individual or collective fanaticisms. Religion and imagination are intervolved (Wordsworth and Blake are in perfect accord on *this*), and whereas Catholicism incites an apocalyptic response:

> Mine ear has rung, my spirit sunk subdued,
> Sharing the strong emotion of the crowd,
> When each pale brow to dread hosannas bowed
> While clouds of incense mounting veiled the rood,
> That glimmered like a pine-tree dimly viewed
> Through Alpine vapours

the Anglican Church, which is the *religio loci* corresponding to the *genius loci* of England, rejects such appalling rites in the hope that nature, man, and God constitute ultimately "one society":

> the Sun with his first smile
> Shall greet that symbol crowning the low Pile:
> And the fresh air of incense-breathing morn
> Shall wooingly embrace it; and green moss
> Creep round its arms through centuries unborn.

Covenant has replaced, as completely as possible, apocalypse: his emblem marries nature, time, and the spirit.

The *Ecclesiastical Sonnets*, from which the above extracts are taken, show Wordsworth is suspicious of everything that could rouse the apocalyptic passions. This is also an important clue to his later politics, which seem illiberal, apostate even; a failure of nerve like his poetry. The evidence against him is indeed black. "That such a man," cries Shelley, "should be such a poet!" Shelley did not know Wordsworth personally, but even the faithful Crabb Robinson, who made all the possible allowances, is compelled to address Dorothy in 1827: "I assure you it gives me a real pain when I think that some further commentator may possibly hereafter write: 'This great poet survived to the fifth decennary of the nineteenth century, but he appears to have died in the year 1814, as far as life consisted in an active sympathy with the temporary [viz. temporal] welfare of his fellow-creatures.' " Only in matters of Church doctrine, as distinguished from Church or national politics, does something of Wordsworth's liberalism remain. His views, says H. N. Fairchild, praising where he thinks to blame, are "wholly consistent with modern Christian liberalism . . . very loose and vague, however, for a nineteenth-century High Churchman."

Wordsworth, it is clear, has passed from the idea that change (let alone revolutionary change) intends a repossession of the earth to the idea that it might cause a greater dispossession than ever. Harper has documented his panic fear of change. It is a deeply emotional and imaginative thing, and has almost no relation to his own very small prosperity. The Reform Bill of 1832, for instance, seems to him to herald a revolt of the masses. He prophesies ruin and destruction to England and thinks of having to leave it. His jeremiads indicate a soul which knows itself too well, and is still afraid in others of those "blasts of music" and "daring sympathies with power" to which he had given ear at the time of the French Revolution.

Dark thoughts—"blind thoughts" as he calls them in "Resolution and Independence"—certainly continue to impinge on him. Yet how deep they lie, almost too deep for notice. They come to the surface only in matters of politics, and in exceptionally self-conscious verses, like those in memory of Chamonix. The most famous of the River Duddon sonnets, the "Afterthought" of the series, runs truer to course. The whole series, less conventional than it seems, participates in the poet's desire to bind together the powers of his mind and of nature; and to know this illumines the character of his final sonnet.

The "After-thought" begins very simply:

> I thought of Thee, my partner and my guide,
> As being passed away.

It makes us wonder, this quiet human directness, whom the poet is addressing, but then Willard Sperry's observation that "his brief for nature's morality was based upon her openness to our address" comes to mind. The more remarkable aspect of the verses is what Wordsworth can have meant by the river "passing away."

He must have recalled the prophecy of streams shrinking in the final fire, of "Old Ocean, in his bed left singed and bare" (*Prelude* V.33). This must have come to him and threatened the entire basis of his sonnets, which is the partnership of mind and nature. Or is it his own death which he foresaw, as in "Tintern Abbey"? But why, in that case, would he talk of Duddon's death rather than of his own?

I suspect, in any case, that the personal fact of his dying seemed to him a small matter compared to the river's loss and the foreboded severing of the loves of man and nature. Duddon is mortal in that it may die in man or to him as he grows older, but especially in that it may die to the human imagination, generally, on Wordsworth's death. For if his special mission among poets is to marry nature to the mind, his death takes on a cosmic meaning. The rest of the poem, of course, dispels his strange fear concerning Duddon:

> —Vain sympathies!
> For, backward, Duddon! as I cast my eyes,
> I see what was, and is, and will abide;
> Still glides the Stream, and shall for ever glide;
> The Form remains, the Function never dies;
> While we, the brave, the mighty, and the wise,
> We Men, who in our morn of youth defied
> The elements, must vanish;—be it so!
> Enough, if something from our hands have power
> To live, and act, and serve the future hour;
> And if, as toward the silent tomb we go,
> Through love, through hope, and faith's transcendent dower,
> We feel that we are greater than we know.

This is pure consolation and too easy. His sympathies (for the stream!) are "vain" because nature outlives man and will continue to inspire him; and because man, too, has the promise, through religion, of an immortality that hopefully does not exclude the tie of nature.

Yet the distance between "Tintern Abbey" and the River Duddon "After-thought" is not great. The primary experience is one of nature, of the Wye or the Duddon or other great presences. In the earlier poems we are told directly of how the cataracts haunted the boy or how the objects of nature "lay upon his mind like substances" and "perplexed the bodily sense." The same kind of perplexity is produced by the appearance of the white doe. The mystery in nature is that of our relation to it, which is darkly sympathetic, so that Goethe calls it "das offenbare Geheimniss," an incumbent natural mystery. But this experience of relationship, open to all, is followed by the further mystery of its diminution, also shared by all. The poet who returns to Tintern Abbey knows his loss; he sees it in the glass of the landscape, darkly; and a prophetic fear, despite nature's continuing importance, leads him to envisage severance and even death. The conclusion that his death may mean the passing away of nature from the human mind is not yet drawn, for he prays that his sister may continue a relationship to which he is dying. But in the "After-thought" his fear touches that furthest point. It does so fleetingly, yet still bespeaks either a delusion of grandeur or a remarkable conviction that man and nature are growing irremediably apart, and that the gap between them, whether a historical error or a providential test, already verges on apocalypse. "The sun strengthens us no more, neither does the moon."

The burden of this secret consciousness in Wordsworth should not be underestimated. It is he who stands between us and the death of nature; and this is also the truest justification for the "egotistical sublime" in his poetry. He values his own lightest feeling for the sufficiencies of mother earth—

> The night that calms, the day that cheers;
> The common growth of mother-earth
> Suffices me—her tears, her mirth
> Her humblest mirth and tears
>   [*Peter Bell*, Prologue]

—because her call to him, unregarded, augurs a loss in our capacity to respond to nature, and hence the virtual opposite of that "great consummation" of which he sings in the verses that preface the 1814 *Excursion*. He feels that he must personally fasten or newcreate the links between nature and the human mind. The "Adonais" Shelley laments is strangely like his own conception of himself.

I may seem to exaggerate Wordsworth's sense of mission; but no one has yet explained the heartsickness and melancholia of the aging poet. These are prompted, of course, by political fears (which are really imaginative fears) and by personal grief, yet do they differ, except in persistence, from earlier dejections? Is his "fixed despondency, uncorrected" human weakness merely, and the effect of old age, or may it not accord with his own younger picture of himself as a "meditative, oft a suffering man"? What his meditations were, and why linked intimately to a certain kind of suffering, may now be clear. The selfhood Wordsworth knew, and which is always related to a fear of the death of nature, is at first alleviated by his sense of special mission, then cruelly confirmed by what he takes to be his growing isolation. At the time of "Michael," he is still thinking "Of youthful Poets, who among these hills / Will be my second self when I am gone"; it is in hope of these that he spins his homely ballads. But he never recognizes Shelley or Keats or any of the following generation as his second self. He is a stubborn, old, opinionated man—perhaps; the fact remains that Shelley and Keats, though concerned with the humanizing of imagination, have greater affinities with the Renaissance poets and that these have greater affinities with one another than Wordsworth has with any of them. Milton, whose sense of mission is as strong as his, could turn to Spenser and even to Virgil; Blake, though almost unknown in his time, thought of himself as continuing or correcting Milton and the Bible; but Wordsworth, despite his love for the older writers, and especially for Milton, can turn to no one in his desire to save nature for the human imagination. He is the most isolated figure among the great English poets.

Wordsworth's Severe Intimations

Paul H. Fry

As I arrive at the period when genres begin to be "naturalized" along with poetic diction, my continuing to read odes as odes may call for a few words of defense. In the eighteenth century the genres still comprised a "cosmic syntax" that had its place in an articulate and more or less legible universe. Generic thinking prevailed in most quarters, even though there was often disagreement about the proper hierarchy of the genres: epic was still highest in the criticism of Pope's followers, but a lively minority from John Dennis to Watts and Bishop Lowth placed the "sacred lyric" highest. Johnson was rather unusual in viewing the genres with some disapproval. He opposed the strict decorum of any generic approach to poetry for fear of encouraging insincerity and distorted observation. As one pieces together his strictures on pastoral and the ode, his defense of Shakespeare's mixed genres, and his attention to the local rather than the larger structural features of poetry in all the modes, one realizes how fully he anticipates Wordsworth (though, of course, in behalf of a far more generalized sense of reality) in viewing poetry as the "real language of men."

The challenge to the taxonomic view of literature arose from a resurgence of epistemological trust in what Gray had contemptuously called the "language of the age." A genre, from Aristotle onward, had always been understood to be a fictive solution to the problem of untidiness in the real world, but no one had ever claimed that "history" is not itself far tidier than life. History was more accurate, perhaps, than poetry; but no critic in the line of Aristotle ever confused verbal representation with objective presentation. As Aristotle himself put the matter in his seminal grammar, the *Categories*, "Substance cannot be predicated." Discourse, in other words, always defers and specie-fies the thing in itself, proceeding nec-

From *The Poet's Calling in the English Ode*. © 1980 by Yale University. Yale University Press, 1980.

essarily in referential categories. Since generic thinking is therefore inescapable, the Aristotelian might argue, it may as well be cultivated, especially
because it does seem to correspond to the several great forms that inhere
in nature. Although in the Neoplatonic variant of this tradition that Sidney
follows, the generic fictions were understood to merge with a transcendental ground (the Ideal) insofar as they purged the dross of their material
ground (the phenomenal apparitions that Plato was right to abuse poets
for imitating); and although even among empiricists opinions differed concerning the degree to which genres should realign the nature of things,
there was still an implicit belief at the root of every generic theory until
1800 that poetic space is what we largely perceive and moderately re-create
according to received models given either by nature or by nature's best
metonym, Homer, whose *Margites* and "Homeric Hymns" made him the
father of every genre that exists.

A Wordsworthian poetics leads to the new conclusion that poetic space
is what we half perceive and half create on the basis of an ad hoc symbiosis
of mind with nature. Thus the cosmic syntax or taxonomy formerly given
ready-formed to the creative faculties of the poet becomes in Wordsworth
a unitary principle that appears in changing ways, according to the pressure
of the moment, at the joining place of mind and nature. This powerful
reduction to "the one Life within us and abroad" (Coleridge) undermines
all gross classification even as it promotes the unique selfhood or substance
of "the meanest flower that blows" within the imagined unity of things.
The atomistic and the cosmic fuse under the pressure of imagination, leaving the illusion of difference to linger only among intermediate quantities:

> the one interior life
> That lives in all things, sacred from the touch
> Of that false secondary power by which
> In weakness we create distinctions, then
> Believe that all our puny boundaries are things
> Which we perceive and not which we have made.
> [from an early notebook for *The Prelude*]

On this view, symbolism is available to all the arts of expression, symbolism
being the making-present of some universal power that is universally absent
until by magic the *nomen* grows numinous. This faith in the symbol is meant
to quiet our obstinate questionings, whether of sense or of the supersen-
suous, by waiving altogether the question of the existence or nonexistence
of the physical referent. The triangulation of word, thing, and spirit by the
"symbol" effaces the thing by sublating its newly glorified selfhood. Only
the symbol, as Coleridge might say, "is that it is," an articulate Presence,
like the Word. This antigeneric faith, be it said now, is none other than—
the faith that typifies the genre called the ode. Were it not antinomian,
defiant of determinacy by externally given origins, this faith would attach
itself to the office of prayer.

When genre theory reappears in the organization and the Preface of

Wordsworth's 1815 *Collected Poems*, it is based in good part on subjective distinctions. The cosmos is still one, but our different faculties (e.g., fancy, imagination) with their different predilections (affection, the need to name, and so on) and phases of perception (e.g., "early youth") will present the "one Life" in various guises that truly are different from each other. Not absolutely but in tendency, Wordsworth transfers the science of genres from cosmology to psychology.

It is only very recently that the idea of a random field of signification, irreducible to any well-ordered syntax of faculties in the conscious subject, has challenged classification of all kinds. According to this view, both objective *and* subjective generic thinking are attributes of a naive epistemology, or rather of the naive faith that an epistemology is possible. I think that this Pyrrhonism has always been perceptibly registered by the presentational lyric, despite its generally idealistic aims. The ode, that Great Auk among the birds that are themselves objects of the obsolete science of ornithology, the ode of all forms, has always known the ruptures of dissemination. The sheer textuality of the ode, its re(com)pression of alien generic structures as the daemonic traces of lyric metaphor, yields a skepticism about the contentments of form that belies both occasion and vocation.

Perhaps there is room for yet another sentence in the current debate about periodization, a sentence that would defend my own approach to literary history: *The theoretical discourse of any period lies waiting and implicit in the discursive forms that precede it.* Thus one could support the observation of Fredric Jameson, for whom origins are material and diachronic agencies, that "the new is to the old as latent content working its way to the surface to displace a form henceforth obsolete." Periodization might properly map the passing over of knowledge from its encodement in structure to the discourse about structures: from code to statement, which in turn becomes a new code, harboring anxieties that will force their way into the open in yet later statements. This dialectic would somewhat exaggerate the incidence of change in the series of poems I am studying, however. The knowledge I am tracing in the ode remains partly encoded and partly discursive knowledge in any ode to this day, but periodic changes in the ode can nevertheless still be recorded as topological shifts, irreducibly different, in the near-utterance or dissemination of the repressed. Thus, concerning the great Romantic odes to which I now turn, it will gradually become apparent that in them the sublime, here understood as the uncanny element of lyric inspiration, has been conceived in a way that differs wholly from its conception in the eighteenth-century ode.

I

Wordsworth's early "Remembrance of Collins" reflects a complex and alert reading of Collins's odes. Beginning as Collins once did with Spenser, Wordsworth's "Glide Gently, thus for ever glide, / O Thames!" recognizes

Collins's desire to write the poem of his own chaste marriage. Very possibly, therefore, Wordsworth numbers among the motives of the mad "Poet's sorrows" (20) the epithalamic failure of Collins's odes. Interweaving images from the Death of Thomson Ode and the "Ode to Evening" (and also from Thomson's "Hymn on Solitude": "Descending angels bless thy train"), Wordsworth tries to purify Collins's typically mysterious haunted moment by arming it with holiness and scattering the daemonic, as did Milton in the Nativity Ode, with a militant poise:

> How calm! how still! the only sound,
> The dripping of the oar suspended!
> —The evening darkness gathers round
> By virtue's holiest powers attended.

Wordsworth's prayer that the "child of song" (19) be attended by a vision that lightens our falling toward darkness, a vision of the high birthplace both of ourselves and of our virtue, is offered in order to restore the otherness and innocence of the past to the odes of Collins; and, on a far more difficult occasion, it is also the prayer of the Intimations Ode.

The happier past, as a sign of poetic election and of life after death, can be recovered only through that most ontologically treacherous of faculties, memory. Recollection in "calm weather" can never be facile; indeed, it may be wise to assume, upon careful reading, that recollection in the Intimations Ode is recognized to be an exhilarating but futile exercise. In itself, however, the quality of difference between present and past that is given by memory as a newly refined poetic topic—"and, oh! the difference to me!"—enables the odes of Wordsworth and his major contemporaries to represent change more plausibly than any of Gray's or Collins's resources had permitted. But only *more* plausibly. The Romantic ode writer hopes that one change—from past to present—will imply the coming of another, the redemption of the present. But the disappointment of that hope cannot be avoided, owing to the continued necessity of repetition, which insists upon the immutability of the present. No naturalizing of vocative devices can ever completely suppress this immutability because, after all, the presupposed existence of some indivisible and unchanging power is just what an ode is written to celebrate. The ode bends the quality of difference in all experience to its mono-myth, which is only speciously genealogical.

All the great odes I shall discuss from now on are evening odes. The veils of Gray and Collins are taken over by the Romantics as a sober coloring of clouds and tropes at sundown that still conceals the "wavy bed" (Wordsworth's "mighty waters") of the sun-poet's origin. That the sense of evening in the Romantic ode is yet more intense than in earlier odes can be shown in a rough way even by comparative biography. Whereas eighteenth-century poets, even Swift, began their careers by assaying the vocational challenge of Pindarism, Wordsworth and Coleridge "began" (if we disregard their school exercises) in the quieter keys of the topographical poem and the slighter lyric modes. M. H. Abrams's inclusion of the Intimations Ode and "Dejection. An Ode" in his persuasively described unifying genre, "the greater Romantic lyric" (encompassing the common themes and structure of the sublime ode and the Conversation Poem), may be questioned simply by appealing to dates. Nearly all the major Conversation Poems of both Wordsworth and Coleridge were written well before the Companion odes that were begun in 1802, begun in response to growing intimations of loss. If the eighteenth-century poet proved himself to be a poet by writing an ode, the Romantic poet proved himself *still* to be a poet by writing an ode, but no longer a poet gifted with unmediated vision. The turning of Wordsworth and Coleridge to the unnatural conventions of ode writing is itself a farewell to the natural holiness of youth.

II

L'ode chante l'éternité, l'épopée sollenise l'histoire, le drame peint la vie. Le caractère de la première poésie est la naïveté, le caractère de la seconde est la simplicité, le caractère de la troisieme, la vérité. . . . Les personnages de l'ode sont des colosses: Adam, Caïn, Noé; ceux de l'épopée sont des géants: Achille, Atrée, Oreste; ceux du drame sont des hommes: Hamlet, Macbeth, Othello. L'ode vit l'idéal.
—VICTOR HUGO, *Préface de Cromwell* (1827)

From its publication to the present, the Intimations Ode has had the reputation of being Wordsworth's most confused poem. In this respect it is appropriately an ode or, more precisely, an irregular Pindaric. What Wordsworth dictated to Miss Fenwick, "To the attentive and competent reader the whole sufficiently explains itself" (*Poetical Works* IV.463), curiously recalls Gray's "vocal to the intelligent alone." . . . From Jonson through Collins, the Pindaric form is a refuge for confusion; it both reflects and deepens uncertainties that will not lend themselves to forthright treatment. As a final preface to the Romantic ode, we may review here, in the form of a summary typology, the confusions that lie beneath the unending hope of the ode to stand purely, through invocation, in the pure presence of what its presentation always stains and darkens.

Here, then, is the normative course of an ode. Some quality of absolute worth is traced back to its conception, where it appears as a fountainhead, sunrise, or new star. But the landscape of dawning, inescapably twilit, is instinct with regional spirits that misbehave and will not be reduced to order. It is impossible for the compressions of syntax and figure to avoid implicating these dark spirits in the urconception of the ode and of its numen alike. Such spirits are "kept aloof" at first, like Collins's "dangerous passions," by the ode's shifting of its etiology from the spiritual to the sublunary plane—from theogony, in other words, to the earliest stages of recorded history or childhood. This descent from the divine is halted and in some measure reversed by the poet's location of a primitive society or early selfhood in a region that he still calls sacred (the magic circle, garland, manger, shrine, or temple). The history of poetry, meanwhile, is imagined as one great ode, sacralized by the analogy between the holy place the ode describes and the circle of its own form. Hence, the transcendent pastness of the past is lost almost completely in the defensive act of exorcizing its false, daemonic, and generically diverse oracles. Once great Pan is pronounced dead, the oracle grows nearly silent, and the vocal occasion of the ode, consecrated to the celebration of the present, is mediated and muted by all the formal defenses that writing ritualizes.

In violent denial of this loss, the ode now loudly reasserts its divine calling: it hazards the frenzied tropes of identification that we call "enthusiastic" and then quickly collapses into self-caricature. This is the brief noontide phase of the ode, envisioned as a Phaeton-myth of flight followed by blindness and a fall into or toward the sea. The sun has been placed once more too squarely in view, so that the excessive bright of its cloudy skirts becomes an ominous darkness, like the darkness of dawn. To avoid the bathos of Phaeton's death, the poet reins in ("Stop, stop, my muse," exclaims Cowley in "The Resurrection," "allay thy vig'rous heat!") and adjusts himself to the light of common day. In the decline of this light toward evening, the ode accepts a diminished calling, often movingly and even cheerfully embraced as the hymning of a favorite name, and never reasserts its enthusiastic mission. Even this denouement is marred, however, by the regathering and haunting of twilit forces.

We may adapt some of these outlines to the Intimations Ode in order to establish a viewpoint from which its confusion may then be reconsidered more carefully. Wordsworth's ode opens with the recollection of a pastoral dawn when the sun, in place of the poet, had a "glorious birth." This happy scene is peopled by the usual denizens of the vernal ode—songbirds, frolicking animals—from whose jubilee the speaker is excluded. In content the scene is that of the "Sonnet on the Death of West" abused by Wordsworth in his 1800 Preface. In earlier life the speaker's spontaneous vision helped "apparel" the scene he now adorns more conventionally. In order to make himself present to his own childhood, as he attempted to do by evoking the Boy of Winander in *The Prelude*, Wordsworth now invokes and petitions the happy voice of the Shepherd-boy. His identification with a better self, which is wholly fitting in an ode, seems for the moment to yield rewards. The Babe leaps up, as Wordsworth's heart had leapt up the day before, to nestle closer to Mother Nature. But—and here the voice of the original four-stanza ode turns downward after the blindly exclamatory "I hear! I hear!"—but, the poet seems to wonder, does paradise have a mother only? The lost Tree and single Field suggest an Eden that was begotten by a Father, and the adult poet can only partly keep from knowing that his visionary birth, though too noble for pastoral, was nevertheless still erotic. The Pansy at his feet recalls Milton's Pensive Nun, who always keeps her head pointed toward, if not in, the sand. Thus far Wordsworth's expression of loss has simply followed the convention of the amorous vernal ode whereby the speaker looks about frantically for his absent mistress.

Wordsworth does have a glimpse of her, though, and is not pleased, as the fifth stanza reveals. The maternal earth from which he feels alienated has "pleasures of her own," and it is her natural yearning to possess her foster child and make him forget his epic and patriarchal origins, "that imperial palace whence he came." Following exactly the scenario presented by Otto Rank, she interferes, in her lowly role, with the poet's myth of his birth as a hero, and her interference is as erotic as that of the Nurse in *Romeo and Juliet*. Even as we pass the poem thus schematically in review, we should note that there is a degree of voluntarism, even relief, in the adult's alienation from his childhood. The "Child of Joy" is given pause in so designating himself, and feels a hint of Gray's "fearful joy." We shall see in the long run, however, that this impure intimation is vastly preferable to those purer ones that come to replace it. From stanza five onward, the poet will strive to imagine a self-conception that is not an earthy anecdote from the pastoral tradition, to imagine a birth-myth that is not an earth-myth or failed autochthony. At first this seems a good idea. By bringing about a reconciliation of his mortal being with "the light of common day," with the ordinariness of earth, the poet can once more invest with the appearance of dialectical truth the assumption that his immortal being must derive from a region that is *not* common; the animation of the soul seems to depend on the disinspiriting of earth.

The figure of the imperial palace carries the sun's "glorious birth" across the increasingly dualistic chasm of the poet's logic while alienating the sun from the landscape it formerly graced. The poet remembering himself as a bright-haired youth or sun-child now identifies with the Father, through the metalepsis "God, who is our home," in a higher region that is set apart from natural kindness as the sublime is set apart from the beautiful. This brief intimation (his first of immortality) makes up the subsumed epic phase of the ode. In Victor Hugo's terms, Adam has become Orestes. Shaking off the mother, by whose possessive kisses he is fretted (like a brook fretting in its channel [line 94], the hero descends from his epic to his dramatic phase, recalling Aristotle's derivation of theatre from child's play in the *Poetics*: "As if his whole vocation / Were endless imitation." Here the Father stands back, the one apart from the many, no longer identified with the son but still tendering the sunlight of his gaze. Now the child becomes the chameleonic Hamlet, trapped in a "prison-house" (68) of nature and changed into a different player by each attention from the mother whose yearnings in her natural kind have caused him so much anxiety. Little actor though he is, however, he is still a solitary and a soliloquist, like John Home in Collins's Scottish Superstitions Ode: "unto this he frames his song." He acts odes.

Hamlet calls the world a "prison" (II.ii); but in *Hamlet* the world is only one of two prisons, the other being identified by the ghost of Hamlet's father: "I am thy father's spirit . . ."

> But that I am forbid
> To tell the secrets of my prison-house,
> I could a tale unfold whose lightest word
> Would harrow up thy soul.
>
> [I.v.9, 13–16]

This discordant intimation Wordsworth records in his next stanza:

> Mighty Prophet! Seer blest!
> On whom these truths do rest,
> Which we are toiling all our lives to find,
> In darkness lost, the darkness of the grave;
> Thou, over whom thy Immortality
> Broods like the Day, a Master o'er a Slave

For the child's domination by Mother Earth, then, there is an equivalent master-slave dialectic between son and father. Immortal regions are suddenly as much like prisons as mortal ones; and the ode's noontide, its most high-flown rhetoric, having seen too much reality, falls back to the theme of blindness, which could be an ode's address, thus stated, to its own self-blighted celebratory mandate:

> Thou little child, yet glorious in thy might
> Of heaven-born freedom [as a Slave?] on thy being's height,
> Why with such earnest pains dost thou provoke
> The years to bring the inevitable yoke,
> Thus blindly with thy blessedness at strife?

In singling out the main point of repetition in this poem (crucial repetition being typically revealed, as we saw in the "Ode to Duty," by a stutter or gaffe like this one about the slave's heaven-born freedom), we have perhaps come to see why no blessedness is visible that is not in some wise tainted. The child must be admitted to know what he is doing in choosing blinders.

Having absorbed the rival genres in the child's progress toward his earthly prison and then reacted frantically back toward its displaced theme of originary magic, only to discover a different prison in that theme, Wordsworth's ode now lapses into its final, elegiac phase, giving notice of this change with a verbal allusion to "Lycidas": "Not for these I raise / The song of thanks and praise." Here begins Wordsworth's evening retrospect and its attempt to overbalance the heavy weight of custom with the philosophic mind's conversion of remembered joy into "natural piety." The ode becomes a song in praise of sublimation, and it has some sublime moments remaining. It distances the Deluge (into which an ode, like Phaeton, is always falling) from the standpoint of calm weather, thus belatedly justifying the suggestion of a covenant in the rainbow that comes and goes; it returns to the vernal festival of earthy childhood "in thought" only; and finally it returns to the landscape of the first line, adding the word "Fountains" to the initial list because, through the sublimation of dangerous waters, the philosophic mind is now able to recognize a seminal source as well as an Edenic foster mother. All these qualified returns make up Wordsworth's "Stand." The irregularity of all the previous stanzas is reduced to uniformity, with the exception of an odd line out that refuses the eclipse it appears in: "Is lovely yet." Wordsworth's hymnic epode, like Collins's homiletic harvest at the end of the "Ode to Evening," joins the common produce of the common day in an order serviceable. The necessary sacrifice of godlike autochthony for natural piety brings on silence, an unutterable pathos that is vastly different from the shouts of the Child of Joy. The question of immortality is mooted in the end, and we must reconsider it if we are to discover why this is so.

III

> *that dubious hour,*
> *That twilight when we first begin to see*
> *This dawning earth.*
> —*The Prelude* V.511–13

Is the Intimations Ode, in Lionel Trilling's deft phrase, about growing old or growing up? It is hard to know how or where to enter this dispute. It seems to me that the poem is about not knowing whether childhood, adulthood, or yet a third state of complete disembodiment is best; that it is, in short, about confusion. In the Fenwick note Wordsworth confesses having experienced the opposite "subjugations" of idealism and materialism in childhood and adulthood, respectively, and seems to imply that the purpose of his poem is to thread its way between prisons, or rather to find a restful expansiveness in their mutual collapse. In this modest aim I think it succeeds, despite serious flaws of coherence that will appear. Deliberately an ode, the poem experiments with presentation, the presentation in this case of an elusive nimbus called a "glory." The experiment fails, but in place of ecstasy the poet gains knowledge, a new awareness of the role played by determinacy in consciousness.

Wordsworth's apology in the Fenwick note for his chosen myth of a prior existence reflects the etiological anxiety of any ode, the fear of dark places, and also recalls the antinomian relation of an ode to orthodoxy. His myth, he says, "is far too shadowy a notion to be recommended to faith." Still, however, as he also clearly implies in the note, he knows no proof of immortality that is not in some way shadowy; this despite the fact that for Wordsworth, as for Coleridge, autonomy of thought cannot be demonstrated without proof of the mind's original participation in an eternal cause. This necessary priority of the spirit is termed by Wordsworth in the note an Archimedean "point whereon to rest" what would be, otherwise, the dreary machine of Associationist psychology.

Although the lack of such proof may cause some anxiousness, it is not really the belief in immortality, however founded, that the ode questions, but rather the nature of immortality. By allusion and repetition, Wordsworth's ode clouds over what in religion are foregone conclusions about the sources of life and death. It is disturbing, for example, that "Nor man nor Boy, / Nor all that is at enmity with joy, / Can utterly destroy . . ." alludes to the speech of Moloch in *Paradise Lost* that calls the Creator a destroyer, like Collins's Fancy. Or again, it is difficult to understand what blindness is if the Child is at once "an eye to the blind" and "blindly with his blessedness at strife." As [is] also apparent in Collins's "Ode on the Poetical Character," a poet cannot merely decree a difference between Vision and vision that his poem fails otherwise to sustain.

To cite another troublesome passage, where is the guilt and on what ground is the misgiving in the following lines?

> Not for these I raise
> The song of thanks and praise;
> But for those obstinate questionings
> Of sense and outward things,
> Fallings from us, vanishings;
> Blank misgivings of a Creature
> Moving about in worlds not realized,
> High instincts before which our mortal Nature
> Did tremble like a guilty thing surprised.

The solipsism of the child is obstinate, and his experience of a lapse is the opposite of Adam's: not a corruption of soul but a falling away of the flesh. Immortality is intimated by the child as a state of emptiness and vertigo, a Melvillean blankness that is duplicitous for all its vacancy, since it has more than one habitation ("worlds")—perhaps a true and a false zone of antimatter. The bodily "Creature" would appear to have been created as a companion for the soul's loneliness. The song that is raised, in sum, shows every sign of being a song of thanks for the gift of mortality.

This is not to imply, however, that the entire burden of the song is a foolish critique of immortality. The main point is, rather, that memory harbors phantoms. Whatever immortality may be like, mortal discourse is confined to what a child can know about it, or, yet more mediately, to what an adult can remember of childhood knowledge. The child's recollections are indeed "shadowy," both because adult memory is busy securing the present by darkening the past (in this sense the poem *is* "about growing up" and being happy with the present) and also because, as "be they what they may" rather sheepishly concedes, what the poet remembers is not really the "high instincts" of childhood but the phantom Underworld of the Greeks. The confessed Platonism of Wordsworth's preexistence myth comes chiefly from the Myth of the warrior Er, who "coming to life related what, he said, he had seen in the world beyond" (*Rep.* 614b). Er describes souls struggling to be born between two worlds, governed, like Wordsworth's Slave, by the Spindle of Necessity. But the feeling of Wordsworth's intimations is, in fact, more Homeric than Platonic; it is "impalpable as shadows are, and wavering like a dream" (Fitzgerald's *Odyssey* XI). Wordsworth's ode may be seen as a moving failure of perspective; called forth to be condemned, mortal Nature reasserts its vital strength and beauty.

By comparison, immortality is a dream. In the third stanza there is a crux of remarkable compression, "The Winds come to me from the fields of sleep." Many a hapless recitation of this line has produced "fields of sheep," a slip that is prompted by the surrounding gleeful pastoral in which no creature sleeps during the rites of spring. The fields of sleep belong to an earlier time and place, the threshold of birth which is, later, "but a sleep and a forgetting." Wordsworth's winds bring news of birth, then, yet seem imagistically to recall an even earlier moment, the classical fields of asphodel and poppy. In contrast with the jollity of a child's landscape, the winds of adult memory recollect the stupor of immortality, or what Homer calls the "shores of Dream" (*Odyssey* XXIV).

In approaching the designedly binding and blinding symbol of the ode, that of the "glory," we must pause over metaphysics a little longer. The prolepsis that the ode never moves beyond is the ambiguous apposition of line 5. Presumably "the glory and the freshness of a dream" modifies "celestial light" in the previous line; but the grammar does not prevent reading the line in apposition to "every common sight." One's total impression of lines 1–5 is that the glory summarily modifies both the common, with which the poem concludes, and the celestial, with which it has begun. Hence either the common itself is glorious, properly viewed (like the cuckoo and the lesser celandine of the 1802 period), or else the glory is a nimbus, a frame of celestial light that leaves the framed common object unilluminated in itself. This sliding apposition looks forward to the confusion of the whole text. The word "dream" belongs to the rhyme group "stream-seem," and thus its presumptive modifying power over "sight" and "light" is further weakened. Having been spread too thin, the glory is only faintly visible. To parrot the inescapable question of Wordsworth interpretation, does the glory come from without or within?

Since the glory is now absent, and since it is recalled by an *ubi sunt* that is also, at the same time, an indirect invocation, this question is doubly difficult. To disregard for the moment where the glory comes from, even though that is the motivating question of any ode and plainly an important one, it may profit to go on asking what it is. Here an answer is forthcoming. The glory is an "Apparel," a dressy appearance that is Wordsworth's equivalent of Gray's tapestries and Collins's veils. It is worn by every common sight as a covering for nakedness: "not in utter nakedness, / But trailing clouds of glory do we come." The glory screens out the indecent as well as the quotidian commonness of things and poses an obstacle to the kindness of natural yearning. Perhaps it is already clear where the glory comes from. Once more the Fall proves indeed fortunate, as it lends a needful covering to an original state of nakedness. In this poem death is not only the context of intimation, but also, it seems, the context of intimacy. By allusion to Collins's "sallow Autumn fills thy lap with leaves," Wordsworth's imagery of mortality turns autumnal long before his evening ear takes command of the ode. "Earth fills her lap with pleasures of her own" is a covering of Eve's nakedness that unites the pleasures of life and the glory of afterlife in a common veil. Man *wears* "Earth" even before we are told that he is her inmate, exchanging as he grows up "the glories he hath known" for new apparel.

If we compare the mortally colored imagery of the celestial that the adult remembers from the time of glad animal movement in early childhood with the otherworldliness of the celestial that he remembers from the time of solipsism in later childhood, we can see the distance between two glories, between the festive dress of a young world and the phantom light of interstellar vacancy. Concerning this second glory: Wordsworth could love a clear sky, and in the second stanza we cannot yet feel uneasy about the sky's undress, as "The Moon doth with delight / Look round her when the heavens are bare." But the region of the Moon is absolutely separate from that of man, and her delight cannot be merged with Earth's pleasures. Later, when pleasure has palled, the bare sky will mirror a blank misgiving. In "Dejection," Coleridge will seem to narrow this gulf by giving the moon her own nimbus from the outset, "a swimming phantom light," and he will transfer Wordsworth's earthly pleasure to the sphere of the moon's delight: "I see the old moon in her lap." In "Dejection," as we shall see, it is not the immortal skies that are lonely, but the poet.

Both "Dejection" and the Intimations Ode sometimes touch upon subjects that are too intimate to remain within a shareable sphere of reference. For both poets, but for Wordsworth especially, the daemon of an ode is an unreconstructed and thus far "strong" egoism. What poet before Wordsworth admitted to being relieved and made strong by his own timely utterance? As we have seen [elsewhere], Akenside read Milton for inspiration, Gray Spenser, and so on. Although the position of the sounding cataracts between "I am strong" and "No more shall grief of mine" might indicate that Wordsworth has found his timely utterance in Revelation, one feels that too many more griefs succeed this one to confirm any gospel. Earlier odes have mottoes chosen from the classics; Wordsworth's utterance and his motto (starting in 1815) are all his own. The drawback of this strength is that Wordsworth's allusion to his own uncanonized oeuvre leaves the ordering of his present text in a muddle. It is not possible to say with certainty what Wordsworth's timely utterance was, nor what his thought of grief was. But if a note on the subject in Wordsworth's own hand were discovered, that would be a positive harm. In the text, the grief and the thought are significant because they are unspecified. They remain simply implied presences, emblems of what Coleridge termed the "flux and reflux" of the whole poem. They are impure signifiers—symptoms. Perhaps their presence in the text can be understood, then, as a near-utterance about the idea of repression, about the apparel of the repressed that veils an ode. To refer again to the Fenwick note, what Wordsworth most vividly remembers about writing his ode is frustration. He needed a fulcrum, a prior content without which his form, "the world of his own mind," would follow its own irresolute course. The preexistence myth provides inadequate leverage, but the timely utterance, because unspecified, can stand behind and beneath the text as a buried originary voice.

One may wonder about the deference of sound to sight in this ode, noting that elsewhere Wordsworth explored aural areas that have more profound mystical roots than does the (mainly Western) visionary idea. Like Dionysus "disguised as man" in Euripides, this written ode travels daily farther from the East because pure voice would be naked, a too immediate experience of "God, who is our home." This is the experience an ode cannot risk. The prophetic child must be "deaf" in order to read "the eternal deep." The visual blankness of eternity is also an "Eternal Silence," and sound is relegated wholly to "our noisy years": birdsong, the tabor that syncopates the vernal heartbeat, the outer-ance of speech that relieves solitude, the trumpets sounding from the Salvator-fringes of the regenerate landscape, the shouts of happiness. After this outburst, there are no more sounds until the pygmy turns actor; however, even his "song," is not sung but written down, "a little plan or chart."

Sound resonates beyond the setting for pastoral joy only once in the poem, at the end of the ninth stanza, in the song of praise for the adult's recollection of the child's recollections:

> Hence in a season of calm weather,
> Though inland far we be,
> Our souls have sight of that immortal sea
> Which brought us hither,
> Can in a moment travel thither,
> And see the Children sport upon the shore,
> And hear the mighty waters rolling evermore.

This magnificent passage, the pivot (or fulcrum) of the poem, culminates in another unspecified utterance. It is also the key to Wordsworth's version of Milton's resurrected Lycidas, the "genius of the shore." It *is* a pivotal passage, yet it is not easy to discover a context for it. It is not clear by what logic the celestial descent has become an aquatic emergence; nor is it clear, though we happily accept the transit, just how we are carried from sight to sound.

I have suggested [elsewhere] that the genealogical phase of the ode before Wordsworth leaves out, or tries to leave out, the Deluge, which appears in nearly every scriptural cosmogony in the history of culture and recurs in Jung's belief that the materials of the dreamwork are oceanic. Until his personal tragedy concerning a death by water in 1805, Wordsworth, unlike his predecessors in the ode, was a willing voyager in strange seas of thought and loved sonorous waters. The dream-vision of *Prelude* V (88–97) offers up the sort of apocalyptic "Ode" that Wordsworth could have been expected to write:

"This," said he,
"Is something of more worth;" and at the word
Stretched forth the shell, so beautiful in shape,
In colour so resplendent, with command
That I should hold it to my ear. I did so,
And heard that instant in an unknown tongue,
Which yet I understood, articulate sounds,
A loud prophetic blast of harmony;
An Ode, in passion uttered, which foretold
Destruction to the children of the earth
By deluge, now at hand.

One might then certainly expect the Intimations Ode, considering its subject, also to leave the shore for deeper waters. But the "Waters" at line 14 are merely lacustrine, and the jolly "sea" of "Land and sea" (30) is, one suspects, only present for the sake of rhyme. For the most part, the movement of this ode is inland and downward, until it comes to rest in a place that is "too deep for tears." Traditionally, the ode takes an aspiring flight but fears Phaeton's plunge, and with partial success avoids the risk of drowning by curbing its flight. Wordsworth's ode bows to this tradition, with the result, however, that this passage, with its seaward direction, seems isolated from the argument of which the passage is meant to be the center.

"Lycidas," not an ode but an elegy, makes room for a drowning. Milton recalls a happy pastoral setting, "by fountain, shade, and rill," to which Wordsworth alludes in lines 1 and 189; but with the death of its pastor, the *locus amoenus* will have fallen silent except for mournful echoes unless Milton can reanimate the strain. Wordsworth's first revision of "Lycidas," then, is to fill his own pastoral site with noise and to locate the noise only there, hoping to imply that the silence of higher places is preferable. However, the errancy of his intimations points to some awareness on his part that Milton was right, as was Sophocles in the *Coloneus*: if the vital and benign genius cannot be given a home within the budding grove, its possible course among the stars can offer little consolation. "Lycidas" announces the return of the genius from water to land through the intercession of one who could not drown. Wordsworth describes the return of memory from land to the shoreline where genius had been left behind.

Or rather, where genius *appears* to have been left behind. Wordsworth's ninth stanza, with its key in "Not for these," begins to look homeward, back toward the starting places of the ode that will be reviewed in stanzas ten and eleven. Wordsworth's journey to the shore begins this review of inland places because, in fact, the journey only seems to have been undertaken. He is and remains inland far; it is only in moments of vacancy, seasons "of calm weather," that he counteracts his fear of the eternal abyss with memories of "sport" among a community of children who have nothing in common with the solitude of infinite space. The children emerge *from* the "immortal sea," happy to be born, and steadily move inland themselves toward the pleasures of the Shepherd-boy. Immured in our adulthood, our souls seem to want something else, something other than what children want, when they listen to the conch shells of their inner ear. They zoom directly back to the sea itself, and only afterward notice the children playing with their backs to the water. Unlike the ignorant child, the soul of the adult has intimations of death; they are not quite the intimations he was meant to have, but they still induce a state of mind that is preferable, as Jonson's Cary-Morison Ode also insisted, to "listlessness" and "mad endeavour."

The soul's hearing death for the first time, then, is an intimation of voice, of aural immediacy, not as a beginning but as an end. The children's audition, which is permitted by the grammar if not by the parallelism of syntax, is quite different; it is not nostalgic but strains forward, and smooths their passage from the deafening roar of death, which they no longer hear as such, to the companionable shouts of their coming joy. Lycidas our Shepherd-boy is not dead, because the morning star of his return replaces the evening star of his having sunk elsewhere. For Wordsworth's Child we rejoice, as in "Lycidas," because he has been born, not because he was previously drowned:

> The Soul that rises with us, our life's Star,
> Hath had elsewhere its setting,
> And cometh from afar:

The child has returned, fortunately, to be Nature's Pastor once more. His "vision splendid" arises from his own glorious birth, when Heaven is no distant bareness of the sky but an immediate environment that "lies about us in our infancy."

"Our birth is but a sleep and a forgetting," the line that precedes those just quoted, wavers uncertainly between two famous counterstatements about life and death in *Measure for Measure*. One of them, Claudio's "Ay, but to die, and go we know not where" (III.i.118–31), is worth quoting at length, not only because it juxtaposes the two prisons of both *Hamlet* and the Intimations Ode, but also because it expresses the fear that Wordsworth's frostlike weight of life is, in fact, a condition of the afterlife as well:

> or to reside
> In thrilling region of thick-ribbèd ice,
> To be imprisoned in the viewless winds
> And blown with restless violence round about
> The pendant world. . . .
>
> . . . .
>
> The weariest and most loathèd worldly life
> That age, ache, penury, and imprisonment
> Can lay on Nature is a paradise
> To what we fear of death.

This is the body of imagery that Wordsworth's shadowy recollections cannot dissolve, however much his ode may aspire to the otherworldly viewpoint of the Duke's counsel about sleep and forgetting:

> Thou hast nor youth nor age,
> But as it were an after-dinner sleep
> Dreaming on both.
>
> [III.i.32–34]

The Duke's utterance is not strong enough to be "timely," though; it is merely Stoical, and itself contains the repetition that negates transcendence: "thy best of rest is sleep, / And that thou oft provok'st, yet grossly fear'st / Thy death, which is no more" (III.i.17–19). Among these less than reassuring attitudes Wordsworth must himself have felt compelled to waver, "when having closed the mighty Shakespeare's page, / I mused, and thought, and felt, in solitude" (*Prelude* VII.484–85).

The conclusion seems inescapable that Wordsworth's Intimations are best forgotten; and forgetting is what the last two stanzas in effect achieve. Stanzas ten and eleven seek images for the continuity that was hoped for in "The Rainbow":

> The Child is father of the Man;
> And I could wish my days to be
> Bound each to each by natural piety.

In these lines, the wish for existential continuity is weakened by having been spoken conditionally, and also by the impious bid for autochthonous independence of being that here and elsewhere undercuts Wordsworth's homage to the adult father. Perhaps these slight discords are enough to warn us that an ode for which such a passage is the best available motto will not be smooth going; but they are nothing to the discords that any ambitious presentational ode will engender in itself. In any case, the poet's days are bound each to each at the close of the Great Ode in an altogether "natural" way that is *pius* if not pious; but his piety is *not* founded in any visionary or eschatological intimation.

From his and Coleridge's Conversation Poems, perhaps from the Meditative Lyric of the seventeenth century, and certainly from instinct, Wordsworth had formed the habit of concluding with a benediction, which typically, as in "Tintern Abbey" or "Dejection," transmits the boon of gladness in nature to a beloved friend who is less burdened than the poet with the heavy weight of adulthood. The hesitation with which the pronoun "my" is introduced in "The Rainbow" may itself imply the replacement of the self by another in a benediction: *my* days and perceptions may prove disjointed, but perhaps yours will not. So in stanza ten of his ode, Wordsworth confers his generalized blessing on unselfconscious youth from the detached and newly acquiescent standpoint of "thought." However successful the tone of this blessing may be thought to be, it must still be stressed that there is no scope for benediction in the cult hymns after which odes model themselves. The ending of a hymn leads by nature in quite another direction, toward a petition. In a hymn the petition may possibly involve the blessing of others, but in an ode it is primarily for the self, a request that the poet's egotistically sublime vocation be confirmed. Not just Wordsworth's but nearly all thoughtful odes, however, swerve away from the formula of petition toward benediction and other forms of self-sacrifice that are all essentially vocational disclaimers. At least in this last respect, then, the endings of hymns and odes are similar.

Wordsworth's heart no longer leaps up; rather it goes out, in "primal sympathy," to others, to the whole sphere of those Creatures whom Coleridge's Ancient Mariner learned to "bless" (see the Intimations Ode, line 37). Henceforth there is little to be heard of the immortality theme and nothing of substance about the "one delight" (192) of joyous childhood that the poet has now "relinquished"—pretending, with the active verb, to have given it up voluntarily. What now appears, rather, is the severer compassion of the Eton College Ode, the "Ode to Adversity," and Wordsworth's "Ode to Duty": "the soothing thoughts that spring / Out of human suffering." As in the "Ode to Duty," the healing power of Nature is itself now hallowed as routine, as Nature's "more habitual sway," and the sober coloring of the clouds no longer needs to serve as a repressive veil, since the troubled mysticism of the poem is now silenced, apparently by choice. Until the final line of Wordsworth's evening ending there is no hint of immortality, no effort even to carry over or restate the phantom imagery of immortality. Natural piety in these lines is a secular reverence moved by the pathos of mutability:

> The clouds that gather round the setting sun
> Do take a sober coloring from an eye
> That hath kept watch o'er man's mortality;
> Another race hath been, and other palms are won.
> Thanks to the human heart by which we live,
> Thanks to its tenderness, its joys and fears,
> To me the meanest flower that blows can give
> Thoughts that do often lie too deep for tears.

This is a grave ending, full of allusions to Gray: to the "race" and the "fearful joy" of the Eton College Ode, to the frail blossoms in the Death of a Favorite Cat. Also, as in so many great odes, there is a final "gathering" of the mind's humbled thoughts now rendered as congregational homilies, a gathering that willingly stands far below the cosmic gathering of clouds or twittering swallows. A conclusion of this sort is a service rendered, a graveside hymn to man's mortality, without intimation but with something that would seem to achieve collective intimacy were it not for "To me," a last gift of special knowledge awarded to the self by the odic voice. To the famous question, "Where is it now, the glory and the dream?" we may answer in behalf of Wordsworth's "me": Aye, where is it? Mortality alone has its music.

Intimations apart, then, the question remains, Which is better, childhood or being grown up? It may be of use to measure the Intimations Ode in this respect against a passage from "In Desolation," by a poet whom Wordsworth would have been less than human not to have reperused attentively in the summer of 1803, his new acquaintance Sir George Beaumont's Renaissance ancestor Sir John Beaumont:

> If solid vertues dwell not but in paine,
> I will not wish that golden age againe,
> Because it flowed with sensible delights
> Of heavenly things.

Like Beaumont, Wordsworth is never quite easy about the glad animal movements of his little pagan selves, though it would be an exaggeration to insist that his nativity ode exorcises them; early childhood, for him, is simply incomplete. The later stages of childhood, however intense, are already projected by present memory toward the double imprisonment of the adult, the state of being shuttled to and fro between the burden and the absence of the flesh; but the difference remains that late childhood lacks the solace of adulthood's deliberative resources. At bottom, as it seems to me, the speaker of the Intimations Ode prefers himself grown up, or just as he is, in fact, at the moment.

Wordsworth's choice of the Pindaric format would mean that he could scarcely have composed the poem on his customary walks, chanting aloud. In attempting the vocality of an ode, Wordsworth would have needed to stay at his desk, weighing meters and blocking stanzas in writing. In facing this paradox, a highly relevant passage may be enlisted from Jacques Derrida: "Writing is that forgetting of the self, that exteriorization, the contrary of the interiorizing memory, or the *Erinnerung* that opens the history of the spirit." Wordsworth's ode is more crucially a forgetting than an attempted reconstitution of any earlier self; it celebrates forgetting in celebrating birth, its own birth ultimately, and does so by entering a poetic shape that imitates the constant discontinuity of being alive and suffering. "Pain," says Nietzsche, "always raises the question about its origin while pleasure is inclined to stop with itself without looking back." Childhood has no myth of childhood, and no fund of suffering to be projected as a benediction. (It goes without saying, I hope, that concerning actual childhood these assertions are probably false; we are speaking here, though, of what the overstrained figures of memory can know about a child's memory in an ode.) The failing powers of adulthood are necessary, like the fading of Shelley's coal and the secondariness of Coleridge's secondary imagination, for the dissemination of voice in the writing of poetry, which starts, like a mortal stroke, as a severance from the Logos, and then, over that very fissure, takes its stand against the "severing of our loves."

IV

To the last point of vision, and beyond,
Mount, daring warbler!—that love-prompted strain

. . . .

Thrills not the less the bosom of the plain:
Yet might'st thou seem, proud privilege! to sing
All independent of the leafy spring.
              —"A Morning Exercise" (1828)

The Intimations Ode is uncharacteristic of Wordsworth. It is a poem that appears openly to espouse the attitudes that partisans of the sophisticated Wordsworth take to be important but only covertly present in his poetry (longing for apocalypse, hatred of nature), but that actually favors, presumably against the poet's design, the wise naturalism that partisans of the Simple Wordsworth take to be everywhere intended: faith in and through nature without clear revelation, whatever "faith" in this context may mean. The Great Ode loses the power of grounding spiritual knowledge in physical experience, the power which had made "Tintern Abbey" a less confused poem, "well pleased to recognize"

> In nature and the language of the sense
> The anchor of my purest thoughts, the nurse,
> The guide, the guardian of my heart, and soul
> Of all my moral being.

This passage, which redeems even the troublesome foster mother of the Intimations Ode, represents what can with most propriety be called Wordsworth's "unified vision," though needless to say there are rifts in the ground near the Wye as well. Speaking only of "vicious" poetry in his "Essay, Supplementary" (1815) to the 1800 Preface, Wordsworth identifies the quality of "confusion" that Cleanth Brooks was the first to emphasize in the Intimations Ode itself: "the realities of the Muse are but shows, and . . . her liveliest excitements are raised by transient shocks of conflicting feeling and successive assemblages of contradictory thoughts." Wordsworth seems to have felt that bad poetry is full of contradictions in terms—oxymorons—yet his own most contradictory poem is his Great Ode. In these concluding remarks I want to reconsider the oxymoron "natural piety" from the standpoint of Wordsworth's lesser odes in order to show that the confusion of all his odes is peculiar to what he would have termed the "mould" in which they are cast (1815 Preface).

It may be remarked, though, before turning to other odes, that Wordsworth could always handle intimations of immortality more positively in poems that were not odes. Unless "The Mad Monk" was written by Wordsworth himself, the clearest forerunner of the Intimations Ode (as of "A Slumber did my spirit seal"), doubtless printed as the first poem in the

1849 edition for this reason, is not an ode but a quieter sort of poem, "Written in Very Early Youth":

> a Slumber seems to steal
> O'er vale, and mountain, and the starless sky.
> Now, in this blank of things, a harmony,
> Home-felt, and home-created, comes to heal
> That grief for which the senses still supply
> Fresh food.

This passage affirms a "blank" vision without being troubled about its blankness; it is quite possibly referred to directly in the compromised affirmation of the Great Ode, lines 145–51, where a blank misgiving condemns the eternally dead to roll round earth's diurnal course with shadows. Another convincingly positive treatment of "this blank of things" appears in an untitled poem of 1800, in which a Solitary forsaken by his beloved exclaims:

> I look—the sky is empty space;
> I know not what I trace;
> But when I cease to look, my hand is on my heart.

This is indeed an intimation, lesser than, but comparable to, the moments of surprised revelation in lassitude that are featured in *The Prelude*. An intimation thus suggestive cannot appear in an ode because its quiet tenor openly founds knowledge in ignorance and avoids afflatus. Perhaps this distinction alone is enough to indicate that an ode can never be characteristic of Wordsworth.

Wordsworth's odes and ode-like poems constantly reject mysterious knowledge. The apostrophe called "To H. C. Six Years Old" (1802), for instance, offers an unambiguous view of the semi-transparent "glory" that confuses the Great Ode:

> O Thou! whose fancies from afar are brought;
> Who of thy words dost make a mock apparel,
> And fittest for unutterable thought.

Here the "glory," like Wordsworth's "home-created" harmony of 1786, is the opaque apparel by expression of sights both common and uncommon. "To a Skylark" (1805) summarizes without reversing the values of the Great Ode: strength of song in despondency, joy divine, the "banqueting place in the sky," "Joy and jollity," and the "hope for higher raptures, when life's day is done." This slight poem, which may play in the background of Keats's Nightingale Ode, petitions the bird to "Lift me, guide me, till I find / That spot which seems so to thy mind," but then admits failure, lacking as it does "the wings of a Faery," and at last reposes solely in hope. In "To the Cuckoo" (23–26 March 1802), which plays in the background of Shelley's Skylark Ode, the poet asks, "shall I call thee Bird, / Or but a wandering Voice?" Clearly the latter, since only when invisible does the bird bring back childhood; the poet listens, "till I do beget / That golden time again." This poem, like the Great Ode, deprives spiritual knowledge of any material ground:

> O blessèd Bird! the earth we pace
> Again appears to be
> An unsubstantial, faery place;
> That is fit home for Thee!

Metric stress drives home the point: for thee, but not for me, and never for both of us at once. Only a much later bird poem, now fully shackled by the sense of "Duty" that overrides an ode's wish for immediacy, can return, though weakly, to the balanced tropes of earthbound freedom that sustain "Tintern Abbey." "To a Skylark" (1825; very possibly written in response to Shelley's "Skylark") concludes with the sort of nonvisionary emblem of continuity that characterizes the later Wordsworth: "Type of the wise who soar, but never roam: / True to the kindred points of Heaven and Home!" Here Donne's compass is lamentably overstretched, as Wordsworth's figure pays homage to the elastic metaphysical grounding that was available to Donne but is now unavailable, given the dualism on which the dialectic of presence and absence in an ode depends.

  In the "Vernal Ode" (1817), a lumbering Pindaric, a "Stranger" descends from the sky and is compared to "the sun, / When it reveals, in evening majesty, / Features half lost amid their own pure light." Hence we are not surprised at his apparel: "there the Stranger stood alone; / Fair as a gorgeous Fabric of the East." This angel then delivers a homily to the harp that exactly recalls the dilemma of perspective in the Intimations Ode; what should have been a condescending account of mortality by an Immortal takes itself by surprise and gives way to envy of the lesser condition:

> Mortals, rejoice! The very angels quit
> Their mansions unsusceptible of change,
> Amid your pleasant bowers to sit,
> And through your sweet vicissitudes to range!

This passage is yet further sullied by its evocation of the tarnished angels (as interpretations of Genesis 6 often made them out to be) who wooed "the daughters of men" before the Flood. The poet tries in vain to undo what the Stranger, perhaps one of those angels himself, has done, and hopes to evoke a "golden time again" by studying the providential anatomy of the bee. But since that time *has*, after all, departed, man's intimations of any higher state are now a mockery, and the angels are perhaps a little too cozy when they appear even in man's least postlapsarian memories:

> We were not mocked with glimpse and shadow then,
> Bright Seraphs mixed familiarly with men;
> And earth and stars composed a universal heaven!

Nothing could confess more clearly what was missing from the "glimpse and shadow" of Wordsworth's earlier intimations.

The last line of the "Vernal Ode," like that of the 1825 Skylark poem, effects a clumsy and confessedly conjectural liaison of ground and sky that is amplified, again within the pleasing chains of Duty, in the long ode "On the Power of Sound" (1828):

> Ye wandering Utterances, has earth no scheme,
> No scale of moral music—to unite
> Powers that survive but in the faintest dream
> Of memory?—O that ye might stoop to bear
> Chains, such precious chains of sight
> As laboured minstrelsies through ages wear!
> O for a balance fit the truth to tell
> Of the Unsubstantial, pondered well!

This passage concedes the necessary failure of vocal poetry to unite the material and the immaterial worlds in the single liberating prison of a secular scripture, a minstrelsy "laboured" as writing but still not absent from vocal sources. The ode concludes hymnically, as the poet defers to a single and inimitable Maker, denying once and for all the priority of vision—which is nevertheless the only intuitive sense at the disposal of man, bounded as he is by space and time:

> A Voice to Light gave Being,
> To Time, and Man his earth-born chronicler;
> A Voice shall finish doubt and dim foreseeing,
> And sweep away life's visionary stir;
>
> . . . .
> O Silence! are Man's noisy years
> No more than moments of thy life?
>
> . . . .
>   No! though earth be dust
> And vanish, though the heavens dissolve, her stay
> Is in the WORD, that shall not pass away.

This poem is yet another critique of the hopes that Wordsworth now imagines his Intimations Ode to have embodied. His critique leads him to give up the idea of an ode altogether and to welcome in its stead the idea of a hymn. Wordsworth plainly understood a hymn to be a collective service, inspired only by faith in common and commonly shared truth. His two "hymns," "Hymn for the Boatmen" (1820), which begins "JESU! bless our slender boat" and ends "All our hope is placed in thee; / *Miserere Domine!*" and his "Labourer's Noon-Day Hymn" (1834), are both written as if for rote use by the unpoetical faithful. In Wordsworth, as in most other ode writers, the idea of a hymn is confined to the end of an ode. So "To the Small Celandine" (30 April 1802) ends by pledging a duty: "I will sing, as doth behove / Hymns in praise of what I love"; and since this flower or its equivalent is the "meanest flower" of the Great Ode, the decision in that poem's close for the renunciations of hymnody may be seen yet more clearly.

In "Composed upon an Evening of Extraordinary Beauty and Splendour" (1818), called an "ode" in Wordsworth's headnote, aural childhood and an obscurely visionary present once more appear contrasted. The "Time"

> when field and watery cove
> With modulated echoes rang

is now supplanted by

> This silent spectacle—the gleam—
> The shadow—and the peace supreme!

On the present evening, the speaker claims to have had an unqualified renewal of Joy, at which he is too surprised not to wonder peevishly about the purpose of the experience: "This glimpse of glory, why renewed?" To prepare him (he may suspect) for some unappareled horror? Or is it rather that he has grown accustomed to his earthly prison, to the "precious chains of sight" required for "laboured minstrelsies," so well accustomed in fact that he actively resents the recurrence of the boundless, of the unutterable sublime that mocks the ever-narrowing boundaries of his craft? Plainly he considers the Intimations Ode, not this one, to have been peevish, and he now accepts visionary loss as a wise Providence protecting him, perhaps, from a dangerous and heretical possession: "Oh, let thy Grace remind me of the light, / Full early lost, and fruitlessly deplored." The Great Ode's lament as much as its petition, he now feels, was fruitlessly undertaken for what already, in "Peele Castle" (1805), he had called "the gleam, / The light that never was."

If, as we now have seen, the dualism of a Wordsworthian ode is given as part of its "mould," so that its oxymorons cannot be sustained or illustrated without turning hymnic, we may reconsider "natural piety" as a gloss on the Intimations Ode, assuming that the oxymoron can be resolved only in ceasing to be a contradiction in terms. Perhaps a literary source for a piety that *is* "natural" can be suggested: *The Aeneid*, by the author from whom Wordsworth took his punning and evasive first motto, *paulo majora canamus*. Wordsworth's sober coloring is quite Virgilian; it consists in the discovery of personal strength through reverence for an absent father who can *only* be revered in strength when he is absent. Wordsworth's tears (still tears, though "too deep" for them) are tears for the passing of *things* in their gay "apparel." In the conversion of spiritual loss to earthly sympathy, Wordsworth's Great Ode stages its limited triumph—and triumph of limits. The watch it keeps over mortality betrays its calling but recovers humanity. The moment when the ode writer crosses from the heroism of *pius Aeneas* to the profounder but far more melancholy heroism of *pater Aeneas*, having left the originary father forever among the Shades, is also the moment of relieved self-conception that purifies the earthly nature of Aeneas's mother, Venus.

Coleridge's "A Light in Sound": Science, Metascience, and Poetic Imagination

M. H. Abrams

In the margin of "The Eolian Harp," as printed in his *Poems* of 1797, Coleridge penciled, "This I think the most perfect poem I ever wrote"; with characteristic self-deprecation he added, "Bad may be the best perhaps." Coleridge's first sentence is justified by the crucial part played by the poem not only in his own poetic development, but as the first and paradigmatic instance of the central Romantic form I have elsewhere called "the greater Romantic lyric" of description and meditation.

In the mid-1790s Coleridge's ambitious longer poems were in the genre he called "the sublimer Ode," in which he imitated the oracular manner and visionary matter of an earlier era when, as he said, "the Bard and the Prophet were one and the same character." Writing amid the hopes and terrors engendered by the turbulent early years of the French Revolution, he had tried—emulating Milton in an earlier period of revolutionary crisis— to endow his poems with a resonant and authoritative public voice, like that of the Biblical prophets, as the sanction for a philosophical, theological, and moral frame of reference that would help his contemporaries keep their bearings in a time of dereliction and dismay. These poems included passages of eloquence, but they manifested a borrowed and unconvincing stance, ill-digested Miltonisms, and a shrill falsetto voice; as Coleridge himself commented, in the effort to dramatize and give "a poetic colouring to abstract and metaphysical truths," his poetry "is crowded and sweats beneath a heavy burthen of Ideas and Imagery! It has seldom Ease."

In "The Eolian Harp" Coleridge establishes the presence of a private person in a localized setting, speaking with a conversational voice in a fluent blank verse that conceals the intricacy of the structure, in which the counter-movements of description and meditation form a double helix. The poem begins with a description of observed details of the outer scene, then turns inward to the play of the observing consciousness; at the same time

From *The Correspondent Breeze: Essays on English Romanticism*. © 1984 by M. H. Abrams. W. W. Norton and Co., Inc., 1984.

the consciousness, freed from time and space, moves out through a sustained evolution of memory, thought, and anticipation, which is controlled throughout by the seemingly casually chosen particulars of the physical setting, rises to a climactic moment of vision beyond sense, then turns again outward and also rounds back to end where it had begun, with a recapitulation of the details of the outer scene. "The Eolian Harp" is a flawed example of this remarkable poetic invention; there are instances of stock diction and standard moral parallels ("Meet emblems they of Innocence and Love!" "such should Wisdom be"), and the concluding verse-paragraph strikes the modern reader as a timid and ineptly managed retreat to religious orthodoxy from the bold speculation of the middle of the poem. Within a few years, however, Coleridge eliminated such weaknesses to achieve a perfection of the circuitous lyric of description and meditation in "Frost at Midnight" (1798).

The standard text of "The Eolian Harp" is usually dated 1795, but is in fact the version that Coleridge published in his collected poems, *Sibylline Leaves*, in 1817. Between 1795 and 1817 the poem was frequently altered and supplemented so that, although it was the first of his conversation poems to be undertaken, it was the last to be completed. The final version is thus a palimpsest that can serve as an index to Coleridge's evolving thought and imagination over a period of twenty-two years—the crucial years between his early and his mature views of the world. I shall sketch the four chief stages of the poem's development; references are to the line numbers in the standard text.

1. The first stage was a manuscript draft of seventeen lines entitled "Effusion 35. Clevedon, August 20th, 1795." It corresponds, though with differences of detail, to the first sixteen and a half lines of the final version. "Effusion" connoted a spontaneous expression of personal circumstances and feelings. On 20 August Coleridge was engaged to marry Sara Fricker, and the poem represents the lovers on a visit to the cottage in Somersetshire that they were about to rent as their first home. The poet is seated by the cottage at evening, his bride leaning against his arm, receptive to the light and scents and sounds of the peaceful scene. In the partly opened window they have placed that favorite Romantic musical instrument, a wind-harp— that is, an oblong sounding box whose strings, in response to the variable touch of the breeze, vibrate into chords of altering pitch and loudness. The lover's consciousness invests the relations of the casement and the harp, the harp and the circumambient breeze, with the posture, languor, and guile of erotic dalliance. In the final rendering of these lines:

> And that simplest Lute,
> Placed length-ways in the clasping casement, hark!
> How by the desultory breeze caress'd
> Like some coy maid half yielding to her lover,
> It pours such sweet upbraiding, as must needs
> Tempt to repeat the wrong!

2. The second chief stage was the first published version, in Coleridge's *Poems on Various Subjects* of 1796. Although still called an "Effusion," the poem has been developed into an obviously artful construction of fifty-six lines; it corresponds to all of the final text except that it lacks lines 26–33. This version is the one that justifies the usual description of "The Eolian Harp" as a wedding or honeymoon poem: Coleridge and Sara, having been married on 4 October 1795, are now living in the cottage at Clevedon. Taking up where the earlier manuscript left off, Coleridge first continues the earlier sexual imagery (the sounds, at the bolder importunities of the masculine wind, "over delicious surges sink and rise"), then introduces a descriptive tour-de-force wherein the witchery of nature's music transforms, to the musing mind, the sights and odors and sounds of this world into a fantasy of "Fairy-Land" or (the subsequent imagery suggests) of an exotic paradise,

> Where Melodies round honey-dropping flowers,
> Footless and wild, like birds of Paradise,
> Nor pause, nor perch, hovering on untam'd wing!

The poet's meditation now shifts (line 34) to recall recurrent occasions in which—not at evening and in the company of the beloved, but alone and while resting from his work at high noon—he lies stretched out on a nearby hillside, watching the dance of sunlight on the sea. In this remembered situation the presently perceived wind-harp remains the vehicle of the metaphoric process of thought, but the poet, when musing in solitude, is preoccupied not with love but with metaphysics. First the sounds of the harp (lines 39–43) become the analogue for the fantasies that, random and various as the breeze, "traverse my indolent and passive brain." Then, in a sudden focus of the random thoughts, the harp modulates into a radical image for the consciousness of all living things, responding with the music of thought to one divine and all-informing breeze:

> And what if all of animated nature
> Be but organic Harps diversely fram'd
> That tremble into thought, as o'er them sweeps
> Plastic and vast, one intellectual breeze,
> At once the Soul of each, and God of all?

The term "plastic" for a formative and organizing principle within nature—derived from Ralph Cudworth and other seventeenth-century Neoplatonists—was widely used in the 1790s, and Coleridge suggested in several other poems written at the time of "The Eolian Harp" that there is in nature an indwelling cause of the organization and consciousness of all individual existents. But he always expressed this concept in a guarded way, and in "The Eolian Harp" he presents it in the mode of a hypothetical question. Even in this form it turns out to be too bold, for even more than in his contemporary poems, it opens up a possibility that filled Coleridge with metaphysical terror: the world-view he called "Pantheism." That is, the passage threatens to absorb a transcendent and personal Creator of the world, without remainder, into an indwelling Soul of Nature, the *Pneuma* or *Spiritus Sacer* or *Anima Mundi* of the Stoics and Neoplatonists, which informs all the material universe and constitutes all modes of consciousness. Furthermore, as in the pagan philosophers who had taken the terms *pneuma*, *spiritus*, and *anima* in the literal sense of "breeze" or "breath," Coleridge's "intellectual breeze" even suggests a regressive form of the religion of Nature in which the unifying presence is a sacred wind or divine breath. The poet therefore represents his hypothetical speculation as having been spoken aloud, so that Sara—the voice of domestic Christian piety, a dramatized aspect of Coleridge's own divided mind—may dispraise such philosophy as "shapings of the unregenerate mind." The lyric speaker precipitately retracts the analogy and instead acknowledges his faith in a Christian Deity capable of yielding, to a sinful and miserable man, a grace beyond his deserts. The listing of these gifts in the concluding line closes the circle of the poem by repeating, in reverse order, the descriptive details of the beginning: "Peace, and this Cot, and thee, heart-honour'd Maid"—ending thus with the "pensive Sara" addressed in the opening phrase.

3. Except that it dropped "Effusion" from the title, Coleridge's *Poems* of 1797 reproduced the version published in 1796. Coleridge introduced the third major change six years later, in his *Poems* of 1803. Here he deleted lines 21–25—the comparison of the music of the wind-harp to the sound of twilight elfins—in order to move directly from the relationship of the two human lovers, as imaged in the erotic interplay between breeze and harp, to an encompassing love that relates the poet to all things in a world where even the silent air is potential music. In the original version of this inserted passage:

> Methinks it should have been impossible
> Not to love all things in a World like this,
> Where e'en the Breezes of the simple Air
> Possess the power and Spirit of Melody!

4. The fourth important change completes the poem as we have it now. In his collected poetry of 1817, *Sibylline Leaves*, Coleridge for the first time entitled the poem "The Eolian Harp." He restored the lines on fairyland and the birds of paradise which he had dropped from the preceding edition, letting them stand between the passage on human love and that on the love for all things. Then, after he had finished correcting the proofs for *Sibylline Leaves*, Coleridge sent the printer a list of Errata in which he included, for insertion immediately after the lines on the birds of paradise, a new quatrain, together with a version of the succeeding passage on the love for all things which he had revised so as to accord with these four new lines. The total insertion, which I reproduce as it was printed in the Errata, constitutes lines 26–33 of the final text:

> O! the one Life, within us and abroad,
> Which meets all Motion and becomes its soul,
> A Light in Sound, a sound-like power in Light,
> Rhythm in all Thought, and Joyance every where—
> Methinks, it should have been impossible
> Not to love all things in a world so fill'd,
> Where the breeze warbles and the mute still Air
> Is Music slumbering on its instrument!

"O! the one Life . . ." The exclamation introduces a moment of vision that every reader feels to be the imaginative climax of the poem. These lines, however, in T. S. Eliot's phrase, communicate before they are understood. In the confidence that they will communicate more subtly and richly after they are understood—and also that to understand them is to understand what is most distinctive in Coleridge's mature thought and imagination—I shall undertake to explicate the passage by seeking answers to four questions: What did Coleridge mean by his allusion to "a light in sound, a sound-like power in light"? How is this allusion related to "the one Life within us and abroad, / Which meets all motion"? In what way does the insight into a light in sound justify the sense of "joyance every where"? And what has this entire complex of a light in sound, the one Life, and universal joyance to do with the relation between the human lovers that precedes it and the culminating love for all things that follows it?

Exploration of the conceptual scheme that underlies this passage involves Coleridge's views about Newton's *Opticks*, Newton's scientific methods and theories, and the post-Newtonian world picture; the new metaphysical system that Coleridge constructed on the basis of his reading in Friedrich Schelling and other German *Naturphilosophen*; concepts that he found in Jacob Boehme and other esoteric thinkers; as well as his interpretation of the Biblical accounts of the creation and the Incarnation; so that I must be very selective. But even a cursory survey of the cognitive infrastructure of the imaginative moment expressed in these eight lines will indicate that they implicate a much heavier "burthen of Ideas" than that under which his early bardic poems had sweated and strained. Coleridge lamented repeatedly that metaphysics and "abstruse thought," to which he had turned for refuge from personal disasters, had depressed or destroyed his power of poetry. Unwanted "metaphysical trains of thought," he wrote in a letter to William Sotheby,

> when I wished to write a poem, beat up Game of far other kind—
> instead of a Covey of poetic Partridges with whirring wings of
> music . . . up came a metaphysical Bustard, urging it's slow,
> heavy, laborious, earth-skimming Flight, over dreary & level
> Wastes.

But less than a week earlier Coleridge had also insisted to the same correspondent that "a great Poet must be, implicitè if not explicitè, a profound Metaphysician. He may not have it in logical coherence. . . . But he must have it by *Tact*." It is because, in the passage of "The Eolian Harp" which is our concern, the burthen of ideas remains largely implicit within the imaginative insight it generates and supports that Coleridge is able to write philosophical poetry with the ease he had earlier sought and here supremely achieved.

I. A LIGHT IN SOUND

What are we to make of the mysterious reference to "a light in sound, a sound-like power in light"? The figures, technically, are oxymorons, and have usually been interpreted as alluding to synesthesia—the phenomenon in which the stimulation of one sense evokes a response involving a different sense. There had during the preceding century been intense interest, among poets and critics as well as philosophers, in such intersensory phenomena, stimulated in part by Newton's analogies in his *Opticks* between the propagation of light and of sound and between the perception of harmony and discord in musical tones and in colors. Coleridge shared this interest in what he called in the *Biographia Literaria* "the *vestigia communia* of the senses, the latency of all in each, and more especially . . . the excitement of vision by sound," and the line "A light in sound . . ." may include the suggestion of such a vestigial common-sensorium as an instance of the universal "latency of all in each" that leads to the poet's invocation of the one Life. But Coleridge's orbit of reference in this line is much wider than the psychology of sense-perception, for it involves a total metaphysic of the constitution of the material universe, of the nature of life, and of the relation of the mind to the universe it perceives.

The quatrain of "The Eolian Harp" on a light in sound was added to the text in a list of Errata to *Sibylline Leaves* that Coleridge composed no earlier than the spring of 1816, and possibly as late as the spring of 1817. This places the writing of the quatrain squarely in the middle of the remarkable span of four years or so when, in a sudden burst of intellectual activity, Coleridge composed his most important works on philosophy and science, including the *Biographia Literaria*, the *Theory of Life*, his two *Lay Sermons*, his radically revised and enlarged version of *The Friend*, and the series of *Philosophical Lectures* that he delivered between December 1818 and March 1819. All these works contain passages relevant to Coleridge's theories of the relations between light, sound, and life, and I shall later cite some of them. Most immediately pertinent and revealing, however, are a series of philosophical letters that Coleridge wrote between November 1816 and January 1818—that is, during and soon after the time when he composed the Errata—which show that he was almost obsessively preoccupied with the ideas that underlie the passage added to "The Eolian Harp."

Thus, Coleridge wrote Ludwig Tieck on 4 July 1817, a few weeks before *Sibylline Leaves* was issued, that the positions taken by Newton in his *Opticks* that "*a Ray* of Light" is a "*Thing*," "a physical *synodical Individuum*," and that "the Prism is a mere mechanic Dissector" of "this complex yet divisible Ray," had always appeared to him "monstrous FICTIONS!" Instead he put forward the view—adopted, he said, "probably from Behmen's Aurora, which I had *conjured over* at School"—"that Sound was = Light under the praepotence of Gravitation, and Color = Gravitation under the praepotence of Light." Above all, two letters that Coleridge wrote shortly thereafter to the Swedenborgian, C. A. Tulk, provide decisive clues not only to the line about light and sound but also (as we shall see) to the entire passage we are scrutinizing. In the first letter, written two months after the publication of *Sibylline Leaves*, Coleridge declared that "the two Poles of the material Universe are . . . Light and Gravitation. . . . The Life of Nature consists in the tendency of the Poles to re-unite, and to find themselves in the re-union." Then:

> Color is Gravitation under the power of Light . . . while Sound
> on the other hand is Light under the power or paramountcy of
> Gravitation. Hence the analogies of Sound to Light.

"A light in sound, a sound-like power in light"—we find in these letters references to the light, sound, and power alluded to in this line, and to the analogies that the line suggests between sound and light, as well as an indicated relation between these matters and life—"the Life of Nature." But what has all this to do with gravitation, the deficiencies of Newton's theory of light, and the polarity of the material universe, and what are we to make of "praepotence"? At first sight these passages, instead of explaining the mystery of a light in sound, seem to wrap it in an enigma. To explain in turn this enigma, we need to glance at some elements in the world-view that Coleridge was evolving in the period 1815–18.

Coleridge's reference of his views on light and sound to Boehme's *Aurora*, it will appear later, has substantial grounds, but it is misleading nonetheless. Coleridge's immediate precedents for the particular terms and metaphysical constructions in these letters were the writings of the contemporary philosopher Friedrich Schelling and, to a lesser extent, the writings of Schelling's fellow workers in *Naturphilosophie*, especially Henrik Steffens. He had begun to study Schelling intensively in about 1808—his burst of philosophical activity in the 1810s is, in considerable part, a result of the exciting possibilities that Schelling's thought opened out to him. For the sake of brevity I shall attend mainly to Coleridge's own views, with only an occasional glance at the German formulations that he adopted but altered to accord with his prior interests and speculations. Our investigation leads us to the center of Coleridge's philosophy of nature. This is an area of his thought that, until very recently, scholars have either discreetly overlooked or else—assessing it as an attempt to achieve by free fantasy what scientists discover by patient experiment—have rejected as "mere abracadabra," "a bizarre farrago of pretentious nonsense." Such judgments are inevitable if we simply apply to Coleridge's scheme of nature the criteria of the philosophical positivism that Coleridge's scheme was specifically intended to dispossess. If our intent, on the other hand, is not to dismiss but to understand an important development in nineteenth-century intellectual history, then we can do no better than to emulate Coleridge's own procedure, which John Stuart Mill found to be so intellectually liberating. Mill pointed out that by Bentham (the great philosophical positivist of his time), men have been led to ask of an opinion, "Is it true?" By Coleridge, they have been led to ask, "What is the meaning of it?" and to answer this question by trying to look at the opinion "from within."

> The long duration of a belief, [Coleridge] thought, is at least proof of an adaptation in it to some portion or other of the human mind; and if, on digging down to the root, we do not find, as is generally the case, some truth, we shall find some natural want or requirement of human nature which the doctrine in question is fitted to satisfy.

Let us then take Coleridge's vision of nature seriously and try to look at it from within, to see what it undertook to accomplish and what natural want it served to satisfy.

Coleridge's aim was not to replace experimental science by speculative science, but instead to develop a counter-metaphysic to the metaphysical foundations of modern science; his philosophy of nature, in short, was not science, nor anti-science, but metascience. By the reference, in his letter to Tieck, to Newton's "monstrous Fictions" in the *Opticks*, he did not mean to oppugn Newton as an experimental physicist, to whose procedures and discoveries he paid spacious tribute. His objection was to Newton as a man whose prestige as a physicist had given impetus to a metaphysics that, in Coleridge's view, permeated and vitiated all areas of thought and culture in the eighteenth century, "the Epoch of the Understanding and the Sense" in philosophy, psychology, politics, religion, and the arts. For despite his reluctance to frame hypotheses, Newton had proposed, in the "Queries" he added to his *Opticks*, that rays of light are "corpuscular," that is, "very small Bodies emitted from shining Substances," and that these bodies in motion excite "Waves of Vibrations, or Tremors" in a hypothetical "aether." This aether, although very "rare and subtile" is nonetheless a material medium that pervades, in varying densities, both space and bodies and serves to explain not only the action at a distance both of light and gravity, but also the refraction and reflection of light, as well as the propagation of light and sound from the eye and ear through the nerves "into the place of Sensation" where they are converted into sight and hearing.

This procedure, Coleridge argues, sets up a logical regress, since it undertakes to solve "Phaenomena by Phaenomena that immediately become part of the Problem to be solved." Worse still, Newton in his famed thirty-first Query had put forward the stark image of a universe whose ultimate elements are indivisible particles of matter capable of motion:

It seems probable to me, that God in the Beginning form'd Matter in solid, massy, hard, impenetrable, moveable Particles, of such Sizes and Figures, and with such other Properties, and in such Proportion to Space, as most conduced to the End for which he form'd them.

And as ultimate reality is thus reduced to masses and motion—for the simple reason that these are the only things that the highly specialized techniques of physical science are capable of managing mathematically—so the Creator of this reality is reconstrued to accord with such a postulated creation. That is, Newton's God is represented as the omnipresent mover of all particles, and also as the infallible seer of the particles in themselves that we are able to see only after they have been translated into the "images" formed by the sense through the intermediation of rays of light. God, Newton says, is "a powerful ever-living Agent, who being in all Places, is . . . able by his Will to move the Bodies within his boundless uniform Sensorium"; he is also the Being

who in infinite Space, as it were in his Sensory, sees the things themselves intimately . . . wholly by their immediate presence to himself: Of which things the Images only carried through the Organs of Sense into our little Sensoriums, are there seen and beheld by that which in us perceives and thinks.

"Sir Isaac Newton's Deity," Coleridge drily remarked, "seems to be alternately operose and indolent," for he undertakes to do everything, yet delegates so much power to "Vice-regent second causes" as "to make it inconceivable what he can have reserved."

Newton's move, as Coleridge saw it, was an immense extrapolation of a working fiction of physical science—what we now call a "conceptual model"—into a picture of the actual constitution of the universe. The "Mechanic or Corpuscular Scheme," Coleridge said, "in order to submit the various phenomena of moving bodies to geometrical construction," had to abstract "from corporeal substance all its *positive* properties," leaving it only "figure and mobility. And as a *fiction of science*, it would be difficult to overvalue this invention." But Descartes and later thinkers "propounded it as *truth of fact*: and instead of a World *created* and filled with productive forces by the Almighty *Fiat*, left a lifeless Machine whirled about by the dust of its own Grinding."

To Coleridge this view of the ultimate structure of reality was both incredible to human experience of the world and intolerable to human needs. As no more than a drastic subtraction from the rich diversity of sense-phenomena, it remains itself phenomenal, the product of what Coleridge repeatedly described as a "slavery" to the senses, especially to the eye. The "needlepoint pinshead System of the *Atomists*" was a fictional product of that "slavery to the eye" which reduces "the conceivable . . . within the bounds of the *picturable*," and excludes "all modes of existence

which the theorist cannot in imagination, at least, *finger* and *peep* at!"
Against this world-picture, in the literal sense of "picture" as something
that can be visualized, Coleridge again and again brought the charge that
it is, precisely speaking, lethal. It has killed the living and habitable world
of ordinary experience, as well as the metaphysical world of the pre-Carte-
sian and pre-Newtonian past, in which the mind of man had recognized
an analogon to itself and to its life, purposes, sentiments, values, and needs;
a world, therefore, in which man was a participant and could feel thoroughly at home. By the translation of the "scientific calculus" from a prof-
itable fiction into ontology, Coleridge claimed in 1817, "a few brilliant
discoveries have been dearly purchased at the loss of all communion with
life and the spirit of Nature." And against this "philosophy of death,"
which leaves only the "relations of unproductive particles to each other,"
he posed his own philosophy of life, in which "the two component counter-
powers actually interpenetrate each other, and generate a higher third,
including both the former."

That is, in radical opposition to the picture of a world composed of
particles of matter in motion, to whose impact an alien mind is passively
receptive, Coleridge sets up what, following Schelling, he calls a "vital,"
or "dynamic," or "constructive" philosophy. The elements of this philosophy are not moving material particles but inherent energies, or "powers,"
that polarize into positive and negative "forces" (also called "thesis and
antithesis") which operate according to "the universal Law of Polarity or
essential Dualism." By this Coleridge means that the generative and sustaining elements of his universe exist only relatively to each other and
manifest an irremissive tendency on the one hand to oppose themselves
and on the other hand to reunite. These powers and forces are not physical
or phenomenal, but metascientific and pre-phenomenal elements (in Coleridge's terms, they are not "real" but "ideal"), hence they cannot be pic-
tured, but only imagined; they do, however, within the phenomenal world
which they bring into being, have especially close and revealing analogues
that Coleridge calls their "exponents." It is only by their "living and generative interpenetration," or "synthesis," that the polar powers and forces
achieve the condition of matter, and so move into the phenomenal realm
available to the senses. "In all pure phaenomena," Coleridge says, "we
behold only the copula, the balance or indifference of opposite energies,"
and "matter" is to be considered "a Product—coagulum spiritûs, the pause,
by interpenetration, of opposite energies."

We are at length ready to turn back to Coleridge's enigmatic statement,
in his letter to C. A. Tulk of September 1817, that "Color is Gravitation
under the power of Light . . . while Sound on the other hand is Light under
the power or paramountcy of Gravitation." "The two Poles of the material
Universe," Coleridge there says, are "Light and Gravitation." Or as he
wrote in a manuscript note:

Well then, I say that all Powers may be reduced, in the first instance, into

Light & Gravity.
But each of these beget two other powers. Under Gravity we place Attraction and Repulsion: and under Light the Powers of Contraction and Dilation.

That is, the two elemental counter-powers that generate the cosmos he calls "light" and "gravity." These are not the light we see nor the weight, or gravitational force, we feel; they exist on a different ontological plane as "speculative" or "ideal" powers of which phenomenal light and weight serve as the closest "exponents" in experience. Each of these two powers evolves two counter-forces, constituting a tetrad of forces that Coleridge represents graphically as a north-south line crossed by an east-west line: gravity involves a pull in and its opposite, a push out, while light pulses radially in all directions and at the same time contracts back to its center. The continuous and incremental syntheses of the two counter-powers of gravity and light constitute the material elements and bodies of everything that exists. The innumerable qualitative differences among existing things, hence among the phenomena perceived by the senses, are determined by which of these two elemental powers—at any given level of their synthesis—is "predominant," in a range of ratios that extends from the extreme predominance of gravity, through a mid-point of "indifference" or "neutralization" between the two powers, to the extreme predominance of light. "That a thing *is*," as Coleridge puts it, "is owing to the co-inherence therein of any two powers; but that it is *that* particular thing arises from the proportions in which these powers are co-present, either as predominance or as reciprocal neutralization." (For "predominance," Coleridge elsewhere uses the alternative expressions "praepotence," "dynasty," "under the power of," or "paramountcy.")

The metaphysical enigma has, I trust, become transparent enough so that we can look through it at the initial mystery of "The Eolian Harp," line 28: "A light in sound, a sound-like power in light." Seated in close communion with his bride and luxuriously open to the light and color and sounds of the outer world, the poet, by a leap of imagination, achieves insight to the common pre-phenomenal powers of which all these phenomena are exponents, and so apprehends the unity within their qualitative diversity—sounds that incorporate the elemental counter-power of light, and light that, appearing as color, incorporates the elemental counter-power of gravity. For as we have seen, the power of gravitation, when predominant over the "co-present" power of light, manifests itself to the senses as sound, and when subordinate to light, manifests itself to the senses as color.

II. THE ONE LIFE

In what Coleridge called his "speculative," as opposed to "empirical," science of nature and life, he "constructs" (in the sense of rendering intelligible by reference to a single genetic principle) the total universe. Driven by their inherent stresses of opposition-in-unity, and manifesting in the struggle diverse degrees of relative "predominance," the powers of light and gravity evolve, by the progressive synthesis of prior syntheses, through the several distinctive orders of organization that Coleridge, following Schelling, calls "potences." At each level of organization, entities are linked by correspondences—according to an equivalence in the predominance of light or gravity—to entities on all other levels. On the first level of potence we get magnetism, electricity, and galvanism (which to Coleridge includes chemical combination), then all the forms of the inorganic world, then the forms of the organic world of plants and animals up to the highest stage of organic life, man; at which point mind, or "consciousness," emerges. This culminating achievement is a radical breakthrough in the developmental process, for consciousness is capable of a reflex act by which—in a continuing manifestation of "the universal Law of Polarity" whereby it counterposes, in order to reconcile, the outer world as "object" to itself as "subject"—it reengenders as knowledge the natural world within which it has itself been engendered, and of which it remains an integral part. Thus man's mind closes the evolutionary circle of polar generation by the powers of light and gravitation, the human and the nonhuman world merging at the focal point of consciousness.

We come to the moment in line 26 of "The Eolian Harp"— "O! the one Life within us and abroad." Coleridge's preoccupation with the one Life as a truth manifested in highest human experience, but alien to the post-Newtonian world-picture, goes back long before 1816 or 1817, when he added this passage to the poem. As early as 1802, for example, he had written to Sotheby that Nature will have her proper interest only to him "who believes & feels, that every Thing has a Life of its own, & that we are all *one Life*." In the Hebrew Psalmists, unlike the mythological poets among the Greeks, you find "genuine Imagination."

> In the Hebrew Poets each Thing has a Life of it's own, & yet they are all one Life. In God they move & live, & *have* their Being—not *had*, as the cold System of Newtonian Theology represents, but *have*.

And in the conversation poems that Coleridge wrote within several years after the 1796 version of "The Eolian Harp," the climax of each meditation on a landscape had been a moment of insight—the sudden awareness of a single Presence behind and within the phenomena of sense. In all these early poems, however, the visionary moment had been described in terms that had long been traditional. In "The Eolian Harp" of 1796, the poet tentatively put forward a latter-day version of the Stoic World-Soul—"one intellectual breeze"—as the principle that makes all animated nature "tremble into thought." In other conversation poems the poet found "religious meanings in the forms of nature!" or discovered that nature was an orthodox "Temple" built by "God" and that the diversified landscape "seem'd like Omnipresence"; or else the landscape manifested itself to be God's veiled self-revelation,

                                          of such hues
As veil the Almighty Spirit, when yet he makes
Spirits perceive his presence;
        ["This Lime-Tree Bower My Prison," 41–43]

or (in the concept that had persisted from early Christian exegetes through Bishop Berkeley) the objects and aspects of the landscape were recognized to be *verba visibilia* in God's Book of Nature,

The lovely shapes and sounds intelligible
Of that eternal language which thy God
Utters.
        ["Frost at Midnight," 59–61]

Now, some fifteen years later, the metascience of nature that Coleridge had evolved from German *Naturphilosophie* provided him with a full and detailed conceptual structure to support and articulate his earlier intuitions. In this scheme, in which all matter and spirit are generated by the interplay of the same elemental powers, there is no gap between the living and the lifeless, nature and man, or matter and mind, but only a distinction of levels of organization. "What is *not* Life," Coleridge asks, "that really *is*?" For "in the identity of the two counter-powers, Life *sub*sists; in their strife it *con*sists: and in their reconciliation it at once dies and is born again into a new form." This "universal life" of ever-renewing strife and reconciliation pulses through all individual forms and all the orders of being, beginning with "the life of metals"—where in "its utmost *latency* . . . life is one with the elementary powers of mechanism"—up through the progressive levels of "individuation" to the human consciousness, which in its living reciprocity with its specific contrary, nature, is capable of achieving the awareness that there is only one Life within us and abroad.

Hence the statement I quoted earlier from Coleridge's letter to C. A. Tulk that "the Life of Nature" consists in the sustained tendency of the poles of "Light and Gravitation" to separate and re-unite. But this same revealing letter, written within a few months of the final version of "The Eolian Harp," makes it plain that Coleridge's intuition of "the one Life within us and abroad" has not merely a metascientific basis, but a Biblical one as well. It will help to clarify this essential aspect of Coleridge's thought—and of the poem—if we turn back to consider the significance of Coleridge's statement to Tieck, that same year, that he had adopted the idea of the relation of light and gravity to color and sound "probably from Behmen's Aurora, which I had *conjured over* at School."

The Aurora, written in 1611–12, was the first of Jacob Boehme's books; it is incomplete, and even more obscure than Boehme's later expositions of his esoteric but very influential doctrines. Through the fantastic terminology and melodramatic narration, however, we can make out its basic concepts and design. Boehme's undertaking is to elucidate the mystery of the creation of the world and of man, as the initial episode in the history of human and cosmic salvation. He bases his account of the creation on the first chapter of Genesis (which he regards as in fact the story of a second creation, intended to repair the wreck of the angelic world occasioned by the fall of the angel Lucifer) and also upon the commentary on the creation in the Gospel of John (on which Boehme largely relies for his account of the first creation of a perfect world). But Boehme claims that he has been inspired by divine grace infused "in my spirit," and that he is therefore able to decipher the spiritual truths concealed within the esoteric sound-symbolism of the literal Biblical narrative. Boehme's symbolic interpretation of the creation (more accurately, of the two creations) turns out, in fact, to be mainly a remarkably elaborated version of the doctrines and terminology he had learned (at this period of his life, at second hand) from the alchemical philosophy of Paracelsus and other Renaissance Hermeticists.

To Boehme, the essential condition for all creativity and progression, both in being and in thinking, is a strenuous tension between contraries, or opposed forces, whose sequential separations and unions give rise to everything that exists. The archetypal struggle in the fallen world is between the contrary forces of good and evil, love and hate, but these are destined to eventuate in the triumph of good and love in the coming redemption. Even the original creation of the angelic world, however, resulted from the energy generated by opponent principles. For God the Father manifests a joyous union of divine powers that Boehme calls, collectively, the "Salliter," or the "Sal-niter." This totality involves seven different *Qualitäten*, which Boehme derives from *Quelle* and *quellen* ("a spring," "to gush forth"), and which are therefore not what we ordinarily call "qualities," but "powers" or "forces" (*Kräfte*). Each one of these elemental powers is a balance of opposing contraries, and each also has its appropriate counterpower. From the divine Salliter, in the successive unions and renewed oppositions of the diverse opponent powers and forces, issues all that constitutes the world, from stones and metals through plants and animals to the body and spirit of man, who as microcosm is the perfect analogue of the world's body and spirit. In Boehme's world there is thus no gap between animate and inanimate, body and mind, conscient and inconscient—all are an emanation of the powers of the one Deity, and throughout all there surges one life, exhibiting itself in the conflict and interpenetration of the same vital forces.

In this great radiation outward from the divine source of all life and being, Boehme puts by far the greatest stress on the role in creation of two elements, sound and light. The reasons for this emphasis are patent. In the Book of Genesis, God's creation is by word, or sound. His first creative sounds are, "Let there be light," which forthwith become light, and His later creative sounds become all forms of life, including man. And in the first chapter of John we find the creative fiat represented as the Word, which is equated with light, and also with life, and finally becomes itself incarnate:

> In the beginning was the Word, and the Word was with God, and the Word was God. . . .
>
> All things were made by him; and without him was not any thing made that was made.
>
> In him was life; and the life was the light of men.
>
> And the light shineth in darkness; and the darkness comprehended it not. . . .
>
> And the Word was made flesh, and dwelt among us.

Boehme repeatedly echoes these passages from Genesis and John (see, for example, chapters 18 and 26). In his symbolic translation of them into a philosophy of nature, light is represented, not as one of the primal powers, but as something which is generated from the ensemble of the seven powers; as Boehme puts it, light is "perpendicular" to the ontological plane of the powers. This light is equated with the Son, as well as with the sun, the "place" of light in the heavens; while in man, the light constitutes his soul and spirit. Sound, on the other hand, is one of the seven elemental powers within the divine Salliter itself; this power Boehme calls "Mercurius" (that is, Mercury or Hermes Trismegistus, the great magus of the Hermetic philosophers). Boehme identifies this "sound" (*Schall*) with the creative voice and with the harmony of the heavenly music; accordingly, from this "sound, tone, tune or noise . . . ensued *speech*, language, and the *distinction* of everything, as also the ringing melody and *singing* of the holy angels, and therein consisteth the forming or framing of all *colours*, beauty and ornament, as also the heavenly *joyfulness*" (*Aurora*, 10.1). In its manifestation as speech, sound serves as the vehicle for the expression of spirit, hence as the vehicle (in God's creative fiat) by which the third aspect of God, the Holy Spirit, expresses itself. Sound, in Boehme's intricate system of analogies and identities, thus is equated with the Word, or divine Logos itself, and so is integral with light and life and the Son, as an element in the triune nature of God which manifests itself throughout the creation.

Whatever the extent of his claimed knowledge of *The Aurora* during his schooldays, we know that Coleridge closely studied and copiously annotated this and other books by Boehme, in the English "Law edition," from the year 1807 on, just prior to and collaterally with his immersion in Schelling and other *Naturphilosophen* during the second decade of the nineteenth century. Coleridge's thinking was inveterately organic and genetic, always traveling back to the radical of a view—or as he called it, to the "seminal" idea—which has proved historically capable of growing into a total metaphysic. It should be clear even from my brief summation that he found a great deal in Boehme's dualistic vitalism that suited his own mature "dynamic" philosophy; and in the letter to Ludwig Tieck, as well as in his private annotations, Coleridge tended to impose on Boehme's inchoate views the terms and structure of the metascience he had developed on the basis of contemporary German thinkers. It was in line with this persistent tendency (and not in order to hide his debt to Schelling) that Coleridge interpreted Boehme's arcane statements about the primary roles of light and sound in nature to accord with his own doctrines about the elemental counter-powers of gravitation and light and their relative "predominance" in the diverse phenomena of sound and color.

But what in Boehme's writings made the greatest appeal to Coleridge, as against Schelling's early *Naturphilosophie*, was that Boehme had derived his scheme of nature from the Biblical accounts of the creation, although Coleridge feared that Boehme had not entirely avoided the "Pantheism" that he found blatantly manifested in Schelling—the assimilation of a transcendent Creator into a religion of Nature. As far back as the letter to Sotheby of 1802, it will be recalled, Coleridge had discovered the sense of "one Life" within all things, specifically, in "the Hebrew poets" of the Old Testament. Now, in a marginal comment on *The Aurora*, he comments on Boehme's treatment of light in the creation and Incarnation:

> That not Heat but Light is the Heart of Nature is one of those truly profound and pregnant Thoughts that ever and anon astonish me in Boehme's writings. . . . The affinity . . . of the Flesh and Blood generally to Light I trust that I shall make clear in my commentaries on the first and sixth chapters of the Gospel of John. Hence in the Logos (distinctive energy) is *Light*, and the Light became the *Life* of Man.

The "commentaries" on John to which Coleridge alludes he planned to include in his *Logosophia*, the comprehensive philosophical work on which he labored for decades but never completed. In this "Opus Maximum," the exposition of his own "Dynamic or Constructive Philosophy" was to be "preparatory" to "a detailed Commentary on the Gospel of St. John," in order "to prove that Christianity is true Philosophy"; and this section was in turn to be followed by a treatise on "the Mystics & Pantheists," including Jacob Boehme.

We return to the indispensible letters that Coleridge wrote to C. A. Tulk in 1817 and early 1818. There he begins his "rude and fragmentary" sketch of "the Science of the Construction of *Nature*" with God, who is the absolute "Identity" or "*Prothesis*" which precedes any polarity between thesis and antithesis; Coleridge comments that to adopt the alternative, the "Lockian, and Newtonian" Creator as "an hypothetical Watch-maker," is in fact to "live without God in the world." And he begins his construction of nature—"the Genesis . . . the *Birth* of Things"—with an interpretation of the opening sentence of the Book of Genesis, "In the beginning God created the Heaven and the Earth." Coleridge's hermeneutics is based on his view that the Bible embodies the ideas of "reason" in the mode of "imagination," hence that it is "a science of realities" expressed in "symbols." His interpretation of the Biblical accounts of the creation, therefore, like Boehme's, is symbolic, although on quite different grounds.

I will not reconstruct the exegetic maneuvers by which Coleridge translates "And the Earth was waste and void . . . and Darkness on the Deep" to signify that what first came into existence was "gravitation," which is best designated by "the combination of the Ideas, Darkness & the Deep or Depth." He continues:

> And God said—Let there be *Light*: and there was *Light*. And God divided the *Light* from the *Darkness*—i.e. Light from Gravitation . . . and the two Poles of the material Universe are established, viz. Light and Gravitation. . . . The Life of Nature consists in the tendency of the Poles to re-unite. . . . God is the Sun of the Universe—it's gravitation or Being by his Omnipresence, it's Light by his only-begotten Son . . . Deus alter et idem!

He also conjoins the account of the creation of light in Genesis with the commentary on the creative Logos in the opening chapter of John:

> God SAID, Let there be Light: and there became LIGHT! In the beginning was the Word. All things *became* . . . through the Word, the living and vivific Word . . . whose Life is the *Light* of men. . . . The Light . . . rose up in the Darkness and in the Depth—and in and with it *became* . . . the two Primary Poles of Nature, Light and Gravitation.

On these grounds Coleridge proceeds to "construct" the orders of being and of sense-phenomena that make up the universe, including, in the passage which is our central concern, the construction of color as "Gravitation under the power of Light" and of sound as "light under the power or paramountcy of Gravitation."

Coleridge's inserted passage in "The Eolian Harp," then, is only the visible tip of a massive complex of submerged ideas, scientific and metascientific, scriptural and theological. We know enough of this substructure to recognize now that the poet's moment of vision is also a theophany, and that the oxymorons in which the moment is expressed signify not only the "law of contradiction," or polarity, on which Coleridge's metascience is based, but also the central Christian mysteries. For in Coleridge's interwoven universe of correspondences and analogues, of exponents and symbols, "a light in sound" is the distant reflection of the light generated by the primal sound, "Let there be light," while "a sound-like power in light" is the distant echo of the creative Word which became flesh and is the Light as well as the Life both of nature and man.

In line 27, this one Life "meets all motion and becomes its soul." In the Newtonian world-picture, motion—as measured by the altering position, through time, of particles of matter in space—had been an elementary postulate. Coleridge, however, by intricate reasoning derives "ideal" (prephenomenal) time and space from his own first premise, or "Prothesis," as the primitive polar opposites whose synthesis constitutes "motion." He conceives motion, that is, as a point moving through space in time, so that it forms, and is represented graphically by, a line; and the bipolar line, in the next synthesis, achieves a third dimension as "depth." Coleridge cryptically summarizes to Tulk the role of these elementary constructs in generating the universe:

> Time × Space = Motion. Attraction × Repulsion = Gravity as Depth.—These are ideal relations. The ideal + real, or rather the Ideal = Real. World arises out of chaos (= Indistinction) or begins, with the creation of Light.

He adds, however, that "a Life, a Power, an *Inside*, must have pre-existed" the ideal dimensions of time, space, motion, and depth, of which "the LIFE *appearing*" in the real, or material, world is the result; and that this process of the "interpenetration of opposite energies," of which matter is a product, sustains itself, as process, to constitute the "spirit" in all matter. Otherwise stated: the elemental rhythm of opposing and interpenetrating polarities in which life consists, when it meets all "ideal" motion, brings it into existence as matter, in which the continuing pulsation of the one Life constitutes the spirit or soul; and this vital outer rhythm, he goes on to say in "The Eolian Harp," has its analogue, in high moments of human consciousness, as a "rhythm in all thought."

III. JOYANCE

Now, what of the "joyance every where" in line 29? "Joy" and "joyance" were specialized terms, used by Coleridge as the emotional index to a particular relationship between the conscious self and the outer world. To clarify its significance in "The Eolian Harp," we need to consider again Coleridge's evolving scale of being, at the point at which the reflexive consciousness emerges in man.

Man, Coleridge says in his letters to Tulk, represents the ultimate product of the two contrary "ends" of the life-process, namely "Individualization, or apparent detachment from Nature = progressive Organization" and "the re-union with Nature as the apex of Individualization." And since, as he says in the contemporary work, the *Theory of Life*, "the form of polarity" applies at this as at every evolutionary stage, "the intensities must be at once opposite and equal," so that the independence of an individual man should ideally be matched by "interdependence" with other men in the social organization, while "as the ideal genius and the originality [i.e., the highest degree of human autonomy], in the same proportion must be the resignation to the real world, the sympathy and the intercommunion with Nature," which exists "in counterpoint to him." But although man is both product and participant in the universal process of life, he is radically different from the rest of nature, in that by achieving consciousness, he also achieves freedom of the will. As Coleridge puts it in the same passage, man "is referred to himself, delivered up to his own charge"; and here things can go drastically wrong. For an excess in the tendency to individuation—especially when fostered by untoward "hardships" and "circumstances"—can force "a man in upon his little unthinking contemptible self," and so cut the individual consciousness off from the sense of its interdependence with other men and of its intercommunion with outer nature.

To be cut off from all relationship to man and nature, to suffer what he called "the evils of separation and finiteness," was to Coleridge as to other Romantic thinkers and poets the radical affliction of the human condition. This is the state to which the Romantic philosopher Hegel gave the name "alienation," and it is, as Coleridge saw it, the inescapable situation of anyone who accepts the Newtonian world-picture, the dead universe of matter in motion, as existential reality. "Joy," on the other hand, is the term Coleridge specifically appropriated to the state of mind in which all alienation is annulled—it is an equipoise of the contrary mental powers, manifested in an inner life so abundant that it breaks through the barrier of self to yield awareness of the one Life that is shared with other selves and with nature. As Coleridge says about "joy" in his *Philosophical Lectures*, with respect to "genius," which is the term he uses for the creative power of the human mind and imagination:

> All genius exists in a participation of a common spirit. In joy individuality is lost. . . . To have a genius is to live in the universal, to know no self but that which is reflected not only from the faces of all around us, our fellow creatures, but reflected from the flowers, the trees, the beasts, yea from the very surface of the [waters and the] sands of the desert.

To this I shall add a contemporary statement by Coleridge in *The Friend* of 1818. This passage, in its context, ascribes the scientific world-picture to an alienation of mind from nature, and counters it, as the premise of philosophy, with the primal intuition of an integrity of the self and not-self, mind and nature, of which the sign in human consciousness is the condition called "joy":

> The ground-work, therefore, of all true philosophy is the full apprehension of the difference between . . . that intuition of things which arises when we possess ourselves, as one with the whole . . . and that which presents itself when . . . we think of ourselves as separated beings, and place nature in antithesis to the mind, as object to subject, thing to thought, death to life. This is abstract knowledge, or the science of the mere understanding. . . . [The former on the other hand] is an eternal and infinite self-rejoicing, self-loving, with a joy unfathomable, with a love all comprehensive.

IV. LOVE

In this intuition of the community of all life, the movement from "a joy unfathomable" to "a love all comprehensive" parallels the movement in

"The Eolian Harp" from "joyance every where" to the universal love described in the next lines, which Coleridge revised and integrated with the added passage on the one Life:

> Rhythm in all thought, and joyance every where—
> Methinks, it should have been impossible
> Not to love all things in a world so filled.

There remains, in conclusion, to show the relation in Coleridge's thinking at this period between all-comprehensive love and the elemental powers of gravity and light, as these manifest themselves in a light in sound.

In this instance, too, the connection is established in one of his letters to C. A. Tulk. There having "constructed," on both metascientific and Biblical grounds, "the two Primary Poles of Nature, Light and Gravitation," he goes on to say that these "correlatives and correspondent Opposites, by and in which the Unity is revealed," are

> (to borrow your happy and most expressive Symbol) the Male and female of the World of Time, in whose wooings, and retirings and nuptial conciliations all other marriages . . . are celebrated inclusively.—These truths it is my Object to enforce in the manner best fitted (alas! how hopeless even the best!) to the present age.

To indicate what lies behind this astonishing attribution of sexuality to all phenomenal nature ("the World of Time") requires another look, from a different vantage point, at Coleridge's metascientific enterprise. The post-Newtonian world-picture repelled him because it had been deliberately stripped bare of any correlative to the life of man and any sanction for human purposes and values. While a young man of thirty Coleridge had written to Southey that "a metaphysical Solution, that does not instantly *tell* for something in the Heart, is grievously to be suspected as apocryphal," and in the *Biographia Literaria*, contemporaneously with the last version of "The Eolian Harp," he extolled Boehme, despite the "delusions" and fantasies he found mixed with his "truths," because he had contributed "to keep alive the *heart* in the *head*; gave me . . . [a] presentiment, that all the products of the mere *reflective* faculty partook of DEATH. Coleridge meant that, as man cannot live by science alone—in his terms, by the evidence of the senses ordered by the "reflective faculty," the "understanding"—neither can he endure a universe constructed to suit the narrow requirements of Newtonian physics rather than the large requirements of human life. Coleridge undertook to develop an alternative world-vision that would suffice to the heart as well as the head, by supplementing science with imagination—as he put it in terms of his faculty-philosophy, the phenomena of "the senses," as classed and ordered by "the understanding," are to be "impregnated" by "the imagination," and so reconciled and mediated to the requirements of the supreme and inclusive power of mind, "the reason."

We can translate Coleridge's terms into the idiom of our own time.

His prime endeavor, like that of his contemporaries, the great German architects of all-inclusive metaphysical "systems," was to assimilate the findings and hypotheses of contemporary science to the inherent demands and forms of the human imagination, in the kind of inclusive vision of man in the world that Northrop Frye calls a "myth of concern." In this undertaking man is put back into nature, from which the sophisticated logic of science had severed him, by applying the primitive imaginative categories of analogy, correspondence, and identity. Through this procedure nature is once more endowed with the inherent energies of life and with humanly intelligible purposes and values, and so constitutes a milieu in which man can fully live and be at home. And since the cultural myth of concern that Coleridge had inherited was the Judeo-Christian one set forth in the Bible, and since Coleridge felt a greater need than contemporary German philosophers to salvage the essentials of its creed of salvation, he undertook explicitly to ground his world-vision on bases common both to the Old and New Testament and to "speculative physics."

No doubt Coleridge would have rejected this description, since it transposes the criterion of his intricately rationalized system from a truth of correspondence to ultimate reality to a truth of correspondence to man's deepest instincts and needs, as these shape the forms of his imagination. But Schelling, I think, might well have accepted it, for Schelling was one of the German philosophers who helped establish the present views, of which Northrop Frye is a distinguished representative, that human needs inevitably compel the creation of a mythology to live by, in civilized no less than in primitive societies. Schelling asserts that in the modern world the mythology of the ancients has been outworn, while "the mythology of Christendom" is unsuitable for valid poetry, so that now "every truly creative individual has to create his own mythology." All these separate creations, however, will prove, in the indeterminate future, to be parts of a single system of myth. The preeminent material for this evolving mythology is contemporary *Naturphilosophie*, such as he has himself developed. It is his conviction, Schelling says, "that in the higher speculative physics is to be sought the possibility of a future mythology and symbolism," which will reconcile the contraries between the pagan and Christian mythologies in one vision of nature; but this achievement, he adds, will be the work not of any one individual, but of "the entire era."

Conspicuous in Schelling's own later *Naturphilosophie* is its tendency to move from abstract concepts to explicitly anthropomorphic and mythical formulations. This tendency is most obvious in the instance of his basic principle of polarity. In his early writings Schelling had based this category on the concepts of bipolarity in recent scientific developments in magnetism and electricity, as well as on Kant's essay of 1786, which undertook a "metaphysical" derivation of the primitive "matter" of Newtonian physics from the elemental "powers" of attraction and repulsion. Coleridge in his turn based his early formulations of the polar-principle on the theory of his scientific friend Humphry Davy that all substances are the product of elementary forces, even before he absorbed the views of Kant and the metaphysical system of Schelling. Coleridge, however, rightly pointed back to a long tradition, from "the Dynamic Theory of the eldest Philosophy" in the pre-Socratic thinkers, through Renaissance Hermeticism, to Jacob Boehme as precedent to Schelling in putting forward "the universal law of polarity." In these earlier thinkers the philosophical representation of an all-originative and sustaining interplay of elemental opposites had not yet completely emerged from its origins in a cosmic myth of universal bisexuality—the myth of male and female divinities or powers, antithetic and warring yet mutually attractive and necessary, which periodically merge in unions that beget the world and all things in it. In its older forms, in other words, universal polarity had been derived from bisexual procreation as its prototype; and it is the sexual dimension of human nature, we may plausibly conjecture, that gives the myth of cosmic bisexuality its persisting hold on imagination even today, in current forms of the "perennial philosophy." After all, as Schelling remarked, human union and procreation is "the single instance in which we are to a certain extent permitted to be witnesses of an original creation."

In his early writings of 1797, Schelling at times referred to the contrary powers of gravity and light as the feminine or "mother-principle" and the masculine or "procreative principle," which are "represented" or "expressed" in the differentiated sexes of the higher organisms. Increasingly after that he dramatized his metaphysics of polarity by endowing it with anthropomorphic features and relationships. He wrote in 1804, for example, that "made pregnant by light, gravity gives birth to the diverse forms of things and delivers them from her fruitful womb to independent life." Driven by the compulsion to progressive individuation, the powers of gravity and light, at the organic stage of evolution, separate first into the bisexual organs in a single plant, then into the separate sexes of the animal and human realms. Yet every individual remains the product of both powers, and each monosexual individual needs its polar opposite in order to fulfill the contrary compulsion of nature toward identity. "This is the secret of eternal love . . . in that each is a whole, yet desires the other and seeks the other." Hence:

> As the being and life of nature rests on the eternal embrace of light and gravity, so the unions of the two sexes, their begetting and propagation of innummerable species, are nothing else than the celebration of the eternal love of those two [powers] which, when they could have been two, yet wanted to be one, and thereby created all of nature.

Such also are the grounds of Coleridge's statement, in his letter to Tulk, that light and gravitation are "the Male and female of the World of Time, in whose wooings, and retirings and nuptial conciliations all other marriages . . . are celebrated inclusively." Like the German *Naturphilosophen*, Coleridge sometimes mythicized his metascience, to humanize his vision of a natural world whose diverse orders of being are linked by familial correspondences to man and mind, and whose processes are compelled by inconscient analogues of love and hate, of oppositions and marriages. Hence those strange passages in Coleridge's speculative natural history that seem to a casual reader to be merely fantasies based on free association. In a manuscript, for example, he declares that, though all the chemical elements contain the two counter-powers, "Gravity and Light with Warmth as the Indifference," yet because of the differing "predominance of some one, Carbon most represents Gravity, Oxygen Light, and Hydrogen Warmth." When, in the sequential combinations of these chemical elements, nature achieves the plant, we find in its generative organ, the flower, "the qualitative product of Oxygen = Light in the outness and splendor of Colors, the qualitative product of Hydrogen = Warmth in the inwardness and sweetness of Fragrance"; and this fragrance Coleridge interprets as the accompaniment of "gentle love," of which the flower serves as a material symbol. And when—in the continuing genetic process of the "interpenetration" of the primal opposites, gravity and light—we reach the level of birds, we find that the colors of their plumage correspond to the colors of the flower, but that a new phenomenon, bird-song, or sound, has replaced the odors of flowers and taken over their biological function in ensuring fertilization. In birds, then, Coleridge says, we have "light in the form (under the power) of Gravity in Color, and Gravity sub formâ et ditione Lucis subditione"—that is, "gravity subordinated to the form and dominion of light"—in the bird-song. The "Sounds and sweet yearning varied by quiet provoking challenging sounds" are thus "the surrogates of the Vegetable Odors—and like these, are the celebrations of the Nuptial moments, the hours of Love.

Such passages provide a bridge between the "sound-like power in light" and the love of all things in the inserted section of "The Eolian Harp." They provide also a broader perspective through which to review the long evolution of that poem between 1795 and 1817, as I described it at the beginning of this essay. In its first short form "The Eolian Harp" had been a love poem which assimilated the relation of the wind and the strings of the harp to the dalliance, the "wooings, and retirings" of the human lovers. It had next been developed into a marriage poem, and also expanded into a metaphysical speculation about "all of animated nature." In its final form it is still a love poem, but a cosmic love poem, in which the love between the poet and his bride becomes the exponent of a universal relationship— the "union of the individual with the Universe" which, Coleridge said, occurs "through love." It is still a marriage poem, too, but one in which the human union becomes, in Coleridge's technical term, an "exponent" of the primal union in which "all other marriages . . . are celebrated inclusively." For in the lines added in 1817 the poet breaks through sensation into vision, in which the phenomenal aspects of the landscape, its colors, music, and odors, are intuited as products and indices of the first manifestations of the creative Word, gravitation and light, in whose multiform unions all nature and life consist; and he goes on to celebrate the world's song of life and joy, which sounds through the wind-harp, in which the silent air is merely music unheard, and of which the subject is the one Life that, in marrying all opposites, also weds the single consciousness to the world without. And however we may judge the metascientific and religious beliefs that engendered the moment of vision, they have in this passage been transformed by the imagination from a creed into the poetry of immediate experience, and so compel our participation independently of either belief or disbelief:

> O! the one Life within us and abroad,
> Which meets all motion and becomes its soul,
> A light in sound, a sound-like power in light,
> Rhythm in all thought, and joyance every where—
> Methinks, it should have been impossible
> Not to love all things in a world so fill'd;
> Where the breeze warbles, and the mute still air
> Is music slumbering on her instrument.

Coleridge, we know, printed this passage as an addendum to a poem already set in type. The insertion throws the whole poetic structure into imbalance by locating the climax of the meditation near the beginning. By 1817, however, Coleridge, though capable of poetic moments, was not capable of sustained poetic endeavor; as he said two years later, "Poeta fuimus," but "the Philosopher, tho' pressing with the weight of an Etna, cannot prevent the Poet from occasionally . . . manifesting his existence by smoke traversed by electrical flashes from the Crater." In succeeding printings of "The Eolian Harp" Coleridge simply transferred the added passage into the text without altering its context. But the poet's retraction of his metaphysical speculations in the original conclusion to the poem had never been at ease with its surroundings either in tone or in idiom, and after this high moment of religious as well as metaphysical imagination, the coda is rendered inconsequent as well as anticlimactic.

"Positive Negation": Threshold, Sequence, and Personification in Coleridge

Angus Fletcher

"It was, I think, in the month of August, but certainly in the summer season, and certainly in the year 1807, that I first saw this illustrious man, the largest and most spacious intellect, the subtlest and the most comprehensive, in my judgment, that has yet existed amongst men." Thus, in an article written some twenty-seven years later, Thomas De Quincey recalled his first encounter with Coleridge. The encounter was somewhat uncanny. Coleridge, one might say, *appeared* to his young admirer.

> I had received directions for finding out the house where Coleridge was visiting; and, in riding down a main street of Bridgewater, I noticed a gateway corresponding to the description given me. Under this was standing, and gazing about him, a man. . . . his eyes were large and soft in their expression; and it was from the peculiar appearance of haze or dreaminess, which mixed with their light, that I recognized my object. This was Coleridge. I examined him steadfastly for a minute or more; and it struck me that he saw neither myself nor any other object in the street. He was in deep reverie; for I had dismounted, made two or three trifling arrangements at an inn door, and advanced close to him, before he had apparently become conscious of my presence. The sound of my voice, announcing my own name, first awoke him: he started, and, for a moment, seemed at a loss to understand my purpose or his situation; for he repeated rapidly a number of words which had no relation to either of us. There was no *mauvaise honte* in his manner, but simple perplexity, and an apparent difficulty in recovering his position amongst daylight realities. This little scene

From *New Perspectives on Coleridge and Wordsworth: Selected Papers from the English Institute.* © 1972 by Columbia University Press.

over, he received me with a kindness of manner so marked it might be called gracious.

Coleridge appeared to De Quincey in the hovering stance of "a solitary haunted by vast conceptions in which he cannot participate," Hartman's romantic "hero of consciousness." He stood on the threshold between a building and a street, a palace and a highway, a temple and a labyrinth. This threshold is an edge at which simultaneous participation in the sacred and the profane becomes available to the hero of consciousness.

THRESHOLDS: A SPENSERIAN ORIGIN

The gateway is a sacred *via transitionae* in all cultures: in our materialist world there are myths of carrying brides over doorsteps, though we no longer break oatcakes over the heads of newlyweds. Thresholds, which are dangerous, have an ancient, rigorous mythography and rite. The Romans consecrated a god of gates, Janus, whose bifrontal face looked opposite ways, in and out of the city, blessing or cursing the passer in his entrance to or exit from the city.

Janus was also a god of beginnings, which suggests that, in any advanced civilization, a genuine beginning always starts from somewhere. Within culture, it would seem, there are no beginnings *ex nihilo*. The scene of the origin is a fountain, a *templum*, a ground made sacred because it is the iconic double of the world conceived as sacred space and therefore, as so frequently in the ancient civilizations, a space formally demarcated by a sacred limit, the so-called *mundus*—the world-wall. Within culture, also, deaths and endings seem to belong to what lies outside the sacred inner-space, an outside archetypally structured as "the labyrinth."

Ancient religious traditions descend and enter into English poetics largely through the imagery of a dialectical opposition between temple and labyrinth. The Romantic fascination with these two great images of life seems to gain its power from the hybrid nature of classical and Christian mythography, as a Christian Humanist combination. The temple and labyrinth are the paradigmatic mythic structures for Biblical, as much as classical, historicity and prophecy. The hybridization of pagan and Christian myth is, at least in this area, entirely conventional.

If temple and labyrinth provide the models of sacred stillness and profane movement, the threshold is the model of the transitional phase that links these two fundamental modes of being. Mythographically thresholds take many forms: Homer's Cave of the Nymphs, Virgil's twin Gates of Horn and Ivory, Dante's Limbo—or, leaping into the modern era, Wordsworthian "spots of time," Conrad's shadow line, Forster's Caves of Marabar. While epic tradition supplies conventional models of the threshold, these conventions are always subject to deliberate poetic blurring, and this shift from the distinct limen to the indistinct serves a double purpose. On the one hand, poets, like painters, may delight in the softening of outline because it permits an intensification of medium: thus Turner's mastery of the indistinct expresses a technical interest in medium which is remarkably parallel to that of his near-contemporary, Coleridge. On the other hand, and this is perhaps the fundamental and more substantial point, poets have wished to subtilize, to dissolve, to fragment, to blur the hard material edge, because poetry hunts down the soul, with its obscure passions, feelings, other-than-cognitive symbolic forms. Spenser, for example, places doormen at the gates of his various temples; Milton stations various guardians of the gates: angels watch over Eden, Heaven, and Hell (including the counterwatch of Sin and Death). Such porters actively frame their universes. Yet despite this hard and obvious utility of suggesting the security force watching over mythic borders, few poets of major stature remain long interested in the material aspect of the threshold. If not always before, at least with the Renaissance there is a poetic commitment to a blurred psychologized threshold. Earlier authors like Virgil and Apuleius appeal to the Renaissance poets partly because this psychological element had been so strong in their earlier rites of passage.

Spenser's thresholds are often occurrences in the minds of his protagonists, changes of mind, rather than transitions of body or thing. At his most powerful, as at the end of Book III of *The Faerie Queene*, Spenser may accommodate a physical and mental crossover, so that the two merge in one single, unbroken psychosomatic drama. Scudamour cannot pass the threshold of Busirane's castle-prison, because his "mind" will not permit the passage, but Britomart can pass over, and when she does, as with her other marvelous psychological breakthroughs, she achieves for Spenser an originating shift within English romantic sensibility. She enacts the exchange of psychic energies.

From Spenser, Milton learns the iconographies of mental shift. Milton takes the mind to be the locus of the symbolic threshold, and he begins his career (after saluting Shakespeare, Donne, and the other Metaphysicals) with shorter works on various rites of passage, among them the "Ode on the Morning of Christ's Nativity," *Comus,* and "Lycidas." The later epic works dramatize cosmic threshold-scenes, but the same sense of dawning animates even the prose works of Milton—his *Areopagitica* breathes light as the form or medium of truth. Milton places dramatic action at the cosmic threshold. For English romantic rites of passage he is a most vocal prophet.

Where this prophetic voicing becomes problematic, however, is not in the discrimination of our romantic interest in it: that we recognize. But threshold becomes a more elusive concept when we stress, as such, the prophetic speech that marks its liminal apprehension. Here both sight and sound tend to create a sense of time, and time is enigmatic.

BETWEENNESS AND TIME

In poetry, as in the Scriptures, one notes at once the temporal aspect of the threshold. Measures of the precise amount of natural light (or artificial light, if you take *The Invisible Man* as the contemporary model) specify the experiencing of a shift from one period to another. The archetypal liminal scene occurs at dawn or dusk (Baudelaire's two *crépuscules*), at the end of a departing year or the start of a new year (January), the end or beginning of an era, a millennium perhaps. Whatever the magnitude of the joined time-frames, however, there seems to be no reason why thresholdness, which its chief modern theorist, Heidegger, would call "betweenness"— *das Zwischen*—could not minimally refer to a crossing from one instant to another. Montaigne, in *Repentance*, when he says "I do not portray being, I portray passing," is assuming the possibility of instantaneous change— "from minute to minute," he says, "my history needs to be adapted to the moment. I may presently change." Indeed, in high Coleridgean fashion, he can conceive that since all things in the world are in constant motion, "stability itself is nothing but a more languid motion."

Montaigne is the philosopher of modern poetry, and the one thinker whom we at once associate with the Shakespearean (and by an extrapolation, with the Coleridgean) enterprise. Montaigne records the way things more and more seem to be staggering with "natural drunkenness." Remarkably, while more extension-conscious than even Descartes himself, Montaigne can speak to Shakespeare because he shares the sense of the dramatic confusions wrought upon us by the "petty pace" of diurnal time.

The slow Cartesian scientific development of a system opposed to Montaigne, the "elimination of time" which Whitrow has shown descending earlier from Archimedes, flowering with Descartes, and culminating with Einstein's "geometrization" of all time and space, makes war upon the poet's sense of time as lived duration, lived succession. "Physics endeavours in principle to make do with space-like concepts alone, and strives to express with their aid all relations having the form of laws." Here "space-like" means, or may be translated to mean, "dimensional." Einstein is not monogamously wedded to space—the great fiddle-player allows time into the cosmic system as long as it can be "space-*like.*" The wars of space and time in modern science are no more monolithic than any other wars fought since the Renaissance. Yet time took refuge, after Descartes and Locke, in the arms of the poets.

Time, of course, had never even seemed neatly or conveniently dimensional. Dimensionally, in terms of measurement, despite natural clocks like the human pulse or the moon and artificial clocks like hour-glasses, time had always been mysterious, which Saint Augustine admitted in Book XI of the *Confessions*. To take only one Augustinian paradox of temporal nondimensionality: "In other words we cannot rightly say that time *is*, except by reason of its impending state of *not* being" (i.e., its falling away into the disappeared past, out of an empty future that is not yet). Rather in the manner of Hamlet, Augustine has just made his famous aside: "What, then, is time? I know well what it is, provided that nobody asks me."

Augustine's epistemological jest reminds us that it has never been difficult for Western man to perceive time as the model of nothingness, with space the model of somethingness. Time in our world displays an instantaneity so perfect in its slippery transit—its slither from one temporal fix to another—that there is nothing to mark, let alone measure, its being, its at-homeness. Like the doomed brother and sister of Coleridge's "Time Real and Imaginary," time's arrow dissolves finally before us into nothingness, as it flies forever outward toward the infinitely going-away horizon we call "space." Time as the creator and destroyer of space is relatively easy for us to imagine. Time, as becoming, is then whatever is not space. Yet the heart only painfully accepts this divorce.

Coleridge, whose heart is so full, if sometimes only of its own emptiness, its desire to be filled, seems fully aware that the betweenness of time-as-moment, pure thresholdness, barren liminality, at least in what Einstein would call a "space-like" way, must be a nothingness. Between the temple and labyrinth there must be a crossing which, viewed from the perspective of time, does not stand, stay, hold, or persist. Yet the poet craves persistence and duration—like Spenser and Milton, Coleridge would dilate the prophetic moment; unlike them he takes opium, with what effects of temporal dilation we can only surmise. So he is caught in a psychosomatic paradox: though the threshold is temporally nonexistent, a phantom-place, the passage across this no-man's-land seems to be more intense, experientially, than life either inside or outside the temple, inside or outside the labyrinth. The threshold unmakes the dialectic of inside and outside, replacing it by an unmediating passage between. Its motto: Readiness is all.

The intensity of the rite of passage, or simply, of Montaigne's "passing," seems with Coleridge to raise an accompanying liminal anxiety—the existential vertigo that led Herbert Read to associate Coleridge and Kierkegaard. This anxiety characteristically feels like a border-crossing emotion. It manifests itself as uncertainty, as fear approaching paranoia, the fear that life processes will be blocked, that one will be arrested, pressed down, or suffocated in the manner of Poe's heroes (with whom Coleridge shares the terror of suffocation). As one approaches the border, this anxiety rises; as one crosses it successfully, the anxiety recedes. While anxiety may also be "free floating," here it tends to focus on the border-scene itself, the moment of crossing the border, with its guards. The moment is finally a dramatic event, as one's actual experience at borders will testify, and in the final stages of this present essay I will consider one aspect of the dramatic nature of the threshold experience, its personifying tendency. Nevertheless, the special, painful uncertainty of thresholdness should first, in a theoretical account, give rise to a connected problem, the problem of sequence, and to this we must now turn in our search for the Coleridgean readiness.

SEQUENCE

In the present context, "sequence" means the process and the promise that something will follow something else. Spatially, sequence means the *suc-*

cessive placement of events which, when they occur "in sequence," will display a one-after-the-otherness. If events occur "in rapid sequence," they come right next to each other. This neighborly aspect of sequence does not necessarily mean that events will always follow one next to the other in a crowded way, each event as it were jammed right up against its neighbor and "predecessor." Predecessors and precursors get linked to their successors, if anything, because there is a strung-out, stretched relation from earlier to later. A sequence is like a line; it has length. Tempted as we may be to argue that two points or events may make a sequence, we perhaps should question whether sequences do not need to be constructed out of three or more points. The initial statement might be made that a sequence is not likely to be a *straight* line or shortest distance between two points. Common experience suggests that sequences are wavy lines, strung out like the linked chains of logical sorites.

Words like "line" and "string" imply a necessarily spatial or "rhopalic" definition of sequence, and yet sequence can also mean what follows logically, and here space is ideal. This logical concatenation might, for example, be represented by the theoretical circles of Boolean algebra or the thickness of lines and points in geometry, that is, a thickness known by its own theoretical absence. Logical space is the space which, "In the beginning," was occupied by the Logos of St. John. Although the readiest terms by which we understand sequence are spatial, there is a question as to what kind of space sequences may be occupying if, as so often in the thought of Coleridge, they are sequences with logical, theoretical, or visionary form.

There is a yet further difficulty, which almost defines the problem of sequence so far as it relates to Coleridge: the fact that serious concern with "what follows" will have to entertain a temporal factor, whether science wishes so or not. Can a poet imagine a sequence that is devoid of any passing of time, when the poem shifts from space to space, point to point, as long as there are more than two points in the diagram? From this question arises the Sisyphian labor of modern philosophy, whether a Jamesian, Bergsonian, Husserlian, or any other phenomenological attempt, to define the role of time-consciousness in the grasp of logical wholes. Under this structure of analysis, our phrase "next door" would have to be replaced by "and then" or simply by "afterwards." In spite of the fact that, in dealing with sequence, we begin spatially, we end on a note of temporal description. God alone has the power to be absolutely timeless. All His acts occur at once. To begin with, "The Infinite I Am" names an entirely spatial mode of being, set off against man's relativistic temporal nature.

The Fourth Gospel counters the utter timelessness of God. To this text Coleridge intended to devote a critical study (which, in effect, he sketched in *The Confessions of an Inquiring Spirit*). Paradoxically, St. John's doctrine of the Logos is the most powerful philosophic machine within Christian culture for the counterattack against the logical annihilation of time. The Incarnate Word is a theoretical notion of man-in-time, and thus Coleridge mythologizes The Word when he reads the Fourth Gospel.

Time and the Logos are, no doubt, violently yoked together. Coleridge, the diachronic thinker, believes in the Johannine Incarnation, *even though* the mystique of The Word sometimes shifts ideas of sequence into a mystique of stillness, which is stated as a numerological mystery leading to the static number symbolism of Revelation. In such static symbolism a sequence "follows" because each element of it is like a natural number, the larger numbers "following" because they contain the smaller numbers. Numerology, if not number theory, suggests a timeless ontology.

Yet the *poetics* of number accept, and do not, under pressure from logic, reject man's time-bound duration. Augustine's *De Musica* conceived poetry as the art of right proportioning (*bene modulandi*), and ultimately as the mirror or *speculum* of the world—an apparently stabilizing, if not static, symbolic system. But poetry moves, and verses turn, as Augustine knew well (the first five books of *De Musica* discuss rhythm and meter). Poets use spatial terms to control changes in time. They spend their lives measuring lines of poetry—we still study metrics—and Coleridge was a notable metrical experimenter, like almost all metaphysical poets in the English tradition. We may conclude that the poetic pursuit of the logos demands a measuring and time-feeling poetic activity. This runs counter to the *contemplation* of number, as the unchanging pattern of the logos, and instead embraces an incarnational notion of the poet as a living, moving, breathing, uttering prophet. Incarnation brings the logos into the world as a living, and dying, man—the Son of Man. It temporalizes and historicizes number.

PATER ON RELATIVISM: A DIGRESSION

The Coleridgean homing on the Fourth Gospel reminds us further that incarnation is a relativistic concept and that, with it in mind, the philosophic poet can introduce relativity—in the form of causal conditions—into the otherwise absolute and timeless mysteries of a Platonic system. It was Walter Pater, the next great English critical theorist after Coleridge, who saw this problem most clearly. His essay *Coleridge* observed by way of introduction to his subject that "modern thought is distinguished from ancient by its cultivation of the 'relative' spirit in place of the 'absolute.' Ancient philosophy sought to arrest every object in an eternal outline, to fix thought in a necessary formula, and the varieties of life in a classification by 'kinds,' or *genera*. To the modern spirit nothing is, or can be rightly known, except relatively and under conditions." Then follows an exquisite description of the delicacy of true scientific observation, which reveals "types of life evanescing into each other by inexpressible refinements of change." We are listening to the doctrine of Impressionism in its most exact refinement. Coleridge, we expect, will be its chief relativistic progenitor.

Yet Pater proceeds to argue the converse: he finds Coleridge the defender, in a lost cause, of the older absolutism. As the greatest English critical impressionist, Pater could make the point. Perhaps today he would speak differently if, like us, he had access to Coleridge's *Notebooks*. Yet he almost seems disingenuous. Pater seems blind to the real Coleridge who appears to us in so many ways the first hero of critical relativism in English literature. When Pater says that "the literary life of Coleridge was a disinterested struggle against the relative spirit," we may wonder if the follower has not falsified his paternity. Pater to the contrary, there is plenty of "the excitement of the literary sense" in Coleridge, and is this sense not relativistic? But what really matters is the framework in which Pater placed his precursor: the conflict between the absolute and relative spirits.

This digression will have reminded the reader that the deep Coleridgean interest in the incarnation of genius amounts to a concern for the activity of man, inspired man, *in time.* Genius for Coleridge is nothing if not relative, and this includes a causal dimension of temporal sequence. Sequence attains relativistic form when it is allowed to show its causal enlinkedness. If sequences of events are "causal sequences," their temporal nature is hedged by those conditional limits which can only be known to Pater's spirit of relative perceptions.

Poets, of course, have always shared with storytellers the knowledge that mythic time is not an absolute and causally blank dimension. Mythmakers know that if you tell a story confidently, no matter how strange its materials, sequence as a causally relativistic set of conditions will begin to arise all by itself. Sequence will arise from the metonymic next-door placement of event after event. The reader imports a hidden causality, though none be present on the surface. If, in a story, one event is told after another, a causal conditionality is very hard *not* to imagine. The imagination, in short, manufactures causes. *Post hoc, ergo propter hoc* is one principle of myth.

What distinguishes Coleridge from Pater is then not a priority of absolute over relative spirit, but rather a different attitude—which Pater did not sufficiently discriminate—toward sequence. Pater displays a synchronous method, while Coleridge is heroically diachronic in his relativisms. Coleridge begins his poetic career wishing to preserve the mythmaker's "story line," because its implicit metaphysic reaffirms his sense of diachronic order. He wants this exactly in proportion to his immense anxiety about its being possible.

SEQUENCE AND SURVIVAL

Coleridge appears to have suffered from the particular fear that sequence might not organize his world. This is not to say that his lifelong interest in, and study of, logic, is a mere defense-mechanism against a malaise which logic should have had the magic power to undo. Nor, necessarily, that his fascination with logical sequence implies the paranoia which Freud supposed might underlie philosophic thought in general. We need not go so far. We can, however, observe that Coleridge appears comforted and reassured by the contemplation of "method," as various recent students of his life and work have shown. His criticism adopts Method as a liturgical ideal; for him method is the expression, and the experience, of grace as it appears in this life. Conversely, like Hamlet he is terrified lest events simply may not follow. His work can be conceived as an intensely interested struggle against this fear.

The great sequences of this struggle are to be found in works of prose, not verse. Prose articulates sequence in grammatical form. The theoretical center for Coleridge is the prose treatise contained in the Essays of *The Friend*, where the critic develops his theory of method. Most perfectly exemplified by Shakespeare, method implies, as a kind of providential order, that the mind keeps moving and shaping simultaneously the conditions of its movement. Thus, in methodical sequence the poet may wander narratively or dramatically with great range, yet will always project the sense of over-all design, a sort of implicit city-plan for his own development in the myth. Shakespeare the model author achieves a balance, since "without continuous transition there can be no method," while "without a preconception there can be no transition with continuity." Method is survival through and beyond continuous uncertain eventualities, achieved because its progression is vital, the reverse of "dead arrangement." Method is inevitably somewhat dramatic and unafraid in spite of the underlying fear that one will lose one's way. Or, more bluntly, method is the expression of courage in the presence of that fear. The literary model of a superordinate structure built on this courageous plan is the whole Shakespearean canon, which for Coleridge has the precise status of a Bible. The model of a subordinate structure of methodical sequence will be the dramatic texture of the poems and plays of Shakespeare, whose genius carries the action careering forward, while judgment continually checks the "Fiery-Four-in-Hand."

The second great document in the Coleridgean pursuit of method is the *Biographia*. Whereas the *Essays on Method* describes the wayward yet ordered sequence of thought that gives Shakespearean drama its "implicit metaphysic," the *Biographia* is more ingenious and ambitious. It does not just describe. It embodies. It enacts, while it narrates, the series of learnings that went into the final providence of the poet's own critical and poetic life. In a way Coleridge one-ups Wordsworth, since his own *Prelude*—the *Biographia*—is written in prose, whereas Wordsworth exploited the method-making powers of the medium of prose only to the extent that prose modulates his blank verse. One other clue to the method underlying the *Biographia* is its epic structure and its final settling upon an agon between Wordsworth and the author, in the concluding chapters. The critical analysis of Wordsworth's theory and practice is not just criticism; it is, more adequately considered, a conceptual myth of the confrontation of two great, jarring, fraternal intellects. Method appears in the *Biographia*, therefore, secondarily in the analysis of mind and imagination as such, and primarily in the dramatic impersonation of that analysis as Coleridge wrestles with his essential adversary, Wordsworth. The critique enacts the biography, and does so methodically, because this is a *literary* biography. In a sense the critique is Shakespearean, since it personifies the critical issues at stake. The *Biographia*, like its double, *The Prelude*, is a myth of imaginative lifestyle.

This lifestyle has two possible poles, one of which might be called operatic. It leads to the plan for the impossible *Magnum Opus*. Its chief yearning is sublimity and unbounded power over vast domains. The Magnum Opus mania drove Coleridge to plot endless impossible projects, most of which envisage the ultimate transformation of some vast labyrinthine body of inchoate materials into an equally vast, but now perfectly lucid and structured, temple of ideal order. With intuitive grace and genius, Coleridge managed to dictate the *Biographia* and to write a number of other extended prose works, so that, in spite of himself, especially through the *Biographia*, he achieved his desired scope—largely because in that and other works he escaped his compulsions, and just played.

The other polarity of lifestyle implicit in Coleridge's "method" is an obverse one, the reduction to the infinitely small, to the instantaneous threshold, where anxiety and uncertainty produce an ideal *reduction* of the *magnum opus* to an *opus minimum*. As Coleridge himself was fond of saying, extremes meet, and here the compulsion to overwhelm with sublimity meets the compulsion to pass lightly over the threshold.

The poetics of threshold require an inversion of the ideal of epic containment, such that the poet now strives for lyric concision, *to act for* the epic scope of his vision. The ideal poem depends in this inverted aesthetic on an art of perfect exclusion. The tradition is thus one of brevity, wit, and metaphysical conceit, of the kind that increasingly fascinated Coleridge as he grew older and more deeply pursued the poetry of Donne, Herbert, Crashaw, and others from his favorite century, the seventeenth. No earlier models, however, could quite predict the varieties of threshold-poem which Coleridge was to achieve.

EMOTIONS AT THE THRESHOLD

To get at this range we need an instrument, the emotive spectrum, which can measure the sense of threshold itself. If readiness is the stance within the doorway, then an attitude of confidence or courage is the ideal mode of readiness. This contrasts with the labyrinth, where the natural emotive state is terror or a generalized anxiety; or perhaps, if life is a Spenserian Wood of Error, then the feeling there is a specifically competitive anxiety, to which Marvell draws attention: "How vainly men themselves amaze / To win the palm, the oak, or bays." Conversely in the temple (or garden) one need not fear, though upon first entering from the labyrinth, one may experience an irrelevant, leftover fear. This is opposed to the controlled sense of trial which often the hero is ritually and penitentially, though not experientially, led through, before his final triumph within the structure of the temple. In the temple, at last, one learns confidence; one's faith triumphs.

At the threshold—between temple and maze—there is a possible range of normal threshold-feelings: anxiety, readiness, blind hope. This continuum measures the degrees of dread, and it refers specifically to a range of feelings aroused by the *sacer*, the taboo, the holy. For if within the temple the holy seems triumphant, in the labyrinth the holy is either lost or irrelevant, whereas at the threshold these differences are exactly what is put into question. The threshold tries the sense of the holy.

Thresholds in Coleridge range widely in the degree of confidence or fear they may generate. "Frost at Midnight," with its emphasis on silence and ministry, identifies the ritual transition with the "secret ministry" of frost hanging up its silent icicles, "Quietly shining in the quiet Moon." Poised, the poet—in his threshold *persona*—may bless the child, asleep in his arms, and while meditating on the "stranger," the film of flame glowing in the fire, he prophesies a hopeful future for the child; he sees the child poised also, but on the threshold of a happier life than what the poet had known when he was a child. "Fears in Solitude" balances liminal feelings, so that it suspends war and human conflict within the scales of "Love, and the thoughts that yearn for human kind." "This Lime-Tree Bower My Prison" suspends the poet on the edge of a perfect templum, yet there is a double threat implicit in his suspended state: the bower, as in Spenser, imprisons, while the beloved friends depart from it, leaving the poet alone. Their leaving him has the effect of making the bower a Goldengrove; the poet still utters a hope: "Henceforth I shall know / That Nature ne'er deserts the wise and pure"—but friends may leave other friends, quite innocently, though accidentally, alone.

The danger in being optimistic about Coleridge's visions of threshold is quite simple: it is absurdly wrong for him, in general. The typical case, for example *The Ancient Mariner*, is infused with terror. This is a holy dread, not useful caution. The poem is an exercise in what Hartman has called the "spectral confrontations" which are the essential moments of liminal experience. The Mariner's tale is set against the framing doorway before the marriage feast—the basic threshold, of house and home—but its myth sweeps us and the Mariner along the corridors of death and time in a terror-driven sequence of liminal passages, as the ship becomes the first vessel to "burst" into the silent sea of transformational rites. Similarly, in "Kubla Khan," there may be a "sunny pleasure-dome" for optimists to dwell on, but the finality of the poem is a meditation on the terrors of prophetic vision as it confronts theological ultimates and the naive simplicity of templar rituals ("Weave a circle round him thrice"), leaving us in some doubt as to how much poison there is in the milk of Paradise. *Christabel*, in another direction, romanticizes erotic anxiety at the moment of most fearsome sexual initiation. Perceived conventionally, the poem is a gothic tale, full of graveyard atmosphere. Within the convention, one notes the importance of the metric invention, to the hesitancy implied by the theme of demonic eros. But *Christabel* denies the catharsis of its gothic convention. It almost immediately insists on the sacred separation of castle and forest. Christabel reaches her fatal crossover, having brought Geraldine back to the Castle with her.

> Christabel with might and main
> Lifted her up, a weary weight,
> Over the threshold of the gate,

and from this moment the poem scarcely pauses in the exploration of the transit between dream and wake, control and abandon, eros and death, taboo and free sexuality, through a vicious regress of antinomies.

Christabel fascinated its early readers especially because it foresaw the world of Victorian inhibition. Isolating sexual boundaries and metamorphoses, it also isolated a growing sexual anxiety. It anticipated the Tennysonian eros. For many years Coleridge insisted that he would finish the poem, but it may be that he hesitated, not because no story could be machined to follow upon Parts I and II, but because the two parts had already adequately set forth their real tenor, the threshold phenomenon itself, and to move along from their unfinished liminality would have been to destroy their perfect readiness by a useful, but merely conventional, narrative ending.

There are times, of course, when Coleridge openly confronts terror as a pure state, that is, as nightmare. In "The Pains of Sleep" the "wide blessing" of deep sleep is subverted by an interim condition of labyrinthine dreams: "For aye entempesting anew / The unfathomable hell within, / The horror of their deeds to view, / To know and loathe, yet wish and do!" As one reflects on these terrible moments in the poet's visionary life, one values more deeply his attachment to the moon, which sustains him in a most extraordinary way, not least because the moon is a primary natural clock older than any chronometric device.

PRAYER AND THE JOURNEYING MOON

The moon has always been known to poets for its changes, its continuous waxing and waning. With Coleridge the moon, among many meanings, enjoys status as an angelic messenger of the possibility of safe crossing, and safe standing at the threshold. As angelic messenger, the moon brings news to the poet by reflecting the sun's light, and other messages depend upon that primary mirroring. Reflected, moonlight is benign, the opposite of that lurid sunset-red Visconti used everywhere in his film "The Damned," which in its original version is called "The Twilight of the Gods." Female, or androgynous, the moon brings happier messages of confident augury. Thus the marginal gloss upon the moon in *The Ancient Mariner*: "In his loneliness and fixedness he yearneth towards the journeying Moon, and the stars that still sojourn, yet still move onward; and everywhere the blue sky belongs to them, and is their appointed rest, and their native country and their own natural homes, which they enter unannounced, as lords that are certainly expected and yet there is a silent joy at their arrival."

The journeying moon is the harbinger of the return of the hero of consciousness. The celestial bodies are like lords "certainly expected," the prodigal sons of heaven. Coleridge, I suppose, wanted to create a myth of expectation. He praised Shakespeare for achieving plots which work, not through surprise, but through fulfilled expectation. His own criticism is more alive than most, mainly because it stands poised and ready to notice, to respond where there is no standard response. He can observe the most delicate verbal, especially syntactic, shifts. Coleridge is the poet-critic of expectancy. Perhaps in order to intensify this method of response, he shifts, in later years, to a mode of poetry quite unlike that practiced in *The Ancient Mariner* or *Christabel*, a poetry, even so, which derives partly from those early poems. As Coleridge the poet becomes increasingly liminal, he seeks poetic prayer—praying being the liturgical form of crossing over once again. The climax of *Mariner* occurs when the Mariner prays—this climax is to become the modal pattern in several later poems, where, however, there is little narrative. Coleridge finally seeks an entente with George Herbert, and especially with the poem "Prayer." Generally *The Temple* creates a structuring dramatic scene of prayer, but in that one lyric the maximum expectancy is reached through a total annihilation of all verbs. No single predominant turn of thought forces itself upon the reader, because the poet allows no constricting verb to push the reader here, there, or anywhere. Verbless, the poem and its reader kneel down, waiting, devoted. Herbert has a formalist importance for Coleridge which Donne, whom he so admires, could never have, for *The Temple* explores the pressures preventing prayer, as much as its amenities and glories. Studying Herbert (and Donne too, one must grant), Coleridge would appear to have sharpened his own skills in addressing the absolute. That, not Pater's notion of "tracking of all questions, critical or practical, to first principles," is the problem solved by *The Temple* and then by Coleridge's later poems. He has to address himself to a frightening sacredness—his "deity."

"LIMBO" AND THE METAPHYSICAL MODE

It is a systematic consequence, therefore, when the finest poems of threshold, "Limbo" and "Ne Plus Ultra," derive from a Herbertian poetic and state the limits of the powers of prayer. "Ne Plus Ultra" is directly imitated from "Prayer," and it too lacks any verb, with the same liminal intensification accruing to it as a result of a syntactic stillness. Yet Coleridge is not easy or very calm in this stillness; it threatens, with short, weighted, magical phrases that portend storms of spirit and destiny. Like Herbert, Coleridge is rather more dramatic than lyrical as he adopts the attitude of prayer. [Walter Jackson] Bate has observed further that "in the better verse of Coleridge from 1817 until his death we find a denseness of thought embodied in an odd, original imagery, frequently homely, occasionally even grotesque." This reborn Metaphysical wit manages such "amalgamation or fusion under pressure" that its philosophical words and phrases become "almost substances for him, thick with emotion and meaning. In these poems, with their dense reflectiveness, their odd, often crowded metaphor, their allusion to the technical vocabulary and conceptualizations of Philosophy, Coleridge creates a mode of poetry entirely his own."

Perhaps the finest example is "Limbo," thought to have been written in the same period as the *Biographia*. "Limbo," more complex in form than its companion piece, "Ne Plus Ultra," is a strange mixture of personification, dramatic monologue, and visionary fugue. Its most prominent feature is a dramatic or melodramatic attitude, while its iconography is variously allusive, including echoes of Dante, Milton, perhaps Shakespeare (Hamlet calls the Ghost "old mole"), more probably Henry Vaughan's "Night" and its portrait of Nicodemus (who could be the model for Coleridge's Human Time). The sense of varied poetic origins reveals the essential Coleridge. He is eclectic, yet single-voiced. Nor does the poem assert a doctrinal or dogmatic view of human salvation. The poet seems mainly interested in the transition between this world and the next. A hesitancy throughout conveys anxiety over the liminal condition itself, rather than a theological debate.

Despite this evanescence of doctrine, however, "Limbo" attempts to define an indefinable, ultimate limit, which the poet calls "positive negation." In so doing he justifies his bizarre method of metaphysical wit and prayer: he personifies a bulk of nothingness. His declamatory style, solidifying horror and anxiety, recovers the primitive, or primary, sources of poetic animation. If to personify is to give soul to an idea or thing, then here the poetry is gaining soul through personification.

Coleridge, we are informed, designed his shorter pieces and then read them in such a way that "the verses seem as if *played* to the ear upon some unseen instrument. And the poet's manner of reciting is similar. It is not rhetorical, but musical; so very near recitative, that for any one else to attempt it would be ridiculous, and yet it is perfectly miraculous with what exquisite searching he elicits and makes sensible every particular of the meaning, not leaving a shadow of the feeling, the mood, the degree, untouched." [Henry Nelson Coleridge, in the *Quarterly Review* (1934)]. This searching, inflecting recitative expresses the animation of the personifying process.

PERSONIFICATION AND NEGATIVITY

A new or renewed Renaissance mode of personification would seem to be the main yield of the poetry of threshold. The need to renew personification was inherited directly from most eighteenth-century verse except the greatest. During that period the older, conventional personified abstractions slowly froze to death, and now poets had to bring the statues back to life. Frank Manuel, like Hartman in his studies of genius, has shown that the pre-Romantics could reanimate a daemonic universe in the mode of "the new allegory." From another point of view personifications could come alive again because there were once again adequate conditions of rumination. As Michel Foucault has said, the celebratory religions of an earlier time now gave place to "an empty milieu—that of idleness and remorse, in which the heart of man is abandoned to its own anxiety, in which the passions surrender time to unconcern or to repetition in which, finally, madness can function freely." Madness is complete personification. Poets need not, though some in fact did, descend into this generative void.

Yet the conditions of madness and a renewed animism still demand the appropriate poetic forms, which Coleridge had to invent. As Huizinga has remarked, personification is a kind of mental play, and this ludic strain is strong in Coleridge's make-up. Formally, we can say that personification is the figurative emergent of the liminal scene. In the temple there appear to be personified abstractions hard at work, virtues and noble essences, while labyrinths are stocked by an equal and opposite number of vices and personified negations—the lions of the Marquess of Bath. Yet these polar opposites perhaps only gain animate life, if they have it, from their participation in the process of passage. Personifications come alive the moment there is psychological breakthrough, with an accompanying liberation of utterance, which in its radical form is a first deep breath. Poetry seeking a fresh animation is poetry seeking to throw off the "smothering weight" of the "Dejection" Ode. Such a poetry must breathe, showing life coming or going away, as in "Limbo."

This breathing may be explained in part, if we reckon with the inner nature of personification. An active, vital, person-making figure must not be a moral cliché. It must not be a machine in a materialist sense. It cannot simply parody the *daimon*. It must be a "real ghost," like the spectral presence of a drug experience or a nightmare or daydream. Hartman has finely observed: "In fact, whenever the question of persona arises in a radical way, whenever self-choosing, self-identification, becomes a more than personal, indeed, prophetic, decision—which happens when the poet feels himself alien to the genius of country or age and determined to assume an adversary role—poetry renews itself by its contact with what may seem to be archaic forces." *This* personifying author will find himself listening, as well as looking, for phantoms.

Above all the phantom must not exist. It must resist existence. To envision and realize the phantom person poetically the poet must empty his imagery of piety and sense, allowing in their place some measure of daemonic possession. The one necessary poetic act will be to utter, to speak, nothingness. To achieve this defining negativity, the poem "Limbo" typically seeks to *posit* negation as the ultimate daemon. By asserting the life of this final nothingness, the poet has reinvented the Ghost of *Hamlet*, the Witches of *Macbeth*, the daemonic powers that abandon Antony, Hermione's statue that comes alive in *The Winter's Tale*. This is a dramatic reinvention; it enghosts and embodies the persons of a play.

The logic of personification requires a phantom nihilism and a return to the heart of drama. This achievement in the later Coleridge depends upon the liminal scene, which permits the greatest experiential intensity at the very moment when the rite of passage denies or reduces the extensity of either the temple or the labyrinth. Drama gets its personifying nothingness—its phantoms—from the making of continuous threshold-scenes. Because the Elizabethan period had so fully subscribed to the norms of drama, its free use of personification—unlike most eighteenth-century personification—goes quite unnoticed. But there is scarcely a line in a Shakespeare sonnet that does not breathe this language of the personified force. Coleridge, in turning to the theme of nothingness, was trying to get back some of that Renaissance utterancy and dramatic presence. Half-brother to Hamlet, he almost succeeded.

THE DRAMATIC PERSONIFICATION

The dramatic or, perhaps more accurately, the melodramatic aspect of the personified "positive negation" must fit a general theory of figurative language. Of late much has been written about the precise differences between metaphor and metonymy. It should by now be clear that the problem of sequence is also a problem of figurative series.

In the modern era, when not only music, but all the arts, have tried to hold their balance while experiencing the loss of tonal center, poets and novelists have testified to the complete loss of cadence within the figurative structures provided by traditional poetics. Atonalism and even aleatory procedures are natural, in an era such as ours. But before its radical breakdowns had occurred, poets could still employ the ancient figurative structures, by bending them.

Such was the Coleridgean scene, where the figurative aspect of threshold and sequence was traditional enough. For the temple and its "timeless" hypotactic structures of sacred being, there was the normal and normative use of part / whole relations, figured in *synecdoche*. For the labyrinth and its unrelieved parataxis the norms were bound to be *metonymic*, as they are in the modern novel, where life is represented in the naturalistic maze of meaningless eventuality. For the threshold the norms were, as the term itself forces us to believe, *metaphoric*. This was the great Romantic rediscovery.

Metaphor has always been the figure of threshold, of passing over. Its symbolic function has always been transfer, transference, metamorphosis, shifting across, through, and over. Metaphor is a semantic process of balancing at the threshold. Metaphor draws the edge of the limen with surgical exactness. When we ally metaphor and the dramatic, we accept the momentary adoption of *an other self*, which the mask of dramatic *persona* makes possible. Significant human integers—men as unique creatures with endowments of a yet universal nature—demand metaphor, because metaphor provides the freedom (not the chaos) of a momentary masking.

The person-making, personifying, gestures of the dramatic poet thus sink down, or fall, to the level of nothingness and ghosts, because at that level of the *ex nihilo* there is a test of the "too, too solid flesh" of man. If a ghost can exist, then so can the hero. If his father has a ghost, Hamlet can avenge (and destroy) him, and *be* Hamlet. Hamlet must personify his father, as it were, in order to be himself. Admiring Shakespeare and identifying with Hamlet, Coleridge brought the study of figurative language into the modern context, by giving it a psycholinguistic basis. This modern grasp of the metaphoric—which Johnson vaguely anticipated in *The Life of Cowley*—seems to require an awareness of the experiential element in the *discordia concors*, an anxiety and liminal trembling which is the experience of living through a metaphor. I have envisaged this tremor as the emergence of a personification, at a threshold. Perhaps these too are "only metaphors." If so, they may illuminate the ludic view of theory-building. Coleridge was in nothing so modern as in his theoretical playfulness.

His instincts naturally led him to center his critical theories on the career of Shakespeare, that is, upon a dramatic or dramatistic center. In part this was bardolatry. But Coleridge had a cosmopolitan range of thought, and in his critical theory of method the dramatic (if not always the drama) has fundamental force. For him the drama is the saving test by which men are discovered in their personhood through dialogue. Essaying a poetry and a critique of the liminal moment, he took up arms against the excessive mass of problems which the modern critic knows only too well— our sea of information. Coleridge wanted to find an All that could be One, believed he found it in the final personification—the Trinity—and failed, if he did fail, because he no more than any other man could prevent life's perverse atomism. If he failed to control the world with his personifying eloquence, we should grant him that person and metaphor are the utterance of the gateway, and most men do not want to be standing in gateways. They would rather be inside, or out in the street.

Coleridge's "Kubla Khan":
The Oriental Idyll

E. S. Shaffer

The romantic epic is the "little epic," the pastoral or "minor epic" to which Porphyry in "The Cave of the Nymphs" had assigned a higher, theological level of meaning. It is concerned with the cosmic etiological drama that is one form of myth. That this level of meaning has been so impressively represented in modern poetry is owing in large part to the reformulation of the significance of myth in the Christian context carried out by the Biblical critics in the 1790s. "Kubla Khan" is one of the first poems to represent the new views of myth and so to usher in a new poetic age.

Lent impetus by Greek studies, the idyll became the most popular form of the eighteenth century, and aesthetic theory confirmed its position. Even major epics, major in length, scope, and intention, tended to have an idyllic core. Schiller spoke of idyll as one of the most characteristic forms of modern poetry, praising Milton's depiction of Adam and Eve as the finest example of it. Its excellence depended not simply on "primaeval communion with the springs of Being," but on suggesting the progress, refinement, and end of Being as well. Schiller suggested the range of the modern poet of idyll:

> Er mache sich die Aufgabe einer Idylle, welche jene Hirtenunschuld auch in Subjekten der Kultur und unter allen Bedingungen des rüstigsten feurigsten Lebens, des ausgebreitetsten Denkens, der raffiniertesten Kunst, der höchsten gesellschaftlichen Verfeinerung ausführt, welche, mit einem Wort, den Menschen, der nun einmal nicht mehr nach *Arkadien* zurück kann, bis nach *Elysium* führt.

Let him [the modern poet] make it his task to create an idyll which

From *"Kubla Khan" and* The Fall of Jerusalem: *The Mythological School in Biblical Criticism and Secular Literature 1770–1880.* © 1975 by Cambridge University Press. Originally entitled "The Oriental Idyll."

carries out that pastoral innocence also in subjects of culture and in all conditions of the most active, passionate life, the most strenuous thought, the most subtle art, the highest social refinement, which, in short, leads man, who cannot any longer return to Arcadia, forwards to Elysium.

["Über Naive und Sentimentalische Dichtung"]

The romantic epic operates through a "picture" technique. This was at first tied to the painterly picturesque, as in Lessing's *Laokoon* and in Uvedale Price's theory, well-known in England in the 1790s; but it rapidly acquired greater freedom.

Coleridge was very familiar with these developments, and practised the picturesque method of Gilpin in his notebook descriptions of Germany. A recent critic has commented:

> The picturesque artists' was the wider range of experience that could be managed by discontinuity and planned irregularity, but they kept to the picture-like single perspective. The interior landscape, however, moves naturally towards the principle of multiple perspectives, as in the first two lines of "The Waste Land," where the Christian Chaucer, Sir James Frazer, and Jessie Weston are simultaneously present.

In fact, the exterior landscape, becoming a mobile location, mobile in time and space, developed "multiple perspectives" and so became capable of serving as an interior landscape. The accomplished interchangeability of exterior and interior landscapes is perhaps the most significant achievement of Biblical Orientalism for poetry in the nineteenth century.

The idyll was indeed to be a major nineteenth-century form; one need think only of those two Victorian "apocalyptic epics," Tennyson's *Idylls of the King* and Hopkins's *The Wreck of the Deutschland*. If Tennyson's idyll is the "miniature epic in a luxuriant natural background," as Douglas Bush puts it, Coleridge's is the most miniature epic in the most luxuriant natural background of all. Coleridge's syncretist use of myth, moreover, is echoed everywhere in Victorian poetry, not in direct emulation, but as a response to the same movements of thought. "Kubla Khan" accomplishes the poetic revolution that in France occupied the period from Chénier's Orphic epic to the "Parnasse." In Germany, not surprisingly, the step from Hölderlin to Rilke scarcely seems to need the mediation of a century.

The visionary tradition had a picturesque perspective built into it. Eichhorn could with justification interpret the Apocalypse as a drama, for, in theory, the visionary prophet is actually seeing the events played out in the heavens, as all events are rehearsed before they take place on earth. The heavens are a stage on which he sees the drama unroll:

> Quod autem in his visorum descriptionibus prophetae legebantur in statu ecstatico in coelum abrepti res futuras, ante eventum ad actum revocatas et repraesentatas, suis oculis obiectas conspexisse,

id hanc vim habuit et effectum, ut ex eo colligeretur, nihil in orbe terrarum evenire et contingere, quod non antea coram Deo coelitumque congressu in theatro.

But that in these descriptions of visions, prophets, rapt into heaven in ecstatic state, were read to have beheld with their own eyes things to come, realized and represented before the event—this had the power and effect that from it could be concluded, nothing happens in the universe which is not first given to be played and watched in the celestial theatre in the presence of God and the heavenly assembly.

[*Commentarius in Apocalypsin Johannis*]

The mythological Bible critics adapted the visionary theatre, in which the seer was to see the future, to the historian's view of the past. As [David Friedrich] Strauss put it,

In the absence of any more genuine account which would serve as a correcting parallel, [the historian] must transplant himself in imagination upon the theatre of action, and strive to the utmost to contemplate the events by the light of the age in which they occurred.

[*The Life of Jesus*, translated by George Eliot]

Coleridge's marginalia on Eichhorn's *Commentarius* cluster about the climactic point in the history, that is, around Rev. 9.13–15, the second of the three woes, when the sixth angel sounds its trumpet. Here the Roman army invades the centre of the city; the destruction of the Temple is imminent, though not to be accomplished until the blaring of the seventh trumpet: "But in the days of the voice of the seventh angel, when he shall begin to sound, the mystery of God should be finished, as he hath declared to his servants the prophets" (Rev. 10.7).

This moment in the Book of Revelation—

"And the sixth angel sounded, and I heard a voice from the four horns of the golden altar which is before God,

"Saying to the sixth angel which had the Trumpet, Loose the four angels which are bound in the great river Euphrates"

—is the "pregnant moment" of Lessing's "picture" technique, when the prophetic Laocoön and his sons are seen not in their death agony, but calm in the very toils of the serpents. We do not see Troy burn; we are not aware that it will burn, though after the fact the fate of Laocoön is an unmistakable portent. So here, the world is for the first and last time on the brink of a destruction that has been accomplished again and again.

At this idyllic moment in the "little epic" vision of Revelation we see the geography of the city whole—its vertical as well as its cross-section— the corrupt city, the place of the imprisonment of the demons and the dead;

the Holy City of men; and the celestial city of the New Jerusalem, which Zechariah and Ezekiel envisoned as preexisting and descending into the earthly city with the Messiah's coming. They are united as never before, yet separating out at the trumpet call to judgment, and signalling their final reunion, the single tripartite cosmos of Dante.

As in Shelley's *Prometheus*, a critic tells us, it is the "fusion of outer and mental worlds that become the Romantic substitute for little epic narrative. For them the arresting of a vivid moment of experience, or 'spot of time' in Wordsworth's phrase, took precedence over any ritual order of events." But in "Kubla" we see that the Romantics did not "substitute" for the little epic narrative—such a substitution would be inexplicable—but transformed the epic narrative itself into a spot of time that stood for and absorbed the whole. Ritual is not so much abandoned as transfixed at the gesture that implies the necessity of its past and future repetition.

Eichhorn's interpretation of these verses, and Coleridge's dissent from it, carry us from the neoclassic epic and the apocalyptic lay to the centre of the sacred geography of "Kubla." Eichhorn gives the historical interpretation: the Roman army enter the *theatrum* and find the "demon" enemy, some of whom they imprison. ("Angel" may be "demon" in Hebrew folklore.) The Jews, then, are imprisoned. In the Euphrates? Eichhorn comments,

> Qui carceris locus soli debetur poetae ingenio, nullamque patitur ex historia excidii Hierosolymitani interpretationem. Poesis enim prophetica postulat, ut singula in carmine declaranda ad loca certa personasque certas revocentur. Quid? quod nec Romanus exercitus, ad Judaos coercendos ab Euphrate progressos dici poterat; is enim ex Achaia profectus Alexandriam petiit et legionibus Ptolemaidis et Caesareae auctus in Judaeam irrupit, vid. Josephus de bello Judaico lib. 3. c. I. 3.

> The place of imprisonment we owe solely to the fancy of the poet, and it allows of no interpretation in accordance with the historical destruction of Jerusalem. Indeed, prophetic poetry postulates that each thing to be declared in the song must be related to specific places and people. Which ones? The Roman army could not be said to have proceeded to surround the Jews from the Euphrates; for it had set out from Achaia, reached Alexandria, and, increased by legions of Ptolemais and of Caesarea, invaded Judea.
> (*Commentarius.* See Josephus, *The Jewish War*, Book 3, chap. I. 3.)

He points out that in Old Testament passages "the Euphrates" appears in apposition with "the great river" (Gen. 15.18; Deut. I.7; Jos. I.4).

Coleridge condemns the method that makes Eichhorn impotent to interpret this and a variety of other passages: "Eichhorn's great error is in carrying his general meanings, & his resolutions of particular passages into mere poetic garnish, to an excess."

Eichhorn, in short, allegorizes too fully in a historical sense, and when allegory fails him, he gives up, and attributes the passage to mere poetic fancy. This misses the real sense and significance of the apocalyptic style.

Coleridge justifies the apocalyptic poet's imagination. He protests:

> I wonder at this assertion from so acute and ingenious a Man as Eichhorn.
>
> First, as I have noted—as Rome was to be symbolized as *Babylon*, the River must be Euphrates. But that the four mighty Destroyers were bound in the great River "up a great River, great as any Sea" is according to the code of popular Beliefs—the bad Spirits are sent bound to the bottom of the Red *Sea*—But a *Sea* would not have been appropriate or designative of the Roman Power—while the Tyber was a perfect Synonime of Rome, and the trite poetic exponent of the Roman Empire—Now the Tyber could not but be changed into the Euphrates—Therefore the ἐπὶ τῷ ποτάμῳ τῷ μεγάλῳ Ἐυφράτῃ is no mere poetic ornature; but a very significant & requisite amplification.
>
> Four giant Dæmons could not be imagined bound or chained up in a vast *City*—this would have been far too indefinite—But neither in any Dungeon or Tower in Babylon—That would have been as much too narrow, & besides too gross an outrage to probability, & above all, too little ghostliness—with great judgement therefore the sublime Seer transfers their prison to the River but amplifies the River into all the magnificence of a Sea for the imagination of the Readers. Only read the Greek words aloud ore rotundo: and you will feel the effect.—Add to this the Hebrew Associations with the Euphrates—Captivity after bloody Wars, and the Siege, Sack, and utter Destruction of their chief City & Temple!—Is it not, I again say, wonderful that Eichhorn should overlook all these so striking and exquisite proprieties in a 'soli debetur poetæ ingenio'!!
>
> [marginal note on the *Commentarius*]

Now it is not impossible that Eichhorn is right. But what Coleridge does here is characteristic of the symbolism of "Kubla." First, the three great sacred cities—Jerusalem, Babylon, and Rome—are blended; the symbolism is not sequential, as in Eichhorn's scheme, but simultaneous. Because Rome too must fall, and the city of wickedness is Babylon, the captive demons in Jerusalem may be imprisoned in "the Euphrates." Coleridge's note exclaims: "As Rome was to be Babylon, the River must of course be Euphrates!" The references are interchangeable, they flow in and out of each other. Geographical mobility is uncannily combined with exact location, timelessness with precise and known history. The superimposition and blending of meaning is perfect.

Nor is the method far from Revelation itself: "And their dead bodies shall lie in the street of the great city, which spiritually is called Sodom and Egypt, where also our Lord was crucified" (Rev. II.8). All great cities are places of corruption, and may be called by their names; and in all places of corruption was, and is, the Lord crucified. This is unstated typology of immense extent.

Especially characteristic of "Kubla" is the way the river expands at a touch into a sea—size is as immaterial as place and time—while retaining all the connotations of that particular named river and acquiring all those of the sea. Both river and sea are prominent in the Apocalypse. Babylon's seat is also "upon many waters" (Jer. 51.13). As Farrer remarks, "we may suppose the side-streams and canals of Euphrates spreading around her." Farrer points out too that John's river of blood at the time of the destruction "even unto the horses' bridles" is a reference to Ezek. 47 and 48.20 where in the vision of Jerusalem the river of life issuing from it is measured, on all four sides equally, by the depth of the stream on the body of a man trying to ford it.

The sea is of course, as [Robert] Lowth put it, the "place where the wicked after death were supposed to be confined; and which, from the destruction of the old world by the deluge, the covering of the Asphaltic vale with the Dead Sea, etc. was believed to be situated *under the waters*" [*Lectures on the Sacred Poetry of the Hebrews*, translated by G. Gregory]. Moreover, the sea is a "ritual name." John's vision begins with a presentation of the great "Sea" of the heavenly temple (Rev. 4.6) which refers to the laver in the Temple, and, in Christianity, to baptism: "Baptism is a 'sea,' indeed, it is the Red Sea water through which the people of God are saved, and separated from heathen Egypt (1 Cor. 10.1–2)."

The Old Testament context of "caves of ice" is even more striking. In the fourth of Herder's *Oriental Dialogues*, which marks the high point in his splendid dithyramb on nature in Oriental poetry, and its dependence on the One God, he shows the connection of God's creativity with His destructive powers, using the Book of Job as his text. The abyss, the unfathomable ocean, is both the place of the dead and the vast region of the unborn. The abyss, or destruction, "hath no covering before Him." "The abyss where light had never pierced, stands uncovered—this is the awful, the dark moment, when CREATION begins." Herder follows the steps of the creation in Job 38: first the founding of the earth, then the formation of the sea:

> The earth is represented as an edifice, founded and measured by the Almighty; and no sooner are its foundations laid, and the corner-stone fixed, than all the *sons* of God and the *morning-stars* raise an acclamation of joy and a song of praise to the great Creator. Now comes the formation of the ocean:
>
>> Who shut up the sea within doors,
>> When it brake forth, as it were, from the womb?

Herder cites the passage, "Hast thou entered into the springs of the sea?
. . . Hast thou entered into the treasures of the snow?"

> Hath the rain a father?
> The drops of the dew, who hath begotten them?
> Out of whose womb cometh forth the ice?
>
> The waters rise into mountains, and become as stone,
> And the surface of the waves is bound in frost.

Herder glosses the passage:

> Above, the light comes forth in streams, and the east-wind carries
> them over the land: the Father of heaven and the earth forms
> canals for the rain and marks out a course for the clouds. Below,
> the waters become a rock, and the waves of the sea are held in
> chains of ice.

The "caves of ice," then, mark a most dramatic moment in the creation:
the emergence at once of solidity and variety out of the sea's abyss. The
primaeval relation between creation and destruction is the main formal
principle of Revelation, as well as of "Kubla." Coleridge, of course, had
no need of Herder to remind him of these passages from the Book of Job.
But Herder sets Coleridge's enterprise in its context, even ending his chapter with poems of Ossian: "To the Setting Sun," "To the Morning Sun,"
"To the Moon," "Address to the Evening Star."

And of course one could go on in this vein: a woman presides over
each phase of Revelation, and in each of her incarnations she is familiar in
the annals of the Old Testament. Jerusalem wails for her imprisoned "demon" leaders (no mere "Gothick" touch this, although "demon-lover" undoubtedly owes something to the vogue for Bürger and perhaps Wieland).
In the note . . . referring to the Jewish leaders, Coleridge spoke of the
Hebrew "Amarus," a link to the "Amahra" of the first draft of "Kubla"
and to Milton's Mt. Amara, which critics have agreed was a major reference
point for "Kubla" (though no such link is needed), as well as connecting
with the sea itself, the bitter waters. The "cedarn" cover of the sacred
mountain of Lebanon is proverbial. The "ancestral voices prophesying war"
are not a trivial detail filched from Purchas about the priests of the Khan,
but the heart of the apocalyptic warning of the seer echoing his great
prophetic forbears Jeremiah and Ezekiel, distant and unattended.

The number symbolism which is so conspicuous a feature of Oriental
systems was also given a Biblical origin or at least sanction: through one
verse from the Apocrypha, Wisd. of Sol. II.21: "omnia in mensura et nu-
mero et pondere disposuisti," "number was sanctified as a form-bestowing
factor in the divine work of creation." The very idea of the Bible as containing all wisdom is a recommendation of brevity. Again the range is from
the popular-sententious—like the numerical apothegm from the *Arabian
Nights*, "Always use the toothpick for two and seventy virtues lie therein"—

to the systematic holy mystification of the prophets. "Kubla Khan" contains a considerable amount of sacred numerology, though in a very refined form. The main examples—"So twice five miles of fertile ground / With walls and towers were girdled round" and "Five miles meandering with a mazy motion"—may well have been suggested by Ezekiel's measurements of the Holy City.

In apocalyptic mysticism, the Book of Ezekiel, with its vision of the throne-chariot in the first chapter, and its measurements of the celestial city in the last, was of particular importance. Indeed, St Jerome mentions a Jewish tradition which forbids the study of the beginning and the end of the Book of Ezekiel before the completion of the thirtieth year. It is, of course, the model for the New Jerusalem of Revelation. In Coleridge's Notebooks for May 1799 appears the significant collocation of "The Tarter Chan" and "The Fable of the Four Wheels," that is, the chariot from Ezekiel.

> [Y]e shall offer an oblation unto the Lord, an holy portion of the land: the length shall be the length of five and twenty thousand reeds, and the breadth shall be ten thousand. This shall be holy in all the borders thereof round about.
>
> 2. Of this there shall be for the sanctuary five hundred in length, with five hundred in breadth, square round about; and fifty cubits round about for the suburbs thereof.
>
> 3. And of this measure shalt thou measure the length of five and twenty thousand, and the breadth of ten thousand: and in it shall be the sanctuary and the most holy place.
>
> (45.1–3)

The incantatory numbers, based on five, continue throughout the measuring of the sacred river waters on the body of the prophet:

> 15. And the five thousand, that are left in the breadth over against the five and twenty thousand, shall be a profane place for the city, for dwelling, and for suburbs: and the city shall be in the midst thereof . . .
>
> 20. All the oblation shall be five and twenty thousand by five and twenty thousand: ye shall offer the holy oblation foursquare, with the possession of the city.
>
> 21. And the residue shall be for the prince, on the one side and on the other of the holy oblation, and of the possession of the city, over against the five and twenty thousand of the oblation toward the east border, and westward over against the five and twenty thousand toward the west border, over against the portions for the prince: and it shall be the holy oblation; and the sanctuary of the house shall be in the midst thereof.
>
> (48.15–21)

It is not surprising that this obsessive five, a holy number, ambiguously indicating the sanctuary and in the centre the most holy place, the city and the suburbs, and then the entire surrounding area of land, in the prophet who provided the pattern for the Book of Revelation, should be used by Coleridge as a sign of the tradition of the coming of the New Jerusalem.

To go on allegorizing "Kubla" in this vein would not be quite futile, for the Christianized Old Testament context was certainly the primary one for Coleridge. Nevertheless, it is inadequate to the poem, as all interpretations of "Kubla" have been, for it fails to take account of the method of simultaneous Oriental contexts developed in half a century of Biblical and literary studies. In rejecting our simple allegory of Revelation, we shall see the process by which the renascence of allegory in Biblical criticism modulated into Romantic symbolism.

The impetus to a new mythological understanding came from many sides: from explorers' and travellers' reports, from Sir William Jones's *Asiatick Researches*, from the *philosophes'* speculations on the nature of primitive man. But the most profound alteration in attitudes and ideas was brought about when Christianity faced the fact of its own mythological character. The Biblical critics' new views of myth, clearly stated by Eichhorn and Gabler in the 1790s, represent the most subtle and influential, if desperate, Christian apologetics. In myth, the legendary, the monstrous, and the traditional could be accommodated by historical scholarship; in myth, "fact" and "fiction" could be merged into a new form of truth.

The visionary Oriental landscape of poetry bears the traces of this whole difficult history; it emerges at the end of the century in a new form, nowhere so fully or so gracefully achieved as in "Kubla Khan." Far from reflecting ignorance about the Orient, far from any mere search for the exotic, the ornamental, or the artificial, far from being a mere "expressive" reaction in favour of the primitive, the new mythical landscape has absorbed the vast quantity of new information and the insights of an Oriental scholarship gradually freed, almost against its will, from the literalism both of inherited tradition and of rationalist historicizing.

As the new view of myth began to emerge, the Edenic scene intensified in significance through the multiplication of simultaneous reference: the primordial myths persist not only through all the stages of Christian thought, dressed up anew at each major religious metamorphosis, they appear in all religions and nations. "Kubla" represents in its eighteenth-century form the great primordial myth of the origin and end of civilization in the religious spirit of man.

What "spot" is it we actually see in "Kubla" at the pregnant visionary moment? The landscape of Revelation is there, certainly: the sacred river, the fountain, the sea where the forces of darkness are imprisoned, the woman both holy and demonic, the sacred enclosure of the Temple. But the immediate impression is of course primarily pastoral, paradisaical, and Oriental, and the imagery has always been felt, rightly, to have been displaced from the undeniable Biblical base. Yet the first clues are in the Bible.

Goethe reminds us that "Da wir von orientalischer Poesie sprechen, so wird notwendig, der Bibel, als der ältesten Sammlung, zu gedenken." "In speaking of Oriental poetry, we must take note of the Bible, as the oldest collection." One of Goethe's favourite books of the Bible was the Book of Ruth, the "lieblichste kleine Ganze das uns episch und idyllisch überliefert worden ist," "the most charming little unity, epic and idyll, that has been handed down to us." ["Hebräer," Notes to Der West-östlicher Divan].

One of the most charming little epic-idylls of the eighteenth century was the pastoral poet Salomon Gessner's Der Tod Abels, The Death of Abel, a poem to which Coleridge often referred admiringly. It is a good poem, deserving of the vast popularity it enjoyed in Germany and in England; even in the poor English translation by Mrs Collyer, in its ninth edition by 1768, something of its virtue is preserved. Gessner made a skillful fusion of the religious epic, the idyll, and the Oriental setting.

Just before the most likely date for the composition of "Kubla Khan," November 18, 1797, Coleridge and Wordsworth on their walking tour planned to make the Valley of Stones the scene of a prose tale in the manner of Gessner's Death of Abel, and probably within a few days The Wanderings of Cain was begun and, as a collaborative enterprise, abandoned. At the same time, certainly in the course of the tour, the idea of the Lyrical Ballads was conceived. Coleridge retired to the farm between Porlock and Linton with the setting of the Biblical idyll and the idea of the lyrical ballad uppermost in his mind.

The setting has much in common with that of the Song of Songs, as Goethe described it (and for that matter with the Book of Ruth):

> Durch und durch wehet eine milde Luft des lieblichsten Bezirks von Kanaan; ländlichtrauliche Verhältnisse, Wein-, Garten- und Gewürzbau, etwas von städtischer Beschränkung, sodann aber ein königlicher Hof mit seinen Herrlichkeiten im Hintergrunde. Das Hauptthema jedoch bleibt glühende Neigung jugendlicher Herzen, die sich suchen, finden, abstossen, anziehen, unter mancherlei höchst einfachen Zuständen.

> Through and through the poem wafts the mild breeze of the loveliest district of Canaan; rural circumstances of mutual trust, vineyards, gardens, groves of spices, something of urban confinement too, but then a king's court with its formal splendours in the background. The main theme nevertheless remains the burning love of two young hearts, who seek, find, repel, and attract one another amid circumstances of exceedingly great simplicity.

> ["Hebräer"]

This landscape, at once rural arcadia, city, and court, is an archetype of Oriental poetry.

These descriptions of the small "city-kingdom" (Newton's phrase) are a commonplace of the numerous eighteenth-century efforts to write a complete universal history of civilization, sacred and profane. Newton, Vico, Boulainvilliers began with a universal pre-history based on the old notion of "the four ages of the world." They mused on the condition of the first men after the Flood, prior to the founding of cities.

> The first men after the flood lived in caves of the earth & woods & planes well watered by rivers for feeding their herds & flocks, such as were the planes of Babylonia, Assyria, & Egypt. By degrees they cut down the woods & learnt to build houses & towns of brick in the planes of Assyria, Babylonia & Egypt. Thence men spread into places less fertile.
>
> [Newton]

They described the gradual formation of human communities, from the isolated units of the mobile desert patriarchs through the establishment of religious centres and the agglomeration into large urban, national, and finally the vast imperial monarchies of Egypt, Assyria, Persia, and Greece. All empires were held to have shown the same pattern of growth. Newton, equally interested in precise calculations and in general laws of development, tried to plot the size of the ancient city-kingdoms, and he held them to have been very small, comparable with contemporary English villages and corporation towns. He computed that before the victory of the Israelites there had been about one thousand walled cities in the land, the large number indicative of their puny dimensions. He illustrates the particulate origin of empires by "the small size of the army, hardly more than a collection of retainers, that Father Abraham had arrayed against the kings of Sodom and Gomorrah."

On the one hand, these were scientific descriptions, laws of growth, intended as a counterpart to the physical history of the world; on the other, they were celebrated, as De Bougainville, secretary of the Académie des Inscriptions et Belles-Lettres, celebrated Newton's, as "l'histoire de l'esprit humain." A modern treatment like Lewis Mumford's *The City in History* is remarkably similar in spirit and in detail to its eighteenth-century forerunners.

In Gessner's poem, we find the ancient city-kingdom described at the point of its Biblical origin: the settlement built by Adam and Eve after their expulsion from Eden. We are shown the still lovely landscape of a holy mountain, reminiscent of Eden, still visited by spirits, yet new and bleak, a wholly human settlement, a raw stockade barely maintained against the wilderness, an altar visited as much in despair as in reverence. Adam and Eve echo their situation, wonderfully combining their original patriarchal dignity, simplicity, and virtue with new labours, plaints, and pains. Gessner with great success and delicacy created a world half original paradise, half fallen nature.

Just this landscape, combining still-remembered paradise, wilderness, enclosed city, and cultivated court, is captured in "Kubla." City and country, rural yet populous, idyllic yet threatening, holy yet secular, sacred yet fallen, court and cot—it is tempting to see the stereotypes of the eighteenth century merging into those that will dominate the nineteenth. Just for this moment, in this exotic setting, they exist simultaneously, and express a permanent condition of man.

In the Biblical poems of the eighteenth century, this primaeval Oriental scene recurs in a dazzling variety of forms. "Eden" was an immensely diversified scene, a mobile location, not merely of the Creation and the Fall, but of that characteristically eighteenth-century *topos*, the founding state of civilization in general, the centre of *Urmonotheismus*, archetypal monotheism. Typically, as in Gessner, the scene was paradise displaced, paradise already lost though still visible, paradise beset by the ambiguities of human culture. Only with the Fall could civilization begin and develop. Eden had taken on new significance for a century that liked to believe in the progress of civilization and yet profoundly knew its corruption.

After the first night spent outside Paradise, Adam gathers new courage:

Seest thou, EVE, that river, which, like a huge serpent, winds in bright slopes through the meadows? The hill on its bank, seems, at this distance, like a garden full of trees, and its top is cover'd with verdure.

Adam and Eve approach the brilliant scene:

We now advanc'd to the eminence. Its gentle ascent was almost cover'd with bushes and fertile shrubs. On the summit, in the midst of fruit-trees, grew a lofty cedar, whose thick branches form'd an extensive shade, which was render'd more cool and delightful, by a limpid brook, that ran in various windings among the flowers. This spot afforded a prospect so immense, that the sky was only bounded by the dusky air; the sky forming a concave around us, that appear'd wherever we turn'd, to touch the distant mountains.

Here, then, are two natural domes, suggesting the presence of a celestial infinity, in a spot which, as Adam says, is "a faint shadow of Paradise, whose blissful bowers we must never more behold." He concludes: "Receive us, majestic cedar, under thy shade." Coleridge had a wealth of fully developed and directly relevant poetic description of fallen paradises at hand.

If Gessner maintained a sense of the patriarchal dignity of Adam and Eve even in their fallen state, Klopstock in *Der Tod Adams, The Death of Adam*, made palpable the fear of what must happen to the race when the memory of paradise is finally extinguished. In the morning the Angel of Death appears to Adam and tells him that he will die that day when the sun sinks onto the cedar forest that covers the slopes of Eden. The geography is exactly and imposingly generalized: on one of the mountain peaks surrounding that of Eden, the altars of the fallen Adam and Eve still face, over the chasm, a dimming Eden. Adam addresses Seth:

Es ist fürchterlich, Sohn! Zwar diese kühle Erde, in der auch die duftende Rose und die schattende Zeder wächst, ist es nicht! Aber hier soll ich verwesen!

> How dreadful looks this earth, my son! no more
> That fertile earth, which I of late beheld
> O'erspread with roses, or in whose deep bosom
> The branching cedars struck fantastic root.

Adam looks in the direction of Eden, no longer able to see it:

Ihr schönen Gefilde! Ihr hohen quellvollen Berge! Ihr schattenden kühlen Täler, und ihr Kinder der Berge und der Täler! die ihr euch unter dem Fusse des Wandrers biegt, oder eure Gipfel über die hohe Wolke emporhebt! ihr segenvollen Gefilde, wo ich gewandelt, wo ich Leben und Freude eingeatmet, wo ich all meine Kinder, so viele Lebendige um mich gesehen habe! . . . Ich will mich wegwenden, mein Sohn, denn ich kann den Strom kaum mehr von der Ebne unterscheiden.

> O ye happy plains,
> Ye lofty mountains, where a thousand springs
> Rise; and, with streams luxurious, pour down
> The steep declivities; ye vales eternal,
> With cooling shades and laughing verdure crown'd
> . . . Let us depart,
> My son; my feeble sight can scarce discern
> Distinctly ought, nor from the river's stream
> Knows the firm earth.

These "Forests elder than the Sun," as Coleridge called them, become an obsessive image in the poem. Adam, looking in the direction of Eden:

ADAM. Hast du die Sonne gesehn, da du zurückkamst?
SETH. Sie war mit Wolken bedeckt, doch war sie nicht ganz
    dunkel eingehüllt. Wenn mich mein Auge nicht trügt; so
    war sie—weit heruntergestiegen!
ADAM. Weit herunter.—Sieh aus, mein Sohn, ob die Wolken
    nicht weg sind?

> *Adam.*   Alas, my child,
>   I see them not. The sun perhaps with clouds
>   Is darken'd o'er.
> *Seth.* The clouds are thick; yet shade not
>   All the sun's brightness.
> *Adam.* From the cedar's forest,
>   Seems it far distant yet?

Again, in Act III, Seth looks out towards Eden:

SETH. Die Sonne steigt hinunter! die Zedern fangen schon an
zu decken. Gib uns deinen Segen, mein Vater!
ADAM. Sie steigt hinunter?

> *Seth.* The sun declines apace and the tall cedars
>   Fade on the eye:—oh father, father, bless us.
> *Adam.* The sun already at the cedar's forest!

Thus Eden, now screened by the cedars' cover and veiled by failing vision, becomes the seal of death for the fallen Adam.

This mountainous, cedar-covered scene is, of course, the Hebraic, the Palestinian paradise reflected in Coleridge's lines:

> And here were forests ancient as the hills
> Enfolding sunny spots of greenery.

> But oh! that deep romantic chasm which slanted
> Down the green hill athwart a cedarn cover!

In Klopstock's *Messias*, there is a transcendent or astronomical Eden, based, in its locale at least, on Young. The eternal Idea of Eden exists on another star. God descends, pausing to view His works, among them a star where lives a race of rational, unfallen men, an innocent Adam and Eve. In Klopstock's best "Hebraic" style, Adam utters an invocation to the presence of God in Eden:

> Sprich, Ceder, und rausche!
>   Reissender Strom, steh!
> Steh dort! Denn da ging er hinüber. Du sanfteres Athmen.

> Stille Winde, lisple von ihm, wie du lispelst, als Er,
> Ach der Unendliche! lächelnd von jenen Hügeln herab kam!
> Steh vor ihm, Erd', und wandle nicht fort, wie ehmals du
>   standest,
> Als er über dir ging, als sein erhabneres Antlitz
> Wandelnde Himmel umflossen, als sein göttlich Rechte
> Sonnen hielt, und wog, und Morgensterne die Linke!

Speak, ye cedars, rustling speak—speak, for under your branches I saw him walk! Stay, thou rapid stream—stay, for there I saw him pass thy waves! Whisper, ye gentle gales, as when with smiling grace he descended from those towering hills! Stand still before him, O earth, and suspend thy course, as once thou stoodst still, when he passed over thee; when round his face sublime the moving heavens flowed! when his right hand poised the glowing suns, and in his left he held the revolving planets!

As popular as the creation story was its repetition in reverse at the time of the Flood, when degraded civilization was destroyed and patriarchal simplicity restored. More than one theorist of the origins of religion chose this as the crucial historical moment: whether in Vico's compelling descriptions of the distressed state of postdiluvian man, out of which rose his worship of ferocious gods, or in Boulanger's mild, suffering, melancholy, and beneficent postdiluvian primitive, this second Fall seemed to usher history in, to be a testing-place for man's secular psychology when the last authentic memory of prelapsarian Eden had been dispersed. "Kubla," with its perfected simultaneities of reference, shows us both: the Eden of the first creation and the Eden of God's wrath on the rising verge of the Flood waters, where the ancestral voices prophesy in vain.

J. J. Bodmer, the translator of *Paradise Lost* into German, wrote an epic, *Noah*, which attempted to depict the rise of civilizations after the Fall and their decline to the Deluge. It so roused Southey's enthusiasm even in translation that he declared his intention to learn German, write on the subject of the Deluge, and so "take my seat with Milton and Klopstock." The myth of the Flood is still treated literally. But there is a real feeling in the poem for the glory of the decadent civilizations and their monuments that strew the plains round the lost Eden. How can the flowering of civilization be so vile? This puzzle of the theodicies exercised Bodmer, and he makes an almost Byronic lament over the deserted great cities after the Flood recedes. The evil city of Thamista, dwelling-place of Og, goes down thus: "Now was the city encompass'd by the prevailing flood, and the lustre of its structures of polish'd marble, amidst the turbid deep, resembled the silver moon, in a gloomy sky."

Bodmer attempted to map literally the geographical multiplicity of the complex set of centres of civilization on the eve of the Flood. Noah and his three sons live in a displaced Eden at the foot of the mountain of Eden; unknown to them, the true Eden still exists. As the poem opens, a path from the foot of the mountain becomes visible to Japhet and he follows it back to Eden, where he discovers the sage Sipha (Noah's wife's brother) and his three daughters. This is the scene adapted by Wieland in his chivalric Oriental tale of *Oberon*, also known to Coleridge, probably in the original. In Book II, Noah is taken by Raphael on a lightning tour of all the degraded kingdoms; like the hidden Eden, the true lore is everywhere enslaved by "hell-born superstition," yet still survives in a higher sense.

Eden is never wholly lost in this poem—that is the reward of Noah—but as the Deluge comes, Eden perforce takes new forms. The dome of the ark is lined inside with divine paintings, a revelation of a future Eden:

The ceiling seem'd to rise into a lofty dome, in the centre of which, was a wheel'd throne of sapphire, animated by an indwelling spirit, attended by cherubs. The wheels were studded with glittering beryl, and between them, fire blazed prompt for vengeance. On the throne sat a judge, arm'd with thunder; terrible his visage, terrible the front of his throne, and terrible the thundering wheels, whence, with irresistible rapidity issu'd destruction, hurling down myriads of beings, for whom open'd a flaming abyss, while round the judge, flew multitudes of bright spirits, shining with all the effulgence of celestial glory.

Among these unfamiliar forms, Noah catches sight of a radiant figure:

How my heart beats, surely this is the precious Redeemer, and each piece in prophetic painting, displays the glorious work of redemption. Oh what comforts shall I receive in the rolling ark, when encompassed with the waters of the deluge, if the benevolent angel . . . will instruct me, by explaining these hidden mysteries!

In all these poems, the Old Testament setting has got to be linked with the New, and the means taken are usually unsatisfactory. Here the vision has to be literally pictorial for the Enlightenment poet; but it is symbolically vivid as well. We may perhaps think of Kubla's "stately pleasure-dome" riding upon the shadow of the waters as carrying a revelation and a ravishment as great at least, and scarcely more exotic and obscure, than Noah's at these scenes of a future unknown to him yet stirring him to recognition. The patristic and medieval rhetorical technique of *figura*—the prefiguration of the New by the Old Testament—amplified and extended to other mythologies, and removed from time and space, is just discernible at the heart of the new mythological poetics.

There is yet another vision of Eden in Bodmer's poem: Japhet's prophetic dream of the garden of unborn souls. He sees an Eden-like scene:

a plain, profusely adorn'd with flowers; streams clearer than crystal water'd the luxuriant soil, and a grove laden with all the rich exuberance of autumn, spread along the sloping hills, receiving the morning's genial light.

This dream-light, in which he sees the unborn souls of various leaders, is "bright day," and when the dream-day wanes, he wakes. Bodmer's is clearly a classical scene, a Platonic "soul-dwelling"; Eden is projected backwards and forwards, before and after human time.

There was a lively argument among theologians as to whether the scene of the creation was spring or autumn. The two versions of Genesis, separated out by Jean Astruc, who noted in his *Conjectures* of 1753 that some parts of Genesis are devoted to a god "Jahweh" and others to a god "Elohim," give opposing pictures, the one based on the Babylonian spring at the recession of the flood waters, the other on the fertile and moist harvest season of Palestine after the parched summer. "Kubla," without specifying the season, clearly represents both these Oriental seasons: the waters are both rising and receding. The superimposition of two unfamiliar and opposed seasons breeds timelessness more effectively than Bodmer's autumnal dream-light.

A vision in a dream of Eden as the New Jerusalem is granted to John, ending Book 12 of the *Messias*. John is transported by his guardian angel, first to Lebanon, where cedars wave, on a beautiful morning, when the purling of the brook in the vale below was as sweet as the music of the temple. Then he hears the celestial harmony; and in a darkened grove he sees a huge cedar cut down and fashioned into a cross; but then it shoots forth palms. He is transported again, to Eden:

> Da war der Jünger nicht mehr in Libanons Haine.
> Ach, er war in Eden, und sah von dem Himmel ihm glänzen
> Mehr, also Purpur und Gold, und vernahm er erhabnere
>   Chöre,
> Und es schlug ihm das Herz von der Wonne vollem Gefühle.

The scene of the disciple's vision was now removed from Lebanon to Eden, where he beheld a celestial glory that infinitely exceeded the splendour of gold and purple. He now heard more sublime choirs, and his heart was filled with the sweetest sensations of joy.

In a dazzling variety of forms, then, Eden appears in eighteenth-century poetry, a highly specified physical scene, yet a highly mobile one, whose marks and meanings can be transferred to a Platonic pre-world, to outer space, or to a ceiling painting.

This Oriental scene of the origin of civilization, already so mobile, was gradually released from its Jewish, Christian, and Greek moorings and located in Mohammedan and Hindu settings. The most striking example is William Beckford's "Arabian tale" *Vathek* (1782), whose scrutiny of this scene, at once Voltairean and sensuous, consciously organizes a large body of scholarly and literary material in which these familiar motifs are brilliantly reinforced in the exotic imagery of Islamic faith and superstition. The Caliph Vathek had a pleasure-palace upon a mountain; down the "green declivity" of the mountain near four fountains, was a "dreadful chasm," a "vast black chasm" in the plain, where the Giaour, or Infidel, appears to the Caliph and "in accents more sonorous than thunder" promises to bring him to the Palace of Subterranean Fire, which holds the "talismans that control the world." Vathek is commanded to go from his city of Samarah to the ruined city of Istakhar, or ancient Persepolis. After making his way, with great vicissitudes, through the forests of cedar and the waste mountains, he finds in the ruins of great civilization a Hell that evokes "l'ambiance persane de l'Arabie sous la dynastie des Abbassides, l'atmosphère même de *Vathek* tout entier" and yet is instantly recognizable to the Christian reader. Beckford's Hell is justly renowned for the Miltonic sublimity of its satanic ruler Eblis, the fallen angel of Islam, and the Dantesque vision of the tortured worshippers of the dark powers of knowledge whose hearts are perpetually aflame in their transparent breasts, chief among them the

Princess Carathis, the Caliph's mother, whose demonic arts earn for her a perpetual circean whirling that renders her invisible.

Throughout the century Islam had continued to be considered a Christian heresy; so in *Vathek* the familiar motifs are printed in the negative. This negative printing has given *Vathek* a special place in Romantic poetry, admired as it was by the masters of the darker vein, Byron, Poe, Swinburne, Mallarmé, and echoed in *Les Fleurs du mal* and the Carthage of Flaubert's *Salammbô*. In the ironic mode perfected since Bayle, the heretical context makes possible a free reference back to Christianity. Thus in *Vathek*, if Mohammedanism is a Christian heresy, by the powerful and unexpected superimposition of motifs, and their culmination in a mutual hell, Christian civilization is itself revealed as a heresy.

Ambition and lust had been seen as the ruling traits of Mohammed throughout the century. As [Humphrey] Prideaux had written (defending Anglicanism against the deists):

> It is to be observed that *Mahomet* began the *Imposture* about the same time that the *Bishop of Rome* first assumed the title of *Universal Pastor* . . . so that *Antichrist* seems at the time to have set both his feet upon *Christendom* together, the one in the *East* and the other in the *West*.
>
> [*The True Nature of Imposture Fully Display'd in the Life of Mahomet*]

In *Vathek*, the devils of Mohammed figure as the authors of civilization, which originates in the insatiable craving to grasp the roots of cosmic power. Religious civilization is Hell; and there is no alternative to it in Beckford's world but the gratifications of the childlike Gulchenrouz, whose innocence resembles Rousseau's pleasurable state after first being chastised by his nurse. As Raymond Schwab has said, "La Renaissance orientale est l'avènement de l'humanisme intégrale," but already its integrity is threatened from within.

Sir William Jones further extended, indeed systematized, the mobility of the primeval scene, first in his translations of poems from several Oriental languages, already published when *Vathek* was written, then in his own free imitations of them, and in his *Asiatick Researches* (1794), and finally in his brilliant letters from India of the end of the century; and he gave new scholarly grounding to the Biblical critics' insistence on the "Oriental" nature of the Scriptures. The fantastic, as [André] Parreaux has noted, moved in the same direction as erudition and philology. The work of Jones was of particular importance, as Schelling later acknowledged in the *Philosophie der Mythologie*, in the development of the syncretic view of mythology.

Jones was a representative and to some extent a victim of the crosscurrents of the 1790s. His interests were primarily secular: law, poetry, Oriental languages; his enthusiasm for Persian and Arabic poetry and for the refinements of Hindu thought carried him very far from any orthodox Christian concerns. Yet he was aware of the bearing his researches had on his religion, and while insisting on untrammelled historical and linguistic investigation, on an "analytic" method as opposed to Jacob Bryant's "synthetic" one, the *Researches* nevertheless culminate in a defence of the traditional valuation of the Bible as superior in antiquity, in wisdom, and in literary value to the sacred writings of any other nation. He is aware of the revolutionary implications of his work on the antiquity of Hindu civilization and on the parallelism of mythologies, but rejects them. His resolutions of difficulties are often altogether too facile, yet lacking in conviction. His work is a strange mixture of a new and self-professed accuracy, geographical, linguistic, historical, with unfounded traditional views.

Jones's wide-ranging mind and graceful, flowing prose create a sense of the immediacy, accessibility, and disposability of the whole of Asia:

> When I was at sea last August, on my voyage to this country, which I had long and ardently desired to visit, I found one evening, on inspecting the observations of the day, that *India* lay before us, and *Persia* on our left, whilst a breeze from *Arabia* blew nearly on our stern.

In this same easy manner he commands all of Asia, from whatever centre he chooses:

> Considering *Hindustan* as a centre, and turning your eyes in idea to the North, you have on your right, many important kingdoms in the Eastern peninsula, the ancient and wonderful empire of China with all her Tartarian dependencies, and that of Japan, with the cluster of precious islands, in which many singular curiosities have too long been concealed: before you lies that prodigious chain of mountains, which formerly perhaps were a barrier against the violence of the sea, and beyond them the very interesting country of Tibet, and the vast regions of Tartary, from which, as from the Trojan horse of the poets, have issued so many consummate warriors, whose domain has extended at least from the banks of the Ilissus to the mouths of the Ganges: on your left are the beautiful and celebrated provinces of Iran or Persia, the unmeasured, and perhaps unmeasurable deserts of Arabia, and the once flourishing kingdom, of Yemen . . . ; and farther westward, the Asiatick dominions of the Turkish sultans, whose moon seems approaching rapidly to its wane.

Jones prefers the term "Asiatick" to "Oriental," which is a merely relative term "and though commonly used in Europe conveys no very distinct idea."

Yet his combination of traditional doctrine with the new historical accuracy is nowhere more striking or more influential than in his nomination of a candidate for the geographical centre and origin of monotheism.

Examining in turn the Hindus, the Arabs, the Tartars, the Persians, the Chinese, and "the Borderers, Mountaineers, and Islanders of Asia," he reached the conclusion that the Hindus, Arabs, and Tartars are three separate races by whom most of Asia has been peopled; the other Asians are mixtures of these races. He nevertheless held to the traditional view that there was an original primitive monotheism which deteriorated into polytheism, and to the view that there was one literal geographical centre in which this first arose. Opposing Baillie's theory that the seat of civilization was Tartary, mainly on the grounds that its cold climate rendered it unfit, he opts for Iran as the centre from which all other civilizations radiated: Persia, the home of that refined and elegant poetry he so loved.

> We may therefore hold this proposition firmly established, that *Iran*, or *Persia* in its largest sense, was the true centre of population, of knowledge, of languages, and of arts; which, instead of travelling westward only, as it has been fancifully supposed, or eastward, as might with equal reason have been asserted, were expanded in all directions to all the regions of the world, in which the Hindu race had settled under various denominations.

This solution of course presents difficulties: for one, Jones adduces as proof that "mother" Sanskrit was present in Iran, as were the other two "independent" languages, Arabic and Tartar. In what sense can there be "one" geographical centre from which everything emanated and "one" mother language when there are by his own reckoning three races independent racially and linguistically?

Whatever the awkwardness of the theory, however, it incomparably enriched the idea of the single monotheist centre for civilization, by exploring the whole range of actual locations for such a centre and then selecting the most inclusive of them. It proved decisive for the Romantic epic. The excitement aroused, especially in Germany in the 1790s, by Jones's *Asiatick Researches* and by his translation of the *Sakuntala* (and later by the publication of the *Ramayana* and the *Mahabarata*) maintained Herder's emphasis on the "original" religious epic of mankind. The notion of Sanskrit as the general Indo-European mother language was turned to nationalist purposes in the search for the "Indo-Germanic" epic, located with exhilarated inaccuracy in the *Nibelungenlied*. As Heine remarked drily of the German Romantic school, in particular Friedrich Schlegel, "In the *Mahabarata* and the *Ramayana*, they saw a Middle Ages in the shape of an elephant."

Although Jones opted for Iran, his own remarks support another possibility: Abyssinia, the scene of Milton's false paradise, Mt. Amara. "Ethiopia and Hindustan were peopled or colonized by the same extraordinary race," the people said by Apuleius to have "received the first light of the rising sun." Jones cites the tradition (treated by D'Herbelot as a fable, but by Newton as genuine) that colonists from Edom had carried the arts and sciences of astronomy, navigation, and letters into Italy; and since the invention and propagation of letters and astronomy were widely agreed to be of Indian origin, the Idumeans must have been a branch of the Hindu race. The "goddess with many arms," representing the powers of Nature, dominated both Egypt (as Isis) and Bengal (as Isani).

Abyssinia was noted for its wisdom; Aesop was an Abyssinian, and his apologues are related to the Hindu. Lowth and Eichhorn both credited the great culture of the Book of Job to its origin in Idumea, "von jeher der Sitz morgenländische Weisen," as Eichhorn put it, "from time immemorial the seat of Oriental sages" [*Einleitung in das Alte Testament*]. The links of Abyssinia with the Bible were stronger still: for many had argued in the eighteenth century, among them Bishop Warburton, that Moses, for better or for worse, had gleaned all his wisdom from the Egyptian priests. Jones adduces a linguistic connection as well, holding that "the Jews and Arabs, the Assyrians, or second Persian race, the people who spoke Syraick, and a numerous tribe of Abyssinians, used one primitive dialect" which was wholly distinct from that of the first race of Persians and Indians, Romans, Greeks, Goths, Egyptians (or Ethiopians).

If, then, one were seeking a geographical centre of Oriental civilization as closely linked with Mosaic history as possible, Abyssinia would be a more attractive choice than Iran. Coleridge in "Kubla Khan" distributes his favours almost equally between the icy Tartary of the Khan and the Abyssinia of the "damsel with the dulcimer"; Abyssinia as the only actual place named in the poem carries the day. The Christian implication is still uppermost, though deliberately obscured and merged with its equivalent myths:

> A damsel with a dulcimer
> In a vision once I saw:
> It was an Abyssinian maid,
> And on her dulcimer she played,
> Singing of Mount Abora.

The Nile and India were thus connected by a stronger link than "a hook of memory" between two isolated passages of Coleridge's reading; Jones even pays tribute to Bruce's modern description of the Nile, in the course of his discussion of the primal origin of civilization and the reasons for universal moon worship. Coleridge had no need to make "free associations" in the manner of Lowes: the context was well established.

Jones's choice of Iran, one feels, was largely governed by his great love and knowledge of Persian poetry. It is his own imitations and pastiches of it that he offered to Europe as a treasury of new images, rather than the real but difficult splendours of his translation of the Arabian *Mu'allaqât*. The pieces he offered are stylized and schematic summaries of the main topics and images he felt could be most usefully and easily absorbed by European poetry. Although "Kubla" gives Abyssinia precedence over Iran as the origin of civilization, and although the scene of the poem is fundamentally the rugged Palestinian topography of eighteenth-century depictions of the immediate post-Edenic world among the cedar-covered mountains and chasms, there is no doubt it is overlaid and refined by

Jones's exquisite Persian Orientalism, by the beguiling, enamelled landscape of pleasure-dome, fountain, maidens, musky odours, and clear running waters:

> And there were gardens bright with sinuous rills,
> Where blossomed many an incense-bearing tree.

The perfumed trees—"incense-breathing gales perfumed the grove"—are
as obsessive an image in Jones's imitations as the cedarn cover in the Biblical
epics. The range of examples shows once again how Coleridge toned down
any extravagance that would immediately have identified and so limited
him to a particular kind of Oriental poetry: "*Yes, I rejoined*, when those two
damsels departed, musk was diffused from their robes, as the eastern gale
sheds the scent of clove-gillyflowers" ["The Poem of Amriolkais" from
Jones's *Moalla Kat*]. The avoidance of extremes permits simple syncretic
interleaving to pass unremarked.

Jones insisted on the confirmation his purely analytic examination offered to the Mosaic accounts: "We cannot surely deem it an inconsiderable
advantage, that all our historical researches have confirmed the Mosaick
accounts of the primitive world." This is so even if Genesis is merely "a
preface to the oldest civil history now extant"; but if the Bible is inspired,
then his, Jones's, theories are completely confirmed:

> If MOSES then was endued with supernatural knowledge, it is no
> longer probable only, but absolutely certain, that the whole race
> of man proceeded from Iran, as from a centre, whence they mi-
> grated at first in three great colonies; and that those three branches
> grew from a common stock, which had been miraculously pre-
> served in a general convulsion and inundation of this globe.

His reason for holding the Old Testament to be inspired (apart from
the confirmation it lends to his theories) is particularly interesting:

> The connection of the Mosaick history with that of the Gospel by
> a chain of sublime predictions unquestionably ancient, and ap-
> parently fulfilled, must induce us to think the Hebrew narrative
> more than human in its origin, and consequently true in every
> substantial part of it, though possibly expressed in figurative lan-
> guage; as many learned and pious men have believed, and as the
> most pious may believe without injury, and perhaps with advan-
> tage, to the cause of revealed religion.

There is a kind of hedging in this passage which is immediately recognizable
as belonging to the intelligent man of the Enlightenment who has no desire
to undermine Christianity, whatever his appraisal of the worth of its evidences. For Jones, the essential "proof" lies in historical accuracy: if the
Book is literally accurate, then it is genuinely prophetic, i.e. inspired. Jones's
faith has a kind of rationalist pathos about it: the Bible as accurate history,

and prophecy as prediction, was doomed to extinction, in part by his own researches.

The crucial step towards the acknowledgment that the Bible is mythological was being taken at that very moment in Germany, with Eichhorn and Gabler's explication of Genesis as myth. Jones, denying that Genesis is a myth, put clearly what was at stake:

> Either the first eleven chapters of *Genesis*, all due allowance being made for a figurative Eastern style, are true, or the whole fabrick of our national religion is false.

Jones adds that "if any cool unbiased reasoner will clearly convince me, that MOSES drew his narrative through Egyptian conduits from the primeval fountains of Indian literature," he will be prepared to help circulate the truth. But some pages further on he announces:

> There is no shadow then of a foundation for an opinion, that MOSES borrowed the first nine or ten chapters of *Genesis* from the literature of *Egypt*: still less can the adamantine pillars of our *Christian* faith be moved by the result of any debates on the comparative antiquity of the *Hindus* and *Egyptians*, or of any inquiries into the *Indian* Theology.

Eichhorn and his school, including Coleridge, thought otherwise. One feels a kind of constriction as one moves back from the imperial, Enlightened world of Jones, ruler and dilettante, into the world of the German protestant Biblical critics, the academic Orientalists. Yet theirs were the bolder minds, pursuing the implications of their work into the bone and marrow of Christian revelation. As Strauss noted,

> The most hollow natural explanation, did it but retain the slightest vestige of the historical—however completely it annihilated every higher meaning,—was preferable, in the eyes of the orthodox, to the mythical interpretation.
>
> [*Life of Jesus*]

Again the origins of the higher critical analysis lie in literary studies, in the researches of Heyne into classical mythology and of Herder into Persian and Hebrew; and again their analysis issues immediately into literature. Coleridge's scheme for writing hymns on the sun and the moon is one of its fruits.

As early as 1779, Eichhorn had brought Heyne's ideas on myth to bear on Genesis, in his anonymous *Urgeschichte*, published in his *Repertorium für biblische und morgenländische Literatur*. His pupil, Johann Philipp Gabler, published a new edition of it in 1790–93, with a lengthy introduction and full commentary, which greatly extended its influence, and ushered in the mythological analysis of the rest of the Old Testament and the New.

It was, of course, nothing new to trace all religion to worship of the heavenly bodies; indeed, it was a stock Enlightenment procedure. Jones wrote:

> Although I cannot believe with NEWTON, that ancient mythology was nothing but historical truth in a poetical dress, nor, with BACON, that it consisted solely of moral and metaphysical allegories, nor with BRYANT, that all the heathen divinities are only different attributes and representations of the Sun or of deceased progenitors, but conceive that the whole system of religious fables rose, like the *Nile*, from several distinct sources, yet I cannot but agree, that one great spring and fountain of all idolatry in the four quarters of the globe was the veneration paid by men to the vast body of fire, which 'looks from his sole dominion like the God of this world;' and another, the immoderate respect shown to the memory of powerful or virtuous ancestors, especially the founders of kingdoms, legislators, and warriors, of whom the *Sun* or the *Moon* were wildly supposed to be the parents.

In "On the Gods of Greece, Italy, and India" Jones gave a more cautiously eclectic summary of the "four principal sources of all mythology":

> I. Historical, or natural, truth has been perverted into fable by ignorance, imagination, flattery, or stupidity . . . II. The next source . . . seems to have been a wild admiration of the heavenly bodies, and, after a time, the systems and calculations of Astronomers . . . III. Numberless divinities have been created solely by the magick of poetry; whose essential business it is, to personify the most abstract notions, and to place a nymph or a genius in every grove and almost in every flower . . . IV. The metaphors and allegories of moralists and metaphysicians have been also very fertile in Deities.

Coleridge was well acquainted too with Dupuis's reduction of Jesus to a solar myth, the twelve apostles to twelve astrological "houses." Moreover, there had been a century of active speculation in many quarters about the motivation and degree of comprehension of primitive man in arriving at his earliest religious conceptions. But what was new was the attempt to harmonize these diverse accounts through the application of Heyne's view of mythology, gleaned from Greek literature, to the Bible considered as literature. The result was a deepened mythological hermeneutics that touched all literature.

One of Heyne's principles was: "Man versetze sich ganz in das Zeitalter der Geschichte," "Transplant yourself wholly into the period of the story." Eichhorn developed this, demanding of the reader of Genesis:

> Vergiss das Jahrhundert, in dem du lebst, und die Kenntnisse, die es dir darbietet, und kannst du das nicht, so lass dir nicht träumen, dass du das Buch im Geiste seines Ursprunges geniessen werdest.

Das Jugendalter der Welt, das es beschreibt, erfordert einen Geist
in seine Tiefe herabgestimmt; die ersten Strahlen des dämmernden
Lichtes der Vernunft vertragen das helle Licht ihres vollen Tages
nicht; der Hirte spricht nur einem Hirten, und der uralte Morgenländer nur einem anderen Morgenländer in die Seele.

Forget the century in which you live and the knowledge it offers
you, and if you cannot do that, do not imagine that you can savour
the Book in the spirit of its origin. The youth of the world which
it describes demands a spirit steeped in its depths; the first rays
of the dawning light of reason cannot bear the bright light of its
full day; the shepherd speaks only to the soul of a shepherd, and
the ancient Oriental only to the soul of another Oriental.

[*Einleitung in das Alte Testament*]

A second principle of Heyne, equally familiar to us from its Biblical
critical use, the "necessary unity," "nothwendige Einheitlichkeit," of interpretation, was used to unify the two originals that had been discerned
in Genesis.

In Heyne's view, clearly formulated in a lecture to the Göttinger Aka-
demie in 1764, myths were philosophemes about the cosmos. Thus far they
were philosophical, even metaphysical; but in primitive times there was
no adequate conceptual language in which to express these insights; they
had to be expressed in the language of the senses, the *Bildersprache* that
became a byword of Herder's. *Homo mythicus* had a native idea of God,
however undeveloped. Heyne offered a psychological explanation of the
process, similar to Kant's in his *Beobachtungen über das Gefühl des Schönen
und Erhabenen, Observations on the Feeling of the Sublime and Beautiful* and
equally derived from the Longinian revival: the immensity of nature places
primitive man in a state of religious awe, and in this emotional state his
imagination becomes active and forms his objective perceptions into an
imaginative construction.

As Eichhorn paraphrased Heyne's version:

Die Einbildungskraft bleibt nicht in den engen Grenzen der münd-
lichen Überlieferungen stehen, sie schweift noch weiter ins Reich
der Möglichkeiten aus und erhöht vieles, was sie im Nebel der
Zeit sieht bis zu einer Riesengrösse und verwandelt also Sagen in
wahre Zauberideen.

The imagination does not remain within the narrow bounds of the
oral transmission, it ranges yet further in the realm of possibilities
and raises much of what it glimpses in the mists of time to gigantic
proportions and transforms sagas into truly magical ideas.

[*Einleitung in das Alte Testament*]

The foundation of mythology is ignorance of the causes of the appearances; whatever needs explanation, every event, order and, especially,

disorder in nature and the psyche are attributed to the direct intervention of God. But the note of Enlightened condescension begins to disappear: of the causes of appearances, the "witnesses" are always ignorant.

Heyne harmonized the two major and conflicting views of myth: that it is intellectual in character and that it originates in primitive ignorance. Myth was genuinely intellectual, he affirmed; yet allegorical exegesis was improper unless it was clearly indicated by the author as his intention, and we must always remember that we do not have the myths in their original form. Myth was genuinely primitive; yet it was not ignoble, not beast worship or fetishism, not the result of fear and "superstition," nor was it imposed by unscrupulous priests or kings. Moreover, while Heyne's view lends itself to transcendentalist theories of perception, it had the virtue of appearing not as philosophy or psychology, but as a canon of criticism.

Heyne very well represents the early stage of the transition from Enlightenment ideas of an abstract natural religion indwelling in all men to Romantic views of mythical symbolism as the paradigm for all thought. His sense of the philosophical nature of mythical expression which nevertheless takes a form quite different from abstract rationalism became both the problem and the solution for the new philosophy.

The Biblical critics tried, by applying Heyne's analysis of the mythic mode of thought, to reconstruct the process by which the Biblical "histories" had been arrived at. For them, the important thing in Heyne's view of myth was that myth was no longer mere fable, unworthy fiction, or even poet's fiction in the sense of departure from truth; myth was "the oldest history and the oldest philosophy," and one could respectably call, as Gabler did, for a "mythologica sacra," a higher, or Biblical mythology.

Eichhorn and Gabler had at first retained some elements of Genesis as historical (the eating of a poisoned fruit; the existence of a tree), in order, as they afterwards admitted, to make their analysis more palatable to the public; but in the new edition, Genesis I-3 was stated to be, in Heyne's sense, a purely philosophical myth, that is, one in which "the historical" is merely a vestment for the philosophical idea. The systematic comparison of extra-Biblical myths with Biblical ones, and the application of the principle of unified interpretation, made it impossible to maintain any element of historical fact whatsoever in Genesis. Thus the treatment of the Old Testament as Oriental literature led logically to the full relinquishing of the claim to historical factuality.

Herder had pointed out that there were four Oriental *Wundergeschöpfe* in Genesis, the two trees, the talking snake, and the cherub. Eichhorn had already explained the cherub and the tree of life as mythical. Gabler went further:

Und nun sollen doch die damit genau verbundenen zwei übrigen Wundergeschöpfe, der schädliche Baum, der ohnehin nach seiner offenbar mythischen Schilderung als Weisheitsbaum das unverkennbare Gepräge asiatischer Dichtung an sich trägt, und die

Schlange, die als redend vorgestellt, offenbar auch ein Produkt der asiatischen Phantasie ist, im Paradies *wirklich* existiert haben?

And now should the other two marvels that are closely connected with them nevertheless be held *really* to have existed in Paradise, the injurious tree, which, according to its manifestly mythical description as a tree of wisdom, bears the unmistakable stamp of Asiatic poetry, and the snake which is represented as speaking, manifestly also a product of the Asiatic fantasy?

[*Urgeschichte*]

The reference to familiar Greek literature emboldened the critics; as Gabler put it:

Sucht wohl ein Heyne mühsam den Prometheus, Epimetheus, die Pandora und ihre Büchse zu retten, und nur das notwendig-mythische von ihnen abzustreifen; oder hebt er nicht vielmehr den Hauptsatz der zum Grunde liegt: 'Mit den Künsten kommt Ungemach und Elend in die Welt' aus dem ganzen Mythos heraus und erklärt alles Übrige für nichts als für mythische Philosopheme, da ja selbst Prometheus, Epimetheus und Pandora offenbar etymologische Wesen sind? Sehen nun nicht Adam (Mann) und Eva (Männin) ebenso etymologisch aus, wie Prometheus und Pandora? Hat wohl je ein verständiger Ausleger der griechischen Mythen die Götterspeisen Nektar und Ambrosia so in Schutz genommen, wie der Theologe sich der Elohimspeisen, des Weisheits-und Lebensbaumes, annimmt?

Does a Heyne really seek laboriously to salvage Prometheus, Epimetheus, Pandora and her box, and to strip away only the necessary mythical trappings from them; or does he not rather lift out of the myth as a whole the principle that lies at the base of it: 'With the arts disorder and suffering come into the world', and declare all the rest nothing but a mythical philosopheme, since even Prometheus, Epimetheus, and Pandora are clearly etymological beings? Do not Adam (Man) and Eve (Woman) look just as etymological as Prometheus and Pandora? Has any reasonable interpreter of the Greek myths ever defended (as real) the divine diet of nectar and ambrosia as the theologian defends the food of the Elohim, the tree of wisdom and life?

[*Urgeschichte*]

Gabler puts the fateful question: *"Is not the primitive world everywhere the same?"* *"Ist die Urwelt nicht überall gleich?"* The myths of the Bible have no claim to special protection.

The approach to full mythologizing was made step by step during the 1790s. Immediately following the republication of the *Urgeschichte*, Eichhorn began to apply his method to the New Testament, in a series of papers: the "Versuch über die Engelserscheinungen in der Apostelgeschichte," "Essay on the Appearances of the Angels in the Acts of the Apostles"; the "Ausgiessung des Geistes am Pfingstfest," "The Outpouring of the Holy Ghost at Pentecost"; and, especially, an essay on the "Versuchungsgeschichte Jesu," the "Temptation of Jesus," which rapidly became a model for mythological exegesis. Eichhorn's method was to select the incidents most obviously dictated by preexistent mythological explanation and to reconstruct from the situation of the narrative the corresponding underlying natural process. He is most successful, as Sachs has noted, when he can provide a psychological motivation which is transposed, in accordance with the mythical outlook of Jesus's time, into the miraculous or supernatural. Each element of the narrative is given a naturally understandable psychological equivalent. In short, this is a thoroughly rationalistic method, though an "advanced" one, in that mythical expressions are understood as historically necessary, rather than as the result of error, superstition, or deception.

Strauss, in the history of the mythological approach to the Bible that forms the introduction to *Das Leben Jesu*, summed up Eichhorn's achievement:

> The mythological researches of a Heyne had so far enlarged his circle of vision as to lead Eichhorn to perceive that divine interpretations must be alike admitted, or alike denied, in the primitive histories of all people. It was the practice of all nations, of the Grecians as well as the Orientals, to refer every unexpected or inexplicable occurrence immediately to the Deity.

Indeed, the celebrated *Das Leben Jesu* which created a scandal all over Europe on its publication in 1835 was only an uncompromising extension of Eichhorn's method to the whole fabric of the New Testament.

During the 1790s, Gabler published his own series of papers; he did not go beyond Eichhorn's method, but openly formulated their common canons of interpretation. Gabler pointed out explicitly that the method was not really conducing, as Eichhorn had hoped, to a critically sharpened conception of the *Tatsächliche*, of actual fact, but was postulating a narrative art "bei welcher Objektiv-Tatsächliches und subjektives Räsonnement darüber eine ungeschiedene Einheit bilden," "in which the objectively factual and the subjective rationale for it form an undifferentiated unity." The higher criticism had already moved from a mythology of history to a history of mythology.

This radical shift was nevertheless still grounded in Orientalism; the new narrative art, according to Gabler, was precisely the Oriental mode of thought:

> Es liegt in dem Charakter des Orientalers, eine Begebenheit nie nackt zu erzählen, sondern so, wie er sich dachte, dass es dabei

zugegangen oder wie sie erfolgt sein möchte. *Räsonnement war immer in Geschichte eingeschlossen, und wurde selbst als Faktum dargestellt;* weil der Orientaler sichs gar nicht denken konnte, dass etwas anders vorgefallen sein konnte als er sichs gerade vorstellte. Das Faktum und die Art, sich das Faktum zu denken, floss bei dem Morgenländer in Ein unzertrennliches Ganze zusammen.

It is rooted in the character of the Oriental never to relate an event barely, but rather as he supposed that it happened or might have happened. *Rationale was always included within the story, and was itself represented as fact;* for the Oriental could not imagine that something could take place otherwise than just as he conceived it to himself. The fact and the way of conceiving the fact flowed together for the Oriental into an inseparable whole.

[*Neuestes Theologisches Journal*]

There is no mistaking the still rationalist primitivism of this description of the Oriental mind, much inferior to Herder's insights into the Christian Orientalism of the Evangelist. The decisive step had nevertheless been taken; the symbolist mythographers would now hold that not only was the Bible completely mythological, but that "the Oriental mind" was the mind of Everyman.

Coleridge recalled his youthful enthusiasm for the mythological poetry of Genesis:

I interpreted the Chapter as a Morning Hymn, in which the Creation is represented under the analogy of the daily emergence of visible Nature out of Night thro' all the successive appearances till full Sun rise and thence explained the posteriority of the Sun & the visible Orb, to the Light, it's far earlier Harbinger.

[marginal note in Eichhorn]

This may represent Coleridge's earliest view of the matter, in its straightforward Enlightenment pungency, its rational "natural" explanatory power, and its Herderian affirmation that the Book is a set of Oriental songs. It is worth noticing, however, that Coleridge again finds means to resist the disintegrative effects of Biblical criticism through subtler modes of interpretation which themselves become part of his canon of criticism, sacred and secular. There are not necessarily two different accounts of the Creation merged in Genesis 1–3, Coleridge is saying, providing one applies Eichhorn's tools less crudely than Eichhorn does. He notes that Eichhorn would find his own interpretation "too refined":

surely Eichhorn would denounce the separation of the Vegetable from the Animal Creation by an intermediate Creation of the present Solar System, Forests elder than the Sun, as a Chimaera κατ' ἔμφυσιν.

[marginal note]

Indeed, Coleridge is only applying more strictly one of Eichhorn's own rules: primitive man explained phenomena in the order of their sensuous appearance, not in order of their logical causes. "Forests elder than the Sun" are not *Wundergeschöpfe*, nor are they signs of an overlapping of two Creation accounts, they are the great primeval trees that rise up in the early morning light to the eye of ancient man before he sees the actual orb of the sun come over the heavily wooded horizon. Again the poet's mind is able to credit the myth fully; and therefore he straightaway bounds ahead of the painful, crabwise progress of Eichhorn towards a grasp of the Bible as a whole as myth.

Coleridge takes Genesis as a proof of the high possibilities in primitive man, against those debunkers who insisted on his savage state. He inveighs against the

> arbitrary and in many respects improbable Hypothesis, that the Human Race commenced in Savagery. Most unscriptural at all events is the Supposition: and in my humble opinion not less unphilosophical. If we credit the Book of Genesis (& what other historic document have we that comes near to it in age & authenticity?) we must admit, that the most important of the Arts were discovered or invented before the Flood and that a Monarch had risen before the dispersion of the Human Race. I can find nothing in Job, that might not have been written by a contemporary of Abraham: tho, if I were to fix on any period, it would be between the times of Joseph and Moses.
>
> [marginal note]

In Coleridge there is no trace of the rationalist contempt for the "Oriental mind" that still lingered in Gabler and Eichhorn even while they placed that mind at the basis of their own religious culture.

Coleridge's rejection of the notion of primitive *Spracharmut*, the poverty of language attributed to early man, made it possible for *Bildersprache* to attain the full reach of allegory. Gabler wrote, restating Heyne's view:

> *Bildersprache ist noch lange nicht Allegorie*—nur dann konnte sich aus Bildersprache Allegorie bilden, als die Bildersprache nicht mehr *unvermeidliche* Folge der Spracharmut war, sondern üppiger poetischer Schmuck, freier Erguss des überströmenden Witzes und *absichtliches* Kunstwerk einer reichen Dichterfiktion wurde.

> *The language of images is very far from being allegory*—allegory could take shape from the language of images only when the language of images was no longer the *unavoidable* consequence of poverty of language, but had become *deliberate* poetic ornament, the free outpouring of a brimming intellect and the intentional artifact of a rich poetic fiction.
>
> [*Urgeschichte*]

For Coleridge, the capacity for allegory was not confined to rational man; rational man simply made the mistake of using it in isolation from the spontaneous creative power of the *Bildersprache*.

The history of the development of the concept of the Logos (to Unitarians, the prime example of Oriental thought within Christianity) that Coleridge gave in the Introduction to his MS "Logic" attempts to show how the poetic primitive transforms itself into the philosophical and finally the theological insight, producing along the way all literary genres.

The method and tone of this Introduction, although it is attached to much later thinking about transcendental logic, are quite distinct from that thinking and hark back to the mythological speculations of the 1790s. Coleridge gave a splendid description of the unmethodical, "promiscuous" learning of childhood and of primitive communities. All that we need to know comes to us in

> a gay & motley chaos of facts & forms, & thousand-fold experiences, the origin of which lies beyond memory, traceless as life itself & finally passing into a part of our life more naked than would have been compatible with distinct consciousness and with a security beyond the power of choice! Or shall we call this genial Impulse a Will *within* the Will, that forms the basis of choice and the succedaneum of instinct, which the conscious choice will perfect into knowledge?

For individuals and communities, "This is the happy delirium the healthful fever of the physical, moral & intellectual being,—nature's kind & providential gift to childhood."

In the *Aids to Reflection*, Coleridge, discussing the element of Oriental allegory in Genesis, makes it clear that primitive "spontaneity" in no way precludes complexity of conception:

> As to the abstruseness and subtlety of the Conceptions, this is so far from being an objection to this oldest *Gloss* on this venerable Relic of Semitic, not impossibly ante-diluvian, Philosophy, that to those who have carried their researches farthest back into Greek, Egyptian, Persian and Indian Antiquity, it will seem a strong confirmation. Or if I chose to address the Sceptic in the language of the Day, I might remind him, that as Alchemy went before Chemistry, and Astrology before Astronomy, so in all countries of civilized Man have Metaphysics outrun Common Sense.

Coleridge's view is like Herder's both in its acclaim for the spontaneous motley of the primitive condition and in the subtlety with which the primitive state is made the foundation of all further development: as the "Oriental tales" of the early Gospels are woven into and raised to a higher power by "John," so a philosophical etymology of the Logos, the prime theological concept of St. John, generates poetry. For Coleridge, myth could not be, as for critics tied to Heyne, an inarticulate allegory, for primitive language was supremely rich and ready; it is much more an implicit, an evolving allegory, as for Kant the aesthetic idea is always asymptotic to logical expression. "Kubla Khan" renders the primitive language of myth in the form of a poetic artifact: poetry is not rationalizing and ornamental, but the achievement without loss of the evolution of the human race.

Herder, in his popular *Oriental Dialogues*, showed how the mobile location could be used as a method of literary criticism, how, that is, the myth as historical milieu could mediate between literal event and free allegory. Herder tried to establish a general context and landscape for "Oriental poetry," extending Lowth's work on Hebrew poetry to Persian and Arabic poetry as well. He regularly illustrated his points both from the Old Testament and from Persian poetry; indeed, he sometimes illustrated points about Hebrew religious views from Persian poetry. Ultimately, his purpose was to show what a modern German poetry must be, and how it could escape from sterile imitations of classical or Oriental models by translating their spirit fully into the modern world.

He composed a generalized description of Paradise, which even in the Arabian and Persian bards expresses the ideal "of human joy and felicity." In response to Alchipron's objection that the scenery is no doubt enchanting, but is it not likely to attach men too much to the pleasure of the senses? Eugenius replies:

> On the contrary, I feel a sincere delight, when I find the eastern Bards, in their national songs, representing the verdant plains, the trees that project a deep and refreshing shade, the crystal lakes and purling streams, as the remains of the ancient Paradise, and the presage of its restoration in a future scene, which they call the *land of Eden*, the happy region of tranquillity and contentment. How different are these views of a future destination from the sordid notions of those northern Bards, the sons of *Edin*, who place their departed heroes in lofty halls, daubed with gold, and loaded with hogsheads of metheglin and beer, which they swill out of the skulls of their slaughtered enemies!

We must give up trying to choose among the multitudinous traditions of the location of Paradise, Herder concluded, and instead adopt Moses's own representation of it "as a sort of *enchanted land*, unknown to him."

Although Palestine, Persia, and Abyssinia were the heartland of Orientalism for Coleridge, he drew examples for his "enchanted land" from further afield. On the extreme western edge of the Orient is another example of the sacred landscape. Jotted down in his notebooks while reading *A Relation of a Journey begun An: Dom: 1610. Foure Bookes. Containing a description of the Turkish Empire, of Aegypt, of the Holy Land, of the Remote parts of Italy, and Islands adjoining* is a reference to this passage by Sandys, the translator of Ovid's *Metamorphoses*, as of the Psalms of David:

> And as the Papists attribute an extraordinary holiness to *Rome*, so doe the Greekes unto *Athos*, a mountaine of *Macedonia*; so named

of *Athon* the sonne of *Neptune*, dekt with still-flourishing trees, and abounding with fountaines; called also The Holy Mountaine by the Christians. A place from the beginning dedicated to Religion: lying directly West from Lemnos; and so high, that though it be seven hundred furlongs distant; yet it is said a little before the setting of the Sunne to cast a shadow on that Island. Whereupon the proverbe: 'Aspiring Athos hides / The Lemnian heifers sides."

Of all the forms of Oriental thought, Coleridge had least sympathy with Hinduism, at least in his later years. The familiar passages in the *Philosophical Lectures*, probably echoing Friedrich Schlegel's polemic in *Die Weisheit der Inder* (1808), *The Wisdom of the Indians*, are confirmed in later manuscripts. Yet even in his last writings, in the midst of attacking Sir William Jones for comparing the *Bhagavad-gita* with Milton, this *topos* retained its power for him:

> Their next neighbours of the North the temple-throned infant of Thibet with the Himala behind and the cradle of the Ganges at his feet, convey to my mind an impressive likeness, seems to me a pregnant symbol, of the whole Brahman Theosophy.
>
> [MS "Divine Ideas"]

Here is that same Oriental landscape again, the landscape of "Kubla": the temple with the sacred mountain behind and the sacred river at its feet.

We have, then, in "Kubla Khan" a perfectly generalized Oriental setting. It was not Coleridge's "association" of isolated patches of reading that merged these Oriental landscapes into one, but a recognized literary technique. The "picture" method employed upon an existing, in principle locatable, but invisible, natural landscape created an interchangeably internal and external vision.

The generalized Oriental setting achieved for Coleridge's poem what he admired as the chief technical virtue of *The Faerie Queene*: that it is enacted "truly in the land of Faery, that is, of mental space." This was Spenser's means of achieving unity and "harmonizing his descriptions of external nature and actual incidents with the allegorical character and epic activity of the poem." His images are not picturesque, but are "composed of a wondrous series of images, as in our dreams," and these images exist "in the marvellous independence and true imaginative absence of all particular space and time."

Herder pointed to the meaning of the unity achieved in this way. Ultimately, the superimposition of Oriental images depends on loosing the myth of the founding of civilization from specificities of date and place. Speaking of the "essential and distinctive character of Man, and that which places him above all classes of beings merely animal, that he is *susceptible of religion*," Herder showed how man's religious susceptibility made possible the development of knowledge itself. The idea of the unity of God led men to look for unity of design, for general laws of nature, and so delivered them again from "polytheistical disorder and anarchy." Hebrew poetry, through its method of "the parallelism of heaven and earth," was the "first bulwark against idolatry."

But Herder failed, in Coleridge's view, to live up to his own insight. Herder's Oriental landscape was avowedly merely human, merely poetic, merely an "Arabian tale" (or a Hebrew one) after all. The atmosphere of charmed sleep in Spenser existed not for itself, Coleridge pointed out, but to enable the allegory to work. Coleridge defended allegory in the Bible against Herder's disposition to interpret it all as *menschlich*, as if, Coleridge tartly remarks, we were to interpret "Plato Kant Leibnitz, etc" as "Esop's Fables for Children":

> How can Herder have the effrontery to assert that there is no Tone of ALLEGORY in the Tree of *Life*, and the Tree of the Knowledge of Good and Evil—& a talking Serpent—&c &c. If these do not possess all the marks of Eastern Allegory, of allegory indeed in genere, what does? And why should not Moses introduce historical Persons in an allegory, as well as the Author of the Book of Job?— History was for instruction—no such cold Divisions then existed, as *matter of fact* Chronicles, & general Gleanings of the Past, such as those of Herodotus.
>
> [marginal note in Herder]

Coleridge here is making it very clear that the equality of all mythologies does not reduce them to a merely "human" story; on the contrary, it must give rise to the profound sense for their spiritual truth that the Hellenistic age experienced. History itself must be understood anew in this light. For finally what was significant about the Oriental *topos* was not that being "exotic" it could lend itself to mental topography, but that having acquired the status of mental topography, it was not absolved from the encounter with facts of time and place.

The way "historical persons" are absorbed into mythical significance becomes plain in Coleridge's discussion of Origen's allegory of Genesis. In the notebooks where Coleridge discussed most searchingly various issues arising out of Eichhorn's work, he offered a profounder view than Herder, Gabler, or Eichhorn of the nature of myth and its application to Genesis. We are dealing now with the later Coleridge, Coleridge writing in full knowledge of Creuzer's *Symbolik* (1808–12) and of Schelling's early "Über Mythen, Philosophemen, und Sagen" (1793), "On Myths, Philosophemes, and Sagas," and the splendid essay, "Die Gottheiten von Samothrake" (1815), "The Gods of Samothrace." Coleridge's early grasp of myth matured into a conception of intellectual activity as myth-making.

He criticized an anonymous German writer on the pagan Mysteries for rendering Origen's μύθους καὶ γράμματα as

> fables and letters, instead of symbolic Stories and sacred Books— from not knowing the true import of *Mythes* or Philosophemes,

which Sallust, the Greek Platonist, happily conveys when he describes the Kosmos or Material Universe as the μυθος κατ' εξοχήν—and the creative Logos as *mythologizing*.

[MS Notebook]

Coleridge's knowledge of Origen undoubtedly goes back to the earliest period of his intellectual life; the Church fathers, with the Neoplatonists, were among his earliest reading. His Hellenistic orientation is an historical construction in an almost Hegelian sense; but it is also a specific and learned reference to the authentic roots of Christian exegesis. Origen's criticism indeed throws light on Coleridge's. His strong doctrine of the inspiration of the Bible and his strong doctrine of the "accommodation" of the Biblical revelation to the capacities of the audience make equally, though in opposite directions, for the strenuous application of allegorical techniques of interpretation. Ultimately, the conviction of the plenary inspiration of the Bible depends (wonderfully covertly) on the force and subtlety of the interpretation. Origen exemplifies in an earlier form the mutual dependence of the critical and the constructive that we have noted as characteristic of the higher criticism. Origen undertook to defend the Bible against pagan charges of crude and fabulous simplicity by developing a highly refined allegory. Coleridge, absorbing the historical–critical fragmentation of the Bible text, reasserted the substantial spiritual unity of the Bible through the idea of communal experience. Looking away from the historical situation of the two men, we may discover the necessary circularity of the commentator on a sacred text: he must find difficulties in it—inconsistencies, incoherences, barbarisms, absurdities—and having pointed them out, he must overcome them. For the best critic of Holy Writ, sacred or secular, to discover faults is to proclaim inspiration.

Coleridge went on to speak of the later chapters of Genesis, of Adam and Eve as a myth:

> Thus too in Origen's belief the transgression of Adam and Eve was a Muthos, εν γραμμασι εβραίκοις—an Idea shadowed out in an individual Instance, imaginary or historical—The truth remains the same. It did take place—and the Individuals, in whom it first took *place* (realized itself in space, & a fortiori in *time*, *place* implying both: for space cannot be particularized but in connection with Times, as the sole Measure of Space) where Adam and Eve—'In Adam we all die'—or Adam and Eve were the Individuals, in whom it *first* took place: in this alone different from all other Men and Women / In the former the Individuality is rightfully assumed—in the second, it is recorded—the Truth is the same in both, and both alike are Mythic, and belong to Mythology.

[MS Notebook]

This is a brilliant solution: the radical dissolution of time and space, far more radical than in Herder, is converted into a defence of the historicity of mythological characters and events. The wheel comes full circle: when history is fully understood as myth, then myth can be rediscovered as history.

Coleridge's reference to Origen's controversial views on Genesis is as much an interpretation as a quotation of authority—as indeed quotation by Coleridge always is. Did Origen intend to jettison the literal sense of the story of Adam and Eve, as Philo had done, comparing the talking serpent with "bogies and monsters"? Origen cited as a parallel the myth of the conception of Eros in Zeus's garden in the *Symposium*, suggesting that Plato may have learnt the myth from Jewish savants when he visited Egypt. As Hellenistic allegory derived from Greek reinterpretations of Homer after the attacks by Plato, the use by Biblical critics of methods developed for Greek literature was time-honored but dangerous practice, subject to the same charges of unorthodoxy that have again and again been levelled at Origen. Christian defenders of Origen have sometimes tried to argue that he never sacrificed the literal meaning of the text to his allegorical interpretation; Coleridge, on the contrary, admits that Origen's passage on Genesis is spiritual allegory of the kind that is concerned with permanent meaning rather than historical literalism, praises him for it, and adopts it as a precedent for the equation of myth and history. This is typical of Coleridge's supposed orthodoxy: he embraces heresy and elevates it into tradition.

The crucial point, however, is the nature of the distinction between "allegory" and "*muthos*." On the one hand, it is clear that Hellenistic allegory was an extremely important source for Heyne and the Biblical critics who adopted his method, and that this helps to explain the revival of allegory in the eighteenth century and its long survival into the Romantic period. On the other hand, it is clear that "myth" as used by the new critics was substantially different from allegory; and the difference lay precisely in its ability to mediate between the timeless moral or spiritual allegorization and the specific historical milieu in which a myth has its roots. The myth critics do not abandon but incorporate the historical interpretation of the Bible. Yet the "historical milieu" becomes itself a mobile location like the paradise of the epics: it is a product of the historical experience not of one place and time but of the entire Christian community, and like an allegory, can be reconstructed and transported over the whole range of that experience.

Thus Coleridge:

> The whole Jewish history, indeed, in all its details, is so admirably adapted to, and suggestive of, symbolical use, as to justify the belief that the spiritual application, the interior and permanent sense, was in the original intention of the inspiring Spirit, though it might not have been present, as an object of distinct consciousness, to the inspired writer.

> [*Notes on English Divines*]

Daniélou has written that it is possible to hold to the historical reality of the events, "because typology consists precisely in showing that it is the history itself that is figurative, and not in substituting allegory for history." Eichhorn and Gabler banned *figura*: the Old Testament did not pre-figure the New. But they developed a new kind of *figura*: the New Testament contained the whole of the Old Testament. This was historically rational; yet it preserved the traditional fictional possibilities. Now they take their start in Revelation after the fact, in short, in apocalypse, not in "prophecy." Prophecy is no longer the prediction of actual events to come, but the renewed vision of the meaning of the past for the future. Within the New Jerusalem is contained the progressive history of Eden from the Creation. This conception of *figura*, by renewing the typically figurative blend of historical reality and spiritual interpretation, pointed the way from allegory to symbolism.

Schelling, whose very earliest writings, in 1792, demonstrate his intimate knowledge of the work of Heyne, Herder, and Eichhorn, in his *Philosophie der Mythologie* extended and summed up the development of Biblical Orientalism. Mythology is the mark of humanity; without it, no community, no people can exist, for a people is "die Gemeinschaft des Bewusstseyns," " a community of consciousness." Poetry, he said, does not give rise to mythology, but mythology to poetry:

> Poesie [ist] wohl das natürliche Ende und selbst das nothwendig unmittelbare Erzeugniss der Mythologie, aber als wirkliche Poesie . . . nicht der hervorbringende Grund, nicht die Quelle der Göttervorstellungen seyn könnte.

> Poetry is indeed the natural end and even the necessary direct product of mythology, but, as genuine poetry, . . . cannot be the cause nor the source of conceptions of the gods.

Poetry, then, is the higher stage of mythology; and Schelling's own conception of symbol is such that the fullness and perfection of any potentiality depends on and embraces the "abyss" from which it evolved.

Schelling reviewed the history of the movement. Before Hume, it had been assumed that monotheism was original, by revelation, and that polytheism arose only through corruption and falling away from revelation. Hume's view that polytheism, based on the animation of nature, was the source of the conception of God, was combated in various ways.

Lessing in *Die Erziehung des Menschengeschlechts, Education of the Human Race*, attributed polytheism to the exercise of reason which "zerlegte den einzigen Unermesslichen in mehrere Ermessliche," "analysed the single uncommensurable object into several measurable ones." G. Voss thought the gods of all nations were euhemerized in the Old Testament, a modern version of the theory that all genres were to be found in the Bible, which if not the origin of all mythologies, was a compendium and synthesis of them. This theory was systemized through Baillie's idea that all peoples had split off from an *Urvolk*. But such an *Urvolk*, with an *Uroffenbarung*, Schelling says, cannot be one nation, but must in some way stand for all mankind; the Hebraic teaching must be pieced out with the various mythologies of other nations. The first to do this was William Jones.

Herder's attempt to describe a generalized Oriental landscape, then, was not merely a literary and critical device, it was part of the much larger undertaking to show that all human society is founded on the same religious need or instinct, a sense for God without which it would be impossible to see gods in nature at all; the undertaking to piece together the one *Urvolk* again.

Schelling was able to reconcile the notion of natural polytheism with the notion of original revelation: the first monotheism was only a potentiality, still unconscious, a "relative monotheism," a servitude from which polytheism liberated men by teaching them to discriminate and to seek the enduring amidst alteration. Original monotheism was not a revelation for all time, but the beginning of the long process of education of the race; and the medium of that education was mythology.

Like Schiller, Schelling held that one does not and cannot find or explore the religious consciousness simply by going back to a primitive state of man; revelation is a process taking place in history, not a single event taking place at the commencement of the race, though it culminates in Christ. It teaches the race not only its origins, but its end, what Kant called our "moral destination." Mythology is the preparation for religious revelation, both historically and psychologically; the taste—or the distaste—for the bizarre or passionate primitive is irrelevant. "Das Heidenthum ist uns innerlich fremd, aber auch mit dem unverstandenen Christenthum ist zu der angedeuteten Kunsthöhe nicht zu gelange." "Paganism is inwardly alien to us, yet with an uncomprehended Christianity we can never attain to the highest level of art." Not only the underlying unity of the religious sense, but the many forms it takes must be honored. Although we seek the reason of things, we must not merely allegorize them. "Die Absicht muss vielmehr seyn, dass auch die Form als eine nothwendige und insofern vernunftige erscheine." "We must rather consider the form too as necessary and therefore rational."

Schelling, although in the *Philosophie der Kunst* (1802–1803) he rejected the notion that allegory was the essence of mythology, which he defined as a form of symbolic thought attributing to the gods an independent value, still maintained that Christian thought was allegorical. This last vestige of Christian privilege is banished in the *Philosophie der Mythologie*, apparently in reaction against Creuzer, whose *Symbolik* maintained a dualism of sense and sign that went against the grain of Schelling's idealism. Schelling was dissatisfied even with the term "symbol," which he thought suggested the dissociation of image and sense almost as much as allegory, and adopted instead Coleridge's conception of tautegory, which he quoted in a long footnote: in that mythology is not allegoric, but tautegoric, the gods do not signify anything outside of themselves, but simply what they are. All revelation by the same token is tautegory.

The result of this levelling of Christianity to mythology is the triumph of critical apologetics: for now Christ is endowed with an historical reality again, the Incarnation is to be taken at face value, the bread and wine are not symbols but the flesh and blood of Jesus. The new mythological truth of Christianity is immediate, unconditional, "lived"; it is the reality not of representation of doctrine, but of a train of historical events which have truly taken place, even if they have existed only in the history of consciousness.

The literal historical event in the sense of the Enlightenment—which it had become abundantly clear the Christian story was not—was effectively transformed into a metaphysical event. For Schelling this carried the implication that ritual, rite, the reenacting of the metaphysical event, took precedence over doctrine; for Coleridge, as in his interpretation of the Genesis myth, the metaphysical event enacts its doctrinal significance. Schelling continued to stress the difference between myth and poetry, because he had still to combat the school of Heyne and Eichhorn, for whom poetry itself, artificial, intellectual, was tied to the allegorical tradition. But Coleridge identified poetry with myth; this being so, he could absorb allegory into his scheme of development, not as characterizing Christian thought as against myth, but as one legitimate phase of mythological poetry. This, of course, does not mean that poetry reproduces primitive myth, but rather that it creates, at each stage of the development of consciousness, the metaphysical event.

The old attempt to demonstrate the priority and superiority of Judeo-Christian revelation through the comparison of the religious imagery of the Greeks, the Hebrews, the Egyptians, the Persians, the Indians, became the attempt to comprehend the fundamental psychology of the human race. Man looking into his primeval religious history finds the depths of his present psyche. At the same time, though only by an immense expansion of Christian terms of reference and a complete recasting of the meaning of historicity, symbolic mythologists could defend Christianity as the culmination and expression of the whole range of human religious demands.

Schelling expressed the insight of the universality of the original significance of mythology in these Romantic terms:

> Man konnte die Mythologie etwa auch mit einem grossen Tonstück vergleichen, das eine Anzahl Menschen, die allen Sinn für den musikalischen Zusammenhang, für Rhythmus und Tact desselben verloren hatten, gleichsam mechanisch fortspielte, wo es dann nur als eine unentwirrbare Masse von Misstönen erscheinen konnte, indess dasselbe Tonstück, Kunstgemäss aufgeführt, sogleich seine Harmonie, seinen Zusammenhang und ursprünglichen Verstand wieder offenbaren würde.

> We can compare mythology with a great musical composition, which a number of men who had lost all sense for musical connexion, for rhythm and for measure kept on playing as if me-

chanically, so that only an inextricably confused mass of discords could result, whereas the same composition, artistically performed, would at once reveal again its harmony, its connexion, and its original meaning.

[*Einleitung in die Philosophie der Mythologie*]

Coleridge in "Kubla Khan," having not yet reached his own mature views of the nature of symbolic unity, was able to use the syncretist technique of "piecing out" from a diversity of culturally uprooted mythologies to create a unity of superimposed, overlapping images whose not quite exact correspondence sets their edges shimmering and revives each nation's failing gods into authentic universal life. In "Kubla," Coleridge gives us both the echo of the half-forgotten meaning of the races of the world, and a sense for the whole composition fully harmonized.

In his critical remarks on Cottle's epic *Messiah*, made in 1815, just after preparing the new preface to "Kubla Khan" for the first publication of the poem, Coleridge expressed fully the Romantic theory of the fragment as genre. The union of essential epic brevity with universal scope that he had described as the Miltonic idea of his own proposed epic in 1797 reappears, in the wake of his reading of Schelling, as a fully formulated aesthetic defence of the epic fragment:

> The common end of all *narrative*, nay, of *all*, Poems is to convert a series into a Whole: to make those events, which in real or imagined History move on in a strait Line, assume to our Understandings a *circular* motion—the snake with it's Tail in it's Mouth. Hence indeed the almost flattering and yet appropriate Term, Poesy—i.e. poiesis = *making*. Doubtless, to *his* eye, which alone comprehends all Past and all Future in one eternal Present, what to our short sight appears strait is but a part of the great Cycle—just as the calm Sea to us appears level, tho' it be indeed only a part of a globe. Now what the Globe is in Geography, *miniaturing* in order to *manifest* the Truth, such is a Poem to that Image of God, which we were created into, and which still seeks that Unity, or Revelation of the *One* in and by the *Many*, which reminds it, that tho' in order to be an individual Being it must go forth from God, yet as the *receding from him* is to *proceed* towards Nothingness and Privation, it must still at every step turn back toward him in order to *be* at all—Now a straight Line, continuously retracted forms of necessity a circular orbit. Now God's Will and Work CANNOT be frustrated.

History "real or imagined" is a linear series of metaphysical events bent by ultimate ends into the cyclical form that assures those ends.

The original monotheistic unity, loosed from time and space, formally achieves the status of symbol; but it refuses the title as long as "symbol" does not maintain a link, however tenuous, with an "event." Schelling redefined symbol, through Coleridge's "tautegory," so that it would do just that; and this too is the sense of the "reality" which in Coleridge's familiar definition of symbol is visible through its translucence. The achievement of "mental space" controlled by a firm unity that is a reminiscence of an only-just-abandoned claim to literalness depended on an Orientalism evolved through the exigencies of the higher criticism.

Kathleen Raine has said that with "the Hellenistic revolution" set in train by Thomas Taylor and culminating in Shelley,

> Polytheism had become the natural language of English poetry, not in the purely decorative sense in which Pope or Dryden adorned country squires and their elegant daughters with the names of gods and nymphs, but as a language of qualitative and metaphysical discourse.

This is half right. It was indeed a language of qualitative and metaphysical discourse; but it was so precisely because it was not the language of polytheism (any more than Plato's mythological language was). The new mythology, while honouring and incorporating the diversity of forms, specifically denigrated polytheism and sought a basis, historical and psychological, for an underlying "monotheism" or unity of numina.

Mythological interpretation depends on an already existing tradition whose terms can be used to "place" new events. Scholem, in *On the Kabbalah and its Symbolism*, points out that this is true of the whole mystical tradition—that whether it presents itself as radically reforming or as confirming ancient authority, its revelations are always in terms of its orthodox tradition. To put it crudely, Buddhists do not have visions of the Virgin Mary. Strauss falls back heavily on Jewish tradition for his explanation of the events of the life of Jesus. No one in England did more than Coleridge to show the nineteenth century the way to its form of vision: the imaginative renewal and maintenance of the past. But the dependence on tradition for explanation leaves its real sources obscured and finally buries the tradition itself. Coleridge's strong objections to Eichhorn's referring the art of John solely to preexisting usage in the other books of the Bible display his intense certainty that the springs of mythology must always rise freshly from the experience of the single seer.

As Empson has said of pastoral, "It is felt that you cannot have a proper hero without a proper people, even if the book only gives him an implied or magical relation to it." Coleridge carried pastoral to its outward bound, for the "hero" is the visionary poet who renews and reminds a people of the mythology without which they are not a people at all, but tribes of animals. And "the people" in this instance is humanity, the original humanity before the polytheistic dispersion. Traditionally, the hero was "half outside morality, because he must be half outside his tribe in order to mediate between it and God, or it and nature." The element of magic is inherent in this relation. "Magic" was whatever could restore humanity's sense of its own nature, which was bound up with its sense of the supernatural. This lost, the entire edifice of civilization, including the prized rationality, comes tumbling down.

Coleridge's syncretism, even working within the bounds of Christianity, gave him a range and depth and sympathy hardly to be found in any orthodoxy. It is just possible that a Buddhist might have a vision of the Virgin Mary—or of an Abyssinian maid. In that primitive yet cosmopolitan dawn just before the beginning of the nineteenth century it was not so evidently necessary that "The gods of China are always Chinese," as Wallace Stevens put it for our own tribal times in "Two or Three Ideas." Coleridge's transcendental enterprise was to lay bare the source of mythology, the sense for a God in the human race. In "Kubla Khan" we see the enterprise making its earliest and most attractive appearance, as we find there the sense for a God in its first pristine form, before articulation, before all tradition. It is first revelation, as it is last.

The Two Eternities: An Essay on Byron

G. Wilson Knight

A poet's work may often appear to contradict his life. With Lord Byron this is not so. He is, as a man, a vital embodiment of post-Renaissance poetry: a proud individualist, asserting the primacy of instinct through an agonized self-conflict. His social sympathies are violently given to causes of liberty. He incurs charges of immorality. He lives what others so often write, leaving his native land somewhat as Timon leaves Athens. That insistent aspiration, that aristocracy of spirit, met with variously in fiction after fiction, is here incarnate: more, it is given, as in Shakespeare's plays, an outward formulation in aristocracy of birth. Such aristocracy may be used in poetry to materialize an inner, spiritual, royalty, as in *Tess of the D'Urbervilles*: and Byron is so much the more effective, as a dramatic figure, by reason of his title. In close alliance he shows an ingrained Shakespearean respect for tradition, for history, increasing the agony and tension of revolt. He has weakness, and is tortured by a sense of sexual sin. The vice, weakness, and nobility behind all high literary adventures are his, as a man. How slight some famous poets might appear should we choose to scrutinize their apparent littleness, their failure to match in life the spectacular essences of their work. A slight shift of perspective and Wordsworth looks like an old maid; Coleridge becomes a not very pleasant blend of talkative don and dope-fiend; Keats an adolescent; Shelley a seraphic blur. But Byron has warm flesh and color. His life itself falls into poetic and tragic form. Mediterranean coasts are perennially fertilizing forces to northern poetry. Italy floods the Renaissance and particularly the Shakespearean consciousness; poets from Chaucer and Milton to Browning and Lawrence have travelled there; and many have managed to die there, or thereabouts. But Byron does it all more superbly than any. Greece—to put a subtle matter crudely—seems for some time to have been challenging our traditional

From *The Burning Oracle*: *Studies in the Poetry of Action*. © 1939 by Oxford University Press.

Christian culture, many poets offering an Olympian or Dionysian theology as co-partners with the Christian. Moreover, liberty—of spirit, mind, body, and community—has been for centuries a widening and pressing imaginative demand. Our dominant personal and communal poetic directions from Marlowe and Milton through Pope to Shelley, Browning, and Lawrence are, I should suppose, (i) something closely related to erotic instincts, and (ii) the cause of liberty. Byron suffers social ostracism and banishment for the one and death for the other. Incest, says Shelley, is a very poetical thing: presumably since every act of artistic creation involves a kind of incestuous union within the personality. Byron is suspected of it in actual fact. Next, he dies fighting for the perfect sacrificial cause: the liberty of Greece. He lives that eternity which is art. He is more than a writer: his virtues and vices alike are precisely those entwined at the roots of poetry. He is poetry incarnate. The others are dreamers: he is the thing itself.

His literary work (our only present concern) is continuous with these impressions. He did not at first see himself as a poet, as an early preface shows; and when he did start writing in earnest, went after stories of color and action. His human understanding is glamorous, his incidents well costumed. Piratical adventure mixes with passionate love; there is the flash of steel and smell of powder. His is a cruel, yet romantic, world where blood flows hot. It is objectively conceived. Byron can lose himself in creation of emotional shapes outside his direct experience. He will use a reverential Christianity for his purpose; but can equally well salute a dying Moslem in *The Giaour* with the consummate technical ease of:

> But him the maids of Paradise
>   Impatient to their halls invite,
> And the dark heaven of Houris' eyes
>   On him shall glance for ever bright.

This is a truly Shakespearean power, one with the impersonal historical interest of *Childe Harold* and his love of peoples and places generally. A strong sense of a particular and honorable past lingers round each person or place he touches. He is poetically sensitive to variations in human tradition and culture. He is cosmopolitan and extroverted. And yet his tales also express a certain violent and recurring psychological experience with mysterious depths of passion and guilt variously hinted or revealed. To this I give my primary attention.

The Giaour is a powerful example. The inside of mental agony is revealed, Byron's poetry piercing and twisting into its center:

> The mind, that broods o'er guilty woes,
>   Is like the Scorpion girt by fire;
> In circle narrowing as it glows,
> The flames around their captive close,
> Till inly search'd by thousand throes,

> And maddening in her ire,
> One sad and sole relief she knows,
> The sting she nourish'd for her foes,
> Whose venom never yet was vain,
> Gives but one pang and cures all pain,
> And darts into her desperate brain

The rhetorical tension is maintained with a never-failing grip. Each word is charged, each sentence tight. What universes are here housed in the tiny yet deadly form of the scorpion: its own venomous nature makes its agony the more terrifying. The little drama symbolizes the horror, which is one with the energies, of biological existence: it gets at the very nerve behind ecstasy and anguish alike. Byron's in-feeling into animal life and energy is from the start distinctive. *The Giaour* is rich with it:

> Go when the hunter's hand hath wrung
> From forest-cave her shrieking young,
> And calm the lonely lioness:
> But soothe not—mock not, my distress!

He continually attributes sensitive nerves and minds to the animal creation; or may delight in its more lyric vitalities, as when he sees a butterfly

> rising on its purple wing
> The insect queen of eastern spring

being chased by a boy, and makes subtle comparison between this and love. Either the fleeting loveliness rises far above the "panting heart," or, if caught

> With wounded wing, or bleeding breast,
> Ah! where shall either victim rest?
> Can this with faded pinion soar
> From rose to tulip as before?

See the choice placing of a well-considered diction; also the peculiarly soft use of consonants. Stern as are his tales, Byron's poetry masters with equal ease a lyric grace and wrenching guilt: and through all burns deep sympathy for animals, often small ones (as in Pope); which is again one with his penetration to the central energies, the springs of action, in beast or man. The two are continuous. The hero of *The Giaour* is typical of Byron's tales, a man in hell, yet unbowed, and with a certain obscurity as to the dark cause of his suffering:

> Wet with thine own best blood shall drip
> Thy gnashing tooth and haggard lip;
> Then stalking to thy sullen grave,
> Go—and with Ghouls and Afrits rave;
> Till these in horror shrink away
> From spectre more accursed than they!

This ends a passage of towering satanic virulence; and its compressed explosiveness must surely win respect even from those whose direct response will be most impeded by the traditionally modelled—though pulsing—phraseology. Though the hero retires to a monastery where it "soothes him to abide," for "some dark deed without a name," he nevertheless "looks not to priesthood for relief." The balance of some irreligious passion against orthodox Christianity approaches in tone that of *Eloisa to Abelard*; while the rejection of religious assistance as powerless to ease the dark anguish and alter an inevitable course recalls *Faustus, Wuthering Heights,* and Byron's own *Manfred.* The close is subdued:

> I would not, if I might, be blest;
> I want no paradise, but rest.

He would be buried with no record but a simple cross. The Moslem's hatred for the infidel is here burningly proud and fierce; but Christianity is also at the last reverenced. Such opposites of pagan fire and Christian gentleness are characteristically Byronic; and they are to be in poem after poem subdued, as here, to an eternal peace.

Perhaps Conrad in *The Corsair* is the finest of his early human studies:

> Lone, wild, and strange, he stood alike exempt
> From all affection and from all contempt.
>
> (I.11)

The narratives revolve generally on an inward psychic, or spiritual, conflict. Though Conrad is a pirate chief of stern and ruthless action, his is a deeply spiritual bitterness. His anguish is almost brutally revealed:

> There is a war, a chaos of the mind,
> When all its elements convulsed, combined,
> Lie dark and jarring with perturbed force,
> And gnashing with impenitent remorse.
>
> (II.10)

The lines suit Macbeth: and though we may be reminded of Crabbe the Byronic hero has a tragic direction not found in *Peter Grimes.* He is noble and Miltonic:

> His was the lofty port, the distant mien,
> That seems to shun the sight—and awes if seen:
> The solemn aspect, and the high-born eye,
> That checks low mirth, but lacks not courtesy
>
> (I.16)

No captive girls ever seduce his attention from Medora. "None are all evil" (I.12), we are told, and at the core of his personality is a love, a "softness"; this word, or "soft," recurring throughout Byron's work with the deepest central significance. In this very poem Antony is the "soft triumvir" (II.15). Conrad is, however, a grim figure; and his endurance whilst awaiting torture is given terrible poetic disclosure. Yet he refuses to save himself by a cowardly murder and is nauseated by a woman, Gulnare, doing it for him. Indeed, all horrors of his wide piratical experience or natural imagination are shown as nothing to that arising from this desecration of feminine gentleness. From none

> So thrill'd, so shudder'd every creeping vein,
> As now they froze before that purple stain.
>
> (III.10)

The passage is most powerful, tracing territories explored in the conception of Lady Macbeth. The hero suffers originally through determination to save women from his own piratical massacre: which, though perhaps irrational, is intensely Byronic. Frequently we come across such ruthless evil and cynical callousness enshrining a strangely soft, almost feminine, devotion. Conrad's heart "was form'd for softness, warp'd to wrong" (III.23). The poem's conclusion holds a reserved depth of feeling reminiscent of Pope. He finds Medora dead:

> He ask'd no question—all were answered now
> By the first glance on that still, marble brow.
>
> (III.21)

Notice how strongest emotion is uttered through a simple statement: "all were answer'd now"; and how that makes of one human death a vast eternity, almost an assurance. So

> his mother's softness crept
> To those wild eyes, which like an infant's wept
>
> (III.22)

Yet he is not sentimentalized. As in *Macbeth*, the poet dares to end with a condemnation, leaving the human delineation to plead its own cause:

> He left a Corsair's name to other times,
> Link'd with one virtue, and a thousand crimes.
>
> (III.24)

From the start, the central complex of loneliness and cruelty is undefined. The same figure recurs in *Lara*. Though cold, ruthless, and with a smile "waned in its mirth and wither'd to a sneer" (I.17) the hero is yet one "with more capacity for love than earth bestows" (I.18) on most men. The dark mystery shrouding his past is never lifted. They are all, like Heathcliff and Captain Ahab, personalities tugged by some strange evil between time and eternity.

The poetic vigour of each narrative, depending on choice and exact statement rather than abstruse analogy or magic sound, never fails. Subtle rhythmic variation may finely realize description, as this of a floating corpse, from *The Bride of Abydos*:

> As shaken on his restless pillow
> His head heaves with the heaving billow.
>   (II.26)

Continually a fine thing is said as a way to realize some great feeling. Especially strong are the darkest moments, as "I want no paradise, but rest" and "This brow that then will burn no more" from *The Giaour*. The decasyllabic couplets of *The Corsair* hold an equal tragic force:

> Oh! o'er the eye Death most exerts his might,
> And hurls the spirit from her throne of light.
>   (III.20)

Verbs play a major, often a dominating part, as in the remorseless beat of the line "Eternity forbids thee to forget" (I.23) from *Lara*. The diction accepts personifications of a vast yet simple and un-ornate kind, and traditionally "poetic" words of various sorts. These, as in Pope, are chosen to express a ready-made fusion of the particular and general. The influence of Pope may be at times very obvious, too, in couplet-modulation, as—to take random examples from a wide field—in *The Corsair*, I.11, and the lines beginning "No danger daunts . . ." from *The Bride of Abydos*, II.20. As in Pope, each word is exactly used but loaded with more than its natural maximum of force. The lines cry to be uttered and can be understood, if not fully appreciated, at once. The emotional precision is unerring, defined yet never metallic: like the twang of a taut string.

However perfect the control, the energies—spiritual or physical—set in action are striking. Many fine animal creations are symptomatic of the Byronic mastery of the vital and organic, as in the wild Tartar horse of the later story *Mazeppa* with the "speed of thought" in his limbs, and the other thousand with

> Wide nostrils never stretch'd by pain
> Mouths bloodless to the bit or rein
>   (XVII)

Byron feels in and with the animal. There is the "stately buffalo" with his "fiery eyes" and stamping hoofs attacked by wolves in *The Siege of Corinth* (XXIII); the insect stinging to save its property (compare the wren in *Macbeth*) and the adder seeking vengeance when trodden on, in *The Corsair* (I.13–14). The end of *The Prisoner of Chillon* provides perhaps the best; where the hero, after an eternity of dark imprisonment, has actually made such friends with the spiders of his dungeon and so long loved the mice at their "moonlit play" that he is reluctant to leave; and I doubt if the whole range of Byron's work provides a sweeter instance of his uncanny penetration into the most secret chambers of a mind in agony and loneliness. The moon in Byron has elsewhere such tragic associations. Continuous with these animal intuitions is the Shakespearean feeling for human personality, characterized by ability and desire to give vital action and project figures of innate dignity—quite apart from their ethical standing—and blazing courage; and women, including Gulnare in *The Corsair*, of an utterly instinctive, yet magnificent, devotion.

The tales are characterized by (i) vivid and colourful action, and (ii) a recurring psychological conflict normally related to some feminine romance-interest. You may get mainly action, as in *The Bride of Abydos* and the nightmare frenzy of the ride of *Mazeppa*; or mainly a psychological study, as in *Lara*. *The Corsair* I think the finest in its balance of both. The atmosphere of *The Giaour* is powerfully realized, but the hero's remorse seems disproportionate to the occasion. The central guilt-complex is, of course, always best left without premature definition, as in *Hamlet* and *Macbeth*. We can feel the poet aiming at a story-action that fits his intuition. However, in the tightly woven and sustained power of *Parisina* a short plot is cleverly devised to condition logically the mind-state of the Byronic hero, the story stopping where he begins. The perfect fusion of inward experience and active plot is never perhaps quite mastered. There is no deeply significant outer conflict, no clash of universal forces, unless the balance of religions in *The Giaour* might so qualify. Profundities are found in most searching human comment continually, but the action is not by itself profound. A bridge of some sort is needed; a conduit to flood the whole setting with something of the hero's tragic power. The narratives are to this extent slightly inorganic in comparison with Shakespeare: they have a hero, but no heart. A field of dramatic meaning has not been generated—an individual psychological and spiritual study, however deep, cannot quite do this—and the incidents and persons accordingly lose generalized significance and stature: though the tragic direction generally works to create a sense of some mysterious eternity at the close. Only a judgment most insensitive to the deadly marksmanship of Byron's peculiar excellences would stigmatize them as "melodramatic."

These tales of action and geographic color are strung together by a central, expressly personal, experience. The human penetration, the revelation of mental suffering, is always primary. But *Childe Harold* is more consistently extraverted, though it has a similar twofold appeal, with, again, a separateness: nature-descriptions, however, doing something towards a fusion, as I shall show. A series of meditations on places and events is given unity by the shadowy conception of Harold, that is, Byron. Yet, this once forgiven, we are struck by the amazing vitality of creation. Byron is the only poet since Shakespeare to possess one of Shakespeare's rarest gifts: that of pure artistic joy in the annals—after searching I can find no better word—of human action; in close association, moreover, with places. He feels the tingling nearness of any heroic past. Gray had something of this; so had Scott; and Hardy gets it in his *Dynasts* as a whole, perhaps, if not in the parts. This is something quite beyond our contemporary sophistication. It is an ability to love not mankind, as did Shelley, but men; and men—or women—of various sorts, places, and times:

> Is it for this the Spanish maid, aroused,
> Hangs on the willow her unstrung guitar
>
> (I.54)

Or, of Waterloo:

> And wild and high the 'Cameron's gathering' rose!
> The war-note of Lochiel, which Albyn's hills
> Have heard, and heard too have her Saxon foes—
> How in the noon of night that pibroch thrills
>
> (III.26)

And this of the dying gladiator:

> He reck'd not of the life he lost nor prize,
> But where his rude hut by the Danube lay
>
> (IV.141)

He is fascinated with the persons of one scene or event after another. The scattered incidents are given a sincere unity by the autobiographical thread; this extraverted interest, almost love, being integral to the Byronic imagination.

But the suffering behind every glamorous association is not forgotten. Historic excitement is often one with a condemnation of history: since a fundamental love of men is involved and history often cruel. For example:

> Ah, monarchs! Could ye taste the mirth ye mar,
> Not in the toils of glory would ye fret;
> The hoarse dull drum would sleep, and Man be happy yet!
>
> (I.47)

There is no facile militarism: but rather an opposition to the clang and fury of world affairs of simple—and often, as here, sensuous—joys. On the eve of Waterloo a "heavy sound" of cannon breaks short the pleasures of the dance. Then are there

> cheeks all pale, which but an hour ago
> Blushed at the praise of their own loveliness;
> And there were sudden partings, such as press
> The life from out young hearts, and choking sighs
>
> (III.24)

I point not merely to verbal excellences but to the especially impersonal, yet warm, sympathy with human instincts. So from "Beauty's circle" they are shown next in "battle's magnificently proud array"; and finally hurled, horse and rider, friend and foe, "in one red burial." The fervor which so admires courage and battle-finery is one with that which pities the transition from dance to slaughter. It is a total awareness of the Shakespearean sort. Byron can start to describe a bull-fight in a glamorous stanza (I.73) of steeds and spurs and ladies' eyes; only to give a poignant sympathy to the suffering of bull and horse in a "brutal" sport. The same sympathy is accorded the dying gladiator in Book IV butchered for Rome's enjoyment: yet this does not preclude a feeling for Rome's imperial greatness. The poet is aware of emotional opposites involving each other, or rather of a single emotion taking opposite forms of assertion and pathos: just as the agonized conflicts and evil passions of his heroes are somehow one with their instincts of chivalry and tenderness. So he lets himself be, as it were, annihilated continually before each splendor and pathos in turn.

His feeling for human nobility past and present is also one with his acceptance of a traditional poetic diction. This repays our close attention. Few poets have accomplished so much effortless force in single lines, as, for example:

> Stop!—for thy tread is on an Empire's dust!
> (III.17)

Or

> The spouseless Adriatic mourns her lord
> (IV.11)

Or

> Oh Time! the beautifier of the dead
> (IV.130)

The utterance is weighty yet carried easily: the thing said seems to be all in all, with no attempt at original expression. There is a play of metaphor and often what Ruskin—in a confused and misleading essay—named the "pathetic fallacy": but such call no attention to themselves and are accompanied by no especial excitement. The style here, as in the tales, is peculiarly assured, involving a use of words where the fusion of general and particular, philosophic meditation and objective description, has already been performed; though in *Childe Harold* both the general scheme and stanza form alike demand a more fluid and less packed and explosive language. No effort is expended on abstruse comparison or the jerking of word or image from its habitual use or associative value. Personifications and abstractions are frequent but never cloudy, denoting concepts generally accepted. They are always words of an adequate syllabic weight; words, as it were, tested in the past and found to ring true; words of poetic lineage. In the first two lines just quoted "tread," "dust," "spouse," "mourns," all strike me as examples of what might be called a middle diction, a workmanlike poetic, but not too poetic, manner. This may rise even to

> Their praise is hymn'd by loftier harps than mine
> (III.29)

without loss of sincerity. So we have strong nouns, plain, usually active, verbs, sentences cleanly turned out, well drilled, and marching to their purpose. No verbal magic is allowed at the expense of clarity. Similarly,

Byron's religious intuitions are based on a preliminary acceptance of the conventional, seen in the robust Johnsonian phraseology—as well as thought—of

> I speak not of men's creeds: they rest between
> Man and his Maker.
>
> (IV.95)

As a rule every accent is poetically distinguished with none superlative: nor meant to be. But the thing said, or the object seen, may be of superlative grandeur, as this, of Rome:

> The Niobe of nations! There she stands,
> Childless and crownless, in her voiceless woe.
>
> (IV.79)

The sympathy with the present pathos of ruins cannot be detached from that acceptance of the one-time historic splendor which also chooses well-worn associations such as the splendor of "nations," the awe of crowns, the traditional poetic appeal of a word such as "woe." Byron likes, as a poet, what is already warm with human contact. He injects into it his own vitality, whether in admiration or rebellion. He likes human society and its history: which is but a surface effect of that deeper infeeling into animal or human vitality that enables him to display both convincing action and a moving pathos.

And yet again he stands outside the world he writes of, balancing human purpose against human futility. *Childe Harold* is a lamentation in noble phrases over the widespread ruins of a dead chivalry and a dead tyranny. Byron is superbly conscious of the whole of Europe. But he also sees it as one vast theater of tombstones: though at his touch the dead are temporarily raised, and in the poetry there is no futility. He ranges across the centuries accepting and cherishing a past—or recent present—which he simultaneously repudiates and regrets. So he hymns empires whilst hating the wrongs of tyranny; recognizes the "lion" in Napoleon whilst decrying servility to "wolves" (III.19); glories in patriot battlefields though attacking the iniquities of wars by which monarchs "pave their way with human hearts" (I.42); at the limit, he praises life whilst entranced by death. He is a militant pacifist, exposing the fallacies of ambition (I.42–4). The tragic notes are his surest, the richer for the human excellences apprehended. The whole poem is written from a vast eternity-consciousness to which historic events, as events, are the negative symbols of its expression. There is thus a very "life" in "despair," a mysterious "vitality of poison" (III.34). Particulars are vivid chiefly by reason of their felt transience. Somehow their transience *is* their eternity:

> Far other scene is Thrasimene now
>
> (IV.65)

Or, when we come to Rome, the mystery of time itself takes ghostly form, entwined with infinite space and natural magic:

> But when the rising moon begins to climb
> Its topmost arch, and gently pauses there;
> When the stars twinkle through the loops of time,
> And the low night-breeze waves along the air
> The garland-forest, which the gray walls wear,
> Like laurels on the bald first Caesar's head;
> When the light shines serene but doth not glare,
> Then in this magic circle raise the dead:
> Heroes have trod this spot—'tis on their dust ye tread.
>
> (IV.144)

The grandeur of Rome lives most in its ruins. After visiting the Coliseum and wandering through memories of a dead empire we come to St. Peter's, which strikes from the poet both a magnificent religious fervor and subtle architectural appreciation in living terms, characteristically, of the *human* mind unable to take in the whole splendor with a single glance, yet at last distended to eternal comprehension; and end with the great invocation to the sea, imperial beyond all empires—

> Roll on, thou deep and dark blue Ocean—roll!
> Ten thousand fleets sweep over thee in vain.
>
> (IV.179)

With what sureness are handled, as in Gray's "Elegy," the noble platitudes so often composing the greatest poetry. "Assyria, Greece, Rome, Carthage, what are they?" he asks. Their life was conditioned by that spirit (he calls it "freedom" but perhaps we should give it a wider name) that alone can preserve, without which they are dust. That spirit is reflected by both (i) the poet's ranging consciousness—the "eternal spirit of the chainless mind" of his Chillon sonnet—autobiographical soliloquy significantly alternating with the scenic progress and reaching its culmination in the great personal apologetic and satiric outburst near the close; and (ii) the sea, unfettered by temporal law.

> Time writes no wrinkle on thine azure brow:
> Such as creation's dawn beheld, thou rollest now.

This vast unfathomable interlocks itself with that humanism, that social and historic sympathy, so dearly deep in Byron; something other, drawing him near the awestruck naturalism of Wordsworth.

Childe Harold has, continually, passages of more elemental sort, with also a continual swerve in comment from particular to general. My remarks on diction do not say the whole truth. Often a metaphor may start up with at once surface flash and revealing psychological depth, the more vivid for the generally level style:

And how and why we know not, nor can trace
Home to its cloud this lightning of the mind.

(IV.24)

Natural immensities fill out wide areas of the later Cantos III and IV, acting
as a bridge between the hero and his world: his own consciousness is shown
as, personally, more akin to them than to the human drama that was his
first story. The process reflects that dissociation found first in *Timon of
Athens* and urgent since: but no other poet of Byron's period shows a range
of sympathy sufficient to include both sides of the opposition. So the sea
is felt as a bounding freedom (as in *The Corsair*), especially freedom from
stifling human contacts (III.2,3). He now invokes "maternal Nature"
(III.46). That other vastness of mountains so weightily insistent in the imagination of Byron's day is duly honoured:

> Not vainly did the early Persian make
> His altar the high places, and the peak
> Of earth-o'ergazing mountains.
>
> (III.91)

Such an association may be referred back to both Wordsworth and Coleridge. But there are passages more finely detailed, more energy-striking
than this: as that describing the roar and hell-cauldrons of a "Kubla Khan"
mountain waterfall, the rising mist above, the ever fertilized green turf,
the peaceful river of the plain; and, as we look back, an Iris rainbow shot
through the dreadful waters, still and brilliant above agonized distraction,
like "Love watching Madness with unalterable mien" (IV.69–72): a line
whose depth and fervency of human—or other—understanding shows the
author to be, potentially, a tragic artist of Shakespearean stature. Often
such a swift transition transfixes its mark with quivering intensity: Byron's
nature-images are, normally, made to serve, or at least blend into, some
human purpose. But they are also great in their own right: so we have
"shaggy summits" (IV.73) where, when storm and darkness riot, there are
flashes lovely as—typically—a woman's "dark eye," as

> From peak to peak, the rattling crags among
> Leaps the live thunder!
>
> (III.92)

"Live": a living ecstasy continually energizes Byron's work. But he can also
treat of mighty glaciers or the placid Rhone with immediate descriptive
force. All such vast natural symbols objectify that in himself that demarks
him from men's society. Any man "who surpasses or subdues mankind"
is as a mountain looking on the hate of those below (III.45). Himself he is
a "portion" of that nature "around" him, rejecting the agonies of human
society, finding life in natural kinship with the "mountains, waves, and
skies," as "part" of his soul, and looking to death for cosmic freedom
(III.71–75). He knows the secrets of "pathless woods" and "lonely shore"

(IV.178). They and their eternity are the watch-towers from which he looks down on the rise and fall of empires. But he never for long forgets man. "I love not man the less but nature more" (IV.178) is really an overstatement. All his finest nature-impressions up-pile to blend with the supreme human grandeur of Rome. His mind outdistances his companions, that is all: if he could put all of himself into one word, that word were "lightning" (III.97). The choice is exact: and the image can be reversed. His brow, like that of his own Azo ploughed by the "burning share" of sorrow (*Parisina*, 20), may be, metaphorically, felt kin also to that of Milton's Satan which "deep scars of thunder had intrench'd"; or the She-wolf of his own description, the "thunder-stricken nurse of Rome" whose limbs lightning has blackened (IV.88); or, best of all, the bust of Ariosto "doubly sacred" by the thunder-flame that stripped it of its crown (IV.41).

Few poets show so instinctive a human insight: yet he is being forced against his will into the individualism of Wordsworth and Shelley. Yet there is a difference. He assimilates, but is not subdued by, the splendors of nature. He has been blamed for lightly and theatrically making poetic gestures not deeply felt; and it is true that certain lines in *Childe Harold* appear to merit the charge. Sometimes the transition from the more Augustan diction of the tales (mostly written before the latter Cantos of *Childe Harold*) to a newly vital nature-imagery is not perfect. Byron seems to gather in his new material with something of too sweeping a gesture, too aristocratic a superiority: he takes it for his own, more human, purpose. He is not, any more than Shakespeare, subdued to nature-mysticism. Yet he can, when he cares to, turn it to a far finer, because more human, account, as in the image of love and madness recently noticed, than any poet of his day. He is always above, not below, his contemporaries. The others rave over cataracts and mountains: and he too goes to mountains for inspiration. As it happens, they serve him magnificently: probably as a man, certainly as a poet. But they do not rank so importantly with him as that other more Shakespearean vastness, the sea. That from *The Corsair* (which contains some fine sea-poetry) to *The Island* and *Don Juan* is a permanent possession, whereas mountains affect him deeply only now, in mid-career. No English poet has written more finely of the sea, as in the rolling volumes—got by *o*-sounds—of

> Thou glorious mirror, where the Almighty's form
> Glasses itself in tempests; in all time,—
> Calm or convulsed, in breeze or gale or storm,
> Icing the pole, or in the torrid clime
> Dark-heaving—boundless, endless, and sublime,
> The image of eternity, the throne
> Of the Invisible; even from out thy slime
> The monsters of the deep are made; each zone
> Obeys thee; thou goest forth, dread, fathomless, alone.
>
> (IV.183)

"The image of eternity": the concept pulses throughout Byron's work. Contrast this with his great denunciatory and prophetic passage (IV.133–37) where he piles on the heads of mankind his curse of "forgiveness"; next strikes the exact note and manner of Pope's satiric epistles ("petty perfidy," "the small whisper of the as paltry few," "venom," "reptile"); and finally asserts the undying powers ("something unearthly") of his poetry to reassert his rights. You can see how the two elements—objective human interest and lonely individualism—of the early narratives are rending apart. He is torn between history and tragic insight, mankind and lonely self-conflict, time and eternity. The disparity is bridged by sea and mountains, infinite expanse and lifting mass, each at once symbols of both the natural and the eternal.

Byron: Troubled Stream from a Pure Source

Leslie Brisman

The conception of a true *world, the conception of morality as the essence of the world (these two most malignant errors of all time!) were once again, thanks to a wily and shrewd skepticism, if not provable, at least no longer* refutable. *Reason, the* right *of reason, does not extend that far. Reality had been reduced to mere "appearance," and a mendaciously fabricated world, the world of being, was honored as reality.*
—NIETZSCHE, *The Antichrist*

I tell you: one must still have chaos in one, to give birth to a dancing star.
—NIETZSCHE, *Thus Spake Zarathustra*

In his 1821 diary, Byron waives questions about origins with the studied nonchalance typical of the narrator of *Don Juan*: "If, according to some speculations, you could prove the World many thousand years older than the Mosaic Chronology, or if you could knock up Adam and Eve and the Apple and Serpent, still what is to be put up in their stead? or how is the difficulty removed? Things must have had a beginning, and what matters it *when* or *how*?" To the poet concerned with history, the prehistorical *when* did matter a great deal—if not in literal, calendar chronology, at least in terms of the mythic chronology of the passions, the prohibitions, the guilt. To the poet obsessed with the divorce between the tree of knowledge and the tree of life, it mattered *how* these emblems were represented in allusion and retellings of the myth. Perhaps most of all it mattered that questions of creation be deflected into awareness of the fallen world as we know it. Adam and Eve can scarcely be mentioned without a shift of interest to the apple and serpent, for the creation story remains a distant fiction while the Fall is a present truth. "With a characteristic ellipsis," writes Michael Cooke, "Byron blanks out the supposedly historical perfect world and shows the certified world going from bad to worse."

What Byron "blanks out" remains as much a presence in his poetry as the materials of repression are presences in the psyche generally. In *A Map of Misreading*, Harold Bloom suggests that a poet's greatest moments are related to his powers of repression, and his verse seems daemonized with special energy when presences the poet would rationally or consciously dismiss are given voice while an inner censor sleeps. Calvinist in temperament but no Christian in belief, Byron thought that an undisguised faith in a paradise was at the root of intellectual and social error. Whether

From *Romantic Origins*. © 1978 by Cornell University. Cornell University Press, 1978.

out of rivalry with Shelley on the subject of evil or simply in pursuit of the satirist's antimask, Byron implies that the history of inauthentic poetry—and the progress of the world at large from bad to worse—may be the responsibility of those who have failed to forget the belief in an anterior, perfect world. No doubt he would mock the idea of deep repression as much as he did the failure to put radical innocence out of mind, for Byron makes public the gesture of assigning nostalgias about an unfallen condition their proper place. What for others are the hidden workings of the psychic defenses and tropes of representation are often for him the surface subject or plaything of his verse. Remarkable always is the way he gets us to discard commonplaces about the traumatic or scandalous stuff of repression and to see sexuality and fallen experience as what we find acceptable to expose, while innocence and its priority need to be hidden.

I

Cain, Byron's most successful reworking of Genesis myth, announces from its very title the decentering of myth or the differentiating deferral from prelapsarian origins to fallen experience. Early on, the drama also makes clear a concomitant reversal of our ordinary sense of belatedness: radical innocence, not sexuality or a fall, is what we cover. Oblivious of the loincloth of Christian theology, Cain points to what seem to him to be unaccommodated facts:

> The snake spoke *truth*: it *was* the tree of knowledge;
> It *was* the tree of life: knowledge is good,
> And life is good; and how can both be evil?
>
> (I.i.36–38)

In hushing him, Eve asks Cain to content himself with what is, and let the innocence of his perspective be relegated back in history—and to the back of the mind. Bringing to the surface what Eve has repressed, the devil offers Cain knowledge, leading him to a different sort of statement than the one with which he confronted Eve: "It was a lying tree—for we *know* nothing" (II.ii.366). It is hard to be a devil of stature in the devil's presence, especially when Lucifer is contriving to accentuate his epigone's sense of creatureliness. The full daemonization of Cain depends on Lucifer's being gone, and Cain seems closest to the spirit whose presence he disdains when, away from Hades, he insists grandly on his innocence of the Fall and shares Lucifer's revaluation of temporal and moral priorities.

Byron shares them too. Before the drama proper he prefaces a note that ostensibly belittles a demonic stance: "The assertion of Lucifer, that the pre-Adamite world was also peopled by rational beings much more intelligent than man, and proportionably powerful to the mammouth, etc., etc., is, of course, a poetical fiction to help him make out his case." The particularities of this preexistence may be a "poetical fiction," but the interest in upsetting the priority of the received account is for Byron a most authentic business of poetry. In the play proper Byron dismisses the primacy of the Genesis creation and has Lucifer present visions of anterior worlds. At the same time, he images his own belatedness by centering on a fall after the inherited one, not on Adam but on Cain. References to earlier creation seem designed not for the assertion of temporal priority by itself but for the pressures they place on Cain to bear the burden of new anteriorities, and stand as the focal point on which the turn from the received to the new myth can pivot:

> CAIN: Where dost thou lead me?
> LUCIFER: To what was before thee!
> The phantasm of the world; of which thy world
> Is but the wreck.
> CAIN: What! is it not then new?
> LUCIFER: No more than life is; and that was ere thou
> Or I were, or the things which seem to us
> Greater than either.
>   (II.i.151–56)

If we read just the first two sentences of this exchange, we could entertain, with justified suspicion, the notion of a time machine. And "the phantasm of the world" seems a Luciferic reduction to the level of claptrap of Shelley's magnificent fiction of a shadow world in *Prometheus Unbound*. But contempt for such machinery is undermined when the word "world" is replaced by the word "wreck." If past glories are not as such to be recaptured, ruins of the past can still be very much present; if other worlds are the business of romancers turned science-fiction visionaries, still the belatedness of this world has an authentic ring. Thus, while we can hardly make a significant imaginative gesture toward recapturing the purity of origins—which belong somewhere back in God's country—we can come to recognize that we stand at a significant distance from such things, and can come to see an external Hades or a dark region of the mind haunted by the phantasms of anterior creation.

When Lucifer tells Cain that they are on their way to view shades of pre-Adamite beings, Cain's surprise, "What! is [the world] not then new?" presents the newness of the world balanced, as it were, on the tenuous point of the interrogative. For the moment Cain holds the world up on one questioning finger. Lucifer's casual shrug, "No more than life is," topples that world from its fragile axis. Though the action and reaction are verbal, "In the beginning was the Word," and this verbal exchange seems to demand priority over what is to be seen in space. "Language is properly the medium for this play of presence and absence," writes Derrida: "Is it not within language—is it not language itself that might seem to unify life and ideality?" For Lucifer and for Byron language rather separates present life from preconceptions of ideality, and a particular verbal exchange constitutes a particular victory over both the presence or givenness of spatial reality and the possibility of past spaces and times. At this point in Byron's drama the verbal exchange precedes the sight of anterior creatures and precludes the sight of alternate worlds. Lucifer does not take Cain to other planets but passes them by: "The lights fade from me fast, / And some till now grew larger as we approach'd / And wore the look of worlds" (II.i.167–69).

The experience of passing by these worlds preludes the experience of confronting shadows of the past and introduces the perspective from which dismissals prove more authentic than actual confrontations with preexistents could be. Indeed, Cain finds the trip he does take no match for his anterior and superior desires. But the attitude cultivated in outer space extends to contempt for priority more generally. Lucifer tells Cain,

> Many things will have
> No end; and some, which would pretend to have
> Had no beginning, have had one as mean
> As thou.

> (II.i.156–59)

Beginnings are mean things, and sublimity is to be sought not in the dawning of days or worlds but in what Nietzsche called the twilight of the gods— in grand dismissals of the past. Lucifer is thus educating Cain to the indifference toward beginnings that Byron expressed in his diary entry. Or perhaps more precisely, Lucifer is abetting the process that Byron's diary witnesses by which the sense of creatureliness (of feeling what Milton's Adam felt when he first woke and knew himself *made*) goes underground and is covered by indifference to origins and the posturings of a fallen angel.

Brought back to his own postlapsarian world, Cain finds the price of his proclaimed freedom from the past to be a radical naturalism, knowledge of mortal nature's nothingness regardless of (or repressing knowledge of) its Creator. When Cain's offering of fruits is scattered on the earth, he exclaims, "From earth they came, to earth let them return." This is *radical* innocence because rooted in the earth, ignorant of the fact of human death that lies hidden in the phrase as it lies hidden in Cain's effort to cast down Abel's altar and return it too to the earth. If Abel's piety leads him to acknowledge God as spiritual source, Cain's knowledge of the earth makes him stick to his earthy vision of origins.

"There may be always a time of innocence," Wallace Stevens tentatively proposes in *The Auroras of Autumn*: "There is never a place." Dismissing Jehovah as a bloodthirsty God who delights in sacrifice, Cain could be said to claim both "There never was a time of innocence" and "This must be the place." Insisting on the present time, the present place, he exclaims to Adah before Abel comes on the scene to make his sacrifice, "Why, *we* are the innocent." To make this a place innocent of sacrifice, sublimation, and all experiential orderings of the world into higher and lower, spiritual and earthy, Cain proposes leveling Abel's altar. He asks Abel to "Stand back till I have strew'd this turf along / Its native soil." The intended physical deconstruction of the altar and metaphysical deconstruction of the hierarchies it acknowledges may be taken as an emblem of Byron's lifelong efforts to reduce spiritual pretensions and fictions to their "native soil."

To challenge prevenient mythology, Byron needed to do more than inherit the dichotomies of good and evil, God and Satan, and choose the other side. Nor could he simply adapt the dual vision of man as both creation of God and creature of dust who to dust returns and create a protagonist who is wholly committed to one of these Biblical statements of origins. The conflict between Cain and Abel, while it concerns two views of man's original substance, subsumes an argument between two views of what constitutes original action. For Abel and for the Bible one discovers one's originality in relation to the Originator. For Cain and for Byron one does not discover one's originality in relationship to the Author of Evil; nothing can be thought "original" till it separates itself from relationship to sources. So Byron argues about his Cain in a letter to John Murray:

> Cain is a proud man: if Lucifer promised him kingdom, etc., it would *elate* him: the object of the Demon is to *depress* him still further in his own estimation than he was before, by showing him infinite things and his own abasement, till he falls into the frame of mind that leads to the Catastrophe, from mere internal irritation, not premeditation, or envy of *Abel* (which would have made him contemptible), but from the rage and fury against the inadequacy of his state to his conceptions.

If Cain's action is to be his own, not Satan's, it must be motivated by "internal irritation," not a larger dialectical quarrel with God in which he would be a victim, and no originator. Even envy would not have been sufficiently his own, depending directly as it does on awareness of the priority of the envied. To the scene of the murder Cain brings a preexistent sense of infinite things and a preexistent sense of abasement, of dust-to-dust, both of which have been abetted by Lucifer. Impelled toward both awarenesses, he is now on his own; and if the glory seems a vision borrowed or imposed, the naturalistic dismissal of preexistent sublimity is something experienced as original to the self.

From his flight with Lucifer, Cain returns to his natural existence, his existence as natural man—a paterfamilias, a man of the earth, one who feels his littleness far more native to his consciousness than his memory of "extinguish'd worlds." The glory he could call his own would come from the possibility of transcending memory, transcending the givenness of the past, and striking (if need be, with a deathblow) a point for the originality of the self. Writing of Proust, Gilles Deleuze voices a kind of credo for the mind unextinguished by its immersion in preexistent materials: "It is no longer a matter of saying: to create is to remember—but rather, to remember is to create, to reach that point where the associative chain breaks, leaps over the constituted individual, is transferred to the birth of an individuating world." Blake repeatedly finds this point; Byron repeatedly discovers it to be an illusion. His Cain is disappointed in the possibilities of breaking the chain of the past and attending the birth of an individuating world; he is confronted instead with the natural birth of an individual—his flesh-and-blood son—a birth which, in Byron's telling revisionist chronology, antedates the slaying of Abel. When Adah berates Cain, "Do not whisper o'er our son / Such melancholy yearnings o'er the past," she voices the simple demystification that would put all hankerings for romantic origins in their place. It is the kind of rebuke Byron himself makes of Cain's weak desires, and of his own moments of soft romanticism from the lingering over childhood scenes in *Hours of Idleness* to the moments of innocence in the Haidée episode of *Don Juan*. Adah continues with cheerfulness she seems to have picked up from the end of *Paradise Lost*: "Why wilt thou always mourn for Paradise? / Can we not make another?" But the awareness of death intervenes and keeps Cain (to borrow Byron's own term from the letter) "depressed."

This depression is not simply sadness but the reduction of man to his earthy origins and first nothingness. Tiller of the soil, father of an earthly creature who is overshadowed by cypresses and the fact of death, Cain finds that the awareness of man's grotesque lowness is the concomitant of his sublime ambition to stand original and free. "Nota," says Stevens's rejuvenated Crispin: "His soil is man's intelligence. / That's better. That's worth crossing seas to find." Cain has crossed vast seas of space and thought with Lucifer to find this soil the sum total of his intelligence and knowledge. In a terrible irony, even the soil is alienated from Cain when it absorbs Abel's blood; as a vagabond, Cain will be estranged from the earth he had thought most truly his own.

In Genesis, Cain protests that his burden is too great and that whoever finds him will slay him. In Byron, Adah voices these objections while Cain himself asks to be allowed to die. The visual brand on the forehead is thus all the more imposed and is accompanied by a verbal brand: "Stern hast thou been and stubborn from the womb, / As the ground thou must henceforth till" (III.i.503–4). These signs of separation magically rouse Cain into authentic voice, for he speaks now with Shakespearean power and Miltonic resonance, but comes into his own:

> After the fall too soon was I begotten;
> Ere yet my mother's mind subsided from
> The serpent, and my sire still mourn'd for Eden.
> That which I am, I am; I did not seek
> For life, nor did I make myself; but could I
> With my own death redeem him from the dust—
> And why not so?
>
> (III.i.506–12)

Truer than the plain fact ("I did not seek / For life") is the extraordinary imaginative independence that comes precisely in the diminished idea of causality—the narrowed sense of priority that nevertheless aggrandizes the self. The opening lines of this speech are like those of Shakespeare's Edgar saving for himself what little imaginative freedom is left after the wheels of causality have rolled to this catastrophic point: "The dark and vicious place where thee he got / Cost him his eyes." Asserting the metaphor-making power (the power of localizing a symbolic topos or a time) over the catastrophe from which the need for metaphor springs, these speeches leave the imagination triumphant yet. Byron's Cain seems to surpass Edgar in moving from slender to full-fledged self-assertion: "That which I am, I am." If the power of this seems limited by our awareness that it is borrowed from Milton's Satan (Tennyson's Ulysses will be similarly threatened), it becomes all the more Cain's and Byron's own when compacted with a new, unsatanic—indeed, Christ-like—impulse. Even if it does come from despair, the wish to redeem Abel by sacrificing himself seems to contradict everything Cain stood for in opposing Abel and the sacrifice-loving God Abel worshiped. But instead of a capitulation, these lines, so summarily dismissed by the angel, represent a final fictiveness, a last emblem of the mind's capacity to transcend its circumstances and create its own vision of things.

The power given to the branded Cain is like that Byron gives his Prometheus: "Thou art a symbol and a sign / To mortals of their fate and force." Turned into signs, Cain and Prometheus have restored to them a purity of figuration which asserts both the individual origination of their actions and their special connection with ultimate origins. One's act is divine, one's demonic, but branded forever they share the fate of having their daemonized power abstracted from their persons and made a sign of the human condition. We do not worship, but we "read" or recognize the sign, point to it and say:

> Like thee, Man is in part divine,
> A troubled stream from a pure source;
> And Man in portions can foresee
> His own funereal destiny,
> His wretchedness, and his resistance,
> And his sad unallied existence.
> To which his Spirit may oppose
> Itself.
>
>   ("Prometheus")

II

The idea of a "pure source" can be safeguarded from both the assaults of experience and the jibes of the worldly satirist by appearing to be translated from this earth to some imaginatively anterior one. In the diary entry quoted at the beginning of this chapter, Byron speculates on an original innocence: "I sometimes think that *Man* may be the relic of some higher material being, wrecked in a former world, and degenerated in the hardships and struggle through Chaos into Conformity." The stipulation of *material* being guards the innocence of the idea of preempting the satirist's ammunition and imagining man's faded spirit to have the form, originally, of a more fulfilled natural man. In the context of his satirical poems, Byron makes the anterior world that of sexuality which, he loves to protest too much, he has long renounced. Man's "original" moments, to be recalled but not recovered, are moments of satisfied love:

> No more—no more—Oh! never more on me
> The freshness of the heart can fall like dew,
> Which out of all the lovely things we see
> Extracts emotions beautiful and new.
>
> (*Don Juan*, I.214)

As an addition to the manuscript of *Don Juan*, this little nostalgia for innocence appears mid the flamboyant posturing with something of the air of an aria mid recitatif telling the story of decay.

A similar tone is struck when Byron explains his treatment of Contessa Guiccioli to the Countess of Blessington: "I am worn out in feelings; for, though only thirty-six, I feel sixty in mind, and am less capable than ever of those nameless attentions that all women, but, above all, Italian women, require." (The man who could no more resist adding that last particularizing slur than he could resist sexual objects of any sex, any nationality, was not to be worn out.) Blessington records Byron's myth of imaginative independence as that of an antecedent world from which the imagination, like a Son of God, emerges never to be capable of feeling quite at home with a single, belated Daughter of Man:

> The way in which I account for it [my boorishness, or the "something . . . in the poetical temperament that precludes happiness"] is, that our *imaginations* being warmer than our *hearts*, and much more given to wander, the latter have not the power to control the former; hence, soon after our passions are gratified, imagination again takes wing, and finding the insufficiency of actual indulgence beyond the moment, abandons itself to wayward fancies, and during this abandonment becomes cold and insensible to the demands of affection. . . . It is as though the creatures of another sphere, not subject to the lot of mortality, formed a factitious alliance (as all alliances must be that are not in all respects equal) with the creatures of this earth, and, being exempt from its sufferings, turned their thoughts to brighter regions, leaving the partners of their earthly existence to suffer alone.

Depicting the imagination as a "creature of another sphere," he grants it priority, so that turning away from a particular alliance and letting one's fancy wander back to the brighter regions becomes a matter of visionary loyalty to the mind's original place. Whether the marriage is that of man's spirit to his natural being or more literally the entanglement of a man with an actual lady, the marriage metaphor allows for both the legitimate pull into nature and the legitimized resistance to that pull on the grounds that spirit would be pulled down into unequal alliance. The concept of "factitious alliance" provides a vehicle for the conflicting ideas of origin: spiritual preexistence and demystified naturalism.

Obviously the concept of "factitious alliance" was attractive to Byron the man, allowing him to turn biographical facts into a kind of personal fall myth. The concept also has much to do with the structure of *Don Juan* and the way originality is regained in the love encounters. But let us turn, rather, to a poem whose more muted tones give the romantic alternative to naturalistic origins a better chance.

III

The advertisement to the 1814 edition of *Lara* seems to play coyly with the nature of the "factitious alliance" of the hero and heroine of the poem: "The reader of *Lara* may probably regard it as a sequel to a poem that recently appeared: whether the cast of the hero's character, the turn of his adventures, and the general outline and colouring of the story, may not encourage such a supposition, shall be left to his determination." If we follow these suppositions, Lara and Kaled are Conrad and Gulnare of *The Corsair* now caught in the unequal alliance of preoccupied man and devoted lady. What these identifications tell us about either poem is more difficult to determine. Byron seems to be toying with the concept of origin, as though seeing *Lara* as sequel to *The Corsair* answered questions about the genesis of the poem or about the mysterious preexistence of its hero. But the plot of *Lara* seems to be neither dependent on nor significantly clarified by the story of *The Corsair*, and it is not immediately apparent what insight we gain into one dark hero by the suggestion that he is to be identified with another, equally mysterious character.

The story of *Lara* may be briefly stated. After a long absence, Lara returns to his feudal seat accompanied by his faithful page Kaled. At a party some time later, Lara is recognized by Ezzelin, who, before he can challenge Lara or reveal Lara's past identity or crimes, mysteriously disappears. Hostility to Lara grows, and in an all-out battle Lara is mortally wounded. He is attended in his dying moments by Kaled, whose grief reveals her identity as a woman.

As Byron himself commented on the tale, "it is too little narrative, and too metaphysical to please the greater number of readers." The "metaphysical" quality needs to be discussed, though we may dismiss Byron's habitual protestations that his poetry was carelessly composed and insignificant. There is too little narrative in *Lara* for the "metaphysical" cast not to be a conscious goal, and one belies the work by seeming to discover, as critics have done, the obvious clanking of gothic machinery and the overt resort to mysterious silence.

In general, Byron's fondness for mystery is almost as great as his delight in satiric demystification. The poet of *Don Juan*, for example, toys with the penchant for the secret, protesting that he will, rather, be perfectly open. Introducing Haidée and Zoe, he declares, "I'll tell you who they were," as if to forestall dark conceits about their nature. "Besides, I hate all mystery, and that air / Of clap-trap which your recent poets prize" (II.124). More than an incidental laugh at his own "clap-trap," the dismissal of mystery underlies the genuine effort at the pristine. Not simply gothic trappings but the sophisticated joking about trappings must be gotten out of the way if the Haidée episode is to glimpse an unsophisticated simplicity. Later in *Don Juan* the demystification is less gentle, and it is worth recalling the last episode of that poem to keep in mind how much of what came easiest to Byron had to be laid aside in cultivating the "metaphysical" in *Lara*.

Here is Juan reacting to sounds of the Black Friar ghost's reappearance:

> Were his eyes open?—Yes! and his mouth too.
> Surprise has this effect—to make one dumb,
> Yet leave the gate which eloquence slips through
> As wide as if a long speech were to come.
> Nigh and more nigh the awful echoes drew,
> Tremendous to a mortal tympanum:
> His eyes were open, and (as was before
> Stated) his mouth. What open'd next?—the door.
> (XVI.115)

The listing of opened apertures prepares for the openness of the full naturalistic disclosure to come: the phantom is "her frolic Grace," the very much flesh-and-blood (though not too much flesh, indulged taste makes Byron pause to note) woman. The revelation of Fitz-Fulke is a veritable apotheosis of naturalism, defeating once and for all any pretenses to possible sublimity. What is banished for good is not simply the ghost-as-mystery, but more particularly the Black Friar ghost, the ghost that recalls a lost patrimony and, by extension, betrayed spiritual paternity. It is just those suggestions that *Lara* would explore, raising the metaphysical speculation of whether "some higher material being" and not simply some natural woman may lie at the origin of the story and the center of its mystery. But let me delay our return to *Lara* a little longer to glean from the *Don Juan* stanza a symbol and theme central as well to the earlier poem.

Caught with his mouth open, unable to speak, Juan is comically but significantly restored to an innocence that would fit him not for the degenerate Fitz-Fulke but for the more primary beauty (whose very name suggests beginnings), Aurora. Throughout *Don Juan* speech is the mark of the fall, and the hero's ease at social pleasantries betrays his distance from "higher material being." Aurora disdained Juan's talk, but "approved his silence" (XIV.106). "The ghost at least had done him this much good / In making him as silent as a ghost" (XVI.107). Insofar as the ghost in this ghostly silence is man's ghost or *geist*, his spiritual nature, Juan finds revived in him "the love of higher things and better days," glimpsing thus the vision of preexistent sublimity that haunts Byron, though not usually his hero in *Don Juan*. Aurora herself seems to come from such another world, and is preserved from degeneration by the outward manifestation of spiritual quietude:

> The worlds beyond this world's perplexing waste
> Had more of her existence, for in her
> There was a depth of feeling to embrace
> Thoughts, boundless, deep, but silent too as Space.
>
> (XVI.48)

From her perspective we can look back at the several ladies of the epic and find them measured by their talk. Julia, who has the priority only in terms of biography or biology in Juan's life, falls into the poem's longest speech when first discovered by Alfonso. If nature is thus victorious in Canto I, the Haidée episode images a prenatural sublimity in portraying the lady coping with the pleasing restraint of a language barrier. That Edenic possibility closed, the poem moves to a parody of the speech problem when Gulbeyaz expects Juan to melt by her "merely saying, 'Christian, canst thou love?' " (V.116). From the still more depraved Catherine we get no direct words.

Keeping in mind the Haidée episode, where the language problem is recognized and valorized, we may return to *Lara*, where master and page share memories of a preexistent state under the cloak of a foreign tongue. "Cloak" belies the innocence of their speech, however, for the magic of the former language is that it is spoken not behind doors but in all openness, entrancing its uncomprehending auditors. *Lara* is perhaps Byron's most silent poem, and we stand in relation to it as do the retainers or antagonists of Lara when the communication with Kaled is not to be shared. What Byron says of his hero can thus comment on or forestall what others could say of Byron here: "His silence formed a theme for others' prate" (I.17). We cannot dismiss *Lara* as a simple tale overlaid with mystery, because silence is theme, story but the setting in which the central silence can be examined and admired.

As the poem opens it presents in setting what I have described in theme. Lara is returned, and "The gay retainers gather round the hearth, / With tongues all loudness and with eyes all mirth." The gathering round of loud-tongued retainers is pictorially representable as a magic circle, and it describes in social terms what Wordsworth might have called a central silence at the heart of endless agitation. The potential is all there at this point for a tale like Keats's *Eve of St. Agnes*, or, a little later, *Lamia*. But Byron deliberately suppresses narrative and gives mystery its barest background.

One fact seems both to call for and strangely to defeat further explanation. Since Lara is returned, he does not descend into the poem like a Christ figure into earth, trailing clouds of preexistent glory from the soul's home. The land to which he returns *is* home, and the otherworldliness has been acquired elsewhere, in a place not native to him. In a way this simple story-fact captures all that story can do to dramatize the conflicting claims of natural and supernatural origins. The fatherland seems less one's own than some other land one has made one's own, for natural and spiritual paternities seldom correspond. The question of priority is complicated by the question of whether the fatherland is a place to live or a place to die. Corresponding to the sense that *Lara* has "too little narrative," that the story is essentially over before the poem begins, would be the hero's sense that his life has really been lived elsewhere. He is now but the shadow of himself, a death-in-life figure, or, more accurately, the remains of a figure of spiritual life returned to the death that is natural life.

The conflict between spiritual and natural paternities, or perhaps more accurately between the alternate voids of both failures of relationship, is expressed in the second stanza's description of Lara, "Left by his sire, too young such loss to know / Lord of himself—that heritage of woe." As Byron discovered biographically and dramatized in stories of absent or hostile father figures, one is not simply left to oneself by a father's death; to take the self as one's domain one must both abandon a natural patrimony and seize or create a realm elsewhere. To discover in the self a "heritage of *woe*" one needs to conceive of experiential possibilities as exhausted and one's futurity burdened by belatedness. With all but the woe spent from the self-heritage, Lara returns to the patrimonial heritage, almost knowing, perhaps, that that too will be shortly spent.

In the years away was the domain of self conquered or squandered? One could retreat to the pun on a life "spent" and say simply that the gaining is the spending. Byron gives the two actions just a little more space than they would have in a pun and depicts self-knowledge as the waking from self-indulgence. A manuscript reading, "for his feelings sought / Their refuge in intensity of thought," is corrected to read, "his feelings sought / In that intenseness an escape from thought" (I.8). "Escape" suggests that self-consciousness surrounds indulgence, preceding and following it, and evading questions about anteriority. In lines that follow, however, experience becomes not the void between moments of heightened awareness, but the height from which awareness of the soul's home can spring: "The rapture of his heart had look'd on high, / And ask'd if greater dwelt beyond the sky." Does the question signify assurance and satisfaction, challenging heaven to provide greater pleasures than those enjoyed? Or does the question, disdaining all earthly achievement, point via the appetite's insatiableness to the soul's infinity? The glimmer of ambiguity provides a glimpse at the mystery of *Lara*, the dark relationship between past experience and the kind of alternate celestial worlds Lucifer and Cain passed by.

The mystery is intensified (one cannot really say "explored") in the stanzas that follow. In the portrait gallery, "where his fathers frown'd," Lara's attendants heard "The sound of words less earthly than his own." What or whose words these may be, if they be, "must not be known." To say that mystery here is serving its own purposes is to be on precisely the right track, though to say that mystery without communication is gothic claptrap seems to me to avoid both the intention and achievement of such episodes. Parody of such moments will come soon enough in *Don Juan*; and exploitation of such moments requires more narrative—the kind of mystery that provides significant or misleading clues, not the deliberate paucity of detail we find here. We are given simply the suggestion of voices, "the sound of words" without the words, and the single descriptive detail—always ready, in gothic literature, to turn from adjective to verb—of frowning fathers in the portrait gallery. If those portraits were to respond to Lara, would their frowns or voices be the communication of dead fathers to their heir, or would they be protesting the intrusion of another ghost, another voice out of the past that belongs to Lara alone and not to them? The moment is too tenuous to permit such speculation to take hold, but again a manuscript revision points to Byron's care with suggestive ambiguity. "The sound of words less earthly than his own" was originally written, "The sound of other voices than his own." The original line is closer to claptrap, allowing suggestions of a general communication with the dead or, for possible naturalistic solution, voices of the living; the revised line properly focuses the ambiguity on communication "less earthly" because spoken by a spirit of the earth's past or a spirit from other realms and other skies.

A similar ambiguity attends a fearful call one night when the palace occupants hear a sound that rouses them from their sleep and confronts them with preoccupied Lara's bad dream—or what may be the pre-occupied palace's ghostly Presences:

> 'Twas midnight—all was slumber; the lone light
> Dimm'd in the lamp, as loth to break the night.
> Hark! there be murmurs heard in Lara's hall—
> A sound—a voice—a shriek—a fearful call!
> A long, loud shriek—and silence; did they hear
> That frantic echo burst the sleeping ear?
> They heard and rose, and tremulously brave,
> Rush where the sound invoked their aid to save;
> They come with half-lit tapers in their hands,
> And snatch'd in startled haste unbelted brands.
>
> (I.12)

As in Coleridge's *Christabel*, question and answer suggest the disparity between spiritual quest and the declarative nature of the world we know. When Lara wakes with (or is it "to"?) a shriek and fearful call, the sound of words puzzles his attendants, for the delirious prince speaks in what seem to be "accents of another land" (I.13). Neither attendants nor readers discover what those words are, though it is not difficult to say that they have more to do with the "sound of words less earthly" than with anything explicable in "his native tongue." At this point we are given what comes closest to being a narrative thread to seize on. Lara's words were "meant to meet an ear / That hears him not—alas, that cannot hear!" If we are tired of mystery, we can use this thread to weave the connection between *Lara* and *The Corsair*. Lara would thus have had a dream of his dead love Medora, who "cannot hear," and would be comforted by Gulnare-Kaled, who knows of Medora, can speak her language, and at least quiet the spirit of the man she cannot distract into love.

To say that such are the identifications behind the "mystery" is less to resolve than to deny the mystery and its richness. If we turn back to the dream night we can discover more from the setting, the poetry that lies just outside narrative:

> It was the night, and Lara's glassy stream
> The stars are studding, each with imaged beam;
> So calm, the waters scarcely seem to stray,
> And yet they glide like happiness away;
> Reflecting far and fairy-like from high
> The immortal lights that live along the sky.
>
> (I.10)

A small but not insignificant contribution to the air of romance may be noted in the identification of the stream as "Lara's." The country too is called "Lara's" rather than by any national name, and in general the paucity of proper names or properly externalized events makes one view what story there is as belonging more to the psyche than the person of Lara. The commerce between external and internal nature seems imaged in the lines about reflection. It is not that the mind, like the stream, receives images of external nature; rather, the stream for the moment seems to image a higher spiritual reality represented by the stars. Waters that "glide like happiness away" are easily enough separated from the human emotion they are said to represent. But "The immortal lights that live along the sky" are not so easily divorced from the anthropomorphic, the inspiriting humanization of the verb "live." The adjective "immortal" moves the description into a realm of higher being, thus insulated, as it were, from assaults of self-consciousness about such projections. The riverbed seems a little Eden, complete with flowers and waters "mazy like the snake." To Lara, who feels he is already fallen, such Eden vision is best left alone, for its unadulterated perfection but "mock'd such breast as his." This mockery takes the place of the ordinary mockery satiric naturalism directs at visions of "higher spirit," and at the myths of organized religion generally. Here, where any potential demystifying mockery would have to be spirit's scorn of flesh, "You scarce would start to meet a spirit there."

What kind of spirit? Some daughter of God come down to mingle with the sons of men? Or some ghost of a daughter of man, haunting the consciousness of Lara as fallen son of God? To rephrase, would one imagine such a spirit come from man's mythic, idyllic past, or Lara's biographical, actual past? The alternatives, for the moment, mingle. If stars in water are a visual illusion and spirits in nature a romantic fantasy, the mingling of mythic and personal past is nonetheless a real mingling. Lara is painfully reminded "of other days, / Of skies more cloudless, moons of purer blaze." By itself "other days" most properly belongs to his personal past, while the purified scene belongs to imagination's ideal or anterior world. One can neither scorn Byron's fancied "higher spiritual being" as the delusion of young love nor scorn young love as an inadequate vehicle for the sense of spiritual being. Scorn is preempted by this fallen spirit who remembers what he was yet must endure the descent into nature or the nature of loss.

In a stanza Byron added to the original manuscript, Lara's relationship to his Luciferic literary ancestry is made explicit:

> As if the worst had fallen which could befall,
> He strove a stranger in this breathing world,
> An erring spirit from another hurl'd;
> A thing of dark imaginings.
>
> (I.18)

Taken by themselves, either the implied satanism or the naturalistic pity for lost love would seem self-indulgent. Tenuously identified, the spiritual potential of each is given a local habitation in the other. In *The Corsair*, Conrad is a little too good to be thought capable of grand satanic crimes. *Lara* taints its hero with just a suggestion of something less than sweet. Aloof from others, his mind dwelling "in regions of her own," Lara is capable of fixing himself upon others' memory like a serpent round a tree. The detail may be there to prepare for Ezzelin's recall; more significantly, it keeps the suggestions of spirit menacing as they are attractive. Lara himself is the most menaced, victim of his own power to defy forgetfulness.

The introversion of this power is dramatized in the encounter with Ezzelin, who points to Lara at Otho's party the way Keats's Apollonius stares down the no less serpentine Lamia. These demystifiers would clear away all but memory of the actual, historical past. Yet an incomplete exposure only mystifies further, and Ezzelin leaves Lara with the cryptic warning, "O! never canst thou cancel half her debt, / Eternity forbids thee to forget" (I.23). Is the debt memory's debt to Eternity or Lara's debt to a specific lady? The abstractness or absence of the antecedent for "her" only heightens the thematic mystery concerning antecedence and forgetting. Though the encounter with Ezzelin is as spare of detail and information as was Lara's dream, its very silence tells us more than details of the past could. Ezzelin's questions, "how came he thence?—what doth he here?" (I.22), seem not to demand an account of the slings and arrows of Lara's outrageous fortune but to strip away the accidents of fortune and confront Lara's romantic origins. Robert Gleckner calls the Ezzelin encounter "a transparent device to dramatize the presentness of all the past and the inescapability of one's self, one's inner world." Ezzelin's own mysterious disappearance, while teasing the fancy into inventing story explanations, arouses the imagination to confront Ezzelin as a specter of Lara himself. Instead of asking, "What did they do with Ezzelin?" we are directed to more Wordsworthian intimations: "Whither is fled the visionary gleam? / Where is it now, the glory and the dream?" Not that Ezzelin embodies glory and dream, but his presence marked the presence of the question to Lara. As voiced by the poet, the question asked the next day about Ezzelin teases us out of thoughts about visionary gleam: "But where was he, that meteor of a night, / Who menaced but to disappear with light?" (II.6).

At a moment of visionary failure, Wordsworth looks around him and finds "waters on a starry night / Are beautiful and fair; / . . . But yet I know, where'er I go / That there hath past away a glory from the earth." If we turn back from the night of Ezzelin's disappearance to the night of Lara's dream, we can find in the waters of the starry night reflections of glory past. Lara is a fallen star, and Ezzelin, "meteor of a night," an image of star's fall—its fading into the light of common, naturalistic day. Inasmuch as these star references are images, they suggest that an experiential loss is being treated, under the license of romantic hyperbole, as a Lucifer-like fall from heaven. But in a poem so spare, where these few images are so much the light and the life of the poem, we are thrown back into the romance element with the conviction that story details, experiential losses, can only represent the "starry connaissance" that makes metaphoric language closer to reality than narrative plain song. While the story lasts, the relative claims of starry and earthy realities, spiritual and natural origins, must be kept in balance. The ambiguity is represented, for example, by the description of Lara leaving Otho's party with Kaled. "His only follower from those climes afar, / Where the soul glows beneath a brighter star" (I.25). If "climes afar" describes the ordinary territory of romance, the extent to which this distance is natural or supernatural depends on whether one emphasizes "beneath" or "star." Nature lovers flourish beneath their star, but the star represents all that transcends nature and connects man to primeval glory. Love is, the poet says in *The Giaour*, "A spark of that immortal fire / With angels shared" (lines 1132–33).

Only after Lara's death does the poem return to the night of the encounter with Ezzelin, as if to record that the stars shine still though the flesh is mortal. With the death of Lara the character, the poem can dispense also with the ordinary bounds between man and man or mind and mind that keep one literary figure an antagonist rather than a projection of another. In terms of the story, the demystification of Lara—when our hero is reduced from the ambiguous element Byron elsewhere calls "fiery dust" and is returned to dust—is followed by the demystification of Ezzelin's death. But whether we are wholly in the realm of nature now remains a further mystery. The story of Ezzelin's death is separated from the main narrative by being presented as a peasant's tale. Within that tale comes the poem's most startling detail, all the more prominent if the peasant's tale is read beside Byron's source, where the detail is not to be found. The Serf watches the stream into which a body has been cast:

> He caught a glimpse, as of a floating breast,
> And something glitter'd starlike on the vest;
> But ere he well could mark the buoyant trunk,
> A massy fragment smote it, and it sunk:
> It rose again, but indistinct to view,
> And left the waters of a purple hue,
> Then deeply disappear'd.
>
> (II.24)

If one wishes to see the star here merely as Ezzelin's badge of knighthood, one's desire for naturalistic reduction receives this final dousing. If one sees instead an echo of the night of Lara's dream, one finds Byron approaching, in muted tones, the kind of imaginative triumph Shelley more flamboyantly executed at the end of *Adonais*. For Shelley, the star beacons from on high, while for Byron—building into the image itself its insurance against demystification—the reflection of the star glimmers for a moment from below. If Ezzelin was a pursuing specter to Lara, his death here shadows forth the life of the hero. The mysterious Lara returned to his fatherland is the star "indistinct to view" at second and final remove from its prelapsarian state. In terms of the peasant narrative, the star sinks; in terms of romantic narrative, the star image outlasts Lara's life in nature.

The mystery of *Lara* lies in the strange relationship between narrative and preexistent sublimity revealed at the end. If one believed in the temporal priority of a prenatural state, the fall into narrative—telling the story of a man's loves and losses on earth—would be a fall into nature. In itself, the Byronic speculation about an anterior spiritual state has the same fictive status as naturalistic narrative. But a narrative true to one's sense of fall restores the spiritual sublimity that lies "behind" and thus anterior to the story. Not that romance comes first, satiric reduction next. Byron's revisions, whether on the scale of individual lines of *Lara*, the addition of the romantic stanzas at the end of Canto I of *Don Juan*, or the major reworking of Act III of *Manfred*, show that often the impulse to reduction came first and had to be purged or laid aside to allow for a possible sublimity. Within the achieved fiction, however, one can find restored the primariness of the higher spiritual state and the belatedness of nature. An account of a fall contains no assurance that the prelapsarian condition will convincingly represent a higher spiritual state; neither does satire insure the anteriority of the serious. But if a narrative has earned its emblems of spirit, the degradation of those emblems can authenticate what they once were.

As the poem draws to a close, the very story seems a degradation of the spiritual into the literal. It is one thing to sense that a pure adventure tale is being embroidered by sophisticated innuendos and images, or turned into embroidery by having narrative detail cut out to leave a delicate, lacelike story-fabric. But it is something very different to sense that the literal level has itself descended from the metaphysical and darkly reflects a purer literary origin. With the battle lost, Lara's faithful soldiers see that "One hope survives, the frontier is not far, / And thence they may escape from native war" (II.11). To cross that border would be (or once would have been) to become border figures and haunt the ambiguous geographical spaces that used to be more than geographic. They would "bear within them to the neighboring state / An exile's sorrows or an outlaw's hate." These burdens are theirs proleptically, for the exile's sorrows are the inner sorrows of alienation regardless of where one stands; and the outlaw's hate grew from the mind's war with nature before the war became that of Lara and Otho, or before it could become the war of outcasts and citizens. The geographic border seems a descendant of a temporal one and reminds us of Lara's exile from an original *un*native home, for which a new exile could be but a literalizing repetition.

In abstract terms the significance of such a new border crossing is figured by Foucault, who speaks of the "recession of the origin . . . on the far side of experience." Picture the "far side of experience" literalized geographically; imagine the retreat of origins turned into a military retreat, and one sees Lara's forces traveling backward across the border to the dynasty of archaic or arcadian imaginings, under the government of which the mysteries of life and the simple patterns of life peacefully coexist. But does Byron's "recession of the origin" reach the "dynasty of its own archaism"? Lara and his men look more closely and discover not arcadia—the mythic land of prelapsarian pastoralism—but Otho's men, who have *preempted* the border ground and cut off Lara's forces from retreat. Byron's poised verse matches one preemption with another, first descrying the romantic or "preposterous" perspective of Lara's men, then the realistic fact of Otho's ambush:

> It is resolved, they march—consenting Night
> Guides with her star their dim and torchless flight.
> Already they perceive its tranquil beam
> Sleep on the surface of the barrier stream;
> Already they descry—is yon the bank?
> Away! 'tis lined with many a hostile rank.
> Return or fly!—What glitters in the rear?
> It is Otho's banner, the pursuer's spear!
> Are those the shepherds' fires upon the height?
> Alas! they blaze too widely for the flight.
>
> (II.12)

The star misguides, the *already*s mistake, and those wonderful shepherds' fires come to be seen with greater clarity as fires from the enemy camp.

The plaintive, gentle music of the questions and answers in this stanza forms an equivalent, in narrative voice, of the undertones in Shakespeare's *Antony and Cleopatra*, the sad music of the god Hercules leaving Antony before that star falls. The effect in Byron's stanza is also more particular, for the misprision in the last two lines quoted does more to create a sense of the lost pastoral than could any extended description of shepherds in the beyond-the-border land whence Lara came. These two lines express a further loss, the absence of the particularity in the lines that precede them. By themselves, the last two lines would capture ordinary delusion, the defeat of expectation when an envisioned land of escape turns out to be the enemy's camp. This is what any such loss might be. The lines before, however, depend for their resonance on all that stars and streams have come to be in this poem. The expectation that reflected starlight will appear prelapsarian tumbles when the lights are more clearly descried. Whether or not a prelapsarian state was a tenable myth, the loss of that topos, that expectation, is a real loss, authenticating the imputed anteriority of the preexistent spiritual state. For the moment we are caught expecting stars of redemption—or at least a battle of angels in which the stars throw down their spears and become the fallen angels. But the spears are simply Otho's spears, and the war is not heavenly but corporeal. The weight of allusion is lost; simultaneously, and consequently, the anteriority of the "higher spiritual state" is assured.

As far as the narrator of *Lara* is concerned, "The secret long and yet but half conceal'd" (II.21) is the sex of Kaled. By itself this revelation is so meager that the aura of mystery maintained throughout the poem would be no more than what the *Quarterly Review* found the dream episode to be, "a mere useless piece of lumber." Is the secret wholly demystified, one must ask, when we extrapolate from the revelation of Kaled's sex that she is Gulnare, and that Lara-Conrad has been pining over Medora (first love of the hero of *The Corsair*)? By itself the turn from one set of literary facts to another avails naught. Yet the very inadequacy of such information proves instructive and leads to the recognition that the specific identity of Kaled, like the sex of Kaled and sexuality in general, are not the secrets of poetry but the cover for the mysteries of love, of innocence, and of the priority of spiritual life.

Byron's admission that the secret of Kaled's sex has been but half concealed all along makes public the kind of half concealment characteristic of the workings of repression. In a sense Kaled's devotion to Lara is founded on forgetfulness of Lara's preoccupation with Medora, and Kaled's mystification figures that of the reader. Yet as revelation, the baring of Kaled's breast is as poor a thing as would be the baring of plain facts of past experience to one undergoing psychoanalysis. To represent the fact that nothing has really been revealed, Kaled is seen ever silent while all around demand facts: "Vain was all question ask'd her of the past, / And vain e'en menace—silent to the last." What she has to reveal is love, and that is a significance that has just found public sign, though in an important sense the signs were there all along. What she has to conceal is the daemonic or transcendent rather than purely sexual nature of love, and that is something no physical unveiling could destroy. The preexistence of this bond between Lara and Kaled preempts the status of organized religion's bond between God and man. Dismissing the special sanction of churches, Byron presents Lara resting as much at peace as man could be: "Nor is his mortal slumber less profound, / Though priest nor bless'd, nor marble deck'd the mound." Yet these lines mystify as much as they demystify, for while denying special status to church or fame, they grant special status to the emotions of Kaled, which add to the burial of Lara a special grace.

The literary kinship between *The Corsair* and *Lara* confirmed at this moment also encourages the renewed mystification. We are drawn not to the sexual facts that bind the stories but to the fact of love, which, transcending the single poem, seems to transcend natural life as well and image a source purely "literary" and therefore purely spiritual. The one-sidedness of love—Kaled-Gulnare loves Lara-Conrad who loves Medora—keeps the line of transcendence looking pure, and while ostensibly confronting the fact that Lara is really the old disappointed lover of *The Corsair*, we remember also that Conrad was as much a fallen angel there as Lara is in this poem. "The relic of some higher material being," Byron specified, "wrecked in a former world." One could say that the very entrenchment of the myth of preexistence in nature authenticates it. More accurately, the entrenchment is not in nature but in a previous poem. If Conrad is not Lara but Lara's literary precursor, then the reference *Lara* makes to a preexistent state is both natural (equal fictions represent states on the same plane) and supernatural (the reference to another fictional framework represents the movement outside nature). The preexistence is real, while the knowledge that this realm is but another fiction safeguards such poetry from further demystification.

IV

Granted Byron's enormous skepticism of any romantic assertion, some solution like that discovered in *Lara* is necessary to protect the authenticity of the representation of a higher spiritual state. Unless the poet were to undertake a more strenuous career of poetic remaking—as does Wordsworth, for example, in *The Prelude*—the technical solution found in the relationship of *Lara* to *The Corsair* is a device available only once. What are other possibilities?

Perhaps closest to the play between fictions in the *Tales* is the play with the reader's knowledge within a given fiction. Byron's dramas, in particular, catch the reader in his tendency to draw premature conclusions. When the false prematurity is exposed, one is embarrassed or persuaded into accepting some other figure or story as prelapsarian. *Werner; or The Inheritance*, in which degeneration is literalized (the son *is* more a demon than the father) may be a successful melodramatic representation of achieved anteriority. Act III, Scene 3 takes place in a "secret passage" between Werner's and Stralenheim's chambers, as though spatially representing the mysterious and morally dubious paths between the generations. We are tempted into believing the Gabor's soliloquy precedes the murder of Stralenheim. When we discover later that the murder has already been committed, that the scene of anticipation is in fact belated, the degradation of our sense of time and judgment makes us more willing, in turn, to accept glimpses of fallen angel in Gabor and Werner. Though the terms are those of melodrama, the internal argument is that of, for example, Wordsworth in *Prelude* VI, confronting the fact that he has crossed the Alps before he was aware of it and finding, retrospectively, an unfathered vapor of imagination. Perhaps *Werner* remains, ultimately, the story of a too clearly fathered heritage of woe; but perhaps the very blatancy of the family romance leaves some room for intimations of spirit redeemed from the general curse.

More thematic and less technical solutions to the problem of representing the anteriority of a higher spiritual state may be discovered in Byron's stories of individual or governmental tyranny. If the present state of oppression can be seen as having degenerated from a purer form of nature, then our sense that demystification would parallel or participate in the degeneration helps forestall demystification. In the song at Haidée's banquet in *Don Juan* III, the hypothesized poet sang—or would have sung—of past glory and past song, bemoaning how the lyre "degenerated" into hands like his. "The voices of the dead / Sound like a distant torrent fall," more a part of nature, and for the moment more real, than the artificial aestheticism of the banquet or the lighthearted attitude of the poet of the surrounding stanzas. Having stood for the moment with Lambro discovering what has happened to his island home, we extrapolate on the basis of the degeneration of this paradise from our first view of it to the larger sense of paradise lost in the degeneration of historical Greece. In *The Two Foscari*, Marina exclaims that "this crowd of palaces and prisons is not / A paradise" (III.i.147–48), a remark that has only the pristine perspective of understatement to counter the weight of Venetian corruption and unhappiness. Less ladylike is the Doge's myth of preexistence: "Methinks we must have sinn'd in some old world / And *this* is hell" (II.i.364–65).

Byron's grandest adaptation of imputed anteriority based on a sense of present fallenness is *Manfred*. In other dramas and the tales the myth of preexistence is generally safeguarded by being grounded thoroughly in nature, so that to the skeptical eye there are only two geographies, or two historical periods, or, at most, two poetic fictions. In *Manfred* the concept of an anterior spiritual state is further guarded by the distinction drawn between Manfred's spirit and the world of other spirits, whose authenticity is ultimately denied when their power over Manfred is denied. The kind of ambiguity about spiritual or biographical past, so necessary in *Lara*, is still there: Manfred's longed-for lady is Astarte, her very name suggesting an otherworldly attraction as much as a flesh-and-blood lure. Ultimately the drama distinguishes between Manfred's quest for spiritual originality and the questionable primariness of the supernatural personae.

In his first approach to the "mysterious agency" of spirits, Manfred conjures unsuccessfully with "written charm" and magical signs. Denying the primal quality of this writing scene, the spirits respond rather to a spell "Which had its birthplace in a star condemn'd / The burning wreck of a demolish'd world" (I.i. 44–45). The song of the Seventh Spirit would imply that this is Manfred's star, though he seems both to operate under its influence and to operate its influence. The question of whether the power to raise spirits is Manfred's own or is merely lent him, as the Seventh Spirit claims, "but to make thee mine," is one of a number of questions about the past which need to be demystified rather than simply answered. Another such question concerns forgetfulness "of what—of whom—and why?" as the First Spirit asks. To give particulars about the "what" and "who" is to answer the question—perhaps a necessary stage in the demystification, and one Byron relegates, not without tact, to the confrontation with the Witch of the Alps in Act II. Beyond answers, however, the whole concept of forgetfulness needs to be exposed and perhaps discarded.

Byron was all too fond of the stance urbanely versified in the 1805 poems "To Caroline": "Not let thy mind past joys review—Our only hope is to forget." The passion for forgetfulness marks the turn to more postured Romanticism in the opening of Canto III of *Childe Harold*. Perhaps poems like *Lara* sophisticate the efforts to suppress the past or escape victimization by it. Biographically, the call for forgetfulness seems more self-indulgent. Memory had no pleasure for him, he was fond of confessing, and he expressed the wish "for insanity—anything—to quell memory, the never-dying worm that feeds on the heart, and only calls up the past to make the present more insupportable." It would be too easy to walk away from *Manfred* as from a portrait of man under the weight of his personal burden of the past. Nor can we simply say that forgetfulness is dismissed in the drama. Perhaps the desire for forgetfulness is purged, but only when it is demystified or shown to be a misdirection or a misapprehension of the object of desire.

Already in Act I, Manfred discovers the powerlessness of supernatural agency in his search for oblivion. "I lean no more on super-human aid, / It hath no power upon the past" (I.ii.4–5). At this point the path of the superhuman and the path to power over the past divaricate. Manfred does not immediately pursue either of these paths, however. He turns instead, whether by conscious redirection or the accidents of external nature, to the scene around him, and discovers the beauty of nature. "Why are ye beautiful?" is another misleading question, however, and it takes suicidal thoughts to confront him with the importance of nature: its primariness. Part sublime, part pastoral, the scene is through both attributes primordial, in touch with the sources of power because in touch with the past in a way that has nothing to do with personal memory. "Here," Manfred notes parenthetically, "the patriarchal days are not / A pastoral fable" (I.ii. 310–11).

If it would be too radical a dismissal to say that incest is not Manfred's crime, we could at least say that incest only makes literal a perverted relation to paternity and the past. The scene on the Jungfrau mountain less indulges than purges Byron's tendency to bemoan the burden of experience, and self-dramatization as fallen angel is aborted when Manfred is rescued by the Chamois Hunter. The literalized, dramatic height of the Alps permits the momentary fiction that a suicidal plunge would be a Luciferic fall. This fiction confronts us with a greater truth, that Manfred literally unfallen cannot so melodramatically impute to himself the state of fallen angel. Literally unfallen man is also spiritually unfallen in some sense not yet fully recognized by the abortive suicide but implied in the grand injunction of the hunter: "Stain not our pure vales with thy guilty blood!" (I.ii.372). Not acquiescing to Manfred's self-abnegation, the hunter calls Manfred's blood "guilty" only proleptically. The blood would be guilty of staining the vales which are yet pure. Just as the vales retain the stamp of the primeval, Manfred himself retains contact with the unfallen element of human nature.

"Power upon the past" was a misapprehended object of desire, and questing for it is like the child's questioning whether God could build a mountain he would be unable to move. I compare a quest to a question not for verbal play but to suggest that this is the kind of play Manfred himself is engaged in. When the Witch of the Alps retires, Manfred claims he has one resource left: "I can call the dead / And ask them what it is we dread to be" (II.ii.271–72). Has he himself confused his quest with a question? He needs to learn that the object of his own quest is not power over past or future; the real desire is to be able to approach, in the future, the power *of* the past. The mountain scene was a first contact with the primeval; the colloquy with the spirits in Act II is the second.

When the phantom of Astarte answers Manfred—and she answers only him—she gives not the information Manfred requests, but knowledge nonetheless that he will translate into power. Questions of forgiving or forgetting were misdirected questions, betraying—regardless of their answer—a subjugation to the past. With the information given by Astarte, that he will die the next day, Manfred is forced to analyze or deconstruct into its components the desire to redeem his relationship with Astarte: on the one hand, guilt at violating another can be erased only by passive resignation to the will of another; "forgive me!" is something only the *you* can do for the *me*. On the other hand, the desire to be forgiven or to forget is the desire to restore the primariness of one's own will, the desire to feel one's "original" power unburdened by the past. The component of resignation baffled, Manfred asserts the full power of original will.

The mystification dispelled by the act of will involves the relationship between the past and the supernatural. In a confusion about primariness and power, the supernatural personae had been appealed to; but if they could not dispel the past, Manfred learns that he can dispel them. His was the spell that conjured them, and his is the power to deny their primacy. One's past belongs to one's self, not to any other powers, and demons are de-mans, spirits who come from man and not parental figures who bequeath power to students of the past. Manfred identifies his present power with his skill:

> In knowledge of our fathers when the earth
> Saw men and spirits walking side by side
> And gave ye no supremacy.
>
> (III.iv.377–79)

In this vision of primordial times man is not degenerated from the spirits but an equal with them. Thus dispelling Byron's myth of degeneration, Manfred restores the primariness of his will and lifts the burden of the past. When the "original" in the sense of what took place originally is distinguished from the "original" in the sense of manifested originality, the original moment is no longer in the lost *then* but in the present *now*. Making an end of the demons, Manfred stands like God in the primary act of imagination asserting "I am" and silencing the deep. The mind becomes "its own origin of ill and end."

Byron's "one word":
The Language of Self-Expression
in *Childe Harold* III

Sheila Emerson

In Canto III of *Childe Harold's Pilgrimage*, just after the Alpine storm is hushed into a background music of "departing voices" (96), Byron raises his own in an apparent assault on self-expression:

> Could I embody and unbosom now
> That which is most within me,—could I wreak
> My thoughts upon expression, and thus throw
> Soul, heart, mind, passions, feelings, strong or weak,
> All that I would have sought, and all I seek,
> Bear, know, feel, and yet breathe—into *one* word,
> And that one word were Lightning, I would speak;
> But as it is, I live and die unheard,
> With a most voiceless thought, sheathing it as a sword.
>
> (97)

Thus it is that "what we have of feeling most intense / Outstrips our faint expression" (IV.158); but even so it does not get away without leaving behind some "faint expression" of itself. Byron's feeling becomes increasingly intense between stanzas 92 and 97, as his attention moves from a natural scene to its viewer's reach for self-expression and relief from self, to return again to the landscape. This movement and the gesture of dismissal which concludes it are recurrent in *Childe Harold*; and when studied in the context of similar actions, Byron's taking leave of his stormy mood appears to be complexly politic and by no means out of order, just as phrases like "and yet breathe" or "And that one word were Lightning" seem less melodramatic than they have to many readers and more appropriate to the dramatic hazards of the moment. Byron's moment in III.97 is frustrated by the combination of self-reference and self-concealment, and so is the reader,

From *Studies in Romanticism* 20, no. 3 (Fall 1981). © 1980 by the Trustees of Boston University.

but these impulses to describe himself and to declare himself indescribable work together again and again in Canto III. One way to approach both this collaboration, and the series of engagements between Byron's self-consciousness, to see exactly how reflexive attitudes and attitudes towards reflexiveness express themselves in his language.

For there is a workable analogy between the figure Byron cuts as he regards himself in the world, and the configuration of his reflexive language—language that often is, or is used to explore, the maneuver of an imagination that reflects on itself. In the following essay I will apply the term "reflexive" to images in which something is presented in terms of itself ("Vice, that digs her own voluptuous tomb," I.83) and to syntactical movements which turn back on themselves ("to be trodden like the grass / Which now beneath them, but above shall grow," III.27), as well as to the way such figures may ultimately refer to the speaker who makes them. Before Canto III was published Shelley wrote poetry in which these references are ambivalently positive and negative, suggesting a kinship between the creativity of the reflexive imagination and its self-destructive solipsism. And like Shelley, Byron was of course familiar with the connotations of Milton's reflexive imagery and imagery of recoil, both of which are powerfully infused with the experience of a being whose mind is its own place. Although criticism has dwelt on Byron's celebrated way with the satanic persona, very little has been said about his grasp, in *Childe Harold*, of the way Milton's imagery evokes the closed circuit of self-projection, the enlarging yet confining continuum of inner and outer landscapes.

In fact Byron's positions and movements are far more often tracked in the criticism of Canto III than is the language in which he makes them known. And yet the remarkable persistence of reflexive imagery and syntax is a material witness of particular value in the case of a poet who is himself his own material. Of course this fact does not settle the question of premeditation—always a tricky one with Byron. I will pursue his meditations in the order and in the language in which he presents them, for his language gathers meaning episodically, as does much else that accumulates in *Childe Harold*. By the time Byron reaches stanza 97 the pattern of his self-expression is fully articulated. And the relationship between his verbal strategy and his verbalized experience suggests an important point of negotiation, a promising means of coming to terms with a poet who says repeatedly what he will not say.

I

Four years before he published Canto III Byron wrote that "Passion raves herself to rest, or flies" (I.83), and that "Each has his pang, but feeble sufferers groan / With brain-born dreams of evil all their own" (II.7). The circular action implicit in the first and drawn out in the second of these two comments aptly introduces Byron's shipboard reflections on nature—

which, in turn, are introduced by an image of geographical reflection, as Byron beholds two land masses beholding each other:

> Through Calpe's straits survey the steepy shore;
> Europe and Afric on each other gaze!
> Lands of the dark-ey'd Maid and dusky Moor
> Alike beheld beneath pale Hecate's blaze:
>
> (II.22)

It may be that the Maid and the Moor bring him back to the sense that he is "friendless now," just as the literal reflection he sights gives way to his reflexive image for what he feels within: "The heart, lone mourner of its baffled zeal." Byron laments the fate of lovers whose "mingling souls forget to blend" (II.23), and there is something of the failure to blend in his subsequent attempt to forget his axioms about life on earth while brooding on part of the earth: the maneuver is curious, typical, and predictably doomed. "Thus" as he gazes at the moon's reflection in the waves, his "soul forgets her schemes of Hope and Pride," and dwells on "something dear, / Dearer than self" which nonetheless recalls him to himself with "A flashing pang" (II.24).

Byron is back upon the waves at the beginning of Canto III; and his language at once plunges the reader into a multiple experience of reflection and reflexiveness, as Byron finds himself in Harold and both find themselves in nature and neither—not surprisingly—finds relief for long in either. If he is "as a weed" (III.2) at the mercy of the wind and water, his "theme" (III.3) is at the mercy of his own relentless course of thought. This would seem like double jeopardy for the "One" who has already been tossed about by his own dark fate—or it would, if Byron did not suggest that Harold, "The wandering outlaw of his own dark mind," really has only one dark mind to contend with. What Byron finds in his "Tale" are a seascape and a landscape that are both physical and mental, his and Harold's:

> in that Tale I find
> The furrows of long thought, and dried-up tears,
> Which, ebbing, leave a sterile track behind,
> O'er which all heavily the journeying years
> Plot the last sands of life,—where not a flower appears.
>
> (III.3)

Like the experience which it describes, the image evolves into a vista that is not only imagined by the mind but seems physically to open out within it. There is something like this masterfully grotesque hybrid of vision and literal-mindedness in Canto II, where Byron imagines the "broken arch," "ruin'd wall," and "chambers desolate" within a skull which was, like his own mind, "once Ambition's airy hall, / The dome of Thought, the palace of the Soul" (6). This kind of parallel imagery is developed in III.5, where "thought seeks refuge in lone caves" which are at once Byron's haunts on earth and his own "soul's haunted cell." The "airy images" he seeks recall the "little schemes of thought" (II.36) he derided earlier but which he now substantiates into "A being more intense" (III.6) than anything he projected in Canto II. But if "we endow / With form our fancy" (III.6) partly in order to achieve "Forgetfulness" (III.4), then Harold's virtue may already be compromised beyond redemption. For the worrisome thing about "gaining as we give / The life we image" (III.6) is its being all we gain.

And the "giddy circle" (III.11) of such relationships does not end here, as nature too has imaged itself in legible form: when Harold shares their "mutual language," he is forsaking "the tome / Of his land's tongue" in order to read from "Nature's pages glass'd by sunbeams on the lake" (III.13). Once more the reflection that he sees in nature precedes the re- flexive act of his own imagination: "Like the Chaldean, he could watch the stars, / Till he had peopled them with beings bright / As their own beams. . . ." This is unfortunate not only because the stars are associated with the futility of fame in stanza II, but also because watching stars peopled by human thought can never insure that "human frailties" will be "forgotten quite." Byron observes that if Harold could "have kept his spirit to that flight / He had been happy"; but the reflexive imagery hints that Harold has never really gotten off the ground. In any case, "this clay will sink" (III.14).

Byron admires the way the heart holds out against ordeals like these, "Shewing no visible sign, for such things are untold" (III.33). Like the natural mirrors he finds at sea and in lakes, the heart is itself a mirror that may "break, yet brokenly live on" (III.32). But this kind of vitality might be as "antithetically mixt" as the spirit of Napoleon (III.36)—a spirit whose problem is different in degree but not in kind from the problem of Harold and his creator. If there is a "fever at the core, / Fatal to him who bears" it, then the Napoleonic "fire / And motion of the soul" are essentially self- consuming no matter how far they "aspire" beyond the self (III.42). Byron repeats this conclusion in the next two stanzas, and does it in a way that brings to mind the storm he himself is "riding" at the beginning of the Canto: "Their breath is agitation, and their life / A storm whereon they ride" (III.44).

Images like these help explain why Byron gives two different reasons in stanzas 4 and 6 for writing Canto III. He wants to forget all "agitation," but without any real or imagined "high adventure" (III.42) the cure of quiet will prove as fatal as the disease: the "intense" existence he creates keeps Byron from being "Even as a flame unfed, which runs to waste / With its own flickering, or a sword laid by / Which eats into itself, and rusts inglo- riously" (III.44). As for the actual life of high adventure, Byron banishes those struggles which can neither attain the "sun of glory" nor evade "Contending tempests" (III.45). His declaration that "true Wisdom's world will be / Within its own creation" (III.46) recalls the impulse of Harold's proud desolation to "find / A life within itself" (III.12).

These descriptions of self-sufficiency are, like Byron's rationale for writing, far less ominous than the kind of preying on oneself he describes in stanza 42. But the likeness is troubling regardless of what Byron intends, and the likeness only deepens when he turns back again to the world of "Maternal Nature" (III.46). He now associates "the mountain-majesty of worth" with "immortality" (III.67), and it is fitting that when Lake Leman "woos" him "with its crystal face," there are stars mirrored in the water among the mountains:

> The mirror where the stars and mountains view
> The stillness of their aspect in each trace
> Its clear depth yields of their far height and hue:
>
> (III.68)

But once he has been brought to the water, Byron's own reflection may be what gets in his way; he at once protests that "There is too much of man here, to look through / With a fit mind the might which I behold." The reflection of man's image, displacing that of nature, makes way for the reflexive language of Byron's formula for a life that would be the "survivor of its woe" (III.67):

> keep the mind
> Deep in its fountain, lest it overboil
> In the hot throng, where we become the spoil
> Of our infection.
>
> (III.69)

Thus the mountains become volcanic and may either implode or explode; under the circumstances it may be "better, then, to be alone" (III.71). The solitary bird to which he likens himself two stanzas later may spurn "the clay-cold bonds which round our being cling," but it takes off into some circular syntax—"waxing vigorous, as the blast / Which it would cope with"—that recalls those ill-fated voyagers whose "breath is agitation, and their life / A storm whereon they ride" (III.44). Without access to "the immortal lot" (III.74), these flights, like the mingling in stanza 72, might be "in vain."

It is as a sharer in "the immortal lot" that Byron later celebrates the author of *La Nouvelle Héloïse*, but Rousseau's love of "ideal beauty, which became / In him existence" (III.78) recalls not only the enlivening life Byron breathes into Harold but also the troubling reflexiveness of that creation, "which could find / A life within itself, to breathe without mankind" (III.12). At first the creation of Harold promises to take Byron where he wants to go, but it delivers no more completely than do those Napoleonic figures whose "breath is agitation." The reflexive agitation of Rousseau is mingled with the breath of his inspiration, much as they are in Byron's verse, so that the "breath which made him wretched" (III.77) also "breathed itself to life in Julie" (III.79). But Byron's telling note to stanza 79 lets some of the air out of this mouth-to-mouth resuscitation: he extols Rousseau's description of a kiss, then denies the adequacy of even this superlative expression—and he does it, characteristically, because such words "must be felt, from their very force, to be inadequate to the delineation." As in stanza 97, Byron's dismissal of mere language helps substantiate emotion that is said to be ineffable; but for Byron's Rousseau, the imperfect fit of words and feeling offers no escape from reflexive interchange, which is sustained in hope and frustrated in fact. And if this form of self-expression may bring no relief from self, it may also shorten the lives of those who have mastered it. Although his words start innocently enough as "sunbeams" (III.77), Rousseau is soon said to be "Kindled . . . and blasted" by the "ethereal flame" which, in turn, "teems / Along his burning page" (III.78).

Byron eventually turns back from these to nature's pages as reflected in the purity and stillness of "Clear, placid Leman" (III.85). But the contemplation of nature again comes around to a circular pattern of thought. Glittering in the dark on a hillside, the star-reflecting dews (like the drop that reflexively weeps its own tear in Marvell's "On a Drop of Dew") "All silently their tears of love instil, / Weeping themselves away, till they infuse"—very much in the Shelleyan spirit of *Epipsychidion* (lines 465–69)—"Deep into Nature's breast the spirit of her hues" (III.87). There is something comparable to this kind of interaction in the next stanza, in which man seeks to "read" his fate in the stars to which he has already claimed kinship and after which earthly fortune, fame, power, and life have already "named" themselves. Given the number of stanzas Byron has devoted to the vanity of glory-seeking, this sort of nomenclature may sound a troubling hint of the spells that Rousseau cast. "'Tis to be forgiven," Byron says, that "in our aspirations to be great, / Our destinies o'erleap their mortal state" (III.88), although he once found it hard to forgive the fiery souls who "aspire / Beyond the fitting medium of desire" (III.42). The point is not that Byron is carried away by the "poetry of heaven," but that he carries himself away. And in so doing he brings home to the reader the dangerous glamour of Rousseau, who is very much in Byron's mind when he confronts the storm on the lake where Julie once drew breath.

II

In stanza 89 Byron expands his involvement with the stars into a vision of the involvement of all creation in a single "life intense." Stanza 85 makes way for this imagery of nature "Mellowed and mingling" (III.86), as he sails into Lake Leman and so into the night when heaven and earth are silent as "we" are in "thoughts too deep" to express (III.89). The "feeling infinite" at once "purifies" Byron from self and keeps him company when he is by himself—both soundlessly; for its "tone" is not the familiar harmony of music but its "Eternal" soul and source, a tone which, like "the fabled Cytherea's zone," is impalpable except to the imagination (III.90). But when the sky changes and thunder sounds among "the rattling crags" (III.92), Byron's simile for the scene is suddenly more discordant. In this image—which is glimpsed while the mountains echo and "the lit lake shines" with reflected lightning, "a phosphoric sea" (III.93)—the banks of the Rhone are seen to answer to each other across the water, or rather, it is seen that they once did, for they are

> Heights which appear as lovers who have parted
> In hate, whose mining depths so intervene,
> That they can meet no more, though broken-hearted;
>
> (III.94)

The image recalls those desolate souls Byron thought of as he sailed through Calpe's straits with Europe and Africa on either side (II.22); and like those mourners, these banks seem to be turned back on themselves, left alone, as Byron puts it, "war within themselves to wage" (III.94).

Byron's earlier use of images of reflection makes this cluster of them seem portentous; and the portents do not diminish when a distinction between man and nature develops with the storm, leaving Byron silent in his thoughtfulness while "every mountain now hath found a tongue" (III.92). Now that it is neither moonbeams nor sunbeams that glass nature's image on the lake, Byron seems less fluent in the "mutual language" (III.13) he and Harold share with her. This is perhaps why, although they are already intimate, Byron begs the night to let him be "A sharer in thy fierce and far delight" (III.93). When she expresses herself "With night, and clouds, and thunder" (III.96), nature is personified as a man who behaves "as if he did understand, / That in such gaps as desolation work'd, / There the hot shaft should blast whatever therein lurk'd." These gaps bring to mind not only the so-called desolation of Harold but also the fact that his creator may be "here" in his boat at the cleavage of the banks, where "The mightiest of the storms hath ta'en his stand" (III.95). But even if Byron (who does not choose to specify his whereabouts) is watching the storm from a distance, the dangers the scene presents to its would-be participant are more than theoretical: Byron has already shown how those who climb too high, like Napoleon, are exposed to "The avalanche—the thunderbolt of snow" (III.62), or how those like Rousseau are "On fire by lightning; with ethereal flame / Kindled . . . and blasted" (III.78).

In the stanza between the outbreak of the tempest and the momentous stillness that precedes it, Byron refers to the various ways that men have expressed their emotions in "Nature's realms of worship, earth and air" (III.91). But only "now" (III.97) that the storm is nearly out of earshot does he speak of giving vent to his own feelings. He has staged a confrontation between himself and nature when she is the way he likes her best, "in her features wild" (II.37); and the result—which follows a series of reflexive actions and images—is the climax of the relationship between Byron's attitudes towards self-description and self-control, and that pattern of circular reflections which is both an instance of and a comment on the way he has found to express himself in Canto III.

The force and suddenness of his outburst in stanza 97 imply not only that this impulse has been strong (and perhaps growing) since stanza 93, but also that his desire to be part of the storm has brought him neither direct nor vicarious relief. Meanwhile, the desire itself has been conditioned by Byron's response to the storm, so that it persists only as ambivalence within the conditional mood of stanza 97. This ambivalence informs his choice of words between "Could I" and "I would speak," although his opening verb indicates that under the circumstances Byron's experience (of history, of the scene, of himself) will control his ambition. "Embody" recalls his scheme to "endow / With form our fancy" (III.6), but also the almost palpable way that the night has made itself felt. "Unbosom" relates both to his rationale for writing in stanza 4 and to the uneasy questions which conclude stanza 96. That Byron wants to express his thoughts is nothing new, but his striking use of the verb "wreak" corresponds to the violent self-indulgence—the "fierce and far delight" —with which the tempest "unbosoms" itself. "Throw" in the third line likewise answers to the way the storms "fling their thunder-bolts" (III.95). Since Byron rarely feels anything mildly, "strong or weak" probably refers to the quality rather than the intensity of his emotions, and thereby draws attention to the mixed character of "all I seek." "And yet breathe" may refer to his usual way of surviving his feelings, as in stanza 32; but the words may also function in relation to "could I wreak" in the same way that "into *one* word" relates to "Could I embody."

So Byron may be implying that he will not wreak his thoughts upon expression because he cannot do it "and yet breathe." That this is not his primary emphasis is clear from his placement of italics, but the phrase does contribute to a sense of hazardous extremity, as if Byron were as imperiled by a potential decision as Rousseau was by his overboiling passions. The seemingly perverse insistence on "*one* word" forces the reader back on Byron's previous usage and forward to the conclusion that it was loaded on the negative side. If he had simply wanted to foreclose his option, the "*one* word" would have been enough. But he adds the further condition that "that one word were Lightning," which complicates the case past immediate dismissal. After all, in the implicit parallel between nature's "Sky, mountains, river, winds, lake" (III.96) and Byron's "Soul, heart, mind, passions, feelings" (III.97), the "lightnings" correspond in position to the alternatively "strong or weak." Lightning has the power and beauty to which Byron is drawn in stanza 88; but it is also associated with the image of Rousseau as a tree on fire (III.78). Even this ambivalence would be relatively simple if Byron were not so dazzled by the brilliance of Rousseau's writing, or if he did not think at times of human life as a tree which can only bear "detested fruit" (III.34). The apples on the Dead Sea's shore suggest that man and nature are in a similarly fallen condition, and this is ultimately why Rousseau's outbursts may be related to a storm's. In stanza 96 Byron questions the tempest about the goal of its "departing voices," which he supposes might either return unquietably on the being which produced them, "like those within the human breast," or else might find such respite as eagles do. But this image conjures up both the eagles which fly "unutterably high" around Parnassus (IV. 74) and—from much less far afield—the self-consuming "eagle" Napoleon (III.18).

It is the reduced potential of man and nature that reduces Byron to an unsatisfying choice of the lesser of two evils: "as it is" he avoids the physical and spiritual dangers of lightning, but stanza 97 still seems to fall into silence as stanza 96 fell into doubt. Once again, it is important to note that Byron's gesture of dismissal does not alter his sense of likeness to the storm. As he discovers or details this likeness his wish to participate does not so much diminish as it becomes superfluous, redundant. This is why he denies neither his wish of stanza 93 nor the storm itself but only the lightning-like outbursts of which he may or may not be capable. In refusing, at least poetically, to authorize this ultimate parallel between his own self-expression and the storm's, Byron criticizes a way of life and of writing which would provide him with no escape from his tempestuous emotions. This much may seem simple; but as has already been suggested, the conditional mood of stanza 97 contains both Byron's reservations about the storm and his onrushing impulse to explode. The dramatic result seems to be at once a natural culmination of his uneasiness and an unnaturally strained attempt to deflect the course of impulse.

It is possible that Byron deliberately represents rather than resolves this conflict, deploying italics and punctuation which give weight to the fast-moving lines and put a sort of drag on their meaning. Six nouns and five commas draw out the first line of stanza 96, and it seems appropriate to take in slowly the accumulating subject of the verb "be." But in the next stanza, Byron's "Soul, heart, mind, passions, feelings, strong or weak" are all objects of the verb "throw," which they follow at a surprisingly even pace, so that the syntax which does so much to create the momentum of stanza 97 also slows the speed with which it may be pronounced. The argument and meter of line 6 would have passed more inconspicuously through the narrow space of "a" word; instead both come up against the "*one*" italicized by Byron. But regardless of how long it takes to reach the seventh line, his requirement that his word literally be lightning rather than lightning-like suggests how far out of his way he feels he must go to make the anticlimax seem inevitable.

The same sort of pressure is behind his insisting on just "*one* word." He does not reject all self-expression but refers instead to one particularly explosive mode which he fabricates into what seems to be a highly specific impossibility—which he accordingly finds impossible. This process would loosen logic far enough to draw attention even if it did not end in a non sequitur. But the conclusion that he will "live and die unheard" because he cannot or will not say everything in one word cannot be imputed to petulance. It amounts either to an admission that he cannot do the impossible—which may be reason for self-complacency; or it amounts, metaphorically speaking, to preferring torture by suffocation to torture by inflammation, which is not very far removed from the choice he makes in stanza 69. To put it another way, Byron's blanket statement in the last two lines may be proof that he still has energies that need to be stifled: his decisively ambiguous announcement leaves him with the same problem as before, and no further solution.

Unlike the Byron of stanza 93, the Byron of the end of 97 is sobered rather than exhilarated by nature: his likeness to the world around him no longer seems to constitute a license for flights of the spirit but rather the grounds for self-control. As so often in Canto III, Byron turns from his life among others to his kinship with nature; and—like many people who return with mixed feelings from abroad—his is reminded of himself where he is most at home. But in stanza 97 the pattern of circular returns comes to an almost operatic crisis. The familiar experience of running into himself is sharpened by a sense of dramatic danger, which is part of the role not only of the storm but also of Napoleon and Rousseau, whom its imagery recalls. With "the far roll / Of your departing voices" (III.96), Byron seems to give himself the cue for a solo. But what happens instead is that he drops the voice that rises to a pitch in 97, which accounts for the paradox of his audibly announcing that he is now "unheard." The impression that he has forced himself up to a kind of falsetto suggests that Byron may have conjured up the storm with the purpose of compelling this voice to break. As an attempt at self-definition, stanza 97 operates by contradistinction to the careers of Napoleon and Rousseau. The crescendo of emotion which begins with nightfall involves a Napoleonic reach for the sky as well as a Rousseauan dalliance with lightning. By rehearsing their ascents Byron puts himself in a position to undergo a rhetorical fall which escapes the more fatal falls of his models. Insofar as his leap is a trial run, it is not clear whether Byron is trying to school himself or his readers or both. But if things seem to settle all too soon into their denouement, one of the points of stanza 97 is that a gentle decline is the safer way to go.

So the excess of stanza 97 may be another typically Byronic desperation measure: that is, it may be an instance of Byron's carefully measured use of desperation. Certainly he elaborates his intention in a way that compromises his innocence of self-conscious and even premeditated motives. Regardless of whether Byron means for the reader to associate this "sheathing" with Harold's in stanzas 10 and 15 or the "sword" with Napoleon's in stanza 44, and regardless of whether he assumes that no one will expect him to be "voiceless" for long, his metaphorical resignation seems almost mock-heroic. It is not surprising that Shelley uses the same imagery to make the opposite, dashingly heroic point: "Poetry is a sword of lightning, ever unsheathed, which consumes the scabbard that would contain it." But stanza 97 has its triumph too, and it is more than a matter of getting the last words in. Byron makes a gesture of triumphant self-expression out of the very boundaries that he senses in reflexive thoughts of nature, and out of the very limits that he sets to his speaking of himself. For if "sheathing it as a sword" is an act of self-defense, it is also a form of self-assertion. The life in the poetry unmistakably proclaims that he has got something to sheathe.

III

On the morning after the night before, Byron turns from the "mining depths" of the Rhone to the spot where the river has "spread himself a couch" on which Byron can now muse in peace (III.104). He sees no more or less of himself in the scene than ever, but he sees it somewhat differently. Like Voltaire's, Byron's is a "various" wit, and his having "multiplied himself among mankind" (III.106)—like the "broken mirror" that makes "A thousand images of one that was, / The same" (III.33)—may contain a clue to the riddle of how a man could hypothetically say everything he thinks in *"one* word." But this is no more than a hint, and Byron once more takes leave to "quit man's works, again to read / His Maker's" (III.109)— which he soon turns from in order to read his own.

Byron's reading of *Childe Harold* III is presented in a coda that summarizes important aspects not only of its "theme" but also of its strategy of self-expression. In stanza 111, the patterns of self-concealment and self-reflexiveness converge in a recital of what "we" have been "taught":

> to steel
> The heart against itself; and to conceal,
> With a proud caution, love, or hate, or aught,—
> Passion or feeling, purpose, grief or zeal,—
> Which is the tyrant spirit of our thought,

The rhyme words "feel," "steel," "conceal," "zeal," sound a reminder of elements in stanza 97 which they draw together in ringing affirmation that "We are not what we have been." Although he has repeatedly turned away from the returns of language on its creators, although he has repeatedly given notice that his words may be no more than a "harmless wile" (III.112), still his language of self-protection is a mode of self-confinement, and still this is deliberate. If he is no longer a man "in a shroud" of his own thoughts, he has since "filed" his mind, "which thus itself subdued" (III.113).

But with the reflexive language a belief also persists to which he has not given voice before. "I do believe, / Though I have found them not, that there may be / Words which are things"—words that do not circle him with echoes that enclose him and then fade, words that do not "weave / Snares for the failing" like the "virtues" he suspects (III.114), words that do not just express him but go on—as he means them, and as he means them to—without him. As in stanza 97, Byron's mood is conditional, subjunctive, and as in stanza 97, his language describes the possibility of a condition of language which it denies having discovered. But what Byron gives credence to here are "Words," not *"one* word," "things," not one thing, like lightning. Although the plurals may suggest a way out of the singular rhetorical trap of stanza 97, in the present tense of Canto III it may be that words are things only in a "dream."

And it seems to be from out of a dream, or in waking from a dream, that Byron—who proudly denied that he had "cried aloud / In worship of an echo" (III.113)—now cries aloud to his unseen daughter. The section devoted to Ada dwells on a different sort of offspring from Childe Harold or *Childe Harold's Pilgrimage*; but whatever else she means to him, Ada is also involved in Byron's hope to extend himself beyond his own lifetime. As in the case of his literary hopes in Canto IV (9–10), his confidence in his daughter will (or will not) be realized because she is his daughter and because of self-discipline. His prediction about her is shaped by the same patterns of self-reflexiveness and self-constraint as are his predictions about himself: "of thy sire / These were the elements,—and thine no less. / . . . but thy fire / Shall be more tempered, and thy hope far higher" (III.118). This reference to fire looks back to the untamed lightning bolt of III.97 and forward to the Apollo Belvedere which is informed rather than consumed by flame (IV.163).

Byron concludes with a sigh over the distance that separates him from his daughter. But it is important to remember that like the "voiceless thought" which may be imagined but not heard in stanza 97, even "as it is" (III.97 and III.116) the voice of her father will somehow blend with Ada's "future visions"—a "token and a tone" (III.115), something "more than life" that will persist when his is over (III.117). She may never be what she "might'st have been" to him; but in declaring what he plans to be to *her*, Ada's unseen, unheard father makes us ponder the words which alone can reach her.

IV

The best commentary on the implications of Byron's *"one* word" is Byron's, and it comes, indirectly, in Canto IV: "History, with all her volumes vast, / Hath but *one* page" in stone or in ink (108). The words which disclose "all human tales" are likewise involved in a continuum within which they may refer to themselves or to each other, and may be envisaged as part of a single meaning, or a single meaninglessness. This reunion of far-flung multitudes has about it the spirit of Byron's repeated dismissals of the circlings of language rather than the air of any celebration; but the stanza also points to the coalescence of many words into something which is the opposite of what he mistrusts, something substantial, irreducible, invariable. The alternative Byron proposes to repeating "the same rehearsal of the past" is not no rehearsal but instead *"one"* which is "better written here" and can be recognized anywhere, any time. "Here," as elsewhere in *Childe Harold*, refers to the poem that is written as well as to the place it is written about; and Byron's swift passage between Rome and the page written in Rome presages his equally fluent translations back and forth between audible and legible words, between words which need not be written to be apprehended, and the visible words which he says he can speak on without. And thus, like the "voiceless thought" which is un-sounded in Canto III, the one page which is "better written here" is, by a seeming sleight of mind, suddenly unworded, unread: "Away with words!

draw near, / Admire, exult—despise—laugh, weep,—for here / There is such matter for all feeling" (IV.108–9). In the retrospect of Canto IV, it takes no sleight of mind to see how one word which is written for the future— for Ada, for posterity—may be voiceless, and yet taken to heart: "Something unearthly, which they deem not of, / Like the remembered tone of a mute lyre" (IV.137).

In the meantime, the "clay-cold bonds" (III.73) which encumbered him before are galvanized into an "electric chain wherewith we are darkly bound," as Byron associates, more generally than in Canto III, the "light-ning of the mind" with the reflexive action of "things which bring / Back on the heart the weight which it would fling / Aside for ever" (IV.23–24). But near the end of Canto IV he "steal[s]" from what he may be or has been in order "To mingle with the Universe, and feel / What I can ne'er express, yet can not all conceal" (178). Unlike in III.111, it is now "steal" not "steel" that rhymes with "feel" and "conceal," and the word evokes the Promethean theft which is repaid by the sculptor of the Apollo Bel-vedere in stanza 163. The "blight and blackening" effects of the "lightning of the mind" (IV.24) are countered by the afterglow of "an eternal glory" which "breathes the flame with which 'twas wrought" (IV.163), as Byron develops his ideas about "A being more intense" (III.6) into a theory or hypothesis of salvation by art in its various forms—including the form that is taken by a poem. The "poetic marble" which is "not of human thought" (IV.163) is opposed to the "false creation" of the self-projective imagination, which fondly pursues outside itself the ideal "forms the sculptor's soul hath seized" (IV.122). Yet even while Byron describes the unearthly in-spiration of the statue, a "solitary nymph" appears who has "madden'd in that vision" (IV.162), and if only for a moment her figure touches on the connection between the god who glances "lightnings" (IV.161) and the "nympholepsy of some fond despair" (IV.115). In thinking of the dreams which mortals entertain, Byron still cannot disown that configuration of exhibition and inhibition, of self-projection and self-restraint, by means of which he expresses himself in Canto III. However partial, however fitful, the glimpse of other possibilities comes through his sense of self-impris-onment, in terms of it, as the scent of the ocean comes to a man who feels landlocked:

> Though from our birth the faculty divine
> Is chain'd and tortured—cabin'd, cribb'd, confined,
> And bred in darkness, lest the truth should shine
> Too brightly on the unprepared mind,
> The beam pours in, for time and skill will couch the blind.
>   (IV.127)

Byron moves towards the discriminations on which this outlook is based in III.97 and 104 when he implies that only certain kinds of "beings" of the mind will serve his purpose: they must be disciplined, "purified," tempered by "time and skill" into something timeless, like the ocean. In this long perspective, the "one word" of III.97 comes to suggest not only a kind of writing which does not solve his problems but also a redeeming work of art of which he may not yet be capable. These two readings are not mutually exclusive because the artist who does not control his potential is ultimately in the same boat as the artist who prematurely exploits it: in neither case does the end justify the dangerous means. But when he writes his way into Canto IV, Byron reverses the persistent moods of stanza 97, making declarative his intention to be heard and leaving conditional his suspicion that he might not be. Although twined with longer-winded doubts, a new note of confidence is sounded that recasts Harold's motive to forsake "his land's tongue" (III.13): "I twine / My hopes of being remembered in my line / With my land's language" (IV.9). When he later invokes what has been most within him, it is "a far hour" that "shall wreak" the fullness of his verse rather than his own unmediated impulse that would "wreak / My thoughts upon expression" (III.97). Again rhyming "weak" and "seek," he now denies any implication of weakness if his "voice break forth" and declares that he means to seek "in this page a record" (IV.134). Regardless of its intended meaning or effect—and readers have had reason to question both—it is by "Forgiveness" (IV.135) that Byron seeks to break free of the vicious circle of his circumstances—the very "Torture and Time" which he says his words, if not his life, will outlast: "But there is that within me which shall tire / Torture and Time, and breathe when I expire" (IV.137).

Much as Byron's "one word" eventually compresses a variety of experience and may be read in a variety of ways, a single artifact expresses the variety of the author of *Childe Harold* or *Don Juan*. The words which only "may" be things in *Childe Harold* III.114 most emphatically "are" things in *Don Juan*:

> But words are things, and a small drop of ink,
>   Falling like dew, upon a thought, produces
> That which makes thousands, perhaps millions, think.

The enormity of its spread is all the more impressive as the markedly small drop of "ink" extends itself into "think" with the help of nothing more than the first two letters that spell out a "thought"—a cunning literalization of Byron's next remark:

> 'Tis strange, the shortest letter which man uses
> Instead of speech, may form a lasting link
>   Of ages.
>
> (III.88)

Chosen out of the whole expanse of written language, "the shortest letter" is the most swiftly scanned link between a man and those who come after him, and the link that makes the "ages" look most expansive by contrast. Yet "the shortest letter" is not a *trompe-l'oeil* but a thing like the "one word" that is lightning "Instead of speech" in *Childe Harold*: a striking yet potentially silent thing that is taken in, as it is put out, in almost no time, and whose recurrently visible design outlasts the lifetimes of men.

So Byron's final return to the immutable ocean may suggest the access he has found through art to another "image of Eternity" (IV.183), and artfulness—his own if not other men's—also helps rescue him from foundering in his own time-bound reflections. But before he returns to the "glorious mirror" where it is the Almighty's form that "Glasses itself in tempests" (IV.183), Byron pauses for a stanza at a spot which lacks the glitter of Lake Leman, but which persists in the memory of *Childe Harold's Pilgrimage*—as a reminder not only of Byron's self-entrapment, but also of the strategies of self-expression by which he made his escape:

> Lo, Nemi! navelled in the woody hills
> So far, that the uprooting wind which tears
> The oak from his foundation, and which spills
> The ocean o'er its boundary, and bears
> Its foam against the skies, reluctant spares
> The oval mirror of thy glassy lake;
> And, calm as cherish'd hate, its surface wears
> A deep cold settled aspect nought can shake,
> All coiled into itself and round, as sleeps the snake.
>
> (173)

This passage begins just after Byron refers once more to "the electric chain" of a despair "Whose shock was as an earthquake's" (IV.172)—a reference which circuitously involves Byron's allusions to lightning and his vision of "the long envenomed chain" of the asp that winds around Laocoön (IV.160). So it may come as no surprise that the description of the volcanic Lake Nemi seems to shuffle and reuse the volcanic imagery Byron applies to himself in III.69, or that it recalls the image of Milton's Serpent which Satan finds "fast sleeping . . . / In Labyrinth of many a round self-roll'd." But the Serpent is not harmful at this point in *Paradise Lost*, for Satan has not entered into the shape which he beholds. And at this point in *Childe Harold* the infinite regress of reflexive imagery has been worked into another kind of pattern, as the snake with its Old Testament associations of coldness and hate is wreathed into the tail-eating serpent whose figure is the emblem of eternity. Byron's art may free expression from the circle of mortality, but it leaves the sting in language that recoils upon itself.

The Unpastured Sea:
An Introduction to Shelley

Harold Bloom

It is the unpastured sea hungering for calm.
—*Prometheus Unbound,* Act III, Scene ii

Mesdames, one might believe that Shelley lies
Less in the stars than in their earthy wake,
Since the radiant disclosures that you make
Are of an eternal vista, manqué and gold
And brown, an Italy of the mind, a place
Of fear before the disorder of the strange,
A time in which the poet's politics
Will rule in a poets' world.

—WALLACE STEVENS

I

Percy Bysshe Shelley, one of the greatest lyrical poets in Western tradition, has been dead for more than a hundred and forty years, and critics have abounded, from his own day to ours, to insist that his poetry died with him. Until recently, it was fashionable to apologize for Shelley's poetry, if one liked it at all. Each reader of poetry, however vain, can speak only for himself, and there will be only description and praise in this introduction, for after many years of reading Shelley's poems, I find nothing in them that needs apology. Shelley is a unique poet, one of the most original in the language, and he is in many ways *the* poet proper, as much so as any in the language. His poetry is autonomous, finely wrought, in the highest degree imaginative, and has the spiritual form of vision stripped of all veils and ideological coverings, the vision many readers justly seek in poetry, despite the admonitions of a multitude of churchwardenly critics.

The essential Shelley is so fine a poet that one can feel absurd in urging his claims upon a reader:

I am the eye with which the Universe
  Beholds itself and knows itself divine;
All harmony of instrument or verse,
  All prophecy, all medicine is mine,
All light of art or nature;—to my song
Victory and praise in its own right belong.

That is Apollo singing, in the "Hymn" that Shelley had the sublime

From *The Ringers in the Tower: Studies in Romantic Tradition.* © 1971 by The University of Chicago. The University of Chicago Press, 1971.

audacity to write for him, with the realization that, like Keats, he was a rebirth of Apollo. When, in *The Triumph of Life*, Rousseau serves as Virgil to Shelley's Dante, he is made to speak lines as brilliantly and bitterly condensed as poetry in English affords:

> And if the spark with which Heaven lit my spirit
> Had been with purer nutriment supplied,
>
> Corruption would not now thus much inherit
> Of what was once Rousseau—nor this disguise
> Stain that which ought to have disdained to wear it.

The urbane lyricism of the "Hymn of Apollo," and the harshly self-conscious, internalized dramatic quality of *The Triumph of Life* are both central to Shelley. Most central is the prophetic intensity, as much a result of displaced Protestantism as it is in Blake or in Wordsworth, but seeming more an Orphic than Hebraic phenomenon when it appears in Shelley. Religious poet as he primarily was, what Shelley prophesied was one restored Man who transcended men, gods, the natural world, and even the poetic faculty. Shelley chants the apotheosis, not of the poet, but of desire itself:

> Man, oh, not men! a chain of linkèd thought,
> Of love and might to be divided not,
> Compelling the elements with adamantine stress;
> As the sun rules, even with a tyrant's gaze,
> The unquiet republic of the maze
> Of planets, struggling fierce towards heaven's free
>   wilderness.
>
> Man, one harmonious soul of many a soul,
> Whose nature is its own divine control,
> Where all things flow to all, as rivers to the sea.

The rhapsodic intensity, the cumulative drive and yet firm control of those last three lines in particular, as the high song of humanistic celebration approaches its goal—that seems to me what is crucial in Shelley, and its presence throughout much of his work constitutes his special excellence as a poet.

Lyrical poetry at its most intense frequently moves toward direct address between one human consciousness and another, in which the "I" of the poet directly invokes the personal "Thou" of the reader. Shelley is an intense lyricist as Alexander Pope is an intense satirist; even as Pope assimilates every literary form he touches to satire, so Shelley converts forms as diverse as drama, prose essay, romance, satire, epyllion, into lyric. To an extent he himself scarcely realized, Shelley's genius desired a transformation of all experience, natural and literary, into the condition of lyric. More than all other poets, Shelley's compulsion is to present life as a direct confrontation of equal realities. This compulsion seeks absolute intensity, and courts straining and breaking in consequence. When expressed as love, it must manifest itself as mutual destruction:

> In one another's substance finding food,
> Like flames too pure and light and unimbued
> To nourish their bright lives with baser prey,
> Which point to Heaven and cannot pass away:
> One Heaven, one Hell, one immortality,
> And one annihilation.

Shelley is the poet of these flames, and he is equally the poet of a particular shadow, which falls perpetually between all such flames, a shadow of ruin that tracks every imaginative flight of fire:

> O, Thou, who plumed with strong desire
>   Wouldst float above the earth, beware!
> A Shadow tracks thy flight of fire—
>   Night is coming!

By the time Shelley had reached his final phase, of which the great monuments are *Adonais* and *The Triumph of Life*, he had become altogether the poet of this shadow of ruin, and had ceased to celebrate the possibilities of imaginative relationship. In giving himself, at last, over to the dark side of his own vision, he resolved (or perhaps merely evaded, judgment being so difficult here) a conflict within his self and poetry that had been present from the start. Though it has become a commonplace of recent criticism and scholarship to affirm otherwise, I do not think that Shelley changed very much, as a poet, during the last (and most important) six years of his life, from the summer of 1816 until the summer of 1822. The two poems of self-discovery, of mature poetic incarnation, written in 1816, "Mont Blanc" and the "Hymn to Intellectual Beauty," reveal the two contrary aspects of Shelley's vision that his entire sequence of major poems reveals. The head and the heart, each totally honest in encountering reality, yield rival reports as to the name and nature of reality. The head, in "Mont Blanc," learns, like Blake, that there is no natural religion. There is a Power, a secret strength of things, but it hides its true shape or its shapelessness behind or beneath a dread mountain, and it shows itself only as an indifference, or even pragmatically a malevolence, toward the well-being of men. But the Power speaks forth, through a poet's act of confrontation with it that is the very act of writing his poem, and the Power, rightly interpreted, can be used to repeal the large code of fraud, institutional and historical Christianity, and the equally massive code of woe, the laws of the nation-states of Europe in the age of Castlereagh and Metternich. In the "Hymn to Intellectual Beauty" a very different Power is invoked, but with a deliberate and even austere tenuousness. A shadow, itself invisible, of an unseen Power, sweeps through our dull dense world, momentarily awakening both nature and man to a sense of love and beauty, a sense just beyond the

normal range of apprehension. But the shadow departs, for all its benev-
olence and despite the poet's prayers for its more habitual sway. The heart's
responses have not failed, but the shadow that is antithetically a radiance
will not come to stay. The mind, searching for what would suffice, en-
countered an icy remoteness, but dared to affirm the triumph of its imaginings over the solitude and vacancy of an inadvertent nature. The
emotions, visited by delight, felt the desolation of powerlessness, but dared
to hope for a fuller visitation. Both odes suffer from the evident straining
of their creator to reach a finality, but both survive in their creator's tough
honesty and gathering sense of form.

"Mont Blanc" is a poem of the age of Shelley's father-in-law, William
Godwin, while the "Hymn to Intellectual Beauty" belongs to the age of
Wordsworth, Shelley's lost leader in the realms of emotion. Godwin became
a kind of lost leader for Shelley also, but less on the intellectual than on
the personal level. The scholarly criticism of Shelley is full of sand traps,
and one of the deepest is the prevalent notion that Shelley underwent an
intellectual metamorphosis from being the disciple of Godwin and the
French philosophical materialists to being a Platonist or Neoplatonist, an
all but mystical idealist. The man Shelley may have undergone such a
transformation, though the evidence for it is equivocal; the poet Shelley
did not. He started as a split being, and ended as one, but his awareness
of the division in his consciousness grew deeper, and produced finally the
infernal vision of *The Triumph of Life*.

II

> *But even supposing that a man should raise a dead body to life before our
> eyes, and on this fact rest his claim to being considered the son of God;—
> the Humane Society restores drowned persons, and because it makes no
> mystery of the method it employs, its members are not mistaken for the
> sons of God. All that we have a right to infer from our ignorance of the
> cause of any event is that we do not know it.*
>
> —SHELLEY, *Notes on Queen Mab*

The deepest characteristic of Shelley's poetic mind is its skepticism. Shelley's intellectual agnosticism was more fundamental than either his troubled
materialism or his desperate idealism. Had the poet turned his doubt
against all entities but his own poetry, while sparing that, he would have
anticipated certain later developments in the history of literature, but his
own work would have lost one of its most precious qualities, a unique
sensitivity to its own limitations. This sensitivity can be traced from the
very beginnings of Shelley's mature style, and may indeed have made
possible the achievement of that style.

Shelley was anything but a born poet, as even a brief glance at his
apprentice work will demonstrate. Blake at fourteen was a great lyric poet;
Shelley at twenty-two was still a bad one. He found himself as a stylist in

the autumn of 1815, when he composed the astonishing *Alastor*, a blank verse rhapsodic narrative of a destructive and subjective quest. *Alastor*, though it has been out of fashion for a long time, is nevertheless a great and appalling work, at once a dead end and a prophecy that Shelley finally could not evade.

Shelley's starting point as a serious poet was Wordsworth, and *Alastor* is a stepchild of *The Excursion*, a poem frigid in itself, but profoundly influential, if only antithetically, on Shelley, Byron, Keats, and many later poets. The figure of the Solitary, in *The Excursion*, is the central instance of the most fundamental of Romantic archetypes, the man alienated from others and himself by excessive self-consciousness. Whatever its poetic lapses, *The Excursion* is our most extensive statement of the Romantic mythology of the Self, and the young Shelley quarried in it for imaginatively inescapable reasons, as Byron and Keats did also. Though the poet-hero of *Alastor* is not precisely an innocent sufferer, he shares the torment of Wordsworth's Solitary and, like him,

> sees
> Too clearly, feels too vividly; and longs
> To realize the vision, with intense
> And over-constant yearning;—there—there lies
> The excess, by which the balance is destroyed.

Alastor, whatever Shelley's intentions, is primarily a poem about the destructive power of the imagination. For Shelley, every increase in imagination ought to have been an increase in hope, but generally the strength of imagination in Shelley fosters an answering strength of despair. In the spring of 1815 Shelley, on mistaken medical advice, confidently expected a rapid death of consumption. By autumn this expectation was put by, but the recent imagining of his own death lingers on in *Alastor*, which on one level is the poet's elegy for himself.

Most critical accounts of *Alastor* concern themselves with the apparent problem of disparities between the poem's eloquent Preface and the poem itself, but I cannot see that such disparities exist. The poem is an extremely subtle internalization of the quest-theme of romance, and the price demanded for the internalization is first, the death-in-life of what Yeats called "enforced self-realization," and at last, death itself. The *Alastor* or avenging demon of the title is the dark double of the poet-hero, the spirit of solitude that shadows him even as he quests after his emanative portion, the soul out of his soul that Shelley later called the epipsyche. Shelley's poet longs to realize a vision, and this intense and overconstant yearning destroys natural existence, for nature cannot contain the infinite energy demanded by the vision. Wordsworthian nature, and not the poet-hero, is the equivocal element in *Alastor*, the problem the reader needs to, but cannot, resolve. For this nature is a mirror-world, like that in Blake's "The Crystal Cabinet," or in much of Keats's *Endymion*. Its pyramids and domes are sepulchers for the imagination, and all its appearances are illusive, phantasmagoric, and serve only to thwart the poet's vision, and drive him on more fearfully upon his doomed and self-destructive quest. *Alastor* prophesies *The Triumph of Life*, and in the mocking light of the later poem the earlier work appears also to have been a dance of death.

The summer of 1816, with its wonderful products "Mont Blanc" and the "Hymn to Intellectual Beauty," was for Shelley, as I have indicated, a rediscovery of the poetic self, a way out of the impasse of *Alastor*. The revolutionary epic, first called *Laon and Cythna*, and then *The Revolt of Islam*, was Shelley's first major attempt to give his newly directed energies adequate scope, but the attempt proved abortive, and the poem's main distinction is that it is Shelley's longest. Shelley's gifts were neither for narrative nor for straightforward allegory, and the *terza rima* fragment, *Prince Athanase*, written late in 1817, a few months after *The Revolt of Islam* was finished, shows the poet back upon his true way, the study of the isolated imagination. Whatever the dangers of the subjective mode of *Alastor*, it remained always Shelley's genuine center, and his finest poems were to emerge from it. *Prince Athanase* is only a fragment, or fragments, but its first part at least retains something of the power for us that it held for the young Browning and the young Yeats. Athanase, from a Peacockian perspective, is quite like the delightfully absurd Schythrop of *Nightmare Abbey*, but if we will grant him his mask's validity we do find in him one of the archetypes of the imagination, the introspective, prematurely old poet, turning his vision outward to the world from his lonely tower of meditation:

His soul had wedded wisdom, and her dower
Is love and justice, clothed in which he sate
Apart from men, as in a lonely tower,

Pitying the tumult of their dark estate.—

There is a touch of Byron's Manfred, and of Byron himself, in Athanase, and Byron is the dominant element in Shelley's next enduring poem, the conversational *Julian and Maddalo*, composed in Italy in the autumn of 1818, after the poets had been reunited. The middle portion of *Julian and Maddalo*, probably based upon legends of Tasso's madness, is an excrescence, but the earlier part of the poem, and its closing lines, introduce another Shelley, a master of the urbane, middle style, the poet of the "Letter to Maria Gisborne," the *Hymn to Mercury*, of parts of *The Witch of Atlas* and *The Sensitive Plant*, and of such beautifully controlled love lyrics as "To Jane: The Invitation" and "Lines Written in the Bay of Lerici." Donald Davie, who as a critic is essentially an anti-Shelleyan of the school of Dr. Leavis, and is himself a poet in a mode antithetical to Shelley's, has written an impressive tribute to Shelley's achievement as a master of the urbane style. What I find most remarkable in this mastery is that Shelley carried it over into his major achievement, the great lyrical drama *Prometheus Unbound*, a work written almost entirely in the high style, on the precarious level of the sublime, where urbanity traditionally has no place. The astonishingly original tone of *Prometheus Unbound* is not always successfully maintained, but for the most part it is, and one aspect of its triumph is that critics should find it so difficult a tone to characterize. The urbane conversationalist, the relentlessly direct and emotionally uninhibited lyricist, and the elevated prophet of a great age to come join together in the poet of *Prometheus Unbound*, a climactic work that is at once celebratory and ironic, profoundly idealistic and as profoundly skeptical, passionately knowing its truths and as passionately agnostic toward all truth. More than any other of Shelley's poems, *Prometheus Unbound* has been viewed as self-contradictory or at least as containing unresolved mental conflicts, so that a consideration of Shelley's ideology may be appropriate prior to a discussion of the poem.

The clue to the apparent contradictions in Shelley's thought is his profound skepticism, which has been ably expounded by C. E. Pulos in his study *The Deep Truth*. There the poet's eclecticism is seen as centering on the point "where his empiricism terminates and his idealism begins." This point is the skeptic's position, and is where Shelley judged Montaigne, Hume, and his own older contemporary, the metaphysician Sir William Drummond, to have stood. From this position, Shelley was able to reject both the French materialistic philosophy he had embraced in his youth, and the Christianity that he had never ceased to call a despotism. Yet the skeptic's position, though it powerfully organized Shelley's revolutionary polemicism, gave no personal comfort, but took the poet to what he himself called "the verge where words abandon us, and what wonder if we grow dizzy to look down the dark abyss of how little we know." That abyss is Demogorgon's, in *Prometheus Unbound*, and its secrets are not revealed by him, for "a voice is wanting, the deep truth is imageless," and Demogorgon is a shapeless darkness. Yeats, sensing the imminence of his apocalypse, sees a vast image, a beast advancing before the gathering darkness. Shelley senses the great change that the Revolution has heralded, but confronts as apocalyptic harbinger only a fabulous and formless darkness, the only honest vision available to even the most apocalyptic of skeptics. Shelley is the most Humean poet in the language, oddly as his temperament accords with Hume's, and it is Hume, not Berkeley or Plato, whose view of reality informs *Prometheus Unbound* and the poems that came after it. Even Necessity, the dread and supposedly Godwinian governing demon of Shelley's early *Queen Mab*, is more of a Humean than a Holbachian notion, for Shelley's Necessity is "conditional, tentative and philosophically ironical," as Pulos points out. It is also a Necessity highly advantageous to a poet, for a power both sightless and unseen is a power removed from dogma and from philosophy, a power that only the poet's imagination can find the means to approach. Shelley is the unacknowledged ancestor of Wallace Stevens's conception of poetry as the Supreme Fiction, and *Prometheus Unbound* is the most capable imagining, outside of Blake and Wordsworth, that the Romantic quest for a Supreme Fiction has achieved.

The fatal aesthetic error, in reading *Prometheus Unbound* or any other substantial work by Shelley, is to start with the assumption that one is about to read Platonic poetry. I mean this in either sense, that is, either poetry deeply influenced by or expressing Platonic doctrine, or in John Crowe Ransom's special sense, a poetry discoursing in things that are at any point legitimately to be translated into ideas. Shelley's skeptical and provisional idealism is *not* Plato's, and Shelley's major poems are mythopoeic, and not translatable into any terms but their own highly original ones. Shelley has been much victimized in our time by two rival and equally pernicious critical fashions, one that seeks to "rescue" visionary poetry by reading it as versified Plotinus and Porphyry, and another that condemns visionary poetry from Spenser through Hart Crane as being a will-driven allegorization of an idealistic scientism vainly seeking to rival the whole of experimental science from Bacon to the present day. The first kind of criticism, from which Blake and Yeats have suffered as much as Shelley, simply misreads the entire argument against nature that visionary poetry complexly conducts. The second kind, as pervasively American as the first is British, merely underestimates the considerable powers of mind that Shelley and the other poets of his tradition possessed.

Shelley admired Plato as a poet, a view he derived from Montaigne, as Pulos surmises, and he appears also to have followed Montaigne in considering Plato to be a kind of skeptic. Nothing is further from Shelley's mind and art than the Platonic view of knowledge, and nothing is further from Shelley's tentative myths than the dogmatic myths of Plato. It is one of the genuine oddities of critical history that a tough-minded Humean poet, though plagued also by an idealistic and pseudo-Platonic heart, should have acquired the reputation of having sought beauty or truth in any Platonic way or sense whatsoever. No Platonist would have doubted immortality as darkly as Shelley did, or indeed would have so recurrently doubted the very existence of anything transcendent.

The most obvious and absolute difference between Plato and Shelley is in their rival attitudes toward aesthetic experience. Shelley resembles Wordsworth or Ruskin in valuing so highly certain ecstatic moments of aesthetic contemplation precisely because the moments are fleeting, because they occupy, as Blake said, the pulsation of an artery. For Shelley these are not moments to be put aside when the enduring light of the Ideas is found; Shelley never encounters such a light, not even in *Adonais*, where Keats appears to have found a kindred light in death. There is no ladder to climb in Shelley's poetry, any more than there is in Blake's. There are more imaginative states of being and less imaginative ones, but no hierarchy to bridge the abyss between them.

III

It is no longer sufficient to say, like all poets, that mirrors resemble the water. Neither is it sufficient to consider that hypothesis as absolute and to suppose . . . that mirrors exhale a fresh wind or that thirsty birds drink them, leaving empty frames. We must go beyond such things. That capricious desire of a mind which becomes compulsory reality must be manifested—an individual must be shown who inserts himself into the glass and remains in its illusory land (where there are figurations and colors but these are impaired by immobile silence) and feels the shame of being nothing more than an image obliterated by nights and permitted existence by glimmers of light.

—JORGE LUIS BORGES

It has been my experience, as a teacher of Shelley, that few recent students enjoy *Prometheus Unbound* at a first reading, and few fail to admire it greatly at a second or later reading. *Prometheus Unbound* is a remarkably subtle and difficult poem. That a work of such length needs to be read with all the care and concentration a trained reader brings to a difficult and condensed lyric is perhaps unfortunate, yet Shelley himself affirmed that his major poem had been written only for highly adept readers, and that he hoped for only a few of these. *Prometheus Unbound* is not as obviously difficult as Blake's *The Four Zoas*, but it presents problems comparable to that work. Blake has the advantage of having made a commonplace understanding of his major poems impossible, while Shelley retains familiar (and largely misleading) mythological names like Prometheus and Jupiter. The problems of interpretation in Shelley's lyrical drama are as formidable as English poetry affords, and are perhaps finally quite unresolvable.

It seems clear that Shelley intended his poem to be a millennial rather than an apocalyptic work. The vision in Act III is of a redeemed nature, but not of an ultimate reality, whereas the vision in the great afterthought of Act IV does concern an uncovered universe. In Act IV the imagination of Shelley breaks away from the poet's apparent intention, and visualizes a world in which the veil of phenomenal reality has been rent, a world like that of the Revelation of Saint John, or Night the Ninth of *The Four Zoas*. The audacity of Shelley gives us a vision of the last things without the sanction of religious or mythological tradition. Blake does the same, but Blake is systematic where Shelley risks everything on one sustained imagining.

I think that a fresh reader of *Prometheus Unbound* is best prepared if he starts with Milton in mind. This holds true also for *The Prelude*, for Blake's epics, for Keats's *Hyperion* fragments, and even for Byron's *Don Juan*, since Milton is both the Romantic starting point and the Romantic adversary. Shelley is as conscious of this as Blake or any of the others; the Preface to *Prometheus Unbound* refers to that demigod, "the sacred Milton," and commends him for having been "a bold inquirer into morals and religion." Searching out an archetype for his Prometheus, Shelley finds him in Milton's Satan, "the Hero of Paradise Lost," but a flawed, an imperfect hero, of whom Prometheus will be a more nearly perfect descendant. Shelley's poem is almost an echo chamber for *Paradise Lost*, but all the echoes are deliberate, and all of them are so stationed as to "correct" the imaginative errors of *Paradise Lost*. Almost as much as Blake's "brief epic," *Milton*,

Shelley's *Prometheus Unbound* is a courageous attempt to save Milton from himself, and for the later poet. Most modern scholarly critics of Milton sneer at the Blakean or Shelleyan temerity, but no modern critic of Milton is as illuminating as Blake and Shelley are, and none knows better than they did how omnipotent an opponent they lovingly faced, or how ultimately hopeless the contest was.

Paraphrase is an ignoble mode of criticism, but it can be a surprisingly revealing one (of the critic as well as the work, of course) and it is particularly appropriate to *Prometheus Unbound*, since the pattern of action in the lyrical drama is a puzzling one. A rapid survey of character and plot is hardly possible, since the poem in a strict (and maddening) sense has neither, but a few points can be risked as introduction. Shelley's source is Aeschylus, insofar as he has a source, but his genuine analogues are in his older contemporary Blake, whom he had never read, and of whom indeed he never seems to have heard. Prometheus has a resemblance both to Blake's Orc and to his Los; Jupiter is almost a double for Urizen, Asia approximates Blake's Jerusalem, while Demogorgon has nothing in common with any of Blake's "Giant Forms." But, despite this last, the shape of Shelley's myth is very like Blake's. A unitary Man fell, and split into torturing and tortured components, and into separated male and female forms as well. The torturer is not in himself a representative of comprehensive evil, because he is quite limited; indeed, he has been invented by his victim, and falls soon after his victim ceases to hate his own invention. Shelley's Jupiter, like Urizen in one of his aspects, is pretty clearly the Jehovah of institutional and historical Christianity. George Bernard Shaw, one of the most enthusiastic of Shelleyans, had some illuminating remarks on *Prometheus Unbound* in *The Perfect Wagnerite*. Jupiter, he said, "is the almighty fiend into whom the Englishman's God had degenerated during two centuries of ignorant Bible worship and shameless commercialism." Shaw rather understated the matter, since it seems undubitable that the Jupiter of Shelley's lyrical drama is one with the cheerfully abominable Jehovah of *Queen Mab*, and so had been degenerating for rather more than two centuries.

Prometheus in Shelley is both the archetypal imagination (Blake's Los) and the primordial energies of man (Blake's Orc). Jupiter, like Urizen again, is a limiter of imagination and of energy. He may masquerade as reason, but he is nothing of the kind, being a mere circumscriber and binder, like the God of *Paradise Lost*, Book III (as opposed to the very different, creative God of Milton's Book VII). Asia is certainly not the Universal Love that Shaw and most subsequent Shelleyans have taken her to be. Though she partly transcends nature she is still subject to it, and she is essentially a passive being, even though the apparently central dramatic action of the poem is assigned to her. Like the emanations in Blake, she may be taken as the total spiritual form or achieved aesthetic form quested after by her lover, Prometheus. She is less than the absolute vainly sought by the poet-hero of *Alastor*, though she is more presumably than the mortal Emilia of

Epipsychidion can hope to represent. Her function is to hold the suffering natural world open to the transcendent love or Intellectual Beauty that hovers beyond it, but except in the brief and magnificent moment-of-moments of her transfiguration (end of Act II) she is certainly not one with the Intellectual Beauty.

That leaves us Demogorgon, the poem's finest and most frustrating invention, who has been disliked by the poem's greatest admirers, Shaw and Yeats. Had Shaw written the poem, Demogorgon would have been Creative Evolution, and had Yeats been the author, Demogorgon would have been the Thirteenth Cone of *A Vision*. But Shelley was a subtler dialectician than Shaw or Yeats; as a skeptic, he had to be. Shaw testily observed that "flatly, there is no such person as Demogorgon, and if Prometheus does not pull down Jupiter himself, no one else will." Demogorgon, Yeats insisted, was a ruinous invention for Shelley: "Demogorgon made his plot incoherent, its interpretation impossible; it was thrust there by that something which again and again forced him to balance the object of desire conceived as miraculous and superhuman, with nightmare."

Yet Demogorgon, in all his darkness, is a vital necessity in Shelley's mythopoeic quest for a humanized or displaced theodicy. The Demogorgon of Spenser and of Milton was the evil god of chaos, dread father of all the gentile divinities. Shelley's Demogorgon, like the unknown Power of "Mont Blanc," is morally unallied; he is the god of skepticism, and thus the preceptor of our appalling freedom to imagine well or badly. His only clear attributes are dialectical; he is the god of all those at the turning, at the reversing of the cycles. Like the dialectic of the Marxists, Demogorgon is a necessitarian and materialistic entity, part of the nature of things as they are. But he resembles also the shadowy descent of the Holy Spirit in most Christian dialectics of history, though it would be more accurate to call him a demonic parody of the Spirit, just as the whole of *Prometheus Unbound* is a dark parody of the Christian salvation myth. Back of Demogorgon is Shelley's difficult sense of divinity, an apocalyptic humanism like that of Blake's, and it is not possible therefore to characterize *Prometheus Unbound* as being humanistic or theistic in its ultimate vision. Martin Price, writing of Blake's religion, observes that "Blake can hardly be identified as theist or humanist; the distinction becomes meaningless for him. God can only exist within man, but man must be raised to a perception of the infinite. Blake rejects both transcendental deity and natural man." The statement is equally true for the Shelley of *Prometheus Unbound*, if one modifies rejection of transcendental deity to a skeptical opening toward the possibility of such a Power. Though Demogorgon knows little more than does the Asia who questions him, that little concerns his relationship to a further Power, and the relationship is part of the imagelessness of ultimates, where poetry reaches its limit.

The events of *Prometheus Unbound* take place in the realm of mind, and despite his skepticism Shelley at this point in his career clung to a faith in the capacity of the human mind to renovate first itself, and then the outward world as well. The story of the lyrical drama is therefore an unfolding of renovation after renovation, until natural cycle itself is canceled in the rhapsodies of Act IV. Of actions in the traditional sense, I find only one, the act of pity that Prometheus extends toward Jupiter at line 53 of Act I. Frederick A. Pottle, in the most advanced essay yet written on the poem, insists that there is a second and as crucial action, the descent of Asia, with her subsequent struggle to attain to a theology of love: "Asia's action is to give up her demand for an ultimate Personal Evil, to combine an unshakable faith that the universe is sound at the core with a realization that, as regards man, Time is radically and incurably evil." Behind Pottle's reading is a drastic but powerful allegorizing of the poem, in which Prometheus and Asia occupy respectively the positions of head and heart: "The head must sincerely forgive, must willingly eschew hatred on purely experimental grounds" while the heart "must exorcize the demons of infancy." One can benefit from this provisional allegorizing even if one finds *Prometheus Unbound* to be less theistic in its implications than Pottle appears to do.

Further commentary on the complexities of the poem can be sought elsewhere, but the aesthetic achievement needs to be considered here. Dr. Samuel Johnson still knew that invention was the essence of poetry, but this truth is mostly neglected in our contemporary criticism. It may be justly observed that Shelley had conquered the myth of Prometheus even as he had transformed it, and the conquest is the greatest glory of Shelley's poem. One power alone, Blake asserted, made a poet, the divine vision or imagination, by which he meant primarily the inventive faculty, the gift of making a myth or of so re-making a myth as to return it to the fully human truths of our original existence as unfallen men. If Johnson and Blake were right, then *Prometheus Unbound* is one of the greatest poems in the language, a judgment that will seem eccentric only to a kind of critic whose standards are centered in areas not in themselves imaginative.

IV

Nature has appointed us men to be no base or ignoble animals, but when she ushers us into the vast universe . . . she implants in our souls the unconquerable love of whatever is elevated and more divine than we. Wherefore not even the entire universe suffices for the thought and contemplation within the reach of the human mind.
—LONGINUS, *On the Sublime*

Published with *Prometheus Unbound* in 1820 were a group of Shelley's major odes, including "Ode to the West Wind," "To a Skylark," and "Ode to Liberty." These poems show Shelley as a lyricist deliberately seeking to extend the sublime mode, and are among his finest achievements.

Wallace Stevens, in one of the marvelous lyrics of his old age hears the cry of the leaves and knows "it is the cry of leaves that do not transcend themselves," knows that the cry means no more than can be found "in the final finding of the ear, in the thing / Itself." From this it follows, with massive but terrible dignity, that "at last, the cry concerns no one at all."

This is Stevens's modern reality of *decreation*, and this is the fate that Shelley's magnificent "Ode to the West Wind" seeks to avert. Shelley hears a cry of leaves that do transcend themselves, and he deliberately seeks a further transcendence that will metamorphosize "the thing itself" into human form, so that at last the cry will concern all men. But in Shelley's Ode, as in Stevens's, "there is a conflict, there is a resistance involved; / And being part is an exertion that declines." Shelley too feels the frightening strength of the *given*, "the life of that which gives life as it is," but here as elsewhere Shelley does not accept the merely "as it is." The function of his Ode is apocalyptic, and the controlled fury of his spirit is felt throughout this perfectly modulated "trumpet of a prophecy."

What is most crucial to an understanding of the Ode is the realization that its fourth and fifth stanzas bear a wholly antithetical relation to one another. The triple invocation to the elements of earth, air, and water occupies the first three stanzas of the poem, and the poet himself does not enter those stanzas; in them he is only a voice imploring the elements to hear. In the fourth stanza, the poet's ego enters the poem, but in the guise only of a battered Job, seeking to lose his own humanity. From this nadir, the extraordinary and poignantly "broken" music of the last stanza rises up, into the poet's own element of fire, to affirm again the human dignity of the prophet's vocation, and to suggest a mode of imaginative renovation that goes beyond the cyclic limitations of nature. Rarely in the history of poetry have seventy lines done so much so well.

Shelley's other major odes are out of critical favor in our time, but this is due as much to actual misinterpretations as to any qualities inherent in these poems. "To a Skylark" strikes readers as silly when they visualize the poet staring at the bird and hailing it as nonexistent, but these readers have begun with such gross inaccuracy that their experience of what they take to be the poem may simply be dismissed. The ode's whole point turns on the lark's being out of sight from the start; the poet *hears* an evanescent song, but can see nothing, even as Keats in the "Ode to a Nightingale" never actually sees the bird. Flying too high almost to be heard, the lark is crucially compared by Shelley to his central symbol, the morning star fading into the dawn of an unwelcome day. What can barely be heard, and not seen at all, is still discovered to be a basis upon which to rejoice, and indeed becomes an inescapable motive for metaphor, a dark justification for celebrating the light of uncommon day. In the great revolutionary "Ode to Liberty," Shelley successfully adapts the English Pindaric to an abstract political theme, mostly by means of making the poem radically its own subject, as he does on a larger scale in *The Witch of Atlas* and *Epipsychidion*.

In the last two years of his life, Shelley subtly modified his lyrical art, making the best of his shorter poems the means by which his experimental intellectual temper and his more traditional social urbanity could be reconciled. The best of these lyrics would include "Hymn of Apollo," "The Two Spirits: An Allegory," "To Night," "Lines . . . on . . . the Death of Napoleon," and the final group addressed to Jane Williams, or resulting from the poet's love for her, including "When the lamp is shattered," "To

Jane: The Invitation," "The Recollection," "With a Guitar, to Jane," and the last completed lyric, the immensely moving "Lines Written in the Bay of Lerici." Here are nine lyrics as varied and masterful as the language affords. Take these together with Shelley's achievements in the sublime ode, with the best of his earlier lyrics, and with the double handful of magnificent interspersed lyrics contained in *Prometheus Unbound* and *Hellas*, and it will not seem as if Swinburne was excessive in claiming for Shelley a rank as one of the two or three major lyrical poets in English tradition down to Swinburne's own time.

The best admonition to address to a reader of Shelley's lyrics, as of his longer poems, is to slow down and read very closely, so as to learn what Wordsworth could have meant when he reluctantly conceded that "Shelley is one of the best *artists* of us all: I mean in workmanship of style":

> There is no dew on the dry grass tonight,
>   Nor damp within the shadow of the trees;
> The wind is intermitting, dry, and light;
>   And in the inconstant motion of the breeze
> The dust and straws are driven up and down,
> And whirled about the pavement of the town.
>   ("Evening: Ponte Al Mare, Pisa")

This altogether characteristic example of Shelley's workmanship is taken from a minor and indeed unfinished lyric of 1821. I have undergone many unhappy conversations with university wits, poets, and critics, who have assured me that "Shelley had a tin ear," the assurance being given on one occasion by no less distinguished a prosodist than W. H. Auden, and I am always left wondering if my ears have heard correctly. The fashion of insisting that Shelley was a poor craftsman seems to have started with T. S. Eliot, spread from him to Dr. Leavis and the Fugitive group of Southern poets and critics, and then for a time became universal. It was a charming paradox that formalist and rhetorical critics should have become so affectively disposed against a poet as to be incapable of reading any of his verbal figures with even minimal accuracy, but the charm has worn off, and one hopes that the critical argument about Shelley can now move on into other (and more disputable) areas.

V

Cruelty has a Human Heart,
And Jealousy a Human Face;
Terror the Human Form Divine,
And Secrecy the Human Dress.

The Human Dress is forged Iron,
The Human Form a fiery Forge,
The Human Face a Furnace seal'd,
The Human Heart its hungry Gorge.
        —BLAKE, "A Divine Image"

The Cenci occupies a curious place in Shelley's canon, one that is overtly apart from the sequence of his major works that goes from *Prometheus Unbound* to *The Triumph of Life*. Unlike the pseudo-Elizabethan tragedies of Shelley's disciple Beddoes, *The Cenci* is in no obvious way a visionary poem. Yet it is a tragedy only in a very peculiar sense, and has little in common with the stageplays it ostensibly seeks to emulate. Its true companions, and descendants, are Browning's giant progression of dramatic monologues, *The Ring and the Book*, and certain works of Hardy that share its oddly effective quality of what might be termed dramatic solipsism, to have recourse to a desperate oxymoron. Giant incongruities clash in *Prometheus Unbound* as they do in Blake's major poems, but the clashes are resolved by both poets in the realms of a self-generated mythology. When parallel incongruities meet violently in *The Cenci*, in a context that excludes myth, the reader is asked to accept as human characters beings whose states of mind are too radically and intensely pure to be altogether human. Blake courts a similar problem whenever he is only at the borderline of his own mythical world, as in *Visions of the Daughters of Albion* and *The French Revolution*. Shelley's Beatrice and Blake's Oothoon are either too human or not human enough; the reader is uncomfortable in not knowing whether he encounters a Titaness or one of his own kind.

Yet this discomfort need not wreck the experience of reading *The Cenci*, which is clearly a work that excels in character rather than in plot, and more in the potential of character than in its realization. At the heart of *The Cenci* is Shelley's very original conception of tragedy. Tragedy is not a congenial form for apocalyptic writers, who tend to have a severe grudge against it, as Blake and D. H. Lawrence did. Shelley's morality was an apocalyptic one, and the implicit standard for *The Cenci* is set in *The Mask of Anarchy*, which advocates a nonviolent resistance to evil. Beatrice is tragic because she does *not* meet this high standard, though she is clearly superior to every other person in her world. Life triumphs over Beatrice because she does take violent revenge upon an intolerable oppressor. The tragedy Shelley develops is one of a heroic character "violently thwarted from her nature" by circumstances she ought to have defied. This allies Beatrice with a large group of Romantic heroes, ranging from the Cain of Byron's drama to the pathetic daemon of Mary Shelley's *Frankenstein* and, on the cosmic level, embracing Shelley's own Prometheus and the erring Zoas or demigods of Blake's myth.

To find tragedy in any of these, you must persuasively redefine tragedy, as Shelley implicitly did. Tragedy becomes the fall of the imagination, or rather the falling away from imaginative conduct on the part of a heroically imaginative individual.

Count Cenci is, as many critics have noted, a demonic parody of Jehovah, and has a certain resemblance therefore to Shelley's Jupiter and Blake's Tiriel and Urizen. The count is obsessively given to hatred, and is vengeful, anal-erotic in his hoarding tendencies, incestuous, tyrannical, and compelled throughout by a jealous possessiveness even toward those he abhors. He is also given to bursts of Tiriel-like cursing, and like Tiriel or

Jupiter he has his dying-god aspect, for his death symbolizes the necessity of revolution, the breaking up of an old and hopeless order. Like all heavenly tyrants in his tradition, Cenci's quest for dominion is marked by a passion for uniformity, and it is inevitable that he seek to reduce the angelic Beatrice to his own perverse level. His success is an ironic one, since he does harden her into the only agent sufficiently strong and remorseless to cause his own destruction.

The aesthetic power of *The Cenci* lies in the perfection with which it both sets forth Beatrice's intolerable dilemma, and presents the reader with a parallel dilemma. The natural man in the reader exults at Beatrice's metamorphosis into a relentless avenger, and approves even her untruthful denial of responsibility for her father's murder. The imaginative man in the reader is appalled at the degeneration of an all-but-angelic intelligence into a skilled intriguer and murderess. This fundamental dichotomy *in the reader* is the theater where the true anguish of *The Cenci* is enacted. The overt theme becomes the universal triumph of life over integrity, which is to say of death-in-life over life.

The Cenci is necessarily a work conceived in the Shakespearean shadow, and it is obvious that Shelley did not succeed in forming a dramatic language for himself in his play. Dr. Leavis has seized upon this failure with an inquisitor's joy, saying that "it takes no great discernment to see that *The Cenci* is very bad and that its badness is characteristic." It takes a very little discernment to see that *The Cenci* survives its palpable flaws and that it gives us what Wordsworth's *The Borderers*, Byron's *Cain*, and Coleridge's *Remorse* give us also in their very different ways, a distinguished example of Romantic, experimental tragedy, in which a crime against nature both emancipates consciousness and painfully turns consciousness in upon itself, with an attendant loss of a higher and more innocent state of being. The Beatrice of Shelley's last scene has learned her full autonomy, her absolute alienation from nature and society, but at a frightful, and to Shelley, a tragic cost.

VI

But were it not, that Time *their troubler is,*
All that in this delightfull Gardin growes,
Should happie be, and have immortal blis
—SPENSER

In the spring of 1820, at Pisa, Shelley wrote *The Sensitive Plant*, a remarkably original poem, and a permanently valuable one, though it is little admired in recent years. As a parable of imaginative failure, the poem is another of the many Romantic versions of the Miltonic Eden's transformation into a wasteland, but the limitations it explores are not the Miltonic ones of human irresolution and disobedience. Like all of Shelley's major poems, *The Sen-*

sitive Plant is a skeptical work, the skepticism here manifesting itself as a precariously poised suspension of judgment on the human capacity to perceive whether or not natural *or* imaginative values survive the cyclic necessities of change and decay.

The tone of *The Sensitive Plant* is a deliberate exquisitiveness, of a more-than-Spenserian kind. Close analogues to this tone can be found in major passages of Keats's *Endymion* and in Blake's *The Book of Thel*. The ancestor poet for all these visionary poems, including Shelley's *The Witch of Atlas* and the vision of Beulah in Blake's *Milton*, is of course Spenser, whose mythic version of the lower or earthly paradise is presented as the Garden of Adonis in *The Faerie Queene*, Book III, Canto VI, which is probably the most influential passage of poetry in English, if by "influential" we mean what influences other poets.

The dark melancholy of *The Sensitive Plant* is not Spenserian, but everything else in the poem to some extent is. Like many poems in this tradition, the lament is for mutability itself, for change seen as loss. What is lost is innocence, natural harmony, the mutual interpenetrations of a merely given condition that is nevertheless whole and beyond the need of justification. The new state, experiential life as seen in Part III of the poem, is the world without imagination, a tract of weeds. When Shelley, in the noblest quatrains he ever wrote, broods on this conclusion he offers no consolation beyond the most urbane of his skepticisms. The light that puts out our eyes is a darkness to us, yet remains light, and death may be a mockery of our inadequate imaginations. The myth of the poem—its garden, lady, and plant—may have prevailed, while we, the poem's readers, may be too decayed in our perceptions to know this. Implicit in Shelley's poem is a passionate refutation of time, but the passion is a desperation unless the mind's imaginings can cleanse perception of its obscurities. Nothing in the poem proper testifies to the mind's mastery of outward sense. The "Conclusion" hints at what Shelley beautifully calls "a modest creed," but the poet is too urbane and skeptical to urge it upon either us or himself. The creed appears again in *The Witch of Atlas*, but with a playful and amiable disinterestedness that removes it almost entirely from the anguish of human desire.

The Witch of Atlas is Shelley's most inventive poem, and is by any just standards a triumph. In kind, it goes back to the English Renaissance epyllion, the Ovidian erotic-mythological brief epic, but in tone and procedure it is a new departure, except that for Shelley it had been prophesied by his own rendition of the Homeric *Hymn to Mercury*. Both poems are in *ottava rima*, both have a Byronic touch, and both have been characterized accurately as possessing a tone of visionary cynicism. Hermes and the Witch of Atlas qualify the divine grandeurs among which they move, and remind us that imagination unconfined respects no orders of being, however traditional or natural.

G. Wilson Knight first pointed to the clear resemblance between the tone of *The Witch of Atlas* and Yeats's later style, and there is considerable evidence of the permanent effect of the poem's fantastic plot and properties upon Yeats. Shelley's *Witch* is Yeats's "Byzantium" writ large; both poems deal with Phase 15 of Yeats's *A Vision*, with the phase of poetic incarnation, and so with the state of the soul in which art is created. In a comparison of the two poems, the immediate contrast will be found in the extraordinary relaxation that Shelley allows himself. The nervous intensity that the theme demands is present in the *Witch*, but has been transmuted into an almost casual acceptance of intolerable realities that art cannot mitigate.

The Witch of Atlas, as Shelley says in the poem's highly ironic dedicatory stanzas to his wife, tells no story, false or true, but is "a visionary rhyme." If the Witch is to be translated at all into terms not her own, then she can only be the mythopoeic impulse or inventive faculty itself, one of whose manifestations is the Hermaphrodite, which we can translate as a poem, or any work of art. The Witch's boat is the emblem of her creative desire, and like the Hermaphrodite it works against nature. The Hermaphrodite is both a convenience for the Witch, helping her to go beyond natural limitations, and a companion of sorts, but a highly inadequate one, being little more than a robot. The limitations of art are involved here, for the Witch has rejected the love of every mortal being, and has chosen instead an automation of her own creation. In the poignant stanzas in which she rejects the suit of the nymphs, Shelley attains one of the immense triumphs of his art, but the implications of the triumph, and of the entire poem, are as deliberately chilling as the Byzantine vision of the aging Yeats.

Though the Witch turns her playful and antinomian spirit to the labor of upsetting church and state, in the poem's final stanzas, and subverts even the tired conventions of mortality as well as of morality, the ultimate impression she makes upon us is one of remoteness. The fierce aspirations of *Prometheus Unbound* were highly qualified by a consciously manipulated prophetic irony, yet they retained their force, and aesthetic immediacy, as the substance of what Shelley passionately desired. The ruin that shadows love in *Prometheus Unbound*, the *amphisbaena* or two-headed serpent that could move downward and outward to destruction again, the warning made explicit in the closing stanzas spoken by Demogorgon; it is these antithetical hints that survived in Shelley longer than the vehement hope of his lyrical drama. *The Sensitive Plant* and *The Witch of Atlas* manifest a subtle movement away from that hope. *Epipsychidion*, the most exalted of Shelley's poems, seeks desperately to renovate that hope by placing it in the context of heterosexual love, and with the deliberate and thematic self-combustion of the close of *Epipsychidion* Shelley appears to have put all hope aside, and to have prepared himself for his magnificent but despairing last phase, of which the enduring monuments are *Adonais* and *The Triumph of Life*.

VII

What man most passionately wants is his living wholeness and his living unison, not his own isolate salvation of his "soul." Man wants his physical fulfillment first and foremost, since now, once and once only, he is in the flesh and potent. For man, as for flower and beast and bird, the supreme triumph is to be most vividly, most perfectly alive. Whatever the unborn and the dead may know, they cannot know the beauty, the marvel of being alive in the flesh. The dead may look after the afterwards. But the magnificent here and now of life in the flesh is ours, and ours alone, and ours only for a time.

—D. H. LAWRENCE, *Apocalypse*

Except for Blake's *Visions of the Daughters of Albion*, which it in some respects resembles, *Epipsychidion* is the most outspoken and eloquent appeal for free love in the language. Though this appeal is at the heart of the poem, and dominates its most famous passage (lines 147–54), it is only one aspect of a bewilderingly problematical work. *Epipsychidion* was intended by Shelley to be his *Vita Nuova*, celebrating the discovery of his Beatrice in Emilia Viviani. It proved however to be a climactic and not an initiatory poem, for in it Shelley culminates the quest begun in *Alastor*, only to find after culmination that the quest remains unfulfilled and unfulfillable. The desire of Shelley remains infinite, and the only emblem adequate to that desire is the morning and evening star, Venus, at whose sphere the shadow cast by earth into the heavens reaches its limits. After *Epipsychidion*, in *Adonais* and *The Triumph of Life*, only the star of Venus abides as an image of the good. It is not Emilia Viviani but her image that proves inadequate in *Epipsychidion*, a poem whose most turbulent and valuable element is its struggle to record the process of image-making. Of all Shelley's major poems, *Epipsychidion* most directly concerns itself with the mind in creation. "Mont Blanc" has the same position among Shelley's shorter poems, and has the advantage of its relative discursiveness, as the poet meditates upon the awesome spectacle before him. *Epipsychidion* is continuous rhapsody, and sustains its lyrical intensity of a lovers' confrontation for six hundred lines. The mind in creation, here and in *A Defence of Poetry*, is as a fading coal, and much of Shelley's art in the poem is devoted to the fading phenomenon, as image after image recedes and the poet-lover feels more fearfully the double burden of his love's inexpressibility and its necessary refusal to accept even natural, let alone societal limitations.

There is in Shelley's development as a poet a continuous effort to subvert the poetic image, so as to arrive at a more radical kind of verbal figure, which Shelley never altogether achieved. Tenor and vehicle are imported into one another, and the choice of natural images increasingly favors those already on the point of vanishing, just within the ken of eye and ear. The world is skeptically taken up into the mind, and there are suggestions and overtones that all of reality is a phantasmagoria. Shelley becomes an idealist totally skeptical of the metaphysical foundations of idealism, while he continues to entertain a skeptical materialism, or rather he becomes a fantasist pragmatically given to some materialist hypotheses that his imagination regards as absurd. This is not necessarily a self-contradiction, but it is a kind of psychic split, and it is exposed very powerfully in *Epipsychidion*. Who wins a triumph in the poem, the gambler with the limits of poetry and of human relationship, or the inexorable limits? Space, time, loneliness, mortality, wrong—all these are put aside by vision, yet vision darkens perpetually in the poem. "The world, unfortunately, is real; I, unfortunately, am Borges," is the ironic reflection of a great contemporary seer of phantasmagorias, as he brings his refutation of time to an unrefuting close. Shelley too is swept along by what destroys him and is inescapable, the reality that will not yield to the most relentless of imaginings. In that knowledge, he turns to elegy and away from celebration.

Adonais, Shelley's formal elegy for Keats, is a great monument in the history of the English elegy, and yet hardly an elegy at all. Nearly five hundred lines long, it exceeds in scope and imaginative ambition its major English ancestors, the "Astrophel" of Spenser and the "Lycidas" of Milton, as well as such major descendants as Arnold's "Thyrsis" and Swinburne's "Ave Atque Vale." Only Tennyson's *In Memoriam* rivals it as an attempt to make the elegy a vehicle for not less than everything a particular poet has to say on the ultimates of human existence. Yet Tennyson, for all his ambition, stays within the bounds of elegy. *Adonais*, in the astonishing sequence of its last eighteen stanzas, is no more an elegy proper than Yeats's "Byzantium" poems are. Like the "Byzantium" poems (which bear a close relation to it) *Adonais* is a high song of poetic self-recognition in the presence of foreshadowing death, and also a description of poetic existence, even of a poem's state of being.

Whether Shelley holds together the elegiac and visionary aspects of his poem is disputable; it is difficult to see the full continuity that takes the poet from his hopeless opening to his more than triumphant close, from:

> I weep for Adonais—he is dead!
> O, weep for Adonais! though our tears
> Thaw not the frost which binds so dear a head!

to:

> I am borne darkly, fearfully, afar;
> Whilst, burning through the inmost veil of Heaven,
> The soul of Adonais, like a star,
> Beacons from the abode where the Eternal are.

From frost to fire as a mode of renewal for the self: that is an archetypal Romantic pattern, familiar to us from *The Ancient Mariner* and the Intimations Ode (see the contrast between the last line of stanza VIII and the first of stanza IX in that poem). But *Adonais* breaks this pattern, for the soul of Shelley's Keats burns through the final barrier to revelation only by means of an energy that is set against nature, and the frost that no poetic tears can thaw yields only to "the fire for which all thirst," but which no natural man can drink, for no living man can drink of the whole wine of the burning fountain. As much as Yeats's "All Souls' Night," *Adonais* reaches out to a reality of ghostly intensities, yet Shelley as well as Yeats is reluctant to leave behind the living man who blindly drinks his drop, and *Adonais* is finally a "Dialogue of Self and Soul," in which the Soul wins a costly victory, as costly as the Self's triumph in Yeats's "Dialogue." The Shelley who cries out, in rapture and dismay, "The massy earth and spherèd skies are riven!" is a poet who has given himself freely to the tempest of creative destruction, to a reality beyond the natural, yet who movingly looks back upon the shore and upon the throng he has forsaken. The close of *Adonais* is a triumph of character over personality, to use a Yeatsian dialectic, but the personality of the lyric poet is nevertheless the dominant aesthetic element in the poem's dark and fearful apotheosis.

"Apotheosis is not the origin of the major man," if we are to credit Stevens, but the qualified assertions of Shelley do proclaim such an imaginative humanism in the central poems that preceded *Adonais*. In *Adonais* the imagination forsakes humanism, even as it does in the "Byzantium" poems.

Though *Adonais* has been extensively Platonized and Neoplatonized by a troop of interpreters, it is in a clear sense a materialist's poem, written out of a materialist's despair at his own deepest convictions, and finally a poem soaring above those convictions into a mystery that leaves a pragmatic materialism quite undisturbed. Whatever supernal apprehension it is that Shelley attains in the final third of *Adonais*, it is not in any ordinary sense a religious faith, for the only attitude toward natural existence it fosters in the poet is one of unqualified rejection, and indeed its pragmatic postulate is simply suicide. Nothing could be more different in spirit from Demogorgon's closing lines in *Prometheus Unbound* than the final stanzas of *Adonais*, and the ruthlessly skeptical Shelley must have known this.

He knew also though that we do not judge poems by pragmatic tests, and the splendor of the resolution to *Adonais* is not impaired by its implications of human defeat. Whether Keats lives again is unknown to Shelley; poets are among "the enduring dead," and Keats "wakes *or* sleeps" with them. The endurance is not then necessarily a mode of survival, and what flows back to the burning fountain is not necessarily the *human* soul, though it is "pure spirit." Or if it is the soul of Keats as well as "the soul of Adonais," then the accidents of individual personality have abandoned it, making this cold comfort indeed. Still, Shelley is not offering us (or himself) comfort; his elegy has no parallel to Milton's consolation in "Lycidas":

> There entertain him all the Saints above,
> In solemn troops, and sweet Societies
> That sing, and singing in their glory move,
> And wipe the tears forever from his eyes.

To Milton, as a Christian poet, death is somehow unnatural. To Shelley, for all his religious temperament, death is wholly natural, and if death is dead, then nature must be dead also. The final third of *Adonais* is desperately apocalyptic in a way that *Prometheus Unbound*, Act IV, was not. For

Prometheus Unbound ends in a Saturnalia, though there are darker implications also, but *Adonais* soars beyond the shadow that the earth casts into the heavens. Shelley was ready for a purgatorial vision of earth, and no longer could sustain even an ironic hope.

VIII

Mal dare, e mal tener lo mondo pulcro
ha tolto loro, e posti a questa zuffa;
qual ella sia, parole non ci appulcro.
—Inferno 7:58–60

That ill they gave,
And ill they kept, hath of the beauteous world
Deprived, and set them at this strife, which needs
No labour'd phrase of mine to set it off.
—CARY, *The Vision of Dante*

There are elements in *The Triumph of Life*, Shelley's last poem, that mark it as an advance over all the poetry he had written previously. The bitter eloquence and dramatic condensation of the style are new; so is a ruthless pruning of invention. The mythic figures are few, being confined to the "Shape all light," the charioteer, and Life itself, while the two principal figures, Shelley and Rousseau, appear in their proper persons, though in the perspective of eternity, as befits a vision of judgment. The tone of Shelley's last poem is derived from Dante's *Purgatorio*, even as much in *Epipsychidion* comes from Dante's *Vita Nuova*, but the events and atmosphere of *The Triumph of Life* have more in common with the *Inferno*. Still, the poem is a purgatorial work, for all the unrelieved horror of its vision, and perhaps Shelley might have found some gradations in his last vision, so as to climb out of the poem's impasse, if he had lived to finish it, though I incline to doubt this. As it stands, the poem is in hell, and Shelley is there, one of the apparently condemned, as all men are, he says, save for "the sacred few" of Athens and Jerusalem, martyrs to vision like Socrates, Jesus, and a chosen handful, with whom on the basis of *Adonais* we can place Keats, as he too had touched the world with his living flame, and then fled back up to his native noon.

The highest act of Shelley's imagination in the poem, perhaps in all of his poetry, is in the magnificent appropriateness of Rousseau's presence, from his first entrance to his last speech before the fragment breaks off. Rousseau is Virgil to Shelley's Dante, in the sense of being his imaginative ancestor, his guide in creation, and also in prophesying the dilemma the disciple would face at the point of crisis in his life. Shelley, sadly enough, was hardly in the middle of the journey, but at twenty-nine he had only days to live, and the imagination in him felt compelled to face the last things. Without Rousseau, Shelley would not have written the "Hymn to Intellectual Beauty" and perhaps not "Mont Blanc" either. Rousseau, more even than Wordsworth, was the prophet of natural man, and the celebrator of the state of nature. Even in 1816, writing his hymns and starting the process that would lead to the conception of *Prometheus Unbound*, Shelley fights against the natural man and natural religion, but he fights partly against his own desires, and the vision of Rousseau haunts him still in the "Ode to the West Wind" and in the greatest chant of the apocalyptic fourth act of the lyrical drama, the song of the Earth beginning "It interpenetrates my granite mass." Shelley knew that the spirit of Rousseau was what had moved him most in the spirit of the age, and temperamentally (which counts for most in a poet) it makes more sense to name Shelley the disciple and heir of Rousseau than of Godwin, or Wordsworth, or any of the later French theorists of Revolution. Rousseau and Hume make an odd formula of heart and head in Shelley, but they are the closest parallels to be found to him on the emotional and intellectual sides respectively.

Chastened and knowing, almost beyond knowledge, Rousseau enters the poem, speaking not to save his disciple, but to show him that he cannot be saved, and to teach him a style fit for his despair. The imaginative lesson of *The Triumph of Life* is wholly present in the poem's title: life always triumphs, for life our life is after all what the Preface to *Alastor* called it, a "lasting misery and loneliness." One Power only, the Imagination, is capable of redeeming life, "but that Power which strikes the luminaries of the world with sudden darkness and extinction, by awakening them to too exquisite a perception of its influences, dooms to a slow and poisonous decay those meaner spirits that dare to abjure its dominion." In *The Triumph of Life*, the world's luminaries are still the poets, stars of evening and morning, "heaven's living eyes," but they fade into a double light, the light of nature or the sun, and the harsher and more blinding light of Life, the destructive chariot of the poem's vision. The chariot of Life, like the apocalyptic chariots of Act IV, *Prometheus Unbound*, goes back to the visions of Ezekiel and Revelation for its sources, as the chariots of Dante and Milton did, but now Shelley gives a demonic parody of his sources, possibly following the example of Spenser's chariot of Lucifera. Rousseau is betrayed to the light of Life because he began by yielding his imagination's light to the lesser but seductive light of nature, represented in the poem by the "Shape all light" who offers him the waters of natural experience to drink. He drinks, he begins to forget everything in the mind's desire that had transcended nature, and so he falls victim to Life's destruction, and fails to become one of "the sacred few." There is small reason to doubt that Shelley, at the end, saw himself as having shared in Rousseau's fate. The poem, fragment as it is, survives its own despair, and stands with Keats's *The Fall of Hyperion* as a marvelously eloquent imaginative testament, fit relic of an achievement broken off too soon to rival Blake's or Wordsworth's, but superior to everything else in its own age.

IX

The great instrument of moral good is the imagination.
—*A Defence of Poetry*

Anti-Shelleyans have come in all intellectual shapes and sizes, and have included distinguished men of letters from Charles Lamb and De Quincey down to T. S. Eliot, Allen Tate, and their school in our day. To distinguish between the kinds of anti-Shelleyans is instructive, though the following categories are by no means mutually exclusive. One can count six major varieties of anti-Shelleyans, whether one considers them historically or in contemporary terms:

(1) The school of "common sense"
(2) The Christian orthodox
(3) The school of "wit"
(4) Moralists, of most varieties
(5) The school of "classic" form
(6) Precisionists, or concretists.

It is evident that examples of (1), (2), and (4) need not be confuted, as they are merely irrelevant. We may deal with (3), (5), and (6) in their own terms, rather than in Shelley's, and still find Shelley triumphant.

The "wit" of Shelley's poetry has little to do with that of seventeenth-century verse, but has much in common with the dialectical vivacity of Shaw, and something of the prophetic irony of Blake. If irony is an awareness of the terrible gap between aspiration and fulfillment, then the skeptical Shelley is among the most ironical of poets. If it is something else, as it frequently is in the school of Donne, one can observe that there are many wings in the house of wit, and one ought not to live in all of them simultaneously.

Form is another matter, and too complex to be argued fully here. The late C. S. Lewis justly maintained against the school of Eliot that Shelley was more classical in his sense of form, his balance of harmony and design, than Dryden. One can go further: Shelley is almost always a poet of the highest decorum, a stylist who adjusts his form and tone to his subject, whether it be the hammer-beat low style of *The Mask of Anarchy*, the urbane middle style of the "Letter to Maria Gisborne," or the sublime inventiveness of the high style as it is renovated in *Prometheus Unbound*. Shelley was sometimes a hasty or careless artist, but he was always an artist, a poet who neither could nor would stop being a poet. Dr. Samuel Johnson would have disliked Shelley's poetry, indeed would have considered Shelley to be dangerously mad, but he would have granted that it was poetry of a high if to him outmoded order. Critics less classical than Johnson will not grant as much, because their notions of classical form are not as deeply founded.

The precisionist or concretist is probably Shelley's most effective enemy, since everything vital in Shelley's poetry deliberately strains away from the minute particulars of experience. But this is oddly true of Wordsworth as well, though Wordsworth usually insisted upon the opposite. The poetry of renovation in the United States, in our time, had its chief exemplars in William Carlos Williams and in Wallace Stevens, and it is Stevens who is in the line of both Wordsworth and of Shelley. Williams's famous adage, "no ideas but in things," is the self-justified motto of one valid kind of poetic procedure, but it will not allow for the always relevant grandeurs of the sublime tradition, with its "great moments" of ecstasy and recognition. Wordsworth on the mountainside looks out and finds only a sea of mist, an emblem of the highest imaginative vision, in which the edges of things have blurred and faded out. Stevens, opening the door of his house upon the flames of the Northern Lights, confronts an Arctic effulgence flaring upon the frame of everything he is, but does not describe the flashing auroras. Shelley, at his greatest, precisely chants an energetic becoming that cannot be described in the concrete because its entire purpose is to modify the concrete, to compel a greater reality to appear:

> the one Spirit's plastic stress
> Sweeps through the dull dense world, compelling there,
> All new successions to the forms they wear;
> Torturing th' unwilling dross that checks its flight
> To its own likeness, as each mass may bear;
> And bursting in its beauty and its might
> From trees and beasts and men into the Heaven's light.

Had Shelley been able to accept any known faith, he would have given us the name and nature of that "one Spirit." Unlike Keats, he would not have agreed with Stevens that the great poems of heaven and hell had been written, and that only the great poem of earth remained to be composed. His own spirit was apocalyptic, and the still unwritten poems of heaven and hell waited mute upon the answering swiftness of his own imaginings, when he went on to his early finalities:

> As if that frail and wasted human form,
> Had been an elemental god.

The Role of Asia
in the Dramatic Action
of Shelley's *Prometheus Unbound*

Frederick A. Pottle

Since it is a myth, *Prometheus Unbound* is capable of endless allegorization. Some readers like to work out a detailed and particular allegory for it, others prefer to keep the allegory vague and general. Some even deprecate any attempt to formulate a "second meaning." All readers ought to agree that one should understand the myth as dramatic action on its own terms before one starts allegorizing. It may be legitimate to conclude that Demogorgon is Necessity because he says so-and-so, but until we despair of making dramatic sense out of him, we should not conclude that he says so-and-so because he is Necessity. What *happens* in *Prometheus Unbound*?

Though the opposition counts distinguished names, majority opinion seems agreed that there is only one action in the whole so-called drama, and that that action is completed before the First Act has hardly got under way. Prometheus announces at line 53 that he pities Jupiter; the remaining 2557 lines, it is maintained, consist merely of the unrolling necessary consequences of that action, and of jubilation over those consequences. This does not at all accord with what I find the text saying.

What has happened by the end of Act I? Prometheus, who cursed Jupiter three thousand years ago and has remained till at least very recently in a state of passionate enmity toward him, discovers that he no longer hates his persecutor and repents of his curse. This discovery by no means ends his sufferings or brings any alleviation of them; on the contrary, it precipitates a visitation of the Furies and a particularly horrible train of tortures. His state is then cheered by a chorus of prophetic spirits who announce that the hope, the prophecy they bear begins and ends in him (I.690–91, 706–7). Two things are to be noted about these spirits and their songs. First, it is not intimated that they are now putting in an appearance for the first time as a result of Prometheus's change of heart. On the con-

From *Shelley: A Collection of Critical Essays.* © 1965 by Prentice-Hall, Inc.

trary, one would infer that they have been consoling him all along, just as the Furies have been tormenting him. Secondly, their songs are by no means expressions of unmixed joy and hope: they are as sad as they are sweet. No portion of *Prometheus Unbound* has been so generally ignored as the songs of the Fifth and Sixth Spirits (I.763–79). Ione (I.756–57) characterizes their voices as despair mingled with love, and surely despair is not too strong a word for the sentiments these beautiful beings utter. "Yes," says the Fifth Spirit, "Love exists, I have seen him. But he was closely followed by Ruin." "Ah," rejoins the Sixth Spirit, "it is worse than that. Ruin —or Pain—masquerades as Love to betray the best and gentlest." The Chorus, speaking after Prometheus's recantation, does not deny that this is a true description of things as they still stand, but announces confidently that Prometheus will overcome Ruin: they know it as herdsmen know that the hawthorn will blow when they feel the winds of spring. The winds they have felt breathe from Prometheus:

> Wisdom, Justice, Love, and Peace,
> When they struggle to increase,
> Are to us as soft winds be.
> (I.796–98)

Undoubtedly Prometheus begins the action and will end it; we are told so explicitly. But one can begin and end an action without being able to perform all the middle parts of it. At the end of the First Act Prometheus has realized that only through Love can he be freed. All he can do now is to endure and willingly accept his destiny as "the saviour and the strength of suffering man" (I.816–17). He has passed beyond agony and solace (I.819), and is just as firmly pinned to the crag as he was when he cursed Jupiter. Only love can help, and his beloved is far from him (I.808). And the prophecy of his triumph, though the seasonal metaphor makes it seem more immediate than his own bleak vision of victory after an agony of literally innumerable years (I.424), is actually conditional and ambiguous. Wisdom, Justice, Love, and Peace must go on struggling to increase; even if spring comes, there may be delays and setbacks. Frost may blast the young blossoms.

The First Act is the action of Prometheus, the Second is devoted entirely to the action of Asia. She goes to her spouse in response to a summons— not *his* summons, for he has not consciously issued one, but a summons conveyed in two dreams which Panthea has dreamed at his feet. The first presents Prometheus freed, unscarred and rejuvenated, an ardent bridegroom awaiting his bride. But Asia is not summoned to go to her husband by the direct route that Panthea travels. Panthea's second dream was ostensibly another vision of things as they are, a vision of Ruin dogging the steps of Love. She saw a blasted almond-tree bloom, and the miraculous flowers were immediately thrown down by frost. But the fallen petals in this case bore no message of despair; they were stamped with the hopeful directive FOLLOW. And Asia then remembers that she too had had a dream in which FOLLOW was written across the mountain shadows and the leaves of the plants, and the wind in the pines had taken up the message. Echo-songs in the air now repeat the summons and indicate what is to be followed, whither, and why. Asia is to follow the aerial voices through caverns and forest, by lakes and fountains, through mountains growing ever more rugged, to rents, gulfs, and chasms in the earth (II.i.175–202). She is to do it because

> In the world unknown
> Sleeps a voice unspoken;
> By thy step alone
> Can its rest be broken;
> Child of Ocean!
> (II.i.190–94)

She accordingly sets out, hand in hand with Panthea. The eddies of echoes, we are informed, are actually much more than the mere guide they appear to her to be. They are a positive force attracting and impelling her, and they grow steadily stronger as she yields to their impetus; she half walks, half floats on her way, thinking her motion due to her own limbs (II.ii.41–63). She and Panthea pass through a shady damp forest thronged with nightingales, and are finally borne to the top of a pinnacle of rock among the mountains which they recognize as marking the portal to the abode of Demogorgon, a mysterious power already identified as directing the stream of sound (II.ii.43). As they stand admiring the Alpine landscape, which moves Asia to overt theologizing, the spirits, now for the first time become visible, urge her to put herself utterly into their hands and allow herself to be borne unresisting down to the throne of Demogorgon in an abyss below all natural caverns. A spell is treasured there for her alone (II.iii.88), but she can exert it only by utter surrender:

> We have bound thee, we guide thee;
> Down, down!
> With the bright form beside thee;
> Resist not the weakness,
> Such strength is in meekness
> That the Eternal, the Immortal,
> Must unloose through life's portal
> The snake-like Doom coiled underneath his throne
> By that alone.
> (II.iii.90–98)

The lyric (there are five stanzas in all) is apparently not merely an invitation to the descent but accompanies it. At any rate, when the next scene opens, Asia and Panthea are in the Cave of Demogorgon, and there is no reason to doubt that they got there on the Spirits' terms.

The statements that only Asia can rouse Demogorgon to action, that in Demogorgon's cave is treasured a spell for Asia alone, are as express as the earlier statement that the prophecy of regeneration begins and ends in Prometheus. Why then the critics' reluctance to grant that Asia performs an independent and essential part of the action? Undoubtedly because of her seeming passivity in the first three scenes of the Second Act. She follows, she is borne, she does not resist an invading weakness. Significant action, the critics seem to feel, needs to be embodied in language like that of the First Act, language that testifies to a struggle against resistance, language that asserts difficulty. Now, one very important critic, C. S. Lewis, of course does maintain that difficulty is precisely the subject of these scenes, but I do not see any evidence for thinking that the journey was meant to seem physically arduous. We might take as the norm of a really arduous journey that portion of the Second Book of *Paradise Lost* which deals with Satan's ascent from the gates of Hell up through Chaos. If the Second Act of *Prometheus Unbound* were presenting external or physical difficulty, as the Second Book of *Paradise Lost* is, we should hear of lacerating, almost impenetrable, undergrowth in the forest, or rough stones that draw blood from clinging hands and clambering knees, of abysses that the giddy traveler must hang over with inadequate support, of tunnels and chimneys that narrow and threaten to hold him fast. The forest in *Prometheus Unbound* is damp and very shady, but it has the open pathways between the tree trunks that one would expect in a stand of large evergreens (II.ii.1–2). If the poet had wished us to feel that passage through it was physically difficult, he would not have called its gloom "divine" (II.ii.22), and he would not have devoted seventeen lines to a description of the songs of the nightingales. If Asia and Panthea encounter any physical difficulties in the ascent to the pinnacle, they are not reported or alluded to, while the help they are getting from the stream of sound is insisted on.

Yet no careful reader can feel that Asia is an automaton or even that she is naturally impassive. When we first meet her, she is displaying extreme impatience for Panthea's return. She does not instantly follow the echo guide, but ponders her action and takes time to make up her mind (II.i.188–89, 207–8). She says nothing further to indicate that she is on the alert, but the spirits, in everything *they* say, assume that her assent is not irrevocable, that she might balk at any moment. In short, she wills to follow, she wills to continue to follow, and that constitutes her action in these scenes. *Pace* Professor Lewis, her progress is not physically difficult but rather the opposite: it is so easy and pleasant as to raise doubts whether it can possibly conduct to an heroic goal. Asia's difficulty in these scenes is to overcome the scruples that would keep her from surrendering herself to a duty which is disquietingly pleasant. And this difficulty, which I feel to be real, is expressed only indirectly.

This may be considered too subtle for drama. Drama is the most primitive of all literary forms, and our own dramatic tradition is especially committed to physical violence. It has, indeed, often been stated as a truism that physical non-resistance is essentially undramatic. That seems to me simply not true. Willing, not muscular action, is the essential of drama. A physical non-resistance which we see to be gravely and consciously willed, though not the usual stuff of drama in our tradition, will function dramatically in our experience if we will allow it to.

Difficulty in the Fourth Scene is of a more obvious sort, and is expressed directly in Asia's speeches. In the Cave of Demogorgon she performs an action parallel to and of equal importance with that of Prometheus in the First Act. He forgave Jupiter, she works her way to the word that will topple Jupiter from Olympus. In a way, the action is more difficult than his. He had to struggle with excruciating pain, both physical and mental, but it does not appear that he had to struggle with his hatred in order to overcome it. Reaching for it one day, he found it evaporated (I.53). On the other hand, we see her in the agony of struggling through and out of some of her most passionately held attitudes.

One should not speak too confidently of "understanding" this pregnant and subtle colloquy, but two remarks concerning it seem warranted. Demogorgon, though definitely a mighty power who can tell Asia all she dares ask (II.iv.7), always in fact answers her in her own terminology and at the level of her own understanding. We are not to assume that she is merely talking to herself, but she certainly gets no answers she has not herself thought her way to. Secondly, because Demogorgon adapts his answers to her understanding, his oracular utterances must be taken as provisional and progressive. They are not coordinate articles of a creed, but a progress through dogma to the utterly undogmatic faith which will unloose the Doom sleeping under Demogorgon's throne:

> So much I asked before, and my heart gave
> The response thou hast given; and of such truths
> Each to itself must be the oracle.
>
> (II.iv.121–23)

Prometheus, the god-defier, engages in no theological speculation whatever. To him Jupiter is god and all but omnipotent; Jupiter is wicked, cruel, ungrateful, and unjust; Jupiter will ultimately fall. Until he falls, Prometheus expects to be tortured. To Prometheus evil is a fact of experience. He never asks why evil should exist, or if Jupiter comprehends all the evil there is in the cosmos.

Asia, on the other hand, is a passionate theologian, or to be precise is passionately interested in the problem of evil. On the pinnacle, before descending to the Cave of Demogorgon, she had tentatively suggested that the glories and shortcomings of the physical universe might be explained by assuming that it was the work of some beautiful spirit too weak to prevent evil from invading and staining its work. She says she could worship that kind of Creator (II.iii.11–16). Her cast of mind, we see, leads her to posit creation and a Creator with human attributes, and to repel any suggestion that the Creator of the physical universe may be responsible for evil.

But she is not so sure as to other possible creators, and in the Cave of

Demogorgon she at once begins putting the questions that trouble her profoundly. Who made the *living* world, the world of Mind? Who made thought, passion, reason, will, imagination? Who made the sense of love? Demogorgon, in the tersest possible fashion, replies God, Almighty God, Merciful God. He will later suggest that she relinquish this terminology and some of the concepts associated with it, but the important thing at this stage is to give emphatic confirmation, in such terms as possess reality for her, to her intuition that the world of mind is fundamentally divine, or is like divinity, beneficent divinity. Who then, she continues, made terror, madness, crime, remorse, hate, self-contempt, all the varieties of pain? Demogorgon again uses her implied references, but to cover the facts this time he has to resort to ambiguity. "He reigns" may be taken as a virtual repetition of his previous answer, "Almighty God," or it may mean that the Maker of Evil is a usurper. Actually, it means both things at the same time. "Almighty God," the Primal Power, did not make Evil, but if one is to use this kind of language, he "made" the "evil things" which the malignancy of Jupiter converted into positive evil. Demogorgon at this stage wishes to give emphatic confirmation to Asia's intuition that the world of mind is dominated by an Evil Power which it is possible and proper to dethrone, but also to prepare the ground for his next and final position, which will be that when the usurper goes and the Primal Power alone "reigns," the means or occasion of evil, relative to man, will still inhere in the universe.

Asia not unnaturally takes him to be referring solely to a Usurper, and passionately demands the Usurper's name. The world asks but his name, she says; curses shall drag him down. She of course knows Jupiter's name, though she has not yet spoken it, but she confidently expects a curse already uttered to drag *him* down. Before ever she entered the Cave of Demogorgon she had come to the conclusion that the evil of Jupiter, real and horrible as it is, cannot cover all the evil in the universe. There is, she feels sure, an Evil more radical; Jupiter is only a front man. And Demogorgon, by saying "He reigns" rather than "Jupiter" has told that she is so far on the right track.

Well, who *does* reign? Demogorgon's first three utterances might make us think that we had left Greek theology for the Judeo-Christian, but that would be too hasty. We are still within the Greek system, and in that system the question is highly pertinent. Greek myth records a succession of reigning deities, none of them omnipotent. Jupiter (Zeus) had dethroned Saturn (Kronos), just as Saturn had dethroned Uranus, but Jupiter himself was held to be subject to Fate or Necessity. He took over a created universe, and (in Shelley's version) had made nothing but evil. But he was not the originator of evil. So far as Asia could make out, evil entered the world in the reign of Saturn, when Time first appeared. Evil under Saturn had been negative or privative: men lived in joy but in a calm vegetable joy, denied the knowledge that was their birthright. Positive evil—famine, heat, cold, toil, disease, war, violent death, raging and lacerating passions—arrived with Jupiter, and increased in direct proportion as men received knowledge and skill from Prometheus. Prometheus's gifts were obviously not in themselves evil but glorious. Who then rains down evil? Surely not Jupiter. Prometheus pretty much set him up in business, and he is obviously afraid of Prometheus. He does not act like the Creator of Evil, he acts like some one who takes orders. Who is his hidden master? Is his master perhaps a slave too? Where does it all end?

My paraphrase, though highly speculative in its inferences, has so far been content to base itself on what is explicitly provided by Shelley's text. I want now, however, not merely to read *into* the dialogue, but to read *in* some dialogue, and I shall not be deterred if the result sounds more like Shaw than like Shelley.

ASIA. Who is his master? Is he too a slave?

DEMOGORGON. All spirits who serve evil things are enslaved. You are right in thinking Jupiter enslaved.

ASIA. But how about the Being you called God some lines back? If he made the living world, if he is almighty, must *he* not be the hidden master of Jupiter? If he is using evil, is he not enslaved by it?

DEMOGORGON. I employed the terminology and the concepts you gave me, and am glad to note that you now see some difficulties in them. If you load your questions concerning the Primal Power with demands that that Power be a personal, omnipotent Creator, you are going to run into irresolvable contradictions. And "God" is not a very good term either. I suggest that it had better be left to Jupiter.

ASIA. Very well, I give up those demands, holding on only to your assurance that the universe of mind is god-like and beneficent. But is it not possible to carry Jupiter any farther back? If he is a slave, who is his master?

DEMOGORGON. I said that spirits who serve evil *things* are enslaved; I did not say that Jupiter serves the Evil One. I grant that "slave" implies "master"; all figures from the world of human experience are misleading when applied to ultimates. *The deep truth is imageless.* Would it be at all helpful if I told you that the evil Jupiter serves is not personal, that it is, as you yourself hinted, Time? Time, relative to man, is evil, and Time is a mystery. Everything on earth is subject to Time, but not because of malignancy in the will of some Power superior to Jupiter. The Ultimate Power wishes man well and can and does get through to him. Love is not subject to Time.

ASIA. I have asked these questions before, and you have now

confirmed the answers that my heart gave me. These
truths must not be elaborated, systematized,
institutionalized. In such matters each heart must be its
own oracle. One question more, a question I would not
ask if I had the answer anywhere within my own being.
Prometheus will be freed, but when?
DEMOGORGON. Now.

Prometheus's action was to repent of his curse, to stop hating the
manifested evil he continued unyieldingly to resist. Asia's action is to give
up her demand for an ultimate Personal Evil, to combine an unshakable
faith that the universe is sound at the core with a realization that, as regards
man, Time is radically and incurably evil. That action is now finished.
Demogorgon ascends the car to dethrone Jupiter, Asia rises from the abyss
transfigured by the pouring in of that Eternal Love which is not subject to
Time and Change.

Allegorization of myth has exactly the same values and is subject to
the same dangers as any other kind of paraphrase of poetry. A paraphrase
that is substituted for or imported into a poem is reductive, but a paraphrase
that is annotative or exploratory may lead us deeper into the poem's concreteness. My allegorization of *Prometheus Unbound* will be justified if it
backs up my reading of the action.

Shelley's Prometheus has too often been taken to represent the human
mind, Asia to represent Eternal Love or Intellectual Beauty, and Jupiter to
be the embodiment of merely external evil. Though in one aspect (an important one) Prometheus does seem to symbolize human mind and Asia
Nature, a more profound and consistent reading would regard human mind
as divided between Prometheus, Asia, and Jupiter. Prometheus (whose
name in Greek means "forethought") symbolizes intellect, understanding,
the inventive, rational faculties of mankind. Asia is the affective side of
mind: emotion, passion, imagination. The separation of Asia from Prometheus is a "fall" of the Blakean sort which produced Urizen and Ahania,
Los and Enitharmon. Asia is not Intellectual Beauty or Eternal Love, for
she dwells in, and is wholly subject to, the world of Time and Change,
but she is the chief conduit of Eternal Love into that world. Jupiter does
not represent all the evil of human experience. He is subjective or man-
made evil: custom, reaction, tyranny, superstition, outworn creeds. Man's
intellect gave this kind of evil all its strength and has then been confined
and tortured by it. Intellect of itself is capable of realizing that we make
our own mental tortures by hating what we should merely resist, but
knowledge alone will not bring reform or regeneration. Prometheus will
never get free without help from Asia. "Until," Shelley says in his Preface
to *Prometheus Unbound*, "the mind can love, and admire, and trust, and
hope, . . . reasoned principles of moral conduct are seeds cast upon the
high-way of life." Or again, in *A Defence of Poetry*, "The great instrument
of moral good is the imagination" (paragraph 13).

But not the unregenerate Imagination. Asia must go down to the Cave of Demogorgon, the affections must sink back on themselves down into the unconscious depths of being and be made over. Specifically, the affections must exorcize the demons of infancy, whether personal or of the race, and must rebuild themselves in accord with a mature theology. But is not this to turn matters precisely upside down? Surely it is the function of the heart to forgive and of the head to construct theologies? No, would certainly be Shelley's firm rejoinder. The head must sincerely forgive, must willingly eschew hatred on purely experimental grounds. "Revenge, retaliation, atonement, are pernicious *mistakes*" [Preface to *The Cenci*, emphasis added]; intellect must "discover the *wisdom* of universal love" ["Essay on Christianity," emphasis added]. And since the evidence on which all religions are founded is revealed to the heart and does not have the character of experimental verifiability which the intellect demands for its operations, intellect, to be true to itself, must remain scrupulously agnostic. If it does apply the operations of logic to the content of revelation, it produces precisely Jupiter. Theology, in the form of concrete poetic speculation, is the domain and the duty of the imagination.

The Imagination will not get a mature theology and a right religion until, as I have said, it is able to reconcile an unshakable but unelaborated faith that the universe is good and radically beneficent with a calm acceptance of the fact that when all man-made evil is cast off, men will still be confronted by chance and death and mutability.

And a right religion is essential for the overthrow of man-made evil. *Prometheus Unbound* is not humanist in its implications. The power we need to help ourselves is not our own but comes from on high, and will be granted if we make ourselves receptive of it. Eternal Love will stream with increasing power through us to reform the world, not merely the world of mind but also the world of matter. Human intellect thus empowered will build a new heaven and a new earth. The action which began in Prometheus will end in him.

Shelley Disfigured:
The Triumph of Life

Paul de Man

*while digging in the grounds for the new foundations, the broken
fragments of a marble statue were unearthed. They were submitted to
various antiquaries, who said that, so far as the damaged pieces would
allow them to form an opinion, the statue seemed to be that of a mutilated
Roman satyr; or, if not, an allegorical figure of Death. Only one or two
old inhabitants guessed whose statue those fragments had composed.*
—THOMAS HARDY, "Barbara of the House of Grebe"

Like several of the English Romantics' major works *The Triumph of Life*,
Shelley's last poem, is, as is well known, a fragment that has been
unearthed, edited, reconstructed and much discussed. All this archeological
labor can be considered a response to the questions that articulate one of
the text's main structures: " 'And what is this? / Whose shape is that within
the car? and why—' " ([lines] 177–78) [All quotations from *The Triumph of
Life* are from *Shelley's* The Triumph of Life, *A Critical Study*, edited by Donald
H. Reiman. University of Illinois Press, 1965]; later repeated in a more
subject-oriented, second-person mode: " 'Whence camest thou? and
whither goest thou?/ How did thy course begin,' I said, 'and why?' " ([lines]
296–97); finally repeated again, now in the first person: " 'Shew whence I
came, and where I am, and why—' " ([line] 398). These questions can easily
be referred back to the enigmatic text they punctuate and they are characteristic of the interpretive labor associated with Romanticism. In the case
of this movement, they acquire an edge of urgency which is often lacking
when they are addressed to earlier periods, except when these periods are
themselves mediated by the neo-Hellenism, the neo-medievalism or the
neo-Baroque of the late eighteenth and the early nineteenth century. This
is not surprising, since they are precisely the archeological questions that
prompt us to deduce present from the identification of the more or less
immediately anterior past, as well as from the process that leads from then
to now. Such an attitude coincides with the use of history as a way to new
beginnings, as "digging in the grounds for the new foundations." Much
is invested in these metaphors of architecture and of statuary on which
seems to hinge our ability to inhabit the world. But if this curiosity about
antecedents has produced admirable philological results and allowed, as

From *Deconstruction and Criticism*. © 1979 by The Continuum Publishing Company. Originally entitled "Shelley Disfigured."

in the case of *The Triumph of Life*, for the establishment of texts whose unreliability is at least controlled by more reliable means, the questions which triggered all this industry remain more than ever in suspense: What is the meaning of *The Triumph of Life*, of Shelley and of Romanticism? What shape does it have, how did its course begin and why? Perhaps the difficulty of the answers is prefigured in the asking of the questions. The status of all these where's and what's and how's and why's is at stake, as well as the system that links these interrogative pronouns, on the one hand, to questions of definition and of temporal situation and, on the other hand, to questions of shape and of figure. Such questions allow one to conclude that *The Triumph of Life* is a fragment of something whole, or Romanticism a fragment, or a moment, in a process that now includes us within its horizon. What relationship do we have to such a text that allows us to call it a fragment that we are then entitled to reconstruct, to identify and implicitly to complete? This supposes, among other things, that Shelley or Romanticism are themselves entities which, like a statue, can be broken into pieces, mutilated or allegorized (to use Hardy's alternatives) after having been stiffened, frozen, erected or whatever one wants to call the particular rigidity of statues. Is the status of a text line the status of a statue? Yeats, one of Shelley's closest readers and disciples, wrote a fine poem about history and form called "The Statues," which it would be rewarding to read in conjunction with *The Triumph of Life*. But there are more economic ways to approach this text and to question the possibility of establishing a relationship to Shelley and to Romanticism in general. After all, the link between the present I and its antecedents is itself dramatized in the poem, most explicitly and at greatest length in the encounter between the narrator and the figure designated by the proper name Rousseau, who has himself much to say about his own predecessors.

II

The unearthed fragments of this fragment, the discarded earlier versions, disclose that the relationship between Shelley and Rousseau, or between Rousseau and his ancestors, underwent considerable changes as the composition of the poem progressed. Consider, for instance, the passage in which the poet, guided at this moment by Rousseau, passes judgment upon his contemporaries and immediate predecessors, including the openly alluded to Wordsworth, with such vehemence that he condemns them all to oblivion. He is reproached for this by Rousseau who intervenes to assert that he himself, as well as Voltaire, would have ascended to "the fane / Where truth and its inventors sit enshrined," if they had not been so fainthearted as to lack faith in their own intellectual labor as well as, by implication, that of their ancestors. Those encrypted statues of Truth are identified as "Plato and his pupil" (presumably Aristotle) who "Reigned from the center to the circumference" and prepared the way for Bacon and modern science. Rousseau's and Voltaire's capitulation is not a sheer loss however, since Rousseau has gained insight that he is able to communicate in turn to the young Shelley. Donald H. Reiman, the editor of *The Triumph of Life*, glosses the passage as follows:

> Rousseau . . . tries to impress on the Poet that it was exactly this attitude toward the past struggle of great men that led him and Voltaire to abandon their reforming zeal and succumb to life. Thus the poet's contemptuous allusion to Wordsworth turns against him as Rousseau endeavors to show the Poet how the mistakes of those who have preceded him, especially idealists like himself, can serve as a warning to him: Rousseau and Voltaire fell because they adopted the contemptuous attitude toward history that the poet now displays; the child *is* father of the man, and Shelley's generation, representing the full mastery of the age that dawned in the French Revolution, can learn from the mistakes of that age's earlier generations (those of Rousseau and Voltaire and of Wordsworth).

Although this is certainly not presented as an interpretation of the entire text, but only of this discarded passage, it remains typical of the readings generally given of *The Triumph of Life*, even when they are a great deal more complicated than this straightforward statement. It is a clear example of the recuperation of a failing energy by means of an increased awareness: Rousseau lacked power, but because he can consciously articulate the causes of his weakness in words, the energy is preserved and recovered in the following generation. And this reconversion extends back to its originators, since the elders, at first condemned, are now reinstated in the name of their negative but exemplary knowledge. The child *is* father of the man, just as Wordsworth lucidly said, both humbling and saving himself in the eyes of his followers. This simple motion can take on considerable dialectical intricacy without altering its fundamental scheme. The entire debate as to whether *The Triumph of Life* represents or heralds a movement of growth or of degradation is part of this same genetic and historical metaphor. The unquestioned authority of this metaphor is much more important than the positive or negative valorization of the movement it generates.

The initial situation of Rousseau—allied with Voltaire and Wordsworth in a shared failure, as opposed to Plato, Aristotle and Bacon, and as opposed, by implication, to Shelley himself—changes in later versions. In the last available text, itself frozen into place by Shelley's accidental death, the hierarchy is quite different: Rousseau is now set apart quite sharply from the representatives of the Enlightenment (which include Voltaire next to Kant and Frederick the Great) who are condemned with some of the original severity, without Rousseau reproving him for it. No allusion to Wordsworth is included at this point, though Wordsworth is certainly present in other regions of the poem. Rousseau is now classified with Plato and Aristotle, but whereas these philosophers were held up as untarnished images of

Truth in the earlier version, they are now fallen and, in the imagery of the poem, chained to the chariot of Life, together with "the great bards of old" (line 247). The reasons for their fall, as well as the elements in their works and in their lives that both unite and distinguish them from Rousseau, are developed in passages that are not difficult to interpret from a thematic point of view. The resulting hierarchies have become more complex: we first have a class of entirely condemned historical personages, which includes representatives of the Enlightenment as well as the emperors and popes of Christianity (lines 281 ff.); on a distinctly higher level, but nevertheless defeated, we find Rousseau, Plato, Aristotle and Homer. As possibly exonerated from this defeat, the poem mentions only Bacon, a remnant from the earlier passage who now has lost much of his function, as well as "the sacred few" (line 128) who, unlike Adonais in the earlier poem, had no earthly destiny whatsoever, either because, by choice or destiny, they died too early or because, like Christ or Socrates, they are mere fictions in the writings of others. As for Shelley himself, his close proximity to Rousseau is now more strongly marked than in the earlier passage; the possibility of his escape from Rousseau's destiny has now become problematic and depends on one's reading of Rousseau's own story, which constitutes the main narrative sequence of the poem.

Lengthy and complex as it is, Rousseau's self-narrated history provides no answer to his true identity, although he is himself shown in quest of such an answer. Questions of origin, of direction and of identity punctuate the text without ever receiving a clear answer. They always lead back to a new scene of questioning which merely repeats the quest and recedes in infinite regress: the narrator asks himself " 'And what is this?' " (line 177) and receives an enigmatic answer (" 'Life!' ") from an enigmatic shape; once identified as Rousseau, the shape can indeed reveal some other names in the pageant of history but is soon asked, by the poet, to identify itself in a deeper sense than by a mere name: " 'How did thy course begin . . . and why?' " Complying with this request, Rousseau narrates the history of his existence, also culminating in an encounter with a mysterious entity, " ' A shape all light' " (line 352) to whom, in his turn, he puts the question " 'whence I came, and where I am, and why—.' " As an answer, he is granted a vision of the same spectacle that prompted the poet-narrator's questioning in the first place; we have to imagine the same sequence of events repeating themselves for Shelley, for Rousseau and for whomever Rousseau chose to question in his turn as Shelley questioned him. The structure of the text is not one of question and answer, but of a question whose meaning, as question, is effaced from the moment it is asked. The answer to the question is another question, asking what and why one asked, and thus receding ever further from the original query. This movement of effacing and of forgetting becomes prominent in the text and dispels any illusion of dialectical progress or regress. The articulation in terms of the questions is displaced by a very differently structured process that pervades all levels of the narrative and that repeats itself in the main sequences as well as in what seem to be lateral episodes. It finally engulfs and dissolves what started out to be, like *Alastor*, *Epipsychidion* or even *Prometheus Unbound*, a quest (or, like *Adonais*, an elegy), to replace it by something quite different for which we have no name readily available among the familiar props of literary history.

Whenever this self-receding scene occurs, the syntax and the imagery of the poem tie themselves into a knot which arrests the process of understanding. The resistance of these passages is such that the reader soon forgets the dramatic situation and is left with only these unresolved riddles to haunt him: the text becomes the successive and cumulative experience of these tangles of meaning and of figuration. One of these tangles occurs near the end of Rousseau's narration of his encounter with the "shape all light" assumed to possess the key to his destiny:

> "as one between desire and shame
> Suspended, I said . . .
>
> . . . .
> 'Shew whence I came, and where I am, and why—
> Pass not away upon the passing stream.'
>
> " 'Arise and quench thy thirst' was her reply.
> And as a shut lily, stricken by the wand
> Of dewy morning's vital alchemy,
>
> "I rose; and bending at her sweet command,
> Touched with faint lips the cup she raised,
> And suddenly my brain became as sand
>
> "Where the first wave had more than half erased
> The track of deer on desert Labrador,
> Whilst the fierce wolf from which they fled amazed
>
> "Leaves his stamp visibly upon the shore
> Until the second bursts—so on my sight
> Burst a new Vision never seen before.—"
>
> [ll. 398–410]

The scene dramatizes the failure to satisfy a desire for self-knowledge and can therefore indeed be considered as something of a key passage. Rousseau is not given a satisfactory answer, for the ensuing vision is a vision of continued delusion that includes him. He undergoes instead a metamorphosis in which his brain, the center of his consciousness, is transformed. The transformation is also said to be the erasure of an imprinted track, a passive, mechanical operation that is no longer within the brain's own control: both the production and the erasure of the track are not an act performed by the brain, but the brain being acted upon by something else. The resulting "sand" is not, as some commentators imply, an image of drought and sterility (this is no desert, but a shore washed by abundant waters). "My brain became as sand" suggests the modification of a knowledge into the surface on which this knowledge ought to be recorded. Ought to be, for instead of being clearly imprinted it is "more than half erased" and covered over. The process is a replacement, a substitution, continuing the substitution of "brain" by "sand," of one kind of track, said to be like that of a deer, by another, said to be like that of a wolf "from which [the deer] fled amazed." They mark a stage in the metamorphosis of Rousseau into his present state or shape; when we first meet him, he is

> . . . what I thought was an old root which grew
> To strange distortion out of the hill side . . .
>
> And . . . the grass which methought hung so wide
> And white, was but his thin discoloured hair,
> And . . . the holes he vainly sought to hide
>
> Were or had been eyes.
>
> [ll. 182–88]

The erasure or effacement is indeed the loss of a face, in French *figure*. Rousseau no longer, or hardly (as the tracks are not all gone, but more than half erased), has a face. Like the protagonist in the Hardy story, he is disfigured, *défiguré*, defaced. And also as in the Hardy story, to be disfigured means primarily the loss of the eyes, turned to "stony orbs" or to empty holes. This trajectory from erased self-knowledge to disfiguration is the trajectory of *The Triumph of Life*.

The connotations of the pair deer/wolf, marking a change in the inscriptions made upon Rousseau's mind, go some way in explaining the presence of Rousseau in the poem, a choice that has puzzled several interpreters. The first and obvious contrast is between a gentle and idyllic peace pursued by violent aggression. Shelley, an assiduous reader of Rousseau at a time when he was being read more closely than he has been since, evokes an ambivalence of structure and of mood that is indeed specifically Rousseau's rather than anyone else's, including Wordsworth's. Rousseau's work is characterized in part by an introspective, self-reflexive mode which uses literary models of Augustinian and pietistic origin, illustrated, for instance, by such literary allusions as Petrarch and the *Astrée* and, in general, by the elements that prompted Schiller to discuss him under the heading of the contemporary idyll. But to this are juxtaposed elements that are closer to Machiavelli than to Petrarch, concerned with political power as well as with economic and legal realities. The first register is one of delicacy of feeling, whereas a curious brand of cunning and violence pervades the other. The uneasy mixture is both a commonplace and a crux of Rousseau interpretation. It appears in the larger as well as the finer dimensions of his writings, most obviously in such broad contrasts as separate the tone and import of a text such as *The Social Contract* from that of *Julie*. That the compatibility between inner states of consciousness and acts of power is a thematic concern of *The Triumph of Life* is clear from the political

passages in the poem. In the wake of the in itself banal passage on Bo-
naparte, the conflict is openly stated:

> much I grieved to think how power and will
> In opposition rule our mortal day—

> And why God made irreconcilable
> Good and the means of good;
>
> [ll. 228–31]

Rousseau is unique among Shelley's predecessors not only in that this
question of the discrepancy between the power of words as acts and their
power to produce other words is inscribed within the thematics and the
structure of his writings, but also in the particular form that it takes there.
For the tension passes, in Rousseau, through a self which is itself experienced as a complex interplay between drives and the conscious reflection
on these drives; Shelley's understanding of this configuration is apparent
in this description of Rousseau as "between desire and shame /
Suspended."

The opposition between will and power, the intellectual goal and the
practical means, reappears when it is said, by and of Rousseau, that "my
words were seeds of misery—/ Even as the deeds of others" (lines 280–81).
The divergence between words and deeds (by way of "seeds") seems to
be suspended in Rousseau's work, albeit at the cost of, or rather because
of, considerable suffering: "I / Am one of those who have created, even /
If it be but a world of agony" (lines 294–95). For what sets Rousseau apart
from the representatives of the Enlightenment is the pathos of what is here
called the "heart" ("I was overcome / By my own heart alone."). The
contrast between the cold and skeptical Voltaire and the sensitive Rousseau
is another commonplace of popular intellectual history. But Shelley's intuition of the "heart" in Rousseau is more than merely sentimental. Its
impact becomes clearer in the contrast that sets Rousseau apart from "the
great bards of old," Homer and Virgil, said to have "inly quelled / The
passions which they sung" (lines 274–75), whereas Rousseau has "suffered
what [he] wrote, or viler pain!" Unlike the epic narrators who wrote about
events in which they did not take part, Rousseau speaks out of his own
self-knowledge, not only in his *Confessions* (which Shelley did not like) but
in all his works, regardless of whether they are fictions or political treatises.
In the tradition of Augustine, Descartes, and Malebranche, the self is for
him not merely the seat of the affections but the primary center of cognition.
Shelley is certainly not alone in thus characterizing and praising Rousseau,
but the configuration between self, heart and action is given even wider
significance when Rousseau compares himself to the Greek philosophers.
Aristotle turns out to be, like Rousseau, a double structure held together
by the connivance of words and deeds; if he is now enslaved to the eroding
process of "life," it is because he does not exist singly, as pure mind, but
cannot be separated from the "woes and wars" his pupil Alexander the

Great inflicted upon the world. Words cannot be isolated from the deeds they perform; the tutor necessarily performs the deeds his pupil derives from his mastery. And just as "deeds" cause the undoing of Aristotle, it is the "heart" that brought down Plato who, like Rousseau, was a theoretician of statecraft and a legislator. Like Aristotle and like Rousseau (who is like a deer but also like a wolf) Plato is at least double; life "conquered [his] heart" as Rousseau was "overcome by [his] own heart alone." The reference to the apocryphal story of Aster makes clear that "heart" here means more than mere affectivity; Plato's heart was conquered by "love" and, in this context, love is like the intellectual eros that links Socrates to his pupils. Rousseau is placed within a configuration, brought about by "words," of knowledge, action and erotic desire. The elements are present in the symbolic scene from which we started out, since the pursuit of the deer by the wolf, in this context of Ovidian and Dantesque metamorphoses, is bound to suggest Apollo's pursuit of the nymphs as well as scenes of inscription and effacement.

The scene is one of violence and grief, and the distress reappears in the historical description of Rousseau with its repeated emphasis on suffering and agony, as well as in the dramatic action of defeat and enslavement. But this defeat is paradoxical: in a sense, Rousseau has overcome the discrepancy of action and intention that tears apart the historical world, and he has done so because his words have acquired the power of actions as well as of the will. Not only because they represent or reflect on actions but because they themselves, literally, are actions. Their power to act exists independently of their power to know: Aristotle's or Plato's mastery of mind did not give them any control over the deeds of the world, also and especially the deeds that ensued as a consequence of their words and with which they were directly involved. The power that arms their words also makes them lose their power over them. Rousseau gains shape, face or figure only to lose it as he acquires it. The enigma of this power, the burden of whatever understanding Shelley's poem permits, depends primarily on the reading of Rousseau's recapitulative narrative of his encounter with the "Shape all light" (lines 308–433).

III

Rousseau's history, as he looks back upon his existence from the "April prime" of his young years to the present, tells of a specific experience that is certainly not a simple one but that can be designated by a single verb: the experience is that of forgetting. The term appears literally ([line] 318) and in various periphrases (such as "oblivious spell," [line] 331), or in metaphors with a clear analogical vehicle such as "quell" ([line] 329), "blot [from memory]" ([line] 330), "trample" ([line] 388), "tread out" ([line] 390), "erase" ([line] 406), etc. It combines with another, more familiar metaphorical strain that is present throughout the entire poem: images of rising and waning light and of the sun.

The structure of "forgetting," in this text, is not clarified by echoes of a Platonic recollection and recognition (anamnesis) that enter the poem, partly by way of Shelley's own Platonic and Neoplatonic readings, partly by way of Wordsworth's "Immortality" Ode whose manifest presence, in this part of the poem, has misled even the most attentive readers of *The Triumph of Life*. In the *Phaedo* (73) and, with qualifications too numerous to develop here, in Wordsworth's Ode, what one forgets is a former state which Yeats, who used the same set of emblems, compares to the Unity of Being evoked in Aristophanes' *Symposium* speech as the mainspring of erotic desire. Within a Neoplatonic Christian tradition, this easily becomes a fitting symbol for the Incarnation, for a birth out of a transcendental realm into a finite world. But this is precisely what the experience of forgetting, in *The Triumph of Life*, is not. What one forgets here is not some previous condition, for the line of demarcation between the two conditions is so unclear, the distinction between the forgotten and the remembered so unlike the distinction between two well-defined areas, that we have no assurance whatever that the forgotten ever existed:

> "Whether my life had been before that sleep
> The Heaven which I imagine, or a Hell
>
> Like this harsh world in which I wake to weep
> I know not."
>
> [ll. 332–35]

The polarities of waking and sleeping (or remembering and forgetting) are curiously scrambled, in this passage, with those of past and present, of the imagined and the real, of knowing and not knowing. For if, as is clear from the previous scene, to be born into life is to fall asleep, thus associating life with sleep, then to "wake" from an earlier condition of non-sleeping into "this harsh world" of life can only be to become aware of one's persistent condition of slumber, to be more than ever asleep, a deeper sleep replacing a lighter one, a deeper forgetting being achieved by an act of memory which remembers one's forgetting. And since Heaven and Hell are not here two transcendental realms but the mere opposition between the imagined and the real, what we do not know is whether we are awake or asleep, dead or alive, forgetting or remembering. We cannot tell the difference between sameness and difference, and this inability to know takes on the form of a pseudo-knowledge which is called a forgetting. Not just because it is an unbearable condition of indetermination which has to be repressed, but because the condition itself, regardless of how it affects us, necessarily hovers between a state of knowing and not-knowing, like the symptom of a disease which recurs at the precise moment that one remembers its absence. What is forgotten is absent in the mode of a possible delusion, which is another way of saying that it does not fit within a symmetrical structure of presence and absence.

In conformity with the consistent system of sun imagery, this hovering motion is evoked throughout the poem by scenes of glimmering light. This very "glimmer" unites the poet-narrator to Rousseau, as the movement of the opening sunrise is repeated in Rousseau's encounter with the feminine shape, just as it unites the theme of forgetting with the motions of the light. The verb appears in the opening scene:

> a strange trance over my fancy grew
> Which was not slumber, for the shade it spread
>
> Was so transparent that the scene came through
> As clear as when a veil of light is drawn
> O'er the evening hills they *glimmer*;
> [ll. 29–33, *emphasis added*]

and then again, later on, now with Rousseau on stage:

> The presence of that Shape which on the stream
> Moved, as I moved along the wilderness,
>
> More dimly than a day-appearing dream,
> The ghost of a forgotten form of sleep,
> A light from Heaven whose half-extinguished beam
>
> Through the sick day in which we wake to weep
> *Glimmers*, forever sought, forever lost.—
> So did that shape its obscure tenour keep.
> [ll.425–32, *emphasis added*]

It is impossible to say, in either passage, how the polarities of light and dark are matched with those of waking and sleep; the confusion is the same as in the previously quoted passage on forgetting and remembering. The light, in the second passage, is said to be like a dream, or like sleep ("the ghost of a forgotten form of sleep"), yet it shines, however distantly, upon a condition which is one of awakening ("the sad day in which we wake to weep"); in this light, to be awake is to be as if one were asleep. In the first passage, it is explicitly stated that since the poet perceives so clearly, he cannot be asleep, but the clarity is then said to be like that of a veil drawn over a darkening surface, a description which necessarily connotes covering and hiding, even if the veil is said to be "of light." Light covers light, trance covers slumber and creates conditions of optical confusion that resemble nothing as much as the experience of trying to read *The Triumph of Life*, as its meaning glimmers, hovers and wavers, but refuses to yield the clarity it keeps announcing.

This play of veiling and unveiling is, of course, altogether tantalizing. Forgetting is a highly erotic experience; it is like glimmering light because it cannot be decided whether it reveals or hides; it is like desire because, like the wolf pursuing the deer, it does violence to what sustains it; it is like a trance or a dream because it is asleep to the very extent that it is conscious and awake, and dead to the extent that it is alive. The passage that concerns us makes this knot, by which knowledge, oblivion and desire hang suspended, into an articulated sequence of events that demands interpretation.

The chain that leads Rousseau from the birth of his consciousness to his present state of impending death passes through a well-marked succession of relays. Plato and Wordsworth provide the initial linking of birth with forgetting, but this forgetting has, in Shelley's poem, the glimmering ambivalence which makes it impossible to consider it as an act of closure or of beginning and which makes any further comparison with Wordsworth irrelevant. The metaphor for this process is that of "a gentle rivulet . . . [which] filled the grove / With sound which all who hear must needs forget / All pleasure and all pain" (lines 314–19). Unlike Yeats's, Shelley's river does not function as the "generated soul," as the descent of the transcendental soul into earthly time and space. As the passage develops, it enters into a system of relationships that are natural rather than esoteric. The property of the river that the poem singles out is its sound; the oblivious spell emanates from the repetitive rhythm of the water, which articulates a random noise into a definite pattern. Water, which has no shape of itself, is moulded into shape by its contact with the earth, just as in the scene of the water washing away the tracks, it generates the very possibility of structure, pattern, form or shape by way of the disappearance of shape into shapelessness. The repetition of the erasures rhythmically articulates what is in fact a disarticulation, and the poem seems to be shaped by the undoing of shapes. But since this pattern does not fully correspond to what it covers up, it leaves the trace which allows one to call this ambivalent shaping a forgetting. The birth of what an earlier Shelley poem such as "Mont Blanc" would still have called the mind occurs as the distortion which allows one to make the random regular by "forgetting" differences.

As soon as the water's noise becomes articulated sound it can enter into contact with the light. The birth of form as the interference of light and water passes, in the semi-synaesthesia of the passage, through the mediation of sound; it is however only a semi-synaesthesia, for the optical and auditory perceptions, though simultaneous, nevertheless remain treated in asymmetrical opposition:

> A Shape all light, which with one hand did fling
> Dew on earth, as if it were the dawn
> Whose invisible rain forever seemed to sing
>
> A silver music on the mossy lawn
> *And still* before her on the dusky grass.
> Iris her many-coloured scarf had drawn.
>   [ll. 352–57, *emphasis added*]

The water of the original river here fulfills a double and not necessarily complementary action, as it combines with the light to form, on the one hand, Iris's scarf or rainbow and, on the other hand, the "silver music" of oblivion. A traditional symbol of the integration of the phenomenal with the transcendental world, the natural synthesis of water and light in the rainbow is, in Shelley, the familiar "dome of many-coloured glass" whose "stain" is the earthly trace and promise of an Eternity in which Adonais's soul is said to dwell "like a star." As such, it irradiates all the textures and forms of the natural world with the veil of the sun's *farbiger Abglanz,* just as it provides the analogical light and heat that will make it possible to refer to the poet's mind as "embers." The metaphorical chain which links the sun to water, to color, to heat, to nature, to mind and to consciousness, is certainly at work in the poem and can be summarized in this image of the rainbow. But this symbol is said to exist here in the tenuous mode of insistence, as something that *still* prevails (line 356) despite the encroachment of something else, also emanating from water and sun and associated with them from the start, called music and forgetting. This something else, of which it could be said that it wrenches the final statement of *Adonais* into a different shape, appears in some degree of tension with the symbol of the rainbow.

The entire scene of the shape's apparition and subsequent waning (line 412) is structured as a near-miraculous suspension between these two different forces whose interaction gives to the figure the hovering motion which may well be the mode of being of all figures. This glimmering figure takes on the form of the unreachable reflection of Narcissus, the manifestation of shape at the expense of its possession. The suspended fascination of the Narcissus stance is caught in the moment when the shape is said to move

> with palms so tender
> Their tread broke not the mirror of its billow
> [ll. 361–62]

The scene is self-reflexive: the closure of the shape's contours is brought about by self-duplication. The light generates its own shape by means of a mirror, a surface that articulates it without setting up a clear separation that differentiates inside from outside as self is differentiated from other. The self that comes into being in the moment of reflection is, in spatial terms, optical symmetry as the ground of structure, optical repetition as the structural principle that engenders entities as shapes. "Shape all light" is referentially meaningless since light, the necessary condition for shape, is itself, like water, without shape, and acquires shape only when split in the illusion of a doubleness which is not that of self and other. The sun, in this text, is from the start the figure of this self-contained specularity. But the double of the sun can only be the eye conceived as the mirror of light. "Shape" and "mirror" are inseparable in this scene, just as the sun is inseparable from the shapes it generates and which are, in fact, the eye, and just as the sun is inseparable from itself since it produces the illusion of the self as shape. The sun can be said "to stand," a figure which assumes the existence of an entire spatial organization, because it stands personified

> amid the blaze
> Of his own glory.
>
> [ll. 349–50]

The sun "sees" its own light reflected, like Narcissus, in a well that is a mirror and also an eye:

> the Sun's image radiantly intense
> Burned on the waters of the well that glowed
> Like gold.
>
> [ll. 345–47]

Because the sun is itself a specular structure, the eye can be said to generate a world of natural forms. The otherness of a world that is in fact without order now becomes, for the eye, a maze made accessible to solar paths, as the eye turns from the blank radiance of the sun to its green and blue reflection in the world, and allows us to be in this world as in a landscape of roads and intents. The sun

> threaded all the forest maze
> With winding paths of emerald fire.
>
> [ll. 347–48]

The boldest, but also the most traditional, image in this passage is that of the sunray as a thread that stitches the texture of the world, the necessary and complementary background for the eye of Narcissus. The water and pupil of the eye generate the rainbow of natural forms among which it dwells in sensory self-fulfillment. The figure of the sun, present from the beginning of the poem, repeats itself in the figure of the eye's self-erotic contact with its own surface, which is also the mirror of the natural world. The erotic element is marked from the start, in the polarity of a male sun and a feminine shape, eye or well, which is said to

> bend her
> Head under the dark boughs, till like a willow
> Her fair hair swept the bosom of the stream
> That whispered with delight to be their pillow.—
>
> [ll. 363–66]

Shelley's imagery, often assumed to be incoherent and erratic, is instead extraordinarily systematic whenever light is being thematized. The passage condenses all that earlier and later poets (one can think of Valéry and Gide's Narcissus, as well as of the *Roman de la Rose* or of Spenser) ever did with light, water, and mirrors. It also bears witness to the affinity of his imagination with that of Rousseau, who allowed the phantasm of language born rhapsodically out of an erotic well to tell its story before he took it all away. Shelley's treatment of the birth of light reveals all that is invested in the emblem of the rainbow. It represents the very possibility of cognition, even for processes of articulation so elementary that it would be impossible to conceive of any principle of organization, however primitive, that would not be entirely dependent on its power. To efface it would be to take away the sun which, if it were to happen to this text, for example, would leave little else. *And still*, this light is allowed to exist in *The Triumph of Life* only under the most tenuous of conditions.

The frailty of the stance is represented in the supernatural delicacy which gives the shape "palms so tender / Their tread broke not the mirror of [the river's] billow" and which allows it to "glide along the river." The entire scene is set up as a barely imaginable balance between this gliding motion, which remains on one side of the watery surface and thus allows the specular image to come into being, and the contrary motion which, like Narcissus at the end of the mythical story, breaks through the surface of the mirror and disrupts the suspended fall of its own existence. As the passage develops, the story must run its course. The contradictory motions of "gliding" and "treading" which suspended gravity between rising and falling finally capsize. The "threading" sunrays become the "treading" of feet upon a surface which, in this text, does not stiffen into solidity. Shelley's poem insists on the hyperbolic lightness of the reflexive contact, since the reflecting surface is never allowed the smooth stasis that is necessary to the duplication of the image. The water is kept in constant motion: it is called a "billow" and the surface, although compared to a crystal, is roughened by the winds that give some degree of verisimilitude to the shape's gliding motion. By the end of the section, we have moved from "thread" to "tread" to "trample," in a movement of increased violence that erases the initial tenderness. There is no doubt that, when we again meet the shape (lines 425 ff.) it is no longer gliding along the river but drowned, Ophelia-like, below the surface of the water. The violence is confirmed in the return of the rainbow, in the ensuing vision, as a rigid, stony arch said "fiercely [to extoll] the fortune" of the shape's defeat by what the poem calls "life."

This chain of metaphorical transformations can be understood, up to this point, without transposition into a vocabulary that would not be that of their own referents, not unlike the movement of the figure itself as it endeavors to glide incessantly along a surface which it tries to keep intact. Specifically, the figure of the rainbow is a figure of the unity of perception and cognition undisturbed by the possibly disruptive mediation of its own figuration. This is not surprising, since the underlying assumption of such a paraphrastic reading is itself one of specular understanding in which the text serves as a mirror of our own knowledge and our knowledge mirrors in its turn the text's signification. But we can only inadequately understand in this fashion why the shaped light of understanding is itself allowed to wane away, layer by layer, until it is entirely forgotten and remains present only in the guise of an edifice that serves to celebrate and to perpetuate its oblivion. Nor can we understand the power that weighs down the seductive grace of figuration until it destroys itself. The figure of the sun, with all its chain of correlatives, should also be read in a non-phenomenal way, a necessity which is itself phenomenally represented in the dramatic tension of the text.

The transition from "gliding" to "trampling" passes, in the action that is being narrated, through the intermediate relay of "measure." The term actively reintroduces music which, after having been stressed in the previous scene (lines 354–55), is at first only present by analogy in this phase of the action (lines 359–74). Measure is articulated sound, that is to say language. Language rather than music, in the traditional sense of harmony and melody. As melody, the "song" of the water and, by extension, the various sounds of nature, only provide a background that easily blends with the seduction of the natural world:

> all the place
>
> Was filled with many sounds woven into one
> Oblivious melody, confusing sense
> Amid the gliding waves and shadows dun.
>> [ll. 339–42]

As melody and harmony, song belongs to the same gliding motion that is interrupted only when the shape's feet

> to the ceaseless song
>
> Of leaves and winds and waves and birds and bees
> And falling drops moved in a measure new.
>> [ll. 375–77]

The "tread" of this dancer, which needs a ground to the extent that it carries the weight of gravity, is no longer melodious, but reduces music to the mere measure of repeated articulations. It singles out from music the accentual or tonal punctuation which is also present in spoken diction. The scene could be said to narrate the birth of music out of the spirit of language, since the determining property is an articulation distinctive of verbal sound prior to its signifying function. The thematization of language in *The Triumph of Life* occurs at this point, when "measure" separates from the phenomenal aspects of signification as a specular *representation*, and stresses instead the literal and material aspects of language. In the dramatic action of the narrative, measure disrupts the symmetry of cognition as representation (the figure of the rainbow, of the eye and of the sun). But since measure is any principle of linguistic organization, not only as rhyme and meter but as any syntactical or grammatical scansion, one can read "feet" not just as the poetic meter that is so conspicuously evident in the *terza rima* of the poem, but as any principle of signification. Yet it is precisely these "feet" which extinguish and bury the poetic and philosophical light.

It is tempting to interpret this event, the shape's "trampling" the fires of thought "into the dust of death" (lines 388), certainly the most enigmatic moment in the poem, as the bifurcation between the semantic and the non-signifying, material properties of language. The various devices of articulation, from word to sentence formation (by means of grammar, syntax, accentuation, tone, etc.), which are made to convey meaning, and these same articulations left to themselves, independently of their signifying constraints, do not necessarily determine each other. The latent polarity implied in all classical theories of the sign allows for the relative independence of the signifier and for its free play in relation to its signifying function. If, for instance, compelling rhyme schemes such as "billow," "willow," "pillow" or transformations such as "thread" to "tread" or "seed" to "deed" occur at crucial moments in the text, then the question arises whether these particularly meaningful movements or events are not being generated by random and superficial properties of the signifier rather than by the constraints of meaning. The obliteration of thought by "measure" would then have to be interpreted as the loss of semantic depth and its replacement by what Mallarmé calls "le hasard infini des conjonctions" (*Igitur*).

But this is not the story, or not the entire story, told by *The Triumph of Life*. For the arbitrary element in the alignment between meaning and linguistic articulation does not by itself have the power to break down the specular structure which the text erects and then claims to dissolve. It does not account for the final phase of the Narcissus story, as the shape traverses the mirror and goes under, just as the stars are conquered by the sun at the beginning of the poem and the sun then conquered in its turn by the light of the Chariot of Life. The undoing of the representational and iconic function of figuration by the play of the signifier does not suffice to bring about the disfiguration which *The Triumph of Life* acts out or represents. For it is the alignment of a signification with any principle of linguistic articulation whatsoever, sensory or not, which constitutes the figure. The iconic, sensory or, if one wishes, the aesthetic moment is not constitutive of figuration. Figuration is the element in language that allows for the reiteration of meaning by substitution; the process is at least twofold and this plurality is naturally illustrated by optical icons of specularity. But the particular seduction of the figure is not necessarily that it creates an illusion of sensory pleasure, but that it creates an illusion of meaning. In Shelley's poem, the shape is a figure regardless of whether it appears as a figure of light (the rainbow) or of articulation in general (music as measure and language). The transition from pleasure to signification, from the aesthetic to the semiological dimension, is clearly marked in the passage, as one moves from the figure of the rainbow to that of the dance, from sight to measure. It marks the identification of the shape as the model of figuration in general. By taking this step beyond the traditional conceptions of figuration as modes of representation, as polarities of subject and object, of part and whole, of necessity and chance or of sun and eye, the way is prepared for the subsequent undoing and erasure of the figure. But the extension, which coincides with the passage from tropological models such as metaphor, synecdoche, metalepsis or prosopopoeia (in which a phenomenal element, spatial or temporal, is necessarily involved) to tropes such as grammar and syntax (which function on the level of the letter without the intervention of an iconic factor) is not by itself capable of erasing the figure or, in the representational code of the text, of drowning the shape or trampling out thought. Another intervention, another aspect of language has to come into play.

The narrative sequence of Rousseau's encounter, as it unfolds from the apparition of the shape (line 343) to its replacement (line 434) by a "new vision," follows a motion framed by two events that are acts of power: the sun overcoming the light of the stars, the light of life overcoming the sun. The movement from a punctual action, determined in time by a violent act of power, to the gliding, suspended motion "of that shape which on the stream / Moved, as I moved along the wilderness" (lines 425–26) is the same motion inherent in the title of the poem. As has been pointed out by several commentators, "triumph" designates the actual victory as well as the *trionfo*, the pageant that celebrates the outcome of the battle. The reading of the scene should allow for a more general interpretation of this contradictory motion.

We now understand the shape to be the figure for the figurality of all signification. The specular structure of the scene as a visual plot of light and water is not the determining factor but merely an illustration (*hypotyposis*) of a plural structure that involves natural entities only as principles of articulation among others. It follows that the figure is not naturally given or produced but that it is posited by an arbitrary act of language. The appearance and the waning of the light-shape, in spite of the solar analogon, is not a natural event resulting from the mediated interaction of several powers, but a single, and therefore violent, act of power achieved by the positional power of language considered by and in itself: the sun masters the stars because it *posits* forms, just as "life" subsequently masters the sun because it posits, by inscription, the "track" of historical events. The positing power does not reside in Rousseau as subject; the mastery of the shape over Rousseau is never in question. He rises and bends at her command and his mind is passively trampled into dust without resistance. The positing power of language is both entirely arbitrary, in having a strength that cannot be reduced to necessity, and entirely inexorable in that there is no alternative to it. It stands beyond the polarities of chance and determination and can therefore not be part of a temporal sequence of events. The sequence has to be punctured by acts that cannot be made a part of it. It cannot begin, for example, by telling us of the waning of the stars under the growing impact of the sun, a natural motion which is the outcome of a mediation, but it must evoke the violent "springing forth" of a sun detached from all antecedents. Only retrospectively can this event be seen and misunderstood as a substitution and a beginning, as a dialectical relationship between day and night, or between two transcendental orders of being. The sun does not appear in conjunction with or in reaction to the night and the stars, but of its own unrelated power. *The Triumph of Life* differs entirely from such Promethean or titanic myths as Keats's *Hyperion* or even *Paradise Lost* which thrive on the agonistic pathos of dialectical battle. It is unimaginable that Shelley's non-epic, non-religious poem would begin by elegiacally or rebelliously evoking the tragic defeat of the former gods, the stars, at the hands of the sun. The text has no room for the tragedy of defeat or of victory among next-of-kin, or among gods and men. The previous occupants of the narrative space are expelled by decree, by the sheer power of utterance, and consequently at once forgotten. In the vocabulary of the poem, it occurs by *imposition* (line 20), the emphatic mode of positing. This compresses the prosopopoeia of the personified sun, in the first lines of the poem, into a curiously absurd pseudo-description. The most continuous and gradual event in nature, the subtle gradations of the dawn, is collapsed into the brusque swiftness of a single moment:

> Swift as a spirit hastening to his task
> . . . the Sun sprang forth
> . . . and the mask
>
> Of darkness fell from the awakened Earth.
> [ll. 1–4]

The appearances, later in the poem, of the Chariot of Life are equally brusque and unmotivated. When they occur, they are not "descendants" of the sun, not the natural continuation of the original, positing gesture but positings in their own right. Unlike night following day, they always again have to be posited, which explains why they are repetitions and not beginnings.

How can a positional act, which relates to nothing that comes before or after, become inscribed in a sequential narrative? How does a speech act become a trope, a catachresis which then engenders in its turn the narrative sequence of an allegory? It can only be because we impose, in our turn, on the senseless power of positional language the authority of sense and of meaning. But this is radically inconsistent: language posits and language means (since it articulates) but language cannot posit meaning; it can only reiterate (or reflect) it in its reconfirmed falsehood. Nor does the knowledge of this impossibility make it less impossible. This impossible position is precisely the figure, the trope, metaphor as a violent— and not as a dark—light, a deadly Apollo.

The imposition of meaning occurs in *The Triumph of Life* in the form of the questions that served as point of departure for the reading. It is as a questioning entity, standing within the pathos of its own indetermination, that the human subject appears in the text, in the figures of the narrator who interrogates Rousseau and of Rousseau who interrogates the shape. But these figures do not coincide with the voice that narrates the poem in which they are represented; this voice does not question and does not share in their predicament. We can therefore not ask why it is that we, as subjects, choose to impose meaning, since we are ourselves defined by this very question. From the moment the subject thus asks, it has already foreclosed any alternative and has become the figural token of meaning, "Ein Zeichen sind wir/ Deutungslos" (Hölderlin). To question is to forget. Considered performatively, figuration (as question) performs the erasure of the positing power of language. In *The Triumph of Life*, this happens when a positional speech act is represented as what it resembles least of all, a sunrise.

To forget, in this poem, is by no means a passive process. In the Rousseau episode, things happen because the subject Rousseau keeps forgetting. In his earliest stages, he forgets the incoherence of a world in which events occur by sheer dint of a blind force, in the same way that the sun, in the opening lines, occurs by sheer imposition. The episode describes the emergence of an articulated language of cognition by the erasure, the forgetting of the events this language in fact performed. It culminates in the appearance of the shape, which is both a figure of specular self-knowledge, the figure of thought, but also a figure of "thought's empire over thought," of the element in thought that destroys thought in its attempt to forget its duplicity. For the initial violence of position can only be half erased, since the erasure is accomplished by a device of language that never ceases to partake of the very violence against which it is directed. It seems to extend the instantaneousness of the act of positing over a series of transformations, but this duration is a fictitious state, in which "all seemed as if it had been not" (line 385). The trampling gesture enacts the necessary recurrence of the initial violence: a figure of thought, the very light of cognition, obliterates thought. At its apparent beginning as well as at its apparent end, thought (i.e., figuration) forgets what it thinks and cannot do otherwise if it is to maintain itself. Each of the episodes forgets the knowledge achieved by the forgetting that precedes it, just as the instantaneous sunrise of the opening scene is at once covered over by a "strange trance" which allows the narrator to imagine the scene as something remembered even before it could take place (lines 33–39). Positing "glimmers" into a glimmering knowledge that acts out the aporias of signification and of performance.

The repetitive erasures by which language performs the erasure of its own positions can be called disfiguration. The disfiguration of Rousseau is enacted in the text, in the scene of the root and repeats itself in a more general mode in the disfiguration of the shape:

> The fair shape waned in the coming light
> As veil by veil the silent splendor drops
> From Lucifer, amid the chrysolite
>
> Of sunrise ere it strike the mountain tops—
>
> [ll. 412–15]

Lucifer, or metaphor, the bearer of light which carries over the light of the senses and of cognition from events and entities to their meaning, irrevocably loses the contour of its own face or shape. We see it happen when the figure first appears as water-music, then as rainbow, then as measure, to finally sink away "below the watery floor" trampled to death by its own power. Unlike Lycidas, it is not resurrected in the guise of a star, but repeated on a level of literality which is not that of meaning but of actual events, called "Life" in Shelley's poem. But "Life" is as little the end of figuration as the sunrise was its beginning. For just as language is misrepresented as a natural event, life is just as falsely represented by the same light that emanates from the sun and that will have to engender its own rainbow and measure. Only that this light destroys its previous representation as the wolf destroys the deer. The process is endless, since the knowledge of the language's performative power is itself a figure in its own right and, as such, bound to repeat the disfiguration of metaphor as Shelley is bound to repeat the aberration of Rousseau in what appears to be a more violent mode. Which also implies, by the same token, that he is bound to forget him, just as, in all rigor, *The Social Contract* can be said to erase *Julie* from the canon of Rousseau's works, or *The Triumph of Life* can be said to reduce all of Shelley's previous work to nought.

IV

The persistence of light-imagery, in the description of the Chariot of Life as well as in the inaugural sunrise, creates the illusion of a continuity and makes the knowledge of its interruption serve as a ruse to efface its actual occurrence. The poem is sheltered from the performance of disfiguration by the power of its negative knowledge. But this knowledge is powerless to prevent what now functions as the decisive textual articulation: its reduction to the status of a fragment brought about by the actual death and subsequent disfigurement of Shelley's body, burned after his boat capsized and he drowned off the coast of Lerici. This defaced body is present in the margin of the last manuscript page and has become an inseparable part of the poem. At this point, figuration and cognition are actually interrupted by an event which shapes the text but which is not present in its represented or articulated meaning. It may seem a freak of chance to have a text thus molded by an actual occurrence, yet the reading of *The Triumph of Life* establishes that this mutilated textual model exposes the wound of a fracture that lies hidden in all texts. If anything, this text is more rather than less typical than texts that have not been thus truncated. The rhythmical interruptions that mark off the successive episodes of the narrative are not new moments of cognition but literal events textually reinscribed by a delusive act of figuration or of forgetting.

   In Shelley's absence, the task of thus reinscribing the disfiguration now devolves entirely on the reader. The final test of reading, in *The Triumph of Life*, depends on how one reads the textuality of this event, how one disposes of Shelley's body. The challenge that is in fact present in all texts and that *The Triumph of Life* identifies, thematizes and thus tries to avoid in the most effective way possible, is here actually carried out as the sequence of symbolic interruptions is in its turn interrupted by an event that is no longer simply imaginary or symbolic. The apparent ease with which readers of *The Triumph of Life* have been able to dispose of this challenge demonstrates the inadequacy of our understanding of Shelley and, beyond him, of Romanticism in general.

For what we have done with the dead Shelley, and with all the other dead bodies that appear in romantic literature—one thinks, among many others, of the "dead man" that " 'mid that beauteous scene / Of trees and hills and water, bolt upright / Rose, with his ghastly face" in Wordsworth's *Prelude* (V.448–50)—is simply to bury them, to bury them in their own texts made into epitaphs and monumental graves. They have been made into statues for the benefit of future archeologists "digging in the grounds for the new foundations" of their own monuments. They have been transformed into historical and aesthetic objects. There are various and subtle strategies, much too numerous to enumerate, to accomplish this.

Such monumentalization is by no means necessarily a naive or evasive gesture, and it certainly is not a gesture that anyone can pretend to avoid making. It does not have to be naive, since it does not have to be the repression of a self-threatening knowledge. Like *The Triumph of Life*, it can state the full power of this threat in all its negativity; the poem demonstrates that this rigor does not prevent Shelley from allegorizing his own negative assurance, thus awakening the suspicion that the negation is a *Verneinung*, an intended exorcism. And it is not avoidable, since the failure to exorcise the threat, even in the face of such evidence as the radical blockage that befalls this poem, becomes precisely the challenge to understanding that always again demands to be read. And to read is to understand, to question, to know, to forget, to erase, to deface, to repeat—that is to say, the endless prosopopoeia by which the dead are made to have a face and a voice which tells the allegory of their demise and allows us to apostrophize them in our turn. No degree of knowledge can ever stop this madness, for it is the madness of words. What *would* be naive is to believe that this strategy, which is not *our* strategy as subjects, since we are its product rather than its agent, can be a source of value and has to be celebrated or denounced accordingly.

Whenever this belief occurs—and it occurs all the time—it leads to a misreading that can and should be discarded, unlike the coercive "forgetting" that Shelley's poem analytically thematizes and that stands beyond good and evil. It would be of little use to enumerate and categorize the various forms and names which this belief takes on in our present critical and literary scene. It functions along monotonously predictable lines, by the historicization and the aesthetification of texts, as well as by their use, as in this essay, for the assertion of methodological claims made all the more pious by their denial of piety. Attempts to define, to understand or to circumscribe Romanticism in relation to ourselves and in relation to other literary movements are all part of this naive belief. *The Triumph of Life* warns us that nothing, whether deed, word, thought or text, ever happens in relation, positive or negative, to anything that precedes, follows or exists elsewhere, but only as a random event whose power, like the power of death, is due to the randomness of its occurrence. It also warns us why and how these events then have to be reintegrated in a historical and aesthetic system of recuperation that repeats itself regardless of the exposure of its fallacy. This process differs entirely from the recuperative and nihilistic allegories of historicism. If it is true and unavoidable that any reading is a monumentalization of sorts, the way in which Rousseau is read and disfigured in *The Triumph of Life* puts Shelley among the few readers who "guessed whose statue those fragments had composed." Reading as disfiguration, to the very extent that it resists historicism, turns out to be historically more reliable than the products of historical archeology. To monumentalize this observation into a *method* of reading would be to regress from the rigor exhibited by Shelley which is exemplary precisely because it refuses to be generalized into a system.

Keats: Negative Capability

Walter Jackson Bate

From the time he set out in April [of 1817] to begin his long poem, Keats had thought of the year's effort as one of plowing and sowing a field from which he hoped to reap a harvest before autumn closed. Though the slow start of the first few weeks had shaken him badly, the summer had been propitious and September bountiful. Yet from September on he had been feeling that the only good he could expect from all this labor was the "fruit of Experience."

By winter some of the gains were becoming apparent, and the next half year was to reveal more. One enormous gain was that any tendency toward paralysis before the empty page was permanently removed. From here until the end he was to compose with a speed few major poets have matched, at least since the time of Dryden. Even the most condensed of his great lyrics a year or so hence were written rapidly; and though they were extensively revised, the revision itself was done with dispatch—often immediately after a line or passage was written and before he began the next.

While learning the value of momentum, he was also learning what not to do—and by an active self-criticism that would have been impossible had he "been nervous about [*Endymion's*] being a perfect piece . . . & trembled over every page," in which case the poem "would not have been written" at all. "The Genius of Poetry must work out its own salvation in a man: It cannot be matured by law & precept, but by sensation and watchfulness— That which is creative must create itself." By this leap "headlong into the Sea," he had learned at first hand "the Soundings, the quicksands, & the rocks," and knew them in a way he could never have done if he had "stayed upon the green shore, and piped a silly pipe, and took tea & comfortable advice."

From *John Keats*. © 1963 by the President and Fellows of Harvard College. The Belknap Press of Harvard University Press, 1963. Originally entitled "Negative Capability."

One of the first results of this active self-criticism and self-redirection is to be seen in the way in which he swings back from the dilution of style that the practice of writing verse epistles and the influence of Hunt's idiom had encouraged and that *Endymion* greatly increased; and the distinguishing quality of his writing within less than a year is its massive condensation. Another reaction was his strong dislike henceforth of forcing himself to write for the mere sake of writing. He could now indulge this, to be sure, only because *Endymion* was behind him. The helpful habits gained from that gymnastic exercise were already secured. For the same reason he was henceforth to feel freer, if a longer poem was not developing the way he hoped, to leave it unfinished and turn to something else; and his eagerness to publish subsided until, by contrast, it almost approached indifference. While copying *Endymion* for the press, he was developing some new "Axioms" for the writing of poetry, which he describes in a famous letter to his publisher (February 27), and with a candid admission "how far I am from their Centre":

> 1ˢᵗ I think Poetry should surprise by a fine excess and not by Singularity—it should strike the Reader as a wording of his own highest thoughts, and appear almost a Remembrance—2ⁿᵈ Its touches of Beauty should never be half way therby making the reader breathless instead of content: the rise, the progress, the setting of imagery should like the Sun come natural to him—shine over him and set soberly although in magnificence leaving him in the Luxury of twilight—but it is easier to think what Poetry should be than to write it—and this leads me on to another axiom. That if Poetry comes not as naturally as the Leaves to a tree it had better not come at all.

He even began to think, within a month or so after finishing *Endymion*, of the desirability of slow development. He was not being sardonic about poor Charles Cripps, the artist he and Bailey were trying to help, when he told Bailey "I have the greater hopes of him because he is so slow in development." The same day (January 23) he wrote his brothers:

> Nothing is finer for the purposes of great productions, than a very gradual ripening of the intellectual powers—As an instance of this—observe—I sat down to read King Lear once again the thing appeared to demand the prologue of a sonnet.

The implication here and in the sonnet, "On Sitting Down to Read King Lear Once Again," is that something has been happening that could actually be called a development, "a very gradual ripening," but not at all what he had been thinking about when he had first outlined his year's project back in the spring. It seemed gradual because it had been so undeliberate; and what began it, as he now looked back, must have been operating subterraneously. He had bought the copy of Shakespeare in order to steel himself for the "test" of *Endymion*. But that constant recourse to Shakespeare—

beginning with the trustful commitment, the gift of the engraving of Shakespeare, the "daring" hope that he might view Shakespeare as "Presider" over this adventure—had been proving formative in another development with which *Endymion* itself appeared to have little in common except in what it showed of personal courage and of occasional power of phrase.

Within another two months he himself was beginning to feel that this more general development, rather than *Endymion* itself, had been the primary gain. If the four thousand lines of *Endymion* could serve simply as a "Pioneer"—and he uses it in its older sense of a foot soldier, a digger of trenches—"I ought to be content. I have great reason to be content, for thank God I can read and perhaps understand Shakespeare to his depths." As for his long poem, which he is "anxious" to have "printed that I may forget it and proceed," he feels that he has moved only "into the Go-cart from the leading strings."

II

A few days after Keats returned to Hampstead, George and Tom left for Devonshire in the hope that Tom might profit from the change. Tom was becoming very frail; he was spitting blood; the symptoms were far from reassuring to his brothers. George, despite his restiveness and his feeling that he must get started on a career, was willing once again to take charge of things for a while. Keats himself was by no means eager to leave, though he was expected to join them in time. Some changes certainly had to be made in *Endymion*, and a clean copy prepared.

At the same time, John Reynolds, who had been writing the dramatic reviews for the *Champion*, wanted to go to Exeter just after Christmas for a holiday. He was courting Eliza Drewe, who lived there and whom he eventually married. He was also intending to leave the *Champion* anyway in January. With the encouragement of his friend James Rice, he had begun to study law in November. Rice was getting him a position in the law office of Francis Fladgate, had paid for him the fee of £110, and was later to arrange to take Reynolds into partnership in the law firm of himself and his father. Keats, thought Reynolds, could take his place on the *Champion*, and write a review. Although Keats's knowledge of the theater was limited, he had delighted in what he had the chance to see of it. He had been reading the dramatic criticism of Reynolds' own model, William Hazlitt. Edmund Kean, whose gusto Keats admired, would probably be returning to the stage after an illness of a few weeks. Before Reynolds left for Exeter, Keats, as a trial experiment, brought out a review, "Mr. Kean," in the *Champion* (December 21, 1817), written with the rapid verve, the darting impressionism, of Hazlitt's manner. Then, for the January 4 issue of the *Champion*, after Reynolds had left for Exeter, Keats wrote reviews of the play "Retribution" and a pantomime, "Harlequin's Vision."

George and Tom had been gone about a week when Keats, alone in the upstairs lodgings in Hampstead shortly before Christmas, wrote them one of the most quoted, yet one of the most puzzling, of all his letters: quoted—and puzzling—because of the cryptic references to "Beauty" and to "Truth," because of the curious phrase, "Negative Capability," and because it is felt that Keats is now at a level of speculation from which he is beginning to touch on some of the highest functions of poetry.

III

The letter distills the reactions of three months to the dimension of thinking that had opened to him in September. A background that helps to clarify these rapid, condensed remarks is provided by the long letter written to Bailey only a month before, just after Keats had arrived at Burford Bridge determined to "wind up" the last five hundred lines of *Endymion*.

For weeks the ideal of "disinterestedness" about which they had talked at Oxford had eluded his impulsive efforts to apply it to his own personal experience. Given the complexities, the unpredictable problems even in one month of one life, no simple formula could serve. But perhaps that realization was itself a further argument for the need of "disinterestedness" and a further indication of the futility, in a universe of uncertainties, of the brief, assertive postures we assume. The result, as he told Bailey, was a healthful increase in "Humility and the capability of submission." The significant word is "capability," not "submission." "Negative" was to be the next word he would apply to the "capability" he had in mind—"submission" could have very different connotations—though even "negative" would still be far from adequate. Meanwhile he goes on:

> I am certain of nothing but of the holiness of the Heart's affections and the truth of Imagination—What the imagination seizes as Beauty must be truth—whether it existed before or not—for I have the same Idea of all our Passions as of Love they are all, in their sublime, creative of essential Beauty . . . The Imagination may be compared to Adam's dream [*Paradise Lost*, VIII.452–490]—he awoke and found it truth. I am the more zealous in this affair, because I have never yet been able to perceive how any thing can be known for truth by consequitive reasoning—and yet it must be—Can it be that even the greatest Philosopher ever arrived at his goal without putting aside numerous objections—However it may be, O for a Life of Sensations rather than of Thoughts!

Two general premises interweave here. Though they were common enough in the more thoughtful writing of the period, Keats has acquired them partly through self-discovery. Hence, far from being what Whitehead calls "inert ideas," they are invested with possibilities. The first is the premise of all objective idealism: what the human mind itself contributes to what it assumes are direct perceptions of the material world—supplementing, channeling, even helping to create them—is not, as the subjective idealist argues, something imposed completely *ab extra*, something invented or read into nature that is not really there. Instead, this cooperating creativity of the mind has, to use a phrase of Coleridge's, "the same ground with nature": its insights are to this extent a valid and necessary supplement in attaining the reconciliation or union of man and nature that constitutes knowledge. Keats, of course, knew nothing of contemporary German idealism, objective or subjective. He had dipped into a little of Coleridge: Bailey had been reading the *Lay Sermons*, and Keats in early November borrowed the *Sibylline Leaves* from Charles Dilke. But he seems to have caught very little from Coleridge at this point, and associated him a month later with an "irritable reaching after fact and reason" that contrasts with the ideal he is naively but brilliantly evolving throughout the next half year.

It is primarily from Wordsworth that Keats has picked up enough hints to enable him to go ahead with this "favorite Speculation," as he calls it. He was naturally unaware of the massive treatment of man's relation to nature in the *Prelude*, into which Wordsworth was putting so much that he was never satisfied that it was ready for publication. But what Keats had read of Wordsworth he had recently approached in a very different spirit from the way he had been reading poetry the year before. He was quicker to note what he was beginning to call the "philosophical" implications of poetry. By now this speculation about the mind's creativity has become peculiarly his own, and to such an extent that he has begun to toy with the possible antecedence or foreshadowing, through imaginative insight, "of reality to come." The mention of this and of "Adam's dream" introduces

> another favorite Speculation of mine, that we shall enjoy ourselves here after by having what we called happiness on Earth repeated in a finer tone and so repeated—And yet such a fate can only befall those who delight in sensation rather than hunger as you do after Truth—Adam's dream will do here and seems to be a conviction that Imagination and its empyreal reflection is the same as human Life and its spiritual repetition. But as I was saying—the simple imaginative Mind may have its rewards in the repeti[ti]on of its own silent Working coming continually on the spirit with a fine suddenness.

IV

The second general premise involves the familiar Romantic protest on behalf of concreteness and the conviction that the analytic and logical procedures of what Keats calls "consequitive reasoning" violate the organic process of nature. They abstract from the full concreteness, reduce the living process to static concepts, and substitute an artificial order.

Here again the immediate suggestions have come to Keats from Wordsworth but are further substantiated by what he has been reading of Hazlitt. More than any other literary critic of his day, Hazlitt continued the brilliant psychological tradition of eighteenth-century British empiricism, rephrasing and supplementing a descriptive study of the imagination that had been developing for at least sixty years, and applying it even more suggestively to genius in the arts, especially poetry. The great contribution of English psychological criticism throughout the later eighteenth century had been to describe and justify confidence in the imaginative act—an act whereby sensations, intuitions, and judgments are not necessarily retained in the memory as separate particles of knowledge to be consulted one by one, but can be coalesced and transformed into a readiness of response that is objectively receptive to the concrete process of nature and indeed actively participates in it. This entire approach to the imagination naturally involved a corollary protest against the sort of thing implied in Wordsworth's famous phrase, the "meddling intellect." The protest anticipates Whitehead's remarks on the "fallacy of misplaced concreteness": abstraction by its very nature fails to conceive the full concreteness; it draws out particular elements for special purposes of thought; and the "misplaced concreteness" comes when these necessary "short-cuts" in thinking—as Hazlitt calls them—are regarded as equivalent to the concrete reality.

Keats had just begun to catch some of the implications of these ideas during his Oxford visit. Hazlitt's *Essay on the Principles of Human Action* had lit up a large zone of possibilities. Its persuasive argument on the possible "disinterestedness" of the mind, and its brilliant treatment of the sympathetic potentialities of the imagination, had especially won him. But it is enough for the moment to point out how quickly it led him to read other works of Hazlitt. Within a few weeks after he wrote this letter to Bailey, he was telling both Haydon and his brothers that "the three things to rejoice at in this Age" were Wordsworth's *Excursion*, Haydon's pictures, and "Hazlitt's depth of Taste." Hazlitt, by now, had completely replaced Hunt in the triumvirate of the year before.

Finally, Hazlitt's constant use of the word "sensations" in the traditional empirical sense—as virtually equivalent to concrete experience—added a new term to Keats's own habitual vocabulary (hence the remark at the moment about the "Life of Sensations": the bookish Bailey, inclining more toward philosophical analysis, "would exist"—says Keats—"partly on sensation partly on thought"). "Consequitive reasoning" applies to the piecemeal, step-by-step procedures of the analytic and selective intelligence. But though Keats himself cannot perceive how truth can be known by this reductive means, and wonders whether the most astute reasoner "ever arrived at his goal without putting aside numerous objections," he is far from pushing the matter, and grants that it "must be" possible.

V

This letter to Bailey, written at Burford Bridge as he begins his determined seven-day effort to complete *Endymion*, has a sequel of its own. For Bailey seems to have been a little disturbed by portions of it—at least by the speculation about an afterlife in which the "old Wine of Heaven" may consist of "the redigestion of our most ethereal Musings on Earth," and "what we called happiness on Earth repeated in a finer tone and so repeated." Bailey saw Keats in London in January and may have talked with him about the letter. If not, he certainly wrote to him in some detail, and may have taken some time to do so.

At all events, the matter is picked up again in a letter Keats wrote to him on March 13. This letter gives every indication that Keats has been trying to think over some of the remarks he had made before. What he is most eager to state is that he is not a dogmatist in his skepticism—that he is not, as he thinks, a complete skeptic at all. He wishes he could "enter into" all of Bailey's feelings on the matter, and write something Bailey would like (Keats was too "transparent," said Bailey, ever to be able to hide anything); and if he had appeared to be substituting the poetic imagination for religion as a means of arriving at truth, he is now beginning to have moments of doubt about poetry itself.

Then he turns to what he had been trying to express about the validity of the imagination's own contribution to its perception. Some things, certainly "real," may not require this "greeting of the Spirit" from the human mind or heart. But others—at least "things semireal"—do require that greeting, that contribution, for their fulfillment; and this union of the perceiving mind and the perceived object should not be confused with mere "Nothings" that are solely the product of human desires. He begins:

> You know my ideas about Religion—I do not think myself more in the right than other people and that nothing in this world is proveable. I wish I could enter into all your feelings on the subject merely for one short 10 Minutes and give you a Page or two to your liking. I am sometimes so very sceptical as to think Poetry itself a mere Jack a lanthern to amuse whoever may chance to be struck with its brilliance—As Tradesmen say every thing is worth what it will fetch, so probably every mental pursuit takes its reality and worth from the ardour of the pursuer—being in itself a nothing—Ethereal thing[s] may at least be thus real, divided under three heads—Things real—things semireal—and no things— Things real—such as existences of Sun Moon & Stars and passages of Shakspeare—Things semireal such as Love, the Clouds &c which require a greeting of the Spirit to make them wholly exist— and Nothings which are made Great and dignified by an ardent pursuit—Which by the by stamps the burgundy mark on the bottles of our Minds, insomuch as they are able to *"consec[r]ate what'er they look upon."*

The theme of much of the greater poetry to come—certainly of the "Ode on a Grecian Urn" and the "Ode to a Nightingale"—may be described as the drama of the human spirit's "greeting" of objects in order "to make them wholly exist"—a drama in which the resolutions are precarious, as in life itself, and the preciousness of the attainment ultimately crossed by tragedy. But for the moment he is unable to go further, and least of all to go further theoretically. In his remarks to Bailey, particularly about the "semi-real" as distinct from "Nothings," he is trying to grope toward a distinction that Locke could not make and that Hume thought it impossible to make. He can end only with a plea for openness, and by recurring to a thought that has been growing on him for some time: that the heart's hunger for settlement, for finality, cannot be answered unless we shut ourselves off from the amplitude of experience, with all its contradictory diversity. All he can do is to proceed honestly and empirically in this adventure of speculation, of openness, and (as he later phrased it) of "straining at particles of light in the midst of a great darkness."

Quite plainly he will "never be a Reasoner"; every point of thought quickly opens some further unexpected vista; and how could he be confident therefore of "the truth of any of my speculations"? His comic sense is suddenly aroused by the ineffectiveness of his discourse, which he burlesques for a moment; and he ends with a characteristic pun.

VI

The "Negative Capability" letter is best understood as another phrasing of these thoughts, with at least three further extensions. First, the problem of form or style in art enters more specifically. Second, the ideal toward which he is groping is contrasted more strongly with the egoistic assertion of one's own identity. Third, the door is further opened to the perception— which he was to develop within the next few months—of the sympathetic potentialities of the imagination.

He begins by telling his brothers that he has gone to see Edmund Kean, has written his review, and is enclosing it for them. Then on Saturday, December 20, he went to see an exhibition of the American painter, Benjamin West, particularly his picture, "Death on the Pale Horse." Keats was altogether receptive to any effort to attain the "sublime," and West's painting had been praised for succeeding. Yet it struck Keats as flat—"there is nothing to be intense upon; no women one feels mad to kiss; no face swelling into reality." Then the first crucial statement appears:

> The excellence of every Art is its intensity, capable of making all disagreeables evaporate, from their being in close relationship with Beauty & Truth—Examine King Lear & you will find this exemplified throughout; but in this picture we have unpleasantness without any momentous depth of speculation excited, in which to bury its repulsiveness.

In the active cooperation or full "greeting" of the experiencing imagination and its object, the nature or "identity" of the object is grasped so vividly that only those associations and qualities that are strictly relevant to the central conception remain. The irrelevant and discordant (the "disagreeables'') "evaporate" from this fusion of object and mind. Hence "Truth" and "Beauty" spring simultaneously into being, and also begin to approximate each other. For, on the one hand, the external reality—otherwise overlooked, or at most only sleepily acknowledged, or dissected so that a particular aspect of it may be abstracted for special purposes of argument or thought—has now, as it were, awakened into "Truth": it has been met by that human recognition, fulfilled and extended by that human agreement with reality, which we call "truth." And at the same time, with the irrelevant "evaporated," this dawning into unity is felt as "Beauty." Nor is it a unity solely of the object itself, emerging untrammeled and in its full significance, but a unity also of the human spirit, both within itself and with what was at first outside it. For in this "intensity"—the "excellence," he now feels, "of every Art"—we attain, if only for a while, a harmony of the inner life with truth. It is in this harmony that "Beauty" and "Truth" come together. The "pleasant," in the ordinary sense of the word, has nothing to do with the point being discussed; and to introduce it is only to trivialize the conception of "Beauty." Hence Keats's reference to *Lear*. The reality disclosed may be distressing and even cruel to human nature. But the harmony with truth will remain, and even deepen, to the extent that the emerging reality is being constantly matched at every stage by the "depth of speculation excited"—by the corresponding release and extension, in other words, of human insight. "Examine King Lear and you will find this exemplified throughout."

Hazlitt's short essay "On Gusto" had aroused his thinking about style when he read it at Oxford in the *Round Table*; and what he is saying now is partly the result of what he has assimilated from Hazlitt. By "gusto," Hazlitt means an excitement of the imagination in which the perceptive identification with the object is almost complete, and the living character of the object is caught and shared in its full diversity and given vital expression in art. It is "power or passion defining any object." But the result need not be subjective. By grasping sympathetically the overall significance of the object, the "power or passion" is able to cooperate, so to speak, with that significance—to go the full distance with its potentialities, omitting the irrelevant (which Keats calls the "disagreeables"), and conceiving the object with its various qualities coalescing into the vital unity that is the object itself. One result is that the attributes or qualities that we glean through our different senses of sight, hearing, touch, and the rest are not presented separately or piecemeal, but "the impression made on one sense excites by affinity those of another." Thus Claude Lorrain's landscapes, though "perfect abstractions of the visible images of things," lack "gusto": "They do not interpret one sense by another . . . That is, his eye wanted imagination; it did not strongly sympathise with his other faculties. He saw the atmosphere, but he did not feel it." Chaucer's descriptions of natural scenery have gusto: they give "the very feeling of the air, the coolness or moisture of the ground." "There is gusto in the colouring of Titian. Not only do his heads seem to think—his bodies seem to feel."

VII

This interplay and coalescence of impressions was to become a conscious aim in Keats's own poetry within the next six months, and, by the following autumn, to be fulfilled as richly as by any English poet of the last three centuries. Meanwhile, only a few days before he wrote the "Negative Capability" letter to his brothers, he had followed Hazlitt's use of the word "gusto" in his own review "On Edmund Kean as a Shakespearian Actor" (though he later returns to the word "intensity"—"gusto" perhaps suggesting a briskness or bounce of spirit he does not have in mind). He had been trying in this review to describe how "a melodious passage in poetry" may attain a fusion of "both sensual and spiritual," where each extends and declares itself by means of the other:

> The spiritual is felt when the very letters and points of charactered language show like the hieroglyphics of beauty;—the mysterious signs of an imortal free-masonry! . . . To one learned in Shakespearian hieroglyphics,—learned in the spiritual portion of those lines to which Kean adds a sensual grandeur: his tongue must seem to have robbed "the Hybla bees, and left them honeyless."

Hence "there is an indescribable gusto in his voice, by which we feel that the utterer is thinking of the past and future, while speaking of the present."

Keats is here extending the notion of "gusto" in a way that applies prophetically to his own maturer style—to an imaginative "intensity" of conception, that is, in which process, though slowed to an insistent present, is carried in active solution. So with the lines he had quoted a month before to Reynolds as an example of Shakespeare's "intensity of working out conceits":

> When lofty trees I see barren of leaves
> Which erst from heat did canopy the herd,
> And Summer's green all girded up in sheaves,
> Borne on the bier with white and bristly beard.

Previous functions, and the mere fact of loss itself, are a part of the truth of a thing as it now is. The nature of the "lofty trees" in this season, now "barren of leaves," includes the fact that they formerly "from heat did canopy the herd"; nor is it only the dry, completed grain of the autumn that is "girded up in sheaves," but the "Summer's green" that it once was. This entire way of thinking about style is proving congenial to Keats in the highest degree; for though it has independent developments, it has also touched and is giving content to the ideal briefly suggested a year before in *Sleep and Poetry*—even before he saw the Elgin Marbles for the first time: an ideal of poetry as "might half slumb'ring on its own right arm." The delight in energy caught in momentary repose goes back to the idea he had "when a Schoolboy . . . of an heroic painting": "I saw it somewhat sideways," he tells Haydon, "large prominent round and colour'd with magnificence—somewhat like the feel I have of Anthony and Cleopatra. Or of Alcibiades, leaning on his Crimson Couch in his Galley, his broad shoulders imperceptibly heaving with the Sea." So with the line in *Henry VI*, "See how the surly Warwick mans the Wall." One of the comments he wrote in his copy of Milton during the next year gives another illustration:

> Milton in every instance pursues his imagination to the utmost—he is "sagacious of his Quarry," he sees Beauty on the wing, pounces upon it and gorges it to the producing his essential verse. . . . But in no instance is this sort of perseverance more exemplified than in what may be called his *stationing or statu[a]ry*. He is not content with simple description, he must station,—thus here, we not only see how the Birds *"with clang despised the ground,"* but we see them "under *a cloud in prospect.*" So we see Adam *"Fair indeed and tall—under a plantane"*—and so we see Satan *"disfigured—on the Assyrian Mount."*

The union of the ideal of dynamic poise, of power kept in reserve, with the ideal of range of implication suggests one principal development in his own style throughout the next year and a half. The very triumph of this union—as triumphs often tend to do—could have proved an embarrassment to later ideals and interests had it become an exclusive stylistic aim. However magnificent the result in the great odes, in portions of *Hyperion*, or in what Keats called the "colouring" and "drapery" of the *Eve of St. Agnes*, it carried liabilities in both pace and variety that would have to be circumvented for successful narrative and, above all, dramatic poetry. But even at the moment, and throughout the next year, what he calls "intensity"—the "greeting of the Spirit" and its object—is by no means completely wedded to a massive centering of image through poise and "stationing." If his instinctive delight in fullness was strengthened in one direction by the Elgin Marbles—which he still made visits to see—other, more varied appeals to his ready empathy were being opened and reinforced by his reading of Shakespeare.

VIII

The second and longer of the crucial parts of the "Negative Capability" letter is preceded by some more remarks about what he has been doing since his brothers left, and the remarks provide a significant preface. He had dinner—"I have been out too much lately"—with "Horace Smith & met his two Brothers with [Thomas] Hill & [John] Kingston & one [Edward] Du Bois."

Partly because he himself was so direct and—as Bailey said—"transparent," he was ordinarily tolerant of the more innocent affectations by which people hope to establish superiority. Moreover, such affectations appealed to his enormous relish for the idiosyncratic. As the next year passed, the very futility of such brief postures—the pointless intricacy of these doomed stratagems—against the vast backdrop of a universe of constantly unfolding "uncertainties, Mysteries, doubts," was also to take on a pathos for him. In fact, only a month after he tells his brothers about this dinner with Horace Smith and his literary friends, he was to write Bailey, speaking of "Reynolds and Haydon retorting and recriminating—and parting for ever—the same thing has happened between Haydon and Hunt":

> Men should bear with each other—there lives not the Man who may not be cut up, aye hashed to pieces on his weakest side. The best of Men have but a portion of good in them—a kind of spiritual yeast in their frames which creates the ferment of existence—by which a Man is propell'd to act and strive and buffet with Circumstance.

Even so, during these important transitional months he is entering, moments inevitably occur when the familiar comic sense and the deepening charity are suspended. Affectations particularly bother him at such moments. It is a great pity, as he tells Haydon (March 21), that "people should by associating themselves with the fine[st] things, spoil them—Hunt has damned Hampstead [and] Masks and Sonnets and [I]talian tales—Wordsworth ha[s] damned the lakes," and so on. Hazlitt is "your only good damner." because he damns in a different spirit. And Keats was enormously—almost amusingly—disturbed when Reynolds told him that his self-defensive Preface to *Endymion* savored of "affectation" in its own way. Keats kept protesting that, whatever else it showed, it certainly did not show "affectation," though he at once began anxiously to rewrite it.

So at Horace Smith's dinner, which he describes to George and Tom, where he met five other men of literary interests. Their entire way of talking about literature fatigued him for the moment. The possible uses of literature seemed frozen into posture, into mannerism. Given his attempts to approach his new ideal of "disinterestedness," and the thoughts of "Humility" and of openness to amplitude that had become more specific, even more convinced, within the last few months, the gathering typified the exact opposite of what was wanted:

> They only served to convince me, how superior humour is to wit in respect to enjoyment—These men say things which make one start, without making one feel, they are all alike; their manners are alike; they all know fashionables; they have a mannerism in their very eating & drinking, in their mere handling a Decanter— They talked of Kean & his low company—Would I were with that company instead of yours said I to myself! I know such like acquaintance will never do for me.

But his humor was to return when he found himself again in Kingston's company at Haydon's a week and a half afterwards. The "mannerism" in the "mere handling a Decanter" had caught his fancy as a symbol of the entire evening. At Haydon's, as he gleefully told George and Tom, "I astonished Kingston at supper . . . keeping my two glasses at work in a knowing way."

Shortly after Smith's literary party, he went to the Christmas panto-mime at Drury Lane with Charles Brown and Charles Dilke. Walking with them back to Hampstead, he found himself having

> not a dispute but a disquisition with Dilke, on various subjects; several things dovetailed in my mind, & at once it struck me, what quality went to form a Man of Achievement especially in Literature & which Shakespeare possessed so enormously—I mean *Negative Capability*, that is when man is capable of being in uncertainties, Mysteries, doubts, without any irritable reaching after fact & rea-son—Coleridge, for instance, would let go by a fine isolated veri-similitude caught from the Penetralium of mystery, from being incapable of remaining content with half knowledge. This pursued through Volumes would perhaps take us no further than this, that with a great poet the sense of Beauty overcomes every other con-sideration, or rather obliterates all consideration.

Using what we know of the background, we could paraphrase these famous sentences as follows. In our life of uncertainties, where no one system or formula can explain everything—where even a word is at best, in Bacon's phrase, a "wager of thought"—what is needed is an imaginative openness of mind and heightened receptivity to reality in its full and diverse con-creteness. This, however, involves negating one's own ego. Keats's friend Dilke, as he said later, "was a Man who cannot feel he has a personal identity unless he has made up his Mind about every thing. The only means of strengthening one's intellect is to make up ones mind about nothing—to let the mind be a thoroughfare for all thoughts. . . . Dilke will never come at a truth as long as he lives; because he is always trying at it." To be dissatisfied with such insights as one may attain through this openness, to reject them unless they can be wrenched into a part of a systematic structure of one's own making, is an egoistic assertion of one's own identity. The remark, "without any irritable reaching after fact and reason," is often cited as though the pejorative words are "fact and reason," and as though uncertainties were being preferred for their own sake. But the significant word, of course, is "irritable." We should also stress "capable"—"capable of being in uncertainties, Mysteries, doubts" without the "irritable" need to extend our identities and rationalize our "half knowledge." For a "great poet" especially, a sympathetic absorption in the essential significance of his object (caught and relished in that active cooperation of the mind in which the emerging "Truth" is felt as "Beauty," and in which the harmony of the human imagination and its object is attained) "overcomes every other consideration" (considerations that an "irritable reaching after fact and rea-son" might otherwise itch to pursue). Indeed, it goes beyond and "oblit-erates" the act of "consideration"—of deliberating, analyzing, and piecing experience together through "consequitive reasoning."

IX

Such speculations could hardly be called more than a beginning. Taken by themselves they could lead almost anywhere. That, of course, was one of their principal assets. Even so, the need for at least some specific and positive procedures, helpful at any period of life, is particularly pressing at twenty-two. Keats understandably wavered throughout the next few months in trying to interpret whatever premises he had attained thus far—premises that were hardly more than the penumbra of the idea of "disinterestedness" as it touched his concrete experience. Such shadows at least involved extensions of a sort; and the thought of this was to give him some consolation as time passed.

But meanwhile he had moments when something close to mere passivity appealed strongly; and the image of the receptive flower, visited and fertilized by the bee, caught his fancy. The relentless labor of writing *Endymion* was producing a natural reaction. Insights, reconsiderations, "speculations" (to use his own word) overlooked during that huge scurry, were now presenting themselves more abundantly than ever before. Because the gains in having written the poem were becoming assimilated, they were at times almost forgotten. Slow development, maturity, rooted strength, leisure for growth, took on a further attraction. But in the very act of urging eloquently—and justly—the virtues of something not far from Wordsworth's "wise passiveness" the limitations would suddenly disclose themselves to him. He would begin to feel that this was not what he meant, or wanted, at all. At least it was not enough by itself. A letter to John Reynolds (February 19) finely illustrates the course of one "speculation." He starts with a now-favorite thought of his that any one point may serve as a fruitful beginning. A man could "pass a very pleasant life" if he sat down each day and

> read a certain Page of full Poesy or distilled Prose and let him wander with it, and muse upon it, and reflect from it, and bring home to it, and prophesy upon it, and dream upon it—untill it becomes stale—but when will it do so? Never—When Man has arrived at a certain ripeness in intellect any one grand and spiritual passage serves him as a starting post towards all "the two-and-thirty Pallaces."

The result would be a genuine "voyage of conception." A doze on the sofa, a child's prattle, a strain of music, even "a nap upon Clover," could all engender "ethereal finger-pointings." It would have the impetus, the strength, of being self-directive. "Many have original Minds who do not think it—they are led away by Custom." This insight, substantiated by his own experience, leads him next to turn upside down the old fable of the spider and the bee, especially as Swift used it. The appeal of the spider as a symbol is that the points of leaves and twigs on which it begins its work can be very few, and yet it is able to fill the air with a "circuiting." "Now it appears to me that almost any Man may like the Spider spin from his own inwards his own airy Citadel," which will then be creatively meaningful—it will be "full of Symbols for his spiritual eye." Of course his starting-points, his "circuiting," and the achieved "space for his wandering," would all differ from that of others. If we wish to be militant, complications would result. Here Keats comes to the heart of his thought:

> The Minds of Mortals are so different and bent on such diverse Journeys that it may at first appear impossible for any common taste and fellowship to exist between two or three under these suppositions—It is however quite the contrary—Minds would leave each other in contrary directions, traverse each other in Numberless points, and all [at] last greet each other at the Journeys end—A old Man and a child would talk together and the old Man be led on his Path, and the child left thinking—Man should not dispute or assert but whisper results to his neighbour, and thus by every germ of Spirit sucking the Sap from mould ethereal every human might become great, and Humanity instead of being a wide heath of Furse and Briars with here and there a remote Oak or Pine, would become a grand democracy of Forest Trees.

At no later time would he have disagreed with what he has just said. But he carries the ideal of receptivity further in sentences that are sometimes separated from context and interpreted as a new, fundamental credo:

> It has been an old Comparison for our urging on—the Bee hive—however it seems to me that we should rather be the flower than the Bee . . . Now it is more noble to sit like Jove tha[n] to fly like Mercury—let us not therefore go hurrying about and collecting honey-bee like, buzzing here and there impatiently from a knowledge of what is to be arrived at: but let us open our leaves like a flower and be passive and receptive—budding patiently under the eye of Apollo and taking hints from every noble insect that favors us with a visit.

In this spirit he has just written the fine unrhymed sonnet, "What the Thrush Said," with its refrain "O fret not after knowledge." He had been "led into these thoughts . . . by the beauty of the morning operating on a sense of Idleness—I have not read any Books—the Morning said I was right—I had no Idea but of the Morning and the Thrush said I was right."

But as soon as he copies the poem for Reynolds, he becomes "sensible all this is a mere sophistication, however it may neighbour to any truths, to excuse my own indolence." There is not much chance of rivaling Jove anyway, and one can consider oneself "very well off as a sort of scullion-Mercury or even a humble Bee." Two days later he also tells his brothers that "The Thrushes are singing"; but he himself is now "reading Voltaire and Gibbon, although I wrote to Reynolds the other day to prove reading was of no use."

X

Wherever the more general implications might lead, he was clearer and more certain in his growing interest in the impersonality of genius, "especially in Literature." For here the ideal of "disinterestedness" directly touched an internal fund both of native gift and (considering his age) accumulated experience.

What strikes us most in his capacity for sympathetic identification, starting with the schooldays at Enfield, is its inclusiveness. This is not the volatile empathic range of even the rare actor. For the range is vertical as well as horizontal, and is distinguished more by an adhesive purchase of mind than by volubility. He might, in describing the bearbaiting to Clarke, instinctively begin to imitate not only the spectators but the bear, "dabbing his fore paws hither and thither," and, in diagnosing Clarke's stomach complaint and comparing the stomach to a brood of baby-birds "gaping for sustenance," automatically open his own "capacious mouth." But emphatic expressions of this sort were mere side-effects—like the self-forgetful fights at Enfield—of an habitual capacity for identification that went deeper. When he picked up styles in the writing of poetry, it was not as a mimic or copyist but as a fellow participator identified even more with the other's aim and ideal than with the individual himself. If, when still a student at Guy's Hospital, he caught elements of Felton Mathew's style, he dignified them; and the result, poor as it is, transcends anything Mathew wrote. So later with Hunt. Except at the very start, and except for a few isolated passages afterwards, we have nothing of the routine mechanism of a copy. If anything, he brings Hunt more to life. Still later, in *Hyperion*, he was to write within little more than two or three months the only poem among all the Miltonic imitations in English that Milton himself might not have been ashamed to write.

Discussion of these larger manifestations would lead to a summary of his entire development as illustration. We can, however, linger for a moment on his delight in empathic imagery itself. For here, quickly and vividly, his ready sympathy appears long before anyone could have called his attention to such a thing or given him a vocabulary with which to describe it. We think back to Clarke's account of the lines and images that most caught Keats's imagination when they first read together at Enfield. Doubtless feeling the weight of the parting billows on his own shoulders, he "*hoisted* himself up, and looked burly and dominant, as he said, 'what an image that is—*sea-shouldering whales.*' " Much later there was the memorable introduction to Chapman's Homer, and the passage in the shipwreck of Ulysses that brought "one of his delighted stares": "Down he sank to death. / The sea had soak'd his heart through." His reading of Shakespeare, now that he was about to write with less sense of hurry, was beginning to encourage his gift for empathic concentration of image; and within two years this was to develop to a degree hardly rivaled since Shakespeare himself. Among the passages he excitedly copied out for Reynolds, a month before the "Negative Capability" letter, is the description of the trembling withdrawal of a snail into its shell:

> He has left nothing to say about nothing or any thing: for look at Snails, you know what he says about Snails, you know where he talks about "cockled snails"—well . . . this is in the Venus and Adonis: the Simile brought it to my Mind.

> Audi—As the snail, whose tender horns being hit,
>   Shrinks back into his shelly cave with pain,
>   And there all smothered up in shade doth sit,
>   Long after fearing to put forth again.

So with the comment he later wrote in his copy of *Paradise Lost* (IX.179–91):

> Satan having entered the Serpent, and inform'd his brutal sense— might seem sufficient—but Milton goes on *"but his sleep disturb'd not."* Whose spirit does not ache at the smothering and confine- ment—the unwilling stillness—the *"waiting close"*? Whose head is not dizzy at the possible speculations of satan in his serpent prison—no passage of poetry ever can give a greater pain of suffocation.

Finally, before turning to the impact of Hazlitt, we may glance back a few months to Severn's account of his walks with Keats on Hampstead Heath during the preceding summer, while Keats was still working on Book II of *Endymion*. Nothing could bring him so quickly out of "one of his fits of seeming gloomful reverie" as his vivid identification with organic motion in what he called "the inland sea"—the movement of the wind across a field of grain. He "would stand, leaning forward," watching with a "serene look in his eyes and sometimes with a slight smile." At other times, "when 'a wave was billowing through a tree,' as he described the uplifting surge of air among swaying masses of chestnut or oak foliage," or when he would hear in the distance "the wind coming across woodlands,"

> "The tide! the tide!" he would cry delightedly, and spring on to some stile, or upon the low bough of a wayside tree, and watch the passage of the wind upon the meadow-grasses or young corn, not stirring till the flow of air was all around him.

Severn, who tended rather toward revery and vagueness, was repeatedly "astonished" at the closeness with which Keats would notice details, until Severn himself began to catch a little of it:

> Nothing seemed to escape him, the song of a bird and the un- dernote of response from covert or hedge, the rustle of some an- imal, the changing of the green and brown lights and furtive shadows, the motions of the wind—just how it took certain tall

flowers and plants—and the wayfaring of the clouds: even the features and gestures of passing tramps, the colour of one woman's hair, the smile on one child's face, the furtive animalism below the deceptive humanity in many of the vagrants, even the hats, clothes, shoes, wherever these conveyed the remotest hint as to the real self of the wearer.

Severn's notice of Keats's delight in whatever conveyed "the remotest hint as to the real self of the wearer" carries us forward to the Chaucerian relish of character that we find increasingly in the longer letters and even in the mere underlinings and marginal notes of Keats's reading. "Scenery is fine," he writes to Bailey (March 13, 1818), "but human nature is finer—The Sward is richer for the tread of a real, nervous [E]nglish foot." Reading a month or so later in an old copy (1634) of Mateo Aleman's *The Rogue: or, the Life of Guzman de Alfarache*, which James Rice had just given him, he underlines the words, "his voice lowd and shrill but not very cleere," and writes in the margin: "This puts me in mind of Fielding's Fanny 'whose teeth were white but uneven'; it is the same sort of personality. The great Man in this way is Chaucer."

XI

A fairly large internal fund was thus available to be tapped when Keats read, undoubtedly at Bailey's suggestion, Hazlitt's *Essay on the Principles of Human Action*, and bought a copy that was still in his library at his death.

Hazlitt's aim in this short book—his first published work—was to refute the contention of Thomas Hobbes and his eighteenth-century followers that self-love, in one way or another, is the mainspring of all human action, and to prove instead, as the subtitle states, "the Natural Disinterestedness of the Human Mind." Since British philosophy for a century had devoted more speculation to this problem than to any other, Hazlitt's youthful aim was quite ambitious (he began the book in his early twenties, and was twenty-seven when it appeared). His procedure was ingenious, and to some extent original. Moralists trying to disprove Hobbes had for fifty years or more been stressing the sympathetic potentialities of the imagination. Adam Smith's influential *Theory of Moral Sentiments* (1759) is the best-known example. The interest spread to the critical theory of the arts; and well over a century before German psychology developed the theory of *Einfühlung*— for which the word "empathy" was later coined as a translation—English critical theory had anticipated many of the insights involved. It was the peculiar fate of many psychological discoveries of the English eighteenth century to be forgotten from the 1830s until the hungry theorization of the German universities in the late nineteenth century led to a rediscovery and a more systematized and subjective interpretation.

In his *Principles of Human Action*, Hazlitt went much further than Adam Smith's *Theory of Moral Sentiments*. His hope was to show that imaginative sympathy was not a mere escape hatch from the prison of egocentricity, but something thoroughgoing, something indigenous and inseparable from all activities of the mind. Sympathetic identification takes place constantly—even if only with ourselves and our own desired future. Hazlitt's psychology, in effect, is a more dynamic version of Locke's. Instead of the image of the mind as a *tabula rasa* on which experience writes, we have an image of it as something more actively adhesive and projective: equally dependent on what is outside itself for its own coloration, so to speak, but actively uniting with its objects, growing, dwindling, even becoming poisoned, by what it assimilates. Hazlitt's argument turns on the nature of "identity." Suppose that I love myself in the thoroughgoing way that the Hobbists claim—that everything I do, or plan, or hope, is in order to help myself or avoid pain in the future: that even what we call generous acts are done solely (as the Hobbists maintained) because I wish to be praised, or because I wish to get along with others, or because I wish—at least—to be able to live with myself. But how can I know, how especially can I "love," this "identity" that I consider myself? If we look at the problem with empirical honesty, we have to admit that any feeling we have that we are one person, the same person, from one moment to the next (that we have, in short, an "identity") comes directly through two means only—"sensation" and "memory." A child who has burned his finger knows only through "sensation" that it is he and not someone else who has done so. In a similar way, he knows only through "memory" that it was he and not someone else who had this experience in the past. If our identities until now depend on sensation and memory, what can give me an interest in my future sensations? Sensation and memory are not enough. I can picture my future identity only through my *imagination*. The child who has been burned will dread the prospect of future pain from the fire because, through his imagination, he "projects himself forward into the future, and identifies himself with his future being." His imagination "creates" his own future to him.

In short, I can "abstract myself from my present being and take an interest in my future being [only] in the same sense and manner, in which I can go out of myself entirely and enter into the minds and feelings of others." The capacity for imaginative identification, in other words, is not instinctively or mechanically obliged to turn in one direction rather than another: the sole means by which "I can anticipate future objects, or be interested in them," throwing "me forward as it were into my future being" and anticipating events that do not yet exist, is equally able to "carry me out of myself into the feelings of others by one and the same process . . . I could not love myself, if I were not capable of loving others." If stronger ideas than those of one's own identity are present to the mind, the imagination can turn more easily to them. Hazlitt here develops the belief of the associationist psychologists of the time, in whom he was widely read, that the mind instinctively follows and "imitates" what is before it. He expands the attitude of his old college tutor, Joseph Priestley, though Hazlitt is less of a mechanist than Priestley, and stresses the creative activity of the mind in its sympathetic and projective functions. Following Locke, Priestley had argued that, since the mind, as a *tabula rasa*, is conscious only of "the ideas that are present to it, it must, as it were, *conform* itself to them." In other words, since the mind receives everything from experience alone, it adapts itself to the character of what it receives, and does it

> so instantaneously and mechanically, that no person whatever hath reflection . . . to be upon his guard against some of the most useless and ridiculous effects of it. What person, if he saw another upon a precipice and in danger of falling, could help starting back, . . . as he would do if he himself were going to fall? At least he would have a strong propensity to do it. And what is more common than to see persons in playing at bowls, lean their own bodies, and writhe them into every possible attitude, according to the course they would have their bowl to take? . . . The more vivid are a man's ideas, and the greater is his general sensibility, the more intirely, and with the greater facility, doth he adapt himself to the situations he is viewing.
>
> [*Course of Lectures on Oratory and Criticism*]

The argument for "the natural disinterestedness of the mind" is not, of course, that most people are really disinterested, but that there is no mechanical determinism, such as Hobbes and his followers assumed, toward self-love. The disinterestedness exists as far as the *potential* development of the mind is concerned. Knowledge can direct and habituate the imagination to ideas other than that of our own identity. We commonly see that long acquaintance with another increases our sympathy, provided undesirable qualities in the other person, or sheer monotony, do not work against it. If the child is unsympathetic to others, it is not from automatic self-love but because of lack of knowledge—a lack that also prevents him from identifying himself very successfully with his own future interests. Greatness in art, philosophy, moral action—the "heroic" in any sense— involves losing the sense of "our personal identity in some object dearer to us than ourselves."

Hazlitt never developed the psychological implications of his theory much further. A practicing journalist forced to dash off articles and reviews in order to make ends meet, he looked back nostalgically on his *Principles of Human Action* as typical of work he hoped to resume. But the years passed; and the habit of more rapid, less analytic writing became ingrained. His concept of the sympathetic character of the imagination, however, serves as a general premise to much of his literary criticism, especially his writing on Shakespeare. It underlies his conception of the drama as the most objective and therefore the highest form of poetry. It is much in his mind when he turns to the poetry of his own day. Sensing more clairvoyantly than any other English critic of the time the large subjective movement taking place in the arts, of which Romanticism constituted the first stage, he feared a growing split between artist and society through the narrowing (even though partly in self-defense) of the artist's sympathies. His harsher criticism of his own contemporaries—including poets as diverse as Words-worth and Byron—turns on what he feels to be an obtrusion of the poet's personal feelings, interests, defenses, and the danger of losing that "high and permanent interest beyond ourselves" to which art should aim.

XII

Less than three weeks after Keats wrote the "Negative Capability" letter to his brothers around Christmastime, Hazlitt began a course of lectures at the Surrey Institution, just south of Blackfriars Bridge, every Tuesday evening at seven o'clock. These were the famous *Lectures on the English Poets*, the first of which was on January 13 and the last on March 3. Keats looked forward to hearing them all, and, as far as we know, missed only one ("On Chaucer and Spenser," January 20), when he arrived too late. A few sentences at the start of the third lecture, "On Shakespeare and Milton" (January 27), which Keats told Bailey he definitely planned to attend, may have especially struck him. Shakespeare, said Hazlitt,

> was the least of an egotist that it was possible to be. He was nothing in himself; but he was all that others were, or that they could become. He not only had in himself the germs of every faculty and feeling, but he could follow them by anticipation, intuitively, into all their conceivable ramifications, through every change of fortune, or conflict of passion, or turn of thought. . . . He had only to think of anything in order to become that thing, with all the circumstances belonging to it.

By contrast, much modern poetry seems to have become engaged in a competition to "reduce" itself "to a mere effusion of natural sensibility," surrounding "the meanest objects with the morbid feelings and devouring egotism of the writers' own minds."

The immediate effect of Hazlitt's lectures was to open Keats's eyes much sooner than would otherwise have happened to the limitations of the prevailing modes of poetry—limitations that were far from obvious to most writers until a full century had run its course. But the ideal of the "characterless" poet, touching as it did qualities and habits of response intrinsic to himself, gradually took a secure hold of his imagination through-out the months ahead, though still later it was to appear to him as something of an oversimplification. The extent to which it became domesticated in his habitual thinking is shown by a letter the following autumn, at the begin-ning of the astonishing year (October 1818 to October 1819) when his great-est poetry was written. He is writing to Richard Woodhouse (October 27):

> As to the poetical Character itself, (I mean that sort of which, if I am anything, I am a Member; that sort distinguished from the

wordworthian or egotistical sublime; which is a thing per se and stands alone) it is not itself—it has no self—it is everything and nothing—It has no character—it enjoys light and shade; it lives in gusto, be it foul or fair, high or low, rich or poor, mean or elevated—It has as much delight in conceiving an Iago as an Imogen. What shocks the virtuous philosop[h]er, delights the camelion Poet. It does no harm from its relish of the dark side of things any more than from its taste for the bright one; because they both end in speculation. A Poet is the most unpoetical of any thing in existence; because he has no Identity—he is continually in for—and filling some other Body—The Sun, the Moon, the Sea and Men and Women who are creatures of impulse are poetical and have about them an unchangeable attribute—the poet has none; no identity—he is certainly the most unpoetical of all God's Creatures. . . . When I am in a room with People if I ever am free from speculating on creations of my own brain, then not myself goes home to myself: but the identity of every one in the room begins to press upon me [so] that I am in a very little time annihilated— not only among Men; it would be the same in a Nursery of children.

Woodhouse, who by now had acquired a close knowledge of Keats, found these remarks a good description of Keats's own bent of mind, and wrote to John Taylor,

> I believe him to be right with regard to his own Poetical Character— And I perceive clearly the distinction between himself & those of the Wordsworth School. . . . The highest order of Poet will not only possess all the above powers but will have [so] high an imag^n that he will be able to throw his own soul into any object he sees or imagines, so as to see feel be sensible of, & express, all that the object itself wo^d see feel be sensible of or express—& he will speak out of that object—so that his own self will with the Exception of the Mechanical part be "annihilated."—and it is [of] the excess of this power that I suppose Keats to speak, when he says he has no identity—As a poet, and when the fit is upon him, this is true. . . . Shakesp^r was a poet of the kind above ment^d—and he was perhaps the only one besides Keats who possessed this power in an extr^y degree.

Keats had talked with Woodhouse about the subject before, and had thrown himself into it with the fanciful exuberance he found irresistible when he was among serious people. For Woodhouse adds the comment noticed earlier: "He has affirmed that he can conceive of a billiard Ball that it may have a sense of delight from its own roundness, smoothness volubility & the rapidity of its motion."

XIII

We have been anticipating, of course: the implications of the "Negative Capability" letter have encouraged us to look ahead a few months. Back in December, as he felt himself emerging onto this new plateau of thinking, the memory of *King Lear* kept recurring. When he had begun *Endymion* at the Isle of Wight, it was the sea—remembered from the cliff near Margate the summer before (1816)—that had led him to return to the play on this second venture: "the passage . . . 'Do you not hear the Sea?' has haunted me intensely." Now that *Endymion* was finished, and a third venture or transition lay ahead, he was remembering the play somewhat differently. It was probably in December, certainly by early January, that he bought a copy of Hazlitt's *Characters of Shakespear's Plays* (published late in 1817). With only one exception, all his underscorings and marginal comments are concentrated in the chapter on *Lear*. They provide in their own way a further gloss to that "intensity" of conception—that identification and "greeting of the Spirit"—of which he had been thinking when he wrote to George and Tom ("Examine King Lear & you will find this exemplified throughout"): an identification especially prized when—as Hazlitt said in a passage Keats underlines—"the extremest resources of the imagination are called in to lay open the deepest movements of the heart." "The greatest strength of genius," said Hazlitt, "is shown in describing the strongest passions: for the power of the imagination, in works of invention, must be in proportion to the force of the natural impressions, which are the subject of them." Double-scoring this in the margin, Keats writes:

> If we compare the Passions to different tuns and hogsheads of wine in a vast cellar—thus it is—the poet by one cup should know the scope of any particular wine without getting intoxicated—this is the highest exertion of Power, and the next step is to paint from memory of gone self storms.

And beside another passage he draws a line, underscoring the italicized words, and writes "This passage has to a great degree hieroglyphic visioning":

> We see the ebb and flow of the feeling, its pauses and feverish starts, its impatience of opposition, its accumulating force when it has time to recollect itself, *the manner in which it avails itself of every passing word or gesture, its haste to repel insinuation, the alternate contraction and dilatation of the soul.*

Endymion, which he began to copy and correct for the press during the first week of January, seemed remote indeed from the thoughts that now preoccupied him. So in fact did romances generally, though he was to write two more (*Isabella* and the *Eve of St. Agnes*). On Thursday, January 22, he finished copying the first book of *Endymion*; and then, as he told his brothers the next day, "I sat down . . . to read King Lear once again the thing appeared to demand the prologue of a Sonnet, I wrote it & began to read." It is hardly one of his best sonnets—he never even bothered to publish it—but the occasion meant something to him. For he was approaching the play with a new understanding of how much lay beyond the "old oak Forest" of "Romance."

It was only another beginning, and it would have to proceed much more slowly than the other beginnings. But he was prepared, he thought, for "a very gradual ripening of the intellectual powers"; and all he can say now is that "I think a little change has taken place in my intellect lately." Then he turns to the sonnet, copies it out for George and Tom, and adds: "So you see I am getting at it, with a sort of determination & strength, though verily I do not feel it at this moment—this is my fourth letter this morning & I feel rather tired & my head rather swimming."

Keats: The Negative Road

Paul de Man

In the course of time, the reputations of the main English Romantic poets have undergone considerable and revealing fluctuations. It would nowadays be considered eccentric to rate Byron above Wordsworth or Blake, yet during his lifetime Byron's fame far surpassed that of his contemporaries. Not till the end of the nineteenth century did Blake begin to receive full recognition, and we are now no longer surprised to find critics give him a central position that none of his contemporaries would have remotely suspected. We may have some difficulty in sharing the excitement with which the young Yeats discovered the audacities of Shelley's more speculative poems, but, on the other hand, Arnold's judgment in rating Wordsworth above Spenser, Dryden, Pope and Coleridge might again find some support, albeit for reasons that have little in common with Arnold's.

These fluctuations reflect changes in critical temper that are themselves the result of a continued reinterpretation of Romanticism. Time and again, literary and critical movements set out with the avowed aim of moving beyond Romantic attitudes and ideas; in America alone, Pound's imagism, Irving Babbitt's neo-humanism and the New Criticism of T. S. Eliot are relatively recent instances of such a trend; the same anti-Romantic (or anti-idealist) bias underlies neo-Realist and neo-Marxist tendencies here and abroad. But time and again, it turns out that the new conceptions that thus assert themselves were in fact already present in the full context of European Romanticism; instead of moving beyond these problems, we are merely becoming aware of certain aspects of Romanticism that had remained hidden from our perception. We certainly have left behind the Victorian image of Wordsworth, but Wordsworth himself is far from having been fixed and determined by a poetic or critical itinerary that went beyond him. What

From *John Keats: Selected Poetry.* © 1966 by Paul de Man and © 1986 by Patricia de Man. New American Library, 1966. Originally entitled "Introduction."

sets out as a claim to overcome Romanticism often turns out to be merely an expansion of our understanding of the movement, leading inevitably to changes in our images of individual poets.

The poetry of Keats is no exception. As the amount of biographical and critical studies augments in quantity and in quality, our knowledge of Keats has increased considerably, yet many questions remain unresolved, as if the work had not yielded all the possibilities of significance that it may contain. The curve of his reputation shows perhaps less dramatic ups and downs than in the case of Blake or even Shelley: it has constantly risen since his death at the age of twenty-five in 1821. He had already earned the enthusiastic appreciation of several close and loyal friends during his lifetime, but his career was too short to give him the real critical recognition that would have been so useful: Wordsworth paid little attention to him; for all his apparent sympathy, Shelley was deeply uncongenial and remained aloof; Coleridge was already in the decline and Keats hardly knew him; Hazlitt was the object of his admiration rather than a full admirer, and even Hunt's ultimate loyalty went to Shelley rather than to the earlier disciple. Later in the century, the Victorians were never able to forgive Keats his plebeian birth and the unbridled erotic despair of the love letters to Fanny Brawne; Arnold has to strain a great deal to find in the life and letters traces of the moral high-seriousness that he cannot fail to detect in the greater poems. Some of this Victorian snobbishness still echoes in Yeats's reference to Keats as a "coarse-bred son of a livery-stable keeper" who made "luxuriant song" out of his frustrations. But the poetry had always found considerable appreciation, not only for its decorative aspects that so delighted the pre-Raphaelites, but for its thematic depth as well. In our own century, when the relationship between life and work is understood in a somewhat less literal manner, a considerable exegetic effort has been directed especially toward the elucidation of the shorter poems. Continued interest in the biography and in the letters—a new edition of the letters edited by Hyder E. Rollins appeared in 1958 and W. J. Bate's biography appeared in 1963—indicates that the problem that preoccupied the Victorians, the contrast between the banality of Keats's life and the splendor of his work, has not been fully resolved. Arnold's remarks about an element of vulgarity in Keats have cut so deep that recent biographers are still writing polemically in an effort to dispel their effect. This almost always results, even among Keats's warmest admirers, in a trace of condescension or defensiveness, as if one were forced to look for attenuating circumstances. The facts are distorted either by making the life appear darker and more tragic than it was, or by exalting Keats's very genuine courage and self-sacrifice to the point where it obscures his poetry. Except for the last few months, the life is in fact more banal than tragic; it is one of Keats's most engaging traits that he resists all temptation to see himself as the hero of a tragic adventure. The unfavorable circumstances of his birth—he was the eldest of four orphaned children cheated out of their modest inheritance by an unscrupulous guardian—were such that he lived almost always oriented toward the future, keeping his capacity for personal happiness in reserve, so to speak, for the better days he saw ahead. The pathos, of course, is that he never reached these days, but he was no longer able to write by the time he realized this. In reading Keats, we are therefore reading the work of a man whose experience is mainly literary. The growing insight that underlies the remarkably swift development of his talent was gained primarily from the act of writing. In this case, we are on very safe ground when we derive our understanding primarily from the work itself.

The pattern of Keats's work is prospective rather than retrospective; it consists of hopeful preparations, anticipations of future power rather than meditative reflections on past moments of insight or harmony. His poems frequently climax in questions—"Was there a poet born?," "Did I wake or sleep?"—or in statements such as: "and beyond these / I must not think now . . . ," "but now no more, / My wand'ring spirit must not further soar"—that suggest he has reached a threshold, penetrated to the border-line of a new region which he is not yet ready to explore but toward which all his future efforts will be directed. *I Stood Tiptoe* announces *Endymion*, *Endymion* announces *Hyperion*, *Hyperion* prefigures *The Fall of Hyperion*, etc.; Keats is steadily moving forward, trying to pull himself up to the level and the demands of his own prospective vision. None of the larger works—and we know that the larger works mattered most to him—can in any sense be called finished. The circle never seems to close, as if he were haunted by a dream that always remains in the future.

The dream is dramatically articulated from the very start, in a naive but clear mythological outline that even the awkward diction of the early poems cannot altogether hide from sight. It reveals Keats's original conception of the poet's role and constitutes the thematic center around which the history of his development is organized.

In one of Keats's longer early poems, the title line as well as the last word suggest a soaring, Icarus-like urge to "burst our mortal bars" and leave the human world behind. But nothing could be less like Shelley's skylark, a "scorner of the ground," than Keats's young poet. Icarus's rise as well as his fall are acts of overbearing that destroy balance and "burst" beyond natural limits. Even in the earliest poems, Keats never conceives of poetry in this manner: to the contrary, poetry is always the means by which an excess is tempered, a flight checked, a separation healed. In terms of the material sensations toward which Keats's imagery naturally tends, this tendency is expressed in the impression of a temperate breeze that cools excessive heat, but never chills—a sensation so all-pervading throughout the early poems that it cannot be considered merely conventional or derivative:

> pebbly beds;
> Where swarms of minnows show their little heads,
>
> . . . .
> To taste the luxury of sunny beams
> Tempered with coolness.
>
> (*I Stood Tiptoe*, ll. 71 ff.)

Where had he been, from whose warm head outflew
That sweetest of all songs, that ever new,
That aye refreshing, pure deliciousness
                                    (*Idem.*, ll. 181 ff.)

The breezes were ethereal, and pure,
And crept through half-closed lattices to cure
The languid sick; it cooled their fevered sleep
                                    (*Idem.*, ll. 221 ff.)

The early Keats discovers the narrative equivalence of this restoring, balancing power of poetry in the Greek myths, which he interprets at the time as tales in which the distance between mortals and immortals is overcome by an act of erotic union. As a story of love between a goddess and a mortal shepherd, Endymion attracts him even more than Psyche or Narcissus, and he announces it as his main theme before embarking on the narrative poem *Endymion* itself. But the symbolic function of the poet as a narrator of myths immediately widens in significance: since he can "give meek Cynthia her Endymion," he not only restores the natural balance of things, but his exemplary act extends to the whole of mankind. The union between the goddess and the shepherd prefigures directly the communal celebration of mankind liberated from its suffering. By telling "one wonder of [Cynthia's] bridal night," the poet causes the "languid sick" to awake and

Young men, and maidens at each other gazed
With hands held back, and motionless, amazed
To see the brightness in each other's eyes;
And so they stood, filled with a sweet surprise,
Until their tongues were loosed in poesy.
Therefore no lover did of anguish die:
But the soft numbers, in that moment spoken,
Made silken ties, that never may be broken.
                                    (*Idem.*, ll. 231 ff.)

Here we have Keats's original dream in all its naive clarity: it is a dream about poetry as a redeeming force, oriented toward others in a concern that is moral but altogether spontaneous, rooted in the fresh sensibility of love and sympathy and not in abstract imperatives. The touching tale of a lovelorn goddess replaces the Ten Commandments, a humanized version of Hellenic myth replaces Biblical sternness, in an optimistic belief that the universe naturally tends toward the mood of temperate balance and that poetry can always recapture the freshness of ever-rising springs.

The optimism of this myth is tempered, however, by the negative implications it contains: if poetry is to redeem, it must be that there is a need for redemption, that humanity is indeed "languid sick" and "with temples bursting." The redemption is the happier future of a painful present. One of the lines of development that Keats's poetry will follow reaches a deeper understanding of this pain which, in the earlier texts, is merely a feverish restlessness, a discordance of the sensations that creates a tension between warring extremes of hot and cold. Some of his dissatisfaction with the present is transposed in Keats's image of his own situation as a beginning poet on the contemporary literary scene: the greatness of the major predecessors—Spenser, Shakespeare and Milton—measures his own inadequacy and dwarfs the present:

> Is there so small a range
> In the present strength of manhood, that the high
> Imagination cannot freely fly
> As she was wont of old?
>
> (*Sleep and Poetry*, ll. 162 ff.)

Totally oriented toward the future, Keats cannot draw strength from this past grandeur; his use of earlier models will always be more a sympathetic imitation than a dialogue between past and present, as between Milton and Wordsworth in *The Prelude*. Hence that Keats's use of earlier poets is more technical than thematic: however Spenserian or Miltonic the diction of *The Eve of St. Agnes* and *Hyperion* may be, Spenser and Milton are not present as such in the poems; Keats has to derive all his power from energy he finds in himself or in his immediate vicinity. But he experiences his own times as literarily deficient: a curious passage from *Sleep and Poetry*, where the entire movement of the poem, as well as the allegiance to Leigh Hunt, would demand the unmixed praise of contemporary poetry, turns into a criticism of Byron and Wordsworth for failing to deliver the message of hope that Keats would like to hear. As a criticism of *The Excursion* the observation would be valid enough, but it is presented instead as a source of personal discouragement. A certain form of despondency and stagnation seems to threaten Keats from the start and forces him to take shelter in falsely idyllic settings like the one at the end of *Sleep and Poetry*, where the problem that concerns him can be temporarily forgotten but not resolved.

Retreats of this kind recur throughout the work, but they gain in poetic significance as the predicament from which he retreats grows in universality. This progression can be traced in the changed use of Ovidian myth from *Endymion* on, as compared to the earliest poems. Originally, the myths serve to gain access to the idyllic aspects of nature: they are "delightful stories" about "the fair paradise of Nature's light." The sad tales alternate with joyful ones merely for the sake of variety. This, of course, is by no means the dominant mood in Ovid himself, who often reports acts of refined cruelty with harsh detachment. From *Endymion* on, the movement of mythical metamorphosis, practically absent from the early poems, achieves a striking prominence that will maintain itself to the end; the very narrative pattern of *Endymion*, of *Lamia* and, in a more hidden way, of *Hyperion* and the Odes, is based on a series of transformations from one order of being into another. The various metamorphic combinations between the inanimate, the animal, human and divine world keep appearing, and the moment of transformation always constitutes the dramatic climax toward which the story is oriented. Far from being merely picturesque, the metamorphoses acquire an obsessive intensity in which one recognizes a more mature version of the original, happy dream of redemption.

The erotic contact between the gods and man in Ovid is anything but the idyllic encounter between Cynthia and Endymion in *I Stood Tiptoe*; it results instead in the brutal degradation of the human being to a lower order of life, his imprisonment in the rigid forms of the inanimate world: Niobe's "very tongue frozen to her mouth's roof" (*Metamorphoses*, VI, [line] 306), Daphne's "swift feet grown fast in sluggish roots" (I, [line] 551), Myrrha, the mother of Adonis, watching her skin change to hard bark (X, [line] 494). This state of frozen immobility, of paralysis under the life-destroying impact of eternal powers, becomes the obsessive image of a human predicament that poetry is to redeem. A long gallery of human beings thus caught in poses of frozen desire appear throughout the work: the lovers in Book III of *Endymion* imprisoned in a sea cave "vast, and desolate, and icy-cold" (III, [line] 632), the figures on the Grecian Urn, the knight-at-arms of "La Belle Dame sans Merci" caught "On the cold hillside," the knights and ladies at the beginning of *The Eve of St. Agnes* "sculptured dead, on each side, [who] seem to freeze, / Emprisoned in black, purgatorial rails," Saturn at the beginning of *Hyperion* "quiet as a stone, / Still as the silence round about his lair." There hardly exists a single of Keats's important poems in which a version of this recurrent theme fails to appear, though the outward form may vary. It is most frequently associated with the sensation of cold, as if the cooling breeze of *I Stood Tiptoe* heralding the benevolent arrival of the gods had suddenly turned icy and destructive. The myth is a paradoxical version of the mutability theme: the passage of time, the loss of power, death, are the means by which the gods announce their presence; time is the only eternal force and it strips man of his ability to move freely in the direction of his own desire; generations are wasted by old age, "youth grows pale, and specter-thin, and dies" and "Everything is spoiled by use" ("Fancy," [line] 68). Under the impact of this threat, mankind is made powerless in the stagnation that Keats felt at times in himself and saw around him. Mutability causes paralysis.

His dream then becomes a kind of reversal of the Ovidian metamorphosis, in which man was frozen into a natural form: the poet is the one who can reverse the metamorphosis and reanimate the dead forms into life. Again, Book III of *Endymion* gives a clear mythological outline of this process: by a mere touch of his wand, warmth is restored to the frozen lovers and the reanimated figures rejoice in an exact repetition of the redemption scene from *I Stood Tiptoe* (*Endymion*, III, [lines] 780 ff.). This dream, by which dead nature is restored to life and refinds, as it were, the human form that was originally its own, is Keats's fondest reverie. A large measure of his poetical power stems from this. It allows him to give nature such an immediate and convincing presence that we watch it take on effortlessly human form: the ode "To Autumn" is the supreme achievement of this Ovidian metamorphosis in reverse. His ability to make his conceits and metaphors spring out of a genuine identity of nature with man, rather than out of an intellectual awareness of an analogy between both, is also rooted in this dream. It is so strong that it forces itself upon the narrative of his longer poems, even when the original story does not allow for it. In *Hyperion*, one can never conceive of Apollo as the warring opponent of the Titans. Instead, the story inevitably turns toward a repetition of the Glaucus episode in *Endymion*: Apollo tends to become the young man whose task it is to free and rejuvenate Saturn, the victim of old age. We are dealing with still another version of Keats's humanitarian dream. He will reach maturity at the end of a rather complicated itinerary, when the last trace of naiveté is removed from this vision.

The power by means of which the poet can redeem the suffering of mankind is called love, but love, in Keats, is a many-sided force. On the simplest level, love is merely the warmth of sensation: Endymion's ardor is such that it seems to melt the curse of time away at sheer contact. Till the later "Ode to Psyche" when love has been internalized to such an extent that it bears only the remotest relationship to anything physical, the epithet "warm," associated with Eros, preserves the link with sensation in a world that is otherwise entirely mental.

> A bright torch, and a casement ope at night,
>   To let the warm Love in!
>   ("Ode to Psyche," ll. 66–67)

The importance of sensuality to Keats has been abundantly stressed; when some biographers, with the laudable intention of rescuing Keats from the Victorian reproach of coarseness, have tried to minimize the importance of erotic elements in his poetry, they present an oddly distorted picture. Yet, even his most straightforward eroticism easily turns into something more than sensation. First of all, sensuous love for him is more readily imagined than experienced; therefore it naturally becomes one of the leading symbols for the workings of the imagination. One of his most elaborate conceits on the activity of the mind, the final stanza of the "Ode to Psyche," spontaneously associates Eros with fancy; the same is true of the poem "Fancy," in which Eros is present as an activity of the mind. Moreover, since Keats is the least narcissistic of Romantic poets, love is easily transferred by him to others and becomes a communal bond: one remembers how the union of Cynthia and Endymion spontaneously turns into a public feast, the kind of Rousseauistic brotherhood that recurs in Romantic poetry as a symbol of reconciliation. In *Endymion* also, one passes without tension from love to a communal spirit of friendship with social and political overtones; something of the spirit of the French Revolution still echoes in these passages. In the optimistic world of *Endymion*, love and history act together as positive forces and historical redemption goes hand in hand with sensuous fulfillment.

Another aspect of the love experience, however, leads to more complex involvements. Aside from sensation, love also implies sympathy, a forgetting of the self for the sake of others, especially when the other is in a state of suffering. In the earlier poems, when the poet's sympathy goes out to Narcissus, to Psyche or to Pan, or even when Endymion is moved to tears over the sad fate of the wood-nymph Arethusa, these movements of the heart could still be considered a conventional form of sensibility. But in the recurrent image of frozen immobility, the suffering is not just an arbitrary trick of fate or a caprice of the gods: it becomes the generalized statement of the human predicament, man stifled by the awareness of his mortality. Sympathetic understanding of these threatened figures, the attempt "To think how they may ache in icy hoods and mails" (*Eve of St. Agnes*, line 18), tears us away from the safety of everyday experience and forces us to enter a realm that is in fact the realm of death. The ordinary life of consciousness is then suspended and its continuity disrupted. Hence that the experience can only be expressed in metaphors such as "trance" or "sleep," suspended states of consciousness in which the self is momentarily absent. The "romantic" setting of certain dream episodes in *Endymion* or in "La Belle Dame sans Merci" should not mislead us into misunderstanding the connection between love and death that prevails here: love is not a temptation to take us out of the finite world of human experiences, still less an impulse toward a Platonic heaven. Keats's love impulse is a very human sense of sympathy and pity, chivalrous perhaps, but devoid of transcendental as well as escapist dimensions. Endymion cannot resist the "sorrow" of the Indian maiden, Glaucus is taken in by the feigned tears of Circe, the knight of "La Belle Dame Sans Merci" is definitely lulled to sleep only after his lady has "wept, and sighed full sore," and Lamia, also, woos her lover Lucius by appealing to his pity as well as to his senses. Keats's imagination is fired by a mixture of sensation and sympathy in which the dual nature of love is reunited. The sympathy, however, is even more important than the sensation: love can exist without the latter but not without the former, and some of Keats's heroes are motivated by sympathy alone. This adds an important dimension to our understanding of the relationship between love, poetry, and death in his work: because poetry is essentially an act of sympathy, of human redemption, it must move through the death-like trances that abound in Keats. One misunderstands these moments altogether if one interprets them as a flight from human suffering; to the contrary, they are the unmistakable sign of a sympathetic identification with the human predicament. There are moments of straightforward escape in Keats: we mentioned the end of *Sleep and Poetry* as one instance; several of the more trivial poems fulfill the same function. But the "tranced summer night" of *Hyperion*, the Cave of Quietude in Book IV of *Endymion*, the "drowsy numbness" of the Nightingale Ode, the "cloudy swoon" of *The Fall of Hyperion*, do not stand in opposition to human sympathy; as the subsequent dramatic action of these poems indicates, they represent a necessary first step toward the full unfolding of humanitarian love as it grows into a deeper understanding of the burden of mortality.

This expansion of the theme of love, which takes place without entering into conflict with the other, sensuous aspect of love, leads to a parallel deepening of the theme of history. In the easy simplicity of *Endymion*, Keats can herald, at the opening of Book II, the "sovereign power of love" over history: love suffices to bring about universal reconciliation and to make the slow labor of history superfluous. By the time of *Hyperion*, a considerable change has already taken place: the myth of the defeat of the Titans by a new generation of gods is interpreted as the very movement of history. Oceanus's speech (*Hyperion*, III, [lines] 114 ff.) as well as Mnemosyne's initiation of Apollo to

> Names, deeds, gray legends, dire events, rebellions,
> Majesties, sovran voices, agonies,
> Creations and destroyings
>
> (*Hyperion*, III, ll. 114 ff.)

make very clear the increased importance of the theme. But it is not till the late *Fall of Hyperion* that Keats's historical consciousness is fully developed. In *Hyperion*, it remains obscure why the knowledge of the historical past which "pours into the wide hollows of [Apollo's] brain" suffices to "make a god of [him]." The corresponding scene in *The Fall of Hyperion* may be confused in some respects, but not as far as the poet's attitude toward history is concerned: history, in its most general aspects, is for him a privileged subject, because the gift of sympathy which he possesses to a larger degree than any other man allows him to understand the sacrificial nature of all historical movement, as epitomized in the downfall of Saturn. Far from reasserting the consoling law stated by Oceanus "That first in beauty should be first in might" (*Hyperion*, II, line 229), the historical awareness in *The Fall* returns to the deeper theme of man's temporal contingency. The poet is the chosen witness of the damage caused by time; by growing in consciousness he gains no new attributes of beauty or might, merely the negative privilege of witnessing the death of those who surpassed him in greatness. The suggestion of a conquering, youthful Apollo has entirely disappeared. The dynamic thrust of history itself is frozen into immobility by the deadly power of time and the poet now has to expand his capacity for sympathy until it encompasses the full range of this tragedy:

> Without stay or prop
> But my own weak mortality, I bore
> The load of this eternal quietude,
> The unchanging gloom
>
> (*The Fall of Hyperion*, I, ll. 388 ff.)

History can only move by becoming aware of its own contingency. From his earliest poems on, Keats had conceived of his own work as a movement of becoming, a gradual widening of his consciousness by successive stages.

The pattern is present in the prefigured outline of his own career in *Sleep and Poetry*, in the structure of *Endymion* which, for all its apparent disorder, is nevertheless organized as a consistent "growth of a poet's mind," in the famous letter to Reynolds of May 3, 1818, on the poet's progress from the thoughtless Chamber to the "Chamber of Maiden-Thought." This prospective scheme now no longer appears as a reassuring projection, since every step in the progression takes on the form of a tragedy beyond redemption, though not beyond the power of understanding. Nowhere does Keats come closer to a historical consciousness that recognizes and names the full power of negativity. Traveling entirely by his own pathways, he comes upon some of the insights that will shape the destiny of the nineteenth and twentieth centuries.

Yet it seems that Keats never achieves an authority that is commensurate with the quality of this perception. The conception of the poet's role, in *The Fall of Hyperion*, appears at once so lofty in its impersonality and disinterestedness, yet so humane in its concern for the grief of others, that we would expect a more serene tone in Keats's later work. Instead, he frequently sounds the strident note of someone who sees through the fallacy of his own certainties. There seems to be little room for self-deception in the stern wisdom of *The Fall of Hyperion*; where are we to find the point where Keats lies open to his own reproof?

Nothing could be more genuine than the positive aspect of Keats's concern for others: neither in the poetry nor in the letters can one discover a jarring tone that would reveal the presence of affectation or pose in his humanitarian attitude. Keats's generosity is total and all the more admirable since it is never based on an idealization of himself or of others, or on an attempt to emulate a chosen mode. Perfect good faith, however, does not shelter us from the intricacies of moral inauthenticity. Keats's gift for sympathy has a negative aspect, and the significance of his complete evolution can only be understood if one takes this into account.

Already in *Endymion*, when Keats is speaking of love and friendship as central formative experiences, he refers to these experiences as "self-destroying":

But there are

> Richer entanglements, enthrallments far
> More self-destroying, leading, by degrees,
> To the chief intensity: the crown of these
> Is made of love and friendship
> (*Endymion*, I, ll. 797 ff.)

"Self-destroying" is obviously used in a positive sense here, to designate the moral quality of disinterestedness—yet "destroying" is a curiously strong term. The phrase is revealing, for a recurrent pattern in the poetry indicates a strong aversion to a direct confrontation with his own self; few poets have described the act of self-reflection in harsher terms. For Endymion, the most miserable condition of man is that in which he is left to consider his own self in solitude, even when this avowedly takes him close to teaching the "goal of consciousness" (II, line 283):

> There, when new wonders ceased to float before,
> And thoughts of self came on, how crude and sore
> The journey homeward to habitual self!
> A mad pursuing of the fog-born elf,
> Whose flitting lantern, through rude nettle-brier,
> Cheats us into a swamp, into a fire,
> Into the bosom of a hated thing.
>
> (*Idem.* II, ll. 274 ff.)

The inward quest for self-knowledge is described here in the very terms used by Milton to represent the triumph of satanic temptation (*Paradise Lost*, IX, line 633 ff.). The "hated thing" to which Keats refers is the situation, rather than the content of his own consciousness: the condition of the "sole self" is one of intolerable barrenness, the opposite of all that imagination, poetry and love can achieve. The experience of being "tolled back to one's sole self" is always profoundly negative. He almost succeeds in eliminating himself from his poetry altogether. There is, of course, much that is superficially autobiographical in *Endymion* and even in *Hyperion*, but one never gains an intimate sense of Keats's own selfhood remotely comparable to that conveyed by other romantic poets. The "I" of the Nightingale Ode, for instance, is always seen in the movement that takes it away from its own center. The emotions that accompany the discovery of the authentic self, feelings of guilt and dread as well as sudden moments of transparent clarity, are lacking in Keats. Poetic "sleep" or "trance" is a darkening, growing opacity of the consciousness. Suffering plays a very prominent role in his work, but it is always the suffering of others, sympathetically but objectively perceived and so easily generalized into historical and universal pain that it rarely appears in its subjective immediacy: a passage such as the opening scene of *Hyperion* gains its poetic effectiveness from the controlled detachment of an observer who is not directly threatened. The only threat that Keats seems to experience subjectively is that of self-confrontation.

Keats's sympathetic love thus appears less simple than it may seem at first sight: his intense and altogether genuine concern for others serves, in a sense, to shelter him from the self-knowledge he dreads. He is a man distracted from the awareness of his own mortality by the constant spectacle of the death of others. He can go very far in participating in their agony: he is indeed one "to whom the miseries of the world / Are misery and will not let [him] rest" (*Fall of Hyperion*, I, lines 148–49). But the miseries are always "of the world" and not his own, a distinction that should disappear when the suffering referred to is so general that it designates a universal human predicament. Although it would be entirely false to say of Keats that he escaped out of human suffering into the idealized, trance-like condition of poetry, one can say, with proper caution, that he moves away from the burden of self-knowledge into a world created by the combined powers of the sympathetic imagination, poetry and history, a world that is ethically impeccable, but from which the self is excluded.

The tension resulting from this ambivalence does not remain entirely hidden. It comes to the surface, for instance, in the difficult choice he has to make in his literary allegiances, when he has to reconcile his admiration for Shakespeare and Milton with his consideration for Wordsworth, whom he considered his greatest contemporary. His own term for the "self-destroying" power of the poetic imagination is "negative capability," the ability of the mind to detach itself from its own identity, and he associates this characteristic of the poetic temperament primarily with Shakespeare. It is typical, in this respect, that he would consider Shakespeare's life as exemplary: "Shakespeare led a life of Allegory . . ." (letter to George Keats, February 19, 1819) in the full figural and Christian sense of the term, when it is precisely a life so buried under the wealth of its own inventions that it has ceased to exist as a particular experience. This stands, of course, in total contrast to what we find in Wordsworth, for whom the determining moment occurs when the mind exists in and for itself, in the transparency of an inwardness entirely focused upon the self. Even in the absence of the posthumously published *Prelude*, Keats knew the direction of Wordsworth's thought and felt the challenge it offered to his own orientation. Walter Jackson Bate, in his biography of Keats, has well seen the decisive importance of this confrontation when, in the letter of May 3, 1818, to Reynolds, Keats rates Wordsworth above Milton ("who did not think into the human heart") because he is the poet of the conscious self. But Keats did not choose, at that time, to follow Wordsworth into the "dark passages" which he had begun to explore. The poem that stems from these meditations, the first *Hyperion*, is certainly not Wordsworthian and not altogether Miltonic either: the emphasis on characterization, the deliberate variety of tones, the pageant-like conception of history, are all frankly Shakespearean, and in many ways *Hyperion* resembles an optimistic, humanized version of *Troilus and Cressida* more than *Paradise Lost*. It definitely is a poem founded on negative capability. The sense of human sympathy has grown considerably since *Endymion*, but we are even further removed from real self-awareness than in the early poem. Only at the very end of his career will these unresolved tensions come fully into the open and disrupt the continuity of his development—but this happened, not as a result of literary influence but under the pressure of outward circumstances.

Interpreters of Keats have difficulty agreeing on the significance of his latest work: after the almost miraculous outburst of creative activity in May, 1819, when he wrote practically all the great odes in quick succession, there still followed a period of nearly six months until the final onset of his illness. *The Fall of Hyperion*, *Lamia* and several other shorter poems were written at that time. There is some logic in considering the entire period from June till the end of the year as one single unit—the "late" Keats—that includes the poems to Fanny Brawne, dating from the fall of 1819, and frequently considered as poetically unimportant and slightly embarrassing documents written when he was no longer in full control of his faculties. In truth, it is from *The Fall of Hyperion* on that a sharp change begins to take place; it is also from that moment on that the differences among the commentators begin to increase. For all the divergences in the interpretation of the main odes, there exists a clear consensus about the general meaning and merit of these poems; the differences refer to matters of detail and are certainly to be expected in the case of rich and complex poems studied in such great detail. But *The Fall of Hyperion* is considered by some as "the culmination of Keats's work" and the dialogue between Moneta and the poet as a "dialectical victory" over Moneta's attack on poetry; for others, however, the same passage is read as symbolizing "exhaustion and despair" at "seeing the world of poetry doomed to destruction." *Lamia* has also given rise to incompatible readings and to general puzzlement. The hesitations of the critics are the unmistakable sign of a change that is so far-reaching that it requires a radical readjustment on the part of the readers. The particular difficulty and obscurity of *The Fall of Hyperion* and *Lamia* stems from the fact that they are works of transition toward a new phase that is fully revealed only in the last poems Keats wrote.

The striking fact about Keats's last poems is that they contain an attack on much that had been held sacred in the earlier work; one is reminded, at moments, of Yeats's savagely derisive treatment of his own myths in some of the *Last Poems*. There is something indecorous in the spectacle of a poet thus turning against himself and one can understand the desire of commentators to play down this episode in Keats's history, all the more since illness, poverty and increased bitterness invaded his life at the time, offering a convenient explanation for this radical change in tone. It would be a reflection, however, on the strength of Keats's earlier convictions if they had not been able to stand up under the pressure of these events, however damaging they may have been. Even among his near contemporaries—one thinks of Hölderlin, Maurice de Guérin and Gérard de Nerval—some of the most assertive poems are written in a comparable state of physical and mental distress. We must understand that, far from detracting from his stature, the negativity of Keats's last poems shows that he was about to add another dimension to a poetic development that, up till then, had not been altogether genuine.

We can take as an example the poem dated October, 1819, and entitled "To ———," sometimes referred to as "Ode" or "Second Ode to Fanny Brawne." The term "Ode" in the title is fitting, for the dramatic organization of the poem is very similar to that of the famous great odes; it is, in fact, the exact negative counterpart of the "Ode to a Nightingale." The paradox that was partly concealed by the richness of the language in the earlier odes is now fully revealed: the poems in fact set out to destroy the entities they claim to praise; or, to put it less bluntly, the ambiguity of feeling toward these entities is such that the poems fall apart. In the October poem, the absurdity of the dramatic situation is apparent from the first lines, in which Keats begs Fanny to assist him, by her presence, in curing a suffering of which this very presence is the sole cause:

> What can I do to drive away
> Remembrance from my eyes? for they have seen,
> Aye, an hour ago, my brilliant queen!
> Touch has a memory. O say, love, say,
> What can I do to kill it and be free
> In my old liberty?
>
> ("To ——," ll. 1 ff.)

The prospective character of Keats's poetry, which we stressed from the start, stands out here in its full meaning. The superiority of the future over the past expresses, in fact, a rejection of the experience of actuality. Memory, being founded on actual sensations, is for Keats the enemy of poetic language, which thrives instead on dreams of pure potentiality. In the last stanzas, the poem turns from past to future, with all the ardor of the sensuous desire that tormented Keats at the time, and with an immediacy that produces the kind of language that already proved so cumbersome in the erotic passages of *Endymion*:

> O, let me once more rest
> My soul upon that dazzling breast!
> Let once again these aching arms be placed,
> The tender gaolers of thy waist!
>
> . . . .
> Give me those lips again!
>
> (*Idem.*, ll. 48 ff.)

The interest of the passage is that the desire it names has already been canceled out by the statement made at the onset of the poem. The passion that produces these lines is precisely what has been rejected at the start as the main obstacle to the "liberty" of poetic creation. Before Fanny's presence had put the poet within "the reach of fluttering love," his poetic faculties could grow unimpaired:

> My muse had wings
> And ever ready was to take her course
> Whither I bent her force,
>
> (*Idem.*, ll. 11 ff.)

This belongs to a past that preceded his involvement; the movement toward the future is checked by the awareness of a contradiction that opposes love to poetry as memory is opposed to dream. Contradicting the prayer for her return, the poem concludes by stating a preference for imaginary passion over actual presence:

> Enough! Enough! it is enough for me
> To dream of thee!

It is certainly true that the poem destroys itself in a hopeless conflict between temptation and rejection, between praise and blame, that no language can hope to resolve. What is so revealing, however, is that the contradiction so crudely manifest here is potentially present in the earlier odes as well.

The difference in situation between this late poem and the odes "On a Grecian Urn" and "To a Nightingale" is obvious enough: the urn and the nightingale are general, impersonal entities, endowed with significance by an act of the poet's imagination; Fanny Brawne, on the other hand, is a highly distinct and specific person whose presence awakens in him an acute sense of threatened selfhood. The temptation she incarnates clashes directly with his desire to forget his own self. In the earlier odes, this conflict is avoided by keeping carefully apart what the urn and the nightingale signify for Keats himself, and what they signify for Keats in relation to humanity in general. The poetic effectiveness of the odes depends entirely on the positive temptation that emanates from the symbolic entities: the world to which they give access is a world of happiness and beauty, and it is by the suggestive evocation of this world that beauty enters the poems. This, in turn, allows for the dramatic contrast with the world of actual experience, caught in the destructive power of mutability and described throughout, in the Grecian Urn as well as in the Nightingale Ode, in terms that appeal directly to our moral sympathy:

> Here, where men sit and hear each other groan;
> Where palsy shakes a few, sad, last gray hairs,
> Where youth grows pale, and specter-thin, and dies;
> Where but to think is to be full of sorrow
> And leaden-eyed despairs
> ("Ode to a Nightingale," ll. 24 ff.)

The mixture of emotions, in these texts, is subtle and self-deceiving. On the one hand, the poet's sympathy for the suffering of mankind gives him the kind of moral authority that allows him to call authoritatively for a lucid acceptance of human limitations. It is this morally responsible voice that warns his fellow men against the danger of giving in to the deceptive quality of poetic symbols: they "tease" and "deceive" in foreshadowing an eternity that is not within our reach; the urn and the nightingale finally act as powers of death and, in that sense, these poems are also written against the objects they set out to praise. But Keats does not remain in the barren, impoverished world of human contingency, the world of gray rocks and stones that is the landscape of Wordsworth's *Prelude*. As a poet, he does not seem to share in the torments of temporality. The youth that "grows pale, and specter-thin, and dies" in Stanza 3 of the Nightingale Ode could not possibly be the same voice that evokes so magnificently the change that comes over the world by losing oneself in the "embalmed darkness" of the bird's song:

> I cannot see what flowers are at my feet,
>   Nor what soft incense hangs upon the boughs,
> But, in embalmèd darkness, guess each sweet
>   Wherewith the seasonable month endows
> The grass, the thicket, and the fruit-tree wild
>
>   (*Idem.*, ll. 41 ff.)

The richness of these most un-Wordsworthian lines can only come into being because Keats's self is in fact dissociated from the suffering mankind with which he sympathizes. As a humanist, he can lay claim to a good conscience and write poems that have reassured generations of readers, willing to be authoritatively told about the limits of their knowledge ("that is all / Ye know on earth, and all ye need to know"); but as a poet, he can indulge in the wealth of a soaring imagination whose power of metamorphosis knows no limits. The poet of the Grecian Urn would hardly be able to evoke the happy world on the urn if he were himself the creature "lowing at the skies" about to be sacrificed.

We can see, from the poem "To ——" what happens when this distance between the private self and its moral stance vanishes: the late poem is the "Ode to a Nightingale" with the metamorphic power of the imagination destroyed by a sense of real selfhood. This destruction now openly coincides with the appearance of love on the scene, in an overt admission that, up to this point, the moral seriousness of the poems had not, in fact, been founded on love at all:

> How shall I do
> To get anew
> Those molted feathers, and so mount once more
> Above, above
> The reach of fluttering Love
> And make him cower lowly while I soar?
>
>   ("To ——," ll. 18 ff.)

The violence of the feeling is reminiscent of the hostile language in which Endymion refers to solitary self-knowledge. In the experience of love, the self comes to know itself without mask, and when this happens the carefree movement of the poetic imagination falters. Before, as we know from the Nightingale Ode, the intoxication of the imagination, like that of wine, was able to fuse the familiar Keatsian tension between heat and cold into one single sensation:

> O, for a draught of vintage! that hath been
>   Cooled a long age in the deep-delved earth,
> Tasting of Flora and the country green,
>   Dance, and Provençal song, and sunburned mirth!
>
>   ("Ode to a Nightingale," ll. 11 ff.)

But now, in a world ruled by the law of love, such easy syntheses are no longer within our power:

> Shall I gulp Wine? No, that is vulgarism,
> A heresy and schism,
>> Floisted into the canon law of love;—
> No—wine is only sweet to happy men;
>> ("To ——," ll. 24 ff.)

Consequently, the metamorphosis of the landscape, achieved in Stanza 5 of the Nightingale Ode under the impact of the trancelike song, fails, and we are confronted instead with the bleakness of a totally de-mythologized world:

> That monstrous region, whose dull rivers pour,
> Ever from their sordid urns unto the shore,
> Unowned of any weedy-hairèd gods;
> Whose winds, all zephyrless, hold scourging rods,
> Iced in the great lakes, to afflict mankind;
> Whose rank-grown forests, frosted, black, and blind,
> Would fright a Dryad; whose harsh herbaged meads
> Make lean and lank the starved ox while he feeds;
> There bad flowers have no scent, birds no sweet song,
> And great unerring nature once seems wrong.
>> (*Idem.*, ll. 34 ff.)

The landscape, at last, is that of Keats's real self, which he had kept so carefully hidden up till now under poetic myth and moral generosity. It is still an imagined landscape, but rooted this time in an experience that is both intimate and painful: his brother's financial disaster near the very "Great Lakes" here evoked was caused by such a landscape and it is certain that Keats equated his own miseries with the calamitous misadventures of his brother in America. This does not make this landscape less "symbolic" than the world of the nightingale or the Grecian Urn, but it dramatizes the distinction between a symbol rooted in the self and one rooted in an abstract dream.

The power which forces a man to see himself as he really is, is also called "philosophy" in the later Keats; the term receives the same ambiguous value-emphasis as does the word "love." In the same poem "To ——," the previous poetry, written when he was free of the burden of love, is called "unintellectual" and the confining power of self-awareness is stressed again in the rhetorical question:

> What seabird o'er the sea
> Is a philosopher the while he goes
> Winging along where the great water throes?
>> (*Idem.*, ll. 15 ff.)

We have come a long way since the early days of *Endymion* when Keats thought of philosophy as a means to help him carry out his generous dream of human redemption. Apollonius, the philosopher in *Lamia*, has all the outward attributes of villainy, yet there can be no doubt that truth is on his side: Lucius is about to mistake the seductiveness of a serpent for real love and it is, after all, his own weakness that is to blame for his inability to survive the revelation of the truth. In this poem, Truth and Beauty are indeed at odds, but one may well conjecture that, as Keats's sense of truth grew, he would have been able to discover a beauty that would have surpassed that of Lamia. Fanny Brawne may well have looked to him more like Móneta than like La Belle Dame sans Merci.

With the development that stood behind him, this final step could only take the violently negative form of his last poems. It is morally consistent that he would have rebelled against a generosity that offered more protection than it cost him. After having acted, in all his dreams of human redemption, as the one who rescues others from their mortal plight, his last poem reverses the parts. Taking off from an innocuous line in *The Fall of Hyperion* ("When this warm scribe my hand is in the grave") he now offers his hand no longer in a gesture of assistance to others, but as the victim who defies another to take away from him the weight of his own death:

> This living hand, now warm and capable
> Of earnest grasping, would, if it were cold
> And in the icy silence of the tomb,
> So haunt thy days and chill thy dreaming nights
> That thou wouldst wish thine own heart dry of blood
> So in my veins red life might stream again,
> And thou be conscience-calmed—see here it is—
> I hold it towards you.
>
> ("This Living Hand," ll. 1–8)

Romantic literature, at its highest moments, encompasses the greatest degree of generality in an experience that never loses contact with the individual self in which it originates. In the *Confessions*, Rousseau tells how an injustice committed at his expense during his youth awakened within him a universal moral sense: "I feel my pulse quicken as I write this; I shall never forget these moments if I live a hundred thousand years. This first experience of violence and injustice remained so deeply engraved on my soul that all ideas related to it take me back to this initial emotion; this experience which, at its origin, existed only for me, has acquired such a strong consistency in itself, and has grown so far away from my own self-interest, that my heart flares up at the sight or at the report of an unjust deed, committed anywhere at anyone's expense, as if it concerned me personally." It is the scope of this generalized passion which makes it possible for Rousseau to be at the same time the poet who wrote *Julie* and the moral philosopher who wrote the *Social Contract*. The same scope is present in Wordsworth and also, at times, in Blake and Coleridge. Nowadays, we are less than ever capable of philosophical generality rooted in genuine self-insight, while our sense of selfhood hardly ever rises above self-justification. Hence that our criticism of Romanticism so often misses the mark: for the great Romantics, consciousness of self was the first and necessary step toward moral judgment. Keats's last poems reveal that he reached the same insight; the fact that he arrived at it by a negative road may make him all the more significant for us.

Keats: Romance Revised

Harold Bloom

Paul de Man engagingly remarks that "it is one of Keats's most engaging traits that he resists all temptation to see himself as the hero of a tragic adventure." De Man says also of Keats that "he lived almost always oriented toward the future," the pattern of his work being thus "prospective rather than retrospective." These are moving observations, and I honor them. They surmise a Keats whose vision "consists of hopeful preparations, anticipations of future power rather than meditative reflections on past moments of insight or harmony." As does Angus Fletcher, de Man sees Keats as one of the *liminal* visionaries, akin surely to Coleridge, to Hart Crane, perhaps to an aspect of Stevens. De Man points to all those phrases in Keats's poems and letters "that suggest he has reached a threshold, penetrated to the borderline of a new region which he is not yet ready to explore but toward which all his future efforts will be directed." If de Man were wholly right, then Keats ought to be happily free of the Shadow of Milton and of Wordsworth, the composite precursor that both inspired and inhibited him. There can be no more extreme posture of the spirit, for a strong poet, than to take up, perpetually, a prospective stance. I regret taking up a more suspicious or demystifying stance than de Man does, but Keats can charm even the subtlest and most scrupulous of deconstructors. No strong poet, of necessity, is wholly liminal in his vision, and Keats was a very strong poet, greatly gifted in the revisionary arts of misprision. I begin therefore by suggesting that de Man's observation accurately describes one of Keats's prime composite tropes, but also declines (on de Manian principle, of course) to examine the psychic defenses that inform Keats's liminal trope.

Keats no more resembles Nietzsche's Zarathustra than Nietzsche him-

From *Poetry and Repression: Revisionism from Blake to Stevens.* © 1976 by Yale University. Yale University Press, 1976.

self did. I myself, perhaps wrongly, tend to read Zarathustra as a highly deliberate Nietzschean parody of the prospective stance that frequently distinguishes the High Romantic poet. Nietzsche had read and brooded upon Shelley, and also upon that indeliberate parodist, Poe. The contrary to prospective vision, in Blakean rather than Nietzschean terms, is the cycle of the being Blake called Orc, who would like to tear loose from Nature's wheel but cannot. Nietzsche dreamed an antithetical vision, the Eternal Return of the Same, which is transumptive in stance. But these dialectical resources, whether Blakean or Nietzschean, were not congenial to Keats's genius. He was an experiential or retrospective poet at least as much as he was visionary or prospective, and as a poet who lived fully the life of poetry, and very little life of any other kind, he was compelled to one of the fiercest and most problematic struggles with the Covering Cherub of poetic influence that the language affords us.

My primary text in this discourse will be the second and greater of Keats's *Hyperion* fragments or heroic torsos, *The Fall of Hyperion*. I must remark, before commencing a reading of the poem, that here I cannot agree with de Man at all, for in *The Fall of Hyperion* Keats does yield to the temptation to see himself as the hero of a romance that is in the process of turning into tragedy. By the point at which the fragmentary *Fall of Hyperion* breaks off, Keats (perhaps despite himself) has become the quest-hero of a tragic adventure.

Certainly he had resisted such a temptation for nearly the whole of his writing-life, consciously opposing himself in this to Byron and to Shelley, and emulating the precursor he shared with them. Wordsworth, who had made an aesthetic and moral choice against tragedy, and who had refused to identify himself with his own isolate selfhood, the Solitary of *The Excursion*. But in *The Fall of Hyperion*, and perhaps only there, Keats did write at least the sketch of a tragic romance, a prophetic sketch in that the poem has vital descendants both direct and indirect. A dance-play like Yeats's savage *A Full Moon in March* is a direct descendant, while Hart Crane's *The Bridge* is an indirect but remarkably close descendant, and so, I begin to suspect, is Stevens's *Esthétique du Mal*.

In reading Keats as having been a revisionist of Romance, I need to commence by revising the way I have read him in the past, for he too has suffered, and from other critics as well as myself, by the kinds of misreading that canon-formation enforces. In the past, I would have given an account of Keats's development somewhat as follows: after the subjectivizing disorders that rhetorically disfigured *Endymion*, Keats returned to the austere program of his own *Sleep and Poetry*, by attempting to write in what he himself disarmingly called "the more naked and Grecian manner" of the first *Hyperion*. But he discovered that his supposedly more objective epic could not be freed of the not-so-naked and not-so-Grecian manner of *Paradise Lost*, and so he broke off, on the polemical plea that, as he put it: "English must be kept up." His rallying cry became the rather transparent self-deception of: "Back to Chatterton!" which of course turned out to mean:

"Back to Wordsworth!" Turning to the not un-Wordsworthian Cary translation of the *Purgatorio*, Keats then attempted his own purgatorial vision in *The Fall of Hyperion*, and did not so much break that off as discover, quite suddenly, that he had finished the poem as much as it could be finished. This canonical or Bloomian misreading traced a kind of cycle, in which Keats went from Romantic subjectivism to a kind of "Modernist" reaction against Wordsworthian internalization, only to discover at last that the Wordsworthian mode was the authentic and inescapable one for the would-be strong poet. Though I would still have found a critique of Wordsworthianism in *The Fall of Hyperion*, I would have centered any reading of the poem in the movement of a return to Wordsworth, under whatever cover and with whatever saving difference.

So once I would have thought, but now no more. I don't know if I have submitted to a new control, but I do think my sense of how poems make us read them has undergone a distress in which the reader's soul too is humanized, and made more aware of the necessity of error. Keats could not read Milton or Wordsworth without troping what he read, and we do the same to Keats.

Like Shelley, Keats is a poet of the transumptive mode, which is necessarily both retrospective and prospective, as I have been trying to show. In my Shelley chapter in *Poetry and Repression* I emphasized Shelley's radical development of the prime Western poetic image of transumption, the *Merkabah*. In tracing the conflict between fire as the prime image of perspectivizing and the chariot as the image of overcoming belatedness, I concluded that Shelley's yielding to the chariot is equivocal, and unwilling. His heart remained in and with the Condition of Fire; the Fire, he insisted, for which all thirst. Keats, as I surmise we will see, gives himself more graciously to the chariot, to the great image of human and poetic continuity. Here is Keats's own early version of the chariot, from *Sleep and Poetry*, the programmatic poem he wrote at the hopeful age of twenty-one. After a passage of cheerfully erotic wish-fulfillments, involving at least three "white-handed nymphs in shady places," Keats addresses himself to higher things:

> And can I ever bid these joys farewell?
> Yes, I must pass them for a nobler life,
> Where I may find the agonies, the strife
> Of human hearts: for lo! I see afar,
> O'er sailing the blue cragginess, a car
> And steeds with streamy manes—the charioteer
> Looks out upon the winds with glorious fear.

The chariot is the throne-world in motion, but here the throne-world is that of Apollo, or rather of the Apollo of Collins, the Apollo of Sensibility, and not the High Romantic Apollo of Nietzsche. Keats's oxymoron of "glorious fear" suggests Collins's use of fear as a psychic defense and rhetorical trope, of "fear" as the repression of the daemonic force of a belated creativity that needs to forget that it knows itself as a belatedness. "Glorious fear," in Keats or Collins, therefore means a creative repression, as here in Collins's "Ode to Fear":

> Dark power, with shuddering meek submitted thought,
> Be mine to read the visions old,
> Which thy awakening bards have told.

We associate Shelley with rhetorical speed and glancing movement, while Keats, like Collins, is deliberately slow-paced, at times approaching a stasis. The chariot or throne-in-motion is therefore less congenial to Keats than a stationary throne-world, and so his prime transumptive image returns us to the source of Ezekiel's *Merkabah* in the throne-vision of Isaiah. Keats's version of the *Hekhaloth* or heavenly halls has been too little admired, or studied. Here are Book I, lines 176–200, of the first *Hyperion*:

>   His palace bright
> Bastioned with pyramids of glowing gold,
> And touched with shade of bronzèd obelisks,
> Glared a blood-red through all its thousand courts,
> Arches, and domes, and fiery galleries;
> And all its curtains of Aurorian clouds
> Flushed angerly: while sometimes eagle's wings,
> Unseen before by Gods or wondering men,
> Darkened the place; and neighing steeds were heard,
> Not heard before by Gods or wondering men.
> Also, when he would taste the spicy wreaths
> Of incense, breathed aloft from sacred hills,
> Instead of sweets, his ample palate took
> Savour of poisonous brass and metal sick:
> And so, when harboured in the sleepy west,
> After the full completion of fair day,—
> For rest divine upon exalted couch
> And slumber in the arms of melody,
> He paced away the pleasant hours of ease
> With stride colossal, on from hall to hall;
> While far within each aisle and deep recess,
> His wingèd minions in close clusters stood,
> Amazed and full of fear; like anxious men
> Who on wide plains gather in panting troops,
> When earthquakes jar their battlements and towers.

Partly, Keats is writing in the mode of Walter Savage Landor here, a mode of marmoreal reverie, but partly he evokes (consciously, I think) the omen-ridden world of Shakespeare's Roman tragedies, particularly *Julius Caesar*. But these surface similarities or allusions induce no anxieties in Keats, and so do little to determine the tropes and images of the first *Hyperion*. The true precursor-text is the vision of Heaven in *Paradise Lost*, a Heaven in which the impending Fall of Satan and his Host is scarcely a major disturbance, in which the actual War between the faithful and the rebels is at most a minor annoyance for God, the smashing of a few Divine breakfast dishes. The passage that I have just quoted from *Hyperion* is a misprision of the Miltonic Heaven, but it is not itself a Miltonic kind of misprision, in that it is not transumptive; that is, it does not project the Miltonic Heaven into belatedness, while establishing instead its own earliness. It fails to do to Milton's Heaven what Milton did to the Olympus of Homer, and this failure is at the heart or one might say nerve of its powerful uneasiness, an uneasiness that has a thematic function, certainly, but that transcends even thematic necessity. The tropes of this passage (lines 176–200) are all tropes of representation, and yet they overrepresent.

Let me return to, and now adumbrate, a distinction I ventured in *A Map of Misreading*, between ratios (tropes, defenses, images) of limitation and ratios of representation. I said there that "limitations turn away from a lost or mourned object towards either the substitute or the mourning subject, while representations turn back towards restoring the powers that desired and possessed the object. Representation points to a lack, just as limitation does, but in a way that *re-finds* what could fill the lack. Or, more simply: tropes of limitation also represent, of course, but they tend to limit the demands placed upon language by pointing to a lack both in language and the self, so that limitation really means recognition in this context. Tropes of representation also acknowledge a limit, point to a lack, but they tend to strengthen both language and the self."

I quote this gnomic passage because I am now ready to unpack it, to illustrate it by the passage of *Hyperion* under consideration and, I hope, to illuminate Keats's lines by the application of my distinction. But I want to return my distinction to its Kabbalistic source, in order to be reminded that "limitation" and "representation" are highly dialectical terms in the context of poetic interpretation. The Lurianic *zimzum* is not so much a contraction or a withdrawal as it is a concentration upon a point, a kind of intensification of God as he takes a step inside himself. A poetic image of limitation tends to cluster in three areas: presence and absence, fullness and emptiness, insideness and outsideness. In the dialectic of rhetorical irony or of defensive reaction-formation, absence tends to dominate over presence, yet this is more a pointing to an absence or a lack, in language or the self, than it is itself a state of absence. Similarly, in the metonymic reductiveness from images of fullness to those of emptiness, these defensive undoings, regressions, and isolations indicate more a *recognition* of emptiness, whether of the empty word or the empty self, than they actually mean an emptiness itself. Most crucially, in the sublimating perspectivism of metaphorical images, though the emphasis in poems tends most often to be upon the outsideness of objects, sharply distinguished from the inwardness of subjective consciousness, the ratio or trope does not so much limit meaning to the aching sense of a loss of inwardness, but rather concentrates attention upon the process of perspectivizing itself. The Lurianic *zimzum*, as a master, composite ratio or trope of limitation, betrays in its most problematic kinds of meaning its usefulness as a paradigm for all tropes of limitation. *Zimzum* is the ultimate *askesis* because it is God's own *askesis*, His self-truncation, but paradoxically it strengthens rather than weakens God, by concentrating Him, and by making Creation possible. The great Renaissance common-place, most beautifully phrased by Tasso and by Sidney, that only the poet truly merited the term of Creator, as God did, took on a special force in the context of Lurianic Kabbalah, which is I think why figures like Bruno and Pico were so enraptured by Kabbalah.

But this digression has gone out and away, apparently, from the passage of Keats's *Hyperion* in question, for there I said we meet only tropes of representation, even of overrepresentation, which I think is largely true of the first *Hyperion* as a poem, and is another indication of why the earlier *Hyperion* is so much less moving and magnificent than its replacement in *The Fall of Hyperion*. Though tropes of representation also acknowledge limits, and point to lacks, primarily they tend to strengthen limits, and point to lacks, primarily they tend to strengthen both language and the self. Can we not say of the first *Hyperion*, and not just of its single passage under discussion, that the poem's language tries to be stronger than the poem's language can sustain being, and also that Keats's own poetic self is being put under too strong a burden throughout, both as the impersonal narrator and as the Apollo of the fragmentary third book? Too much is being refound, and nearly all at once, throughout the first *Hyperion*, and the poem as a whole, at least as it stands, implies and even exemplifies too sharp a turning-back towards restoring our mutilated human powers, powers for not only desiring a totality, but even for hoping to possess the object of such desire. The function of images or tropes of limitation is to turn us away from the lost or mourned object, and so to bring us back to either a sublimated substitute for the object or, more crucially, a reconsideration of ourselves as mourning subjects. In the first *Hyperion*, Keats took up too directly the burden of Miltonic representation, with a mass of universalizing synecdoches, Sublime hyperboles, and—as we will see— transumptive or metaleptic reversals of tradition. To recognize himself again, Keats had to write *The Fall of Hyperion* and his five great odes, and both the *Fall* and the Odes do follow the structure or pattern of ratios that Wordsworth and most strong post-Wordsworthian poets have followed.

I return, at last, to lines 176–200 of Book I of *Hyperion*, to demonstrate some of these conclusions, after which I will proceed to the main business of this discourse, which is to give a full antithetical reading of *The Fall of Hyperion*, and by it come back full circle to the starting point of my dissent from de Man, which was my insistence that Keats was as much a retrospective as a prospective poet, and also that in his last major work he was compelled, despite himself, to see himself as a hero of quest-romance on the very threshold of becoming a tragic hero. It was a threshold that he did not cross, in poetry or in life, and I hope to surmise before I end this chapter why he would (or could) not cross it in the poem.

When we first confront Hyperion in the earlier poem, he is remarkably balanced between Sublime and Grotesque representation, a balance that, I hasten to add, belongs to Keats's art alone, and not to Hyperion himself, for Hyperion is suffering what we tend to call a failure of nerve, or even a nervous breakdown. At this point Hyperion as Sun God reminds us too well that Freud's formulation of the defense of repression centers it in the psychic area of hysteria. We see and hear a Sublime being, but we are aware, all too uneasily, that this hyperbolical sublimity is founded upon a really fierce repression:

> Blazing Hyperion on his orbèd fire
> Still sat, still snuffed the incense, teeming up
> From man to the sun's God; yet unsecure:
> For as among us mortals omens drear
> Fright and perplex, so also shuddered he—
> Not at dog's howl, or gloom-bird's hated screech,
> Or the familiar visiting of one
> Upon the first toll of his passing-bell,
> Or prophesyings of the midnight lamp;
> But horrors, portioned to a giant nerve,
> Oft made Hyperion ache.
>
> (166–76)

A God who shudders at divinations is in the process of ceasing to be a God, and too nervous a God is a grotesque God. The meaning of Hyperion's repression here rises from its interplay with the grand repressive God of Book III of *Paradise Lost*. From the first moment we see him, Milton's God, unlike Milton's Satan, has no relation whatsoever to the stance and condition of being a poet. From our first encounter with him, Keats's Hyperion is a touch closer to Milton's Satan than Keats would care for him to have been, since like Satan Hyperion is not so much a God in dread of losing his kingdom as he is a poet in dread of losing his poetic powers or mortal godhead. An obsession with divination, a fear of futurity, is the mark of Hyperion, of Satan, and of Blake's Urizen, and its human meaning is the peculiar poetic property not so much of Milton as of Wordsworth, a truth that Keats knew perhaps better than we can know it.

I come now to the particular passage of the first *Hyperion* that I have been circling in upon, the *Hekhaloth* or heavenly halls of the nervous Hyperion, in the Sublime pathos that will be almost the last of his glory. Here I will want to start with a formula that sums up the revisionary element in lines 176–200: Keats gives us *an earliness that works as a lateness*, almost the reverse of the Miltonic scheme of transumptive allusion. Milton knowingly sacrifices the living present, the moment of his empirical being as he writes, in order to achieve an ontological earliness that triumphs over almost the entire tradition that produced him, and makes us see that tradition as being belated in contrast to him. I do not think that Keats, any more than Milton or Wordsworth, ever sought that all-but-impossible union between the ontological and empirical self, *in a poem*, that became the peculiarly American tradition of Romantic poetry, from Emerson and Whitman on to Hart Crane and A. R. Ammons. But, in the first *Hyperion*, Keats is not yet the master of transumptive allusion that, following Milton, he was to become. We can date the transition to Keats's maturity as a poet very precisely, since it was by April 1819 that he gave up the first *Hyperion* for good, and it was during the month from April 20 to May 20, that he fully found himself in the writing of the "Ode to Psyche."

Let us examine Hyperion's palace. Its characteristic imagery is of height and depth, but we may be reminded by it of Blake's comment upon Dante: "In equivocal worlds up & down is equivocal." Hyperion is still sitting exalted, but he acts like ourselves, beings *beneath* the sun. His Shakespearean palace, at once Roman and exotically Eastern, is both "glowing" and "touched with shade," the light also showing an equivocal height and depth. The images of what ought to be earliness crowd upon us: a rising sun; clouds accompanying Aurora, goddess of the dawn; eagles never seen before, and horses never heard before, whether by Gods or men. But all these have to be taken on the lateness of "the sleepy west," of incense turned to "savour of poisonous brass." The Sun God, moving through his domain, is imaged lastly by his angelic attendants or minor Titans, who are waiting for the final lateness of an apocalyptic earthquake. Keats has achieved a surprising immediacy here, but at a triple cost: the only future is a final fall, or utter projection; there is no past surviving into the present, except for a grotesque parody of the Sublime; and the present is introjected as a pure anxiety. I suggest that a full-scale reading of the first *Hyperion* would show that this passage is a part standing for the whole of the fragment. There are essentially only two ratios in the first *Hyperion*, and they are a *kenosis* and a *daemonization*, in uneasy alternation. The fragment vacillates between a defensive isolation of Sublime tradition, through metonymic reduction, and a powerful repression of the Sublime that fails to make the passage from hyperbole to a metaleptic reversal, that is to say from a perpetually mounting force of still greater repression to a stance finally the poet's own.

In contrast, I turn at last to *The Fall of Hyperion*, which is at once Keats's revision of romance and also his acceptance of the necessity of internalizing romance. This supposed fragment is an entire poem, showing the total structure of misprision, the complete patterning of images that Romantic or belated poetry demands. It is not accidental that, of all the Great Odes, the "Ode to Psyche" most resembles *The Fall of Hyperion*, for it was in the "Ode to Psyche" that Keats, with high good humor, came to terms with his own belatedness. As I have sketched an antithetical reading of the "Ode to Psyche" in *A Map of Misreading*, I will leap over that poem here and take its pattern of misprision as a prelude to the richer working-out of the same pattern in *The Fall of Hyperion*.

The fundamental principle of an antithetical or Kabbalistic criticism is that, in poetic texts, tropes are best understood as psychic defenses, because they *act as defenses*, against the tropes of anteriority, against the poems of the precursors. Similarly, in poetic texts, the poet's (or his surrogate's) psychic defenses are best understood as tropes, for they trope or turn against anterior defenses, against previous or outworn postures of the spirit. I shall illustrate this principle by contrasting the opening lines of *The Fall of Hyperion* to part of the opening passage of Wordsworth's *The Excursion*, Book I, lines 77 ff., that describes the Wanderer:

> Oh! many are the Poets that are sown
> By Nature: men endowed with highest gifts,
> The vision and the faculty divine;
> Yet wanting the accomplishment of verse
>
> . . . .
>
> Nor having e'er, as life advanced, been led
> By circumstances to take unto the height
> The measure of themselves, these favoured Beings,
> All but a scattered few, live out their time,
> Husbanding that which they possess within,
> And go to the grave, unthought of.

The first verse-paragraph of *The Fall of Hyperion* may be thought of as a *clinamen* away from this passage of Wordsworth, among others, one of which might be *The Excursion*, Book IV, lines 1275 ff., yet another panegyric in praise of (let it be admitted) that egregious bore, the Wanderer or the censorious Wordsworthian superego:

> Here closed the Sage that eloquent harangue,
> Poured forth with fervour in continuous stream,
> Such as, remote, 'mid savage wilderness,
> An Indian Chief discharges from his breast
> Into the hearing of assembled tribes,
> In open circle seated round, and hushed
> As the unbreathing air, when not a leaf
> Stirs in the mighty woods.—So did he speak:
> The words he uttered shall not pass away
> Dispersed like music that the wind takes up
> By snatches, and lets fall, to be forgotten.

Behind both Wordsworthian passages is an anxiety of Wordsworth's, that the part of his mind represented by the Wanderer may be inimical to poetry, as opposed to the more dangerous part represented by the Solitary, who in Shelley and in the Keats of *Endymion* becomes a figure nearly identical with poetry itself. I think we have underestimated Keats's savagery in *The Fall of Hyperion*, and that he begins the poem with a very bitter rhetorical irony that is his psyche's reaction-formation to this Wordsworthian anxiety:

Fanatics have their dreams, wherewith they weave
A paradise for a sect; the savage too
From forth the loftiest fashion of his sleep
Guesses at Heaven; pity these have not
Traced upon vellum or wild Indian leaf
The shadows of melodious utterance.
But bare of laurel they live, dream, and die;
For Poesy alone can tell her dreams,
With the fine spell of words alone can save
Imagination from the sable charm
And dumb enchantment. Who alive can say,
Thou art no Poet—mayst not tell thy dreams?
Since every man whose soul is not a clod
Hath visions, and would speak, if he had loved,
And been well nurtured in his mother tongue.
Whether the dream now purposed to rehearse
Be poet's or fanatic's will be known
When this warm scribe my hand is in the grave.

(1–18)

What is present, and what is absent in these lines, and why does Keats commence his poem with them? "Fanatics" here mean believing Christians, and so "dreams" here mean religious conceptualizations of a heavenly paradise, or else yet more "primitive" mythologies of paradise. Keats's distinction is between dreams and the telling of dreams, which he defines as poetry. Keats's irony, the *clinamen* directed against Wordsworth, is that fanatic and savage alike are present only as dreamers, but absent as poets, and by Keats's allusive implication Wordsworth's Wanderer, who is all but one with the poet writing most of *The Excursion*, is at once fanatic and savage, a complex dreamer but not a poet. But there is a deeper irony here, though it is still a figuration, still a saying of one thing while meaning another. Keats's concern is purgatorial and self-directed; is *he* present only as dreamer, and absent as poet? He is to rehearse a dream for us, but is he poet or fanatic? Can he tell his dream, which must mean something beyond a rehearsal, or will *The Fall of Hyperion* fail even as *Hyperion* failed? As he says himself, the answer came after he was in the grave, and never more greatly than from this poem. But I need to digress here, as few poems open more profoundly than this does, or confront a reader with so problematic a distinction.

The problem of the status and significance of poetry must be resolved at last in the area where our understanding of the following will meet: dreaming, and the telling of dreams in poetry, and the analogy: sex, and the telling of sex in love. The dialectic of Romantic love, which involves dream and identity, is the core problem. In *The Fall of Hyperion*, Keats moves himself and Moneta from one state of Identity to another state, still of Identity, but involving a self less insistent and more given to the sympathetic imagination. The first state is that of the dream, the second that of the dream's telling.

Geza Roheim, the most interesting speculative mind to arise on the Freudian Left, thought that there was only one basic dream, and that all we needed to understand, finally, was our motive for telling it. Wittgenstein in effect says that the dream and the motive alike cannot be spoken of; for him there is only the telling of dreams. To Freud, it does not matter whether the telling is "accurate" or not, just as it does not matter that the therapeutic image is intruded into the patient's consciousness by the analyst. But it matters to a poet that he get his "dream" right, and matters even more that he draw inevitable images *out of* the consciousness of his proper readers, whether in his own time or afterwards. It is because *pleasure* is legitimately one of his criteria, that the poet has his advantage. Perhaps the Stevensian criteria for poetry as the Supreme Fiction can be modified, to be more active: it must abstract, or withdraw perception from belatedness to earliness; it must *cause* change; it must *create* pleasure; it must humanize; all of these appropriate criteria also, surely, for the other Supreme Fiction— Romantic Love.

Is there an analogy between the strong poet's desire for priority and the motives or necessity for *telling*, whether of dreams in poetry or sexuality in love? We border on the realm of solipsism again; priority perhaps means not being first, but being alone, and is the demonic form of the apocalyptic impulse to be integrated again. "I sure should see / Other men here," Keats says to Moneta, and then adds: "But I am here alone." Yet he has not come to tell her his dreams, but to listen to hers, or rather to hear her study the nostalgias. I will return to this stance of faithful listening to the Muse when it comes to dominate the poem, but for now I return to the poem's opening, this time to map it through to the end.

Let us call the opening verse-paragraph, with its reverberations directed against Wordsworth's Wanderer, Keats's poetic reaction-formation against the anxiety of Wordsworthian presence, a conscious *illusio* that knows at once that Keats is an elected poet, but also that in this poem of trial he will not be free to tell his deepest dreams. The answering restitution or representation is in the noble synecdoche of the next, long verse-paragraph, lines 19–80, where Keats antithetically completes both Book V of *Paradise Lost* and his own "Ode to Psyche." Notice that there is no entrance into this movement of the poem except for the abrupt "Methought I stood," and it is this unmerited and unexplained re-entry into the earthly paradise which is the only dream that Keats will tell in this poem. The recall of lines 60–63 of the "Ode to Psyche" establishes the new poem's largest difference from earlier Keats; the "wreathed trellis of a working brain" there has been externalized here just as the Miltonic dream of Angels and humans feasting together is seen here as belonging to a naturalistic and recent past. Keats stands in a microcosm of the poet's paradise, drinks the honey of Eden, and enters what would be a dream-within-a-dream if it were not so insistently and persuasively a vision of Instruction. When he wakes from his swoon, he is in a poet's purgatory, a ruined sanctuary of every dead faith, and defensively he is turned dangerously against himself, without as yet overtly knowing it.

To stand before the purgatorial stairs is to stand in the realm of displacements, where the center of a dream lances off into indirect byways, into reductions and emptyings-out of things into aspects of things. Rhetorically this is the realm of metonymy, an object-world where there are no resemblances but only contiguities. In lines 81–181 of *The Fall of Hyperion* Keats confronts his Muse in a state of heightened awareness, but also in a state of reified vulnerability. The Keatsian *kenosis* is neither a Wordsworthian regression nor a Shelleyan undoing, but rather resembles Stevens, Keats's descendant, in being a radical isolation. The passage begins just after a repetition of the "Ode to Psyche"'s reduction of dead religion to a metonymic catalog, and continues in a curious tone of the cataloger of contiguities, who cannot summon haste or urgency even to ward off his own destruction until the last possible moment. I will concentrate in this movement upon one moment only, where Keats nearly undoes himself. Moneta has just spoken, with the bitter eloquence that marks her, not so much warning the poet as harshly proclaiming the quick death she confidently expects for him. The purgatorial steps, she says, are immortal, but Keats is only so much dust and sand, a mass of displacements. The poet who had preached disinterestedness is at first so disinterested that he almost fails to move in time. Characteristically, he is roused only by hearing his own involuntary shriek, a rousing or being stung that sets him moving:

> I heard, I looked: two senses both at once,
> So fine, so subtle, felt the tyranny
> Of that fierce threat and the hard task proposed.
> Prodigious seemed the toil; the leaves were yet
> Burning—when suddenly a palsied chill
> Struck from the pavèd level up my limbs,
> And was ascending quick to put cold grasp
> Upon those streams that pulse beside the throat:
> I shrieked, and the sharp anguish of my shriek
> Stung my own ears—I strove hard to escape
> The numbness; strove to gain the lowest step.
> Slow, heavy, deadly was my pace: the cold
> Grew stifling, suffocating, at the heart;
> And when I clasped my hands I felt them not.
> One minute before death, my iced foot touched
> The lowest stair; and it touched, life seemed
> To pour in at the toes

This is, at the least, a strong revision of a romance commonplace; the quester's ordeal of recognition, which is not so much a crisis of self-recognition as it is the agony of being brought to what Yeats called "the place of the Daemon." Keats describes in himself a suffering that is at the threshold of strength, even a pragmatic weakness that becomes a poetic power. This is a quester so detached that he broods first on the fineness and subtlety of his own hearing and seeing, before he bothers to consider the danger he confronts. It is as though various reductions of himself—hearing, sight, chilled limbs, tubercular symptoms—were contiguous with the emblems of danger—the harsh voice of the seeress, the burning leaves, the stairs— but so displaced from a universe of resemblances that the contiguity assumed a solitary emphasis as a characteristic. But why does Keats, as a poet, so empty himself out here? Why does he station himself so deliberately, as though he were one more falsely reified entity in a world of such entities, so that the prophetess Moneta becomes yet another such, and so a kind of false prophetess? Freud tells us that the dreamworld necessarily involves displacement, which rhetorically becomes the mode of metonymy, of so troping or turning from the literal that every complex thing is replaced by a simple, salient aspect of that thing. Keats enters his own poem in the self-proclaimed role as poet, indeed as *the* poet of his own time. Why should he have to undergo such an emptying-out of the poetic self in what is, after all, his annunciation as a strong poet?

I suggest that Keats, a startlingly clear intellect, had a proleptic understanding that there is no breakthrough to poetic strength without a double distortion, a distortion of the precursors and so of tradition, and a self-distortion in compensation. There is no growth into poetic strength without a radical act of interpretation that is always a distortion or misprision and, more subtly, without the necessity of so stationing the poet's ontological self that it too is held up to an interpretation that necessarily will also be distortion or misprision. Keats differs only in degree from previous strong poets by his *acceptance* of these necessities. The prime function of Moneta in the poem is to *misinterpret* Keats, but by so misinterpreting she canonizes him, in a dialectical reversal of her attitude that I now would say does not leave her at the end misunderstanding him any less radically than she misunderstands him when first he stands before her purgatorial stairs. As the Muse, Moneta presides over the canon of poetry and mythology and dead religion, but the canon is a grand ruin, as the poem makes clear. The great sanctuary of Saturn is a wreck, and to be accepted by Moneta as the properly qualified quester is to join an enterprise of disaster. By courteously troping or turning the harsh Muse into accepting him, Keats wins a dubious blessing, as he well knows. It is as though romance is poised already on the verge of what it will become in Tennyson's *The Holy Grail*, where Percivale's quest will destroy everything it touches, or in Browning's *Childe Roland to the Dark Tower Came*, where just the quester's glance will be enough to deform and break all things it views.

We have reached that point in *The Fall of Hyperion* where Keats, mounting up into the shrine of Moneta, mounts up into the Sublime, through the characteristic, paradoxical defense of repression, and by the trope of hyperbole, a trope of excess, of the violent overthrow. A theoretical digression opens before me, in which I hope to clarify not only the poem, but my own antithetical theory of poetry, or rather of the antithetical element in post-Enlightenment poetry.

Richard Wollheim, in his book *On Art and the Mind*, reminds us that Freud knew his favorite models differed in their own purposes from the purposes of art. Freud's models were the dream, the neurotic symptom, the tendentious joke, and all of these have a directness and an immediacy that art fortunately does not have and does not seek. A poem, as Freud well knew, was not a dream, nor a joke, nor a symptom. But Freud, as a humanistic scientist, and Wollheim, as an analytical philosopher, do not know that a poem *is* a kind of error, a beautiful mistake or open lie, that does have the function of, somehow, *telling a dream*. Wollheim, following and expounding Freud, says that a poem does not avail itself of a drop in consciousness or attention in order to become the sudden vehicle of buried desires. But here I think Wollheim is not close enough to what poems actually do, perhaps because he is more interested in the visual arts and less in poetry. Poems, I would insist, indeed do just the reverse of what Wollheim says they don't do, but as this is a dialectical reversal it too is frequently reversed, and so poems do refute Wollheim, not in theory but in the ways they behave. It is by the mode of sublimity that poems suddenly do become the vehicle of buried desires, by violent heightenings of consciousness or attention. But these heightenings can drop away just as suddenly, and abandon us to the consequences of repression, a process rhetorically manifested through the substitution of the trope of litotes for that of hyperbole, by a turning to an underthrow of language that plunges us from the Sublime down into its dialectical brother, the Grotesque.

I would say then that Wollheim, following Freud, is only partly right, because Freud was only partly right, about poetry. Poetic meaning, or the absence of it, exists in the psychic and linguistic gap that separates repression from sublimation. It is true that art, for Freud, does not link up directly with wish and impulse expressing themselves in neurosis, but it does link up, for Freud, and I think in actuality, with defense, and psychic defense need not be or become neurotic, though sorrowfully it usually is or does. Wollheim wisely says that when you abandon the false and non-Freudian equation, neurosis = art, you lose all justification for thinking of art as showing a single or unitary motivation, since except for the relative inflexibility of a neurosis there is no single, unchanging, constant form that our characters or temperaments assume, but rather endless vicissitudes of impulse and feeling, constant formings and re-formings of fantasy, and while there *are* patterns in these, they are as flexible as those of art. I accept Wollheim's formulation of this principle, but with a vital, antithetical proviso—these patterns in feeling and fantasy are frequently defensive without being neurotic, and there are patterns in poetic imagery, rhetoric, and stance that are also defensive, without being neurotic. Wollheim says that art for Freud was constructive as well as expressive, and I would add that what poetry constructs can be a healthy defense against the real dangers of both the inner and the outer life.

Wollheim usefully adds that there is a gap in Freud's account of art, a gap that I think a more antithetical criticism of poetry can help to fill. Freud's vision or poem of the mind developed (as Wollheim indicates) through three stages: first, one in which the unconscious was identified with repression; second, one in which the unconscious was seen as the primary process of mental functioning; third, one in which the unconscious attained a function that went beyond defense, and beyond the ongoing functions of the mind. In this third and final stage, Freud's vision is surprisingly close to Blake's, for the unconscious plays its part as what Blake called the Devourer, binding energy and so building up the ego, the role Blake assigned to Urizen, so that in Freud's final stage the unconscious has turned potentially reasonable. The defenses of projection and introjection are seen by Freud as capable of being transformed beyond defense into a healthful, constructive, ongoing process of *identification*, a Freudian vision in which he again followed the poets, as I have been trying to show, with my emphasis upon schemes of transumption as the characteristic post-Miltonic poetic mode for successfully concluding poems. Wollheim remarks: "In a number of celebrated passages Freud equated art with recovery or reparation on the path back to reality. But nowhere did he indicate the mechanism by which this came about. By the time he found himself theoretically in a position to do so, the necessary resources of leisure and energy were, we must believe, no longer available to him."

It is in the absence of this third-stage Freudian model that I have proposed a Kabbalistic model or paradigm for the image-patterning, for the movement of tropes and defenses towards the strengthening of the poetic ego, that I think is characteristic of the major poets of the last several centuries. But Keats in particular, and in *The Fall of Hyperion* more than anywhere else, gives us yet another critical reason for following Gnostic or Kabbalistic paradigms of belatedness rather than hypothesizing what a mature Freudian psychoesthetics might have become. Most students of Freud would agree that for him the dream and/or the unconscious are at once three things—a representation, a staged scene, and a distortion. But a poem is all three at once also, and we can distinguish between a poem and a dream or unconscious process, simply by remarking that the dream or unconscious process is overdetermined in its *meanings*, since we are discovering, if I am right, that belated poems suffer an increasing overdetermination in *language*, but an increasing *under-determination in meaning*. The dream or the symptom has a redundancy of meaning, but the Wordsworthian or modern poem has an apparent dearth of meaning, which paradoxically is its peculiar strength, and its demand upon, and challenge to, the interpretative powers of the reader.

I return to Keats confronting Moneta. Poetic images are not just condensations or displacements of signs, which would make all poetic images either metaphors or metonymies, and hence all *images-of-limitation*. Poetic images, whether as synecdoches, hyperboles, or transumptions, also transform signs, whether by antithetical completion, by heightening, or by the final illusion of making the sign appear to be earlier than it actually is. But whatever the images of a dream may try to be, they *do* tend to be only images of limitation, and so the dream-tropes are irony, metonymy, metaphor, or in Freudian language: distortion, displacement, condensation. To understand a dream, the dreamer must tell it as a text, which means that he must translate or interpret it into either the language of Freudian reduction, or into the restituting language of poetry, as Keats does. In the scene we have now reached, with Keats facing Moneta after ascending the purgatorial stairs, the language joins the issue for us, between the Freudian, reductive view of repression, and the poetic or Sublime translation or interpretation of repression.

According to Freud, repression is a *failure in translation*, and since I would insist that a strong poem is a triumph of repression, and *not* of sublimation, then I would acknowledge that there must be *some* failure in translation or interpretation in order for a dream to become a poem, which is another way of stating the necessity of *misreading*, if strong poems are to be written or indeed if they are to be read. Just as no dream has a meaning except in relation to other dreams, so that in some clear sense the meaning of a dream can be only another dream, so also poems behave in relation to other poems, as my theory hypothesizes. I want now to break back into Keats's text, at line 134, by venturing this new antithetical formula: *Within a poem the Sublime can only result when translation fails, and so when misprision is heightened, through hyperbole, to a daemonic climax.* The great climax of *The Fall of Hyperion* will be seen to be a revision of the Wordsworthian version of romance, a revision dependent upon an even greater repression than Wordsworth had to accomplish.

The dialogue between Keats and Moneta concerns the problematic of poetic identity, which is an extreme form of the idea of an autonomous ego. Keats, in his speculation upon identity, is part of a very complex nineteenth-century questioning of the notion of a single, separate self, a questioning that culminated in the analytics of Nietzsche, Marx, and Freud, but which may be stronger in the poets even than it was in the great speculators. Is the poetic identity or autonomous ego only a reification? Emerson, who identified the power of poetry with what he called unfixing and clapping wings to solid nature, certainly rejects any notion of a fixed poetic identity or of a single, confined human ego. Neitzsche, on more language-centered grounds, did the same in denying what he called the unnecessary hypothesis of the human subject. There are insights in Keats that may be more subtle than all but a few in nineteenth-century traditions, and these insights tend to cluster around the image of the sole self or poetic identity as a negation of the human. In *Endymion*, Keats had celebrated love and friendship for their work in destroying the autonomy of the self, and had called "crude and sore / The journey homeward to habitual self." But Keats, I think, protested too much his zeal to overcome self-concern, and I think also that Keats has deceived his critics into literalizing his figuration of destroying the self. I am very startled when a critic as demystifying and demystified as Paul de Man says of Keats: "He almost succeeds in eliminating himself from his poetry altogether," or again that "the only threat that Keats seems to experience subjectively is that of self-confrontation." I would venture the paradox that Shelley, who so overtly dramatizes himself in his poetry, is nevertheless far more authentically selfless than Keats in poetry, as he was in life. Keats's speculations on selfhood and identity are not so much deceptive or even self-deceiving as they are evidences of a remarkable repression of anxiety, and also of a will-to-poetic power, and simply cannot be read and accepted at anything near face-value.

Shall we not call Moneta the Muse of repression? Criticism has not explained, nor even attempted to explain, her initial hostility to Keats. It is more than haste that Keats represses as he approaches her altar; it is the highest kind of poetic ambition, which is the dream of an active divination, of the poet becoming a god. All through Keats's poetry, critics rightly have seen different aspects of the same situation recur: a mortal, human male quester-poet confronts an immortal, divine, female Muse-principle, and almost always in a context in which the quester-poet is threatened by death, a death marked by privation, particularly by the cold. But Moneta paradoxically is at once the most ultimately benign and the most immediately hostile of these Muses. Keats asks her the wholly modest question, "What am I that should so be saved from death?" And she snaps that all he has done is "dated on" his doom. When Keats says that he is "encouraged by the sooth voice of the shade," he does *not* mean "consoling" but "truthful," for while he is as courteous as she is abrupt, the truth is that he is now as harsh as she is, because it is harsh to confront truth so directly, or at least what one takes to be truth. What could be harsher, or more apparently un-Keatsian, than the shocking hyperbole that Keats allows himself here?

> Then shouted I
> Spite of myself, and with a Pythia's spleen,
> 'Apollo! faded! O far flown Apollo!
> Where is thy misty pestilence to creep
> Into the dwellings, through the door crannies
> Of all mock lyrists, large self worshippers
> And careless Hectorers in proud bad verse.
> Though I breathe death with them it will be life
> To see them sprawl before me into graves.
> (202–10)

These are not the accents of a poet who has eliminated himself from his own poetry, or for whom self-confrontation is the only subjective threat. What is audible here is spleen all right, and I am afraid that this rancor, from our perspective, is precisely the "good will" on Keats's part that Moneta praises and reciprocates. Keats has done something audacious and only dubiously successful; he purports to speak for Apollo, and to have Moneta speak for all the dead gods of poetry. It is from *that* undemonstrable perspective that Keats so cruelly condemns Shelley, Wordsworth, and Byron, and so it is by being as cruel as Moneta, but towards *other poets*, that Keats has found acceptance by her.

There is no reason to condemn the prevalent critical idolatry of Keats, which as I have remarked elsewhere is a rather benign literary malady. But I do think that such idolatry has blinded us from seeing just what is happening in *The Fall of Hyperion*, and perhaps also in *Lamia*. We have over-canonized Keats, and so we do not read him as he is, with all his literary anxieties and all his high and deep repression plain upon him. From the hyperbolical Sublime of Pythian spleen that he shares with Moneta, Keats attempts the great description of Moneta's face in lines 256–81, which may be the most remarkable extended metaphor in his poetry. I will not analyze it here, except to observe that it fails grandly just as all High Romantic inside/outside metaphors fail, because in attempting to overcome a subject-object dualism it instead extends such dualism. Yet the passage is terribly moving because it persuades us that Keats at last has fulfilled his quest, and has seen what he always wanted to see. He has revised romance, even his own kind of romance, by reconciling and almost integrating the quester and the object of quest. He is no knight-at-arms pining for a Belle Dame, not even the quester after the Melancholy whose "soul shall taste the sadness of her might, / And be among her cloudy trophies hung." Yet his Muse suffers "an immortal sickness which kills not," and is so oxymoronically described that we are bewildered by the shifts-in-perspective that Keats himself cannot control. "Death is the mother of beauty" in Keats's disciple, Stevens, because nothing can be beautiful that does not change, and the final form of change is death. But Keats defies this obvious wisdom, since the "immortal sickness" works a constant change that does not end with death, however unhappy. Earlier in the poem, Keats has referred to his own oxymoronic sickness as being "not ignoble," and we can surmise therefore that Moneta's "immortal sickness" is the fearful repression that results in the poetry of the Sublime, which is Keats's own, overt "illness."

What remains in *The Fall of Hyperion* are traces of a scheme of transumption that Keats sketches without fully working it through. It emerges in two passages of belatedness reversed into earliness:

> whereon there grew
> A power within me of enormous ken
> To see as a god sees, and take the depth
> Of things as nimbly as the outward eye
> Can size and shape pervade . . .
>
> . . . .
>
> —Now in clear light I stood,
> Relieved from the dusk vale. Mnemosyne
> Was sitting on a square-edged polished stone,
> That in its lucid depth reflected pure
> Her priestess-garments.—My quick eyes ran on.

The second of these passages seems to allude to an image in Cary's translation of the *Purgatorio* 9:85–87: "The lowest stair was marble white, so smooth / And polish'd, that therein my mirror'd form / Distinct I saw." As we would expect in the trope of metalepsis, Keats tropes upon his own earlier trope (and Dante's) of the purgatorial stairs. What earlier menaced Keats, the cold stairs that nearly killed him, is now a further means to vision as Keats projects the past, introjects the future, and stands knowingly in a moment that is no moment, a negation of present time. But a transumptive stance, whether in Milton or in Keats, is not simply a prospective one. Its emphasis is not upon a time-to-be, but on the loss-of-being that takes place in present experience.

What then would an antithetical as opposed to a canonical reading of *The Fall of Hyperion* be? All canonical readings (my own earlier one included) have *naturalized* the poem; an antithetical reading would abstract the poem from the irrelevant context of nature, in every sense of "nature." Poems are not "things" and have little to do with a world of "things," but I am not endorsing either the Stevensian notion that "poetry is the subject of the poem." There is no subject *of* the poem or *in* the poem, nor can we make the poem into its own subject. There is a dearth of meaning in a strong poem, a dearth so great that, as Emerson says, the strong poem forces us to invent if we are to read well, or as I would say, if we are to make our misreading stronger and more necessary than other misreadings. *The Fall of Hyperion* is a very strong poem because it impels every reader to return upon his or her own enterprise as a reader. That is the challenge Keats gives us: his stance in relation to Moneta, which means to tradition, which means in turn to the composite precursor, becomes the inevitable paradigm for our stance as readers in relation to his text.

Let me return to the question of a dearth-in-meaning, and elaborate upon it. Only a strong poet can make a dearth-in-meaning, a *zimzum* or limitation that compels subsequent substitution and the *tikkun* or restitution of poetic representation. Any poetaster or academic impostor can write a poem for us that oozes a plenitude of "meaning," an endless amplitude of significances. This late in tradition, we all come to one another smothered in and by meaning; we die daily, facing one another, of our endlessly mutual interpretations and self-interpretations. We deceive ourselves, or are deceived, into thinking that if only we could be interpreted rightly, or interpret others rightly, then all would yet be well. But by now—after Nietzsche, Marx, Freud, and all their followers and revisionists—surely we secretly—all of us—know better. We know that we must be misinterpreted in order to bear living, just as we know we must misinterpret others if they are to stay alive, in more than the merely minimal sense. The necessity of misreading one another is the other daily necessity that accompanies sleep and food, or that is as pervasive as light and air. There is no paradox in what I am saying; I but remind myself of an obvious truth, of *Ananke*, or what Emerson called the Beautiful Necessity.

Keats, revising his lifelong obsession with romance, confronts Moneta as the final form of romance, and sees in her more-than-tragic face the Beautiful Necessity. Of what? Of a mode of repetition in self-destroyings, I think, and a repetition also in the redefinition of romance. I conclude then by asking two questions, both of them in the antithetical context of *The Fall of Hyperion*: what is romance? and what is the repetition of romance?

Freud once described repression as being only a middle stage between a mere, reflex-like defense and what he called an *Urteilsverwerfung* or moral judgment of condemnation. There may be a connection between this description, as Anthony Wilden suggests in his *System and Structure*, and Freud's very difficult essay on "negation," with its much-disputed key sentence: "Through the mediation of the symbol of negation, thought frees itself from the consequences of repression and enriches itself with a content necessary for its accomplishment." Thus freed by negation from the reign of the pleasure-principle, thought (according to Freud) is able to attain the more fixed or devouring forms of the reality-principle or, as Freud says elsewhere, thought at last is enabled to free itself from its sexual past. I would transpose Freud's formula of negation into the realm of poetry, and specifically into the context of *The Fall of Hyperion*, by suggesting that, in Keats's poem, Moneta, as what Freud calls the symbol of negation, mediates for Keats not so as to free his thought from the consequences of repression but so as to show him that his thought cannot be so liberated, if it is to remain *poetic* thought. When she has shown Keats this, then it is his heroism that permits him to accept such dark wisdom. Romance, as Keats teaches us to understand it, cannot break out of the domain of the pleasure-principle even though that means, as Keats knows, that romance must accept the vision of an endless entropy as its fate.

If this is Keatsian or revised romance, then what is the repetition of romance, which is the actual mode of *The Fall of Hyperion* from its first until its final vision of Hyperion: "On he flared"? Though Kierkegaard joked that the dialectic of repetition is easy, he employed his customary rhetorical irony in so joking. At the center of his idea of repetition is the problem of continuity for the individual, a problem that he believed could be solved only by first arriving at a decision, and then by continually renewing it. The best analogue he could find for his vision was the Christian idea of marriage, which he exalted, but pathetically recoiled from personally. Only Christian marriage could give the daily bread that could undergo the severities of repetition, and so finally repetition became meaningless without the perpetual and difficult possibility of *becoming* a Christian.

In Keats, the repetition of romance becomes the perpetual and difficult possibility of *becoming* a strong poet. When Keats persuaded himself that he had mastered such repetition, *as a principle*, then *The Fall of Hyperion* broke off, being as finished a poem as a strong poem can be. Keats had reached the outer threshold of romance, and declined to cross over it into the realm of tragedy. Poised there, on the threshold, his stance is more retrospective than he could have wanted it to be, but there he remains still, in a stance uniquely heroic, in despite of itself.

Chronology

1757   William Blake born November 28 in London.

1770   William Wordsworth born April 7 at Cockermouth in Cumberland.

1772   Samuel Taylor Coleridge born October 21 in the vicarage at Ottery, St. Mary, Devonshire.

1783   Blake's *Poetical Sketches* published, containing poems written 1769–78.

1788   George Gordon, Lord Byron born January 22 in London.

1789   Blake completes engraving of *Songs of Innocence* and *The Book of Thel*.

1790   Blake writes *The Marriage of Heaven and Hell* at the Christological age of thirty-three.

1791   Printing of Blake's *The French Revolution* by left-wing publisher Joseph Johnson, but the poem abandoned in proof sheets.

1792   Percy Bysshe Shelley born August 4 at Field Place, Horsham, Sussex.

1793   Blake finishes the engravings of *America* and *Visions of the Daughters of Albion*.
Wordsworth publishes *An Evening Walk* and *Descriptive Sketches*.

1794   Blake finishes engravings of *Songs of Experience*, *Europe*, and *The Book of Urizen*.
Coleridge publishes *The Fall of Robespierre* (with Robert Southey).

383

1795   John Keats born October 31 at 24 Moorfields Pavement Row, London.
Blake finishes *The Book of Los*, *The Song of Los*, and *The Book of Ahania*.

1796   Coleridge publishes *Poems on Various Subjects* and edits the March–May issues of *The Watchman*.

1796–97   Wordsworth composes *The Borderers*, which is not published until 1842.

1797   Coleridge composes *The Rime of the Ancient Mariner*.

1798   Wordsworth and Coleridge publish *Lyrical Ballads*.

1799   Wordsworth completes first version of *The Prelude*, in two parts.

1800   Second edition of *Lyrical Ballads* published, with a preface by Wordsworth.

1802   Third edition of *Lyrical Ballads* by Wordsworth and Coleridge.

1804   Blake dates the composition of *Milton* and *Jerusalem* from this year, but they are believed to have been finished later.

1805   *The Prelude*, in thirteen books, finished, but Wordsworth chooses not to publish it.

1806   Byron's first poems, *Fugitive Pieces*, privately printed.

1807   Wordsworth publishes *Poems in Two Volumes*.
Byron publishes *Hours of Idleness*.

1809   Blake writes *A Descriptive Catalogue*, containing his remarkable criticism of Chaucer, to accompany an exhibition of his paintings.
Byron publishes *English Bards and Scotch Reviewers* in retaliation against the *Edinburgh Review*.

1810   Shelley publishes *Zastrozzi*, a Gothic novel, followed by *Original Poems by Victor and Cazire*, written with his sister.

1811   Shelley expelled from Oxford on March 25 for writing pamphlet *The Necessity of Atheism*.

1812   Byron publishes first two cantos of *Childe Harold's Pilgrimage*.

1813   Coleridge's early play *Osario*, revised as *Remorse*, performed at Drury Lane Theatre in London.
Shelley publishes *Queen Mab*.
Byron publishes first Oriental tales, *The Giaour* and *The Bride of Abydos*.

1814   Wordsworth publishes *The Excursion*.
        Byron publishes *The Corsair* and *Lara*.
        Keats, age 18 or 19, writes his first poems.

1815   Wordsworth publishes two volumes of *Miscellaneous Poems*.

1816   Coleridge publishes *Christabel and Other Poems*.
        Byron publishes Canto III of *Childe Harold*.
        Shelley publishes *Alastor*.

1817   Coleridge publishes *Biographia Literaria*, *Sibylline Leaves*, and
        his two *Lay Sermons*.
        Keats publishes a volume entitled *Poems*, including his first
        sonnets and *Sleep and Poetry*.

1818   Byron publishes *Beppo* and Canto IV of *Childe Harold* and be-
        gins *Don Juan*.
        Keats publishes *Endymion*, which is attacked by critics. Begins
        Hyperion (abandoned the next year).
        Shelley publishes *The Revolt of Islam* and begins *Prometheus
        Unbound*.

1819   Wordsworth publishes *Peter Bell* and *The Waggoner*.
        Byron's *Mazeppa* and Cantos I and II of *Don Juan* published.
        Shelley writes "Ode to the West Wind" and begins *A Philo-
        sophical View of Reform* (published 1920). Publishes *The Cenci*
        and *Peter Bell the Third*.
        Keats's *annus miribilis*: writes *The Eve of St. Agnes*, "The Eve
        of St. Mark," "Vale of Soul-Making" letter, and "La Belle
        Dame Sans Merci." Writes odes—Psyche, Nightingale, Gre-
        cian Urn, Melancholy, Indolence, and Autumn. Writes *Lamia*
        and begins *The Fall of Hyperion*. Writes *Otho the Great* (with
        Charles Brown), fragment of "King Stephen," and "The Cap
        and Bells." Gives up on *The Fall of Hyperion*.

1820   Shelley publishes *Prometheus Unbound*; writes *The Witch of Atlas*
        from August 14 to 16.
        Keats gravely ill with tuberculosis. His third book published—
        Lamia, Isabella, The Eve of St. Agnes, and Other Poems.
        Blake completes woodcuts to Virgil's *Pastorals*.

1821   Keats dies February 23 and is buried in the Protestant Cem-
        etery in Rome.
        Byron publishes *Cain* and Cantos III, IV, and V of *Don Juan*.
        Shelley writes *A Defence of Poetry* between February and March
        and publishes *Adonais* and *Epipsychidion*.

1822   Shelley works on *The Triumph of Life* during May and June.
        On July 8 Shelley drowns at Lerici.
        Byron publishes *The Vision of Judgment*.

1823   Byron publishes Cantos VI to XIV of *Don Juan*.

1824   Cantos XV and XVI of *Don Juan* published. Byron dies April 19th.

1825   Blake completes engravings for *The Book of Job*.
         Coleridge publishes *Aids to Reflection in the Formation of a Manly Character*.

1826   Blake completes illustrations to Dante.

1827   William Blake dies August 12.

1828   Coleridge's *Poetical Works* published.

1830   Coleridge's *On the Constitution of Church and State* published.

1834   Coleridge dies July 25 at the residence of Dr. James Gillman, Highgate, London.

1840   Coleridge's *Confessions of an Enquiring Spirit* published posthumously.

1850   Wordsworth dies April 23 at Rydal Mount. *The Prelude*, in fourteen books, published posthumously.

Contributors

HAROLD BLOOM, Sterling Professor of the Humanities at Yale University, is the author of *The Anxiety of Influence, Poetry and Repression,* and many other volumes of literary criticism. His forthcoming study, *Freud: Transference and Authority,* attempts a full-scale reading of all of Freud's major writings. A MacArthur Prize Fellow, he is general editor of five series of literary criticism published by Chelsea House.

NORTHROP FRYE is University Professor Emeritus at the University of Toronto. He is the principal literary theorist of our century. His major works include *Fearful Symmetry, Anatomy of Criticism,* and *The Great Code: The Bible and Literature.*

THOMAS WEISKEL taught at Yale University until his tragic accidental death. His masterly book, *The Romantic Sublime,* first appeared in 1976, and is currently being reissued.

FREDERICK A. POTTLE is Sterling Professor of English Emeritus at Yale University. He is best known as the editor and biographer of James Boswell.

GEOFFREY H. HARTMAN is Karl Young Professor of English and Comparative Literature at Yale University. Besides his writings on Wordsworth, his books include *Beyond Formalism* and *Saving the Text.*

PAUL H. FRY is Associate Professor of English at Yale University. He is the author of *The Reach of Criticism: Method and Perception in Literary Theory* and *The Poet's Calling in the English Ode.*

M. H. ABRAMS, the most distinguished living scholar of Romanticism, is Class of 1916 Professor of English at Cornell University. His masterwork is *The Mirror and the Lamp,* the definitive study of Romantic critical theory, which should be read in conjunction with his other major books, *Natural Supernaturalism* and *The Correspondent Breeze.*

ANGUS FLETCHER is Distinguished Professor of English and Comparative Literature at Herbert H. Lehman College and the Graduate Center of the City University of New York. His books include *Allegory, The Prophetic Moment,* and *The Transcendental Masque.*

E. S. SHAFFER is a lecturer in Comparative Literature at the University of East Anglia. She is the author of *"Kubla Khan" and* The Fall of Jerusalem.

G. WILSON KNIGHT was Professor of English at the University of Leeds. One of the leading British literary critics of this century, he wrote extensively on both Shakespeare and Byron. His books include *The Wheel of Fire, The Starlit Dome,* and *The Burning Oracle.*

LESLIE BRISMAN is Professor of English at Yale University. He is the author of *Romantic Origins* and *Milton's Poetry of Choice and its Romantic Heirs.*

SHEILA EMERSON is Assistant Professor of English at Tufts University. She has published essays on Wordsworth and Ruskin and is the author of the forthcoming *Ruskin: The Genesis of Invention.*

PAUL DE MAN was Sterling Professor of Comparative Literature at Yale University. His influential theoretical studies are gathered together in *Blindness and Insight, Allegories of Reading,* and *The Rhetoric of Romanticism.*

WALTER JACKSON BATE is University Professor of English at Harvard University. He is renowned for his critical biographies of Dr. Johnson and Keats.

Bibliography

ROMANTICISM AND ROMANTIC POETRY

Abrams, M. H. *The Correspondent Breeze: Essays on English Romanticism*. New York: W. W. Norton & Co., 1984.

———. *The Mirror and the Lamp: Romantic Theory and the Critical Tradition*. Oxford: Oxford University Press, 1953.

———, ed. *English Romantic Poetry*. New York: Oxford University Press, 1960.

Blake Studies, 1968–.

Bloom, Harold. *The Ringers in the Tower: Studies in Romantic Tradition*. Chicago: The University of Chicago Press, 1971.

———. *The Visionary Company*. Rev. ed. Ithaca: Cornell University Press, 1971.

———, ed. *Romanticism and Consciousness: Essays in Criticism*. New York: W. W. Norton & Co., 1970.

Brisman, Leslie. *Romantic Origins*. Ithaca: Cornell University Press, 1978.

Bush, Douglas. *Mythology and the Romantic Tradition in English Poetry*. Rev. ed. Cambridge: Harvard University Press, 1969.

Cooke, Michael G. *Acts of Inclusion: Studies Bearing on an Elementary Theory of Romanticism*. New Haven: Yale University Press, 1979.

Fry, Paul H. *The Poet's Calling in the English Ode*. New Haven: Yale University Press, 1980.

Frye, Northrop. *Fables of Identity: Studies in Poetic Mythology*. New York: Harcourt, Brace & World, 1963.

———. *A Study of English Romanticism*. 1968. Reprint. Chicago: The University of Chicago Press, 1983.

———, ed. *Romanticism Reconsidered*. New York: Columbia University Press, 1963.

Hilles, Frederick W., and Harold Bloom, eds. *From Sensibility to Romanticism*: *Essays Presented to Frederick A. Pottle*. New York: Oxford University Press, 1965.

The Keats–Shelley Journal, 1952–.

Simpson, David. *Irony and Authority in Romantic Poetry*. Totowa, N. J.: Rowman & Littlefield, 1979.

Studies in Romanticism, 1961–.

Weiskel, Thomas. *The Romantic Sublime: Studies in the Structure and Psychology of Transcendence*. Baltimore: The Johns Hopkins University Press, 1976.

The Wordsworth Circle, 1970–1981.

WILLIAM BLAKE

Adams, Hazard. *Blake and Yeats: The Contrary Vision*. New York: Russell & Russell, 1968.

Ault, Donald. *Visionary Physics: Blake's Response to Newton*. Chicago: The University of Chicago Press, 1974.

Beer, John. *Blake's Humanism*. Manchester: Manchester University Press, 1968.

Behrendt, Stephen C. *The Moment of Explosion: Blake and the Illustration of Milton*. Lincoln: University of Nebraska Press, 1983.

Bloom, Harold. *Blake's Apocalypse: A Study in Poetic Argument*. Ithaca: Cornell University Press, 1970.

Bronowski, Jacob. *William Blake and the Age of Revolution*. London: Routledge & Kegan Paul, 1972.

Curran, Stuart, and Joseph Wittreich, Jr., eds. *Blake's Sublime Allegory: Essays on* The Four Zoas, Milton, *and* Jerusalem. Madison: University of Wisconsin Press, 1973.

Damon, Samuel Foster. *William Blake: His Philosophy and Symbols*. Gloucester, Mass.: P. Smith, 1978.

Damrosch, Leopold. *Symbol and Truth in Blake's Myth*. Princeton: Princeton University Press, 1980.

Davis, Michael. *William Blake: A New Kind of Man*. London: Elek, 1977.

Dorfman, Deborah. *Blake in the Nineteenth Century: His Reputation as a Poet from Gilchrist to Yeats*. New Haven: Yale University Press, 1969.

Erdman, David V. *Blake: Prophet Against Empire*. Princeton: Princeton University Press, 1969.

Essick, Robert N. *The Visionary Hand: Essays for the Study of William Blake's Art and Aesthetics*. Los Angeles: Hennesy & Ingalls, 1973.

Fisher, Peter F. *The Valley of Vision*. Edited by Northrop Frye. Toronto: University of Toronto Press, 1961.

Fox, Susan. *Poetic Form in Blake's* Milton. Princeton: Princeton University Press, 1976.

Frosch, Thomas R. *The Awakening of Albion: The Renovation of the Body in the Poetry of William Blake*. Ithaca: Cornell University Press, 1974.

Frye, Northrop. *Fearful Symmetry*: *A Study of William Blake*. 1947. Reprint. Princeton: Princeton University Press, 1974.

————, ed. *Blake*: *A Collection of Critical Essays*. Englewood Cliffs, N. J.: Prentice-Hall, 1966.

Gallant, Christine. *Blake and the Assimilation of Chaos*. Princeton: Princeton University Press, 1978.

George, Diana Hume. *Blake and Freud*. Ithaca: Cornell University Press, 1980.

Gillham, D. G. *William Blake*. London: Cambridge University Press, 1973.

Glechner, Robert F. *The Piper and the Bard*: *A Study of William Blake*. Detroit, Mich.: Wayne State University Press, 1959.

Hagstrom, Jean H. *William Blake*: *Poet and Painter, an Introduction to the Illuminated Verse*. Chicago: The University of Chicago Press, 1964.

Harper, George Mills. *The Neoplatonism of William Blake*. Chapel Hill: University of North Carolina Press, 1961.

Hilton, Nelson. *Literal Imagination*: *Blake's Vision of Words*. Berkeley: University of California Press, 1983.

Howard, John. *Blake's* Milton: *A Study of the Selfhood*. Rutherford, N. J.: Fairleigh Dickinson University Press, 1976.

Jackson, Wallace. *The Probable and the Marvelous*: *Blake, Wordsworth, and the 18th-Century Critical Tradition*. Athens: University of Georgia Press, 1978.

James, David E. "Blake's 'Laocoon': A Degree Zero of Literary Production." *PMLA* 98, no. 3 (March 1983): 226–36.

John, Brian. *Supreme Fictions*: *Studies in the Work of William Blake, Thomas Carlyle, W. B. Yeats, and D. H. Lawrence*. Montreal: McGill-Queens University Press, 1974.

Keynes, Geoffrey. *Blake Studies*: *Essays on His Life and Work*. 2nd ed. Oxford: Oxford University Press, 1971.

Klonsky, Milton. *William Blake*: *The Seer and His Visions*. New York: Harmony Books, 1977.

Lindsay, Jack. *William Blake*: *His Life and Work*. New York: George Braziller, 1979.

Lister, Raymond. *William Blake*: *An Introduction to the Man and His Work*. London: Bell, 1968.

Mellor, Anne Kostelanetz. *Blake's Human Form Divine*. Berkeley: University of California Press, 1974.

Mitchell, W. J. T. *Blake's Composite Art*: *A Study of the Illuminated Poetry*. Princeton: Princeton University Press, 1978.

Nurmi, Martin K. *William Blake*. Kent: Ohio State University Press, 1976.

O'Neill, Judith, ed. *Critics on Blake*. Coral Gables, Fla.: University of Miami Press, 1970.

Paley, Morton D. *Energy and Imagination*: *A Study of the Development of Blake's Thought*. Oxford: Clarendon Press, 1970.

————, ed. *Twentieth-Century Interpretations of* Songs of Innocence and of Experience. Englewood Cliffs, N. J.: Prentice-Hall, 1969.

Pease, Donald. "Blake, Crane, Whitman, and Modernism: A Poetics of Pure Possibility." *PMLA* 96, no. 1 (January 1981): 64–83.

Raine, Kathleen Jessie. *Blake and the New Age*. Boston: George Allen & Unwin, 1979.

———. *William Blake*. London: Thames & Hudson, 1970.

Sabri-Tabrizi, G. F. *The "Heaven" and "Hell" of William Blake*. London: Lawrence & Wishart, 1975.

Schorer, Mark. *William Blake: The Politics of Vision*. New York: Vintage Books, 1959.

Seurat, Denis. *Blake and Milton*. London: S. Nott, 1935.

Van Sinderen, Adrian. *Blake and the Mystic Genius*. Syracuse, N. Y.: Syracuse University Press, 1949.

Vogler, Thomas A. *Preludes to Vision: The Epic Venture in Blake, Wordsworth, Keats, and Hart Crane*. Berkeley: University of California Press, 1971.

Wagenknecht, David. *Blake's Night: William Blake and the Idea of the Pastoral*. Cambridge, Mass.: Belknap Press, 1973.

Witcutt, William Purcell. *Blake: A Psychological Study*. Darby, Pa.: Folcroft Library Editions, 1974.

WILLIAM WORDSWORTH

Abrams, M. H., ed. *Wordsworth: A Collection of Critical Essays*. Englewood Cliffs, N. J.: Prentice-Hall, 1972.

Arac, Jonathan. "Bounding Lines: *The Prelude* and Critical Revision." *Boundary 2* 7, no. 3 (Spring 1979): 31–48.

Averill, James H. *Wordsworth and the Poetry of Human Suffering*. Ithaca: Cornell University Press, 1980.

Baker, Jeffrey. *Time and Mind in Wordsworth's Poetry*. Detroit, Mich.: Wayne State University Press, 1980.

Beer, John Bernard. *Wordsworth and the Human Heart*. New York: Columbia University Press, 1978.

Bialosotsky, Don H. *Making Tales: The Poetics of Wordsworth's Narrative Experiments*. Chicago: The University of Chicago Press, 1984.

Byatt, Antonia Susan. *Wordsworth and Coleridge in Their Time*. London: Nelson, 1970.

Devlin, David Douglas. *Wordsworth and the Art of Prose*. London: Macmillan & Co., 1983.

———. *Wordsworth and the Poetry of Epitaphs*. London: Macmillan & Co., 1980.

Ferguson, Frances. *Wordsworth: Language as Counter-Spirit*. New Haven: Yale University Press, 1977.

Gérard, Albert S. *English Romantic Poetry: Ethos, Structure, and Symbol in Coleridge, Wordsworth, Shelley, and Keats*. Berkeley: University of California Press, 1968.

Grob, Alan. *The Philosophic Mind: A Study of Wordsworth's Poetry and Thought, 1797–1805*. Columbus: Ohio University Press, 1973.

Halliday, F. E. *Wordsworth and His World*. London: Thames & Hudson, 1970.

Hartman, Geoffrey H. *Wordsworth's Poetry*. New Haven: Yale University Press, 1971.

————, ed. *New Perspectives on Coleridge and Wordsworth: Selected Papers from the English Institute*. New York: Columbia University Press, 1972.

Havens, Raymond Dexter. *The Mind of a Poet*. Baltimore: The Johns Hopkins University Press, 1941.

Heffernan, James A. H. *William Wordsworth's Theory of Poetry: The Transforming Imagination*. Ithaca: Cornell University Press, 1969.

Hodgson, John A. *Wordsworth's Philosophical Poetry, 1797–1814*. Lincoln: University of Nebraska Press, 1980.

Jackson, Wallace. *The Probable and the Marvelous: Blake, Wordsworth, and the 18th-Century Critical Tradition*. Athens: University of Georgia Press, 1978.

Jacobus, Mary. *Tradition and Experiment in Wordsworth's* Lyrical Ballads *(1798)*. Oxford: Clarendon Press, 1976.

Johnson, Lee M. *Wordsworth's Metaphysical Verse: Geometry, Nature, and Form*. Toronto: University of Toronto Press, 1982.

Johnston, Kenneth R. *Wordsworth and* The Recluse. New Haven: Yale University Press, 1984.

Jones, Henry John Franklin. *The Egotistical Sublime: A History of Wordsworth's Imagination*. London: Chatto & Windus, 1954.

McConnel, Frank D. *The Confessional Imagination: A Reading of Wordsworth's* Prelude. Baltimore: The Johns Hopkins University Press, 1974.

McFarland, Thomas. *Romanticism and the Forms of Ruin: Wordsworth, Coleridge, and the Modalities of Fragmentation*. Princeton: Princeton University Press, 1981.

Murray, Roger N. *Wordsworth's Style, Figures and Themes in the* Lyrical Ballads of 1800. Lincoln: University of Nebraska Press, 1967.

Onorato, Richard. *The Character of the Poet: Wordsworth in* The Prelude. Princeton: Princeton University Press, 1971.

Parrish, Stephen Maxfield. *The Art of the* Lyrical Ballads. Cambridge: Harvard University Press, 1973.

Perkins, David. *The Quest for Permanence: The Symbolism of Wordsworth, Shelley, and Keats*. Cambridge: Harvard University Press, 1959.

————. *Wordsworth and the Poetry of Sincerity*. Cambridge, Mass.: Belknap Press, 1964.

Pirie, David. *William Wordsworth: The Poetry of Grandeur and of Tenderness*. London and New York: Methuen & Co., 1982.

Regueiro, Helen. *The Limits of Imagination: Wordsworth, Yeats, and Stevens*. Ithaca: Cornell University Press, 1976.

Rehder, Robert. *Wordsworth and the Beginnings of Modern Poetry*. Totowa, N. J.: Barnes & Noble, 1981.

Sherry, Charles. *Wordsworth's Poetry of the Imagination*. Oxford: Clarendon Press, 1980.

Simpson, David. *Wordsworth and the Figurings of the Real*. London: Macmillan & Co., 1982.

Watson, J. R. *Wordsworth's Vital Soul: The Sacred and the Profane in Wordsworth's Poetry*. London: Macmillan & Co., 1982.

SAMUEL TAYLOR COLERIDGE

Barfield, Owen. *What Coleridge Thought*. Middletown, Conn.: Wesleyan University Press, 1971.

Beer, John, ed. *Coleridge's Variety*. Pittsburgh: University of Pittsburgh Press, 1975.

Bloom, Harold. *Figures of Capable Imagination*. New York: Seabury Press, 1976.

Boulger, James D. *Coleridge as Religious Thinker*. New Haven: Yale University Press, 1961.

——, ed. *Twentieth-Century Interpretations of* The Rime of the Ancient Mariner. Englewood Cliffs, N. J.: Prentice-Hall, 1969.

Burke, Kenneth. *Language as Symbolic Action: Essays on Life, Literature, and Method*. Berkeley: University of California Press, 1966.

Christensen, Jerome. *Coleridge's Blessed Machine of Language*. Ithaca: Cornell University Press, 1981.

——. "Philosophy/Literature: The Associationist Precedent for Coleridge's Late Poems." In *Literature and Philosophy: New Perspectives on Nineteenth- and Twentieth-Century Texts*, edited by William E. Cain. Bucknell, Penn.: Bucknell University Press, 1983.

——. "Politerotics: Coleridge's Rhetoric of War in *The Friend*." *Clio* 8 (1979): 339–63.

Coburn, Kathleen. *Experience into Thought: Perspectives in the Coleridge Notebooks*. Toronto: University of Toronto Press, 1979.

——, ed. *Coleridge: A Collection of Critical Essays*. Englewood Cliffs, N. J.: Prentice-Hall, 1967.

Crawford, Walter B., ed. *Reading Coleridge: Approaches and Applications*. Ithaca: Cornell University Press, 1979.

Delson, Abe. "The Function of Geraldine in *Christabel*: A Critical Perspective and Interpretation." *English Studies* 61 (1980): 130–41.

de Man, Paul. "The Rhetoric of Temporality." In *Interpretation: Theory and Practice*, edited by Charles Singleton. Baltimore: The Johns Hopkins University Press, 1969.

Ferguson, Frances. "Coleridge and the Deluded Reader: *The Rime of the Ancient Mariner*." *Georgia Review* 31 (1977): 617–35.

——. "Coleridge on Language and Delusion." *Genre* 11 (1978): 191–207.

Hartman, Geoffrey H., ed. *New Perspectives on Coleridge and Wordsworth: Selected Papers from the English Institute*. New York: Columbia University Press, 1972.

House, Humphry. *Coleridge*. The Clark Lectures 1951–52. London: Rupert Hart-Davis, 1953.

Isaacs, J. "Coleridge's Critical Terminology." *Essays and Studies by Members of the English Association* 21 (1936): 86–104.

McFarland, Thomas. *Coleridge and the Pantheist Tradition*. Oxford: Clarendon Press, 1969.

———. *Originality and Imagination*. Baltimore: The Johns Hopkins University Press, 1985.

———. *Romanticism and the Forms of Ruin: Wordsworth, Coleridge, and Modalities of Fragmentation*. Princeton: Princeton University Press, 1981.

Modiano, Raimonda. "Words and 'Languageless' Meanings: Limits of Expression in *The Rime of the Ancient Mariner*." *Modern Language Quarterly* 38 (1977): 40–77.

Parker, Reeve. *Coleridge's Meditative Art*. Ithaca: Cornell University Press, 1975.

Randel, Fred V. "Coleridge and the Contentiousness of Romantic Nightingales." *Studies in Romanticism* 21 (1982): 33–55.

Reed, Arden. *Romantic Weather: The Climates of Coleridge and Baudelaire*. Hanover, N. H.: Brown University Press and University Press of New England, 1983.

Schneider, Elisabeth. *Coleridge, Opium, and "Kubla Khan."* 1953. Reprint. New York: Octagon Books, 1966.

Shaffer, E. S. *"Kubla Khan" and* The Fall of Jerusalem: *The Mythological School in Biblical Criticism and Secular Literature 1770–1880*. Cambridge: Cambridge University Press, 1975.

GEORGE GORDON, LORD BYRON

Blackstone, Bernard. *Byron: A Survey*. London: Longmans Group Ltd., 1975.

Bostetter, Edward Everett. *Twentieth-Century Interpretations of* Don Juan. Englewood Cliffs, N. J.: Prentice-Hall, Inc., 1969.

Bowra, C. M. *The Romantic Imagination*. Cambridge: Harvard University Press, 1949.

Boyd, Elizabeth F. *Byron's* Don Juan: *A Critical Study*. New Brunswick, N. J.: Rutgers University Press, 1945.

Calvert, William. *Byron: Romantic Paradox*. Chapel Hill: University of North Carolina Press, 1935.

Chew, Samuel C. *The Dramas of Lord Byron*. Baltimore: The Johns Hopkins University Press, 1915.

Cooke, Michael G. *The Blind Man Traces the Circle: On the Patterns and Philosophy of Byron's Poetry*. Princeton: Princeton University Press, 1981.

de Almeida, Hermione. *Byron and Joyce Through Homer:* Don Juan *and* Ulysses. New York: Columbia University Press, 1981.

Eliot, T. S. *On Poetry and Poets*. New York: Farrar, Straus & Cudahy, Inc., 1957.

Elledge, W. Paul. *Byron and the Dynamics of Metaphor*. Nashville, Tenn.: Vanderbilt University Press, 1968.

Gleckner, Robert F. *Byron and the Ruins of Paradise*. Baltimore: The Johns Hopkins University Press, 1967.

Joseph, M. K. *Byron the Poet*. London: Victor Gollancz, Ltd., 1964.

Jump, John D. *Byron*. London & Boston: Routledge & Kegan Paul, 1972.

————, ed. *Byron: A Symposium*. London: Macmillan & Co., 1975.

Kernan, Alvin. *The Plot of Satire*. New Haven: Yale University Press, 1965.

Knight, G. Wilson. *The Burning Oracle*. New York: Oxford University Press, 1939.

————. *Byron and Shakespeare*. New York: Barnes & Noble, 1966.

————. *Lord Byron: Christian Virtues*. London: Routledge & Kegan Paul, 1952.

————. *Poets of Action*. London: Methuen & Co., 1967.

Kroeber, Karl. *Romantic Narrative Art*. Madison: University of Wisconsin Press, 1960.

Leavis, F. R. *Revaluation: Tradition and Development of English Poetry*. London: Chatto & Windus, 1936.

Lovell, Ernest J. *Byron: The Record of a Quest*. Austin: University of Texas Press, 1949.

McGann, Jerome J. *The Beauty of Inflections: Literary Investigations in Historical Method and Theory*. Oxford: Oxford University Press, 1985.

————. *Don Juan in Context*. Chicago: The University of Chicago Press, 1976.

————. *Fiery Dust: Byron's Poetical Development*. Chicago: The University of Chicago Press, 1968.

Manning, Peter. *Byron and His Fictions*. Detroit: Wayne State University Press, 1978.

Marchand, Leslie A. *Byron's Poetry: A Critical Introduction*. Cambridge: Harvard University Press, 1968.

Marshall, William H. *The Structure of Byron's Major Poems*. Philadelphia: University of Pennsylvania Press, 1962.

Martin, Philip W. *Byron: A Poet Before His Public*. Cambridge: Cambridge University Press, 1982.

Mellor, Anne K. *English Romantic Irony*. Cambridge: Harvard University Press, 1980.

Praz, Mario. *The Romantic Agony*. London: Oxford University Press, 1933.

Ridenour, George M. *The Style of Don Juan*. New Haven: Yale University Press, 1960.

Robinson, Charles E. *Shelley and Byron: The Snake and the Eagle Wreathed in Flight*. Baltimore: The Johns Hopkins University Press, 1977.

————, ed. *Lord Byron and His Contemporaries: Essays from the Sixth International Byron Seminar*. East Brunswick, N. J.: Associated University Press, 1982.

Rutherford, Andrew. *Byron: A Critical Study*. Stanford, Calif.: Stanford University Press, 1961.

Thorslev, Peter L., Jr. *The Byronic Hero: Types and Prototypes*. Minneapolis: University of Minnesota Press, 1962.

Vassallo, Peter. *Byron*: *The Italian Literary Influence*. New York: St. Martin's Press, 1984.

West, Paul, ed. *Byron*: *A Collection of Critical Essays*. Englewood Cliffs, N. J.: Prentice-Hall, 1963.

————, ed. *Byron and the Spoiler's Art*. London: Chatto & Windus, 1960.

Wilkie, Brian. *Romantic Poets and Epic Tradition*. Madison: University of Wisconsin Press, 1965.

PERCY BYSSHE SHELLEY

Baker, Carlos. *Shelley's Major Poetry*. New York: Russell & Russell, 1961.

Barcus, James E. *Shelley*: *The Critical Heritage*. London & Boston: Routledge & Kegan Paul, 1975.

Barrell, Joseph. *Shelley and the Thought of His Time*: *A Study in the History of Ideas*. Hamden, Conn.: Archon Books, 1967.

Bloom, Harold. *Shelley's Mythmaking*. New Haven: Yale University Press, 1959.

Brailsford, H. N. *Shelley, Godwin, and Their Circle*. Hamden, Conn.: Archon Books, 1969.

Brown, Nathaniel. *Sexuality and Feminism in Shelley*. Cambridge: Cambridge University Press, 1979.

Butler, Peter. *Shelley's Idols of the Cave*. Edinburgh: University of Edinburgh Press, 1954.

————. *The Young Shelley*: *Genesis of a Radical*. London: Victor Gollancz, 1951.

Cameron, Kenneth Neil. *Shelley*: *The Golden Years*. Cambridge: Harvard University Press, 1974.

————, ed. *Romantic Rebels*: *Essays on Shelley and His Circle*. Cambridge: Harvard University Press, 1973.

Campbell, Olwen Ward. *Shelley and the Unromantics*. London: Methuen & Co., 1924.

Cherniak, Judith. *The Lyrics of Shelley*. Cleveland, Ohio: Case Western Reserve University Press, 1972.

Crampton, Margaret. *Shelley's Dream Women*. New York: A. S. Barnes & Co., 1967.

Cronin, Richard. *Shelley's Poetic Thoughts*. London: Macmillan & Co., 1981.

Curran, Stuart. *Shelley's Annus Mirabilis*: *The Maturing of an Epic Vision*. San Marino, Calif.: Huntington Library, 1975.

————. *Shelley's* Cenci: *Scorpions Ringed with Fire*. Princeton: Princeton University Press, 1970.

Dawson, P. M. S. *The Unacknowledged Translator*: *Shelley and Politics*. Oxford: Clarendon Press, 1980.

Grabo, Carl. *The Meaning of* The Witch of Atlas. Chapel Hill: University of North Carolina Press, 1935.

————. Prometheus Unbound *and Interpretation*. Chapel Hill: University of North Carolina Press, 1935.

Hall, Jean. *The Transforming Image: A Study of Shelley's Major Poetry*. Chicago: University of Illinois Press, 1980.

Hoffman, Harold Leroy. *An Odyssey of the Soul: Shelley's* Alastor. New York: Columbia University Press, 1933.

Keach, William. *Shelley's Style*. London: Methuen & Co., 1984.

King-Hale, Desmond. *Shelley: His Thought and Work*. 3rd ed. London: Macmillan & Co., 1984.

Leighton, Angela. *Shelley and the Sublime: An Interpretation of the Major Poems*. London: Cambridge University Press, 1984.

Maurois, André. *Ariel: The Life of Shelley*. Translated by Ella d'Arcy. New York: D. Appleton & Co., 1924.

Norman, Sylvia. *Flight of the Skylark: The Development of Shelley's Reputation*. Norman: University of Oklahoma Press, 1954.

Notopoulos, James A. *The Platonism of Shelley*. Durham, N.C.: Duke University Press, 1949.

Peck, Walter Edwin. *Shelley: His Life and Work*. 2 vols. Boston: Houghton Mifflin Co., 1927.

Power, Julia. *Shelley in America in the 19th Century*. New York: Gordian Press, 1969.

Pulos, C. E. *The Deep Truth: A Study of Shelley's Skepticism*. Lincoln: University of Nebraska Press, 1962.

Reiman, Donald H. *Percy Bysshe Shelley*. New York: Twayne Publishers, Inc., 1969.

Reiter, Seymour. *A Study of Shelley's Poetry*. Albuquerque: University of New Mexico Press, 1967.

Ridenour, George M. *Shelley: A Collection of Critical Essays*. Englewood Cliffs, N. J.: Prentice-Hall, 1965.

Rieger, James. *The Mutiny Within: The Heresies of Percy Bysshe Shelley*. New York: George Braziller, 1967.

Robinson, Charles E. *Shelley and Byron: The Snake and the Eagle Wreathed in Flight*. Baltimore: The Johns Hopkins University Press, 1976.

Sperry, Stuart M. "Necessity and the Role of the Hero in Shelley's *Prometheus Unbound*." PMLA 96, no. 2 (March 1981): 242–54.

———. "The Sexual Theme in Shelley's *The Revolt of Islam*." *Journal of English and Germanic Philology* 82, no. 1 (1983): 32–49.

Wasserman, Earl R. *Shelley: A Critical Reading*. Baltimore: The Johns Hopkins University Press, 1971.

Webb, Timothy. *Shelley: A Voice Not Understood*. Manchester: Manchester University Press, 1977.

White, Newman Ivey. *Shelley*. 2 vols. New York: Alfred A. Knopf, 1959.

Woodman, Ross G. *The Apocalyptic Vision in the Poetry of Shelley*. Toronto: University of Toronto Press, 1964.

JOHN KEATS

Bate, Walter Jackson. *John Keats*. Cambridge: Belknap/Harvard University Press, 1963.

————, ed. *Keats: A Collection of Critical Essays*. Englewood Cliffs, N. J.: Prentice-Hall, 1964.

Bush, Douglas. *John Keats: His Life and Writings*. New York: Macmillan Co., 1966.

Caldwell, James R. *John Keats's Fancy: The Effect on Keats of the Psychology of His Day*. Ithaca: Cornell University Press, 1945.

Dickstein, Morris. *Keats and His Poetry: A Study in Development*. Chicago: The University of Chicago Press, 1971.

Ende, Stuart A. *Keats and the Sublime*. New Haven: Yale University Press, 1976.

Evert, Walter H. *Aesthetic Myth in the Poetry of Keats*. Princeton: Princeton University Press, 1965.

Finney, Claude L. *The Evolution of Keats's Poetry*. 2 vols. 1936. Reprint. New York: Russell & Russell, 1963.

Fitzpatrick, Margaret Ann. "The Problem of 'Identity' in Keats's 'Negative Capability'." *Dalhousie Review* 61, no. 1 (Spring 1981): 39–51.

Fogle, Richard Harter. *The Imagery of Keats and Shelley*. Hamden, Conn.: Archon Books, 1962.

Gittings, Robert. *John Keats*. Boston: Little, Brown & Co., 1968.

Goldberg, M. A. *The Poetics of Romanticism: Toward a Reading of John Keats*. Yellow Springs, Ohio: Antioch Press, 1969.

Hewlett, Dorothy. *A Life of John Keats*. London: Hutchison & Company, 1970.

Hilton, Timothy. *Keats and His World*. New York: Viking Press, 1971.

Jones, James Land. *Adam's Dream: Mythic Consciousness in Keats and Yeats*. Athens: University of Georgia Press, 1975.

Jones, John. *John Keats's Dream of Truth*. London: Chatto & Windus, 1969.

Levine, George R. "The Arrogance of Keats's Grecian Urn." *Essays in Literature* 10, no. 1 (Spring 1983): 39–44.

Little, Judy. *Keats as a Narrative Poet*. Lincoln: University of Nebraska Press, 1975.

Lowell, Amy. *John Keats*. 2 vols. 1925. Reprint. Hamden, Conn.: Archon Books, 1969.

Murry, John Middleton. *Keats*. New York: Noonday Press, 1955.

————. *Keats and Shakespeare*. London: Oxford University Press, 1951.

————. *Studies in Keats*. New York: Haskell House, 1966.

O'Neill, Judith, ed. *Critics on Keats: Readings in Literary Criticism*. London: George Allen & Unwin, Ltd., 1967.

Pope, Deborah. "The Dark Side of the Urn: A Re-evaluation of the Speaker in 'Ode on a Grecian Urn'." *Essays in Literature* 10, no. 1 (Spring 1983): 45–53.

Ridley, M. R. *Keats's Craftsmanship: A Study in Poetic Development*. New York: Russell & Russell, 1962.

Rollins, Hyder Edward, ed. *The Keats Circle*. 2 vols. Cambridge: Harvard University Press, 1965.

Slote, Bernice. *Keats and the Dramatic Principle*. Lincoln: University of Nebraska Press, 1950.

Sperry, Stuart M. *Keats the Poet*. Princeton: Princeton University Press, 1973.

Stillinger, Jack. "The Hoodwinking of Madeline: Skepticism in *The Eve of St. Agnes*." *Studies in Philology* 58 (1961): 533–55.

———, ed. *Twentieth-Century Interpretations of Keats's Odes*. Englewood Cliffs, N. J.: Prentice-Hall, 1968.

Vendler, Helen. *The Odes of John Keats*. Cambridge: Belknap/Harvard University Press, 1983.

Ward, Aileen. *John Keats: The Making of a Poet*. New York: Viking Press, 1963.

Wasserman, Earl R. *The Finer Tone: Keats's Major Poems*. Baltimore: The Johns Hopkins University Press, 1967.

Acknowledgments

"Introduction" (originally entitled "The Internalization of Quest Romance") by Harold Bloom from *The Ringers in the Tower*: *Studies in Romantic Tradition* by Harold Bloom, © 1971 by The University of Chicago. Reprinted by permission of The University of Chicago Press.

"Blake: The Keys to the Gates" (originally entitled "The Keys to the Gates") by Northrop Frye from *Some British Romantics*: *A Collection of Essays* edited by James V. Logan, John E. Jordan, and Northrop Frye, © 1966 by the Ohio State University Press. Reprinted by permission.

"Blake's *Jerusalem*: The Bard of Sensibility and the Form of Prophecy" by Harold Bloom from *The Ringers in the Tower*: *Studies in Romantic Tradition* by Harold Bloom, © 1971 by The University of Chicago. Reprinted by permission of The University of Chicago Press.

"Darkning Man: Blake's Critique of Transcendence" by Thomas Weiskel from *The Romantic Sublime*: *Studies in the Structure and Psychology of Transcendence* by Thomas Weiskel, © 1976 by The Johns Hopkins University Press. Baltimore/London: The Johns Hopkins University Press, 1976. Reprinted by permission.

"The Eye and the Object in the Poetry of Wordsworth" by Frederick A. Pottle from *Yale Review* 40, no. 1 (September 1950), © 1950 by Yale University. Reprinted by permission of *Yale Review*.

"Wordsworth: The Romance of Nature and the Negative Way" (originally entitled "The Romance of Nature and the Negative Way") by Geoffrey H. Hartman from *The Unmediated Vision* by Geoffrey H. Hartman, © 1954 by Yale University and © 1982 by Geoffrey H. Hartman, and from *Wordsworth's Poetry 1787–1814* by Geoffrey H. Hartman, © 1964 by Yale University. Reprinted by permission of Yale University Press.

401

"Wordsworth's Severe Intimations" by Paul H. Fry from *The Poet's Calling in the English Ode* by Paul H. Fry, © 1980 by Yale University. Reprinted by permission of Yale University Press.

"Coleridge's 'A Light in Sound': Science, Metascience, and Poetic Imagination" by M. H. Abrams from *The Correspondent Breeze*: *Essays on English Romanticism* by M. H. Abrams, © 1984 by M. H. Abrams. Reprinted by permission of the author. The footnotes in the original essay have been omitted.

" 'Positive Negation': Threshold, Sequence, and Personification in Coleridge" by Angus Fletcher from *New Perspectives on Coleridge and Wordsworth*: *Selected Papers from the English Institute* edited by Geoffrey H. Hartman, © 1972 by Columbia University Press. Reprinted by permission.

"Coleridge's 'Kubla Khan': The Oriental Idyll" (originally entitled "The Oriental Idyll") by E. S. Shaffer from *"Kubla Khan" and* The Fall of Jerusalem: *The Mythological School in Biblical Criticism and Secular Literature 1770–1880* by E. S. Shaffer, © 1975 by Cambridge University Press. Reprinted by permission of Cambridge University Press and the author.

"The Two Eternities: An Essay on Byron" by G. Wilson Knight from *The Burning Oracle*: *Studies in the Poetry of Action* by G. Wilson Knight, © 1939 by Oxford University Press. Reprinted by permission.

"Byron: Troubled Stream from a Pure Source" by Leslie Brisman from *Romantic Origins* by Leslie Brisman, © 1978 by Cornell University. Reprinted by permission of Cornell University Press.

"Byron's 'one word': The Language of Self-Expression in *Childe Harold* III" by Sheila Emerson from *Studies in Romanticism* 20, no. 3 (Fall 1981), © 1980 by the Trustees of Boston University. Reprinted courtesy of the Trustees of Boston University.

"The Unpastured Sea: An Introduction to Shelley" by Harold Bloom from *The Ringers in the Tower*: *Studies in Romantic Tradition* by Harold Bloom, © 1971 by The University of Chicago. Reprinted by permission of The University of Chicago Press.

"The Role of Asia in the Dramatic Action of Shelley's *Prometheus Unbound*" by Frederick A. Pottle from *Shelley*: *A Collection of Critical Essays* edited by George M. Ridenour, © 1965 by Prentice-Hall, Inc. Reprinted by permission.

"Shelley Disfigured: *The Triumph of Life*" (originally entitled "Shelley Disfigured") by Paul de Man from *Deconstruction and Criticism* edited by

Harold Bloom et al., © 1979 by The Continuum Publishing Company. Reprinted by permission of the publisher.

"Keats: Negative Capability" (originally entitled "Negative Capability") by Walter Jackson Bate from *John Keats* by Walter Jackson Bate; © 1963 by the President and Fellows of Harvard College. Reprinted by permission of The Belknap Press of Harvard University Press.

"Keats: The Negative Road" (originally entitled "Introduction") by Paul de Man from *John Keats: Selected Poetry* edited by Paul de Man, © 1966 by Paul de Man and © 1986 by Patricia de Man. Reprinted by permission of Patricia de Man.

"Keats: Romance Revised" by Harold Bloom from *Poetry and Repression: Revisionism from Blake to Stevens* by Harold Bloom, © 1976 by Yale University. Reprinted by permission of Yale University Press.

Index